T0230245

Lecture Notes in Computer Science   1110

Springer

Berlin
Heidelberg
New York
Barcelona
Budapest
Hong Kong
London
Milan
Paris
Santa Clara
Singapore
Tokyo

Olivier Danvy   Robert Glück
Peter Thiemann   (Eds.)

Partial Evaluation

International Seminar
Dagstuhl Castle, Germany
February 12-16, 1996
Selected Papers

 Springer

Series Editors

Gerhard Goos, Karlsruhe University, Germany

Juris Hartmanis, Cornell University, NY, USA

Jan van Leeuwen, Utrecht University, The Netherlands

Volume Editors

Olivier Danvy
BRICS, Department of Computer Science, Aarhus University
Ny Munkegade, Building 540, DK-8000 Aarhus C, Denmark

Robert Glück
DIKU, Department of Computer Science, University of Copenhagen
Universitetsparken 1, DK-2100 Copenhagen East, Denmark

Peter Thiemann
Wilhelm-Schickard-Institut für Informatik, Universität Tübingen
Sand 13, D-72076 Tübingen, Germany

Cataloging-in-Publication data applied for

Die Deutsche Bibliothek - CIP-Einheitsaufnahme

Partial evaluation : international Seminar, Dagstuhl Castle,
Germany, February 12 - 16, 1996 ; selected papers / O. Danvy ...
(ed.). - Berlin ; Heidelberg ; New York ; Barcelona ; Budapest ;
Hong Kong ; London ; Milan ; Paris ; Santa Clara ; Singapore ;
Tokyo : Springer, 1996
  (Lecture notes in computer science ; Vol. 1110)
  ISBN 3-540-61580-6
NE: Danvy, Olivier [Hrsg.]; GT

CR Subject Classification (1991): D.3.4, D.1.2, D.3.1

ISSN 0302-9743
ISBN 3-540-61580-6 Springer-Verlag Berlin Heidelberg New York

© Springer-Verlag Berlin Heidelberg 1996
Printed in Germany

Typesetting: Camera-ready by author
SPIN 10513217   06/3142 – 5 4 3 2 1 0   Printed on acid-free paper

Preface

Partial evaluation has reached a point where theory and techniques are mature, substantial systems have been developed, and it appears feasible to use partial evaluation in realistic applications. This development is documented in a series of ACM SIGPLAN-sponsored conferences and workshops, Partial Evaluation and Semantics-Based Program Manipulation, held both in the United States and in Europe.

In 1987, the first meeting of researchers in partial evaluation took place in Gammel Avernæs, Denmark. Almost ten years later, the time was due to evaluate the progress that has been achieved during the last decade and to discuss open problems, novel approaches, and research directions. A seminar at the *International Conference and Research Center for Computer Science* at Schloß Dagstuhl [6], located in a beautiful scenic region in the southwest of Germany, seemed ideally suited for that purpose.

The meeting brought together specialists on partial evaluation, partial deduction, metacomputation, program analysis, automatic program transformation, and semantics-based program manipulation. The attendants were invited to explore the dimensions of program specialization, program analysis, treatment of programs as data objects, and their applications. Besides discussing major achievements or failures and their reasons, the main topics were:

- **Advances in Theory:** Program specialization has undergone a rapid development during the last decade. Despite its widespread use, a number of theoretical issues still need to be resolved, including efficient treatment of programs as data objects; metalevel techniques including reflection, self-application, and metasystem transition; issues in generating and/or handwriting program generators; termination and generalization issues in different languages; related topics in program analysis including abstract interpretation, flow analysis, and type inference; the relationships of different transformation paradigms, such as automated deduction, theorem proving, and program synthesis.

- **Towards Computational Practice:** Academic research has thrived in many locations. Broad practical experience has been gained, and stronger and larger program specializers have been built for a variety of languages, including Scheme, ML, Prolog, and C. Work is being initiated to bring the achievements of theory into practical use but a number of pragmatic issues still need to be resolved: progress towards medium- and large-scale applications; environments and user interfaces (*e.g.*, binding-time debuggers); integration of partial evaluation into the software development process; automated software reuse.

- **Larger Perspectives:** We also wanted to critically assess state-of-the-art techniques, summarize new approaches and insights, and survey challenging problems.

This book

All participants were invited to submit a full paper of their contribution for this collection. The submitted papers have been reviewed with outside assistance and each paper read by at least three referees. Technical quality, significance, and originality were the primary criteria for selection. The selected papers cover a wide and representative spectrum of topics and document state-of-the-art research activities in the area of partial evaluation. Three surveys were invited to complete this volume:

- In *What not to do when writing an interpreter for specialization*, Neil Jones carefully reviews the (sometimes non-obvious) pitfalls that must be avoided by the partial-evaluation apprentice in order to successfully generate compilers by partial evaluation,
- In *A comparative revisitation of some program transformation techniques*, Alberto Pettorossi and Maurizio Proietti survey the use of well-known transformation techniques in recent work, and
- in *Metacomputation: Metasystem transition plus supercompilation*, Valentin Turchin provides us with a personal account of the history and the present state of supercompilation and metasystem transitions. Professor Turchin presented his invited lecture on his 65th birthday, during the seminar.

Here is a brief topical summary of the contributions in this volume:

Partial evaluation:

- Thomas Reps and Todd Turndige. *Program specialization via program slicing.* Demonstrates that specialization can be achieved by program slicing. A bridge-building paper between two research areas.
- Torben Mogensen. *Evolution of partial evaluators: Removing inherited limits.* Provides a rationalized, unified, and insightful view of recent developments in partial evaluation.
- Michael Sperber. *Self-applicable online partial evaluation.* Reports the successful self-application of a realistic online partial evaluator. Solves a long-standing problem.
- Alain Miniussi and David Sherman. *Squeezing intermediate construction in equational programs.* Applies specialization of stack-machine code to optimize equational programs.

Imperative programming:

- Mikhail A. Bulyonkov and Dmitrij V. Kochetov. *Practical aspects of specialization of Algol-like programs.* Presents a new technique for decreasing the memory usage in the specialization of imperative programs.
- Alexander Sakharov. *Specialization of imperative programs through analysis of relational expressions.* Presents a powerful optimizer applying techniques from supercompilation and generalized partial computation to improve imperative code, using a dependence graph.

Functional programming:

- John Hughes. *Type specialisation for the lambda calculus.* An elegant step towards solving the (in)famous tagging problem in specializing higher-order interpreters for typed programs.
- Olivier Danvy. *Pragmatics of type-directed partial evaluation.* Extends the author's approach to specialize compiled programs by avoiding computation duplication and making residual programs readable, using type annotations.
- Peter Sestoft. *ML pattern match compilation and partial evaluation.* Applies information-propagation techniques to the compilation of pattern matching. An excellent application of partial evaluation in a compiler.

Logic programming:

- Alberto Pettorossi and Maurizio Proietti. *Automatic techniques for logic program specialization.* Describes a general method to specialize logic programs with respect to sets of partially known data given as a conjunction of atoms. The correctness of the technique is shown by a proof based on unfolding/folding transformations.
- Michael Leuschel and Bern Martens. *Global control for partial deduction through characteristic atoms and global trees.* Describes a global control of partial deduction that ensures effective specialization and fine-grained polyvariance, and whose termination only depends on the termination of the local control component — a significant progress.

Metacomputation by supercompilation:

- Andrei P. Nemytykh, Victoria A. Pinchuk, and Valentin F. Turchin. *A self-applicable supercompiler.* Shows the feasibility of self-application of super-compilers by demonstrating its use with examples. The solution of a long-standing open problem.
- Robert Glück and Morten Heine Sørensen. *A roadmap to metacomputation by supercompilation.* A survey paper with a careful explanation of supercompilation and its application in metacomputation, reporting state-of-the-art techniques and including a comprehensive list of references on the topic.

Generating extensions:

- Jesper Jørgensen and Michael Leuschel. *Efficiently generating efficient generating extensions in Prolog.* Reports the first successful hand-written program-generator generator (cogen) for a logic programming language. Exhibits significant speedups with respect to generic specializers and cogens generated by self-application.
- Scott Draves. *Compiler generation for interactive graphics using intermediate code.* Reports on a hand-written cogen for an intermediate language and its successful application to graphics programming. Includes the possibility of runtime code generation for specialized procedures.

Multi-level systems:

- Flemming Nielson and Hanne Riis Nielson. *Multi-level lambda-calculi: an algebraic description.* Considering the recent surge of interest in multi-level calculi, the authors revisit the "B-level-languages" of their book on two-level functional languages. In this paper, they provide us with a unifying treatment of various different calculi by exhibiting a general algebraic framework which can be instantiated to all other known calculi.
- John Hatcliff and Robert Glück. *Reasoning about hierarchies of online program specialization systems.* Successful self-application and metasystem transition is harder to achieve in online specializers than in offline ones. The paper develops a framework which facilitates metasystem transitions involving multiple levels for online specializers.

Program analyses:

- John Gallagher and Laura Lafave. *Regular approximation of computation paths in logic and functional languages.* Introduces computation paths as a novel means to control the polyvariance and termination of specialization techniques for logic and functional languages.
- Wei-Ngan Chin, Siau-Cheng Khoo, and Peter Thiemann. *Synchronization analyses for multiple recursion parameters.* Extends the tupling transformation to functions with multiple recursion parameters. Develops an original framework to identify synchronous handling of recursion parameters and gives terminating algorithms to perform the tupling transformation.

Applications:

- Sandrine Blazy and Philippe Facon. *An approach for the understanding of scientific application programs based on program specialization.* Applies specialization to understanding and maintaining "dusty deck" FORTRAN programs. The paper extends previous work with an interprocedural analysis.
- Charles Consel, Luke Hornof, Francois Noël, Jacques Noyé, and Nicolae Volanschi. *A uniform approach for compile-time and run-time specialization.* Presents a language-independent partial-evaluation framework which is suited for standard partial-evaluation techniques, as well as for run-time specialization. The major application is run-time specialization of one of the most widely used programming languages: C.

Further Partial-Evaluation Resources

Good starting points for the study of partial evaluation are the textbook by Jones, Gomard, and Sestoft [10], the tutorial notes by Consel and Danvy [3], and the tutorial notes on partial deduction by Gallagher [5]. Further material can be found in the proceedings of the Gammel Avernæs meeting [1,4], in the proceedings of the ACM conferences and workshops on Partial Evaluation and Semantics-Based Program Manipulation (PEPM) [2,7,12,13,15], and in special issues of various journals [8,9,11]. An online bibliography is maintained by Peter Sestoft [14].

Acknowledgements

We wish to thank the staff at Schloß Dagstuhl for their efficient assistance and for making the meeting possible. Thanks are also due to Elisabeth Meinhardt and Gebhard Engelhart for helping us to put this book together. And finally, thanks to all participants for a lively and inspiring meeting.

Olivier Danvy
Robert Glück
Peter Thiemann
March 1996

References

1. Dines Bjørner, Andrei P. Ershov, and Neil D. Jones, editors. *Partial Evaluation and Mixed Computation*, Amsterdam, 1988. North-Holland.
2. Charles Consel, editor. *ACM SIGPLAN Workshop on Partial Evaluation and Semantics-Based Program Manipulation PEPM '92*, San Francisco, CA, June 1992. Yale University. Report YALEU/DCS/RR-909.
3. Charles Consel and Olivier Danvy. Tutorial notes on partial evaluation. In Susan L. Graham, editor, *Proc. 20th Annual ACM Symposium on Principles of Programming Languages*, pages 493–501, Charleston, South Carolina, January 1993. ACM Press.
4. Andrei P. Ershov, Dines Bjørner, Yoshihiko Futamura, K. Furukawa, Anders Haraldsson, and William Scherlis, editors. *Special Issue: Selected Papers from the Workshop on Partial Evaluation and Mixed Computation, 1987 (New Generation Computing, vol. 6, nos. 2,3)*. Ohmsha Ltd. and Springer-Verlag, 1988.
5. John Gallagher. Specialization of logic programs. In Schmidt [13], pages 88–98.
6. Robert Glück, Olivier Danvy, and Peter Thiemann, editors. *Dagstuhl Seminar 9607: Partial Evaluation*, IBFI GmbH, Schloß Dagstuhl, D-66687 Wadern, Germany, February 1996. Seminar report 134.
7. Paul Hudak and Neil D. Jones, editors. *ACM SIGPLAN Symposium on Partial Evaluation and Semantics-Based Program Manipulation PEPM '91*, New Haven, CT, June 1991. ACM. SIGPLAN Notices 26(9).
8. Journal of Functional Programming 3(3), special issue on partial evaluation, July 1993. Neil D. Jones, editor.
9. Journal of Logic Programming 16 (1,2), special issue on partial deduction, 1993. Jan Komorowski, editor.
10. Neil D. Jones, Carsten K. Gomard, and Peter Sestoft. *Partial Evaluation and Automatic Program Generation*. Prentice Hall, 1993.
11. Lisp and Symbolic Computation 8 (3), special issue on partial evaluation, 1995. Peter Sestoft and Harald Søndergaard, editors.

12. William Scherlis, editor. *ACM SIGPLAN Symposium on Partial Evaluation and Semantics-Based Program Manipulation PEPM '95*, La Jolla, CA, June 1995. ACM Press.
13. David Schmidt, editor. *ACM SIGPLAN Symposium on Partial Evaluation and Semantics-Based Program Manipulation PEPM '93*, Copenhagen, Denmark, June 1993. ACM Press.
14. Peter Sestoft. Bibliography on partial evaluation. Available through URL ftp://ftp.diku.dk/pub/diku/dists/jones-book/partial-eval.bib.Z.
15. Peter Sestoft and Harald Søndergaard, editors. *ACM SIGPLAN Workshop on Partial Evaluation and Semantics-Based Program Manipulation PEPM '94*, Orlando, Fla., June 1994. ACM.

Reviewers

We gratefully acknowledge the following outside reviewers for their assistance in evaluating the submitted papers.

Sergei Abramov	Julia L. Lawall
Maria Alpuente	Peter Lee
Peter Holst Andersen	Michael Leuschel
David Basin	Rita Loogen
Silvia Breitinger	Bern Martens
Mikhail Bulyonkov	Torben Mogensen
Wei Ngan Chin	Jens Palsberg
Rowan Davies	Alberto Pettorossi
Danny De Schreye	Germán Puebla
Dirk Dussart	Sergei Romanenko
Yoshihiko Futamura	Erik Ruf
John Gallagher	Alexander Sakharov
Mayer Goldberg	Dietmar Seipel
John Hatcliff	Peter Sestoft
Manuel Hermenegildo	Michael Sperber
Neil D. Jones	Morten Heine Sørensen
Jesper Jørgensen	German Vidal

Contents

An Automatic Interprocedural Analysis for the Understanding of Scientific Application Programs

Sandrine Blazy, Philippe Facon
CEDRIC IIE, 18 allée Jean Rostand, 91 025 Évry Cedex, France
{blazy, facon}@iie.cnam.fr
(home page) http://web.iie.cnam.fr/~blazy/home.html

Abstract

This paper reports on an approach for improving the understanding of old programs which have become very complex due to numerous extensions. We have adapted partial evaluation techniques for program understanding. These techniques mainly use propagation through statements and simplifications of statements.

We focus here on the automatic interprocedural analysis and we specify both tasks (propagation and simplification) for call-statements, in terms of inference rules with notations taken from the formal specification languages B and VDM.

We describe how we have implemented that interprocedural analysis in a tool, and how it can be used to improve program understanding. The difficulty of that analysis is due to the lack of well defined interprocedural mechanisms and the complexity of visibility rules in Fortran.

Keywords: software maintenance of legacy code, program understanding, program specialization, interprocedural analysis, inference rules, natural semantics, formal specification, Fortran.

1 Introduction

Older software systems are inherently difficult to understand (and to maintain). Much of the effort involved in software maintenance is in locating the relevant code fragments that implement the concepts of the application domain. The maintainer is often faced with the problem of locating specific program features or functionalities within a large and partially understood system [19].

First, there exists now a wide range of tools to support program understanding [15]. Either they transform programs given a criteria (for instance they restructure programs) or they represent programs according to various formalisms (for instance graphic formalisms showing data and control flows). Hierarchies constructed by these tools should reflect semantics [14]. Program understanding involves recognizing meaningfull entities and their dependencies: calling relationships between subroutines, data flow relationships between variables, definition relationships between variables and types. They are important for understanding the code, but many of their code is difficult to find because it is often fairly deeply embedded within the program.

Next, such tools are fully automated and not customizable. But, there will always be users who will want something else. No tool can foresee all the situations a user will encounter. Customizations, extensions and new applications inevitably become necessary. Thus, instead of supporting a non flexible builder-oriented approach, a program understanding tool should support diverse user preferences as the users' view of the code.

Last, most market tools apply to whole programs or files. For every large system, the information generated by a tool is often prodigious. Presenting the user with reams of data is insufficient. Only the knowledge of this data is important for the user. In a sense, a key to program understanding is deciding what to look and what to ignore.

Scientific programming is a good example that shows the difficulties of the program understanding task. Many scientific application programs, written in Fortran for decades, are still vital in various domains (management of nuclear power plants, of telecommunication satellites, etc.), even though more modern languages are used to implement their user interfaces. It is not unusual to spend several months to understand such application programs before being able to maintain them. For example, understanding an application program of 120,000 lines of Fortran code took nine months [9]. So, providing the maintainer with a tool, which finds parts of lost code semantics ,enables reducing this period of adaptation.

Such observations in an industrial context [9] led us to develop a sofware maintenance tool to help in understanding scientific application programs. The peculiarities of our tool are the following:

• the tool is adpated to scientific application programs. In such programs, the technological level of scientific knowledge (linear systems resolution, turbulence simulation, etc.) is higher than the knowledge usually necessary for data processing (memory allocation, data representations). The discrepancy is increased by the widespread use of Fortran, which is old for a programming language (it lacks programming structures).

For large scientific application programs, Fortran 77 [8], which is quite an old version of the language, is used exclusively to guarantee the portability of the applications between different machines (mainframes, workstations, vector computers). The tool may analyze any Fortran program, but it simplifies only a subset of Fortran 77. This subset is a recommended standard for developping the scientific applications we have studied. The tool can not cope with EQUIVALENCE statements nor with any GOTO statement (they are not recommended), but only goto statements that implement specific control structures (e.g. a while-loop).

Scientific application programs we have studied have been developed a decade ago. During their evolution, they had to be reusable in new various contexts. For example, the same code implements both general design surveys for a nuclear power plant component (core, reactor, steam generator, etc.) and subsequent improvements in electricity production models. The result of this encapsulation of several models in a single large application domain increases program complexity, and thus amplifies the lack of structures in the Fortran programming language. This generality is implemented by Fortran input variables whose value does not vary in the context of the given application. We distinguish [5] two classes of such variables (data about geometry and control data) and we give in Fig. 1. an example of such variables.

• the tool allows the user to formulate hypotheses about the code and investigate whether they hold or must be rejected. As detailed in [17] such a process is one of the major components of dynamic code cognition behaviors. The tool helps to find parts of lost code semantics. It aims at specializing the application program according to specific values of input variables. For instance, if a team maintains only a specific application program that concerns the geometry detailed in Fig. 1, this team can focus on the application program it maintains (instead of the genaral application program that is used by several teams). Another example is the specialization of a 3D-application program into a 2D-one by setting the value of a co-ordinate.

• the tool does not change the original structure of the application program as explained in [4]. The tool is a polyvariant on-line specializer. It is based on partial evaluation but we have adapted partial evaluation for program understanding. In traditional specialization, call statements are unfolded on the fly: during specialization the call is replaced by a copy of the statements of the called procedure, where every argument expression is substituted for the corresponding formal parameter ([3], [7], [11]). This strategy aims at improving efficiency of programs.

As our goal is to facilitate the comprehension of programs, we do not change their structure (as explained in [4]) and we do not change the arity of called procedures. We do not unfold statements. Thus, the size of the code does not increase. Therefore, we are neither faced with the problem of infinite unfolding and termination of the specialization process nor with the problem of duplication of code (recursion does not exist in Fortran 77).

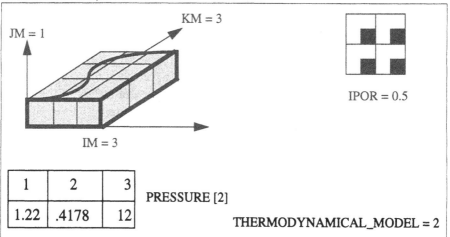

1	2	3
1.22	.4178	12

PRESSURE [2]

THERMODYNAMICAL_MODEL = 2

In this example we consider a liquid flow along the surface of a nuclear power plant component. This component is partitioned along the three axes, with a number of partitions of respectively *IM*, *JM* and *KM*. Moreover, the surface being porous, on a regular basis, *IPOR* is the relative side length of the solid part for each elementary cubic partition. *THERMODYNAMICAL_MODEL* is the number of the law that characterizes the liquid. We also have *PRESSURE*, with integer values that correspond, by a table, to real pressure values, each one with a specific precision.

Fig. 1. Some constraints on input data

Program slicing [18] consists of finding all statements (the slice) in a program that affect the value of a variable occurrence. Static slicing and dynamic slicing have been employed for program understanding. However for code implementing complex functionalities, they produce slices that do not help to understand the code. Other definitions of slicing have been introduced. For instance, quasi static slicing [16] combines together program slicing and partial evaluation, so allowing a better reduction of the program with respect to the slicing criterion.

We have presented in previous papers ([4]-[6]) the development and experiments of a first version of our tool. We give in Fig. 2. (see next page) an example of the program specialization performed by this version. In that first version, no interprocedural analysis was really performed: at each procedure call, the most pessimistic hypothesis about possible changes of variables values was applied and the user had to run the tool on each procedure. As most programs we analyze are large-scale Fortran programs, made of many procedures with complex interactions, that limitation was too severe. Thus we decided to extend the tool by a very precise interprocedural analysis.

Our software maintenance tool must introduce absolutely no unforeseen changes in programs. Therefore, we have first specified the specializer, then we have proven the correctness of that specification with respect to the standard semantics. [6] details this development process in a general framework. This paper describes how we have specified, implemented, and used interprocedural analysis to improve our tool for a better program understanding. Section 2 explains our interprocedural specialization strategy for Fortran programs. Section 3 gives some definitions and shows which data are needed for the specialization of procedures. Section 4 details the interprocedural specialization process. Section 5 is devoted to the implementation of that interprocedural analysis and section 6 offers conclusions and future work.

2 An Interprocedural Specialization Strategy

Fortran 77 [8] characteristics for interprocedural specialization mainly concern static side-effects. Fortran procedures may be subroutines or functions and parameters are passed by reference. In Fortran, variables are usually local entities. However, variables may be grouped in common blocks (a common block is a contiguous area of memory) and thus shared across procedures. Common blocks may also be inherited in a procedure. They have a scope in that procedure but they have not been declared in it.

If a common block is neither declared in the currently executing procedure nor in any of the procedures in the chain of callers, all of the variables in that common block are undefined. The only exceptions are variables that have been defined in a DATA statement (this statement allows initialization of variables) and never changed. Variables and common blocks may be made remanent by a SAVE statement. It specifies that they retain their values between invocations. Constants may also be defined by a PARAMETER statement (for example, PARAMETER pi=3.1416).

Program specialization processes are based on propagation of static data. As far as we

```
IF ( IREX .NE. 0 ) THEN
    DO 111 I = 1 , IM
        X(I) = XMIN + FLOAT(I-1) * DXLU
111 CONTINUE
    DO 112 I = 1 , IM
        DX(I) = DXLU * I
112 CONTINUE
  ELSE
    READ (NFIC11,*, ERR=1103) X
    DO 121 I = 1 , IM
        DX(I) = X(I+1) - X(I)
121 CONTINUE
  ENDIF
  IF ( IMATSO .EQ. 0 .AND. IC .GE. 0) THEN
    ZERO = 0.
    IF ( IC .EQ. 0 ) THEN
        IREGU = 1
    ELSE IF (IC .GE. IM) THEN
        IREGU = 0
    ENDIF
    IF ( IREX .EQ.2 ) THEN
        READ (NFIC11,'(A)',ERR=5,END=5) L
        IF ( INDEX (L,'I') .NE. 0 ) THEN
            IDECRI = 1
        ENDIF
    ELSE
        IDECRI = 2
    ENDIF
    IF ( IDECRI .EQ. 1 ) THEN
        IF ( IREGU .EQ. 0 ) THEN
            IMIN = 2
            IMAX = IM
        ELSE
            IMIN = IM
            IMAX = IM
        ENDIF
    ELSE IF ( IDECRI .EQ. 2 ) THEN
        IF ( IREGU .EQ. 0 ) THEN
            JMIN = 2
            JMAX = JM
        ELSE
            JMIN = JM
            JMAX = JM
        ENDIF
    ENDIF
  ENDIF
ENDIF
```

Initial code

Constraints on input variables:
```
IREX = 1
IC = 0
IM = 20
DXLU = 0.5
```

Constraints on input variables

```
DO 111 I = 1 , 20
    X(I)= XMIN+ 0.5*FLOAT(I-1)
111 CONTINUE
DO 112 I = 1 , 20
    DX(I) = 0.5*I
112 CONTINUE
  IF ( IMATSO .EQ. 0 ) THEN
    ZERO = 0
    IREGU = 1
    IDECRI = 2
    JMIN = JM
    JMAX = JM
  ENDIF
```

Specialized code

Fig. 2. An example of code specialization (without interprocedural analysis)

are concerned, these are variables, parameters or common blocks. Procedure specialization aims at specializing a procedure with respect to static data: static variables (as in specialization of other statements) and also static parameters and static common blocks. The specialization must proceed depth-first to preserve the order of side-effects [2]. This means that a called procedure must be specialized before the statements following its call.

To improve the specialization, specialized procedures and their initial and final static data are kept and reused if necessary. Thus, in a program, when several calls to the same procedure are encountered, at a given call if the set of static data and their values:

• is the *same* as the set of static data (and their values) of a previous call, then the corresponding version is directly reused,

• *strictly includes* in the set of static data (and their values) of a previous call, then the corresponding version is specialized and added to the list of specialized versions. If several versions match, the following selections are successively made: 1) version with the largest set of static data (default strategy), 2) shortest version.

The number of versions of a procedure may theoretically grow exponentially, but our experiments showed that this seldom happens. However, as the number of specialized versions is finite (an option of the specializer enables changing it), if a version must be removed (from the list of versions), either the most restrictive or the most general one is removed. With a general strategy, specialized procedures are more often reused than in the restrictive strategy, but more statements should also be specialized. In a general framework and without any further analysis on the call graph, both strategies are worthwhile, depending on the application to specialize. Thus, an option of the specializer enables changing this strategy and keeping preferably the most general procedures.

A version is characterized by its name, its statements and its initial and final static data. A version name is generated each time a new version is created. The old name is added in the caller as a comment of the call. Fig. 3 (see next page) shows an example of interprocedural specialization. In this figure, ? stands for unknown values of (dynamic) variables.

3 Notations for Specifying Interprocedural Specialization

3.1 Definitions

For a given environment, an expression is static if its subexpressions are all static. The environment is usually a function associating values to variables. For our interprocedural analysis, we need more information than such an environment to take into account side-effects due to parameters and common blocks.

We define in this section some notations, especially set operators, that are useful to specify interprocedural specialization. In these specifications we use maps associating values to identifiers. A map is a finite function. It is represented by a set of pairs of the

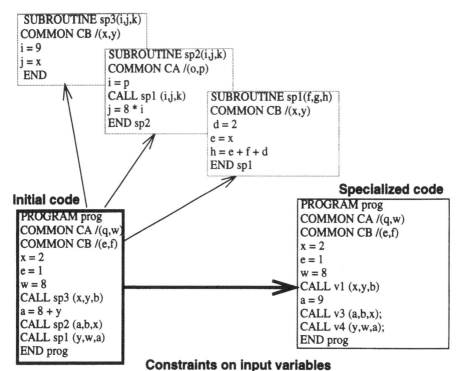

Specialized code

Constraints on input variables

Static Variables: m=2   u=3   v=1   y=5
Common blocks: CA /(q=? , w=8)   CB /(e=1 , f=?)

	Initial static data	Final static data	Version
v1 (sp3)	i=2 j=5 x=1 COMMON CA/ (?,8) COMMON CB/ (1, ?)	i=9 j=1 x=1 COMMON CA/ (?,8) COMMON CB/ (1, ?)	SUBROUTINE v1 (i,j,k) COMMON CB /(x,y) i = 9 j = 1 END v1
v2 (sp1)	f=8 h=9 x=1 COMMONCA/ (?,8) COMMON CB/ (1, ?)	d=2 e=1 f=8 h=11 x=1 COMMON CA/ (?,8) COMMON CB/ (1, ?)	SUBROUTINE v2 (f,g,h) COMMON CB /(x,y) d = 2 e = 1 h = 11 END v2
v3 (sp2)	i=9 k=9 p=8 COMMONCA/ (?,8) COMMON CB/ (1, ?)	i=8 j=64 k=11 p=8 COMMON CA/ (?,8) COMMONCB/ (1, ?)	SUBROUTINE v3(i,j,k) COMMON CA /(o,p) i = 8 CALL v2 (i,j,k) j = 64 END v3
v4 (sp1)	f=1 g=8 h=8 x=1 COMMON CA/ (?,8) COMMON CB/ (1, ?)	d=2 e=1 f=1 g=8 h=4 x=1 COMMON CA/ (?,8) COMMON CB/ (1, ?)	SUBROUTINE v4 (f,g,h) COMMUN CB /(x,y) d = 2 e = 1 h = 4 END v4

Fig. 3. An example of interprocedural specialization

form $x \to y$, where no two pairs have the same first elements. The set of all other possible values is noted *Values*. *Ident* denotes the set of all identifiers. The *Eval* function either yields the value of an expression (if it is static) or gives a residual expression (if it is dynamic).

We introduce a data type constructor named composite type (also called record) and useful set operators, similar to those defined in the formal specification languages B [1] and VDM [10]: mainly domain, $\cup$, override, various forms of restriction, and composition. These operators are written in bold in this paper.

- To create values of a composite type, a "make" function is used, called *mk-T* $(x_1, x_2, ...)$, where the x_i are the appropriate values for the fields and the result is a value of type *T*.

- To access fields of a composite type T, we use the record notation (for instance $T.x_i$).

- The domain (*dom*) operator applies to a map. It yields the set of the first elements of the pairs in the map.

- The union operator $\cup$ is defined only on two maps whose domains are disjoint. Thus it yields a map which contains all pairs of the maps.

- The map override operator $\dagger$ whose operands are two maps, yields a map which contains all of the pairs from the second map and those pairs of the first map whose first elements are not in the domain of the second map.

- The map restriction operator $\triangleleft$ (resp. $\triangleright$) is defined with a first operand which is a set (resp. a map) and a second operand which is a map (resp. a set); the result is all of those pairs in the map whose first (resp. second) elements are in the set.

- When applied to a set and a map, the map deletion operator $\blacktriangleleft$ (resp. $\blacktriangleright$) yields those pairs in the map whose first (resp. second) elements are not in the set.

- The forward composition $r \,; p$ of two maps r and p is the map made of pairs $x \to z$ where there exists some y such that $x \to y \in r$ and $y \to z \in p$.

- Given two maps m, n and a set of pairs of maps s we define *Corres* (m,n) and *GalCorres* (s) such that: *Corres* $(m,n) = m^{-1} \,; n$ and *GalCorres* $(m) = \cup \{Corres\ (x,y) \mid x \to y \in m\}$. *Corres* and *GalCorres* are relations (not necessary maps) but in this paper we use them only in contexts where they are maps. *GalCorres* (m) is only applied to maps *Corres* (x,y) with pairwise disjoint domains.

The two following examples show how both relations are used in the framework of an interprocedural analysis.

Ex1. Let *Formal* = $\{1 \to a,\ 2 \to b\}$ and *LParam* = $\{1 \to x+y,\ 2 \to 27\}$. Then, *Corres* (*Formal*, *LParam*) = *Formal* $^{-1}$; *LParam* = $\{a \to x+y,\ b \to 27\}$. $\qquad \square$

Ex2. Let *ComDecl* = $\{A \to \{1 \to e,\ 2 \to f\},\ D \to \{1 \to l,\ 2 \to m\}\}$ and *ComVal* = $\{A \to \{1 \to 2,\ 2 \to 4\},\ B \to \{1 \to 8,\ 2 \to 1\},\ D \to \{1 \to 5,\ 2 \to 7\}\}$. Then, *Corres* (*ComDecl*, *ComVal*) = *ComDecl* $^{-1}$; *ComVal* = $\{\{1 \to e, 2 \to f\} \to \{1 \to 2,\ 2 \to 4\},$ $\{1 \to l,\ 2 \to m\} \to \{1 \to 5,\ 2 \to 7\}\}$ and *GalCorres* (*ComDecl* $^{-1}$; *ComVal*) = *Corres* ($\{1 \to e, 2 \to f\},\ \{1 \to 2,\ 2 \to 4\}$) $\cup$ *Corres* ($\{1 \to l,\ 2 \to m\},\ \{1 \to 5,\ 2 \to 7\}$) =

$\{e \rightarrow 2, f \rightarrow 4, l \rightarrow 5, m \rightarrow 7\}$. □

3.2 Propagated Data

During interprocedural specialization, data are propagated through statements in order to simplify them. They mainly store definitions of Fortran objects (formal parameters, common blocks, etc.) and relations between variables and values. The values are related to a program point. First, this section details these data. Then, it specifies how they are modified during the specialization of procedures.

Information associated to the current program point consist of:

- an environment (*Env*) providing information that do not change in the program. These are:

  - formal parameters. They are represented by a map *Formal* from integers (the positions in the list of formal parameters) to the names of the corresponding formal parameters. For instance, the map corresponding to the declaration SUBROUTINE SP(a,b,c) is $\{1 \rightarrow a, 2 \rightarrow b, 3 \rightarrow c\}$.

  - declared common blocks. They are similarly represented by a map *ComDecl* from common block names to the maps of their variable names. For instance, the map corresponding to the declarations COMMON A/e,f and COMMON D/l,m is the following map: $\{A \rightarrow \{1 \rightarrow e, 2 \rightarrow f\}, D \rightarrow \{1 \rightarrow l, 2 \rightarrow m\}\}$. The order of variable names associated to common blocks must be kept in the map because of the correspondence between the variables of a common block: the variable names of a same common block may vary from a procedure to another, and their values are passed solely thanks to the position of the variable in the declaration of the common block.

  - saved data. They are represented by a set *SavData* of variables and common block names that have become remanent after a SAVE statement. For instance, the set corresponding to both statements SAVE COMMON A and SAVE X,Y is $\{A, X, Y\}$.

  - initialized data. These are variables defined in a DATA statement and constants defined in a PARAMETER statement. They are represented by a map *InitData* from their names to their initialized values.

  - statements of the program (*Stmts*).

- a state (*State*) representing relations between variables and values. The type of *State* is the composite type *TState* which fields *SV* and *ComVal* are:

  - the mapping (*SV*) from Static variables to their current Values. If interprocedural analysis would not have been performed, only this map would have been used to specialize programs, as it was done in [5].

  - the mapping (*ComVal*) between common block names and the values of their static variables. For instance, in the map $ComVal = \{A \rightarrow \{3 \rightarrow 2\}\}$ the common named *A* is such that its third variable evaluates to 2 and its other variables are dynamic.

• the mapping (*Called*) between names of called procedures and pairs. Such a pair consists of:

  • the environment (*EnvCalled*) of the called procedure,

  • the specialized versions (*Versions*) of the called procedure. This is a set made of quadruples (*Name, Input, Output, V*), where the data type of *Input* and *Output* is *TState*, *V* denotes the whole specialized procedure and *Name* denotes the name of the procedure *V*. The **add** primitive adds a quadruple to a set of versions.

• the inherited common blocks of the current procedure *P*. They are represented by a set *ComInh* of common block names that are declared in one of the procedures of the chain of callers, but not in *P*.

4 Interprocedural Specialization

Our specializer performs two main tasks: data propagation through the code and simplification of statements. Both tasks are detailed in [4] In this section, we specify the propagation through a call-statement and the simplification of a call-statement.

4.1 The Propagation Process

While encoutering a call-statement, the propagation process propagates first the current state of the caller through the called procedure. Then, a most specialized version is selected, yielding an updated state. Last, the code generation process is returned to the calling procedure and the updated state is propagated through the caller, because of side-effects.

In the rest of this paper, *EnvSP* denotes the environment of the current called procedure, that is *EnvSP* Δ *Called(SP).EnvCalled*. During the propagation through the called procedure formal parameters, local variables and common blocks of the called procedure *SP* modifiy the current state:

• If a local variable *V* is initialized in *SP* by a value, this value becomes the new value of *V* whether *V* had a value in the static variables *State.SV* or not. Thus, *State.SV* becomes *State.SV † EnvSP.InitData*.

• Due to correspondences between actual and formal parameters and also between variables of same common blocks, formal parameters and variables of declared common blocks may become static. In this case, they are added in the current state. Thus, the forward propagation updates the current state in the following way. *State.SV* becomes *Input*, with:

$$Input \; \Delta \; (State.SV \; † \; EnvSP. \; InitData) \cup (StaticFormal \; † \; StaticCom)$$

The definitions of *StaticFormal* and *StaticCom* are explained below. As formal (resp. actual) parameters are specified by the map *Formal* (resp. *LParam*) from integers (the ranks of parameters in the list) to the names of parameters, the link between these formal and actual parameters is specified by the map *Corres* (*EnvSP.Formal, LParam*) (see Ex.1 for an example of such a map). Furthermore, only static actual parameters give values to their corresponding static formal parameters. Thus, these static formal parameters are:

$$StaticFormal \, \Delta \, [Corres \, (EnvSP.Formal, LParam) \, ; \, eval \, (State.SV)] \, \triangleright \, Values,$$

where $Corres \, (EnvSP.Formal, LParam) \, ; \, eval \, (State.SV)$ evaluates actual parameters that are expressions, and $\triangleright \, Values$ restricts this result to static formal parameters.

Given a common block C that is declared or inherited in the caller, if V is the n'th variable of C, then its corresponding variable V' in a called procedure SP is the n'th variable of C. If C is declared between the caller and SP (in the chain of callers), the names of V and V' may differ, but these variables share common values. For instance, at the program point call $SP(LParam)$, the value of V is the initial value of V'. Thus, if V is static, then at the entry point of SP, V' is initially static (with the same value of V'). This transmission of values from common blocks of the caller to corresponding common blocks of the called procedure is specified by the map $GalCorres \, (EnvSP.ComDecl^{-1} \, ; \, State.ComVal) \, \triangleright \, Values$.

$$StaticCom1 \, \Delta \, GalCorres \, (EnvSP.ComDecl^{-1} \, ; \, State.ComVal)$$

Ex.3. If the called procedure SP is such as $State.SV = \{i \rightarrow 5, \, j \rightarrow 3, \, a \rightarrow 1\}$ with the following declarations (without initialized data) COMMON A/e, f, g and COMMON D/ 1, m, then $EnvSP.ComDecl = \{A \rightarrow \{1 \rightarrow e, \, 2 \rightarrow f, 3 \rightarrow g\}, \, D \rightarrow \{1 \rightarrow l, \, 2 \rightarrow m\}\}$. If for instance $ComVal = \{A \rightarrow \{1 \rightarrow 2, 2 \rightarrow 4\}, \, B \rightarrow \{2 \rightarrow 1\}, \, D \rightarrow \{1 \rightarrow 5\}\}$, then (from Ex.2) $GalCorres \, (EnvSP.ComDecl^{-1} \, ; \, ComVal) \, \triangleright \, Values \, = \{e \rightarrow 2, f \rightarrow 4, l \rightarrow 5\}$. Thus, $State.SV$ becomes $\{e \rightarrow 2, f \rightarrow 4, l \rightarrow 5, i \rightarrow 5, j \rightarrow 3, a \rightarrow 1, b \rightarrow 3\}$. End of Ex.3 □

Last, common blocks that have a scope in the caller are either declared or inherited in the caller. These are $dom \, (Env.ComDecl) \cup ComInh$. They are inherited by the called procedure SP except if they are re-declared in this procedure. Thus, these common blocks are $ComInh' \, \Delta \, dom \, (Env.ComDecl) \cup ComInh - dom \, (EnvSP.ComDecl)$.

The fields of the state ($State1$) resulting from the propagation through the called procedure are $Input$ and $StaticCom1$, that is $State1 \, \Delta \, mk\text{-}TState \, (Input, StaticCom1)$. After this first propagation, $State1$ and the environment $EnvSP$ of the called procedure are propagated through the statements of the called procedure, yielding a state $State2$ (propagation rule). Then, the propagation through the caller is performed.

As in the propagation through the called procedure, actual parameters, local variables and common blocks of the caller may become static and modify the current state $State2$. In $State2$, the new values of the actual parameters (resp. common blocks) become $StaticActual$ (resp. $StaticCom2$) whether they had a value in the state or not. Thus, $State2.SV$ becomes $State2.SV \, \dagger \, StaticActual \, \dagger \, StaticCom$. This map is restricted to remanent variables: data saved in the called procedure are removed from the current state. Thus, the final state is:

SV' Δ *EnvSP.SavData* $\triangleleft$ *(State2.SV* † *StaticActual* † *StaticCom2).*

The definitions of *StaticActual* and *StaticCom2* are given below. In the called procedure, if a formal parameter is:

• dynamic, then in the state its corresponding actual parameter is suppressed from the static data,

• static, then its value becomes the new value of the corresponding actual parameter, whatever its previous value was.

Corres (LParam, Formal); *eval (State2.SV)* $\triangleright$ *Values* maps actual parameters to the values of their corresponding static formal parameters, as in the definition of *StaticFormal*. As expressions are not handled in static variables maps even if they are static, this map is restricted to identified actual parameters (information such as *x+y* evaluates to *3* are lost). Thus, the static actual parameters are:

StaticActual Δ *ident* $\triangleleft$ *(SV* † *(Corres (LParam, Formal)* ; *eval (State2.SV)* $\triangleright$ *Values)).*

In the caller, the values of some static variables of common blocks are updated in a similar way. These are variables whose value is given by the map *State2.Common*. Thus, in the caller the static variables of common blocks are:

StaticCom2 Δ *GalCorres (Env.ComDecl^{-1}* ; *State2.ComVal).*

Last, in the called procedure, remanent common blocks (*RemCom*) have became remanent by a SAVE statement of the called procedure (they belong to *EnvSP.SavData*), or they exist in the called procedure (either they have been declared in it or they have been inherited from the caller). Thus:

RemCom Δ *dom (EnvSP.ComDecl)* $\cup$ *ComInh'* $\cup$ *EnvSP.SavData.*

State2.ComVal maps static variables of common blocks to their corresponding values. These are common blocks of the caller if remanent common blocks of the called procedure have been removed from the map. Thus, *Env.ComVal* becomes *ComVal'* with *ComVal'* Δ *RemCom* $\triangleleft$ *State2.ComVal.*

The fields of the final state *State'* are *SV'* and *ComVal*, that is *State'* Δ *mk-TState (SV'*, *ComVal').*

Fig. 4. (see next page) recalls whole definitions and the corresponding propagation rule explained in this section. While implementing such rules, variables should be replaced in the rules by their definition.

4.2 Simplification

Recall the interprocedural specialization strategy: while simplifying a call-statement, the specializer checks first whether the called procedure has been specialized in a similar context (that is with the same or less restrictive static data) before. Three situations may happen. They correspond to the three rules of Fig. 5. and are:

• the called procedure *SP* has already been specialized into *V* with the same static data

---

Definitions

$EnvSP \triangle Called(SP).EnvCalled$

Caller → called propagation

$StaticFormal \triangle Corres (EnvSP.Formal, LParam) \,\overset{\bullet}{,}\, eval (State.SV) \triangleright Values$

$StaticCom1 \triangle GalCorres (EnvSP.ComDecl^{-1} ; State.ComVal)$

$Input \triangle (State.SV \dagger EnvSP. InitData) \cup (StaticFormal \dagger StaticCom1)$

$ComInh' \triangle dom (Env.ComDecl) \cup ComInh - dom (EnvSP.ComDecl)$

$State1 \triangle mk\text{-}TState (Input, StaticCom1)$

Called → caller propagation

$StaticActual \triangle ident \triangleleft [Corres (LParam, EnvSP.Formal); eval (State2.SV)] \triangleright Values$

$StaticCom2 \triangle GalCorres (Env.ComDecl^{-1} ; State2.ComVal)$

$SV' \triangle EnvSP.SavData \triangleleft (State2.SV \dagger StaticActual \dagger StaticCom2)$

$RemCom \triangle dom (EnvSP.ComDecl) \cup ComInh' \cup EnvSP.SavData$

$ComVal' \triangle RemCom \triangleleft State2.ComVal$

$State' \triangle mk\text{-}TState (SV', ComVal')$

Propagation rule

$$EnvSP.Env, State1, ComInh', Called \vdash EnvSP.Stmts : State2$$

$$Env, State, ComInh, Called \vdash \textbf{call } SP (LParam) : State'$$

Fig. 4. Propagation of call-statements

(*Input*). Thus, V becomes the specialized procedure of the subject procedure SP (first rule).

• the procedure is not as specialized as wanted (second rule). For instance the last parameter of the procedure to specialize is static, but the last parameter of the most specialized version is dynamic. Then, one of the most specialized versions (*Version*) and its output static data (*Output*) are selected among the versions such that the cardinal of their input static data is the biggest. Note that its static variables and parameters are strictly included in those of the subject procedure, and its common blocks, that have also a scope in the subject procedure, are such that each of their static variables has the same value in both common blocks. Thus, *Version* and *Output* are:

$$Version, Output \Delta \text{ any } V, O \text{ such that } (N, In, O, V) \in Called(SP).Versions \wedge$$
$$Input \subset In \wedge (\nexists (N', J, O, V') \in Called(SP).Versions \text{ such that } Input \subset J \subseteq In)$$

The selected procedure is then specialized (as in the following situation) and the name of the specialized procedure (*NewName*) is selected among the set **NAME** of possible names, that have not been already selected as procedure names.

• the called procedure has not been specialized. A residual procedure is specialized from it, a new name is computed and the current state is modified by the results of the propagation (third rule).

5 Implementation

We have implemented our specification rules as such in our tool where B and VDM operators have been translated into Prolog. This process is the same as those followed in [5] and [13]. The tool is fully automated. A debugger enables apply the rules to be applied step by step. This is useful while trying to understand the behavior of a residual program. For instance, with such a debugger, the user may know at any program point the static values and then understand either why a then-branch of an alternative has been removed and not the else-branch, as he would have thought, or why a function does not yields the expected result.

We have used natural semantics to write our specification rules. Natural semantics gives a formalism to write inference rules, but it does not provide any formalism to describe (and decompose) the environments appearing in the rules. Without interprocedural analysis, such an environment was a single SV-like map. This map was thus a variable in the inference rules. But with an interprocedural analysis, given the environments we propagate, we can not afford to show to the user all the environment variables appearing in the rules.

Environments are pretty-printed in a user-friendly style (which is close to Fortran). Instead of showing directly the mathematical variables that are used in environments, only information that are relevant for the user (e.g. information related to common blocks) are visualized. For instance COMMON A / e = 2, f = u is pretty-printed instead of $Env.ComDecl = \{A \rightarrow \{1 \rightarrow e, 2 \rightarrow f\}\}$, $State.ComVal = \{A \rightarrow \{1 \rightarrow 2, 2 \rightarrow u\}\}$.

6 Conclusion

We have explained how to extend by interprocedural analysis our program specialization technique for program understanding. That analysis is especially difficult in Fortran, due to the lack of well defined interprocedural mechanisms and the complexity of visibility rules. Therefore we have designed these extensions very carefully, starting with a formal specification of the information to be computed. These

---

Definitions

Version, Output Δ any *V, O* such that $(N, In, O, V) \in$ *Called(SP).Versions* $\wedge$

$Input \subset In \wedge \nexists(N', J, O, V') \in$ *Called(SP).Versions* such that $Input \subset J \subset In)$

SelectedNames Δ $\{N \mid (N, I, O, V) \in$ **ran** *(Called).Versions*$\}$

Simplification rules

Rule 1: the called pocedure has already been specialized with the same static data

$$(Name, State1.SV, Out, V) \in \text{Called(SP).Versions}$$

Propagation

$$EnvSP, Output, ComInh', Called \vdash V : State2$$

$$\overline{} \quad (1)$$

$$Env, State, ComInh, Called \vdash \textbf{call } SP (LParam) \rightarrow \textbf{call } NewName (LParam)$$

Rule 2: the called procedure is not as specialized as wanted

$$\{(Name, In, Out, V) \in \text{Called(SP).Versions} \mid State1.SV \subseteq In\} \neq \varnothing$$

$$EnvSP, Output, ComInh', Called \vdash Version \rightarrow SP'$$

Propagation

$$EnvSP, Output, ComInh', Called \vdash SP' : State2$$

$$\textbf{add }((NewName, State.Variables, State2.Variables, SP'), Called(SP).Versions)$$

$$NewName \in \textbf{NAME} - SelectedNames$$

$$\overline{} \quad (2)$$

$$Env, State, ComInh, Called \vdash \textbf{call } SP (LParam) \rightarrow \textbf{call } NewName (LParam)$$

Rule 3: the called procedure has not been specialized

$$\{(Name, In, Out, V) \in \text{Called(SP).Versions} \mid State1.SV \subseteq In\} = \varnothing$$

$$EnvSP, State1, ComInh', Called \vdash EnvSP.Stmts \rightarrow SP'$$

Propagation

$$EnvSP, State1, ComInh', Called \vdash SP' : State2$$

$$\textbf{add }((NewName, State.Variables, State2.Variables, SP'), Called(SP).Versions)$$

$$NewName \in \textbf{NAME} - SelectedNames$$

$$\overline{} \quad (3)$$

$$Env, State, ComInh, Called \vdash \textbf{call } SP (LParam) \rightarrow \textbf{call } NewName (LParam)$$

Fig. 5. Simplification of call-statements

extensions are now integrated in our tool and they allow us to specialize complex programs with much greater precision than previously. Information is propagated along procedure calls, and specialized versions of the called procedures are proposed to the maintainer.

The first experiments with these extensions have given very satisfactory results. Some improvements are now under consideration. For instance a good strategy for reuse of procedure specializations must be developed. Furthermore, the information we compute for interprocedural specialization are of great interest by themselves, in the program comprehension process, independently of its particular use in specialization. Therefore we develop ways to show it in a user-friendly shape.

References

1.   J.R.Abrial *The B method* CNAM lecture notes, 1994

2.   L.O.Andersen *Program analysis and specialization for the C programming language* Ph.D.Thesis, Univ. of Copenhagen, Denmark, DIKU rep. 94/19, 1994.

3.   R.Baier, R.Glück, R.Zöchling Partial evaluation of numerical programs in Fortran ACM SIGPLAN Workshop PEPM, Melbourne, 1994, 119-132.

4.   S.Blazy, P.Facon *Partial evaluation as an aid to the comprehension of Fortran programs* 2nd IEEE Workshop on Program Comprehension, Capri, Italy, July 1993, 46-54.

5.   S.Blazy, P.Facon *SFAC: a tool for program comprehension by specialization* 3rd IEEE Workshop on Program Comprehension, Washington D.C., November 1994, 162-167.

6.   S.Blazy, P.Facon *Formal specification and prototyping of a program specializer* TAPSOFT'95, Aarhus, Denmark, May 1995, LNCS 915, 666-680.

7.   Coen-Porisini, F.De Paoli, C.Ghezzi, D.Mandrioli *Software specializaton via symbolic execution* IEEE Trans. on Soft. Engineering, 17(9), 1991, 884-899.

8.   *FORTRAN.* ANSI standard X3.9, 1978.

9.   M.Haziza, J.F.Voidrot, E.Minor, L.Pofelski, S.Blazy *Software maintenance: an analysis of industrial needs and constraints* IEEE Conf. on Soft. Maintenance, Orlando, 11/1992.

10.   C.B.Jones *Systematic development using VDM* 2nd eds., Prentice-Hall, 1990.

11.   N.D.Jones, C.K.Gomard, P.Sestoft *Partial evaluation and automatic program generation* Prentice-Hall, 1993.

12.   G.Kahn, *Natural semantics* Proc. of STACS'87, LNCS, vol.247, March 1987.

13.   H.Parisot, F.Paumier *Aide à la compréhension et à la maintenance du logiciel: calculs inter-procéduraux pour la maintenance de programmes* MSc. thesis, IIE-CNAM, 06/95.

14.   S.Tilley, K.Wong, M.A.Storey, H.Müller *Programmable reverse engineering* Int. Journal of Soft.Eng.&Knowledge Eng., 4(4), December 1994, 501-520.

15.   H.J.Van Zuylen *Understanding in reverse engineering.* REDO handbook, Wiley, 09/92.

16.   G.A.Venkatesh *The semantic approach to program slicing* Proc. ACM SIGPLAN Conf. on Programming Languages Design and Implementation, Toronto, Canada, 1991, ACM SIGPLAN Notices, 26(6), 107-119.

17.   A.Von Maryhauser, A.M.Vans *Dynamic code cognition behaviors for large scale code* 3rd IEEE Workshop on Program Comprehension, Washington D.C., November 1994, 74-81.

18.   M.Weiser *Program slicing* IEEE Trans. on Soft. Engineering, 10(4), 352-357, 1984.

19.   N.Wilde, M.C.Scully *Software reconnaissance: mapping program features to code* Software maintenance research and practice, vol.7, 1995, 49-62.

Practical Aspects of Specialization of Algol-like Programs

Mikhail A. Bulyonkov and Dmitry V. Kochetov

Institute of Informatics Systems, Novosibirsk, Russia

Abstract. A "linearized" scheme of polyvariant specialization for imperative languages is described in the paper. The scheme is intended for increasing efficiency of specialization. Main properties of the scheme are linear generation of residual code and single memory shared by different variants of specialization process. We sketch a new kind of analysis, called *configuration analysis*, which is aimed on reducing memory usage during specialization. To demonstrate the advantages of the proposed scheme we discuss some benchmarks for the *M2Mix* partial evaluator for Modula-2 language.

1 Introduction

As it was mentioned in [12] "The memory requirements for the specializer are at the moment much too high. We have done some work trying to bring it down but there is still a lot that could be done. It seems that these improvements are necessary to make use of the partial evaluator realistic".

To demonstrate the problem let us assume that we specialize an interpreter with respect to a program. Suppose that there is a procedure in the interpreter for interpretation of statements of the source language. When entering the procedure we need to check for different *configurations*, i. e. static memory state in a point of the program being specialized. The number of configurations is obviously the number of statements in the source program, hence it is linear with respect to its size. If we are using a naive approach, we will store all static memory in each configuration, but static memory includes at least the source program representation. So the amount of information to be stored is quadratic with respect to the size of the source program. To make a partial evaluator a useful instrument we should seek for a "more linear" memory requirements.

The process of specialization has very much in common with processes of interpretation and compilation. The transformation performed by specialization to a large degree consists of these processes: when a specializer is designed as a meta-interpreter, it contains a usual interpreter as its part, and for certain input data a specializer functions like a compiler. But the internal behavior of a specializer is different from that of a traditional compiler.

To increase the efficiency of specialization we need to explicate similarity of these processes in a specialization scheme. From our point of view such an explication with respect to compilation means linear generation of residual code which is similar to linear generation of object code. Under the condition we will not need to keep generated parts of the residual program in the memory, and hopefully we will be able to process programs of realistic size. The similarity with interpretation could lie in the usage of a single memory rather than a number of memory instances generated for different variants of specialization process.

The scheme described below has been developed in the course of two projects: partial evaluator for model *MixLan* language, and ongoing *M2Mix* project — a specializer for Modula-2.

2 Specialization Scheme

Our intention is to have a single shared memory and store additionally only differences between variants which are necessary for switching from one variant to another. In order to provide this, we should put some restrictions on the non-determinism of polyvariant specialization. For example, if we start to construct a specialized procedure body as soon as we meet a call to be specialized, the strategy of memoization will be different from that in the case when we postpone residual procedure construction and proceed with the next statement. In fact, we do not argue that the particular scheme described in the paper is the most efficient, but that reasoning on differences between variants makes sense only if the order of processing is specified.

We presume the binding time analysis to have been done, and since dynamic memory is out of interest in this section we will use the term "memory state" instead of "static memory state".

2.1 Specialization of Sequence

Given a sequence of statements $S_1, \ldots, S_n$ and initial memory state M, we start with processing the statement S_1 on the memory state M. The statement under consideration is not necessarily a simple statement — it could be e. g. a conditional or a while loop. Generally, processing of the first statement can produce a set of different memory states $M_2^1, M_2^2, \ldots$. Next we will process the second statement S_2 on *all* M_2^i, obtaining a set of memory states $M_3^1, M_3^2, \ldots$ as a result. So the main step of the scheme consists in the processing of a statement on a set of memory states as it is shown in Fig. 1.

Given:
   set of memory states $M_i = \{M_i^1, M_i^2, \ldots\}$
   a statement S_i
   $M_{i+1} := 0$
   for each $m \in M_i$ do
      process S_i on m resulting new memory states $\{m_1', \ldots, m_n'\}$
      $M_{i+1} := M_{i+1} \cup \{m_1', \ldots, m_n'\}$
   od.

Fig. 1. Step of sequence specialization

Following this scheme memory overhead is limited mainly by sets of input and output memory states for *one statement*: in most cases we can discard all information about a set of input memory states as soon as we have completed processing of the corresponding statement.

Linear traverse of program resembles the *monovariant* scheme (which was called *strict* in [7]) with the difference that each statement is processed many times before processing of the next one. It allows to append generated pieces of a code to residual program immediately. This is a basis for "linear" code generation.

Improvement of the algorithm is based on the observation that we can *statically* determine potential difference between memory states produced by processing of the current statement. Consider the following sequence of statements:

```
m := 1;
if d then k := k*2 else k := k+2;
m := m+k; k := 2;
```

(Here and further on we will assume that variables k, l, m and n are static, and all others are dynamic. Also since we concentrate on the static actions, we do not show dynamic "decorations" which can appear at any place). Obviously, the first statement in the example always produces a single memory state. The second statement can produce at most two memory states, but we can be sure that they will differ only in (the value of) variable k. When the third statement is processed on a given memory state it produces a single memory state. However, since the statement will potentially be processed on two memory states differing in the variable k the resulting memory states will potentially differ in variables k and m. Finally after execution of the fourth statement only variable m can vary.

Let $Stat$, Var, and Val denote the sets of statements, variables, and values respectively. Formally, we can define function

$$\delta : Stat \longrightarrow (2^{Var} \longrightarrow 2^{Var})$$

where $x \in \delta[S]v$ means that variation of values of variables from $v \subseteq Var$ *before* processing of S implies that x can potentially have different values *after* processing of S. This function allows to annotate statements in a sequence as follows:

$$\Delta[S_1] = \emptyset$$
$$\Delta[S_{i+1}] = \delta[S_i]\Delta[S_i]$$

$\Delta[S_i]$ is a set of variables which can have different values *before* processing of S_i in the course of specialization of sequence $S_1; \ldots; S_n$. For the above sequence we have

$$\Delta[\![m := 1]\!] = \emptyset$$
$$\Delta[\![if\ d\ then\ k:=k*2\ else\ k:=k+2]\!] = \emptyset$$
$$\Delta[\![m:=m+k]\!] = \{k\}$$
$$\Delta[\![k:=2]\!] = \{m,k\}$$

Since values of variables from $\Delta[S]$ can vary before repetitive execution of S, at least these values need to be stored in input memory states for S. However restoring values of variables from $\Delta[S]$ is not sufficient for switching to the next memory state after processing of the previous one: before each but the first iteration of processing of S it is necessary to restore results $\rho[S]$ of statement S. For example, m:=m+k changes the value of m, and hence the value must be restored. On the other hand restoring all the results of S is redundant: it is sufficient to restore only those results of S_i which are at the same time its arguments, $\alpha[S]$. For example, in the following sequence

```
if d then k := k*2 else k := k+2;
l := 2;
m := m+k;
```

l is not an argument of the second statement and so it need not be restored. But m is an argument of the third statement and its value must be restored before each iteration.

Furthermore, a part of the results of a statement S possibly belongs to $\Delta[S]$ and will be restored anyway. Therefore, the set we are looking for is

$$\Gamma[S] = (\rho[S] \cap \alpha[S]) \setminus \Delta[S]$$

Let us define "store" and "restore" operations more formally. Let $Domain(f)$ denote the domain of function f. The "store" operation coincides with the functional operator $|$ of narrowing of function domain:

$$(m|D)(x) = \begin{cases} m(x) & \text{if } x \in D \\ \text{undefined} & \text{otherwise.} \end{cases}$$

The "restore" operation coincides with the functional operator $\oplus$ of union of function domains:

$$(m_1 \oplus m_2)(x) = \begin{cases} m_2(x) \text{ if } m_2(x) \text{ is defined} \\ m_1(x) \text{ otherwise.} \end{cases}$$

From this point we will use a *single* global memory M shared by variants of execution and a set of input memory states will represent differences of variants with respect to M. Now we can define more precisely the main step of the scheme (see Fig 2).

2.2   Specialization of Block Statement

Let us extend the language by block statements. By definition, the Δ-annotation of the first statement in any sequence is *always* empty. It means that each iteration in specialization of a block statement on a set of input memory states consists of two actions. First we restore the current memory state, and then we recursively apply the procedure for specialization of a sequence of statements to the body of the block on the *single* memory state. For example, consider the fragment

---

Given:
memory $M : Var \rightarrow Val$
set of memory states $M_i = \{M_i^1, M_i^2, ...\}$
where $Domain(M_i^j) = \Delta[S_i]$
$M_{i+1} := \emptyset$
$\gamma := M|\Gamma[S_i]$
for each $m \in M_i$ do
  $M := M \oplus m$
  process S_i on M resulting new memory states $\{m'_1, \ldots, m'_n\}$
  $M_{i+1} := M_{i+1} \cup \{m'_1|\Delta[S_{i+1}], \ldots\}$
  $M := M \oplus \gamma$
od.

Fig. 2. Step of sequence specialization using a single memory

```
if d then k := k*2 else k := k+2;
begin
  l := l+k; m := l+2
end;
m := 1;
```

with the following annotation

$$\begin{aligned}
\Delta[\texttt{l:=l+k}] &= \emptyset \\
\Delta[\texttt{m:=l+2}] &= \emptyset \\
\Delta[\texttt{begin l:=l+k; m:=l+2 end}] &= \{k\} \\
\Delta[\texttt{m:=1}] &= \{k, l, m\}
\end{aligned}$$

Had we "unfold" the block, we would be forced to store the various values of l and k before processing of m:=l+2. For the variables which differ after specialization of block $B = \texttt{begin } S_1 \ldots S_n \texttt{ end}$ we have

$$\delta[B]v = \delta[S_n] \ldots \delta[S_1]\, v.$$

If blocks in source language serve also for declaration of local variables, they could be very helpful for a better solution of configuration analysis, since obviously local variables do not appear in configurations outside their scope of declaration. In the following fragment

```
begin
  var k,l;
  begin
    var m;
    if d then m := 1 else m := 2;
    k := m;
  end;
  l := k
end;
```

we have that

$$\Delta[\![\texttt{k:=m}]\!] = \{\texttt{m}\}$$
$$\Delta[\![\texttt{l:=k}]\!] = \{\texttt{k}\}$$

If the inner block were unfolded resulting the statement

```
begin
  var k,l,m;
  if d then m := 1 else m := 2;
  k := m;
  l := k
end;
```

we would have that

$$\Delta[\![\texttt{l:=k}]\!] = \{\texttt{k,m}\}$$

which implies that we need to store values of m before processing of l:=k, even if m is dead at this point. Our experience has shown that in many cases the problem of *dead variables* [11] could be avoided if it were possible to localize dead variables.

2.3 Specialization Points and Configurations

Essentially, the main idea behind block specialization is that specialization of a sequence splitted into blocks may be performed more efficiently then in the case of an unstructured sequence. This is the case when specialization of all statements in a subsequence (except for the last statement) does not lead to several memory states, i. e. for all S

$$\delta[\![S]\!]\emptyset = \emptyset$$

Such splitting can be performed on pre-processing phase. In the following example

```
m := 1;
if d then k := k*2 else k := k+2;
m := m+k; k := 2;
```

the appropriate splitting would look like

```
begin
  m := 1;
  if d then k := k*2 else k:=k+2
end;
begin
  m:=m+k;
  k:=2
end;
```

This transformation can be considered as an imperative analogue of call un-folding analysis in the context of functional languages. The splitting points in a sequence are called *specialization points*, also by analogy with terminology used in specialization of functional languages [10].

Now we can return to specialization of sequences. Let us identify a special-ization point with a statement following the *generating statement S* such that $\delta[S]\emptyset \neq \emptyset$: only processing of generating statements originates several variants. All other statements being processed on a memory variant produce at most one output memory variant. Therefore it is sufficient to keep track of variants at specialization points only. At any specialization point SP corresponding memory instance can be reconstructed from the values of variables from $\Delta[SP]$. We call a pair consisting of specialization point SP and a set of values of variables from $\Delta[SP]$ a *configuration*. $\Delta[SP]$ is called *the set of configurational variables* of the specialization point SP.

2.4 Conditional Statements

Specialization of conditional statement with static test is trivial — it reduces to the specialization of the corresponding branch. For conditional such as $S =$ if E then S_1 else S_2, where E is static, we have[1],

$$\delta[S]v = \begin{cases} v \cup \rho[S_1] \cup \rho[S_2] \text{ if } \alpha[E] \cap v \neq \emptyset \\ \delta[S_1]v \cup \delta[S_2]v. \end{cases}$$

We assume that in the following discussion all conditional statements have dynamic tests. Consider a fragment:

```
k := 0;
l := 0;
if d then k := k+1
else begin k := k*2; l := 3 end;
```

Here we must process *both* branches of the conditional statement. Each branch must be specialized on the same input memory state. Therefore specializer must restore the value of k (result of the first branch) before specialization of the second one. Resulting states can differ only in results of the statement branches, i. e. for conditional statement with dynamic test

$$\delta[S]v = v \cup \rho[S_1] \cup \rho[S_2].$$

In the above example k and l can vary after specialization. The algorithm for specialization of conditional is given on Fig. 3. Note that the algorithm is not symmetrical. If the size of $\rho[S_2] \cap \alpha[S_1]$ is less than the size of $\rho[S_1] \cap \alpha[S_2]$ then it would be better to start with specialization of the else branch.

---

[1] For the sake of simplicity we assume that E is free of side effects.

Given:

memory state $M : Var \rightarrow Val$

statement $S = $ if E then S_1 else S_2

$\gamma := M|(\rho[S_1] \cap \alpha[S_2])$

process S_1 on M resulting new memory states $M_1 = \{m_1^2, \ldots\}$

$M := M \oplus \gamma$

process S_2 on M resulting new memory states $M_2 = \{m_1^2, \ldots\}$

specialization of the whole conditional results in $M_1 \cup M_2$

Fig. 3. Specialization of conditional

2.5 Labels and goto Statements

Undisciplined usage of goto's actually ruins all our attempts for efficient specialization. So we assume that the source language does not allow such nasty features as jumps into compound statements, or in other words that the scope of a label is limited by the sequence where the label appears.

First of all, we want to distinguish between static and dynamic goto's, i. e. between those which can be performed at specialization time and those which have to be done in residual program. When a goto statement is processed, we attempt to interrupt the specialization of all compound statements containing the statement up to the corresponding label level and continue processing from the sequence starting with the label. If interrupted statements require additional actions to complete their specialization, we have to suspend control transfer, i. e. to declare the goto statement dynamic. Otherwise the statement is static. In the following example

```
  k := 0;
  if d1 then goto lab else k := 2;
 lab:
  d2 := k;
```

goto lab is dynamic because conditional statement needs additional actions to complete specialization — processing of the second branch. Therefore, the sequence itself requires analogous steps. Consider another case:

```
  k := 0;
  if d then k := k-1;
  if k>0 then goto lab;
  .....
 lab:
```

Specialization of the second statement generates two configurations. We cannot execute goto lab in the first configuration — to complete the sequence specialization a specializer has to process the second configuration. Hence goto lab is dynamic,even if it is not explicitly located under dynamic test. On the other hand, in the fragment

```
k := 0;
goto lab;
if d then k := k-1;
lab:
```

we do not need to suspend the goto-statement since at this point only one configuration is possible. Hence we classify the statement as static.

We declare a label lab dynamic if there is a dynamic goto lab statement. Furthermore, this makes all jumps to the label dynamic. We introduce a specialization point for each dynamic label, since a specializer will potentially restart processing of a sequence starting with this label for different configurations coming from different —tt goto's. Specialization of a goto statement adds suspended configuration, as it is shown on Fig. 3.

Given:
   memory state $M : Var \rightarrow Val$
   statement $S = $ goto 1
   result is configuration $(1, M | \Delta[1:])$

Fig. 4. Specialization of goto

After specialization of a sequence we must process all suspended configurations related to the sequence's labels. When no new suspended local configurations appear, we discard all local configurations.

Now we determine the variables which must appear in Δ-annotation of labels and whose values have to be stored in suspended configurations in the case when corresponding label is dynamic. In the following fragment lab is static:

```
if d then k := k+1
else k := 0;
if k=0 then goto lab;
k := 3;
lab:
```

Two configurations will be generated after specialization of the first conditional statement. The fragment starting from the second conditional statement will be processed on both configurations but k:=3 will be executed during only one configuration processing. Therefore k can have different values at the point of label lab and must be included in $\Delta[\text{lab}:]$. In general, for any static label lab, $\Delta[\text{lab}:]$ will contain results of all linear fragments delimited by lab itself and a conditional containing jump to lab whose test values differ on different execution variants.

Consider the fragment with dynamic label lab:

```
1 := 0;
lab:
```

```
begin
  m := l+k;
  if d then k := k+1 else goto lab;
end;
l := k-1;
```

There are two specialization points in this fragment: the one before `begin` and the other after `end`. Specialization of `goto lab` will suspend some configuration which will be processed only after `l:=k-1` statement execution. But to resume processing starting from `lab`, we need the previous value of `l`. Therefore we must store the value of `l` in suspended configuration. The same holds for all results of the subsequence starting from `lab`.

In general in configuration associated with dynamic label located in a sequence S, we must store all results of subsequence starting from the first specialization point in S, or from the first statement in S containing a jump to the label. The reason is that we can not determine in advance the order (in terms of labels) in which suspended configurations will be generated and processed.

Such efficiency loss can be compensated by the method already discussed, namely more adequate structuring of program and localization of control. The following fragment will be specialized more efficiently despite of semantic equivalence to the previous one:

```
l := 0;
begin
  lab:
    m := l+k;
    if d then k := k+1
    else goto lab
end;
l := k-1;
```

Here `l` is not a result of the block containing `lab`, and there is no need to store it in suspended configurations. The example illustrates that localization of labels can considerably decrease the amount of stored information.

2.6 Loops

In *MixLan* project loops are preprocessing phase objects . They are translated into `goto`'s, conditionals and blocks. For example

```
for i := E1 to E2 do S
```

is translated into

```
begin
  var i : integer;
  i:=E1;
  lab:
```

```
        if i<=E2 then begin S; i:=i+1; goto lab end
    end;
```

Therefore specialization of loops is expressed as specialization of goto statements. The outer block is very essential: if lab is dynamic, then only loop results will be stored in suspended configuration. With such a translation we do not loose both precision of configuration analysis and efficiency of specialization process.

2.7 Procedures

A procedure body can be divided into static and dynamic parts. If the dynamic part of a procedure is empty, we perform a call at specialization time. Otherwise procedure is called *dynamic*. Processing of a dynamic procedure call consists in evaluating output memory state(s) and constructing residual version of the procedure. We postpone the construction step until specialization of the block containing the procedure declaration is completed. Since during block specialization we do not need bodies of residual procedures, no memory is wasted to store them. In order to collect all input memory states of dynamic procedure, we associate with such a procedure a specialization point. When specializer encounters a dynamic procedure call, it generates a *procedural configuration*. Configurational variables of the specialization point include static formal parameters of the procedure and those global procedure arguments, which may be modified in the time interval starting from generation of the configuration and ending at the moment when specializer extracts the configuration for processing. In the worst case, we have to store values of variables which are modified either

1. in the subsequence starting from the first specialization point in the block where the procedure is declared, or
2. in the subsequence starting from the first call of the procedure, or
3. in the body of any other dynamic procedure declared in the same block.

Consider the following example:

```
begin
  var k,l,n;
  procedure p(m)
    begin
      l := m+n; d := k
    end;
  k := 0; n := 0;
  p(k);
  k := k+1;
  p(l);
end;
```

Specializer will generate two suspended procedural configurations: both configurations contain values of parameter m and global variable k. Therefore, two residual calls will be constructed: p_k0_m0 and p_k1_m0. Note that we do not store the value of n in the configurations.

Summarizing the above discussion we extend the algorithm of block specialization: block's body specialization accumulates the set of configurations for local procedures; when specialization is complete for each configuration it is necessary to construct residual procedure declaration.

To evaluate the set of output memory states for a procedure call we need to execute static part of the procedure. In the case of recursive procedures it potentially leads to non-termination. We can avoid the problem due to the fact that the set of output memory states depends only on the procedural configuration. For each procedural configuration a set of output memory states is collected and reused when specializer encounters the configuration again. Collecting of the set of output memory states requires a fixed point iteration because we could need the set before execution of the procedure body is completed. For example, in the following fragment

```
begin
  var k;
  procedure p(x)
    begin
      if x then
        begin p(x-1); x := x-k; ... end;
      k := 1
    end;
  k := 2;
  p(y);
  write(k);
end
```

when specializer reaches the call p(y), it constructs residual call of p_k2, and then evaluates the set of possible values of k after the call. At the point of recursive call p(x-1) specializer discovers the same configuration, and it tries to fetch the corresponding set of output memory states which is not evaluated yet.

Let us approach the problem more formally. Specializer maintains mapping of the following type:

$$ProcMap = Cfg \longrightarrow 2^M.$$

Let function

$$\Sigma : Stat \longrightarrow Cfg \longrightarrow ProcMap \longrightarrow ProcMap$$

describe the effect of changing this mapping by processing of statement. In particular, if S is a procedure call then

$$\Sigma[\![p(\ldots)]\!] C \pi = fix \lambda \sigma . \pi \cup \Sigma[\![B]\!] (p, [x_1 \mapsto v_1, \ldots, x_n \mapsto v_n]) \sigma,$$

where B denotes procedure body, $v_1, \ldots, v_n$ are values of configurational variables $x_1, \ldots, x_n$ evaluated on the current configuration C, and operation $\cup$ is defined for functions componentwise. In our example we will obtain that

$$\Sigma[\![p(y)]\!] \, (p, [k \mapsto 2]) \bot = [(p, [k \mapsto 2]) \mapsto \{[k \mapsto 1]\}]$$

The approach significantly complicate processing of recursive procedures and requires some extra memory. Had we made all side effects of recursive procedures dynamic, as proposed in [10], the problem would not arise at all. But in many cases such a simplification is unacceptably conservative.

3   Comparison with other analyses

The central issue of the described specialization scheme is *configuration analysis* that determines specialization points and corresponding configurational variables. Configuration analysis is not the only way to reduce memory requirements and it has certain similarities with other analyses.

Configuration analysis singularity consists in the fact that it reflects nonstandard semantics of programs, the order of statements processing according to a particular specialization scheme[2]. This is the reason why we failed to capture the intuitively clear idea of configurational variables with the help of common mod/ref analysis. Below we show that configuration analysis does not coincide with other analyses which are also aimed on reduction of memory consumption.

3.1   Configuration analysis vs. inductive variables analysis

The first one is the inductive variables analysis. A variable is inductive at some program point if has at most one dependence. The following example shows that non-configurational variable is not necessarily inductive.

```
l := 1;
for i := 1 to 10 do
  begin
    m := i - 2;
    if d then
      begin k := i; l := 2 end
    else k := i-1;
    (**)
    write(k)
  end
```

At the point (**) inductive variable k is the configurational one, inductive variable m is not configurational, and configurational variable l is not inductive.

---

[2] As a matter of fact, the same is true for binding time analysis.

3.2 Configuration analysis vs. dead variables analysis

Let us compare configuration analysis with dead variables analysis. Consider the fragment:

```
begin
  var k,l,m;
  k := 1;
  if d then l := 2
  else m := 2;
  (**)
  k := 2;
  l := k+m
end
```

At the point (**) dead variable k is not configurational, alive variable m is configurational, and configurational variable l is dead. So configuration analysis can not be expressed as a form of dead variables analysis. On the other hand, there is no need to store dead variables in configurations, and the example shows that configurational analysis as described above should be complemented by a sort of dead variables analysis.

4 Benchmarks

We had to focus on memory requirements partly because of rather tough computing environment: IBM PC with 33MHz processor, 1MB of RAM. In the *MixLan* project both interpreter and specializer (realized as meta-interpreter) are implemented in Scheme. All examples in the paper are written in *MixLan*. The *M2Mix* project is implemented for Modula-2 in C. Here we used the method of generating extension which is also generated in Modula-2. The benchmarks discussed below are obtained using *M2Mix*.

The advantages of our approach are based on three factors

1. choice of specialization points,
2. storing in configurations only configurational variables instead of all static memory, and
3. possibility to discard configurations when moving to the next statement in a sequence.

To measure the influence of factors 2 and 3 we switched off corresponding actions in generation extension and added calculations of the size of dynamically allocated/disposed memory. These modifications in no way effected residual programs. The result of experiments for two programs is shown in Table 1.

The first program, Splines, is cubic splines interpolation rewritten from Fortran program provided by R. Glück. The second program, Match, is translation of C program for pattern matching provided by L. O. Andersen. In both cases translation was straightforward.

Table1. Memory requirements

	Splines		Match	
	Discard configurations	Keep configurations	Discard configurations	Keep configurations
Store configurational variables only	156	252	261	707
Store all static memory	2288	3696	493	1450

As one could expect, the smallest figures in both cases correspond to *M2Mix* approach and the largest ones — to the naive strategy, when we store all static data in configurations and keep them until the end of residual program generation. So our approach requires 5.56 times less memory in case of Match program, and 23.7 times less in case of Splines. However the impact of each factor depends on particular program. For the Match program we gained more from reducing sizes of configurations, while for the Splines program discarding of configurations is more important.

As for the quality of residual programs, we are quite satisfied with obtained speed-ups: 3 times and 4.99 times for Splines and Match, resp.

5   Related Works

Many ideas which we realized in these projects are based on the old works of Ershov's group [8, 7, 6]. The works of V. Itkin [9] provided a solid theoretical basis for the foundation of our algorithms. A variety of strategies of mixed computation was proposed by B. Ostrovski [13] for a dialect of Pascal. The idea of linearization of mixed computation first appeared in [4].

The most challenging and stimulating was a breakthrough made by L. O. Andersen in specialization of realistic C programs [2, 10]. In particular, he proposed the method of memorizing procedures side effects. This work re-attracted the interest of PE community to the imperative programming; it was followed by considerable success in specialization of Fortran [5, 3] and object-oriented programs [12].

These works have shown that non-trivial partial evaluation of real-life imperative languages is possible in principal. Our work is an attempt to make it practical.

6   Conclusion

We presented a specialization scheme, which while being truly polyvariant takes care not only about the quality of residual programs, but also about the efficiency of the specialization process itself. We believe that a practical specializer for a language should not impose much more requirements than a compiler and/or an interpreter for the language.

We gave only informal outline of the method: limited size of the paper forced out such important issues as binding time analysis, partially static structures, aliasing, external procedures and data explication. Non-trivial treatment of all these issues is crucial for realization of the scheme.

References

1. Andersen, L.O.: *Partial evaluation of C and automatic compiler generation.* LNCS **641** (1992) 251–257.
2. Andersen, L.O.: *Self-applicable C program specialization.* In Procs. of the Partial Evaluation and Semantics-Based Program Manipulation'92 (1992) 54–61.
3. Baier, R., Glück R., Zöchling, R.: *Partial evaluation of numerical programs in Fortran.* In Procs. of the Partial Evaluation and Semantics-Based Program Manipulation'94 (1994) 119–132.
4. Barzdin, G.Ja., Bulyonkov, M.A.: *Mixed computation and compilation: Linearization and decomposition of a compiler.* Computing Center, Siberian Branch of the USSR Academy of Sciences **Preprint 791** (1988) (In Russian).
5. Blazy, S., Facon, P.: *Partial evaluation for the understanding of Fortran programs.* In Procs. of the Software Engineering and Knowledge Engineering'93 (1993) 517–525.
6. Bulyonkov M.A., Ershov, A.P.: *How do ad-hoc compiler constructs appear in universal mixed computation processes?* In Procs. of the Workshop Partial Evaluation and Mixed Computation (1988) 65–81.
7. Ershov, A.P., Itkin, V.E.: Correctness of mixed computation in Algol-like programs. LNCS **53** (1977) 59–77.
8. Ershov, A.P.: Mixed computation: Potential applications and problems for study. Theor. Comp. Sc. **18** (1982) 41–67.
9. Itkin, V.E.: An algebra and axiomatization system of mixed computation. In Procs. of the Workshop Partial Evaluation and Mixed Computation (1988) 209–224.
10. Jones, N.D., Gomard, C.K., Sestoft, P.: *Partial Evaluation and Automatic Program Generation.* Englewood Cliffs, NJ: Prentice Hall, 1993.
11. Jones, N.D.: Automatic program specialization: A re-examination from basic principles. In Procs. of the Workshop Partial Evaluation and Mixed Computation (1988) 225–282.
12. Marquard, M., Steensgaard, B.: Partial evaluation of an object-oriented imperative language. Master's thesis, DIKU, University of Copenhagen, Denmark, April 1992.
13. Ostrovski, B.N.: *Implementation of controlled mixed computation in system for automatic development of language-oriented parsers.* In Procs. of the Workshop Partial Evaluation and Mixed Computation (1988) 385–403.

Synchronization Analyses for Multiple Recursion Parameters

(Extended Abstract)

Wei-Ngan Chin[1] Siau-Cheng Khoo[1] Peter Thiemann[2]

[1] Dept of Info. Systems & Computer Sc., National University of Singapore,
Singapore 119260

[2] Wilhelm-Schickard-Institut, University of Tuebingen, Germany D-72076

Abstract. Tupling is a transformation tactic to obtain new functions, without redundant calls and/or multiple traversals of common inputs. In [Chi93], we presented an automatic method for tupling functions with a single recursion parameter each.

In this paper, we propose a new family of parameter analyses, called *synchronization analyses,* to help extend the tupling method to functions with multiple recursion parameters. To achieve better optimisation, we formulate three different forms of tupling optimisations for the elimination of intra-call traversals, the elimination of inter-call traversals and the elimination of redundant calls. We also guarantee the safety of the extended method by ensuring that its transformation terminates.

1 Introduction

Tupling is a powerful program transformation technique that is capable of obtaining super-linear speedup. A classic example is the naive *fib* function where the presence of redundant calls cause its definition to have exponential time-complexity.

```
fib(0)     = 1;
fib(1)     = 1;
fib(n+2)   = fib(n+1) + fib(n);
```

The automated tupling transformation method of [Chi93] can be used to optimise this function. Initially, a new tuple function of the following form is introduced.

```
fib_tup(n)  = (fib(n+1), fib(n));
```

This can then be transformed to obtain the following program with linear time-complexity.

```
fib(0)      = 1;
fib(1)      = 1;
fib(n+2)    = let (u,v) = fib_tup(n) in u+v;
fib_tup(0)  = (1,1) ;
fib_tup(n+1) = let (u,v)=fib_tup(n) in (u+v,u) ;
```

One serious restriction of the tupling method proposed in [Chi93] is that it can only safely handle functions with a single *recursion parameter* each, such as *fib*. (A recursion parameter is a parameter whose size could progressively decrease via recursive calls of pattern-matching equations. A formal definition is given later.) This limitation excludes many interesting functions with multiple recursion parameters, such as functions *take* and *drop* below:

```
data List a = Nil | Cons(x,xs)
split(n,xs)     = (take(n,xs),drop(n,xs));
take(0,xs)      = Nil;
take(n+1,x:xs)  = x:take(n,xs);
drop(0,xs)      = xs;
drop(n+1,x:xs)  = drop(n,xs);
```

Note that : is an infix notation for *Cons*. Both functions *take* and *drop* have two recursion parameters each. Two of their calls, *take(n,xs),drop(n,xs)*, appear in the RHS of function *split* causing the two input parameters, *(n,xs)*, to be traversed twice. Such multiple traversals are referred to as *inter-call* traversals because the common recursion variables (e.g. *n,xs*) occur across separate recursive calls (e.g. *take* and *drop*). If tupling transformation could be safely extended, these traversals could be eliminated by transforming the definition of *split* (using unfold/fold rules of [BD77]), as follows:

```
Instantiate n=0
split(0,xs)     = (take(0,xs),drop(0,xs))          ; unfold take,drop calls
                = (Nil,xs);
Instantiate n=n+1 and xs=x:xs
split(n+1,x:xs) = (take(n+1,x:xs),drop(n+1,x:xs))   ; unfold take,drop calls
                = (x:take(n,xs),drop(n,xs))          ; abstract take,drop
                = let (ys,zs)=(take(n,xs),drop(n,xs))
                      in (x:ys,zs)                   ; fold split
                = let (ys,zs)=split(n,xs) in (x:ys,zs) ;
```

Another example with multiple recursion parameters is function *zip* below.

```
dup(xs)        = zip(xs,xs);
zip(Nil,Nil)   = Nil;
zip(Nil,y:ys)  = Nil;
zip(x:xs,Nil)  = Nil;
zip(x:xs,y:ys) = (x,y):zip(xs,ys);
```

Note that *zip* is a function with two *list*-type recursion parameters. One of its calls, *zip(xs,xs)*, appear in the RHS of *dup* with two common recursion arguments, *xs*. Here, the multiple traversals occur within the same *zip* function call, as opposed to separate function calls for the previous example. We refer to such multiple traversals as *intra-call* traversals. The two recursion parameters each consumes a *Cons* cell per recursive cycle around the *zip* function. This synchronized consumption of the two parameters allows the intra-call traversals of *zip(xs,xs)* to be eliminated, by transforming *dup* to:

```
dup(Nil)       = Nil ;
dup(x:xs)      = (x,x):dup(xs) ;
```

The main difficulty of extending the tupling method is that not all functions with multiple recursion parameters can be safely transformed. As a counter-example, consider a slightly different *zip2* function:

dup2(xs)	= *zip2(xs,xs)*;
zip2(Nil,Nil)	= *Nil*;
zip2(Nil,y:ys)	= *Nil*;
zip2(x:xs,Nil)	= *Nil*;
zip2(x:xs,y:ys)	= *zip2'(xs,ys,x)*;
zip2'(Nil,ys,x)	= *Nil*;
zip2'(x':xs,ys,x)	= *(x+x',y):zip2(xs,ys)*;

The two mutual recursive functions *zip2* and *zip2'* have two recursion parameters per function. (Though there are three parameters in *zip2'*, only two of them are recursion parameters.) In each cycle around the recursive functions *zip2* → *zip2'* → *zip2*, two *Cons* cells are consumed by the first recursion parameter, and one *Cons* cell is consumed by the second recursion parameter. Hence, the two recursion parameters do <u>not</u> have intra-call synchronized consumption of their inputs for their recursive cycle. If we apply tupling transformation to *zip2(xs,xs)*, we encounter successively larger recursive calls as follows:

$$zip2(xs,xs) \rightsquigarrow zip2(xs,x1:xs) \rightsquigarrow zip2(xs,x1:x2:xs) \rightsquigarrow zip2(xs,x1:x2:x3:xs) \rightsquigarrow \ldots$$

This can cause the tupling method to go into a loop because an infinite number of different *zip2* calls (often called specialisation/folding points) with overlapping recursion arguments are encountered when we attempt to eliminate their intra-call traversals. We regard termination as an important *correctness concern* for automatic transformation methods. This is especially so if the methods are to be safely incorporated into language compilers. (Note that symbol $\rightsquigarrow$ represents a sequence of one or more unfolding steps.)

To solve this problem, this paper proposes a new family of parameter analyses, called *synchronization analyses*, for analysing the interactions between multiple recursion parameters. The proposed analyses can help decide in advance whether it is safe to perform tupling on given functions with multiple recursion parameters.

The proposed extension is also an improvement over an earlier proposal made in [CK93], where some syntactic classification of functions with multiple recursion parameters were introduced. A problem with our earlier proposal is that the syntactic-based approach is rather conservative. Minor syntactic perturbations can cause the older syntactic-based analysis to fail unnecessarily. For example, the following alternative definition of *zip* is not recognized as safe by the older syntactic-based analysis [CK93], but it can be accepted by the new semantics-based analysis to be proposed in this paper.

zip(Nil,ys)	= *Nil*;
zip(x:xs,ys)	= *zip'(xs,ys,x)*;
zip'(xs,Nil,x)	= *Nil*;
zip'(xs,y:ys,x)	= *(x,y):zip(xs,ys)*;

Section 2 reviews the automated tupling method for functions with a single recursion parameter per function. Section 3 considers functions with multiple recursion parameters, together with a framework for synchronization analyses. Section 4 presents the new tupling method in three phases to perform the eliminations of *intra-call traversals*, *inter-call traversals* and *redundant calls*, respectively. Splitting the tupling method into three phases allows more optimisation to be achieved. Related work and conclusion are discussed in Section 5.

2 Tupling Overview

We consider a first-order functional language defined as follows.

Definition 1: *First-Order Language*
The simple language is defined by the following context-free grammar:

$$P ::= [M^+]$$
$$M ::= F^+$$
$$F ::= E^+$$
$$E ::= f(p^*, v^*) = t$$
$$t ::= v \mid C(t^*) \mid f(t^*) \mid let \ \{p = t\}^+ \ in \ t' \mid \perp$$
$$p ::= v \mid C(v^*) \ ;$$

Note that S^* denotes zero or more occurrences of S, while S^+ denotes one or more occurrences.

Each program P is made up of a sequence of one or more mutual-recursive (strongly-connected) sets of functions, M. Each function F is defined by one or more non-overlapping equations, E. Lastly, expressions are made up of variables (v), data constructors (C), functions (f), *let* constructs and a special symbol ($\perp$) for errors. Note that the tuple constructor, $(t_1, \ldots, t_n)$, is regarded as an instance of the more general data constructor, $C(t_1, \ldots, t_n)$.

Each function is defined using a set of complete non-overlapping equations with simple pattern parameters, p^*, and non-pattern parameters, v^*. The use of *simple patterns*, with a single constructor each, does not lose generality. The pattern-matching translation technique of [Aug85] can convert functions with arbitrary nested constructor patterns to those with only simple patterns.

For an example of *complete* non-overlapping equations with simple patterns, we have to rewrite the earlier *take* function as follows:

```
take(0,Nil)    = Nil;
take(0,x:xs)   = Nil;
take(n+1,Nil)  = ⊥;
take(n+1,x:xs) = x:take(n,xs);
```

We abbreviate a sequence of terms $t_1, \ldots, t_n$ by $\vec{t}$, so that a function call $f(t_1, \ldots, t_n)$ can be abbreviated as $f(\vec{t})$ or more precisely as $f(t_i)_{i \in 1..n}$. Also, we abbreviate a set of equations $\{f(\vec{p}_i, \vec{v}_i) = e_i\}_{i \in N}$ by $f \overset{\text{def}}{=} ?\{(\vec{p}_i, \vec{v}_i) \Rightarrow e_i\}_{i \in N}$. To mark the fact that $f \in F$, where F is an arbitrary set of functions, we sometimes annotate its calls using $f^F(\vec{t})$.

We introduce a special context notation with multiple holes.

Definition 2: *Context with Multiple Holes*

A *hole*, $\langle\rangle_m$, is a special variable labelled with a number, m.

A *context*, $\widehat{e}\langle\rangle^F$, is an expression with a finite number of holes, defined by the grammar:

$$\widehat{e}\langle\rangle^F ::= v \mid \langle\rangle_m \mid C(\widehat{e}_i\langle\rangle^F)_{i\in 1..n} \mid f(\widehat{e}_i\langle\rangle^F)_{i\in 1..n} \mid let \; \{p_i = \widehat{e}_i\langle\rangle^F\}_{i\in 1..n} \; in \; \widehat{e}\langle\rangle^F$$
such that $f \notin F$

Note that the context notation is parameterised by a set of functions, F, whose calls must not appear in the context itself. Each expression e can be decomposed into a context $\widehat{e}\langle\rangle^F$ and a sequence of sub-terms $[t]_{i\in 1..n}$ using the notation $\widehat{e}\langle t_i\rangle_{i\in 1..n}^F$. This is equivalent to $[t_i/\langle\rangle_i]_{i\in 1..n}(\widehat{e}\langle\rangle_{i\in 1..n}^F)$ which stands for the substitutions of sub-terms, $t_1, \ldots, t_n$, into their respective holes, $\langle\rangle_1, .., \langle\rangle_n$, for context $\widehat{e}\langle\rangle^F$.

With these notations, we can select all calls of F from an expression e, by:

$$e = \widehat{e}\langle f_i^F(\overrightarrow{t_i})\rangle_{i\in 1..n}^F$$

For example, to select the two *take/drop* calls in the expression $(x{:}take(n,xs), drop(n,xs))$, we use $(x : \widehat{\langle\rangle_1, \langle\rangle_2})\langle take(n, xs), drop(n, xs)\rangle^{\{take,drop\}}$.

Some common predicates on expressions that are used later include:

Definition 3: *Useful Predicates*

The predicate $(t_1 \sqsubseteq t_2)$ is to test if t_1 is a sub-term of t_2, while the proper sub-term relationship is denoted by $(t_1 \sqsubset t_2)$.

The predicate $IsVar(t)$ returns true if t is a variable; false otherwise.

The predicate $IsConst(t)$ returns true if t is a constant expression without any free variables; false otherwise.

2.1 Transformation for SRP-Functions

The tupling method in [Chi93] was formulated for a class of functions with a *single recursion parameter* each, called SRP-functions.

Definition 4: *SRP-Functions*

Consider

$$f^M(p, \overrightarrow{v}) \qquad = \widehat{e}_f\langle f_j^M(tj_0, \overrightarrow{tj})\rangle_{j\in 1..m}^M \; ;$$

This equation is said to be a SRP-equation if the single pattern-parameter, p, is a *recursion* parameter. The pattern-parameter, p, is said to be a *recursion* parameter if the recursion argument, tj_0, for each mutual recursive call, $f_j^M(tj_0, \overrightarrow{tj})$, is a variable taken from p, as follows:

$$\forall j \in \{1..m\}. \; RP\_Cond(p, tj_0)$$
$$\text{where } RP\_Cond(p, t) \equiv IsVar(t) \wedge (t \sqsubseteq p)$$

A function f^M is said to be a SRP-function if all the equations of its M-set are SRP-equations.

Two simple SRP-functions are *deepest* and *depth*.

```
data Tree a = Leaf a | (Tree a) @ (Tree a) ;
deepest(Leaf(a))  = [a];
deepest(l@r)      = if depth(l) > depth(r) then deepest(l)
                    else if depth(l) < depth(r)  then deepest(r)
                    else deepest(l)++deepest(r);
depth(Leaf(a))    = 0 ;
depth(l@r)        = 1+max(depth(l),depth(r)) ;
```

Redundant calls are present in the definition of *deepest*, causing the function to have a time complexity of $O(n^2)$ where n is the size of its input tree. By eliminating the redundant calls, it is possible to reduce the function's time complexity to $O(n)$. An informal tupling algorithm to achieve such an optimisation is given below. (A formal presentation can be found in [Chi95].)

Method 1: Tupling Algorithm, $\mathcal{T}$

Step 0 Decide the set of function calls to tuple, F.

Step 1 Repeatedly *unfold (without instantiation)* each function call of F.

Step 2 Split the F calls to separate tuples based on their sole recursion argument. For each tuple:

Step 3 If the tuple has only one function call, then *terminate*.

Step 4 If the tuple has appeared before, then *fold* against previous definition and *terminate*.

Step 5 Otherwise, introduce a new tuple function definition. This is a *define* step.

Step 6 *Unfold (with instantiation)* any one call of F. Goto Step 1.

2.2 Two Unfold Operations

There are two types of unfolds in the above tupling algorithm, namely:

- Unfolds *without* Instantiation (Step 1)
- Unfolds *with* Instantiation (Step 6)

For example, the call *deepest(l@r)* can be directly unfolded without any instantiation, while the call *deepest(t)* requires its argument t to be instantiated to either *Leaf(a)* or *l@r* before it can be unfolded. As there could be infinitely many different instantiations for recursive types, we shall always apply the *minimal instantiation* needed for unfolding some function call(s).

Notice that Step 6 may involve a non-deterministic choice of F calls to instantiate and unfold. However, it is always followed by Step 1 which repeatedly unfold those F calls which did not require instantiation. This combination of the two steps ensures a deterministic outcome.

To transform the earlier example, we fix $F=\{deepest,depth\}$, and then apply $\mathcal{T}$ to each RHS of their equations. No significant change occur in all equations, except for the second equation of *deepest*. This equation can be written more concisely (using a suitable context $\hat{e}\langle\rangle$) as:

$$deepest(l@r) \quad = \hat{e}\langle depth(l), deepest(l), depth(r), deepest(r)\rangle$$

The tupling algorithm could then be applied, as illustrated below.

$deepest(l@r)$ $= \widehat{e}\langle depth(l), deepest(l), depth(r), deepest(r)\rangle$

Step 2: Gather Calls (according to different recursion arg.)
$= let \; \{(u,v)=(depth(l),deepest(l)); \; (a,b)=(depth(r),deepest(r))\}$
$in \; \widehat{e}\langle u, v, a, b\rangle$

Step 5: Define Tuple Function
$= let \; \{(u,v)=d\_tup(l); \; (a,b)=d\_tup(r)\} \; in \; \widehat{e}\langle u, v, a, b\rangle$

Define
$d\_tup(t)$ $= (depth(t),deepest(t))$

Step 6: Instantiate and unfold depth call
Case $t=Leaf(a)$
$d\_tup(Leaf(a)) = (1,deepest(Leaf(a)))$

Step 1: Unfold deepest call (without instantiation)
$= (1,[a])$;*terminated by Step 3*

Case $t=l@r$
$d\_tup(l@r)$ $= (1+max(depth(l),depth(r)),deepest(l@r))$

Step 1: Unfold deepest call (without instantiation)
$= (1+max(depth(l),depth(r)),$
$= \widehat{e}\langle depth(l), deepest(l), depth(r), deepest(r)\rangle)$

Step 2: Gather Calls
$= let \; \{(u,v)=(depth(l),deepest(l)); \; (a,b)=(depth(r),deepest(r))\}$
$in \; (1+max(u,a),\widehat{e}\langle u, v, a, b\rangle)$

Step 4: Fold with d_tup
$= let \; \{(u,v)=d\_tup(l); \; (a,b)=d\_tup(r)\}$
$in \; (1+max(u,a),\widehat{e}\langle u, v, a, b\rangle)$

2.3 Ensuring Termination

The above tupling algorithm can eliminate both redundant calls and multiple traversals. However, it is possible for the algorithm to be non-terminating for the following reasons:

- Step 1 may unfold (without instantiation) function calls *indefinitely*.
- Step 5 may define new tuple function via *infinitely* many different tuples.

These two potential causes of non-termination can be resolved by two further restrictions on the sub-class of SRP-functions, called the *descending-RP* and the *bounded-arguments* restrictions, respectively.

Definition 5: *Descending-RP Restriction*
Consider a M-set of SRP-functions, $\{f_i\}_{i\in M}$. Build a call-graph where each caller-callee transition of $\{f_i\}_{i\in M}$ is labelled as *descending* or *unchanged*, depending on whether the recursion parameter is decreased or unchanged across its transition[a]. The *descending-RP* restriction is satisfied for $\{f_i\}_{i\in M}$ iff every cycle of call transitions has at least one *descending* transition.

---

[a] There is no need to consider *increasing* transitions since these are disallowed by the SRP-form.

The *descending-RP* restriction can guarantee that there will never be infinite number of unfolds without instantiation. It achieves this by requiring that the mutual-recursive definition do *not* have cyclic caller-callee transitions with non-descending recursion parameter.

The bounded-arguments restriction can prevent infinite number of define steps during tupling. This is achieved by ensuring that there is a bounded number of different tuple function definitions (specialisation/folding points).

Definition 6: *Bounded-Arguments Restriction*
Consider

$$f(p, \vec{v}) \qquad = \hat{e_f} \langle f_j^M(tj_0, \vec{tj}) \rangle_{j \in 1..m}^M \; ;$$

This equation is said to have the *bounded-arguments* restriction if the non-recursion arguments, $\vec{tj}$, from each SRP-call, $f_j^M(tj_0, \vec{tj})$, are either constants or variables from the non-recursion parameters, $\vec{v}$, as follows:

$$\forall j \in \{1..m\}. \forall t \in \{\vec{tj}\}. \; IsConst(t) \vee (t \in \{\vec{v}\})$$

A SRP-function is said to adhere to the *bounded-arguments* restriction if all the equations of its M-set of functions are *bounded-arguments* SRP-equations.

The proposed restrictions (including SRP-form) may appear quite severe. Fortunately, it is possible to use various pre-processing techniques to transform some functions outside these restrictions to equivalent functions within. More details of these two restrictions and their contributions to the termination of tupling method can be found in [Chi93, Chi95].

3   Synchronization Analyses

Functions with multiple recursion parameters can cause new non-termination problems for the tupling method. Apart from the descending-RP and bounded-arguments restrictions, it is also required that multiple recursion parameters be properly synchronized across successive recursive calls. We can extend the sub-class of functions with multiple recursion parameters, as follows:

Definition 7: *MRP-Functions*
Consider an equation with r pattern-parameters:

$$f^M(p_1, \ldots, p_r, \vec{v}) \qquad = \hat{e_f} \langle f_i^M(ti_1, \ldots, ti_r, \vec{ti}) \rangle_{i \in 1..m}^M \; ;$$

This equation is said to be a MRP-equation if all the r pattern-parameters are *recursion* parameters. This condition is expressed as follows:

$$\forall i \in 1..m. \forall j \in 1..r. \; RP\_Cond(p_j, ti_j)$$

A function f^M is said to be a MRP-function if all the equations of its M-set are MRP-equations.

To handle MRP-functions safely, we shall introduce a family of synchronization analyses to determine if their multiple recursion parameters are suitable for either the eliminations of intra-call traversals, inter-call traversals or redundant calls. Our synchronization analyses are based on the function call transitions between MRP-functions. We define:

Definition 8: *Labelled Call Graph*

The *labelled call graph* of a set of MRP-function definitions, M, is a graph whereby each function name from M is a *node*; and each caller-callee transition is represented by an *arrow*, labelled with the *descent* operation on the recursion parameters. Consider each MRP-equation:

$$f^M(\vec{p}, \vec{v}) = \hat{e}_f \langle f_i^M (\vec{di}(p), \vec{ti}) \rangle_{i \in 1..m}^M \ ;$$

To build the graph, we introduce m *caller-callee* transitions, $\{ f \overset{(\vec{di})}{\to} f_i \}_{i \in 1..m}$, labelled by the respective *descent operation* $(\vec{di})$ in tuple form.

The descent operators for each recursion argument are represented as follows. If the LHS pattern parameter is v and the corresponding argument is v, the identity function ID is used as the descent operator since $ID(v) = v$. If the LHS pattern parameter is $c(v_1, \ldots, v_j)$ and its argument is $v_i \in \{v_1, .., v_j\}$, the descent operator $c[i]$ is used where $c[i](c(v_1, \ldots, v_j)) = v_i$. For example, the labelled call graphs for the two versions of *zip* function (from Section 1) are $\{zip \overset{(:[2],:[2])}{\to} zip\}$ and $\{zip \overset{(:[2],ID)}{\to} zip', zip' \overset{(ID,:[2])}{\to} zip\}$, respectively. Note that $:[2]$ is a descent operator to return the second argument of a *Cons* cell.

Call transitions can be composed, as follows:

Definition 9: *Composing Call Transitions*

Given two transitions $f \overset{D_1}{\to} g$ and $g \overset{D_2}{\to} h$, we can compose it as follows:

$$(g \overset{D_2}{\to} h) o (f \overset{D_1}{\to} g) = f \overset{D_2 o D_1}{\to} h.$$

An alternative notation for left-to-right composition is:

$$(f \overset{D_1}{\to} g); (g \overset{D_2}{\to} h) = f \overset{D_1;D_2}{\to} h.$$

We define transitions for both single and multiple recursion parameters.

Definition 10: *RP- and MRP-Transitions*

The transition for a single recursion parameter (e.g. $:[2]$) is known as a *RP-transition*. It is denoted using $d, d1, d2, ..$ or $e, e1, e2, ...$ A sequence of RP-transitions (e.g. $d1; ..; dn$) is denoted using $ds, ds1, ds2, ..$ or $es, es1, es2, ...$

A tuple of RP-transitions (e.g. $(:[2], :[2])$) is known as a *MRP-transition*. It is denoted using $D, D1, D2, ..$ or $E, E1, E2, ..$ A sequence of MRP-transitions (e.g. $D1; ..; Dn$) is denoted using $DS, DS1, DS2, ..$ or $ES, ES1, ES2, ...$

Given a MRP-transition sequence, we can obtain a tuple of RP-transition sequences for the individual recursion parameters via:

$$(d1_1, .., d1_n); ..; (dr_1, .., dr_n) = ((d1_1; ..; dr_1), ..., (d1_n; ..; dr_n))$$

Transition sequences can be compacted (simplified), as follows:

Definition 11: *Compacted Transitions*

Each RP-transition sequence can be compacted using two laws, namely (i)
$d; ID = d$ and (ii) $ID; d = d$.

For each RP-sequence, *ds*, we denote its compacted transition sequence by
compact(ds). MRP-transition sequence can be simplified by compacting its
individual RP-sequences.

To analyse for parameter synchronization around recursive functions, we focus on transition sequences that are cyclic.

Definition 12: *Cyclic Transitions*

A sequence of transitions, $f1 \overset{D_1}{\to} f2 \overset{D_2}{\to} .. \overset{D_{n-1}}{\to} fn \overset{D_n}{\to} f1$, which starts from a
function *f1* and returns back to the same function is called a *cyclic* transition
sequence. The composed version can be abbreviated as $f1 \overset{D_1;..;D_n}{\to} f1$.

Such cyclic transition sequences can be used to analyse how much of a recursion argument is being consumed by each cycle of recursive calls. For example,
the two definitions of *zip* (given in Section 1) have the same (compacted) cyclic
transition sequence, $zip \overset{(:[2]_i:[2])}{\to} zip$.

For each cycle around the recursive function calls, the recursion parameter
must have its size decreased by at least one. This can be guaranteed by ensuring
that all cyclic MRP-transition sequences are *descending* sequences, defined as
follows:

Definition 13: *Descending RP and MRP Transitions*

A RP-transition sequence *ds* is said to be *descending* if $compact(ds) \neq ID$.

A MRP-transition sequence $(\vec{ds})$ is said to be *descending* if

$$\exists ds \in \{\vec{ds}\}.compact(ds) \neq ID$$

Correspondingly, a *M*-set of MRP-functions is said to satisfy the *descending-
MRP restriction* if every of its cyclic MRP-transition sequences is descending.

We are required to handle function calls with either identical, overlapping
or disjoint multiple recursion arguments. Consider two functions *f1, f2* with two
recursion parameters each. The calls {*f1(x1,y1),f2(x1,y1)*} have identical-MRP,
while the calls {*f1(c(x1,x2),y1),f2(x2,y1)*} have overlapping-MRP, but the calls
{*f1(x1,y1), f2(x2,y1)*} have disjoint-MRP. Formally:

Definition 14: *Identical, Overlapping and Disjoint-MRPs*

Two function calls are said to have *identical-MRP* iff every pair of corresponding recursion arguments are identical.

Two function calls are said to have *overlapping-MRP* iff every pair of corresponding recursion arguments have at least one common variable.

Two function calls are said to have *disjoint-MRP* if at least one pair of corresponding recursion arguments does not have any common variable.

To analyse transition sequences, we introduce the following notions of synchronization.

Definition 15: *Synchronization of Call Transitions*

Two compacted RP-transition sequences, *ds* and *es*, are said to be *level 1-synchronized* (denoted by $ds \approx_1 es$) if

$$\exists ds', es'.\,(ds; ds' = es; es')$$

Otherwise, they are said to be *level 0-synchronized* (or *unsynchronized*).

Two compacted RP-transition sequences, *ds* and *es*, are said to be *level 2-synchronized* (denoted by $ds \approx_2 es$) if

$$\exists ds', es'.\,(ds; ds' = es; es') \wedge (ds' = (\vec{ID}) \vee es' = (\vec{ID}))$$

Two compacted RP-transition sequences, *ds* and *es*, are said to be *level 3-synchronized* (denoted by $ds \approx_3 es$) if

$$\exists cs, n, m.\,(ds = cs^n) \wedge (es = cs^m) \wedge (n, m > 0)$$

Note that *cs* is referred to as a *common generator* of the two RP-sequences.

Two compacted RP-transition sequences, *ds* and *es*, are said to be *level 4-synchronized* (denoted by $ds \approx_4 es$) if $ds = es$.

Corresponding notions of *synchronization* apply to compacted MRP-transition sequences. Note that the synchronizations at levels 1 to 4 form a strict hierarchy, with synchronization at level *i* implying synchronization at level *j* if $i > j$. The different notions of synchronization can be used in the following way. Given two calls with identical-MRP. If the two calls follow *level 0-synchronized* (unsynchronized) transition sequences, then their resulting calls will end up with disjoint-MRPs. If the two calls follow transition sequences that are level 4-synchronized, then the resulting calls will have identical-MRP. For level-3 synchronized transitions, the calls will have identical-MRP after traversing every sub-sequence of the common generator. With level 1-synchronized or 2-synchronized sequences, their calls will have overlapping-MRP.

4 Three Phases of Tupling

We now present the tupling method for MRP-functions. In order to obtain better optimisation, we separate this method into three phases, namely:

- Phase 1 - Elimination of Intra-Call Traversals
- Phase 2 - Elimination of Redundant Calls
- Phase 3 - Elimination of Inter-Call Traversals

The three types of eliminations have slightly different (synchronization) requirements. If they were lumped together into a single algorithm, we would need to impose more conservative restrictions to ensure termination. A better result can therefore be obtained if the tupling method were separated into three phases. Each of the three tupling phases will have:

1. a variant tupling algorithm, and
2. its own safe class of transformable functions/calls.

These tupling phases are applied in the above sequence to each set of mutual-recursive functions according to the bottom-up order of the function calling hierarchy. Given mutual-recursive sets of functions, $[M_1, M_2, .., M_n]$, in bottom-up order. We subject a set of function definitions, M_i, to each of the above three phases before proceeding with M_{i+1}. We call this decomposed method, the *three phase tupling* method.

Phases 1 and 3 are applied to appropriate *auxiliary* recursive calls, M_j, in the definition of M_i where $j < i$. Phase 1 is used to eliminate intra-call traversals for certain function calls with common (or overlapping) recursion arguments. Phase 3 is used to eliminate inter-call traversals among separate auxiliary recursive calls with overlapping-MRPs. Phase 2 is to eliminate redundant *mutual* (and *auxiliary*) recursive function calls. Details of the three phases are described in the next three sub-sections.

4.1 Eliminating Intra-Call Traversals

This phase is meant solely for the elimination of intra-call multiple traversals. To formulate a sub-class of functions which are safe for this phase, we introduce the following enhanced form of synchronization:

Definition 16: *Rotate Synchronization*
Two compacted RP cyclic transition sequences, ds, es, are said to *rotate-synchronize* at level-n (denoted by $ds \approx_{n,rot} es$) if:
$$\exists ds_1, ds_2, es_1, es_2. (ds_1; ds_2 = ds) \wedge (es_1; es_2 = es) \wedge (ds_2; ds_1 \approx_n es_2; es_1)$$

The notion of *rotate-synchronization* is to cater to function calls which start at different points of the cyclic transition sequences and yet may synchronize. With this, we define the sub-class of functions safe for Phase 1 tupling as:

Definition 17: *Phase 1 Functions*
A M-set of mutual-recursive functions is said to be *Phase 1* (abbreviated as *P1*) functions if the following conditions are satisfied:

1. Each function satisfy the *descending-MRP* restriction.
2. There exists a sub-set R of two or more parameters that are *rotate-synchronized at level 4* , such that:
$$\exists R. \forall (\vec{ds}) \forall i,j \in R. (ds_i \approx_{4,rot} ds_j)$$
where $(\vec{ds})$ denotes each cyclic MRP-transition sequence.

Such a property would allow each cycle of recursive functions to consume exactly the same number of constructors from each sub-set of the R (level 4 rotate-synchronized) recursion parameters. As a result, a common variable placed among such sub-sets of recursion parameters might re-occur (synchronize) after each cycle of unfolding a recursive function call.

The elimination of intra-call traversals is guaranteed to be safe (terminating) for each P1-function call with common variables among its subset of R parameters. An informal procedure is outlined below.

Method 2: Tupling to Eliminate Intra-Call Traversals

Step 0 Decide the set of safe P1-functions to tuple, F.

Step 1 Repeatedly *unfold without instantiation* all P1-function calls of F.

Step 2 Gather each P1-function call into a single-call tuple. (This is an *abstraction* step.) For each P1-function call:

Step 3 If the P1-call does not have any overlapping R recursion argument, *terminate*.

Step 4 If the P1-call has appeared before, then *fold* against previous definition and *terminate*.

Step 5 Otherwise, generalise the non-R arguments before introducing a new function definition. This is a *define* step.

Step 6 *Unfold* (with minimal instantiations) the P1-function call. Goto Step 1.

The above algorithm allows each argument from R ($\approx_{4,rot}$) parameters to remain in-tact but generalise away the other non-R ($\not\approx_{4,rot}$) arguments at each define step. Also, each tuple consists of only a single call with a subset of common (overlapping) R-arguments. These two tasks are in line with the aim of eliminating intra-call traversals among the R-arguments. To illustrate the tupling procedure, consider the following set of mutual-recursive P1-functions.

$$f1(x1@x2,ys,z1@z2) = \widehat{e_{f1}}\langle f2(x2, ys, z2)\rangle$$
$$f2(x1@x2,ys,z1@z2) = \widehat{e_{f2}}\langle f3(x1, ys, z2)\rangle$$
$$f3(xs,y1@y2,z1@z2) = \widehat{e_{f3}}\langle f4(xs, y1, z2), f2(xs, y1, z1)\rangle$$
$$f4(xs,y1@y2,zs) \quad = \widehat{e_{f4}}\langle f1(xs, y2, zs)\rangle$$

There are two cyclic MRP-sequences, namely $f1 \to f2 \to f3 \to f4 \to f1$ with transition sequence $(@[2], ID, @[2]); (@[1], ID, @[2]); (ID, @[1], @[2]); (ID, @[2], ID)$ and cycle $f2 \to f3 \to f2$ with transition sequence $(@[1], ID, @[2]); (ID, @[1], @[1])$. The compacted representation of these two cycles are $((@[2];@[1]), (@[1];@[2]), (@[2];@[2];@[2]))$ and $(@[1],@[1],(@[2];@[1]))$. We can see that the individual transitions of the first and second parameters are rotate-synchronized at level 4 but not the third parameter. This is so because $@[2];@[1] \approx_{4,rot} @[1];@[2]$ and $@[1] \approx_{4,rot} @[1]$ holds for the two cycles.

Hence, the first two parameters of this M-set of functions could *potentially* allow the elimination of intra-call traversals. As an example consider:

$$main(xs) \quad = \widehat{e_{main}}\langle f1(xs, xs, zs), m(xs, xs, zs)\rangle$$
$$m(xs,y1@y2,zs) = \widehat{e_m}\langle f1(xs, y2, zs)\rangle$$

In the RHS of *main*, there are two auxiliary calls with common R recursion arguments where m is considered to be an intermediate function to the $\{f1,f2,f3,f4\}$ M-set. Both calls are safe to transform. Phase 1 tupling algorithm would define:

$$am(xs,zs) \quad = m(xs,xs,zs)$$
$$n1(xs,zs) \quad = f1(xs,xs,zs)$$

followed by transformation to obtain:

$$main(xs) \quad = \widehat{e_{main}}\langle n1(xs, zs), am(xs, zs)\rangle$$
$$n1(x1@x2,z1@z2) \quad = \widehat{e_{f1}}\langle n2(x2, z2, x1)\rangle$$
$$n2(y1@y2,z1@z2,x1) = \widehat{e_{f2}}\langle n3(y1, z2, x1, y2)\rangle$$
$$n3(y1,z1@z2,x1,y2) = \widehat{e_{f3}}\langle f4(y1, x1, z2), f2(y1, x1, z1)\rangle$$

$$am(x1@x2,zs,x1) \quad = \widehat{e_m}\langle a1(x2, zs, x1)\rangle$$
$$a1(x2,z1@z2,x1) \quad = \widehat{e_{f1}}\langle a2(x2, z2)\rangle$$
$$a2(x1@x2,z1@z2) \quad = \widehat{e_{f2}}\langle a3(x1, z2, x2)\rangle$$
$$a3(x1,z1@z2,x2) \quad = \widehat{e_{f3}}\langle a4(x1, z2), a2(x1, z1)\rangle$$
$$a4(x1@x2,zs) \quad = \widehat{e_{f4}}\langle a1(x2, zs)\rangle$$

Note that the P1-class of functions only guarantees *safe* but not necessarily *effective* elimination of intra-call traversals. In the above example, the intra-call traversals of call $m(xs,xs,zs)$ is effectively eliminated for all the recursive calls. However, the intra-call traversals of function call $f1(xs,xs,zs)$ did not eventually synchronize across the recursive calls since $f2$ and $f4$ calls are still present in the RHS of $n3$. This is so because the rotate-synchronization at level-4 has resulted in calls with *disjoint* (instead of *overlapping*) R recursion arguments. Hence, the *actual* synchronization at level-4 did not materialise for the $f1(xs,xs,zs)$ call. Nevertheless, both P1-calls are safe to transform.

Another point worth noting is that all non-R arguments be generalised by our procedure. As an example, consider the call $f2(xs,xs,xs)$ with three identical recursion arguments. As only the first two arguments are level 4 rotate-synchronized (via $\approx_{4,rot}$), our Phase 1 tupling procedure generalises the last argument to:

$$let\ zs=xs\ in\ f2(xs,xs,zs)$$

This generalisation can help avoid potential non-terminating due to infinite specialisation points (ie. define steps). An example of such non-termination is the $zip2$ function given in Section 1.

Termination Proof There are two potential causes of non-termination.

- Infinite number of unfolding without instantiation (Step 1).
- Infinite number of define steps (Step 5).

Infinite unfolding without instantiation (Step 1) is not possible because the P1-functions have the *decreasing-MRP* restriction. Infinite define of Step 5 is also impossible because there are only a finite number of different single call tuples. Firstly, the non-R arguments are always generalised into variables. Secondly, the size of the R-arguments are bounded. On every cycle, each R-parameter consumes exactly the same number of constructors from each of its recursion argument. Hence, the size of each R-argument during the transition would grow by at most the length of the cyclic MRP-sequence before it is decreased by a corresponding amount in the remaining transitions. As there is a finite number of function names, the number of different tuples which could be encountered is therefore bounded. Hence, infinite number of define steps is not possible since fold transformation (Step 4) will be carried out when a matching call re-appears.

Preservation of Non-Strict Semantics It is easy to show that this tupling phase to eliminate intra-call traversals preserves the non-strict semantics. In particular, the instantiation of recursion parameters occur for only new equations with a single call on their RHS. Since such a call lies in a strict context, its parameter instantiation adheres to the non-strict semantics (see [RFJ89]).

Though preservation of non-strict semantics is simple for this phase, it is not so straightforward for the next two tupling phases. The reason is that the next two phases have to deal with tuples of MRP-function calls. Such calls may have conflicting strictness requirement on the common recursion argument. Under this scenario, an unfold (with instantiation) on one call may indirectly cause another call to violate its non-strict semantics making the latter more strict than should be. Remedies for preserving non-strict semantics will be given in the full paper.

4.2 Synchronization Points

Before describing the analyses and techniques used to eliminate redundant calls or inter-call traversals, we give an enhanced interpretation of the labelled call graph, defined in Definition 8.

We classify the nodes (ie., functions) in the labelled call graph based on the number of its in-coming and out-going (directed) edges: An *intermediate point* is a node that has exactly one in-coming edge and one out-going edge; a *terminal point* is either a sink or a source in the graph; and a *synchronization point* is a *non*-terminal point which has either multiple in-coming edges, or multiple out-going edges, or both.

Synchronization points are potential places where redundant calls within an equation can be detected, and thus effective tupling can take place. In the case of mutual-recursive function definitions, effective tupling are made possible when synchronization (of arguments) can be maintained across recursive function calls. To describe this, we define a *segment* as a sequence of connected edges that link a synchronization point to its neighbouring synchronization point (possibly itself) without visiting any other synchronization points.

Sometimes, an intermediate point in a graph can be viewed as a *pseudo-synchronization* point, which breaks a segment (passing through it) into two sub-segments; this may enable synchronization to be attained independently at each sub-segment. This is useful when the segment itself is not suitably synchronized with any other segment in the graph.

With this classification of nodes, we can easily identify the set of functions eligible for redundant call elimination. This is described in the next section.

4.3 Eliminating Redundant Calls

In this section, we describe the task of redundant call elimination. Firstly, we characterise a class of functions whose redundant calls can be safely eliminated.

Definition 18: *Phase 2 MRP-Functions*
A *M*-set of MRP-functions is said to be *Phase 2* (abbreviated as P2) function if the following conditions are satisfied:

1. Every function satisfies the descending-MRP restriction.
2. The non-recursion parameters satisfy the bounded-argument restriction.
3. Let B be the set of all the segments in the corresponding labelled call graph. Then $Sync(B)$ holds, where

$Sync(B) \equiv \forall i, j \in B. \ (i \approx_0 j) \lor (i \approx_3 j) \lor (|i| > |j| \Rightarrow PseudoSyn(i, j, B)),$

$PseudoSyn(i, j, B) \equiv i \not\approx_3 j \land i \approx_2 j \land (\exists i'.(i = (j; i')) \land Sync((B - \{i\}) \cup \{i'\})).$

(Given a segment i, $|i|$ denotes the number of transitions in i.)

Conditions 1 and 2 help ensure the termination of tupling process. Condition 3 ensures synchronization of the redundant calls. In contrast to the the level-4 rotate-synchronization criteria needed among arguments in the case of Phase-1 tupling, level-3 synchronization between calls suffices for achieving redundant call elimination. In the case where two segments are synchronized at level 2 but not level 3, a pseudo-synchronization point (for the longer segment) is required for synchronization to be obtained at the sub-segments.

Once a M-set of P2 functions is identified, we initiate the transformation by tupling those calls that are located within the same equation and having identical (or overlapping) arguments. If these calls have synchronized cyclic transitions, tupling becomes effective. The Phase-2 algorithm is outlined below:

Method 3: Tupling to Eliminate Redundant Calls

Step 0 Decide a set of mutual-recursive P2-function calls to tuple, F.

Step 1 Repeatedly *unfold without instantiation* each function call of F.

Step 2 Gather each subset of P2-function calls with overlapping-MRP into a tuple. (This is an *abstraction* step.) For each tuple:

Step 3 If the tuple has ≤ 1 function call, then *terminate*.

Step 4 If the tuple has appeared before, then *fold* against previous definition and *terminate*.

Step 5 Otherwise, introduce a new function definition. This is a *define* step.

Step 6 *Unfold* (with minimal instantiation) a P2 call. Goto Step 1.

As an example, consider the following contrived set of functions.

$k1(x1@x2,y1@y2) = \widehat{e_{k1}}\langle k1(x1, y1), k2(x1, y1), k3(x1, y1), k1(x2, y2)\rangle$
$k2(x1@x2,y1@y2) = \widehat{e_{k2}}\langle k2(x1, y1), k2(x2, y2)\rangle$
$k3(x1@x2,y1@y2) = \widehat{e_{k3}}\langle k1(x2, y2)\rangle$

The various segments for these functions are shown in Figure 1. There are six segments altogether (collectively called B), with two synchronization points (represented by two concentric circles): $k1$ and $k2$. For the point $k1$, the cycle (segment) passing through the intermediate point (represented by a cycle) $k3$ synchronizes at level-2 with another cycle ($@[1], @[1]$). Closer investigation reveals that it can be split into two sub-segments: a prefix, ($@[1], @[1]$), and a suffix, ($@[2], @[2]$), such that (i) the prefix is identical to the cycle ($@[1], @[1]$), and (ii) the suffix together with the rest of the segment satisfies the predicate $Sync$. Therefore, $k1$ is a P2 function.

The only equation having calls with identical-MRP is the first equation, which has calls $k1(x1,y1)$, $k2(x1,y1)$, $k3(x1,y1)$. This is the place where potential

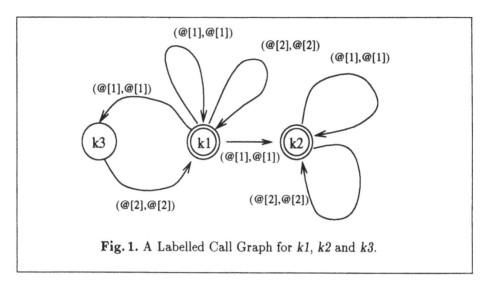

Fig. 1. A Labelled Call Graph for *k1*, *k2* and *k3*.

duplication of function calls could occur. Applying tupling transformation on this set of P2 functions will introduce the following two tuple-functions for the calls with overlapping- (specifically, identical-) MRP.

$$ktup1(x,y) = (k1(x,y),k2(x,y),k3(x,y))$$
$$ktup2(x,y) = (k1(x,y),k2(x,y))$$

The end-result is the following efficient transformed program:

$$
\begin{aligned}
k1(x1@x2,y1@y2) \quad &= \; let \; \{(a,b,c) = ktup1(x1,y1)\} \; in \; \widehat{e_{k1}}\langle a, b, c, k1(x2, y2)\rangle \\
k2(x1@x2,y1@y2) \quad &= \; \widehat{e_{k2}}\langle k2(x1, y1), k2(x2, y2)\rangle \\
ktup1(x1@x2,y1@y2) &= \; let \; \{(a,b,c)=ktup1(x1,y1); \; (d,e)=ktup2(x2,y2)\} \\
&\quad\; in \; (\widehat{e_{k1}}\langle a, b, c, d\rangle, \; \widehat{e_{k2}}\langle c, e\rangle, \widehat{e_{k3}}\langle d\rangle) \\
ktup2(x1@x2,y1@y2) &= \; let \; \{(a,b,c)=ktup1(x1,y1); \; (d,e)=ktup2(x2,y2)\} \\
&\quad\; in \; (\widehat{e_{k1}}\langle a, b, c, d\rangle, \; \widehat{e_{k2}}\langle c, e\rangle)
\end{aligned}
$$

The effect of tupling transformation can also be seen in the resulting labelled call graph (which is omitted here). All the synchronization points in the graph share a common charateristic: Every pair of segments starting from the same synchronization point is unsynchronized. This indicates that redundant calls have been eliminated.

Note that the definition of P2 functions, which was meant for MRP-functions, can also be used to characterise SRP-functions. Specifically, every segment of SRP-functions always satisfies the *Sync* predicate, as it can always be broken into sub-segments which are either unsynchronizing ($\approx_0$) or level-3 synchronizing ($\approx_3$) without encountering level-1 synchronization ($\approx_1$). Hence, the definition of P2 functions, and its corresponding transformation algorithm, can be viewed as a proper MRP extension of the original tupling method based on SRP-functions.

Termination Proof There are only two potential places of non-termination: Infinite application of unfolding without instantiation (Step 1), and infinite number of *define* steps (Step 5).

Infinite application of unfolding without instantiation at (Step 1) is not possible as all P2 functions are required to have descending-MRPs, as implied by

Condition 1 in Definition 18. Infinite *define* at (Step 5) is also impossible because there are only a finite number of different tuples: Firstly, there are finitely many different non-recursion arguments since they can only be drawn from a bounded set of variables and constants. Secondly, there are finitely many different recursion arguments because the size of the recursion arguments is bounded: If two calls come from two cyclic transition sequences which are synchronized at level-3, then (during tupling transformation) the growth of their corresponding recursion arguments is bounded by the maximum length of those synchronized cycles. On the other hand, if two calls are from unsynchronous cyclic transition sequences, then they will be split into separate tuples. Lastly, there is a finite number of function names. These three factors implies that the number of different tuples which can be encountered is bounded.

4.4   Eliminating Inter-Call Traversals

While P2 tupling algorithm eliminates redundant calls appearing within a set of mutual-recursive functions, this section explores the technique for eliminating multiple traversals of data by calls to different functions. Firstly, we define a sub-class of functions applicable to this tupling phase.

Definition 19: *Phase 3 MRP-functions*
A M-set of mutual recursive (and auxiliary) MRP-functions is said to be *Phase 3* (abbreviated as P3) functions if the following conditions are satisfied:

1. Every function satisfies the descending-MRP restriction.
2. For each synchronization point p in the corresponding labelled call graph, let $\mathcal{B}_p$ be the set of segments originated from p. Then, $\forall i, j \in \mathcal{B}_p . (i \approx_0 j)$.
3. Let $\mathcal{B}$ be the set of all the segments in the corresponding labelled call graph. Then $Sync(\mathcal{B})$ holds, where $Sync$ is defined in Definition 18.

Condition 2 above stipulates that no P3 function contains redundant calls. This means a piece of data used as a recursion argument to such a function will not be traversed more than once. We say that the function has *single-traversal* property. This property ensures that the number of calls to be grouped into a tuple never grow. Condition 3 is similar to that defined for P2 functions: It ensures synchronization among multiple traversals.

All P2 functions will become P3 functions after P2 tupling. Furthermore, it is possible to have P3 functions that do not conform to the bounded-arguments restriction. As such, functions with accumulative parameters can be accepted as P3 functions. This is a benefit of splitting tupling method into separate phases.

As every P3 function has single-traversal property, multiple traversal of a piece of data will occur when the data is used as recursion arguments to more than one P3 functions. This is reflected by the existence of two or more calls to P3 functions with overlapping-MRP.

Phase-3 algorithm is similar to Phase-2 algorithm, except that :

1. It is applied to sets of P3 functions, instead of P2 functions.

2. During the abstraction step (*i.e.*, Step 2), it requires the non-recursion arguments to be generalised into values. This is not needed in P2 algorithm because P2 functions satisfy the bounded-argument restriction.

Because P3 functions satisfy the single-traversal property, and non-recursion arguments in the P3-function calls are generalised, we can ensure that only a finite number of different tuples be generated during the tupling process. Together with the requirement that P3 functions have descending-MRPs, we guarantee termination of the tupling process. Detail of the algorithm and the termination proof will be given in the full paper.

5 Related Work and Conclusion

Many techniques have been proposed in the past for avoiding redundant function calls. One of the earliest techniques uses memo-functions [Mic68]. Memo-functions are special functions which remember/store either some or all of their previously computed function calls in a memo-table, so that re-occurring function calls can have their results retrieved from the memo-table rather than re-computed. Though general (with no analysis required), memo-functions suffer from significant table management overheads.

Other transformation techniques (e.g. tupling and tabulation) may result in more efficient programs but they usually require program analyses. One popular approach is to analyse the call dependency graphs (DGs) algebraically. This algebraic approach typically rely on suitable conditions of descent functions to infer redundancy patterns in the DGs. Descent functions are those functions which are applied to the arguments of subsidiary recursive calls. Some common relationships of descent functions which were discovered by Cohen[Coh83] are the *common generator, periodic commutative* and *commutative* redundancy relationships. Though fairly extensive, there are still other classes of programs (e.g. Tower of Hanoi) which are not easily addressed by this algebraic approach. This is due primarily to the difficulty of analysing all possible descent conditions without getting ad-hoc.

Another approach for detecting call redundancy is to make *direct* searches of the DGs. Richard Bird [Bir80] pointed out the possibility of using pebbling game [Pip80] as a general technique for this purpose. This game searches for a suitable pebble placement sequence, using fewest pebbles, to visit the entire graph from the leaves to the root. Similarly, Pettorossi [Pet84] advocated a semi-formal framework for a top-down search of DG to find eureka matching tuples. However, these past proposals are not automatic. Our newly extended tupling method can be seen as an attempt to combine a simple algebraic analyses (on the recursion parameters), together with an automated (search-based) transformation method.

Another related transformation is that proposed by Proietti and Pettorossi [PP91]. They formulated a transformation procedure, called the Elimination Procedure (in short), for eliminating unnecessary variables from logic programs. This procedure is rather powerful because it could perform both fusion [Wad88] and tupling transformations[3] at the same time. The Elimination Procedure is applicable to a class of programs which can be cleanly split into two portions: a *tree-like* sub-program and a *non-ascending* sub-program. In the tree-like sub-program, each clause can be non-linear but each predicate can have at most one parameter. This effectively means that non-linear recursion parameters could only be captured in the tree-like sub-program. Hence, the present restriction allows only predicates corresponding to SRP-functions to be successfully tupled. With the synchronization analyses, our method now works for MRP-functions, as well.

Both our synchronization analyses and Holst's *finiteness analysis* [Hol91] are sophisticated parameter analyses based on function call transitions. Finiteness analysis can detect increasing/decreasing parameters in order to determine if static arguments are safe to specialise. It was formulated to ensure termination of partial evaluators for strict, first-order functional languages. We focus on a different transformation technique, namely tupling. As a result, a new form of parameter analysis is required to ensure that our method is safe.

In this paper, a systematic extension to the tupling method has been proposed. The extended method now works for sub-classes of functions with multiple recursion parameters. To obtain more optimisation, the new method is also structured into three main phases for the elimination of intra-call traversals, inter-call traversals and redundant calls. Like partial evaluation, the extended tupling method is completely automatic with the help of the proposed synchronization analyses.

6 Acknowlegements

This initial ideas for this work were germinated in April-June 1993 during a visit to Chalmers University of Technology by the first author. The author benefited from discussions with John Hughes and Carsten Kehler Holst. Insightful comments by Neil Jones have also helped sharpen the eventual thrust of the paper. Anonymous reviewers also provided helpful comments. The support of NUS research grants, RP920614 & RP930611, are acknowledged.

References

[Aug85] Lennart Augustsson. Compiling pattern-matching. In *2nd ACM Functional Programming Languages and Computer Architecture Conference*, Nancy, France, (Lect. Notes Comput. Sc., vol 201, pp. 368–381) Berlin Heidelberg New York: Springer, 1985.

[BD77] R.M. Burstall and J. Darlington. A transformation system for developing recursive programs. *Journal of ACM*, 24(1):44–67, January 1977.

[Bir80] Richard S. Bird. Tabulation techniques for recursive programs. *ACM Computing Surveys*, 12(4):403–417, December 1980.

---

[3] Tupling requires an additional functionality rule be imposed on predicates to fix the input/output modes of parameters.

[Chi90] Wei-Ngan Chin. *Automatic Methods for Program Transformation.* PhD thesis, Imperial College, University of London, March 1990.

[Chi93] Wei-Ngan Chin. Towards an automated tupling strategy. In *3rd ACM Symposium on Partial Evaluation and Semantics-Based Program Manipulation, ACM Press,* pages 119–132, Copenhagen, Denmark, ACM Press, June 1993.

[Chi95] Wei-Ngan Chin. Tupling: an automatic compile-time memoisation transformation. Technical report, Dept of IS/CS, NUS, May 1995.

[CK93] Wei-Ngan Chin and Siau-Cheng Khoo. Tupling functions with multiple recursion parameters. In *3rd International Workshop on Static Analysis,* Padova, Italy, (Lect. Notes Comput. Sc., vol 724, pp. 124–140) Berlin Heidelberg New York: Springer, 1993.

[Coh83] Norman H. Cohen. Eliminating redundant recursive calls. *ACM Trans. on Programming Languages and Systems,* 5(3):265–299, July 1983.

[Hol91] Carsten Kehler Holst. Finiteness analysis. In *5th ACM Functional Programming Languages and Computer Architecture Conference,* pages 473–495, Cambridge, Massachusetts, August 1991.

[Mic68] Donald Michie. Memo functions and machine learning. *Nature,* 218:19–22, 1968.

[Pet84] Alberto Pettorossi. A powerful strategy for deriving programs by transformation. In *3rd ACM LISP and Functional Programming Conference,* pages 273–281, 1984.

[Pip80] N. Pippenger. Pebbling. Rc 8258 (# 35937), IBM Thomas J Watson Research Centre, May 1980.

[PP91] M. Proietti and A. Pettorossi. Unfolding - definition - folding, in this order for avoiding unnecessary variables in logic programs. In *Proceedings of PLILP,* Passau, Germany, (Lect. Notes Comput. Sc., vol 528, pp. 347–258) Berlin Heidelberg New York: Springer, 1991.

[RFJ89] C. Runciman, M. Firth, and N. Jagger. Transformation in a non-strict language : An approach to instantiation. In *Glasgow Functional Programming Workshop,* August 1989.

[Wad88] Phil Wadler. Deforestation: Transforming programs to eliminate trees. In *European Symposium on Programming,* pages 344–358, Nancy, France, March 1988.

A Uniform Approach
for Compile-Time and Run-Time Specialization

Charles Consel, Luke Hornof, François Noël, Jacques Noyé, Nicolae Volanschi

Université de Rennes / Irisa
Campus Universitaire de Beaulieu
35042 Rennes Cedex, France
{consel, hornof, fnoel, noye, volanski}@irisa.fr

Abstract. As partial evaluation gets more mature, it is now possible to use this program transformation technique to tackle realistic languages and real-size application programs. However, this evolution raises a number of critical issues that need to be addressed before the approach becomes truly practical.

First of all, most existing partial evaluators have been developed based on the assumption that they could process any kind of application program. This attempt to develop *universal* partial evaluators does not address some critical needs of real-size application programs. Furthermore, as partial evaluators treat richer and richer languages, their size and complexity increase drastically. This increasing complexity revealed the need to enhance design principles. Finally, exclusively specializing programs at compile time seriously limits the applicability of partial evaluation since a large class of invariants in real-size programs are not known until run time and therefore cannot be taken into account.

In this paper, we propose design principles and techniques to deal with each of these issues.

By defining an architecture for a partial evaluator and its essential components, we are able to tackle a rich language like C without compromising the design and the structure of the resulting implementation.

By designing a partial evaluator targeted towards a specific application area, namely system software, we have developed a system capable of treating realistic programs.

Because our approach to designing a partial evaluator clearly separates preprocessing and processing aspects, we are able to introduce run-time specialization in our partial evaluation system as a new way of exploiting information produced by the preprocessing phase.

1 Introduction

Partial evaluation is reaching a level of maturity which makes this program transformation technique capable of tackling realistic languages and real-size application programs. However, this evolution raises a number of critical issues which need to be addressed before the approach becomes truly practical.

Universality vs. Adequacy. Until now, most partial evaluators have always been developed based on the assumption that they could process any kind of application programs; they can be seen as *universal* partial evaluators. As partial evaluation addresses more realistic programs, it also faces new challenges when it tackles existing real-size application programs. This new situation reveals that the usual, general-purpose set of analyses and transformations available in traditional partial evaluators falls short of addressing some critical needs of realistic programs.

For instance, not only does a partial evaluator need to offer an extensible set of transformations, but the transformations themselves should be developed based on program patterns found in typical applications programs in a given area.

Need for Design Principles. Furthermore, as partial evaluators treat richer and richer languages, their size and complexity increase drastically. Indeed, programs written in realistic languages like C expose a very wide variety of situations where partial evaluation can be applied. As a result, there is now a clear need to propose design principles to structure the added complexity of the resulting partial evaluators.

Compile-Time Specialization is Limiting. When studying components from real software systems, it becomes apparent that exclusively specializing programs at compile time is limiting. In fact, there exist numerous invariants that are not known until run time and can yet be used for extensive specialization. This situation occurs, for example, when a set of procedures implements session-oriented transactions. When a session is opened, many pieces of information are known, but only at run time. They could be used to specialize the procedures which perform the actual transactions. Then, when the session is closed, the invariants become invalid, therefore the specialized procedures can be eliminated.

Although run-time specialization seems to involve techniques different from compile-time specialization, both forms of specialization are conceptually the same. They should thus be modeled by a unique approach rather than studied separately. Also, when considering realistic languages, the level of effort required to develop a specializer is such that pursuing some uniformity to handle both cases of specialization is critical.

In this paper we present a partial evaluator of C programs, called Tempo[1]. It is based on a general approach capable of handling programs written in a wide variety of languages which spans from the C programming language (in the case of Tempo) to a pure, higher-order dialect of Scheme (in the case of Schism [8, 9]).

A Uniform Approach. This approach is off-line in that it separates the partial evaluation process into two parts: preprocessing and processing [24, 12]. The former part mainly includes a binding-time analysis aimed at determining the static

---

[1] The name Tempo has been previously used for a pedagogical programming language to study binding times and parameter passing concepts [23].

and dynamic computations for a given program and a division (static/dynamic) of its input. Binding-time information is subsequently used by another analysis to assign a *specialization action* (*i.e.*, program transformation) to each construct in the program [10].

The latter part (*i.e.*, processing) performs the specialization for a given action-analyzed program and specialization values. Specialization is then merely guided by the information produced by the preprocessing part. In many regards, this design is very similar to the one used to implement programming languages. For a given program, just like a compiler produces machine instructions, the preprocessing phase produces program transformations. Just like a run-time system executes compiled code, the processing phase (*i.e.*, the specializer) executes the program transformations produced by the preprocessing phase. Just like a compiled code is run many times with respect to different input values, a preprocessed program can be specialized many times with respect to different specialization values. Because specialization has been *compiled*, it is performed very efficiently. Because of the separation between preprocessing and processing, the latter can be implemented in a different language from the former, and thereby facilitate the implementation. More importantly, this design allows one to process action-analyzed programs in many different ways. Indeed, in order to perform compile-time specialization, actions can either be interpreted, or even compiled. The latter form of specialization corresponds to producing a generating extension [2, 21].

Compile-time and Run-time Specialization. More interestingly, actions can be used as a basis to perform run-time specialization. Indeed, actions directly model the shape of residual programs since they express how each construct in a program is to be transformed. In fact, we have developed a strategy to perform run-time specialization based on actions [13]. In essence, an action-annotated program is used to generate automatically source templates at compile time. Then, at run time, the compiled templates are selected and filled with run-time values before being executed. This new approach has many advantages: it is general since it is based on a general approach to developing partial evaluators; it is portable because most of the specialization process is performed at the source level; and it is efficient in that specialization is amortized in a few runs of the specialized code.

An important aspect of our approach is that the preprocessing of a program is identical whether it is specialized at compile time or at run time. This is a direct consequence of the kind of information computed in the preprocessing part of the system.

Adequacy. Tempo has been targeted toward a particular area, namely systems applications. More precisely, the features of Tempo have been guided by program patterns based on actual studies of numerous systems programs and tight collaboration with systems researchers. As a result, the accuracy of critical analyses such as alias analysis and binding-time analysis are adequate for typical systems programs. Also, the program transformations address the important cases in systems programs.

More globally, this new approach to the design of a partial evaluator has had an important consequence; it clearly showed the need for *module-oriented* partial evaluation. Traditional partial evaluators assume they process a complete program. However, systems programs are large enough to reach the limit of what a state of the art analysis, such as an alias analysis, can process [44]. We have therefore developed support to enable one to specialize pieces of a large system.

Summary. This paper makes a series of contributions regarding the design and architecture of a partial evaluator for a real language, applied to real programs. These contributions are as follows.

1. We present an architecture for partial evaluators which is powerful enough to be used for realistic languages and real-size application programs.
2. This architecture has been used to develop a partial evaluator of C programs. Unlike most existing systems, our partial evaluator has been carefully designed to address specific specialization opportunities found in a particular area, namely, systems applications. This strategy allows us to better ensure the applicability of partial evaluation.
3. Although dedicated to a particular application area, the architecture is nonetheless open: new program transformations can easily be introduced at the action analysis level.
4. Last but not least, our architecture has proved its generality in that it allows one to perform both compile-time and run-time specialization. As a consequence, this generalized new form of specialization drastically widens the scope of applicability of partial evaluation.

Outline. In Sect. 2 we explain the preprocessing phase, followed by the different processing phases in Sect. 3. Section 4 then discusses the applications we consider. Related work is addressed in Sect. 5, and finally we give concluding remarks in Sect. 6.

2 Preprocessing

As shown in Fig. 1, the preprocessing part consists of four main phases. It eventually produces transformation operations that must be performed to specialize the subject program.

2.1 Front-End

This phase transforms a C program into a C abstract syntax tree (AST). We have not written a new parser but have rather reused SUIF components [43]. SUIF is a testbed system for experimenting with program optimizations in the context of scientific code and parallel machines. Our abstract syntax is not based

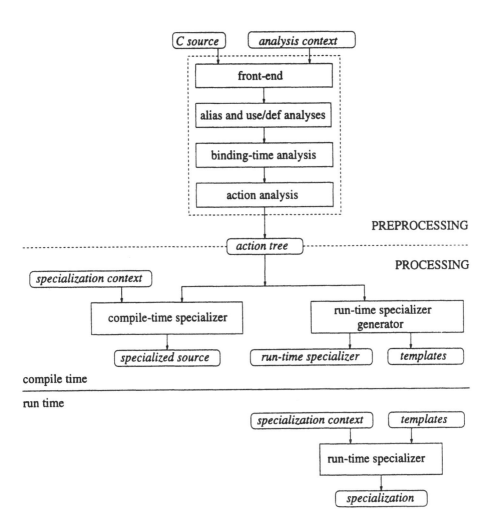

Fig. 1. A general view of Tempo

on the SUIF intermediate format, which is too low-level for our purposes, but on an intermediate representation used by a SUIF program which transforms this format back into C. With a couple of minor modifications to SUIF we are then able to turn C programs into simple high-level ASTs. In particular, our abstract syntax includes a single, **do-while**, loop construct, a single conditional construct, no conditional expression, no comma expression, and no nested type declarations.

Two additional important transformations are applied to the ASTs obtained from SUIF. Firstly, in order to allow for compositional analyses, **goto** statements are eliminated as suggested by Erosa and Hendren [20]. Secondly, renaming makes every identifier unique in order to help building up a flattened static store (see Sect. 3). This renaming also facilitates procedure inlining at postprocessing time.

2.2 Alias and Use/Def Analyses

Because of the pointer facilities offered by the C language, an alias analysis is critical to determine the set of aliases for each variable in a program. This information allows the computation of binding-time properties of variables to take into account side-effects. However, unlike other contexts of use of alias analysis, partial evaluation does not require very accurate information. This situation is essentially due to the kind of static computations that are expected to be performed by partial evaluation. Indeed, based on our experience, static computations rely on invariants whose validity typically follows a very clear pattern. In fact, this is not surprising since invariant behavior must be simple enough to be understandable. Our choice of a context-insensitive analysis is further backed up by the study of Ruf [40] which shows that empirical benefits of a context-sensitive analysis have still to be measured.

Our analysis is very similar to existing ones [16, 40]. It is based on the *points-to* model of aliasing. It is interprocedural, context-insensitive, and flow-sensitive. The analysis takes as arguments a set of procedures, a goal procedure, a description of the initial points-to pairs, and a description of the effect of the external procedures on the points-to relation. The last two arguments make it possible to perform alias analysis in a module-oriented way. This feature is critical to enable one to only specialize parts of a large system. Assuming that programs submitted to specialization are correct, the analysis does not separately deal with *possible* and *definite* points-to pairs (see [7, 40]).

The alias analysis is complemented by a use/def analysis which computes the non-local store affected by each procedure call as well as which procedures are responsible for input/output.

2.3 Binding-Time Analysis

We have developed a binding-time analysis which annotates C programs with their binding times, given a set of procedures, its alias and side-effect information, a goal procedure, and a binding-time description of the context. This context includes the parameters of the goal procedure, a global state, and, as for alias analysis, the external procedures.

Like the alias analysis, the design of the binding-time analysis was driven by the typical specialization opportunities that occur in systems programs. Some of these situations are well-known in the partial evaluation community and are addressed by standard program transformations (*e.g.*, reduction of primitive applications and procedure residualization).

Other situations require new features to be introduced in the binding-time analysis and the subsequent phases. For example, we have found that certain types of variables, such as integers and pointers, are static in some parts of a procedure and dynamic in others. We handle variables of these types in a flow-sensitive manner, giving one binding-time description per variable per program point.

In addition, our analysis offers elaborate strategies to deal with pointers. More precisely, to exploit thoroughly static information included in partially static objects, it is critical to enable static pointers to refer both to static and/or dynamic objects. Indeed, in the case of pointers to structures, references to its static components should be partially evaluated away, whereas references to its dynamic components should be residualized. This situation implies that a single variable must be able to have two binding-time values, depending on the program point: static if used to dereference static objects, and dynamic if used to dereference dynamic objects.

Interestingly, a similar situation occurs when a pointer may refer to more than one memory cell. If some of these memory cells are static and others dynamic, then the same variable should be described by two different binding-time values. Again, the pointer to the static object should be evaluated while the pointer to the dynamic object needs to be residualized.

Previous analyses are not capable of distinguishing the differences between these cases, and therefore conservatively annotate programs with the most approximate information. For example, all these binding-time analyses are flow-insensitive, merging information from all program points together [2, 4, 22]. Further, only one description per variable is available, which may unfortunately residualize some static pointers to static objects [2]. One attempt to resolve this conflict involved splitting structures into static and dynamic parts [2]. This does not work with *module-oriented* partial evaluation, since the interface of a procedure must remain compatible with the interface of the call site.

Another important situation occurs for conditional statements. It has been shown that when conditional statements are processed in a continuation-passing style, the analysis can produce more accurate results [11, 30]. However this strategy might cause code explosion when the test of the conditional statement is dynamic and therefore both branches are residualized.

The analysis of conditional statements via a mixed strategy circumvents the problem. In the case where the test is dynamic, we analyze each branch separately, merge binding-time information at the join point, and then analyze the continuation. On the other hand, if the test is static, then after analyzing each branch separately we analyze the continuation twice, once assuming the true branch will be taken and once assuming the false branch. Since the test is static, the appropriate continuation will be chosen and the useless continuation discarded at specialization time—thus avoiding code explosion.

2.4 Action Analysis

Once the binding-time analysis has been completed, the resulting information is used to determine, for each construct, which specialization *action* (*i.e.,* program transformation) to be performed. This phase comes in addition to the traditional preprocessing phases and has many advantages.

Further compilation of the specialization process. Traditionally, the specializer is directly driven by binding-time information. The complexity of the interpretation of binding-time information depends on the complexity of the binding-time information itself. For realistic languages like the C language, this specialization involves interpreting detailed binding-time information of such objects as data structures. This process can noticeably slow down the specialization phase. In fact, this situation can be improved because binding-time information is available prior to specialization, therefore it can be used to further compile the transformation phase.

More precise definition of the program transformations. Defining specialization actions explicitly forces the designer of the partial evaluator to precisely define the set of program transformations needed for a given language. Not only does this provide better documentation to the user, but it also defines in detail the semantics of the specialization phase.

Better separation between preprocessing and specialization. Because action-analyzed programs capture the essence of the specialization process, they can be exploited in many different ways. In fact, in our partial evaluation system, actions can be both interpreted and compiled, and used for compile-time as well as run-time specialization. This range of applications shows the generality of the information expressed by actions.

Specialization actions for C. Four general transformations are potentially defined for each language construct. Action *reduce* (abbreviated *red*) is assigned to an occurrence of a language construct that can be reduced at specialization time. For example, a conditional statement is reduced when its test expression is static. The action *rebuild* (abbreviated *reb*) annotates a construct that needs to be reconstructed but yet includes some static computations. Action *eval* (abbreviated *ev*) is assigned to an occurrence of a language construct that only consists of purely static components. In other words, it can be completely evaluated away at specialization time. At the other end of the spectrum there is action *identity* (abbreviated *id*) which annotates purely dynamic program fragments.

These transformations are fundamental in the sense that they can be used to define other actions. As an example, consider the case of an *explicated* assignment, *i.e.*, an assignment to a variable which is at the same time static and dynamic. The *explication* of such an assignment can be expressed by combining two actions: an action *ev* indicates that the assignment must be completely evaluated so that the value of the variable be available for the static computations; another action *reb* expresses the fact that the assignment also has to be rebuilt so that the variable can be included in a residual program fragment corresponding to dynamic computations.

3 Processing

There can be various back-ends to an action-analyzed program. By back-ends we mean processing phases. They can be divided into two categories: actions can be exploited for either compile-time or run-time specialization.

3.1 Compile-Time Specialization

Traditionally the result of preprocessing is used for compile-time specialization. Just like machine instructions, produced by a compiler, can be interpreted by a simulator or directly executed by a machine, actions can either be interpreted or compiled. Let us describe these two strategies.

Interpreting Actions. An interpreter of actions corresponds to the usual specializer. It consists of dispatching on each action of a program and executing various operations which perform this action. Because information available prior to specialization has been extensively exploited, the specializer is simple, has a clear structure, and is very efficient.

Conceptually, a specializer combines a standard interpreter to perform the static computations, and a non-standard interpreter to reconstruct program fragments corresponding to the dynamic computations. Unlike standard interpretation, programs may sometimes need to be evaluated speculatively. Typically for conditional statements with a dynamic test expression, both branches need to be partially evaluated since the test expression is unknown at specialization time. A mechanism is thus needed to process the branches independently of each other: they must be processed with the same initial store available before considering the branches. This situation requires to make a copy of the store, and reinstall it at a later stage.

One approach to address this problem is to write a specializer which includes a complete interpreter of C programs. A drawback of this approach is the major development effort that it entails due to the syntactic richness of the C language, and also to the wide range of base types and conversion operations between them (which are sometime machine-dependent!).

Another option is to interface a specializer with an existing C interpreter. However, existing C interpreters do not offer a store model which supports speculative evaluation. Implementing this store copying would require the memory of the interpreter to be tagged in some way and would involve a costly memory traversal.

We have developed a third option which allows us to use a standard compiler to process the static computations, thus preserving the semantics of these computations. The first part of this approach consists of flattening the scope of the static variables of a program. Indeed, only static variables can be involved in static computations. To do so, the idea is to rename all the variables of a program so that they can all be global. Of course, this transformation precludes the specialization of recursive procedures when they are partially static. However, systems programs do not usually exploit this language feature. A consequence of this design is that all static data structures can be allocated contiguously and can be easily copied to implement speculative evaluation. Furthermore, invocations of external procedures (*i.e.*, procedures not processed by the specializer) can be done easily since the store layout is compatible.

The other part of our approach consists of encapsulating purely static (*ev*) fragments in C procedures. These C procedures can be directly compiled by some standard C compiler and linked to the specializer. The specializer thus only concentrates on the operations aimed at reconstructing program fragments. In order to process an *ev* fragment, the specializer simply invokes the C procedure which performs the corresponding computations.

The idea of using a standard compiler to perform part or all of the specialization process is not new. Andersen [2] uses a similar approach in his C partial evaluator (C-Mix) by producing generating extensions. However, his store management is more complex in that each data object is indexed by a version number and has an "object function" that can save and restore its value, and compare it to another copy. These operations are aimed at sharing some copies of the same object (*e.g.*, a matrix) between several static stores. However, in our case, module-oriented specialization greatly reduces the need for such optimizations. Indeed, unlike C-Mix which requires a program to be specialized all at once, Tempo can specialize pieces of a program separately. Furthermore, C-Mix includes a symbolic store used, for instance, when procedures are unfolded, or to manipulate pointers to dynamic objects. In contrast, Tempo's specializer only includes the static C store used by *ev* procedures, and inlining is done as a postprocessing operation for compile-time specialization. This approach greatly simplifies the specializer and does not degrade the quality of the specialized programs.

Compiling Actions. The natural alternative to interpreting actions is to compile them. The same "run-time" system previously described for specialization is reused. Indeed, *ev* fragments can still be packaged up in procedures, as for action interpretation, and thus be directly treated by the C compiler. The main issue when compiling actions is to compile partially static computations, *i.e.*, to reconstruct residual code. A simple action compiler is an almost trivial task to achieve, as shown by Consel and Danvy [10]. A similar compilation process is also known as generating extension [1, 2, 6, 21]. One difference is that this latter approach is directly based on binding-time information and thus far more complicated than an action compiler.

3.2 Run-Time Specialization

Not only can actions be used to specialize programs at compile time but they can also be utilized to perform specialization at run time. In fact, run-time specialization based on actions is just another way of exploiting this information. Indeed, an action describes how to transform a construct and therefore an action tree precisely describes the set of possible specialized programs. This set can be formally defined by a tree grammar.

We have developed an abstract interpreter which produces a tree grammar for a given action-analyzed program. As a simple example of what this analysis produces for an action analyzed program, consider the following action tree fragment:

*reb(*PLUS*(id(*VAR("x")*)*, *ev(...)))*

Assuming an *ev* fragment of type integer, our analysis then produces the tree grammar rule shown below:

L → PLUS(VAR("x"), HOLE(INT))

Once produced, the tree grammar is used to generate templates [25], *i.e.*, source code fragments parameterized with "holes" for run-time values. For the above tree grammar rule, we obtain the following template:

x + *int_hole*

The tree grammar is also used to compile the templates in context, *i.e.*, without loosing control flow information, using a standard compiler. As a result, the quality of the compiled templates is as good as the compiler being used. In fact, in our implementation of the run-time specializer, the GNU C compiler is being used.

One key feature of our approach is that specialization at run-time solely amounts to executing the static computations, selecting templates, filling holes in templates with run-time values, and relocating jumps between templates. The simplicity of these operations makes run-time specialization a very efficient process which on average requires, according to preliminary experiments, specialized code to be run very few times to amortize the cost of specialization.

A complete description of our approach to run-time specialization is presented elsewhere [13].

4 Applications

This section first discusses some generalities regarding the classes of programs which are targeted for specialization. The support for module-oriented specialization is then presented. Finally, typical candidates for specialization in system code are described.

4.1 Classes of Programs Targeted

In recent years, major research projects have been focusing on the design and implementation of operating systems that are both highly-parameterized and efficient. These apparently conflicting goals have led researchers to widen the scope of the techniques which are used in system development. More specifically, programming language techniques have been introduced to perform a critical task, namely, adapting/customizing system components with respect to given parameters. In this context, forms of partial evaluation have become a key technique to develop adaptive operating systems. Examples of such projects include Spin [5], ExoKernel [18], Scout [29], and Synthetix [14, 15].

To validate the applicability of Tempo we have been studying in detail various system components. Some of this work has been done in collaboration with operating system researchers. For example, we have been collaborating with the Synthetix group at Oregon Graduate Institute to apply our approach to file system operations in the Hewlett Packard Unix system [37].

Other areas of current research include inter-process communication (IPC) and remote procedure calls (RPC). In particular, we have been working on fragments of the Chorus operating system [39]. Our goal is to specialize the remote procedure call layer (RPC) with respect to a given RPC stub and server [42].

These studies suggest the following three observations: there is a need for module-oriented specialization, control flow specialization is important, and there are opportunities to specialize with respect to data flow.

4.2 Module-Oriented Specialization

The need for module-oriented specialization appeared obvious when examining any system code. For example, when studying the communication system of Chorus, it turned out that this component was too large to enable one to reason about potential specializations. We therefore concentrated on a specific layer of the protocol stack: the socket level. When isolating this piece of code, we found a great number of global static variables, some deeply embedded in partially static structures. This situation prompted us to work on a tool capable of determining what parts of the global state were needed for a particular piece of code, and assist the programmer to initialize it when performing specialization.

Furthermore, when specializing an isolated piece of code, the partial evaluation system still needs to reason about the unknown used pieces. More precisely, the pieces external to the one considered have to be understood in terms of their side effects. To this end, we are also developing a declaration language which enables the programmer to specify the effects of external pieces.

Another consequence of studying system code is the use of a demand-driven strategy to develop Tempo. Usually, every language feature is being dealt with in a complete way. That is, all possible cases defined for a language feature are handled. This completeness is needed since no specific application is targeted. However for a language like C, this strategy amounts to being very conservative for a number of its features. When a particular kind of programs is targeted, one can observe that language features are seldomly used in their full generality. This situation arises, for example, in the case of the operation **setjump**, which allows programs to exit non-locally. Although this operation has a very unpredictable effect on the control, it is used in a very structured way in system code. In fact, we have characterized the program patterns corresponding to the way it is used, and for these patterns a treatment is proposed.

4.3 Control Flow Specialization

System programs devote much of their time interpreting data structures. These data structures may contain information of the system state or parameters provided by the user. Like any interpreter, these special-purpose interpreters can be specialized with respect to a given program (here, a regular data structure).

This observation can be illustrated, for example, by the communication system we studied. There are some typical interpreting procedures, for instance `udp_usrreq(sock, req, ...)`, at the UDP level, which take a user request and dispatch to the corresponding code. There is also much argument checking performed. For example, for each operation on a socket, the procedure `getsock(fdes)` is called and checks whether the file descriptor is not out of bounds. Still, this information, available when the socket is opened, will not change until it is closed. Run-time specialization can be used in such a situation.

In fact, interpretation is really pervasive in an operating system due to the generality of the services it offers. It is common to observe that some operations devote more than a quarter of their conditional computations to interpret user options or parts of the system state. In this respect, this application area is ideal for partial evaluation.

4.4 Data Flow Specialization

Besides the control flow of a program, specialization can also optimize its data flow. In system code, links between data structures are repeatedly interpreted. For example, the same linked list can be traversed many times, and thus, the pointers linking the elements together are dereferenced repeatedly. Specialization can be used in this situation to optimize the code that traverses such data structures with respect to a given instance. It will eliminate the pointer dereferencing operations.

This idea was originally presented by Massalin [38] and named *executable data structures*. He applied this technique to the task scheduler of the Synthesis operating system. It is a routine which is called when a task switch is needed. To perform this task switch, the scheduler saves the registers of the outgoing task (including the program counter), and then — using a global circular task queue — dereferences a pointer to the next task, loads its registers, and jumps to its saved program counter. To obtain an efficient task switch, prologue and epilogue code are dynamically generated for each task, using some hand-written templates in assembly language. This code only saves the used registers of the old task and loads the needed registers of the new one. This optimization is important when dealing with floating-point registers, whose saving and restoring time is expensive.

The same optimization can be performed using partial evaluation. The prologue and epilogue routines can be derived automatically by specializing a generic task scheduler with respect to a given circular task queue. Let us consider, for simplicity, a non-preemptive scheduler expressed in some pseudo-code. This scheduler is called by a task wishing to give control back to the system:

```
task *crt_tsk;

sched() {
  save_regs(crt_tsk);
  crt_tsk=crt_tsk->next;
  load_regs(crt_tsk);
  jmp_to(crt_tsk->PC);
}

task_1(){
  ...
  sched();
  ...
}
```

It is the second command in procedure **sched** which is important as far as data flow specialization is concerned. It dereferences the pointer to the next task to be activated. Data flow specialization is targeted towards eliminating such operations. Notice that, in contrast, the specialization of the call to the procedure **save_regs** involves control flow specialization.

Once specialized with respect to a given circular list of tasks, the resulting program is:

```
sched_1(){
  save(FP1); save(FP4);
  load(FP2); load(FP3);
  jmp(0x....);
}
```

```
task_1(){
  ...
  sched_1();
  ...
}
```

While this example is overly simplified, it still illustrates how specialization can be applied to complex data structures that are repeatedly interpreted by system code.

5 Related Work

There are already a number of existing imperative partial evaluators [2, 4, 22, 28, 31]. They are either on-line or off-line partial evaluators, and cover a wide range of imperative programming languages, such as C, Pascal, and Fortran. All of these systems are universal in the sense that they offer general solutions. Also, they are all global, requiring the whole program to be processed in order to perform any optimizations. This severely limits real-size applications. Finally, these systems are limited to compile-time optimizations. Run-time information is ignored.

Tempo addresses these shortcomings. By considering specific realistic applications, we make design decisions which allow us to produce a highly effective tool for certain applications. Being module-oriented, Tempo can be applied to smaller parts of large systems, opening up many new opportunities to apply partial evaluation. As well, including a run-time specializer allows new types of optimizations to be performed.

Recently, other forms of run-time specialization have been explored. Some approaches rely on the programmer manually constructing templates, which are then compiled into binary code at run time [17, 19]. With Leone and Lee's approach [26, 27], binding time annotations are explicitly supplied by the user, for each function, using curryfication. A number of compilation operations are then postponed until run time in order to better optimize programs. At the University of Washington, another approach has been proposed, based on user annotations and a modified compiler [3]. All these approaches are error-prone due to the need for user intervention, lose efficiency due to the lack of global perspective, and have not been formalized.

We have addressed each of these issues when developing the run-time specializer for Tempo. The process is automatic and formally defined and proven, guaranteeing a relative degree of safety. Since it is based on the GNU C compiler, we can port our run-time specializer to any architecture which supports this widely available compiler. Finally, efficient code can be created since the templates are all available and compiled before run time, which allows advanced optimizations to be performed.

Current work is also being done on adaptive operating systems [5, 18, 29]. These existing approaches tend to invent new and different technologies in order to provide this adaptiveness.

In contrast, we propose reusing an existing technology, namely partial evaluation, to meet the demands of adaptive operating systems. Our collaboration with the Synthetix group creates a synergistic effect where both groups benefit from the cross-fertilization [37]. The operating systems group identifies where specialization can be applied, and uses our tools to perform their adaptive specialization. By applying Tempo to systems programs, our group can continue refining the tools based on the feedback we receive.

6 Conclusion

We have presented an approach to designing partial evaluators for realistic languages and applied it to real-size applications. Our Tempo system is based on a general approach which consists of separating the process into two parts: a preprocessing phase compiles, after a number of static analyses, input programs into actions, and a processing phase which then executes these actions to perform the actual specialization. As we have shown, this has a number of benefits and, in particular, makes it possible to integrate both compile-time and run-time specialization within the same system.

A second key feature which distinguishes Tempo from standard partial evaluators is the fact that this partial evaluator was developed with a particular domain of applications in mind, namely system code. This decision was based on the belief that a universal partial evaluator would be too general to perform the specific optimizations desired. We have accordingly opted for a bottom-up approach which consists of studying the opportunities for specialization of specific applications and then making design decisions based upon these studies.

Our preliminary experiments, on operating system code, are encouraging. They have shown that partial evaluation can indeed be used to migrate current operating systems towards a new range of adaptive operating systems. These early results have also brought to our attention new concepts and techniques, like module-oriented specialization, which we found necessary to perform the realistic program transformations we desired.

Although much remains to be done, we feel that Tempo is a significant step towards making partial evaluation a practical tool for programming in the large.

Acknowledgements

This research is supported in part by France Telecom/SEPT, ARPA grant N00014-94-1-0845, and NSF grant CCR-92243375. The authors would like to thank Olivier Danvy and Barbara Moura for their comments on drafts of this paper. Thanks are also due to Sandrine Chirokoff, Julia Lawall, Anne-Françoise Le Meur, Jérôme Picault, Vincent Piederriere, and Scott Thibault for their help with the implementation of Tempo.

References

1. L.O. Andersen. – Self-applicable C program specialization. – In *Partial Evaluation and Semantics-Based Program Manipulation*, pages 54–61, San Francisco, CA, USA, June 1992. Yale University, Hew Haven, CT, USA. – Technical Report YALEU/DCS/RR-909.

2. L.O. Andersen. – *Program Analysis and Specialization for the C Programming Language*. – PhD thesis, Computer Science Department, University of Copenhagen, May 1994. – DIKU Technical Report 94/19.

3. J. Auslander, M. Philipose, C. Chambers, S.J. Eggers, and B.N. Bershad. – Fast, effective dynamic compilation. – In PLDI96 [35]. – To appear.

4. R. Baier, R. Glück, and R. Zöchling. – Partial evaluation of numerical programs in Fortran. – In PEPM94 [33], pages 119–132.

5. B.N. Bershad, S. Savage, P. Pardyak, E. Gün Sirer, M.E. Fiuczynski, D. Becker, C. Chambers, and S. Eggers. – Extensibility, safety and performance in the SPIN operating system. – In SOSP95 [41], pages 267–283.

6. L. Birkedal and M. Welinder. – Partial evaluation of Standard ML. – Master's thesis, Computer Science Department, University of Copenhagen, 1993. – Research Report 93/22.

7. D.R. Chase, M. Wegman, and F. Kenneth Zadeck. – Analysis of pointers and structures. – In *Proceedings of the ACM SIGPLAN '90 Conference on Programming Language Design and Implementation*, pages 296–310, White Plains, NY, USA, June 1990. ACM Press. – ACM SIGPLAN Notices, 25(6).

8. C. Consel. – Polyvariant binding-time analysis for applicative languages. – In PEPM93 [32], pages 145–154.

9. C. Consel. – A tour of Schism. – In PEPM93 [32], pages 66–77.

10. C. Consel and O. Danvy. – From interpreting to compiling binding times. – In N.D. Jones, editor, *ESOP'90, 3rd European Symposium on Programming*, volume 432 of *Lecture Notes in Computer Science*, pages 88–105. Springer-Verlag, 1990.

11. C. Consel and O. Danvy. – For a better support of static data flow. – In J. Hughes, editor, *Proceedings of the 5th ACM conference on Functional Programming Languages and Computer Architecture*, volume 523 of *Lecture Notes in Computer Science*, pages 496–519, Cambridge, MA, USA, August 1991. Springer-Verlag.

12. C. Consel and O. Danvy. – Tutorial notes on partial evaluation. – In *Proceedings of the 20th Annual ACM SIGPLAN-SIGACT Symposium on Principles Of Programming Languages*, pages 493–501, Charleston, SC, USA, January 1993. ACM Press.

13. C. Consel and F. Noël. – A general approach for run-time specialization and its application to C. – In POPL96 [36], pages 145–156.

14. C. Consel, C. Pu, and J. Walpole. – Incremental specialization: The key to high performance, modularity and portability in operating systems. – In PEPM93 [32], pages 44–46. – Invited paper.

15. C. Consel, C. Pu, and J. Walpole. – Making production OS kernel adaptive: Incremental specialization in practice. – Technical report, Department of Computer Science and Engineering, Oregon Graduate Institute of Science & Technology, 1994.

16. M. Emami, R. Ghiya, and L.J. Hendren. – Context-sensitive interprocedural points-to analysis in the presence of function pointers. – In *Proceedings of the ACM SIGPLAN '94 Conference on Programming Language Design and Implementation*, pages 242–256. ACM Press, June 1994. – ACM SIGPLAN Notices, 29(6).

17. D.R. Engler, W.C. Hsieh, and M.F. Kaashoek. – 'C: A language for high-level, efficient, and machine-independent dynamic code generation. – In POPL96 [36], pages 131–144.

18. D.R. Engler, M.F. Kaashoek, and J.W. O'Toole. – Exokernel: An operating system architecture for application-level resource management. – In SOSP95 [41], pages 251–266.

19. D.R. Engler and T.A. Proebsting. – DCG: An efficient retargetable dynamic code generation system. – In *Proceedings of the Sixth International Conference on Architectural Support for Programming Languages and Operating Systems (ASPLOS VI)*, pages 263–273. ACM Press, November 1994.

20. A.M. Erosa and L.J. Hendren. – Taming control flow: A structured approach to eliminating goto statements. – In *Proceedings of the IEEE 1994 International Conference on Computer Languages*, May 1994.

21. A.P. Ershov. – On the essence of translation. – *Computer Software and System Programming*, 3(5):332–346, 1977.

22. N.D. Jones, C. Gomard, and P. Sestoft. – *Partial Evaluation and Automatic Program Generation.* – International Series in Computer Science. Prentice-Hall, June 1993.

23. N.D. Jones and S.S. Muchnick. – *TEMPO: A Unified Treatment of Binding Time and Parameter Passing Concepts in Programming Languages*, volume 66 of *Lecture Notes in Computer Science*. – Springer-Verlag, 1978.

24. N.D. Jones, P. Sestoft, and H. Søndergaard. – Mix: a self-applicable partial evaluator for experiments in compiler generation. – *Lisp and Symbolic Computation*, 2(1):9–50, 1989.

25. D. Keppel, S. Eggers, and R. Henry. – Evaluating runtime compiled value-specific optimizations. – Technical Report 93-11-02, Department of Computer Science, University of Washington, Seattle, WA, 1993.

26. M. Leone and P. Lee. – Lightweight run-time code generation. – In PEPM94 [33].

27. M. Leone and P. Lee. – Optimizing ML with run-time code generation. – In PLDI96 [35]. – To appear.

28. U. Meyer. – Techniques for partial evaluation of imperative languages. – In *Partial Evaluation and Semantics-Based Program Manipulation*, pages 94–105, Hew Haven, CT, USA, September 1991. – ACM SIGPLAN Notices, 26(9).

29. A.B. Montz, D. Mosberger, S.W. O'Malley, L.L. Peterson, T.A. Proebsting, and J.H. Hartman. – Scout: A communications-oriented operating system. – Technical Report 94-20, Department of Computer Science, The University of Arizona, 1994.

30. F. Nielson. – A denotational framework for data flow analysis. – *Acta Informatica*, 18(3):265–287, 1982.

31. V. Nirkhe and W. Pugh. – Partial evaluation and high-level imperative programming languages with applications in hard real-time systems. – In *Proceedings of the 19th Annual ACM SIGPLAN-SIGACT Symposium on Principles Of Programming Languages*, pages 269–280, Albuquerque, New Mexico, USA, January 1992. ACM Press.

32. *Partial Evaluation and Semantics-Based Program Manipulation*, Copenhagen, Denmark, June 1993. Yale University, Hew Haven, CT, USA.

33. *ACM SIGPLAN Workshop on Partial Evaluation and Semantics-Based Program Manipulation.* Technical Report 94/9, University of Melbourne, Australia, 1994.

34. *Proceedings of the ACM SIGPLAN '95 Conference on Programming Language Design and Implementation.* ACM Press, June 1995. – ACM SIGPLAN Notices, 30(6).

35. *Proceedings of the ACM SIGPLAN '96 Conference on Programming Language Design and Implementation*, Philadelphia, PA, May 1996. ACM Press. – To appear.

36. *Proceedings of the 23rd Annual ACM SIGPLAN-SIGACT Symposium on Principles Of Programming Languages*, St. Petersburg Beach, FL, USA, January 1996. ACM Press.

37. C. Pu, T. Autrey, A. Black, C. Consel, C. Cowan, J. Inouye, L. Kethana, J. Walpole, and K. Zhang. – Optimistic incremental specialization: Streamlining a commercial operating system. – In SOSP95 [41], pages 314–324.

38. C. Pu, H. Massalin, and J. Ioannidis. – The Synthesis kernel. – *Computing Systems*, 1(1):11–32, Winter 1988.

39. V. Rozier, V. Abrossimov, F. Armand, I. Boule, M. Gien, M. Guillemont, F. Herrmann, C. Kaiser, S. Langlois, P. Léonard, and W. Neuhauser. – Overview of the Chorus distributed operating system. – In *USENIX - Workshop Proceedings - Micro-kernels and Other Kernel Architectures*, pages 39–70, Seattle, WA, USA, April 1992.

40. E. Ruf. – Context-insensitive alias analysis reconsidered. – In PLDI95 [34], pages 13–22. – ACM SIGPLAN Notices, 30(6).

41. *Proceedings of the 1995 ACM Symposium on Operating Systems Principles*, Copper Mountain Resort, CO, USA, December 1995. ACM Operating Systems Reviews, 29(5).

42. E.N. Volanschi, G. Muller, and C. Consel. – Safe operating system specialization: the RPC case study. – In *Workshop Record of WCSSS'96 – The Inaugural Workshop on Compiler Support for Systems Software*, pages 24–28, Tucson, AZ, USA, February 1996.

43. R.P. Wilson, R.S. French, C.S. Wilson, S.P. Amarasinghe, J.M. Anderson, S.W.K. Tjiang, S.-W. Liao, C.-W. Tseng, M.W. Hall, M.S. Lam, and J.L. Hennessy. – SUIF: An infrastructure for research on parallelizing and optimizing compilers. – *ACM SIGPLAN Notices*, 29(12):31–37, December 94.

44. R.P. Wilson and M.S. Lam. – Efficient context-sensitive pointer analysis of C programs. – In PLDI95 [34], pages 1–12. – ACM SIGPLAN Notices, 30(6).

Pragmatics of Type-Directed Partial Evaluation

Olivier Danvy

Computer Science Department
Aarhus University *
(http://www.brics.dk/~danvy)

Abstract. Type-directed partial evaluation stems from the residualization of static values in dynamic contexts, given their type and the type of their free variables. Its algorithm coincides with the algorithm for coercing a subtype value into a supertype value, which itself coincides with Berger and Schwichtenberg's normalization algorithm for the simply typed λ-calculus. Type-directed partial evaluation thus can be used to specialize a compiled, closed program, given its type.

Since Similix, let-insertion is a cornerstone of partial evaluators for call-by-value procedural languages with computational effects (such as divergence). It prevents the duplication of residual computations, and more generally maintains the order of dynamic side effects in the residual program.

This article describes the extension of type-directed partial evaluation to insert residual let expressions. This extension requires the user to annotate arrow types with effect information. It is achieved by delimiting and abstracting control, comparably to continuation-based specialization in direct style. It enables type-directed partial evaluation of programs with effects (*e.g.*, a definitional lambda-interpreter for an imperative language) that are in direct style. The residual programs are in A-normal form. A simple corollary yields CPS (continuation-passing style) terms instead. We illustrate both transformations with two interpreters for Paulson's Tiny language, a classical example in partial evaluation.

1   Introduction

1.1   Background

During partial evaluation [11, 27], parts of a program are evaluated and parts are reconstructed. The parts that are reconstructed yield residual expressions forming the residual program. The parts that are evaluated yield static values. Either of two things can happen to a static value: it may be consumed statically or it may be residualized, *i.e.*, it may be turned into a residual expression whose evaluation will yield a corresponding dynamic value. Sometimes, during partial evaluation, a static value can be both consumed statically and residualized.

---

* Ny Munkegade, Building 540, DK-8000 Aarhus C, Denmark. (danvy@brics.dk)

For example, in the following binding-time annotated Scheme program [8],

```
(lambda (a b c d)
  (let ([r (gensym! "x")])
    `(lambda (,r)
       ,(if (< a b)
            `(r ,(- c) ,c)
            d))))
```

a, b, c, and d denote static integers. The static integers denoted by a and b are consumed statically in the test; the static integer denoted by d is residualized; and the static integer denoted by c is both consumed statically (it is negated) and residualized.

Applying the procedure above to 1, 2, 3, and 4 yields the residual program:

```
(lambda (x6)
  (x6 -3 3))
```

where x6 is a fresh variable.

Had the binding-time analysis been more conservative, and required that static values be exclusively consumed or exclusively residualized, the residual program would be less specialized — namely it would read as follows.

```
(lambda (x6)
  (x6 (- 3) 3))
```

At base type, contemporary partial evaluators do not make this approximation, and thus they allow this double status of static values (*i.e.*, consumable and residualizable). At higher type, however, offline partial evaluators with monovariant binding-time analyses do make this approximation [27]. Lacking a residualization function at higher type, they do not allow the double status of static values. Instead, they favor residualization. Thus the binding-time analysis dynamizes the offending values, and the specializer yields underspecified programs. Better specialization requires the users to "improve the binding times" of their source programs [27, Chapter 12].

This residualization function operating at higher types forms the starting point of "type-directed partial evaluation" [13].

1.2 Type-directed partial evaluation

Type-directed partial evaluation stems from the desire to residualize arbitrary static values in dynamic contexts. Residualizing static values requires knowing the type structure of these values. If these values are higher-order, residualization also requires the type structure of their free variables. Its algorithm parallels the one for source binding-time improvements at higher type [17, 18], and coincides with the coercion algorithm in type systems with subtypes [25, 26], and with a normalization algorithm in proof theory [1] and logical frameworks [35]. This last coincidence suggests that it is possible to specialize compiled programs, by interpreting static expressions as executable code and dynamic expressions as code constructors. We have named this process "type-directed partial evaluation": the specialization of compiled code into the text of its (long $\beta\eta$) normal form [13]. A type-directed partial evaluator is thus unconventional in that it does not process the text of a source program, but its compiled (higher-order) value. The normalization effect is not obtained by symbolic interpretation — it happens *en passant* in the residualization algorithm.

We have described the principles and applications of type-directed partial evaluation elsewhere [13]. In this paper, we investigate some more pragmatic aspects, and merely assume from the reader some rudimentary knowledge of partial evaluation [11, 27] and of the Scheme programming language [8].

1.3 Computation duplication

A type-directed partial evaluator encounters the same problem as all other partial evaluators for call-by-value programs: computation duplication. For example, consider the following procedure (where the type constructor => accounts for Scheme's uncurried procedures, and where a, b, and c denote base types).

```
(define foo       ;;; ((a -> b) a ((b b) => c)) => c
  (lambda (f a k)
    ((lambda (v) (k v v)) (f x))))
```

Let us residualize the value of foo. (Its source text is unavailable: it has been compiled away.)

```
> (residualize foo '(((a -> b) a ((b b) => c)) => c))
(lambda (x0 a1 x2)
  (x2 (x0 a1) (x0 a1)))
>
```

A computation is duplicated: that of the application of the first argument of foo to its second. Sometimes this duplication is of no consequence, *e.g.*, if the function denoted by the first argument of foo is pure (*i.e.*, side-effect free), total, and inexpensive. In general, however, both computation duplication and code duplication are not wanted.

The point of this paper is to remedy this situation. We extend the language of types handled by type-directed partial evaluation to account for impure procedures, whose application should not be duplicated. Our treatment is standard [7] — we insert a residual let expression.

1.4 Let insertion

Let us residualize the value of foo again. This time, we specify that its first argument might perform a side effect (indicated by an annotated arrow -!>).

```
> (residualize foo '(((a -!> b) a ((b b) => c)) => c))
(lambda (x0 a1 x2)
  (let ([b3 (x0 a1)])
    (x2 b3 b3)))
>
```

A residual let expression has been inserted.

This let insertion naturally scales up, yielding residual programs in "CPS without continuations" (a.k.a. "nqCPS", "A-normal forms" [22], "monadic normal forms" [24], *etc.*), as illustrated below.

```
> (residualize (lambda (f x k)
                 ((lambda (v) (k v v)) (f (f x))))
               '(((b -!> b) b ((b b) => c)) => c))
(lambda (x0 b1 x2)
  (let* ([b3 (x0 b1)]
         [b4 (x0 b3)])
    (x2 b4 b4)))
>
```

Residual let expressions can also retain dynamic computations whose result is unused, as illustrated below.

```
> (residualize (lambda (f x y)
                 ((lambda (v) y) (f (f x))))
               '(((b -!> b) b c) => c))
(lambda (x0 b1 c2)
  (let* ([b3 (x0 b1)]
         [b4 (x0 b3)])
    c2))
>
```

The reader should keep in mind that inserting let expressions is something of a challenge, since in contrast to all other existing partial evaluators, we have no access to the text of the source program. In the interactions above, residualize is not a macro — it is a Scheme procedure and thus it processes (compiled) Scheme expressible values.

1.5   Overview

The rest of this paper is structured as follows. We first start with a side issue about naming residual variables (Section 2). This side issue is pragmatically trivial, but solving it does improve the readability of residual programs. Thus equipped, we review the problem of residual computational effects in partial evaluation, and its solutions (Section 3). We then apply Section 3 to type-directed partial evaluation (Section 4). This makes it possible to specialize both a direct-style and a continuation-style interpreter for Paulson's Tiny language (Section 5). As a corollary of Section 4, we outline the CPS transformation of compiled programs in normal form (Section 6). After a comparison with related work (Section 7), we conclude (Section 8).

2 What is in a name?

Under lexical scope, names of local variables do not matter. In practice, though, they contribute to program readability, and thus programmers usually pick "meaningful" identifiers. One reason why automatically generated programs are hard to read is precisely because they have uninformative identifiers. Our strategy for picking residual names is type-directed.

2.1 Implicit naming

The two special forms `define-base-type` and `define-compound-type` are used to declare types. By default, variables of declared types are named after the first letter of the declared type name, catenated with a gensym-generated number. Undeclared variables of compound types start with the letter x followed with a gensym-generated number. We refer to these letters as *name stubs*.

Let us illustrate implicit naming with the first Scheme session of Section 1.

```
> (define-base-type a)
> (define-base-type b)
> (define-base-type c)
> (define-compound-type fun-from-a-to-b (a -> b))
> (define-compound-type Bar ((fun-from-a-to-b a ((b b) => c)) => c))
> (residualize (lambda (f a k)
                  ((lambda (v) (k v v)) (f x)))
              'Bar)
(lambda (f0 a1 x2)
  (x2 (f0 a1) (f0 a1)))
>
```

In this session, a is declared as a base type, and gives rise to the residual variable a1 (the corresponding name stub is a); `fun-from-a-to-b` is declared as a compound type, and gives rise to the residual variable f0 (the corresponding name stub is f); and the residual variable x2 was generated out of the anonymous type (b b) => c (the corresponding name stub is x).

The definition of declared types is substituted for each later occurrence of their name. So for example, the type denoted by Bar is textually the same as the type specified in the first Scheme session of Section 1, modulo the name stubs.

2.2 Explicit naming

Users can specify name stubs in the declaration of a type. Daring users can also specify a full name with a directive `alias`. This may come in handy if no name clash is expected. Name clashes do not occur when there is only one instance of a variable of a declared type. This can happen either statically (the variable is declared at the outset of a residual program) or dynamically (all variables of this type denote a single-threaded value [36]). Both instances are illustrated in Section 5.

2.3 An example

The type (b (c -> b) c) => b denotes an uncurried Scheme procedure with three arguments. We associate the name stub "Y" to the (base) type of the first argument, the name stub "foo" to the (compound) type of the second argument, and the name "Juliet" to the (base) type of the third argument — assuming case sensitivity.

```
> (define-base-type b "Y")
> (define-base-type c "Juliet" alias)
> (define-compound-type f (c -> b) "foo")
> (define-compound-type g ((b f c) => b))
> (residualize (lambda (x y z) (y z)) 'g)
(lambda (Y0 foo1 Juliet) (foo1 Juliet))
>
```

2.4 Summary

Explicit names and name stubs in the types determine the names of residual variables in residual programs.

3 Sound call unfolding under call-by-value

To propagate constants across procedure boundaries, a partial evaluator unfolds calls. Not all parameters may be static, however, and thus under call-by-value, call unfolding is unsound in general. Against this backdrop, and to tame partially static structures, Torben Mogensen suggested to insert a residual let expression for each dynamic parameter, and to pass on the residual identifier naming the dynamic argument instead of the argument itself [31]. As illustrated in Section 1, under call-by-value, let-declared identifiers can be duplicated without compromising the dynamic semantics of source programs.

This simple solution, put at the core of Similix, before it even had partially static values, has scaled up remarkably well, e.g., to solve the thorny problem of automating call unfolding [37], and also to treat dynamic side-effects soundly [7]. Doubled with a variable-splitting mechanism [32], it provides a simple and elegant treatment of both partially static values and higher-order values [4].

In the next section, we adapt this let-insertion technique to type-directed partial evaluation.

4 The particular case of type-directed partial evaluation

Lacking access to the source code, it is impossible to insert residual let expressions at call sites — they are compiled, along with the rest of the source program. However, the only dynamic expressions that should not be duplicated are residual calls to procedures that may perform side effects. Therefore it it sufficient to name these residual calls and return the corresponding (fresh) identifiers to the current context. This follows the spirit of lightweight symbolic values [30], where the only dynamic expressions in the data flow are residual identifiers.

Thus we choose (1) to annotate the type of procedures that may perform side effects, (2) to insert a residual let expression naming their result when one of their calls is unfolded, and (3) to return the residual name to the context of this call. Point (3) requires us to relocate the context of the call in the body of the let expression. This relocation is achieved by abstracting delimited control, for example with shift and reset [14, 15, 19]. This approach is similar to the strategy for continuation-based partial evaluation [6, 29].

The complete specification of type-directed partial evaluation is shown in Figure 1, using the two-level λ-calculus [33], and in Figure 2, using Scheme. Overlined λ's and @'s denote ordinary λ-abstractions and applications. Underlined λ's and @'s denote the corresponding (hygienic) syntax constructors. The domains Value and Expr are defined inductively, following the structure of types, and starting from the same set of (dynamic) base types. TLT is the domain of (well-typed) two-level terms; it contains both Value and Expr.

The down arrow is read *reify*: it maps a static value and its type into a two-level λ-term that statically reduces to the dynamic counterpart of this static value. Reify is applied to types occurring positively in the source type. Conversely, the up arrow is read *reflect*: it maps a dynamic expression and its type into a two-level λ-term representing the static counterpart of this dynamic expression. Reflect is applied to types occurring negatively in the source type.

The generation of residual calls (to pure procedures) reads as follows [13].

$$\uparrow_{t_1 \to t_2} e = \overline{\lambda} v_1 : t_1. \uparrow_{t_2} (e \underline{@} \downarrow^{t_1} v_1)$$

As illustrated in Section 1, we cannot let residual calls to impure procedures flow uncontrolled in the residualization context. Instead, we want (a) to insert a residual let expression naming this residual call and (b) let the freshly declared identifier flow instead. This requires us to abstract the residualization context of impure calls and to relocate it in the body of a residual let expression. (N.B. The residualization context is constructed with the static applications in the definition of reify.) We abstract it with shift, generate a residual let expression naming the residual call with a fresh name, and restore the context in the body of the let expression, providing it with the fresh name, appropriately eta-expanded.

$$\uparrow_{t_1 \xrightarrow{!} t_2} e = \overline{\lambda} v_1 : t_1.\text{shift } \kappa \text{ } \overline{\text{in}} \text{ } \underline{\text{let}} \text{ } x_2 : t_2 = e \underline{@} \downarrow^{t_1} v_1 \text{ } \underline{\text{in}} \text{ } \overline{\text{reset}} (\kappa \overline{@} \uparrow_{t_2} x_2)$$

This technique of abstracting delimited control in a program transformation is getting to be standard by now. It originates in the specification of "one-pass" CPS transformations [14, 15] and is also used today in continuation-based partial evaluation [6, 29]. We illustrate it further in appendix.

Figure 1 is a conservative extension of the original specification [13] — remembering the algebraic property of reset [14, 15]:

Property 1 *For any expression e with no occurrence of shift, reset(e) = e.*

$$t \in \text{Type} ::= b \mid t_1 \times t_2 \mid t_1 \to t_2 \mid t_1 \xrightarrow{\text{!}} t_2$$

$$v \in \text{Value} ::= c \mid x \mid \overline{\lambda} x : t.v \mid v_0 \,\overline{@}\, v_1 \mid$$

$$\overline{\text{pair}}(v_1, v_2) \mid \overline{\text{fst}}\, v \mid \overline{\text{snd}}\, v \mid$$

$$\overline{\text{shift}}\, k : t_1 \to t_2 \,\overline{\text{in}}\, \underline{\text{let}}\, x : t_1 = e_0 \,\underline{@}\, e_1 \,\underline{\text{in}}\, \overline{\text{reset}}_{t_2}\, k \,\overline{@}\, v$$

$$e \in \text{Expr} ::= c \mid x \mid \underline{\lambda} x : t.e \mid e_0 \,\underline{@}\, e_1 \mid$$

$$\underline{\text{pair}}(e_1, e_2) \mid \underline{\text{fst}}\, e \mid \underline{\text{snd}}\, e \mid$$

$$\overline{\text{reset}}_t\, e$$

$$\text{reify} = \lambda t.\lambda v : t.\!\downarrow^t v$$

$$: \ \text{Type} \to \text{Value} \to \text{TLT}$$

$$\downarrow^b v = v$$

$$\downarrow^{t_1 \times t_2} v = \underline{\text{pair}}(\downarrow^{t_1} \overline{\text{fst}}\, v, \downarrow^{t_2} \overline{\text{snd}}\, v)$$

$$\downarrow^{t_1 \to t_2} v = \underline{\lambda} x_1 : t_1.\overline{\text{reset}}_{t_2} \downarrow^{t_2} (v \,\overline{@}\, \uparrow_{t_1}^{t_2} x_1)$$

$$\downarrow^{t_1 \xrightarrow{!} t_2} v = \underline{\lambda} x_1 : t_1.\overline{\text{reset}}_{t_2} \downarrow^{t_2} (v \,\overline{@}\, \uparrow_{t_1}^{t_2} x_1)$$

$$\text{where } x_1 \text{ is fresh.}$$

$$\text{reflect} = \lambda t'.\lambda t.\lambda e : t.\!\uparrow_t^{t'} e$$

$$: \ \text{Type} \to \text{Type} \to \text{Expr} \to \text{TLT}$$

$$\uparrow_b^t e = e$$

$$\uparrow_{t_1 \times t_2}^t e = \overline{\text{pair}}(\uparrow_{t_1}^t \underline{\text{fst}}\, e, \uparrow_{t_2}^t \underline{\text{snd}}\, e)$$

$$\uparrow_{t_1 \to t_2}^t e = \overline{\lambda} v_1 : t_1.\uparrow_{t_2}^t (e \,\underline{@}\, \downarrow^{t_1} v_1)$$

$$\uparrow_{t_1 \xrightarrow{!} t_2}^t e = \overline{\lambda} v_1 : t_1.\overline{\text{shift}}\, \kappa : t_2 \to t \,\overline{\text{in}}\, \underline{\text{let}}\, x_2 : t_2 = e \,\underline{@}\, \downarrow^{t_1} v_1$$
$$\underline{\text{in}}\, \overline{\text{reset}}_t (\kappa \,\overline{@}\, \uparrow_{t_2}^t x_2)$$

$$\text{where } x_2 \text{ is fresh.}$$

Reset and reflect are annotated with the type of the value expected by the delimited context.

$$\text{residualize} = \text{statically-reduce} \circ \text{reify}$$

$$: \ \text{Type} \to \text{Value} \to \text{Expr}$$

Fig. 1. Type-directed residualization with let insertion

In the presence of procedures that may perform side effects, and as illustrated in Section 5, the result of type-directed partial evaluation contains series of flat let expressions. These are characteristic of nqCPS.

```
(define-record (Base name stub))
(define-record (Prod type type stub))
(define-record (Func type type stub))
(define-record (Proc type type stub))

(define residualize
  (lambda (v t)
    (letrec ([reify
               (lambda (t v)
                 (case-record t
                   [(Base name stub)
                    v]
                   [(Prod t1 t2 stub)
                    '(cons ,(reify t1 (car v)) ,(reify t2 (cdr v)))]
                   [(Func t1 t2 stub)
                    (let ([x1 (elaborate-new-name t1)])
                      '(lambda (,x1)
                         ,(Reset (reify t2 (v (reflect t1 x1))))))]
                   [(Proc t1 t2 stub)
                    (let ([x1 (elaborate-new-name t1)])
                      '(lambda (,x1)
                         ,(Reset (reify t2 (v (reflect t1 x1))))))]))]
             [reflect
               (lambda (t e)
                 (case-record t
                   [(Base name stub)
                    e]
                   [(Prod t1 t2 stub)
                    (cons (reflect t1 '(car ,e))
                          (reflect t2 '(cdr ,e)))]
                   [(Func t1 t2 stub)
                    (lambda (v1)
                      (reflect t2 '(,e ,(reify t1 v1))))]
                   [(Proc t1 t2 stub)
                    (lambda (v1)
                      (let ([q2 (elaborate-new-name t2)])
                        (Shift k
                               '(let ([,q2 (,e ,(reify t1 v1))])
                                  ,(Reset
                                     (k (reflect t2 q2)))))))]))])
      (begin
        (reset-gensym!)
        (reify (parse-type t) v)))))
```

Fig. 2. Type-directed partial evaluation with let insertion in Scheme

5   An example: Paulson's Tiny interpreter

Paulson's Tiny language [34] is a classical example in partial-evaluation circles
[4, 7, 10, 27, 32]. Its BNF reads as follows (see Figure 8).

$$
\begin{aligned}
\langle pgm \rangle &::= \textbf{block } \langle decl \rangle^* \textbf{ in } \langle cmd \rangle \textbf{ end} \\
\langle decl \rangle &::= \langle ide \rangle^* \\
\langle cmd \rangle &::= \textbf{skip } | \\
&\qquad \langle cmd \rangle \,; \langle cmd \rangle \;| \\
&\qquad \langle ide \rangle := \langle exp \rangle \;| \\
&\qquad \textbf{if } \langle exp \rangle \textbf{ then } \langle cmd \rangle \textbf{ else } \langle cmd \rangle \;| \\
&\qquad \textbf{while } \langle exp \rangle \textbf{ do } \langle cmd \rangle \textbf{ end} \\
\langle exp \rangle &::= \langle int \rangle \;| \; \langle ide \rangle \;| \; \langle exp \rangle \, \langle op \rangle \, \langle exp \rangle \;| \textbf{ read} \\
\langle op \rangle &::= + \;| - | \times \;| \; = \;| \geq
\end{aligned}
$$

It is a simple exercise to write the corresponding definitional interpreter in
direct style (see Figure 3) or in continuation style (see Figure 4). One can then
apply it to, *e.g.*, the factorial program

```
block res, val, aux
in val  :=  read ; aux  :=  1 ;
   while val > 0  do
      aux  :=  aux * val ; val  :=  val - 1
   end ;
   res := aux
end
```

and residualize the result with either of

```
(residualize (meaning-d fac) 'Type-d)
(residualize (meaning-c fac) 'Type-c)
```

where **meaning-d** and **type-d** are defined in Figures 3 and 9, **meaning-c** and **type-c**
are defined in Figures 4 and 10, and **fac** denotes the parsed factorial program.
Figures 5 and 6 display the corresponding residual programs.

The residual program of Figure 5 is a direct-style Scheme program in A-
normal form, threading the store throughout. The residual program of Figure 6
is a continuation-passing Scheme program, also threading the store throughout.
In both programs, the while loop has been mapped into a fixed-point declaration (reflecting the semantics of while loops in both Tiny interpreters). All the
location offsets have been computed at partial-evaluation time.

The following four facts are worth noting.

1. These residual programs have been generated straight out of the two interpreters of Figures 3 and 4, *i.e.*, with no post-processing.

```
(define meaning-d
  (lambda (p)
    (lambda (add sub mul equ gt read fix true? lookup update)
      (lambda (s)
        (letrec ([meaning-program ...]
                 [meaning-declaration ...]
                 [meaning-command
                  (lambda (c r s)
                    (case-record c
                      [(Skip) s]
                      [(Sequence c1 c2)
                       (meaning-command c2 r (meaning-command c1 r s))]
                      [(Assign i e)
                       (update (r i) (meaning-expression e r s) s)]
                      [(Conditional e c-then c-else)
                       (true? (meaning-expression e r s)
                              (lambda (s)
                                (meaning-command c-then r s))
                              (lambda (s)
                                (meaning-command c-else r s))
                              s)]
                      [(While e c)
                       ((fix (lambda (while)
                               (lambda (s)
                                 (true? (meaning-expression e r s)
                                        (lambda (s)
                                          (while (meaning-command c r s)))
                                        (lambda (s) s)
                                        s)))) s)]))]
                 [meaning-expression
                  (lambda (e r s)
                    (case-record e
                      [(Literal l) l]
                      [(Boolean b) b]
                      [(Identifier i) (lookup (r i) s)]
                      [(Primop op e1 e2) ((meaning-primop op)
                                          (meaning-expression e1 r s)
                                          (meaning-expression e2 r s))]
                      [(Read) (read)]))]
                 [meaning-primop
                  (lambda (op)
                    (case op
                      [(+) add] [(-) sub] [(*) mul] [(=) equ] [(>) gt]))])
          (meaning-program p s))))))
```

Fig. 3. Direct-style Scheme interpreter for Tiny (valuation functions)

```
(define meaning-c
  (lambda (p)
    (lambda (add sub mul equ gt read fix true? lookup update)
      (lambda (s k)
        (letrec ([meaning-program ...]
                 [meaning-declaration ...]
                 [meaning-command
                  (lambda (c r s k)
                    (case-record c
                      [(Skip) (k s)]
                      [(Sequence c1 c2)
                       (meaning-command c1 r s (lambda (s)
                       (meaning-command c2 r s k)))]
                      [(Assign i e)
                       (meaning-expression e r s (lambda (v)
                       (update (r i) v s k)))]
                      [(Conditional e c-then c-else)
                       (meaning-expression e r s (lambda (v)
                       (true? v
                              (lambda (s k)
                                (meaning-command c-then r s k))
                              (lambda (s k)
                                (meaning-command c-else r s k))
                              s k)))]
                      [(While e c)
                       ((fix (lambda (while)
                              (lambda (s k)
                                (meaning-expression e r s (lambda (v)
                                (true? v
                                       (lambda (s k)
                                         (meaning-command c r s
                                           (lambda (s) (while s k))))
                                       (lambda (s k) (k s))
                                       s k)))))) s k)])]
                 [meaning-expression
                  (lambda (e r s k)
                    (case-record e
                      [(Literal l) (k l)]
                      [(Boolean b) (k b)]
                      [(Identifier i) (lookup (r i) s k)]
                      [(Primop op e1 e2)
                       (meaning-expression e1 r s (lambda (v1)
                       (meaning-expression e2 r s (lambda (v2)
                       ((meaning-primop op) v1 v2 k)))))]
                      [(Read) (read k)]))]
                 [meaning-primop ...])
          (meaning-program p s k))))))
```

Fig. 4. Continuation-style Scheme interpreter for Tiny (valuation functions)

```
(lambda (add sub mul equ gt read fix true? lookup update)
  (lambda (s)
    (let* ([n0 (read)]
           [s (update 1 n0 s)]
           [s (update 2 1 s)]
           [s ((fix (lambda (while1)
                      (lambda (s)
                        (let* ([n2 (lookup 1 s)]
                               [n3 (gt n2 0)])
                          (true? n3
                                 (lambda (s)
                                   (let* ([n4 (lookup 2 s)]
                                          [n5 (lookup 1 s)]
                                          [n6 (mul n4 n5)]
                                          [s (update 2 n6 s)]
                                          [n7 (lookup 1 s)]
                                          [n8 (sub n7 1)]
                                          [s (update 1 n8 s)])
                                     (while1 s)))
                                 (lambda (s) s)
                                 s))))) s)]
           [n9 (lookup 2 s)])
      (update 0 n9 s))))
```

This residual program is a specialized version of the Tiny interpreter of Figure 3 with respect to the factorial source program. It is also the textual direct-style version of the residual program of Figure 6.

Fig. 5. Direct-style residual factorial program

2. The two interpreters were compiled with an ordinary Scheme compiler, and the residual programs thus were generated without the usual symbolic interpretation of a partial evaluator (generating extensions nonwithstanding).

3. Thanks to the naming scheme of Section 2, both residual programs are also straightforward to read. Specifically, in Figures 9 and 10,
   - the type of expressible values is declared with the name stub n, to reflect that the corresponding variables are of integer type;
   - the domain of the semantic operator fix is declared with the name stub while, to single out the denotation of source while loops;
   - the type of the semantic operator lookup is declared with an alias, since it is declared globally to the definitional interpreter;
   - the types of the store and of the continuation are declared with an alias, since both are single-threaded in the definitional interpreter.

4. Matching the fact that Figure 4 is the CPS counterpart of Figure 3 [16], Figure 6 is the textual CPS counterpart of Figure 5. This property usually holds modulo renaming, using *e.g.*, Schism or Similix [5, 9].

```
(lambda (add sub mul equ gt read fix true? lookup update)
  (lambda (s k)
    (read (lambda (n0)
    (update 1 n0 s (lambda (s)
    (update 2 1 s (lambda (s)
    ((fix (lambda (while1)
            (lambda (s k)
              (lookup 1 s (lambda (n2)
              (gt n2 0 (lambda (n3)
              (true? n3
                    (lambda (s k)
                      (lookup 2 s (lambda (n4)
                      (lookup 1 s (lambda (n5)
                      (mul n4 n5 (lambda (n6)
                      (update 2 n6 s (lambda (s)
                      (lookup 1 s (lambda (n7)
                      (sub n7 1 (lambda (n8)
                      (update 1 n8 s (lambda (s)
                      (while1 s (lambda (s) (k s)))))))))))))))))))))
                    (lambda (s k) (k s))
                    s
                    (lambda (s) (k s)))))))))) s (lambda (s)
    (lookup 2 s (lambda (n9)
    (update 0 n9 s (lambda (s) (k s)))))))))))))))))))
```

This residual program is a specialized version of the Tiny interpreter of
Figure 4 with respect to the factorial source program. It is also the textual
CPS version of the residual program of Figure 5.

Fig. 6. Continuation-style residual factorial program

The following diagram summarizes the situation. $\mathcal{R}_d$ denotes the residualizing function of Figure 1. $\mathcal{C}$ denotes the CPS transformation. Tiny_d and Tiny_c
denote the text of the direct-style and of the continuation-style Tiny interpreters,
respectively. $[\![\text{Tiny}_d]\!]$ and $[\![\text{Tiny}_c]\!]$ denote their meaning (*i.e.*, compiled code). Finally, fac denotes the source factorial program.

$$
\begin{array}{ccc}
\text{Tiny}_d \text{ (Figure 3)} & \qquad & [\![\text{Tiny}_d]\!]\,\text{fac} \xrightarrow{\ \mathcal{R}_d\ } \text{Figure 5} \\
\Big\downarrow{\scriptstyle\mathcal{C}} & & \Big\downarrow{\scriptstyle\mathcal{C}} \\
\text{Tiny}_c \text{ (Figure 4)} & \qquad & [\![\text{Tiny}_c]\!]\,\text{fac} \xrightarrow[\ \mathcal{R}_d\ ]{} \text{Figure 6}
\end{array}
$$

6 Corollary: CPS transformation of compiled programs

It is very simple to translate nqCPS terms into CPS [12, 23, 28]. Let expressions, for example, in the context of a continuation k, are essentially desugared as follows:

$$\langle\!\langle \text{let } v = f@x \text{ in } e \rangle\!\rangle \, k \;\; = \;\; f@x@(\lambda v.\langle\!\langle e \rangle\!\rangle \, k)$$

This makes it simple to adapt Figure 1 to produce CPS terms. The corresponding program is available through the author's home page.[2] It can be used to perform the following experiment: residualizing the direct-style Tiny interpreter of Figure 3 with respect to the factorial program now yields a continuation-style residual program. This continuation-style residual program textually coincides with the ordinary residualization of the continuation-style Tiny interpreter of Figure 4, provided we relax the alias definition of the compound type CCont in Figure 10.

The following diagram extends the diagram of Section 5 and summarizes the situation. $\mathcal{R}_c$ denotes the new residualizing function.

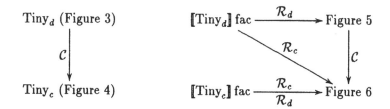

In particular, since all types in the continuation-style Tiny interpreter are pure, residualizing it with either $\mathcal{R}_d$ or $\mathcal{R}_c$ yields the same result.

$\mathcal{R}_c$, however, is not the CPS counterpart of $\mathcal{R}_d$. Furthermore, it does not make sense to CPS transform $\mathcal{R}_d$ as defined in Figure 1 and 2 because source programs in general are in direct style.[3] This makes it a true necessity here to abstract delimited control.

7 Related work

7.1 Partial evaluation

Section 1 has already situated type-directed partial evaluation among related work: it stems from the need to residualize static values in dynamic contexts at higher type; its algorithm coincides with the algorithm for higher-order coercions [25, 26], and also with Berger and Schwichtenberg's normalization algorithm for the simply typed λ-calculus [1]. This coincidence of algorithms shows that there

---

[2] http://www.brics.dk/~danvy
[3] CPS-transforming higher-order programs assumes that their higher-order arguments are also CPS-transformed.

is as much computational power in residualization as in an offline monovariant partial evaluator for the λ-calculus. In particular, and this is the whole point of type-directed partial evaluation, picking a particular representation of staticness (compiled syntax constructions) and of dynamicness (compiled syntax constructors) makes it possible to specialize closed compiled programs, given their type.[4]

The two-level λ-calculus has appeared ideal to express the residualization algorithm. Other unexplored developments include subtyping in the two-level λ-calculus [33].

7.2 Logical frameworks

Users of Frank Pfenning's Elf system [35] are also provided with the ability to associate name stubs to types. The reason is the same as here: readability of generated code in the presence of higher-order abstract syntax.

7.3 Out of control: let insertion vs. disjoint sums

In the POPL'96 proceedings, shift and reset are used to handle disjoint sums [13, Section 3]. This use clashes with the let insertion of Section 4. There is, however, a natural hierarchy in these control abstractions, where the treatment for disjoint sums supersedes the treatment for let insertion. This is thus a case for $shift_2$ and $reset_2$ [14]. We leave this aspect for future work.

7.4 An extensional CPS transformation

In his PhD thesis [21], Filinski defines extensional mappings between monadic values (and programs them in Standard ML). In particular, this makes it possible to define an extensional CPS transformation, in the particular case of the identity monad and of the continuation monad. Composing this extensional transformation with residualization appears to yield the same effect as the CPS transformation of Section 6. The extensional CPS transformation is dashed in the following diagram, which extends the diagram of Section 6.

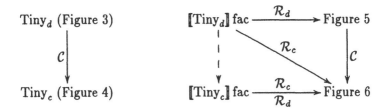

---

[4] One of the referees encouraged us to stress the distinction between constructions and constructors: a constructor generates a construction. This distinction proves essential in the context of program-generating programs.

8 Conclusion and issues

We have extended type-directed partial evaluation with two pragmatic features: the abilities to have a say in residual identifiers and to insert residual let expressions. These make it possible to improve the readability of residual programs, to ensure sound call unfolding, and to specialize direct-style programs containing dynamic computational effects. A simple variant makes it possible to generate residual code in CPS.

These simple steps should contribute to make type-directed partial evaluation more practical. Much work remains to formalize it and make it fit with partial evaluation at large.

Acknowledgements

To Andrzej Filinski, Karoline Malmkjær, and René Vestergaard for their interaction and criticism, and to Julia Lawall, Peter Thiemann, and the anonymous referees for perceptive comments.

This work is supported by BRICS (Basic Research in Computer Science, Centre of the Danish National Research Foundation).

The diagrams were drawn with Kristoffer Rose's X‌Y-pic package and the Scheme sessions were obtained with R. Kent Dybvig's Chez Scheme system.

A Abstracting control with shift and reset

In the following expression, the special form Reset denotes a "prompt" [19], *i.e.*, it delimits the control of its body by supplying it with the identity continuation. The special form Shift abstracts this delimited control into a procedure.

```
(+ 1 (Reset (* 10 (Shift k ...))))
```

The abstracted continuation reads (lambda (v) (* 10 v)). So for example, the expression

```
(+ 1 (Reset (* 10 (Shift k (+ (k 6) (k 4))))))
```

can also be read as

```
(+ 1 (let ([k (lambda (v) (* 10 v))])
        (+ (k 6) (k 4))))
```

and evaluates to 101.

In contrast with call/cc, applying an abstracted continuation here does not "jump out" to yield a final answer. It returns a result at its point of application. This functional behavior makes it possible to compose abstracted continuations [14, 20].

The programming technique used to insert let expressions in Section 4 can be used, for example, to flatten binary trees, as illustrated in Figure 7. The binary tree is traversed depth-first and from left to right, in a delimited context. At every leaf, the traversal is abstracted and the contents of the leaf are cons'ed to the result of the traversal. Procedure flatten-c is the CPS counterpart of Procedure flatten-d. Notice that even though flatten-c is seemingly in "continuation-passing style", it is not tail-recursive. This is the trademark of abstracting delimited control [14, 15, 19].

```
(define-record (Leaf x))
(define-record (Node left-tree right-tree))

(define flatten
  (lambda (t)      ;;; Binary-Tree(X) -> List(X)
    (letrec ([traverse (lambda (t)
                         (case-record t
                           [(Leaf x)
                            (Shift k
                                   (cons x (Reset (k 'dummy))))]
                           [(Node left right)
                            (begin
                              (traverse left)
                              (traverse right))])])
      (Reset (begin
               (traverse t)
               '())))))

(define flatten-c
  (lambda (t k)    ;;; (Binary-Tree(X) (List(X) -> Answer)) => Answer
    (letrec ([traverse (lambda (t k)
                         (case-record t
                           [(Leaf x)
                            (cons x (k 'dummy))]
                           [(Node left right)
                            (traverse left (lambda (dummy)
                                             (traverse right k)))])])
      (k (traverse t (lambda (dummy) '())))))))
```

Fig. 7. Flattening a binary tree

References

1. Ulrich Berger and Helmut Schwichtenberg. An inverse of the evaluation functional for typed λ-calculus. In *Proceedings of the Sixth Annual IEEE Symposium on Logic in Computer Science*, pages 203–211, Amsterdam, The Netherlands, July 1991. IEEE Computer Society Press.

2. Dines Bjørner, Andrei P. Ershov, and Neil D. Jones. *Partial Evaluation and Mixed Computation*. North-Holland, 1988.

3. Hans-J. Boehm, editor. *Proceedings of the Twenty-First Annual ACM Symposium on Principles of Programming Languages*, Portland, Oregon, January 1994. ACM Press.

4. Anders Bondorf. *Self-Applicable Partial Evaluation*. PhD thesis, DIKU, Computer Science Department, University of Copenhagen, Copenhagen, Denmark, 1990. DIKU Report 90-17.

5. Anders Bondorf. Similix manual, system version 3.0. Technical Report 91/9, DIKU, Computer Science Department, University of Copenhagen, Copenhagen, Denmark, 1991.

6. Anders Bondorf. Improving binding times without explicit cps-conversion. In William Clinger, editor, *Proceedings of the 1992 ACM Conference on Lisp and Functional Programming*, LISP Pointers, Vol. V, No. 1, pages 1–10, San Francisco, California, June 1992. ACM Press.

7. Anders Bondorf and Olivier Danvy. Automatic autoprojection of recursive equations with global variables and abstract data types. *Science of Computer Programming*, 16:151–195, 1991.

8. William Clinger and Jonathan Rees (editors). Revised[4] report on the algorithmic language Scheme. *LISP Pointers*, IV(3):1–55, July-September 1991.

9. Charles Consel. A tour of Schism: A partial evaluation system for higher-order applicative languages. In David A. Schmidt, editor, *Proceedings of the Second ACM SIGPLAN Symposium on Partial Evaluation and Semantics-Based Program Manipulation*, pages 145–154, Copenhagen, Denmark, June 1993. ACM Press.

10. Charles Consel and Olivier Danvy. Static and dynamic semantics processing. In Robert (Corky) Cartwright, editor, *Proceedings of the Eighteenth Annual ACM Symposium on Principles of Programming Languages*, pages 14–24, Orlando, Florida, January 1991. ACM Press.

11. Charles Consel and Olivier Danvy. Tutorial notes on partial evaluation. In Susan L. Graham, editor, *Proceedings of the Twentieth Annual ACM Symposium on Principles of Programming Languages*, pages 493–501, Charleston, South Carolina, January 1993. ACM Press.

12. Olivier Danvy. Back to direct style. *Science of Computer Programming*, 22(3):183–195, 1994. Special Issue on ESOP'92, the Fourth European Symposium on Programming, Rennes, February 1992.

13. Olivier Danvy. Type-directed partial evaluation. In Guy L. Steele Jr., editor, *Proceedings of the Twenty-Third Annual ACM Symposium on Principles of Programming Languages*, pages 242–257, St. Petersburg Beach, Florida, January 1996. ACM Press.

14. Olivier Danvy and Andrzej Filinski. Abstracting control. In Mitchell Wand, editor, *Proceedings of the 1990 ACM Conference on Lisp and Functional Programming*, pages 151–160, Nice, France, June 1990. ACM Press.

15. Olivier Danvy and Andrzej Filinski. Representing control, a study of the CPS transformation. *Mathematical Structures in Computer Science*, 2(4):361–391, December 1992.

16. Olivier Danvy and John Hatcliff. On the transformation between direct and continuation semantics. In Stephen Brookes, Michael Main, Austin Melton, Michael Mislove, and David Schmidt, editors, *Proceedings of the 9th Conference on Mathematical Foundations of Programming Semantics*, number 802 in Lecture Notes in Computer Science, pages 627–648, New Orleans, Louisiana, April 1993.

17. Olivier Danvy, Karoline Malmkjær, and Jens Palsberg. The essence of eta-expansion in partial evaluation. *LISP and Symbolic Computation*, 8(3):209–227, 1995. An earlier version appeared in the proceedings of the 1994 ACM SIGPLAN Workshop on Partial Evaluation and Semantics-Based Program Manipulation.

18. Olivier Danvy, Karoline Malmkjær, and Jens Palsberg. Eta-expansion does The Trick. Technical report BRICS RS-95-41, DAIMI, Computer Science Department, Aarhus University, Aarhus, Denmark, August 1995.

19. Matthias Felleisen. The theory and practice of first-class prompts. In Jeanne Ferrante and Peter Mager, editors, *Proceedings of the Fifteenth Annual ACM Symposium on Principles of Programming Languages*, pages 180–190, San Diego, California, January 1988.

20. Matthias Felleisen, Mitchell Wand, Daniel P. Friedman, and Bruce F. Duba. Abstract continuations: A mathematical semantics for handling full functional jumps. In Robert (Corky) Cartwright, editor, *Proceedings of the 1988 ACM Conference on Lisp and Functional Programming*, pages 52–62, Snowbird, Utah, July 1988.

21. Andrzej Filinski. *Controlling Effects*. PhD thesis, School of Computer Science, Carnegie Mellon University, Pittsburgh, Pennsylvania, May 1996.

22. Cormac Flanagan, Amr Sabry, Bruce F. Duba, and Matthias Felleisen. The essence of compiling with continuations. In David W. Wall, editor, *Proceedings of the ACM SIGPLAN'93 Conference on Programming Languages Design and Implementation*, SIGPLAN Notices, Vol. 28, No 6, pages 237–247, Albuquerque, New Mexico, June 1993. ACM Press.

23. John Hatcliff. *The Structure of Continuation-Passing Styles*. PhD thesis, Department of Computing and Information Sciences, Kansas State University, Manhattan, Kansas, June 1994.

24. John Hatcliff and Olivier Danvy. A generic account of continuation-passing styles. In Boehm [3], pages 458–471.

25. Fritz Henglein. Dynamic typing: Syntax and proof theory. *Science of Computer Programming*, 22(3):197–230, 1993. Special Issue on ESOP'92, the Fourth European Symposium on Programming, Rennes, February 1992.

26. Fritz Henglein and Jesper Jørgensen. Formally optimal boxing. In Boehm [3], pages 213–226.

27. Neil D. Jones, Carsten K. Gomard, and Peter Sestoft. *Partial Evaluation and Automatic Program Generation*. Prentice Hall International Series in Computer Science. Prentice-Hall, 1993.

28. Julia L. Lawall. *Continuation Introduction and Elimination in Higher-Order Programming Languages*. PhD thesis, Computer Science Department, Indiana University, Bloomington, Indiana, July 1994.

29. Julia L. Lawall and Olivier Danvy. Continuation-based partial evaluation. In Carolyn L. Talcott, editor, *Proceedings of the 1994 ACM Conference on Lisp and Functional Programming*, LISP Pointers, Vol. VII, No. 3, Orlando, Florida, June 1994. ACM Press.

93

30. Karoline Malmkjær, Nevin Heintze, and Olivier Danvy. ML partial evaluation using set-based analysis. In John Reppy, editor, *Record of the 1994 ACM SIGPLAN Workshop on ML and its Applications, Rapport de recherche N° 2265, INRIA*, pages 112–119, Orlando, Florida, June 1994. Also appears as Technical report CMU-CS-94-129.

31. Torben Æ. Mogensen. Partially static structures in a self-applicable partial evaluator. In Bjørner, Ershov, and Jones [2], pages 325–347.

32. Torben Æ. Mogensen. *Binding Time Aspects of Partial Evaluation*. PhD thesis, DIKU, Computer Science Department, University of Copenhagen, Copenhagen, Denmark, March 1989.

33. Flemming Nielson and Hanne Riis Nielson. *Two-Level Functional Languages*, volume 34 of *Cambridge Tracts in Theoretical Computer Science*. Cambridge University Press, 1992.

34. Larry Paulson. Compiler generation from denotational semantics. In Bernard Lorho, editor, *Methods and Tools for Compiler Construction*, pages 219–250. Cambridge University Press, 1984.

35. Frank Pfenning. Logic programming in the LF logical framework. In Gérard Huet and Gordon Plotkin, editors, *Logical Frameworks*, pages 149–181. Cambridge University Press, 1991.

36. David A. Schmidt. Detecting global variables in denotational definitions. *ACM Transactions on Programming Languages and Systems*, 7(2):299–310, April 1985.

37. Peter Sestoft. Automatic call unfolding in a partial evaluator. In Bjørner, Ershov, and Jones [2], pages 485–506.

```
(define-record (Program names command))

(define-record (Skip))
(define-record (Sequence command command))
(define-record (Assign name expression))
(define-record (Conditional expression command command))
(define-record (While expression command))

(define-record (Literal constant))
(define-record (Boolean constant))
(define-record (Identifier name))
(define-record (Primop op expression expression))
(define-record (Read))
```

Fig. 8. Abstract syntax for Tiny

```
(define-base-type Int n)
(define-base-type Nat n)
(define-base-type Sto s alias)
(define-compound-type CCont (Sto -!> Sto) k alias)
(define-compound-type Add ((Int Int) =!> Int) add alias)
(define-compound-type Sub ((Int Int) =!> Int) sub alias)
(define-compound-type Mul ((Int Int) =!> Int) mul alias)
(define-compound-type Equ ((Int Int) =!> Int) equ alias)
(define-compound-type Gt ((Int Int) =!> Int) gt alias)
(define-compound-type Read (() =!> Int) read alias)
(define-compound-type While (Sto -!> Sto) while)
(define-compound-type Fix
                         ((While -> Sto -!> Sto) -> Sto -!> Sto)
                         fix alias)
(define-compound-type True? ((Int CCont CCont Sto) =!> Sto) true? alias)
(define-compound-type Lookup ((Nat Sto) =!> Int) lookup alias)
(define-compound-type Update ((Nat Int Sto) =!> Sto) update alias)
(define Type-d
  ((Add Sub Mul Equ Gt Read Fix True? Lookup Update) => Sto -!> Sto))
```
Fig. 9. Direct-style Scheme interpreter for Tiny (semantic algebras)

```
(define-base-type Int n)
(define-base-type Nat n)
(define-base-type Ans)
(define-base-type Sto s alias)
(define-compound-type ECont (Int -> Ans) c alias)
(define-compound-type CCont (Sto -> Ans) k alias)
(define-compound-type Add ((Int Int ECont) => Ans) add alias)
(define-compound-type Sub ((Int Int ECont) => Ans) sub alias)
(define-compound-type Mul ((Int Int ECont) => Ans) mul alias)
(define-compound-type Equ ((Int Int ECont) => Ans) equ alias)
(define-compound-type Gt ((Int Int ECont) => Ans) gt alias)
(define-compound-type Read (ECont -> Ans) read alias)
(define-compound-type While ((Sto CCont) => Ans) while)
(define-compound-type Fix
                         ((While -> (Sto CCont) => Ans) -> (Sto CCont) => Ans)
                         fix alias)
(define-compound-type True?
        ((Int ((Sto CCont) => Ans) ((Sto CCont) => Ans) Sto CCont) => Ans)
                         true? alias)
(define-compound-type Lookup ((Nat Sto ECont) => Ans) lookup alias)
(define-compound-type Update ((Nat Int Sto CCont) => Ans) update alias)
(define-compound-type Type-c
  ((Add Sub Mul Equ Gt Read Fix True? Lookup Update) =>
  (Sto CCont) => Ans))
```
Fig. 10. Continuation-style Scheme interpreter for Tiny (semantic algebras)

Compiler Generation for Interactive Graphics Using Intermediate Code

Scott Draves

School of Computer Science
Carnegie Mellon University
5000 Forbes Avenue, Pitsburgh, PA 15213, USA
Home page: http://www.cs.cmu.edu/~spot

Abstract. This paper describes a compiler generator (cogen) designed for interactive graphics, and presents preliminary results of its application to pixel-level code. The cogen accepts and produces a reflective intermediate code in continuation-passing, closure-passing style. This allows low overhead run-time code generation as well as multi-stage compiler generation. We extend partial evaluation techniques by allowing *partially static integers*, conservative early equality, and unrestricted lifting. In addition to some standard examples, we examine graphics kernels such as one-dimensional finite filtering and packed pixel access.

1   Introduction

Interactive graphics is a growing application domain where the demands of latency, bandwidth, and software engineering collide. The state of the art, represented by systems such as QuickDraw GX(R) [44], Photoshop(tm) [42], RenderMan(tm) [52], Explorer(R) [25], and DOOM(tm) [10], is to write in C and assembly language. Programmers use hand-specialized routines, buffering, collection-oriented languages [46], and embedded/dynamic languages, but inevitably we face trade-offs in

program size   Large libraries with many specialized but infrequently used routines waste space.
latency and memory   Using larger batches/buffers reduces interpreter overhead but increases latency and memory traffic.
design time   Optimization requires time and planning that are unavailable to exploratory and evolutionary programmers.

Run-time code generation (RTCG), as exemplified by Common LISP [51], Pike's Blit terminal [43], Masselin's Synthesis operating system [36], researchers at the University of Washington [32], and elsewhere [14][35] is one way to attack this problem. With these systems, one writes programs that create programs. Generating rare cases and fused, one-pass loops as needed directly addresses the program size and latency trade-offs outlined above.

However, RTCG has suffered from a lack of portable, easy-to-use interfaces. Lisp's quasi-quote, Scheme's syntax-rules [5], and parser generators such as YACC [27] automate the mechanics of constructing certain classes of programs, but it remains unclear how we can build an RTCG system that is effective on a wide-range of problems, and is automatic enough that design time and programmer effort can really be reduced.

Partial evaluation (PE) as described in [28] is a semantics-based program transformation. With the cogen approach the programmer can type-check and debug a one-stage interpreter, then by annotation and tweeking, produce an efficient two-stage procedure (a compiler). Binding times manage program division, memoization handles circularities, and the specializer creates variable names and the rest of the mechanics of code construction. The programmer concentrates on higher-level issues such as staging and generalization. Other current attempts to apply PE to RTCG are Fabius [35] and Tempo [8].

This paper explores the application of a directly implemented compiler generator for an intermediate language to pixel-level graphics kernels. The nature of graphics loops is exploited with cyclic integers, which make the remainder (eg modulo 32) of an integer static. A conservative static-equality-of-dynamic-values operator allows static elimination of software caches, thus reducing memory references. The combination of these features allows us to convert bit-level code to word-level code.

For example, say one were converting a packed 24-bit RGB image to 8-bit grayscale. An efficient implementation reads three whole words, breaks them into twelve samples with static shifts and masks, computes the four output bytes, and assembles and writes an output word (see Figure 1) Such a block can make good use of instruction level parallelism. Our objective is to produce residual code like this from a general routine (called say image-op) that can handle any channel organization, bits per pixel, per-pixel procedure, etc.

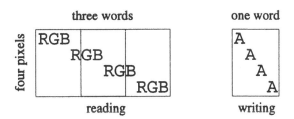

Fig. 1. efficient pixel access

The rest of this paper consists of a system overview followed by a description of cogen, two examples, and experimental results. Sections 6 and 7 place the system in context and conclude. Readers not interested in the intermediate language and its effect on cogen might read only Sections 2, 4.1, and 4.2.2 before skipping to the examples in Section 5.

More discussion but few details can be found in [11]. This paper assumes the reader is familiar with binding times, C compilers, LISP macros, caches, and pixels. [16] provides a good introduction to graphics and [22] to chip architecture.

2 System Overview

Our system is called *Nitrous*; within it, we identify three kinds of program transformers (see Figure 1):

- front ends (traditional and generated) which produce `root` programs from programs in user-defined languages.
- a compiler generator `cogen` for an untyped intermediate language `root`.
- a backend for code assembly and the rest of the run-time system.

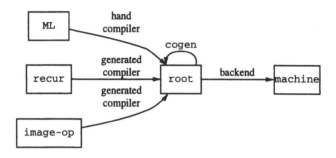

Fig. 2. System Diagram

`root` is a simple abstract machine code, like quad-code [1] with an unlimited number of registers but in continuation-passing closure-passing style (CPS-CPS) [3]. Thus the stack and closures are explicit data structures and all values are named uniformly. The model includes reflection and reification [17], simple data structures, arithmetic, an open set of primitive functions, and represents higher-order values with closures.

`recur` is a sample front end. It is a simple recursive equations language with parallel `let`, `if`, and multi-argument procedures. The `cogen`-created compiler produces straightforward code. It compiles tail-recursive calls without building stack frames, but is otherwise non-optimizing.

`Image-op` is the hypothetical procedure described above. The compiler might be run when the user opens a new file, repositions a window on the screen, chooses a new brush, etc.

A compiler generator transforms an interpreter into a compiler. That is, `cogen` transforms a `root` program and *binding times* (BTs) for its arguments into a *generating extension*. The BTs categorize each argument as static program or dynamic data; essentially they are *types* [21]. The extension consists of a memo table, followed by the static parts of the computation interleaved with instructions that generate residual code (ie do RTCG).

The backend executes `root` programs. We examine current and future backends in Section 5.3.

By supporting reflection we make code-producing functions first class. Nitrous takes this a step further by making the compiler-producing function (cogen) first class: rather than working with files, it just maps procedures to procedures. To facilitate this the back-end supports reification: the root text of any code pointer can be recovered.

Because the compilers produce the same language that cogen accepts, and the root text of the residual programs is easily accessible, multiple layers of interpretation can be removed by multiply applying cogen. The lift compiler (see Section 4.2) works this way; other possibilities include using recur to create input for cogen, or providing a compiler generator as a primitive in the recur language. Such multi-stage application requires that the generated compilers create correctly annotated programs, which can be difficult. In [18] and [19] Glück and Jørgensen present more rigorous and automatic treatments of layered systems using specializer projections and multi-stage binding-time analysis.

3 The Intermediate Language

The core of the system is the intermediate language root. Its formal syntax appears in Figure 3. A program is called a code pointer, or just a code. When a code is invoked, its formal parameter list is bound to the actual arguments. The list of prim and const instructions execute sequentially, each binding a new variable. if tests a variable and follows one of two instruction streams. Streams always terminate with a jump instruction, which transfers control to the code bound to the first argument and passes the rest. Formal semantics can be found in [11].

code ⟶	(code *name args instrs*)	*v* ⟶	*variable*
instr ⟶	(prim *v prim . args*)	*instrs* ⟶	*instr* list
	(const *v constant*)	*args* ⟶	*variable* list
	(if *v true-branch*)	*true-branch* ⟶	*instrs*
	(jump *v . args*)	*prim* ⟶	*primitive operation*

Fig. 3. root syntax

Structured higher-order control flow is managed with closure-passing [3]. A closure pairs a code pointer with its bound variables, and is invoked by jumping to its car and passing itself as the first argument. Normal procedure call passes the stack as the next argument. The stack is just the continuation, which is represented with a closure. See Figure 4 for an example.

Factors that weight in favor of an intermediate language like root include: root 1) makes cogen smaller and easier to write; 2) provides target for a range of source languages; 3) provides an interface for portability; 4) opens opportunity to schedule large blocks and utilize instruction level parallelism; 5) exposes language mechanism (such as complex optional arguments and method lookup) to partial evaluation; 6) reduces as-

```
append(k l m) {                 cont(self r) {
   if (null? l) (car k)(k m) a     (k l m) = (cdr self)   c
   frame = (list k l m)            nr = (cons (car l) r)
   cl = (close cont frame)   b     (car k)(k nr)
   append(cl (cdr l) m)         }
}
```

Fig. 4. root code for append, in sugary-syntax. Notes: *a* return by jumping to the car of k, passing k and m as arguments. *b* close is like cons, but identifies a closure. *c* destructuring assignment.

sembly overhead because it is essentially an abstract RISC code; 7) allows expressing optimizations not possible in a High Level Language.

And against: 1) types would simplify the implementation and formalization; 2) good loops (eg PC-relative addressing) are difficult to produce; 3) explicit stacks and exceptions would reduce consistency requirements and make optimization easier; 4) using a language like GCC [49], OmniVM [48], or the G-machine [29] would leverage existing research.

4 The Compiler Generator

cogen is directly implemented (rather than produced by self-application), polyvariant (allows multiple binding time patterns per source procedure), handles higher-order control flow, and is based on abstract interpretation. This section summarizes how cogen and its extensions work, in theory and practice. The subsections cover binding times, cyclic integers, lifting, termination, and special primitive functions in greater detail.

cogen converts a code and a binding-time pattern to an extension. An extension is identified with the name of the code pointer and the BT pattern, for example append(D S D).

The extensions memoize on static values to produce programs with loops. Arbitrary dynamic control flow can be produced: a recursive equations language can specify any graph. The interaction between cyclic arithmetic and memoization can result in a least common multiple (LCM) computation.

To support variable splitting and inlining the extension renames the variables in the residual code and keeps track of the *shapes* (names and cons structure) of the dynamic values. The shape of a dynamic value is the name of its location. Shapes are part of the key in the static memo table; two shapes match if they have the same aliasing pattern, that is, not only do the structures have to be the same, but the sharing between parts of the structures must be the same. The effect of variable splitting is that the members of a structure can be kept in several registers, instead of allocated on the heap (abstracted into one register).

Inlining is controlled by the dynamic conditional heuristic [4], but setting the special $inline variable overrides the heuristic at the next jump.

In CPS-CPS continuations appear as arguments, so static contexts are naturally propagated. Figure 5 shows the translation of (+ S (if D 2 3)) into root. The extension dyn-if(D S D) calls the extension cont(($\widetilde{close}$ S ($\widetilde{list}$ D S D)) D).

```
dyn-if(k s d) {                     cont(self r) {
    frame = (list k s d)               (k s d) = (cdr self)
    cl = (close cont frame)            rr = r + s
    if (d) (car cl)(cl 2)              (car k)(rr)
    (car cl)(cl 3)                  }
}
```

Fig. 5. Propagating a static context past a dynamic conditional.

4.1 Binding Times

Binding times are the *metastatic* values from self-applicable PE. They represent properties derived from the interpreter text while a compiler generator runs. Primarily they indicate if a value will be known at compile time or at run-time, but they are often combined with the results of type inference, control flow analysis, or other static analyses.

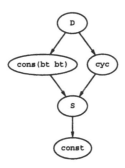

Fig. 6. Lattice Order. ($\widetilde{const}$ c) $\sqsubseteq$ S $\sqsubseteq$ cyc $\sqsubseteq$ D

cogen's binding-time lattice appears in Figure 6. Cons cells are handled with graph grammars as in Mogensen [37]: pairs in binding times are labeled with a 'cons point'. If the same label appears on a pair and a descendant of that pair then the graph is collapsed, perhaps forming a circularity. An annotation may provide the label, much like a type declaration.

We denote a pair $(\widetilde{cons}\ bt\ bt)$ (the label is invisible here). $(\widetilde{list}\ x\ y\ \ldots)$ abbreviates $(\widetilde{cons}\ x\ (\widetilde{cons}\ y\ \ldots\ (\widetilde{const}\ \text{nil})))$. In the lattice, $S \sqsubseteq (\widetilde{cons}\ bt\ bt) \sqsubseteq D$. We use familiar type constructors to denote circular binding times. Figure 7 depicts several useful examples.

For example, a value with BT D list has no static value, but its shape is a list of variable names. The dynamic values are placed in registers as space permits.

As in Schism [6], control flow information appears in the binding times. cogen supports arbitrary values in the binding times, including code pointers, the empty list, and other type tags. Such a BT is denoted $(\widetilde{const}\ c)$, or just c.

Closures are differentiated from ordinary pairs in the root text, and this distinction is maintained in the binding times. Such a binding time is denoted $(\widetilde{close}\ bt\ bt)$.

An additional bit on pair binding times supports a sum-type with atoms. It is not denoted or discussed further.

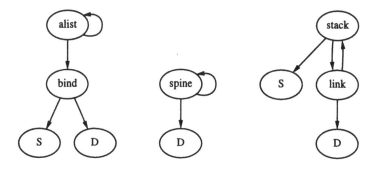

Fig. 7. Three binding times: (S * D) list is an association list from static keys to dynamic values, D list is a list only whose length is static, *stack-bt* is the binding time of a control stack.

Cyclic Integers There are many ways of dividing integers. Nitrous can break an integer into static base, dynamic quotient, and static remainder[1]: $i = bq + r$. Such a binding time is denoted cyc. If b is a power of two (eg 32) then we have a static bit field (eg the 5 low bits are static). In the lattice, $S \sqsubseteq cyc \sqsubseteq D$.

We have to make special cases of all the primitives that handle cyclic values. The easiest are addition and multiplication. The static code works like this:

```
v = (+ s (cyclic b q r)) → v = (cyclic b q (+ s r))
v = (* s (cyclic b q r)) → v = (cyclic (* s b) q (* s r))
v = (+ s d) → v = (cyclic 1 d s)
v = (* s d) → v = (cyclic s d 0)
```

---

[1] Here's another way to divide integers: a static bitmask divides the bits into static and dynamic.

On the left is a source instruction with binding times, on the right is the code in the extension. No case has any dynamic component; because the quotient passes through unchanged we can just copy the shape (q). Rules for (+ cyc cyc) and (* cyc cyc) might also be useful, but are not explored in this paper.

zero?, imod, and idiv are more compicated because the binding time of the result depends on the static value. For zero?, if the remainder is non-zero, then we can statically conclude that the original value is non-zero. But if the remainder is zero, then we need a dynamic test of the quotient. This is a conjunction short-circuiting across binding times. It makes direct use of polyvariance.

```
v = (zero? (cyclic b q r))  →  if (zero? (imod r b))
                                  emit v = (zero? q)
                                  v = #f
```

See Section 4.2.2 for a brief description of the other affected primitives.

Note that the rule given for addition doesn't constrain the remainder to $0 \leq r < b$ by overflowing into the quotient as one would expect. Instead, the congruence modulo b is maintained only at memo points: this is *late normalization* of cyclic values. The extra information propagated by this technique (early-equality across cycles) is required to handle multiple overlapping streams of data.

Thus when the compiler begins to make a dynamic code block, all cyclic values are normalized by adjusting r to satisfy $0 \leq r < b$. This is done by emitting counter-acting additions to q. The sharing between these values must be maintained across this adjustment.

4.2 Lifting

Lifting is generalization, or 'abstracting away' information. If we abstract away the right information the compiler will find a match in its memo table, thus proving an inductive theorem. The simplest lift converts a known value to an unknown value in a known location (virtual machine register). Lifting occurs when

- a metastatic code is converted to a static value. It is replaced with its extension, this requires a binding time.
- a prim has arguments of mixed binding time, causing all the arguments to be lifted.
- a jump has dynamic target, causing all the arguments to be lifted.
- a label repeats in a binding-time grammar, causing its collapse.
- a lift directive appears, generally the result of manual annotation.

Lifting is inductively defined on the binding times. The base cases are:

1. $S \to D$ allocates a dynamic location and initializes it to the static value.
2. $cyc \to D$ emits a multiplication by the base (unless it is one) and addition with the remainder (unless it is zero).
3. $S \to cyc$ results from an annotation used to introduce a cyclic value. The conversion is underconstrained; currently a base of one is assumed.
4. $(\widetilde{cons}\ D\ D) \to D$ emits a dynamic cons instruction.

5. $(\widetilde{close}\ (\widetilde{const}\ p)\ frame) \rightarrow D$ generates and inserts a call to $p\,(\,(\widetilde{close}\ D\ x)$ D D . . .) (all but the first argument are D), then emits the cons.

6. $(\widetilde{close}\ S\ frame) \rightarrow D$ same as the previous case, but the extension has already been computed, so just emits a call and a cons.

Case 5 is particularly interesting. Any static information in *frame* is saved by *reassociating* it into the code pointer before it is lifted. This introduces a complication, as explained in Section 4.3 below. The lift compiler handles applying these cases to structured and circular binding times.

Manual lifting is supported in root with an instruction understood by cogen but ignored by the root semantics:

instruction $\longrightarrow$ ... | (lift *v*) | (lift *v bt*) | (lift *v* (*args*) *proc*)

The variable *v* is lifted to D, unless the target *bt* is given. Any legal lift is supported, including lifting to/from partially static structures with loops and closures. Instead of giving a binding time *bt*, one can give a procedure *proc* which is executed on the binding times of *args*. This provides a rudimentary lift language.

Lifting Structures If a lift isn't one of the base cases outlined above, then the *lift compiler* is invoked to create a procedure that takes the value apart, applies simple lifts at the leaves, and reassembles the structure. cogen inserts a call to this procedure into the source program, and recurses into it.

For example, consider the lift (S * D) list→D. The compiler has a list of values and a list of variable names. It recurses down the lists, and emits a const and a cons instruction (making a binding) for each list member. At the base it recovers the terminator, then it returns up and emits cons instructions that build the spine.

It turns out that this lift compiler can be created by cogen itself. The meta-interpreter is just a structure-copy procedure that traverses the value and the binding times in parallel. A *delayed lift* annotation is used where the BTs indicate a simple lift. Specializing this to the binding times results in a copy function with lifts at the leaves. The value passed to the copy function *has* the binding time that was just a static value. When the continuation is finally called the remaining static information is propagated. The copy function may contain calls to itself (where the BT was circular) or to other extensions (to handle higher-order values).

This is an example of multi-stage compiler generation because the output of a generated compiler is being fed into cogen. The implementation requires care as cogen is being used to implement itself, but the possibility of the technique is encouraging.

Special Primitive Functions cogen treats some primitive functions specially, generally in order to preserve partially static information. Figure 8 gives the improved binding times possible, and in what situations they occur. Notes:

a implement copy propagation by just copying the shape.
b because root is untyped.
c for variable splitting.

d the result is metastatic if the pair has never been summed with an atom. `null?` and `atom?` are also supported.

e `apply` takes two arguments: a primitive (in reality, a C function) and a list of arguments. If the primitive and the number of arguments are static, then the compiler can just generate the primitive instead of building an argument list and generating an `apply`. This supports interpreters with an open set of primitives or a foreign function interface. Notice this doesn't improve the binding times, it just generates better code.

f extensions for both S and D are created, the compiler chooses one statically (see Section 4.1.1).

g the source instruction on the left produces the static code on the right. Rather than the error, one could take a dynamic path, as does case *e* above.

```
v = (imod (cyclic b q r) s)  →  if (zero? (imod b s))
                                    v = (imod r b)
                                 error
```

h like `imod` but

```
v = (idiv (cyclic b q r) s)  →  if (zero? (imod b s))
                                    v = (cyclic (idiv b s) q r)
                                 error
```

Note that it is necessary that the division primitive round down even for negative inputs, ie `(idiv -1 10)` → `-10`.

i `early=` conservative static equality of dynamic values, see Section 5.1.

			(+ cyc S)	cyc	
(identity *x*)	*x*	*a*	(* cyc S)	cyc	
(cons S S)	S	*b*	(+ D S)	cyc	
(cons S D)	($\widetilde{cons}$ S D)		(* D S)	cyc	
(cons D D)	($\widetilde{cons}$ D D)	*c*	(zero? cyc)	both	*f*
(car ($\widetilde{cons}$ x y))	*x*		(imod cyc S)	S	*g*
(pair? ($\widetilde{cons}$ _ _))	S	*d*	(idiv cyc S)	cyc	*h*
(apply S (D list))	D	*e*	(early= D D)	S	*i*

Fig. 8. See the text for notes.

4.3 Details and Complications

Static Control Stacks Because the stack is an explicit argument, when cogen encounters a static recursion the same label will eventually appear on two stack frames. In theory, because $(\widetilde{const}\ x) \sqcup (\widetilde{const}\ y) = S$, when this loop is collapsed the metastatic continuations would be lifted to static, thereby converted to extensions and forming a control stack in the compiler. However, to simplify the implementation cogen uses a special lift that supplies the return BT(s) and sets up the stack:

instruction $\longrightarrow$ ... | (lift v stack *ret-bt* ...)

This causes the lift ($\widetilde{close}$ p *frame*) $\to$ *stack-bt* and uses extension p (($\widetilde{close}$ S *frame*) *ret-bt* ...) to create the extension for the continuation.

For example, consider append(D S D)[2], with lift directives as it shown in Figure 8. The key sequence of extensions and lifts that create the recursion appears in Figure 9. cogen could avoid producing the (probably over-) specialized entry/exit code by checking for the end of the stack explicitly.

```
append(k l m) {
    if (null? l)  (car k)(k m)
    frame = (list k l m)
    cl = (close cont frame)
    lift cl stack dynamic
    append(cl (cdr l) m)
}

cont(self r) {
    (k l m) = (cdr self)
    nr = (cons (car l) r)
    lift nr
    (car k)(k nr)
}
```

Fig. 9. Annotated code for a static recursion.

```
append(D S D)
(close cont (list D S D))
    → stack-bt
cont((close S (list D S D)) D)

append(stack-bt S D)
cont((close S (list
    stack-bt D S)) D)
```

Fig. 10. Building a static recursion.

Shape un/lifting and Sharing Here we consider lift case 5 from Section 4.2 in greater detail. Say f has one argument besides itself. Then lifting ($\widetilde{close}$ f *frame*) $\to$ D creates a call to the extension f (($\widetilde{close}$ D *frame*) D). The extension is used to fold the static part of *frame* into f. The problem is, according to its binding-time pattern, the extension expects the dynamic part of the frame to be passed in separate registers (because of variable splitting), but at the call site the value is pure dynamic, so they are all stored in one register.

---

[2] Only a more complex recursion really requires this, but append is easier to understand.

Nitrous uses special code at the call site to save (lift) the shape, and in the extension wrapper to restore (unlift) the shape. This code optimizes the transfer by only saving each register once, even if it appears several times in the shape (typically a lexical environment appears many times, but we only need to save the subject-values once). The same optimization prevents a normal jump from passing the same register more than once.

Dynamic Control Stacks How do we extract the dynamic stack of a recur program from the stack in the recur interpreter? Say cogen encounters do-call(*stack-bt* S S *alist-bt*) (see Figure 10). When cl is lifted we compute cont(($\widetilde{close}$ S ($\widetilde{list}$ *stack-bt* S)) D). We want to generate a procedure call where cont jumps to apply, so inlining is disabled and we lift the stack (k) to D, invoking lift base case 4. The problem is the extension was made assuming the code pointer would be static, but now it will be dynamic. The unlift code inserts an additional cdr to skip the dynamic value, thus allowing an irregular stack pattern to be handled.

```
do-call(k fn exp env) {        cont(self arg) {
   frame = (list k fn)            (k fn) = (cdr self)
   cl = (close cont frame)        lift k
   lift cl stack dynamic          $inline = #f
   eval(cl exp env)    a          apply(k fn arg)
}                              }
```

Fig. 11. annotated code to produce a dynamic stack frame. Notes: *a* the call to evaluate the argument is inlined.

Alternative Representations of Cyclic Values Cyclic values as described in Section 4.1 are inadaquate for the filter example described below. The problem is the addresses are cyclic values so before you can load a word the address must be lifted, resulting in a dynamic multiplication and addition. The way to solve this is to use a different representation: rather than use q as the dynamic value, one can use bq. This is *premultiplication*. On most RISC architectures the remaining addition can be folded into the load instruction.

The disadvantage of premultiplication is that multiplication and division can no longer maintain sharing information. Which representation is best depends on how the value is used. A simple constraint system should suffice to pick the correct representation.

5 Experiments

This section presents examples of the code transformations possible with Nitrous, and measures their effect on time consumed. Two graphics examples are examined in the subsections, then the benchmark data is presented.

These examples make novel use of partial evaluation to optimize memory access by statically evaluating alignment and cache computations. Thus code written using a load-nybble procedure (with bit pointers) can be converted to code that uses load-word and static shifts and masks.

5.1 Sequential Nybble Access

Say we sequentially access the elements of a vector of packed sub-word-sized *nybbles*[3]. Figure 12 gives code for reducing a vector of nybbles. The code on the right is specialized to 8 bits per nybble and a bit vector length to zero mod 32. There are three things going on:

- Because the loop index is cyclic, three zero? tests are done in the compiler before it reaches an even word boundary and emits a dynamic test. These adjacent iterations of the loop can run in parallel.
- The shift offset is static because (imod cyc S) is static. Shifts with constant offsets generally take one fewer register of space and one fewer cycle in time.
- Redundant loads are eliminated by inserting a static cache: we use the procedure load-word_c instead of the load-word primitive.

The hard part is making the cache work: the cache-present test has dynamic arguments, but it must be eliminated. This is exactly the purpose of early=, it returns true if the compiler can prove the values are equal (are aliases). Since the shapes track the locations of the dynamic values, this is accomplished just by testing them for equality. Note how this equality information is propagated through the idiv primitive.

Note that in the actual implementation, a store is threaded through the code to provide the state for the memory and its cache.

Even if the index were completely dynamic we could still use this fast loop by applying the Trick to make it cyclic.

5.2 1D Filtering with Software Cache

A one-dimensional finite-response filter transforms an input stream of samples into an output stream by taking a sliding dot-product with a constant kernel-vector (see Figure 14). If the kernel has length k then each word is loaded k times. If one makes the outer loop index be cyclic base k, then in the residual code the loop is expanded and the loads are shared. A window on memory is kept in registers but rather than rotating it, we rotate the code around it.

As before, this can be done using a caching load procedure, though the cache now must maintain several values. A cache has BT (cyc * S * D) list, the tuple is of the address, the dirty bit (or other cache control information), and the word from memory. The length of the list controls the cache's size, this must be set manually. The cache

---

[3] Historically 'nybble' means precisely four bits. I have adopted the term to mean anything from one to thirty-one bits.

```
i = cyclic; sum = D
while (i) {
  i = i - bpn
  nyb = load-nybble(i bpn)
  sum += nyb
}

load-nybble(i bpn) {
  addr = i / 32;
  offset = i % 32;
  word = load-word_c(addr)
  return w2n(word bpn offset)
}
```

```
while (iq) {
  iq = iq - 1
  w = load_word(iq)
  sum += (w >> 24) & 255
  sum += (w >> 16) & 255
  sum += (w >>  8) & 255
  sum += (w >>  0) & 255
}
```

Fig. 12. General and specialized code to reduce a vector of nybbles. For simplicty, this code doesn't handle nybbles that overlap words.

```
load-word_c(cache)(addr) {
  if (early= addr cache.addr)
    w = cache.word
    w = (load-word addr)
  cache = (list addr w)
  return w
}
```

```
w2n(w bpn ny) {
  mask = ((1 << bpn) - 1)
  r = mask & (w >> (ny * bpn))
  return r
}
```

Fig. 13. Helper functions.

is managed with the Least Recently Used (LRU) policy. The entry code that 'fills the pipeline' is produced automatically because the memo-test doesn't hit until the cache gets warm.

This example was the motivation for the late normalization described above. The address p is kept premultiplied to avoid a dynamic multiplication when it is lifted at every load.

5.3 Implementation, Backend, and Benchmarks

cogen is written in Scheme48 [30], which compiles an extended Scheme to bytecode[4]. cogen is 2000 lines, supported by 4000 lines of utilities, the virutal root backend, the compiler to GCC, examples, test cases, etc. It has not yet been optimized for speed (eg it doesn't use hashing or union-find). The source code and transcripts of sample runs are available from http://www.cs.cmu.edu/ spot/nitrous.html.

---

[4] In fact the bytecode interpreter is written in Pre-Scheme [31] and compiled to C.

```
                                       w0 = load-word(p)
                                       w1 = load-word(p-1)
  stride = S; kernel = S               w2 = load-word(p-2)
  p = cyc; q = D; klen = S             sum = 2*w0+5*w1+2*w2
  while (p) {                          store-word(q sum)
    dp = dot(0 p kernel klen)          p -= 3; q++
    store_word(q dp)                   while (p-=3) {
    p -= stride                          w0 = load-word(p)
    q--                                  sum = 2*w1+5*w2+2*w0
  }                                      store-word(q sum)
                                         w1 = load-word(p-1)
  dot(sum i j n) {                       sum = 2*w2+5*w0+2*w1
    while (n--)                          store-word(q+1 sum)
      sum += load-word_c(i++)            w2 = load-word(p-2)
            * load-word_c(j++)           sum = 2*w0+5*w1+2*w2
    return sum                           store-word(q+2, sum)
  }                                      q += 3;
                                       }
```

Fig. 14. General and specialized finite filter code. The kernel is [2 5 2] and the stride is one.

Except for the lift compiler (see Section 4.2) the only working front end is a macro assembler, using Scheme as the macro language. So far the code fed to cogen has been written in root (with lift annotations) by hand. The recur compiler produces good code but is unfit for use as a front end because it does not yet produce annotated code.

The hypothetical ideal backend performs register allocation, instruction selection and scheduling, dead-code elimination, constant sharing, and linking to convert this language into executable code. I am budgeting about 2000 instructions to produce each dynamic instruction.

The backend used to produce these benchmarks translates a whole root program to a single GCC [49] function which is compiled, run, and timed using ordinary Unix(tm) tools. The run-time is just 350 lines of C and does not support garbage collection. These times are on a 486DX4/75 running linux (x86), and a 150Mhz R4400 SGI Indy (mips).

Support for reification and reflection is trivial in the interpreted virtual machine, but non-existent in the GCC backend. The ideal backend would support reflection either by transparent lazy compilation or with a 'compiling eval' procedure in the run-time. Reification could be supported by keeping a backpointer to the intermediate code inside each code segment (unless proven unnecessary).

The benchmark programs are summarized below:

recur the front end described in Section 2 run on three simple programs. atree performs a mixture of arithmetic and procedure calls, even tests the parity of 100 by mutual recursion, append a list of length 5 in the usual way.

nybble reduce a vector of nybbles as above, but handles nybbles that cross word boundaries. Ran on 2500 bytes with nybbles of size 4 and 12.

filter a vector of integers, kernel size 3 and 7.

In the nybble and filter examples, the nitrous-int code uses calls to the cached memory operations, but the cache size is set to zero. The manual-int code uses ordinary loads.

The numbers are reported in Figure 15. Appreciable speed-ups are achieved in most cases. The hand-written C code is about twice as fast as the compiled `root` programs. We speculate that this is because we use 'computed goto' and the && operator for all control flow.

	mips				x86			
	nitrous		manual		nitrous		manual	
	int	spec	int	spec	int	spec	int	spec
recur atree	100	2.5			600	15		
recur even	1900	3.7			11000	13		
recur append	150	3.6			710	23		
nybble 4	12000	160	380	140	64000	460	1500	380
nybble 12	4700	77	180	59	25000	210	680	170
filter 3	6500	140	400	45	53000	620	650	230
filter 7	13000	380	880	68	760	1400	450	

Fig. 15. Benchmark data, times in microseconds, two digits of precision. All time trials run five times; best time taken. The 'int' columns are for the general interpreters; and 'spec' for the specialized residual code. The 'nitrous' columns are for code written in `root` and produced by `cogen`, and 'manual' for normal C code written by hand.

6 Related Work and Alternate Paths

This section places Nitrous in context of computer graphics systems practice, and other research in partial evaluation and RTCG. First, we list the standard approaches to the generality/performance trade-off with a collection of examples of each.

custom hardware Blitters, MPEG codec chips. Provides the highest performance at the highest price with the greatest design time and least flexibility.

programmable hardware DSP chips, MediaProcessor(tm) [38]. Require assembly language and special tools to fully utilize them, but they can run C.

application specific compilers MINT [53], Apply [20], Cellang [13]. Usually compile to C and run on stock hardware.

dynamic linking Photoshop(tm) [42], Netscape(tm) [39]. Known as 'plug-ins'. The application dynamically loads code modules adhering to published interfaces.

batching/buffering APL, RenderMan(tm) [52], fnord [12]. Rather than applying an interpreter and one program to each of many data, a batch interpreter sequences vector primitives over the data, thus reducing interpreter overhead. Strip-mining and tiling [55] is necessary if the data don't fit in the cache.

embedded/dynamic languages Emacs lisp [50], Tcl/Tk [40], Microsoft's Visual Basic(tm) [54], PostScript(tm) [24], ScriptX [45], etc. The dynamic language sequences routines implemented with a static languages.

Hardware support for byte-pointers and an on-chip cache have similar effect as our loop optimizations (the hardware repeats the computation, but the hardware is very fast). However, note that the Alpha [47] doesn't support byte pointers, and DSP chips sometimes provide an addressing mode for on-chip SRAM bank, rather than a cache. This is an application of RISC philosophy (factoring from hardware into the compiler to increase the clock rate).

Similix [4] is a sophisticated, freely-available compiler generator. It uses a type-inference BTA, supports higher order Scheme-like language with datatypes and an open set of prims. It supports partially static structs, simple manual lifts, and is monovariant. It produces small programs and runs fairly quickly. It's file-based interface could be combined with a Scheme compiler (provided it had the right interface) to do RTCG. Schism [7] is similar but nicer.

DCG [14] and [33] provide C-callable libraries for RTCG. They use typical C-compiler intermediate language for portable construction and fast compilation with 'rudimentary optimization'. The ratio of static instructions used per dynamic instruction produced is 300 to 1000.

'C [15] augments C with backquote-like syntax to support manual RTCG. It provides a nice interface to DCG, and can handle complex interpreters (eg Tiny-C). By re-targetting C-mix [2] to 'C one might be able to combine the strengths of these systems (constraint-based BTA, fast code generation, a popular language).

Fabius [35] is a compiler generator for a simplified first-order ML-like language. The programmer uses curry notation to specify the program division, and a BTA completes it. This is a very natural means of annotation. The compilers produce machine code directly, thus they are very fast; its ratio is about 7.

Tempo [8] is a off-line, template-based specializer for C aimed at operating systems code. It contains sophisticated pointer analyses and other features to make it work on 'real' systems. So far no results are available.

Staging transformations [26], ordered rewriting [9], program slicing [23], and metaobject protocols [34] contain related ideas from other parts of the language research community.

7 Conclusion and Future Directions

We have described Nitrous, a run-time code generation system for interactive graphics. It uses compiler generation of intermediate code to provide sophisticated transformations with low overhead. It augments standard partial evaluation techniques with new annotations and binding times. While the preliminary results from the graphics kernels are

112

promising, the front and backend are still too incomplete to conclusively demonstrate the utility of this approach. Besides the immediate goals of fleshing out the system and scaling up the experiments, we hope to

- formalize the binding-time lattice in Elf [41] and develop a constraint based analysis.
- merge the static and shape environments, if possible.
- reduce unnecessary memoization.
- reduce the size of the extensions by improving lifting.
- return to self-application.
- bootstrap the system by compiling the experiments (and ultimately itself) with a generated compiler.
- when shape un/lifting data, use vectors instead of lists.
- automatically pick the right representation (pre/post multiplied) of cyclic values.
- can dynamic just be a special case of cyclic (when base is one)?

8 Acknowledgments

This paper was partially written and researched while visiting DIKU and DAIMI with funding from the Danish Research Council's DART project. I would like to thank Olivier Danvy, Nick Thompson, and the anonymous reviewers for their comments on drafts of this paper, and Peter Lee for his continuing feedback, faith, and support.

References

1. A V Aho, R Sethi, J D Ullman. *Compilers: Principles, Techniques, and Tools*. Addison-Wesley 1986.
2. Lars Ole Andersen. *Program Analysis and Specialization for the C Programming Language*. DIKU 1994.
3. Andrew Appel. *Compiling with Continuations*. Cambridge University Press 1992.
4. A Bondorf, O Danvy. Automatic Autoprojection of Recursive Equations with Global Variables and Abstract Data Types. *Science of Computer Programming*16:151-195.
5. William Clinger, Jonathan Rees. Revised[4] Report on the Algorithmic Language Scheme. *LISP Pointers*IV:1-55.
6. Charles Consel. Binding Time Analysis for Higher Order Untyped Functional Languages. *ACM Conference on Lisp and Functional Programming*, 1990.
7. Charles Consel. New Insights into Partial Evaluation: The Schism Experiment. *European Symposium on Programming*, 1988.
8. Charles Consel, Luke Hornof, Francois Noël, Jacque Noyé, Nicolae Volanschi. A Uniform Approach for Compile-Time and Run-Time Specialization. *Dagstuhl Workshop on Partial Evaluation*, 1996.
9. N Dershowitz, U Reddy. Deductive and Inductive Synthesis of Equational Programs. *Journal of Symbolic Computation*15:467-494.
10. DOOM. id Software 1993.
11. Scott Draves. Lightweight Languages for Interactive Graphics. CMU-CS-95-148.
12. Fnord: a Visualization System for Differential Geometry. Brown University 1991.

13. Cellang. ? 1995.

14. Dawson Englar, Todd Proebsting. DCG: An Efficient, Retargetable Dynamic Code Generation System. *ASPLOS*, 1994.

15. Dawson Engler, Wilson Hsieh, M Frans Kaashoek. 'C: A Language for High-Level, Efficient, and Machine-independent Dynamic Code Generation. *Conference on Programming Language Design and Implementation*, 1995.

16. Foley, Feiner, Andries van Dam, John Hughes. *Computer Graphics: Principles and Practice*. Addison-Wesley 1990.

17. Daniel P Friedman, Mitchell Wand. Reification: Reflection without Metaphysics. *ACM Conference on Lisp and Functional Programming*, 1984.

18. R Glück, J Jørgensen. Generating Optimizing Specializers. *IEEE Computer Society International Conference on Computer Languages*, 1994.

19. R Glück, J Jørgensen. Efficient Multi-Level Generating Extensions for Program Specialization. *Programming Language Implementation and Logic Programming*, 1995.

20. L G C Hamey, J A Webb, I-Chien Wu. An Architecture Independent Programming Language for Low-Level Vision. *Computer Vision, Graphics, and Image Processing*48?:.

21. Fritz Henglein. Efficient Type Inference for Higher-Order Binding-Time Analysis. *International Conference on Functional Programming Languages and Computer Architecture*, 1991.

22. John L Hennessy, David A Patterson. *Computer Architecture: A Quantitative Approach*. Morgan Kaufmann 1990.

23. Susan Horwitz, Thomas Reps. The Use of Program Dependence Graphs in Software Engineering. *ICSE*, 1992.

24. Adobe Systems, Inc. *PostScript Language Reference Manual*. Addison-Wesley 1990.

25. IRIS Explorer. Numerical Algorithms Group, Ltd 1995.

26. Ulric Jørring, William Scherlis. Compilers and Staging Transformations. *Principles of Programming Languages*, 1986.

27. Stephen C Johnson. YACC - Yet Another Compiler-Compiler. Bell Labs 1975.

28. N Jones, C K Gomard, P Sestoft. *Partial Evaluation and Automatic Program Generation*. Prentice-Hall 1993.

29. Simon L Peyton Jones. *The Implementation of Functional Programming Languages*. Prentice-Hall 1987.

30. Richard Kelsey, Jonathan Rees. A Tractable Scheme Implementation. *Lisp and Symbolic Computation*?:?.

31. Richard Kelsey. Pre-Scheme: A Scheme Dialect for Systems Programming. ?.

32. D Keppel, S J Eggers, R R Henry. A Case for Runtime Code Generation. UW-CSE-91-11-04.

33. D Keppel, S J Eggers, R R Henry. Evaluating Runtime-Compiled Value-Specific Optimizations. UW-CSE-91-11-04.

34. Gregor Kiczales. Towards a New Model of Abstraction in the Engineering of Software. *IMSA*, 1992.

35. Mark Leone, Peter Lee. Lightweight Run-Time Code Generation. *Partial Evaluation and Semantics-Based Program Manipulation*, 1994.

36. Henry Massalin. *Efficient Implementation of Fundamental Operating System Services*. Columbia 1992.

37. Torben Mogensen. *Binding Time Aspects of Partial Evaluation*. DIKU 1989.

38. John Moussouris, Craig Hansen. Architecture of a Broadband Media Processor. *Microprocessor Forum*?:?.

39. Netscape Navigator. Netscape Communications Corporation 1995.

40. John Ousterhout. *Tcl and the Tk Toolkit*. Addison-Wesley 1994.

41. Frank Pfenning. Logic Programming in the LF Logical Framework. *Logical Frameworks*, 1991.

42. PhotoShop 3.0. Adobe Systems, Inc 1995.

43. Rob Pike, Bart Locanthi, John Reiser. Hardware/Software Trade-offs for Bitmap Graphics on the Blit. *Software-Practice and Experience* 15:131-151.

44. QuickDraw GX. Apple Computer, Inc 1995.

45. ScriptX. Kaleida Labs, Inc 1995.

46. Jay M Sipelstein, Guy E Blelloch. Collection-Oriented Languages. *Proceedings of the IEEE*?:?.

47. Richard L Sites. Alpha AXP architecture. *CACM* 36:?.

48. Colusa Software. Omniware: A Universal Substrate for Mobile Code. *WWW*, 1995.

49. R M Stallman. *Using and Porting GNU CC*. Free Software Foundation 1989.

50. Richard Stallman. *GNU Emacs Manual*. Free Software Foundation 1987.

51. Guy Steele. *Common Lisp the Language*. Digital Press 1990.

52. Steve Upstill. *The RenderMan Companion: A Programmer's Guide to Realistic Computer Graphics*. Addison-Wesley 1989.

53. J E Veenstra, R J Fowler. MINT: a front end for efficient simulation of shared-memory multi-processors. *Modeling and Simulation of Computers and Tlecommunications Systems*, 1994.

54. Visual Basic v3.0 for Windows. Microsoft 1995.

55. Michael Wolf, Monica Lam. A Data Locality Optimizing Algorithm. *Conference on Programming Language Design and Implementation*, 1991.

Regular Approximation of Computation Paths in Logic and Functional Languages

John Gallagher and Laura Lafave

Department of Computer Science, University of Bristol, Bristol BS8 1TR, U.K.
{john,lafave}@cs.bris.ac.uk

Abstract. The aim of this work is to compute descriptions of successful computation paths in logic or functional program executions. Computation paths are represented as terms, built from special constructor symbols, each constructor symbol corresponding to a specific clause or equation in a program. Such terms, called *trace-terms*, are abstractions of computation trees, which capture information about the control flow of the program. A method of approximating trace-terms is described, based on well-established methods for computing regular approximations of terms. The special function symbols are first introduced into programs as extra arguments in predicates or functions. Then a regular approximation of the program is computed, describing the terms occurring in some set of program executions. The approximation of the extra arguments (the trace-terms) can then be examined to see what computation paths were followed during the computation. This information can then be used to control both off-line or on-line specialisation systems. A key aspect of the analysis is the use of suitable *widening* operations during the regular approximation, in order to preserve information on determinacy and branching structure of the computation. This method is applicable to both logic and functional languages, and appears to offer appropriate control information in both formalisms.

1 Introduction

Information about the control flow of program is useful for guiding partial evaluation. In off-line partial evaluation methods, control information is collected during a separate analysis phase; this is then used to drive the specialisation phase. In on-line approaches, control information is gathered dynamically while partial evaluation is actually being performed. The aim of this paper is to compute descriptions of successful computation paths in logic or functional program executions. An approach covering both logic and functional programs is sought, so as to uncover the common principles governing specialisation in both formalisms.

The proposal put forward in this paper is to try to capture the *shape* of computations, including the branching, looping, determinacy and non-determinacy in a set of computations. This information is useful in making decisions about control and polyvariance.

Computation paths are represented as terms, built from special constructor symbols, each constructor symbol corresponding to a specific clause or equation in a program. Such terms, called *trace-terms*, are abstractions of computation trees, which capture information about the control flow of the program. A method of approximating trace-terms will be described, based on well-established methods for computing regular approximations of terms.

Trace-terms could also be used in conjunction with existing methods of generating control information, especially termination analyses. The paper contains examples of combining trace-terms with *process trees* [SG95b] or *m-trees* [MG95].

Related ideas are already in the literature; these include *neighbourhoods* based on computational *histories* [Tur88] and *characteristic trees* [GB91, Leu95]. The aim of both these approaches is to use computational behaviour as an abstraction: two atoms or terms that give rise to similar computations are regarded as identical from the point of view of partial evaluation.

Trace-terms seem to offer a refinement of these notions, allowing more flexible treatment and more precise control than previously. The idea of regular approximation of trace-terms also appears to be related to more recent work by Turchin on *walk grammars* [Tur93, Tur96], though the exact connections have still to be studied. Trace-terms may offer a uniform treatment of all these ideas.

2 Representing Computation Paths

In this section we introduce a representation of (successful) computation paths. The idea is very similar in logic and functional programming, but some of the formal details differ. The idea is to record the clauses or statements used at each step in a computation. We wish to do this independently of any particular computation rule or reduction strategy. In logic programming we may think of this approximately as an AND-parallel computation where all atoms in a goal are simultaneously resolved upon. We can define an AND-tree capturing this directly. In functional programming this is not directly possible, but we can extract order-independent representations from a computation that was constructed using a specific reduction strategy.

2.1 Trace-terms in Logic Program Computations

The idea of using traces of logic program derivations has appeared in various forms, e.g. [Gal86], [Sha87], [GB91] but these representations employed sequences of clauses used in SLD derivations. Thus the SLD computation rule was also encoded in these representations. The method to be described here is independent of the computation rule, and this has certain advantages as will be seen.

Definition 1. clause identifiers
   Let P be a definite program. Let $\{c_1, \ldots, c_n\}$ be the set of clauses in P. Let a_j, $0 \leq j \leq n$ be the number of atoms in the body of the jth clause. Let $\{\varphi_1/a_1, \ldots, \varphi_n/a_n\}$ be a set of n distinct functors (not in the language of P),

where for each j, φ_j is a functor of arity a_j. That is, each clause in P is associated with a functor whose arity is equal to the number of atoms in the body of the clause. These functors will be called *clause identifiers*.

These functors will be used to represent the structure of successful computations. A successful computation in a definite logic program P is represented as an AND-tree, defined as follows.

Definition 2. AND-tree

An AND-tree (for program P) is a tree each of whose nodes is labelled by an atom and a clause, such that

1. each non-leaf node is labelled by a clause $A \leftarrow A_1, \ldots, A_k$ and an atom $A\theta$ (for some substitution θ), and has children $A_1\theta, \ldots, A_k\theta$,
2. each leaf node is labelled by a clause $A \leftarrow true$ and an atom $A\theta$ (for some θ).

Lemma 3. *(Stärk)*

Let P be a program and $\leftarrow A$ be a goal. Then θ is a correct answer for $P \cup \{\leftarrow A\}$ if and only if there is an AND-tree (for P) with root node labelled by $A\theta$.

Furthermore, a successful SLD-derivation with computation rule R can be transformed into an AND-tree. Since AND-trees are independent of the computation rule, AND-trees offer a more abstract characterisation of successful computations than SLD derivations.

Each AND-tree can be associated with a term constructed entirely from clause identifiers.

Definition 4. trace-term corresponding to an AND-tree

Let T be an AND-tree; define $\alpha(T)$ to be either

1. φ_j, if T is a single leaf node labelled by the unit clause identified by φ_j; or
2. $\varphi_i(\alpha(T_1), \ldots, \alpha(T_{a_i}))$, if T is labelled by the clause identified by φ_i/a_i, and has immediate subtrees $T_1, \ldots, T_{a_i}$.

Note that α may map more than one AND-tree to the same term. In fact, the main idea is to use the term $\alpha(T)$ as an abstraction of the AND-tree T. The idea is thus similar in its aims to the idea of *histories* [Tur88], and, more closely, *characteristic paths and trees* [GB91], [Leu95]. The main advantage of this formulation over the techniques just mentioned is that it abstracts away the computation rule, and it is in a much more convenient form for performing analysis of computations, since we can adapt well-established techniques for approximating term structures to approximate terms representing AND-trees. Trace-terms differ from characteristic trees also in that they represent complete answer traces rather than partial unfolding traces.

Example: Let P be the following program:

```
rev([],[]) <- true.
rev([X|Xs],Ys) <- rev(Xs,Zs), append(Zs,[X],Ys).

append([],Ys,Ys) <- true.
append([X|Xs],Ys,[X|Zs]) <- append(Xs,Ys,Zs).
```

Assign the functions $rev1/0, rev2/2, app1/0, app2/1$ to the above four clauses respectively. Consider the goal <- rev([a,b],W). The trace-term for the computation of this goal is $rev2(rev2(rev1, app1), app2(app1))$. Note that the computation of the goal <- rev([c,d],W) would have exactly the same trace-term, since the list elements play no role in the control.

Now consider the goal <- append(U,V,[a,b]). This is non-deterministic and has a set of trace-terms, namely $\{app1, app2(app1), app2(app2(app1))\}$ each of which represents a successful computation.

3   Incorporating Trace-terms in Logic Programs

Trace-terms can easily be added to logic programs, so that the computation returns a trace term as well as its normal result. Let P be a program and let the ith clause be $p(\bar{t}) \leftarrow q_1(\bar{t}_1), \ldots, q_{a_i}(\bar{t}_{a_i})$. Let φ_i/a_i be the trace function symbol associated with the ith clause. Transform each such clause to $p(\bar{t}, \varphi(y_1, \ldots, y_{a_i})) \leftarrow q_1(\bar{t}_1, y_1), \ldots, q_{a_i}(\bar{t}_{a_i}, y_{a_i})$, where $y_1, \ldots, y_{a_i}$ are distinct variables not occurring elsewhere in the clause.

Finally, transform each atomic goal $\leftarrow q(\bar{s})$ to $\leftarrow q(\bar{s}, w)$, where w is a variable not occurring elsewhere in the goal. (Consider only atomic goals without loss of generality).

Example: let P be the reverse program, as in the previous example. It is transformed into the following clauses.

```
rev([],[],rev1) <- true.
rev([X|Xs],Ys,rev2(Y1,Y2)) <- rev(Xs,Zs,Y1), append(Zs,[X],Ys,Y2).

append([],Ys,Ys,app1) <- true.
append([X|Xs],Ys,[X|Zs],app2(Y1)) <- append(Xs,Ys,Zs, Y1).
```

The goal <- reverse([a,b],W) becomes <- reverse([a,b],W,U), which returns the answer W = [b,a], U = rev2(rev2(rev1, app1),app2(app1)). Similarly the goal append(U,V,[a,b],Y) returns three answers, where Y returns the appropriate trace-term corresponding to each answer.

It is obvious that the transformation has no effect on the answers computed for the original program.

Note also that the trace-term can be used to drive the computation as well as record it, since the trace-term uniquely identifies the clause to be resolved at each step. The goal reverse(X,Y,rev2(rev2(rev1, app1),app2(app1))) returns the answer X = [U,V], Y = [V,U], which is the most general substitution associated with that trace-term.

3.1 Trace Terms in Functional Programming

The use of trace-terms to represent computations, and give control information in both logic and functional programming, underlines the connections between specialisation in logic and functional programming. Such connections have already been pointed out by Jones, Glück and Sørensen in their work on supercompilation, driving, deforestation and partial evaluation [SGJ94, SG95b, GS94]. Positive driving, a variant of driving developed by Glück and Sørensen, has been shown to be equivalent to partial deduction in logic languages.

The Simple Functional Language $\mathcal{M}$ In order to discuss representing functional computations precisely, we will employ a simple functional language $\mathcal{M}$ [GK93, SGJ94, GS94, SG95b].

Definition 5. Language $\mathcal{M}$

$$d ::= f \, v_1 \ldots v_n \to t$$
$$| \quad g \, p_i \, v_1 \ldots v_n \to t_i, for \, 1 \le i \le m$$
$$t ::= b \, | \, f \, b_1 \ldots b_n \, | \, g \, t \, b_1 \ldots b_n \, | \, \textbf{if} \, b_1 = b_2 \, \textbf{then} \, t_1 \, \textbf{else} \, t_2$$
$$b ::= v \, | \, c \, b_1 \ldots b_n$$
$$p ::= c \, v_1 \ldots v_n$$

The following restrictions exist for this language:

- Function definitions may have no more than one argument defined on patterns, which must be non-nested and linear.
- Function calls cannot occur as arguments in other function calls unless the function call is the first argument of a g-function call.
- All variables in the right side of a definition occur on the left side and the left side of a definition is linear (i.e. no variable occurs more than once).

In addition, it is clear from the definition of the language that functions are not permitted to be arguments of a constructor. These restrictions of the language guarantee that the results of computations are independent of the order of evaluation. Finally, for the language $\mathcal{M}$ we will specify the data structure for lists, an infix notation $a : as$ to denote the concatenation of a with as, and the terms $[], [x_1, \ldots, x_n]$ to represent Nil and $x_1 : \ldots : x_n : Nil$ respectively.

Incorporating Trace Terms with Computations In order to incorporate trace terms into these programs, we create constructor terms to represent the statements in the program.

Definition 6. statement identifiers

Let p be a program in the language $\mathcal{M}$. Let $\{s_1, \ldots, s_n\}$ be the set of statements in p defining a function h. Associate distinct constructors of the form φ/a (where a is the arity of φ), not in the language of $\mathcal{M}$, to the statements, according to the following two rules:

- If $s_i = h\,x_1, \ldots, x_n \to$ **if** $b = b'$ **then** t **else** t', then associate with s_i the constructors φ_i^T/a_i^T and φ_i^F/a_i^F, such that a_i^T is the number of function occurrences in t, and a_i^F is the number of function occurrences in t'. φ_i^T/a_i^T and φ_i^F/a_i^F are associated with the **then** and **else** branches respectively of the conditional statement.
- Otherwise, if the right hand side of s_i is either a constructor term, a f-function or a g-function, associate with s_i the constructor φ_i/a_i where a_i is the number of function occurrences in the right hand side of s_i.

These constructors will be called *statement identifiers*.

For example, examine the program which finds the last element of a list:

$$
\begin{array}{lll}
last\,(x : xs) & \to check\ xs\ x & < last1/1 > \\
check\,[\,]\ x & \to x & < check1/0 > \\
check\,(z : zs)\ x & \to check\ zs\ z & < check2/1 >
\end{array}
$$

For the ground term $last(A : B)$, the computation is:

$$last\,(A : B) \to check\ B\ A \to check\,[\,]\ B \to B$$

We assign three statement identifiers $last1/1, check1/0$, and $check2/1$ to each of the statements in the program, as noted to the right of the program.

Definition 7. labelled computation

A *labelled computation* S' for the computation $S = t_0, \ldots, t_m$, $m > 0$, is a sequence of ordered pairs $(t_j, \varphi_k/a_k)$ where t_j is reduced to t_{j+1} in S using the statement (or conditional branch of the statement) identified by φ_k/a_k and the last member of the sequence is (t_m, Nil) where Nil indicates the empty statement identifier.

We now define a trace-term associated with a labelled computation. The trace-term should be independent of the computation rule, just as in the logic programming case. There is nothing in functional programs directly equivalent to the AND-tree of logic programs, so the contruction of the trace-term is not quite so direct.

Let $S = (t_0, si_0), \ldots, (t_m, Nil)$, $m > 0$, be a computation where t_m contains no function symbols. During the computation, every function occurring in a term in S is reduced at some point in the computation. Let f be (an occurrence of) a function in t_j; that occurrence appears in $t_j, t_{j+1}, t_{j+2}, \ldots$ until some term t_{j+d} $(d \geq 0)$, at which that occurrence of f is reduced. We define $red(f)$ to be $j + d$ in this case. That is, $red(f)$ is the index of the step at which f is reduced in the computation. For every such occurrence of a function symbol in S, red is uniquely defined. Notice that the restrictions on $\mathcal{M}$ ensure that red is well-defined.

Definition 8. Let $S = (t_0, si_0), \ldots, (t_m, Nil)$ be a labelled computation where t_m contains no function symbols.

Define a trace term associated with each functional subterm occurring in S, by induction on the length of the computation.

1. Let $m = 1$. The only functional term is $t_0 = t_{m-1}$. The trace term associated with t_{m-1} is $\varphi_m/0$ (this must have arity 0 since otherwise t_m would contains a function symbol).

2. If $m > 1$, let $f t_1 \ldots t_s$ be a subterm occurring in t_k, $k < m - 1$. Let $red(f) = k + d$, $d \geq 0$. Suppose the $k + d^{th}$ pair in S is $(t_{k+d}, \varphi_{k+d}/a_{k+d})$, where $t_{k+d} = e[r]$ and $r = f t'_1 \ldots t'_s$. Suppose the right hand side, **then**, or **else** part (as appropriate) of the statement identified by φ_{k+d}/a_{k+d} is $\bar{\iota}$. Then t_{k+d+1} is $e[\bar{\iota}\theta]$ for some substitution θ. Suppose $\langle \beta_1, \ldots, \beta_{a_{k+d}} \rangle$ is the tuple of trace-terms associated with the functional terms in $\bar{\iota}\theta$. Then the trace-term associated with the original term $f t_1 \ldots t_s$ occurring in t_k is $\varphi_{k+d}(\beta_1, \ldots, \beta_{a_{k+d}})$.

Different labelled computations may have the same trace-term, and thus a trace-term is an abstraction of a computation. Returning to the example program, the labelled computation with root node $t_0 = last(A : B)$ is:

$$(last\,(A : B), last1/1) \to (check\,B\,A, check2/1) \to (check\,[]\,B, check1/0) \to (B, Nil)$$

and the computed trace term for t_0 is $last1(check2(check1))$, since $t_3 = B$, the trace term associated with $t_2 = check\,[]\,B$ is $check1$. Similarly, the trace term associated with $t_1 = check\,B\,A$ is $check2(check1)$, which follows from the definition with $k = 1$ and $d = 0$. Repeating this procedure until t_0 results in the trace term for t_0. Finally, we notes that the independence of trace-terms from the reduction order is not illustrated in this example since all trace-term contructors are unary.

4 Approximation of Sets of Trace-Terms

Once trace-terms are incorporated into the program, they can be treated like any other piece of data. Given a program P and a goal or term t where P and t are transformed to include trace-terms, it is of interest for specialisation purposes to find out the set of all the trace-terms arising from the computation of t in P, since the specialised program need follow only the successful computation paths and can precompute sections of computation that are determined.

In general, there can be an infinite number of distinct trace-terms associated with a goal or term. In fact an infinite number of answers is normal for specialisation since usually the input data needed to drive the computation to termination in a recursive program is missing.

There are a number of static analysis techniques available for computing finite descriptions of infinite sets of terms. Usually, of course, such finite descriptions represent approximations of the infinite set. One such technique which is well-understood and has been successfully implemented is the method of *regular approximation* [GdW94], [HCCar], [BJ92], [Hei92], [FSVY91]. In functional languages, a method for deriving regular tree-automata approximations of programs was developed by Jones [Jon87]. The aim of this analysis technique is to compute for each argument position in the program a regular description of the set of values that can appear at that position in successful computations. Properties of regular descriptions ensure that it is decidable whether a given values is or is not a member of the set that is described.

We describe two approaches to computing an approximation of the set of trace terms associated with a computation.

- Enumerate the set of completed computations using a fixpoint algorithm, with widening to ensure termination.
- Obtain a finite description of the set of possible computations using any other technique, and then extract from it a recursive description of the set of associated trace-terms.

5 Fixpoint Algorithm for Regular Approximation

The first approach is described for the logic programming case. The method used is the procedure for regular approximation of definite programs developed by Gallagher and de Waal [GdW94], which has been used in several experiments [dWG94], [SG95a].

Regular approximations of sets of terms are represented as regular unary logic programs (RUL programs) [YS90], which consist of clauses of the form

$$t_0(f(x_1, \ldots, x_n)) \leftarrow t_1(x_1), \ldots, t_n(x_n)$$

where $x_1, \ldots, x_n$ are distinct variables. A regular approximation of a predicate p/n is an RUL program containing a clause $approx(p(x_1, \ldots, x_n)) \leftarrow t_1(x_1), \ldots, t_n(x_n)$. The predicates $t_1(x_1), \ldots, t_n(x_n)$ give the approximations for each of the arguments of p/n.

The algorithm computes a monotonically increasing sequence of RUL programs bottom-up, that is, propagating approximations from the body of a clause to the head. The procedure terminates when a fixed point is found. Termination is ensured by a so-called *widening* procedure, which introduced recursive unary predicates when some "looping" criterion is detected. (Methods of widening seem to be the main difference between the various techniques for regular approximation of logic programs).

5.1 Widening Techniques

As mentioned above, a critical part of the approximation procedure is a suitable *widening* operation. The essence of this operation is that some RUL program is transformed to another RUL program incorporating a new recursive predicate. The new RUL program is "bigger" in the sense that any goal that succeeds with the original RUL program also succeeds in the new one.

The widening rule employed in our current approximation procedure is as follows.

Definition 9. simple widening

Let R be an RUL program containing predicates t_1 and t_2, where t_2 depends on t_1 (that is, t_1 calls t_2, possibly via other predicates). If the set of function symbols in the heads of the clauses defining t_1 and t_2 are the same, then a new recursive predicate, say t_3 is formed, which is the union of t_1 and t_2, and t_3 replaces occurrences of both t_1 and t_2.

Example: Let R be the following RUL program.

```
p(f(X)) <- q(X).          r(f(X)) <- s(X).
p(a) <- true.             r(a) <- true.

q(g(X)) <- r(X).          s(b) <- true.
```

In R, p depends on r, and both predicates contain the same set of functions ($f/1$ and $a/0$) in their clause heads. Widening is performed, introducing a recursive predicate t.

```
t(f(X)) <- u(X).          u(g(X)) <- t(X).
t(a) <- true.             u(b) <- true.
```

This widening operation ensures an upper bound on the size of RUL programs (over a finite set of function symbols). However, it introduces imprecision into the approximation, which though acceptable for many applications like regular type-checking, reduces its usefulness for program specialisation.

Example: Given the trace-term $app2(app2(app1)))$ from the *reverse* program shown above, the corresponding RUL program is

```
t_0(app2(X)) <- t_1(X).
t_1(app2(X)) <- t_2(X).
t_2(app1) <- true.
```

In this program t_0 depends on t_1 and both contain just the function $app2/1$ in their clause heads. Hence widening is applied, giving the recursive RUL program

```
t_3(app2(X)) <- t_3(X).
t_3(app1) <- true.
```

The first RUL program represented a single deterministic computation, while the second represents an infinite set of computations. In other words, a two-element list has been generalised into a list of arbitrary length.

5.2 Improved Widening Operators For Approximating Trace-Terms

Given that one of the main aims of analysing control flow for specialisation is to detect determinacy, another widening operator is now considered. The general aim is to ensure termination of the regular approximation procedure, but to retain as much information as possible about deterministic sections of the computation.

Definition 10. A predicate is called *determinate* if it contains one clause in its definition. It is called *non-determinate* if it contains more than one clause in its definition.

The essential idea of widening operators is to identify a unary predicate which depends on a "similar" predicate. In the simple cases seen so far, the notion of similarity is based on examining the function symbols occurring in the head of the clauses defining the two predicates. The similarity is then strengthened into identity by creating a single recursive predicate to replace both. Refinements of this idea are possible, based on more detailed definitions of "similarity". Similarity based on comparing the function symbols in clause heads can be generalised by looking at the function symbols at a number of levels.

5.3 Similarity with Determinacy to a Fixed Depth

To capture determinacy, we would like to compare the trace-terms defined by regular predicates up to the depth corresponding to the level of determinacy in the predicates. Predicates defined by only one clause are called *determinate predicates*. Let R^0 be an RUL program containing some determinate predicates. Let R^1 be the program obtained by unfolding (once) all calls to determinate predicates in the clause bodies, except self-unfolding (unfolding some body atom using the clause being unfolded). Let R^k be the result (if it is possible) of applying this operation k times. The process may terminate before k is reached, that is, R^m might not contain any unfoldable determinate predicates in clause bodies, for some m (including 0). In this case $R^m = R^{m+1} = \ldots = R^k$.

Example: Let R be the following RUL program.

```
t(f(X)) :- r(X).          s(h(X)) :- q(X).
t(g(X,Y)) :- s(X),s(Y).   q(f(X)) :- p(X).
r(f(X)) :- t(X).          p(a).
```

R^1 and R^2 are shown in Figure 1. There are no determinate predicates in clause

`t(f(f(X))) :- t(X).`	`t(f(f(X))) :- t(X).`
`t(g(h(X),h(Y))) :- q(X),q(Y).`	`t(g(h(a),h(a))) :- true.`
`r(f(X)) :- t(X).`	`r(f(X)) :- t(X).`
`s(h(f(X))) :- p(X).`	`s(h(f(a))) :- true.`
`q(f(X)) :- p(X).`	`q(f(a)) :- true.`
`p(a).`	`p(a).`
R^1	R^2

Fig. 1. Unfolding determinate predicates

bodies of R^2, so all the determinacy has been made explicit.

R^k makes explicit the determinacy in R up to k levels. In R^k, clause heads contain function symbols nested. Given a predicate t, we can speak of the *terms* in the heads of the clauses defining t, rather than just the function symbols as before. A widening operator (parameterised by k) based on this notion is now proposed.

Definition 11. determinacy-based widening

Let t_1 and t_2 be two predicates in an RUL program R, where t_1 depends on t_2. Let R^k be obtained from R as described above. Then apply widening to these two predicates if both t_1 and t_2 contain the same terms (modulo variable renaming) in their clause heads.

This widening is illustrated in the next section.

6 Example: String-Matching

These ideas are illustrated by applying them to the problem of specialising a naive string-matching procedure with respect to a given string but unknown text. The clauses of the procedure are as follows.

```
c0: match(P,T) <- m(P,T,P,T).

c1: m([],_,_,_) <- true.
c2: m([X|P],[X|T],P1,T1) <-
        m(P,T,P1,T1).
c3: m([X|_],[Y|_],P1,[_|T1]) <-
        X \= Y,
        m(P1,T1,P1,T1).
```

It is well-known that this program can be specialised with respect to a known ground first argument (such as match([a,a,b],_)) to yield an efficient matching procedure (like the Knuth-Morris-Pratt string matching procedure) that does not backtrack on the text string.

There are two important aspects of a successful specialisation of this program. Firstly, polyvariance is essential: the procedure m/4 is replicated into several versions, one for each character in the string. Too much polyvariance is not necessarily bad but is inelegant. Too little polyvariance will not achieve the required result. Secondly, the right amount of unfolding is needed. Too little unfolding can yield a program that still backtracks on the text string when a mismatch occurs. Too much unfolding can give a program that "looks ahead" in the text string more than necessary.

Trace-terms can help to find the right amount of polyvariance and unfolding. The clause c0 can be ignored for brevity, and we consider the goal <- m([a,a,b],_,[a,a,b],_). There are obviously an infinite number of trace terms associated with successful computations of this goal. They can be enumerated (by some means not discussed here). The enumeration begins as shown in Figure 2, corresponding to the string being found in the text starting at the first four positions. The different trace-terms at a given position correspond to the different mismatches that can occur on the way to finding the match. (The character * stands for a character other than a. The character ℚ stands for any character other than a and b. In the trace terms, a right square bracket is a "super-bracket" closing all unclosed left brackets).

Trace-term	Position where string occurs	text string
c2(c2(c2(c1]	1	[a,a,b,...]
c3(c2(c2(c2(c1]	2	[*,a,a,b,...]
c2(c2(c3(c2(c2(c2(c1]		[a,a,a,b,...]
c3(c3(c2(c2(c2(c1]	3	[*,*,a,a,b,...]
c3(c2(c2(c3(c2(c2(c2(c1]		[*,a,a,a,b,...]
c2(c3(c3(c2(c2(c2(c1]		[a,*,a,a,b,...]
c2(c2(c3(c2(c2(c3(c2(c2(c2(c1]		[a,a,a,a,b,...]
c3(c3(c3(c2(c2(c2(c1]	4	[*,*,*,a,a,b,...]
c3(c3(c2(c2(c3(c2(c2(c2(c1]		[*,*,a,a,a,b,...]
c3(c2(c3(c3(c2(c2(c2(c1]		[*,a,*,a,a,b,...]
c3(c2(c2(c3(c2(c2(c3(c2(c2(c2(c1]		[*,a,a,a,a,b,...]
c2(c3(c3(c3(c2(c2(c2(c1]		[a,*,*,a,a,b,...]
c2(c3(c3(c2(c2(c3(c2(c2(c2(c1]		[a,*,a,a,a,b,...]
c2(c2(c3(c2(c3(c3(c2(c2(c2(c1]		[a,a,ℚ,a,a,b,...]
c2(c2(c3(c2(c2(c3(c2(c2(c3(c2(c2(c2(c1]		[a,a,a,a,a,b,...]

Fig. 2. Trace-terms for the Match procedure

A program describing this set of trace-terms is given in Figure 3. Determinate predicates in program are unfolded as explained in Section 5.2.

Here t0 depends on t2 and both have identical clause heads, so we create a recursive definition merging these two predicates (and renaming t2 as t0). The result is in Figure 4. More answers are needed, beyond those tabulated in Figure 2, in order to obtain further widening. After more answers have been derived, the procedures for t3 and t8 will be merged, since they will both have the same terms in their clause heads. Notice that although t7 also depends on t3, it will not be merged with it since its clause heads remain different. In fact t1 will be merged with t7 and t0 will be merged with t6.

The final description of trace terms is in Figure 5. The three predicates in the program essentially determine three distinct versions of the m/4 procedure. They are worth distinguishing, from the point of view of partial evaluation, since they behave differently in the computation. Of course, this is an approximation of the set of trace-terms actually derived; every one of the trace-terms tabulated above is described by this program.

Stability occurs when the set of trace-terms represents a complete set of answers. This can be determined by iterative fixed point techniques and is beyond

```
t0(c2(X)) :- t1(X).          t13(c2(c1)).
t0(c3(X)) :- t2(X).          t13(c3(c2(c2(c2(c1))))).

t1(c2(X)) :- t3(X).          t3(c2(c1))).
t1(c3(c3(X))) :- t6(X).      t3(c3(c2(X))) :- t7(X).

t6(c2(c2(X)) :- t10(X).      t5(c2(c2(X)) :- t12(X).
t6(c3(c2(c2(c2(c1))))).      t5(c3(c2(c2(c2(c1))))).

t10(c2(c1)).                 t7(c2(X)) :- t8(X).
t10(c3(c2(c2(c2(c1))))).     t7(c3(c3(c2(c2(c2(c1)))))).

t2(c2(X)) :- t4(X).          t8(c2(c1)).
t2(c3(X)) :- t5(X).          t8(c3(c2(c2(X))) :- t9(X).

t4(c2(X)) :- t11(X).         t9(c2(c1)).
t4(c3(c3(c2(c2(c2(c1))))))). t9(c3(c2(c2(c2(c1))))).

t11(c2(c1)).                 t12(c2(c1)).
t11(c3(c2(c2(X))) :- t13(X). t12(c3(c2(c2(c2(c1))))).
```

Fig. 3. Program Describing Trace-Terms for Match Program (after unfolding determinate predicates)

```
t0(c2(X)) :- t1(X).          t3(c2(c1))).
t0(c3(X)) :- t0(X).          t3(c3(c2(X))) :- t7(X).

t1(c2(X)) :- t3(X).          t7(c2(X)) :- t8(X).
t1(c3(c3(X))) :- t6(X).      t7(c3(c3(c2(c2(c2(c1)))))).

t6(c2(c2(X)) :- t10(X).      t8(c2(c1)).
t6(c3(c2(c2(c2(c1))))).      t8(c3(c2(c2(X))) :- t9(X).

t10(c2(c1)).                 t9(c2(c1)).
t10(c3(c2(c2(c2(c1))))).     t9(c3(c2(c2(c2(c1))))).
```

Fig. 4. Regular Program after Widening t0 and t2

```
t0(c2(X)) :- t1(X).          t3(c2(c1))).
t0(c3(X)) :- t0(X).          t3(c3(c2(X))) :- t1(X).

t1(c2(X)) :- t3(X).
t1(c3(c3(X))) :- t0(X).
```

Fig. 5. Final Description of Trace-Terms

the scope of this presentation.

A specialised program can be built directly from the regular program describing the trace-terms. Three version of **m/4** are generated, renamed appropriately. The trace-terms are used to decide how to unfold the clause bodies for each version.

```
match(X,T) :- m1(X,T,X,T).


m1([X|P],[X|T],P1,T1) :- m2(P,T,P1,T1).
m1([X|_],[Y|_],P1,[_|T1]) :- X \== Y, m1(P1,T1,P1,T1).


m2([X|P],[X|T],P1,T1) :- m3(P,T,P1,T1).
m2([X|_],[Y|_],[U|P1],[_,W|T1]) :- X \== Y, U \== W,
        m1([U|P1],T1,[U|P1],T1).


m3([X],[X|_],_,_).
m3([X|_],[Y|_],[U|P1],[_,U|T1]) :- X \== Y,
        m2(P1,T1,[U|P1],[U|T1]).
```

This program is in fact more general than needed for matching the pattern [a,a,b]. In fact, it handles any pattern of the form [X,X,Y] where X is different from Y. A version specialised to [a,a,b] could easily be obtained from the program above by constant propagation.

7 Associating Trace-Terms with Process Trees in Functional Programming

We now consider an alternative way to use trace-terms to give control information. In Section 3.1 we showed how to associate a trace-term to a labelled computation. For non-ground terms, say *last (A:B:xs)*, it is possible to generate a labelled *process tree* representating a (possibly infinite) set of labelled computations. The notion of a process tree has been introduced for program specialisation in [SG95b]. Since process trees may be infinite, we generalise the labelled process tree to a finite tree, and finally extract the labels from the tree to obtain a recursively-defined set of trace-terms corresponding to the computations in the process tree.

Definition 12. labelled process tree

A *labelled process tree* T' is a (possibly infinite) process tree T such that for a node s in T:

– if s has edges leading to nodes $t_1, \ldots t_n$, $n \geq 1$, then there is a corresponding node s' in T' where s' is s annotated with the set of statement identifiers $\{\varphi_1/a_1, \ldots, \varphi_n/a_n\}$ where φ_i/a_i identifies the statement (or branch of the conditional) used to reduce s to t_i, $1 \leq i \leq n$.

– if s is the last node of a branch of T, there is a corresponding node s' in T' where s' is s annotated with the empty set to indicate the empty statement identifier.

For example, the labelled process tree for *last (A:B:xs)* is shown in Figure 6. For the following examples, we have used a simple generalisation rule for obtaining partial process trees from process trees: create a loop back to a previous node in a branch of the process tree if the two nodes are syntactially equivalent (modulo renaming). This generalisation rule does not ensure a finite partial process tree, but more powerful generalisation algorithms [SG95b] can be substituted for this simple generalisation rule.

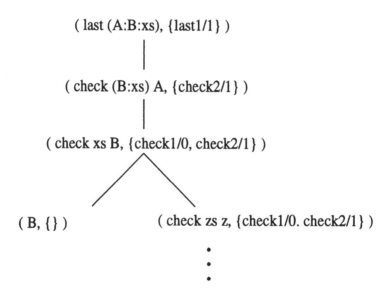

(last (A:B:xs), {last1/1})

(check (B:xs) A, {check2/1})

(check xs B, {check1/0, check2/1})

(B, {})   (check zs z, {check1/0. check2/1})

Fig. 6. The labelled process tree for *last (A:B:xs)*

Finally, we extract the trace-term tree from the labelled partial process tree in the following manner.

Definition 13. trace-term tree

A *trace-term tree* V is the tree obtained from a labelled partial process tree T such that for a node s in T

– if s is annotated with the set $\{\varphi_1/a_1, \ldots, \varphi_n/a_n\}$, then the corresponding node s' in V has n edges such that edge i is labelled with φ_i.
– if s is annotated with the set $\{\}$ and there is no edge leading from s to an ancestor of s in T, there is a node s' which is a leaf node.

– if s is annotated with the set $\{\}$ and there is an edge leading from s to t, an ancestor of s in T (indicating a loop), there is a corresponding edge in V leading from the corresponding node s' to t', the corresponding ancestor node in V.

The labelled partial process tree and trace-term tree for *last (A:B:xs)* are shown in Figure 7.

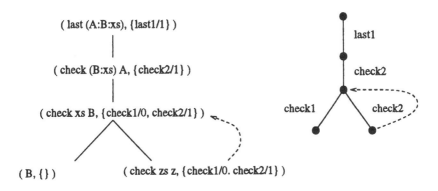

Fig. 7. The labelled partial process tree and trace-term tree for the term *last (A:B:xs)*

7.1 Pattern Matching Example

The pattern-matching example of Section 6 is now discussed in the context of functional programming. A process tree will be constructed, and descriptions of trace-terms extracted from it. The general tail-recursive pattern matching program p, written in the syntax of the language $\mathcal{M}$:

match p s	*loop p s p s*	$< m1/1 >$
loop $[]$ *ss op os*	$\rightarrow$ *True*	$< lo1/0 >$
loop $(p:pp)$ $[]$ *op os*	$\rightarrow$ *False*	$< lo2/0 >$
loop $(p:pp)$ $(s:ss)$ *op os* $\rightarrow$ if $p = s$ then *loop pp ss op os* else *next op os*		
next op $[]$	$\rightarrow$ *False*	$< n1/0 >$
next op $(s:ss)$	$\rightarrow$ *loop op ss op ss*	$< n2/1 >$

Assign the constructors $m1/1$, $lo1/0$, $lo2/0$, $lo3^T/1$, $lo3^F/1$, $n1/0$, $n2/1$, where $lo3^T/1$ represents the statement

$$loop\,(p:pp)\,(p:ss)\,op\,os \rightarrow loop\,pp\,ss\,op\,os$$

and $lo3^F/1$ represents the corresponding statement for the else branch. Then, the trace term for *match A:A:B A:A:A:A:B:u* is:

$$m1(lo3^T(lo3^T(lo3^F(n2(lo3^T(lo3^T(lo3^F(n2(lo3^T(lo3^T(lo3^T(lo1])$$

Similarly, the trace term for the ground term $match\ A : A : B\ A : A : A$ is a single term.

$$m1(lo3^T(lo3^T(lo3^F(lo3^T(lo3^T(lo2])$$

As we noted for logic programs, enumerating these trace terms for successful computations in a program p will result in a set of trace terms from which the non-determinism in p can be identified.

Alternatively, we can construct the labelled process tree (Figure 8) and the corresponding trace-term tree (Figure 9) for the non-ground term $match\ A : A : B\ u$.

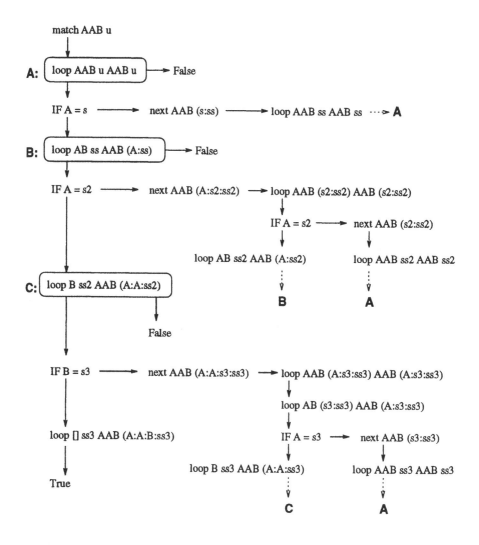

Fig. 8. The labelled partial process tree.

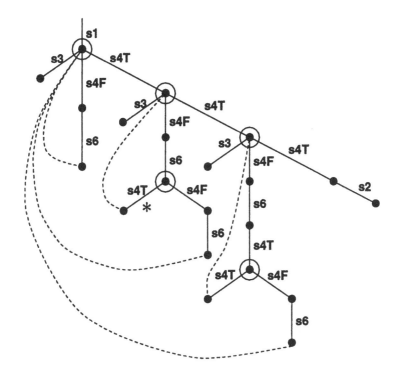

Fig. 9. The corresponding trace-term tree.

Each of the choice points (circled nodes) of the trace-term tree indicates potential polyvariance in the final specialised program. Because positive driving was used to contruct the process tree, the full specialisation needed to achieve the Knuth-Morris-Pratt style pattern matcher is not achieved. Applying the widening technique discussed in Section 5.2 would merge the two uppermost circled nodes in the trace-term tree. However, with negative driving, the arc marked with an asterisk would be eliminated, and the required polyvariance is achieved. As a final footnote, there is slightly more polyvariance in the functional version than in the logic version, since the functional version deals explicitly with match failure. In the logic version, failure to find a match just means that the computation fails.

8 Using Trace-Terms to Detect Control Dependencies

Another use of trace-terms is to help decide when to unfold non-determinate atoms in logic programs. Unfolding too much non-determinism can cause an great increase in program size, with no computational benefits. On the other hand, sometimes unfolding non-deterministic atoms is the key to achieving the desired specialisation. If we are to unfold a non-deterministic choice, therefore, we want some indication that some useful specialisation results.

A simple example is given by the standard *solve* interpreter.

```
solve(true).
solve((x,y)) <- solve(x), solve(y).
solve(x) <- clause(x,y), solve(y).
```

An object program is represented, as usual, as a set of facts of form `clause(h,b)` where h is the clause head and b is the body. A simple propositional example is as follows:

```
clause(r, true).
clause(r, (r,a)).
clause(a, true).
clause(a, a).
```

Partially evaluating with respect to `solve(r)` the obvious required specialisation is to unfold the calls to `clause(x,y)`. The desired specialised program is

```
solve(r).
solve(r) <- solve(r), solve(a).
solve(a).
solve(a) <- solve(a).
```

The predicate `clause` is unfolded and eliminated from the specialised program. How can we detect that it is useful in this case to unfold the calls to `clause(x,y)`, which are non-deterministic?

Add trace-terms to the program, defining function symbols $s1/0$, $s2/2$, $s3/2$ representing the three `solve` clauses, and $c1/0$, $c2/0$, $c3/0$ and $c4/0$ the four `clause` facts. Answers derived using the third `clause` will have trace-terms of the form $s3(u, v)$, where u is one of the `clause` identifiers and v is one of the `solve` identifiers. Examining these, we will see that trace-terms are of one of the following forms: $s3(c1, s1)$, $s3(c2, s2(y, z))$, $s3(c3, s1)$ or $s3(c4, s3(w, z))$. In other words, we can see that the choice for `clause` (the first argument of $s3$) determines the choice for `solve` (the second argument). This indicates that unfolding `clause` will allow further specialising of the call to `solve`. If `clause(x,y)` were not unfolded in the third clause, then the call to `solve(y)` following it could not be specialised, since we can see from the trace-terms that all three clauses for `solve` are applicable to it.

9 Discussion

The idea of trace-terms has been defined in the context of logic and functional programming. Safe approximation of the set of trace-terms associated with a set of computations can be used to determine polyvariance and assist in the control of unfolding.

As noted above, trace-terms are similar in some ways to characteristic trees and histories. The main difference is that trace-terms relate to the *complete answers* to a goal, whereas chararacteristic trees and histories are based on some partial finite number of computation steps. In theory, therefore, trace-terms should give more precise information. However, more refined widening operators than the one presented here may need to be developed to take advantage of this. A second difference is that trace-terms do not depend on the computation rule. Examination of trace-terms can yield information such as dependencies between subgoals in a clause body (or subterms in a definition), as sketched in Section 8.

The practicalities of using trace-terms have not been fully discussed in this paper. One important question which has to be studied is: how should trace-terms be enumerated? There are different possibilities. The most likely ones seem to be goal-oriented fixpoint methods like OLDT in logic programming [TS86] and minimal function graphs in functional programming [JM86]. Complexity issues have not been studied carefully yet either.

The widening operator discussed in Section 5.2 is effectively a generalisation operator, since it introduces recursive descriptions of trace-terms. There appear to be useful possibilities in combining trace-term generalisation with other methods based on termination analysis. This ideas was implicit in the treatment of the functional pattern-match program, in which as finite process tree was first contructed. An example of related structures in logic programming are m-trees [MG95] The methods described by Leuschel and Martens [LM96] make use of characteristic trees in a generalisation technique controlled by *homeomorphic embeddings*. It would be interesting to study the behaviour of trace-terms instead of characteristic trees in this approach. Trace-terms have a different structure to characteristic trees and are like to give different embeddings.

Control based on termination analysis, generally speaking, produces the greatest possible unfolding of a computation. Recursive descriptions of sets of trace-terms can be extracted from structures built based on termination analysis, such as m-trees and process trees, and then widening can be applied to decide on suitable polyvariance. This idea might be useful where m-trees or process-graphs, though finite, contain "too much" polyvariance; trace-terms can be used to capture the "useful" polyvariance.

Note that extracting trace-terms from (branches of) such structures as m-trees and process-trees is essentially no different than getting them from individual concrete computations. The only information required is the identification of statements with arcs of the graphs or trees. Backward arcs in these structures translate directly to recursive descriptions of set sof trace-terms.

Comparison of the application of these techniques to logic and functional programs should yield some interesting comparisons. Capturing determinacy has been a concern of logic program specialisation for some time. In the functional setting, control flow information yielded by trace-terms may provide more flexible control than that given by binding-time analyses, since "static" seems to correspond roughly to "determinate" in functional languages (though not in relational languages). Furthermore, cases where determinacy is obtained with partially static data should also emerge. In new integrated functional and logic languages such as Escher [Llo95] which allow computation with partly instantiated terms, an analysis of control covering both logic and functional features is desirable.

Acknowledgements

We would like to thank the referees for helpful comments, and the participants at the Dagstuhl Seminar on Partial Evaluation for stimulating discussions.

References

[BJ92]   M. Bruynooghe and G. Janssens. Deriving descriptions of possible values of program variables by means of abstract interpretation. *Journal of Logic Programming*, 13(2&3):205–258, 1992.

[dWG94] D.A. de Waal and J. Gallagher. The applicability of logic program analysis and transformation to theorem proving. In *Proceedings of the 12th International Conference on Automated Deduction (CADE-12), Nancy*, 1994.

[FSVY91] T. Frühwirth, E. Shapiro, M.Y. Vardi, and E. Yardeni. Logic programs as types for logic programs. In *Proceedings of the IEEE Symposium on Logic in Computer Science, Amsterdam*, July 1991.

[Gal86] J. Gallagher. Transforming logic programs by specialising interpreters. In *Proceedings of the 7th European Conference on Artificial Intelligence (ECAI-86), Brighton*, pages 109 122, 1986.

[GB91]   J. Gallagher and M. Bruynooghe. The derivation of an algorithm for program specialisation. *New Generation Computing*, 9(1991):305–333, 1991.

[GdW94] J. Gallagher and D.A. de Waal. Fast and precise regular approximation of logic programs. In P. Van Hentenryck, editor, *Proceedings of the International Conference on Logic Programming (ICLP'94), Santa Margherita Ligure, Italy*, MIT Press, 1994.

[GK93]   Robert Glück and Andrei V. Klimov. Occam's razor in metacomputation: the notion of a perfect process tree. In G. Filè P.Cousot, M.Falaschi and A. Rauzy, editors, *Static Analysis. Proceedings*, pages 112–123, Springer-Verlag, 1993.

[GS94]   Robert Glück and Morten Heine Sørensen. Partial deduction and driving are equivalent. In M. Hermenegildo and J. Penjam, editors, *Programming Language Implementation and Logic Programming*, pages 165–181, Springer-Verlag, 1994.

[HCCar] P. Van Hentenryck, A. Cortesi, and B. Le Charlier. Type analysis of prolog using type graphs. *Journal of Logic Programming*, (to appear).

[Hei92]   N. Heintze. Practical aspects of set based analysis. In K. Apt, editor, *Proceedings of the Joint International Symposium and Conference on Logic Programming*, pages 765–769, MIT Press, 1992.

[JM86]   N. Jones and A. Mycroft. Dataflow analysis of applicative programs using minimal function graphs. In *Proceedings of Principle of Programming Languages (POPL'86)*, ACM Press, 1986.

[Jon87]   N. Jones. Flow analysis of lazy higher order functional programs. In S. Abramsky and C. Hankin, editors, *Abstract Interpretation of Declarative Languages*, Ellis-Horwood, 1987.

[Leu95]   M. Leuschel. Ecological partial deduction: preserving characteristic trees without constraints. In M. Proietti, editor, *Proceedings of the 5th International Workshop on Logic Program Synthesis and Transformation*, Springer-Verlag (to appear), 1995.

[Llo95]   J.W. Lloyd. *The Programming Language Escher*. Technical Report CSTR-95-013, Dept. of Computer Science, University of Bristol, 1995.

[LM96]   M. Leuschel and B. Martens. Global control for partial deduction through characteristic atoms and global trees. In O. Danvy, R. Glück, and P. Thiemann, editors, *Proc. of the Dagstuhl Seminar on Partial Evaluation*, Springer-Verlag, 1996.

[MG95]   B. Martens and J. Gallagher. Ensuring global termination of partial deduction while allowing flexible polyvariance. In L. Sterling, editor, *Proc. International Conference on Logic Progrmaming, (ICLP'95), Tokyo*, MIT Press, 1995.

[SG95a]   H. Sağlam and J. Gallagher. *Approximating Constraint Logic Programs Using Polymorphic Types and Regular Descriptions*. Technical Report CSTR-95-17, University of Bristol, Department of Computer Science, 1995.

[SG95b]   Morten Heine Sørensen and Robert Glück. An algorithm of generalization in positive supercompilation. In J. W. Lloyd, editor, *International Logic Programming Symposium*, page to appear, MIT Press, 1995.

[SGJ94]   Morten Heine Sørensen, Robert Glück, and Neil D. Jones. Towards unifying partial evaluation, deforestation, supercompilation, and GPC. In *ESOP*, Springer-Verlag, 1994.

[Sha87]   E.Y. Shapiro. Or-parallel prolog in flat concurrent prolog. In E.Y. Shapiro, editor, *Concurrent Prolog: Collected Papers (Volume 2)*, MIT Press, 1987.

[TS86]   H. Tamaki and T. Sato. OLDT resolution with tabulation. In E.Y. Shapiro, editor, *Proc. 3rd ICLP, London*, Springer-Verlag, 1986.

[Tur88]   V. Turchin. The algorithm of generalization in the supercompiler. In D. Bjørner, A.P. Ershov, and N.D. Jones, editors, *Proc. of the IFIP TC2 Workshop, Partial Evaluation and Mixed Computation*, pages 531–549, North-Holland, 1988.

[Tur93]   V. Turchin. Program transformation with metasystem transitions. *Journal of Functional Programming*, 3(3):283–313, 1993.

[Tur96]   V. Turchin. Metacomputation: MST plus SCP. In O. Danvy, R. Glück, and P. Thiemann, editors, *Proc. of the Dagstuhl Seminar on Partial Evaluation*, Springer-Verlag, 1996.

[YS90]   E. Yardeni and E.Y. Shapiro. A type system for logic programs. *Journal of Logic Programming*, 10(2):125–154, 1990.

A Roadmap to Metacomputation by Supercompilation

Robert Glück & Morten Heine Sørensen

DIKU, Department of Computer Science, University of Copenhagen
Universitetsparken 1, DK-2100 Copenhagen Ø, Denmark
E-mail: {glueck,rambo}@diku.dk

Dedicated to V.F. Turchin on the Occasion of his 65th Birthday

Abstract. This paper gives a gentle introduction to Turchin's super-compilation and its applications in metacomputation with an emphasis on recent developments. First, a complete supercompiler, including positive driving and generalization, is defined for a functional language and illustrated with examples. Then a taxonomy of related transformers is given and compared to the supercompiler. Finally, we put supercompilation into the larger perspective of metacomputation and consider three metacomputation tasks: specialization, composition, and inversion.

Keywords: Program transformation, supercompilation, driving, generalization, metacomputation, metasystem transition.

1 Introduction

Over the years a number of automatic program transformers from Burstall and Darlington's unfold/fold framework [11] have been devised and implemented. The most popular is *partial evaluation* which performs *program specialization*. The possibility, in principle, of partial evaluation is contained in Kleene's *s-m-n* Theorem [47]. The idea to use partial evaluation as a *programming tool* can be traced back to work beginning in the late 1960's by Lombardi and Raphael [58, 57], Dixon [18], and Chang and Lee [12]. Important contributions were made in the seventies by Futamura [23, 24], by Sandewall's group [6], by Ershov [19, 20], and later by Jones' group [45, 46]. In the eighties program specialization became a research field of its own, *e.g.* [8, 14, 16, 44, 53].

Supercompilation [87], conceived by Turchin in the early seventies in Russia for the programming language Refal, achieves the effects of partial evaluation as well as more dramatic optimizations. Turchin formulated the transformations necessary for supercompilation, including the central *rule of driving* and the *outside-in strategy*, in 1972 [80, 81] and the main results concerning self-application, *metasystem transition*, in 1973. The book [96] defined all three *Futamura projections* in terms of metasystem transition. In the English language, the work on supercompilation was first described in [83, 84, 85, 86] and then developed further in [87, 89, 93, 99]. For more historical details, see Turchin's personal account [95]. Despite these remarkable contributions, supercompilation has not found recognition outside a small circle of experts.

This paper gives a gentle introduction to the principles of supercompilation in terms of a *positive supercompiler* [34, 73, 74, 75, 76] comprising two components, *driving* (Sect. 2) and *generalization* (Sect. 3). The supercompiler is compared to related program transformers (Sect. 4), and put into the larger perspective of metacomputation (Sect. 5). We give references to the literature throughout the text, which can hopefully be used as a starting point for further reading. The bibliography contains a comprehensive list of Russian and English titles.

1.1 Object Language

We are concerned with a first-order functional language; the intended operational semantics is normal-order graph reduction to weak head normal form [7].

The syntax of our language appears in Fig. 1 (where $m > 0, n \geq 0$). We assume denumerable, disjoint sets of symbols for variables $v \in \mathcal{V}$, constructors $c \in \mathcal{C}$, and functions $f \in \mathcal{F}$ and $g \in \mathcal{G}$; symbols all have fixed arity. A given program makes use of a finite number of different symbols.

$$
\begin{array}{llll}
\mathcal{Q} \ni q & ::= & d_1 \ldots d_m & \text{(program)} \\[4pt]
\mathcal{D} \ni d & ::= & f\, v_1 \ldots v_n \overset{\triangle}{=} t & \text{(f-function definition, no patterns)} \\[4pt]
& | & g\, p_1\, v_1 \ldots v_n \overset{\triangle}{=} t_1 & \\
& & \quad\quad \vdots & \text{(g-function definition with patterns)} \\
& & g\, p_m\, v_1 \ldots v_n \overset{\triangle}{=} t_m & \\[4pt]
\mathcal{T} \ni t & ::= & v & \text{(variable)} \\
& | & c\, t_1 \ldots t_n & \text{(constructor)} \\
& | & f\, t_1 \ldots t_n & \text{(f-function call)} \\
& | & g\, t_0\, t_1 \ldots t_n & \text{(g-function call)} \\
& | & \text{if } t_1 = t_2 \text{ then } t_3 \text{ else } t_4 & \text{(conditional with equality test)} \\[4pt]
\mathcal{P} \ni p & ::= & c\, v_1 \ldots v_n & \text{(flat pattern)}
\end{array}
$$

Fig. 1. Syntax of programs, definitions, terms, and patterns.

A program $q \in \mathcal{Q}$ is a sequence of function definitions $d \in \mathcal{D}$ where the right side of each definition is a term $t \in \mathcal{T}$ constructed from variables, constructors, function calls, and conditionals. We require that no two patterns p_i and p_j in a g-function definition contain the same constructor c, that no variable occur more than once in a pattern, and that all variables on the right side of a definition be present in its left side. Figure 2 shows the function a for appending two lists, using the short notation $[\,]$ and $(x : xs)$ for the list constructors *nil* and *cons x xs*.

$$
\begin{array}{ll}
a\, [\,]\, ys & \overset{\triangle}{=} ys \\
a\, (x : xs)\, ys & \overset{\triangle}{=} x : a\, xs\, ys
\end{array}
$$

Fig. 2. Example program *append*.

Our language contained case-expressions in [76, 74], because the connection between positive supercompilation and deforestation is clearest for case-expressions. However, g-functions [21] lead to a simpler presentation of generalization.

2 Driving

Driving takes a term and a program and constructs a possibly infinite *process tree*, representing all possible computations with the term, in a certain sense. Figure 3 shows part of the infinite process tree for the term a (a xs ys) xs (note the repeated variable xs). Each node contains a term t and its children contain

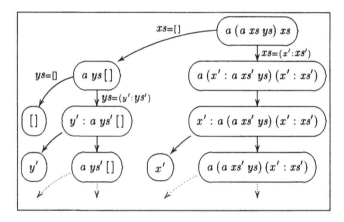

Fig. 3. Example process tree for a (a xs ys) xs.

the terms that arise by one *normal-order reduction* step from t. Whenever the reduction step has different possible outcomes there are several children so as to account for all possibilities. For instance, the topmost branching in Fig. 3 corresponds to the cases $xs = [\,]$ and $xs = (x' : xs')$. Note how the terms in the rightmost branches continue to grow due to the unification-based information propagation of driving, *e.g.* xs is replaced by $(x' : xs')$.

In Sect. 2.1 we define normal-order reduction, and in Sect. 2.2 we introduce process trees and define driving.

2.1 Normal-Order Reduction

A *value* is a term built exclusively from constructors and variables. An *observable* is either a variable or a term with a known outermost constructor. Any term which is not an observable can be decomposed into the form $e[r]$ where the *redex* r is the outermost reducible subterm and the *evaluation context* e is the surrounding part of the term.

More precisely, define *values*, *observables*, *redexes*, and *evaluation contexts* by the syntactic classes $\mathcal{B}, \mathcal{O}, \mathcal{R}$ and $\mathcal{E}$, respectively, as in Fig. 4. Define $e[t]$ to be the result of substituting t for the "hole" $\diamond$ in e.

$$
\begin{array}{llll}
\mathcal{B} \ni b & ::= & v \mid c\, b_1 \ldots b_n & \text{(value)} \\
\mathcal{O} \ni o & ::= & v \mid c\, t_1 \ldots t_n & \text{(observable)} \\[4pt]
\mathcal{R} \ni r & ::= & f\, t_1 \ldots t_n & \text{(redex)} \\
& \mid & g\, o\, t_1 \ldots t_n & \\
& \mid & \text{if } b_1 = b_2 \text{ then } t_1 \text{ else } t_2 & \\[4pt]
\mathcal{E} \ni e & ::= & \diamond & \text{(evaluation context)} \\
& \mid & g\, e\, t_1 \ldots t_n & \\
& \mid & \text{if } d = t_2 \text{ then } t_3 \text{ else } t_4 & \\
& \mid & \text{if } b = d \text{ then } t_3 \text{ else } t_4 & \\
d & ::= & e \mid c\, b_1 \ldots b_{i-1}\, d\, t_{i+1} \ldots t_n &
\end{array}
$$

Fig. 4. Values, observables, redexes, evaluation contexts.

Lemma 1 (the unique decomposition property). For any $t \in \mathcal{T}$ either $t \in \mathcal{O}$ or there exists a unique pair $(e, r) \in \mathcal{E} \times \mathcal{R}$ such that $t \equiv e[r]$.

Figure 5 shows example decompositions. In (1) the outermost call to the f-function f can be unfolded; the evaluation context is empty. In (2) the call to f has to be unfolded (the call to the g-function g cannot be unfolded because the term $f\, t$ does not have a known outermost constructor). In (3) the call to f has to be unfolded; both sides of an equality test must be values.

	t	e	r
(1)	$f\,(g\,t)$	$\diamond$	$f\,(g\,t)$
(2)	$g\,(f\,t)$	$g\,\diamond$	$f\,t$
(3)	if $x=c\,(f\,t)$ then t' else t''	if $x=c\,\diamond$ then t' else t''	$f\,t$

Fig. 5. Examples of decomposition into redex and evaluation context.

The rules for *normal-order reduction* are given by the map $\mathcal{N}$ from terms to ordered sequences $\langle t_1, \ldots, t_n \rangle$ of terms in Fig. 6. The rules of $\mathcal{N}$ are mutually exclusive and together exhaustive by the unique decomposition property.

Notation: the expression $t\{v_i := t_i\}_{i=1}^n$ denotes the result of simultaneously replacing all occurrences of v_i by the corresponding term t_i where $1 \le i \le n$. The expression $\lceil b, b' \rceil$ denotes an idempotent most general unifier $\{v_i := t_i\}_{i=1}^n$ of b and b' if it exists, and *fail* otherwise, where we stipulate t *fail* $\equiv t$. A value is *ground* if it contains no variables. To avoid name capture, the variables occurring in definitions, like $f\, v_1 \ldots v_n \triangleq s$ in the third clause, must be fresh.

Note the substitutions in the two last clauses. The assumed outcome of the test is propagated to the terms resulting from the step. We call this *unification-based* information propagation (*cf.* Sect. 4).

2.2 Process Trees

A *process tree* is a tree where each node is labeled with a term t and all edges leaving a node are ordered. Every node may have an additional *mark*.

t	$\mathcal{N}[\![\,t\,]\!]$
x	$\langle\,\rangle$
$c\,t_1\ldots t_n$	$\langle t_1,\ldots,t_n\rangle$
$e[f\,t_1\ldots t_n]$	$\langle e[s\{v_i:=t_i\}_{i=1}^n]\rangle \quad$ if $f\,v_1\ldots v_n \triangleq s$
$e[g\,(c\,t_1\ldots t_i)\,t_{i+1}\ldots t_n]$	$\langle e[s\{v_i:=t_i\}_{i=1}^n]\rangle \quad$ if $g\,(c\,v_1\ldots v_i)\,v_{i+1}\ldots v_n \triangleq s$
$e[g\,x\,t_1\ldots t_n]$	$\langle(e[s_1\{v_i:=t_i\}_{i=1}^n])\{x:=p_1\},\ldots,(e[s_m\{v_i:=t_i\}_{i=1}^n])\{x:=p_m\}\rangle$
	if $g\,p_1\,v_1\ldots v_n \triangleq s_1;\ \ldots\ ;\,g\,p_m\,v_1\ldots v_n \triangleq s_m$
$e[\text{if }b{=}b'\text{ then }t\text{ else }t']$	$\begin{cases}\langle e[t]\rangle & \text{if } b,b' \text{ are ground, } b \equiv b' \\[4pt] \langle e[t']\rangle & \text{if } b,b' \text{ are ground, } b \not\equiv b' \\[4pt] \langle(e[t])\lceil b,b'\rceil, e[t']\rangle & \text{if } b,b' \text{ are not both ground}\end{cases}$

Fig. 6. Normal-order reduction step.

Definition 2. Let T be a process tree and $\textcircled{t}$ an unmarked leaf node in T. Then $UNFOLD(T,\textcircled{t})$ is the process tree obtained by marking $\textcircled{t}$ and adding n unmarked children labeled $t_1,\ldots,t_n$, where $\mathcal{N}[\![\,t\,]\!] = \langle t_1,\ldots,t_n\rangle$.

Driving is the action of constructing process trees using two essential principles: normal-order strategy and unification-based information propagation.

Algorithm 3 (driving.)

1. INPUT $t_0 \in \mathcal{T}, q \in \mathcal{Q}$
2. LET T_0 be the process tree with unmarked node labeled t_0. SET $i = 0$.
3. WHILE there exists an unmarked leaf node N in T_i:
   (a) $T_{i+1} = UNFOLD(T_i, N)$
   (b) SET $i = i + 1$
4. OUTPUT T_i

3 A Positive Supercompiler

In the previous section we used driving to construct a potentially infinite process tree. The purpose of *generalization* is to ensure that one constructs instead a finite *partial process tree* from which a new term and program can be recovered.

The idea is that if a leaf node M has an ancestor L and it "seems likely" that continued driving will generate an infinite sequence $L,\ldots,M,\ldots$ then M should not be driven any further; instead we should perform *generalization*. In Sect. 3.1 we define a criterion, a so-called *whistle*, that formalizes the decision when to stop. In Sect. 3.2 we introduce some notions that are used in Sect. 3.3 to define generalization. This culminates in a definition of a *positive supercompiler*.

3.1 When to Stop?

We stop driving at a leaf node with label t if one of its ancestors has label s and $s \trianglelefteq t$, where $\trianglelefteq$ is the *homeomorphic embedding relation* known from term algebra [17]. Variants of this relation are used in termination proofs for term rewrite systems [17] and for ensuring local termination of partial deduction [9]. After it was taken up in [76], it has inspired more recent work [5, 55, 94, 95].

The rationale behind this relation is that in any infinite sequence $t_0, t_1, \ldots$ that arises during driving of a program, there *definitely* exists some $i < j$ with $t_i \trianglelefteq t_j$, so driving cannot proceed infinitely. Moreover, if $t_i \trianglelefteq t_j$ then all the subterms of t_i are present in t_j embedded in extra subterms. This suggests that t_j might arise from t_i by some infinitely continuing system, so driving will be stopped for a good reason.

The *homeomorphic embedding* $\trianglelefteq$ is the smallest relation on $\mathcal{T}$ satisfying the rules in Fig. 7, where $h \in \mathcal{X} \cup \mathcal{C} \cup \mathcal{F} \cup \mathcal{G} \cup \{\textbf{ifthenelse}\}$, $x, y \in \mathcal{X}$, and $s, s_i, t \in \mathcal{T}$.

Variable	Diving	Coupling
$x \trianglelefteq y$	$\dfrac{s \trianglelefteq t_i \text{ for some } i}{s \trianglelefteq h\,(t_1, \ldots, t_n)}$	$\dfrac{s_1 \trianglelefteq t_1, \ldots, s_n \trianglelefteq t_n}{h\,(s_1, \ldots, s_n) \trianglelefteq h\,(t_1, \ldots, t_n)}$

Fig. 7. Homeomorphic embedding.

Diving detects a subterm embedded in a larger term, and *coupling* matches the subterms of two terms. Some examples and non-examples appear in Fig. 8. It is not hard to give an algorithm $WHISTLE(M, N)$ deciding whether $M \trianglelefteq N$.

$b \trianglelefteq a(b)$	$a(c(b)) \ntrianglelefteq c(b)$
$c(b) \trianglelefteq c(a(b))$	$a(c(b)) \ntrianglelefteq c(a(b))$
$d(b, b) \trianglelefteq d(a(b), a(b))$	$a(c(b)) \ntrianglelefteq a(a(a(b)))$

Fig. 8. Examples and non-examples of embedding.

3.2 Most Specific Generalization

We define the generalization of two terms t_1, t_2 as the most specific generalization (msg) $\lfloor t_1, t_2 \rfloor$. A well-known result in term algebra states that any two $t, s \in \mathcal{T}$ have an msg which is unique up to renaming. Examples are shown in Fig. 9.

s t	t_g	θ_1	θ_2
$b \trianglelefteq a(b)$	x	$\{x := b\}$	$\{x := a(b)\}$
$c(b) \trianglelefteq c(a(b))$	$c(x)$	$\{x := b\}$	$\{x := a(b)\}$
$c(y) \trianglelefteq c(a(y))$	$c(x)$	$\{x := y\}$	$\{x := a(y)\}$
$d(b, b) \trianglelefteq d(a(b), a(b))$	$d(x, x)$	$\{x := a(b)\}$	$\{x := a(b)\}$

Fig. 9. Examples of most specific generalization.

Definition 4 (instance, generalization, msg, distinct). Given $t_1, t_2 \in \mathcal{T}$.

1. An *instance* of t_1 is a term of the form $t_1\theta$ where θ is a substitution.
2. A *generalization* of t_1, t_2 is a triple $(t_g, \theta_1, \theta_2)$ where $t_g\theta_1 \equiv t_1$ and $t_g\theta_2 \equiv t_2$.
3. A generalization $(t_g, \theta_1, \theta_2)$ of t_1 and t_2 is *most specific* (msg) if for every generalization $(t'_g, \theta'_1, \theta'_2)$ of t_1 and t_2 it holds that t_g is an instance of t'_g.
4. Two terms t_1 and t_2 are *disjoint* if their msg is of the form (x, θ_1, θ_2).

Algorithm 5 (msg.) An msg $\lfloor s, t \rfloor$ of $s, t \in \mathcal{T}$ is computed by exhaustively applying the rewrite rules in Fig. 10 to the initial triple $(x, \{x := s\}, \{x := t\})$:

$$
\begin{pmatrix} t_g \\ \{x := h(s_1, \ldots, s_n)\} \cup \theta_1 \\ \{x := h(t_1, \ldots, t_n)\} \cup \theta_2 \end{pmatrix} \rightarrow \begin{pmatrix} t_g\{x := h(y_1, \ldots, y_n)\} \\ \{y_1 := s_1, \ldots, y_n := s_n\} \cup \theta_1 \\ \{y_1 := t_1, \ldots, y_n := t_n\} \cup \theta_2 \end{pmatrix}
$$

$$
\begin{pmatrix} t_g \\ \{x := s, y := s\} \cup \theta_1 \\ \{x := t, y := t\} \cup \theta_2 \end{pmatrix} \rightarrow \begin{pmatrix} t_g\{x := y\} \\ \{y := s\} \cup \theta_1 \\ \{y := t\} \cup \theta_2 \end{pmatrix}
$$

Fig. 10. Computing most specific generalizations.

3.3 Partial Process Trees

A *partial process tree* differs from a process tree in that it may contain an extra kind of nodes, *generalization-nodes*, with label of form let $x_1 = t_1 \ldots x_n = t_n$ in t and $n+1$ children labeled $t_1, \ldots, t_n, t$, respectively, where $x_1, \ldots, x_n$ do not occur in $t_1, \ldots, t_n$. This kind of node has the distinct feature that the $n + 1$'st edge may go to an ancestor of the node instead of going to a child; such an edge is called a *return edge*. We regard a partial process tree as an acyclic graph by ignoring return edges, so *ancestor, leaf, etc.* apply only to non-return edges. The labels on generalization nodes are unrelated to all other labels wrt. $\trianglelefteq$.

The operations in the following definition, inspired by [59], appear in Fig. 11.

Definition 6. Let T be a partial process tree with node (t) with ancestor (s).

1. If t is an instance of s, i.e. $t \equiv s\{x_1 := t_1, \ldots, x_n := t_n\}$, then $FOLD(T, (s), (t))$ is the tree obtained as follows. Replace (t) by $(\text{let } x_1 = t_1 \ldots x_n = t_n \text{ in } s)$ which is marked, has return edge to (s), and n unmarked children $(t_1), \ldots, (t_n)$.
2. If $\lfloor s, t \rfloor = (t_g, \{x_1 := t_1, \ldots, x_n := t_n\}, \theta)$, then $GENERALIZE(T, (s), (t))$ is the partial process tree obtained as follows. Delete all descendants of (s), and replace (s) by $(\text{let } x_1 = t_1 \ldots x_n = t_n \text{ in } t_g)$ with a mark and $n + 1$ unmarked children $(t_1), \ldots, (t_n), (t_g)$. Return edges from (s) or its descendants are erased.
3. If $t \equiv ht_1 \ldots t_n$ then $SPLIT(T, (s), (t))$ is the partial process tree obtained as follows. Let $t' \equiv h\, x_1, \ldots, x_n$ where $x_1, \ldots, x_n$ are new variables, replace (t) by $(\text{let } x_1 = t_1 \ldots x_n = t_n \text{ in } t')$ which has a mark and $n + 1$ unmarked children $(t_1), \ldots, (t_n), (t')$.

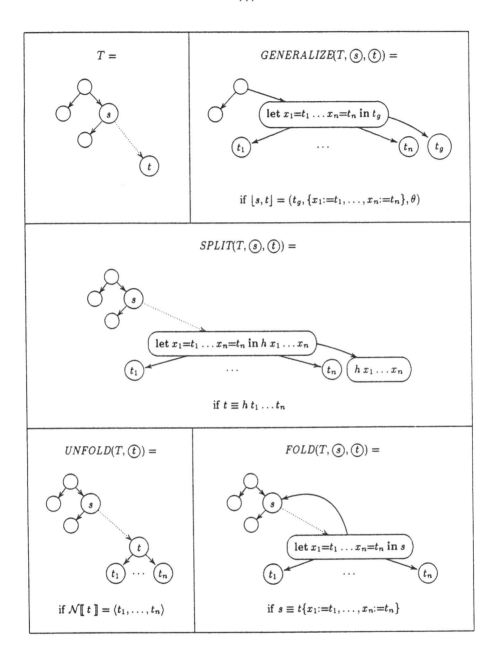

Fig. 11. Operations on partial process tress.

Algorithm 7 (positive supercompilation.)

1. INPUT $t_0 \in \mathcal{T}, q \in \mathcal{Q}$
2. LET T_0 be the partial process tree with unmarked node labeled t_0. SET $i := 0$.
3. WHILE there exists an unmarked leaf node N in T_i:
   (a) IF there exists no ancestor M such that $WHISTLE(M, N)$
       THEN $T_{i+1} := UNFOLD(T_i, N)$
       ELSE
         i. LET M be an ancestor such that $WHISTLE(M, N)$
         ii. IF node N is an instance of M THEN $T_{i+1} := FOLD(T_i, M, N)$
             ELSE IF N and M are disjoint THEN $T_{i+1} := SPLIT(T_i, M, N)$
             ELSE $T_{i+1} := GENERALIZE(T_i, M, N)$
   (b) SET $i := i + 1$
4. OUTPUT T_i

Theorem 8. *Algorithm 7 always terminates.*

The theorem comprises two important facts. The first, a consequence of Kruskal's Tree Theorem, see [17], is that driving a branch cannot go on indefinitely without interruption by generalization. The second fact is that whenever generalization happens, the new nodes are all smaller in a certain order (involving term size and number of occurrences of the same variable) than the one they replace. This would not be the case if the *GENERALIZE* operation were performed when the two compared nodes have labels that are disjoint terms.

As for correctness, it is easily proved that each step of the transformation rules preserves normal-order graph reduction semantics; extending rigorously the proof to account for folding is more involved. A general technique due to Sands [71] can be used to prove this for (positive) supercompilation, see [70].

3.4 Discussion of the Algorithm

A number of choices are left open or settled in an arbitrary way in our algorithm.

First, our algorithm follows Turchin's *generalization principle* [89] which states that a generalization between two terms has a meaning only in the context of the computation process in which they take part. Indeed, our algorithm searches only the ancestors of a leaf node. However, to avoid the generation of duplicate definitions one might imagine searching across different branches; see *e.g.* [38].

Second, our algorithm does not specify a particular strategy for *selecting unmarked leaf nodes*. One may chose a breath-first or depth-first strategy.

Third, in case driving stops the algorithm may employ different strategies for *selecting ancestors* for generalization. For instance, one may choose the closest ancestor, or the ancestor that gives the most specific generalization.

Fourth, when we perform a $GENERALIZE(T, M, N)$ step we replace node M. Instead one could replace N, since this avoids destroying the whole subtree with root M; other branches from M can be retained with no loss of information.

Fifth, the operator $\lfloor \bullet, \bullet \rfloor$ and the stop criterion can be varied (as in [55]). The operation $SPLIT(T, s, t)$ may be refined to split t in another way; *e.g.* if $s \equiv h\, x$

and $t \equiv l\,(k\,(h\,y))$ then split such that $t' \equiv l\,(k\,z)$ (Turchin's algorithm [89] maintains a stack structure of common contexts to determine split points).

Finally, one can imagine various optimizations of which we will discuss only one, namely *transient reductions*. A term of the form $e[g\,x\,t_1 \ldots t_n]$ is *non-transient*, all other terms are *transient*. The optimization consists in adding the disjunction "or the label of N is transient" to the condition in (3a) of Algorithm 7. So only terms that require a choice at run-time are compared to ancestors for whistling in the partial process tree. The rationale is that any loop in the program must pass through a choice point unless there is an unconditional loop in the program. However, this means that the partial process tree in principle can be infinite—a risk considered worth taking in the area of partial evaluation [44]. An alternative to transient reductions that gives similar residual programs, and at the same time retains the guarantee that the constructed partial process trees are finite, are *characteristic trees, e.g.* [55].

The partial process tree for $a\,(a\,xs\,ys)\,xs$ using transient reductions appears in Fig. 12.

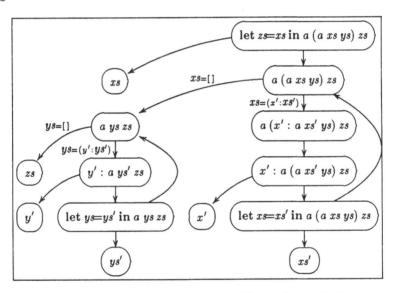

Fig. 12. Example partial process tree with transient reductions.

From this tree one can generate the term $a'\,xs\,ys\,xs$ and a new program (Fig. 13). This transformation is noteworthy because the initial term requires passing the list xs twice, whereas the new term passes xs only once.

$$
\begin{aligned}
a'\,[\,]\,ys\,zs &\triangleq a''\,ys\,zs \\
a'\,(x:xs)\,ys\,zs &\triangleq x:a'\,xs\,ys\,zs \\[4pt]
a''\,[\,]\,zs &\triangleq zs \\
a''\,(y:ys)\,zs &\triangleq y:a''\,ys\,zs
\end{aligned}
$$

Fig. 13. More efficient double append program.

3.5 Comparative Remarks

From its very inception, supercompilation has been tied to a specific programming language, called *Refal* [78], a language inspired by Markov algorithms. A Refal program is a sequence of rewrite rules, used to transform data in the form of associative and possibly nested symbol strings and offers certain advantages for programming, *e.g.* [90, 62]. Running interpreters were available by the end of the 1960's [22]; different versions of the language were implemented [96, 50, 90, 40].

Driving and generalization for our language are simplified considerably due to simpler data structures, untyped variables, and flat patterns (essentially *elementary contractions* [89]). Due to Refal's data structure most general unifiers do not always exist; a *generalized matching algorithm* is defined in [84, 87]. An optimization technique for pattern matching in Refal was developed in [51].

We should note that supercompilation is a normal-order transformation that can be applied to programs with call-by-value semantics, and that transformed programs can be interpreted call-by-value, as done by Turchin. As a result, supercompilation may make programs terminate more often. Here supercompilation is used to transform programs with normal-order graph reduction semantics into programs with the same semantics and the same termination properties.

Process trees correspond to Turchin's *graph of states* [85] (sometimes called Refal graphs or pattern matching graphs [95]). Driving was used in the seventies in a system for inverse computation, called URA (*cf.* [65]; Sect. 5.2), an application that has been suggested earlier in [80]. *Neighborhood analysis* [84] uses driving to determine sets of data that pass through a computation process in identical ways; suggested for generalization [89] and program testing [2, 3]. Several supercompilers have been developed for Refal [39, 49, 67, 89, 98, 99] including several experimental systems by the Refal group in Moscow (mostly unpublished, except [4]). The first 'non-Refal' supercompiler was [34].

4 Related Program Transformers

In this section we compare positive supercompilation briefly to *partial evaluation*, *deforestation*, *partial deduction*, *perfect supercompilation*, and *generalized partial computation*. First we introduce a number of axes along which transformers can be compared, and then enter the coordinates of the above transformers.

4.1 Some Dimensions in Automatic Program Transformation

Information propagation. Every program transformer maintains a certain level of information propagation; we consider *constant propagation*, *unification-based information propagation*, and *constraint-based information propagation*. The three levels differ in how much information is recorded about pattern matching and tests, corresponding to the transformation rules in Fig. 14.

In constant propagation the outcome of tests are ignored. In unification-based propagation substitutions into the transformed terms are used to represent

	$T[\![$ if $u{=}v$ then t else s $]\!] =$	information propagation
(a)	if $u{=}v$ then $T[\![\,t\,]\!]$ else $T[\![\,s\,]\!]$	constant propagation
(b)	if $u{=}v$ then $T[\![\,t\{u{:=}v\}\,]\!]$ else $T[\![\,s\,]\!]$	unification-based
(c)	if $u{=}v$ then $T[\![\,t\,]\!]\{u = v\}$ else $T[\![\,s\,]\!]\{u \neq v\}$	constraint-based

Fig. 14. Information propagation.

the outcome of tests. In constraint-based propagation the transformer explicitly maintains sets of constraints recording previous tests (*restrictions* [84, 34]). Depending on the programming language other abstract properties may be propagated, *e.g.* [72, 15, 77, 43].

Evaluation strategy. One can view a program transformer as an extension of an interpreter, *e.g.* [34, 31, 61, 74]. This implies that the transformer has an *evaluation strategy* that it inherits from the underlying interpreter. More concretely, the transformer processes nested function calls in some order. We consider transformers that use *inside-out* (or *call-by-value* or *applicative order*) and *outside-in* (or *call-by-name* or *normal-order*).

Control restructuring. Control restructuring is concerned with the relationship between program points in the subject and the residual program [10, 69]:

Monovariant: any program point in the subject program gives rise to zero or one program point in the residual program.

Polyvariant: any program point in the subject program can give rise to one or more program points in the residual program.

Monogenetic: any program point in the residual program is produced from a single program point of the subject program.

Polygenetic: any program point in the residual program may be produced from one or more program points of the subject program.

4.2   A Taxonomy of Transformers

Deforestation, due to Wadler [100], performs *program composition* by eliminating intermediate data structures. Deforestation performs, as a special case, program specialization (see [75]). Deforestation is very similar to positive supercompilation except that it uses constant propagation rather than unification-based information propagation. Also, it does not incorporate generalization during transformation. In the original version, deforestation is guaranteed to terminate for a certain class of programs without generalization. Later extensions use annotations computed by a static analysis to guide generalization.

   Partial evaluation performs *program specialization* and, as presented in [44], uses only constant propagation [34, 75, 74]. This limitation applies to all variants of partial evaluation: offline and online approaches with and without partially static structures. The usual evaluation strategy for partial evaluators is applicative-order, see [61].

   Partial deduction, as in [56, 52, 26], and positive supercompilation have essential aspects in common [38]: the way in which goals are unified and how the resulting substitutions are applied to the goals in the next transformation step (construction of a partial SLDNF tree), is much like in the clauses of driving.

Since in logic programs predicates cannot occur inside predicates, there is no direct correspondence to the rules for nested function calls which achieve deforestation. However, local variables in logic programs often represent intermediate data structures that could be removed by more sophisticated techniques. Partial deduction in logic programming is not capable of removing them; this requires an extension of the techniques, see *e.g.* [63, 54, 33].

Turchin's supercompiler [87] and our positive supercompiler are identical with respect to the propagation of positive information, except for certain trivial differences. The main difference between the two is that the former also maintains *negative information, i.e.* the information that a test failed, and this is maintained in the form of constraints (see *perfect driving* [34]).

Generalized partial computation (GPC), due to Futamura [25], has a similar effect and power as supercompilation, but has arbitrary tests rather than just patterns and equality tests. The underlying logic for the tests can be any logic system, for example predicate logic, and may be undecidable for certain logic formulas. In this view, positive supercompilation can be seen as propagating structural predicates that can always be resolved. Abstract interpretation can be used to propagate additional information, *e.g.* [43, 64].

These observations are summarized in Fig. 15. For a more detailed discussion on information propagation see [34, 75, 38, 74, 76], and for more on evaluation strategies see [13, 61]. These papers also give examples of optimizations that require the transformer to use a specific evaluation strategy or level of information propagation. For instance, to pass the so-called *KMP-test* [75], at least unification-based propagation is required; to eliminate intermediate data structures in general, normal-order strategy is required.

transformer	information propagation	evaluation strategy	control restruct. variant	control restruct. genetic	KMP test	elim. struct.
Partial evaluation	constant	in-out	poly	mono	–	–
Deforestation	constant	out-in	poly	poly	–	+
Partial deduction	unification	unspecified	poly	mono	+	–
Positive SCP	unification	out-in	poly	poly	+	+
Perfect SCP	constraint	out-in	poly	poly	+	+
GPC	constraint	out-in	poly	poly	+	+

Fig. 15. A taxonomy of transformers.

5   Larger Perspectives of Supercompilation

Supercompilation achieves program specialization, but is not limited to this application: it is a much wider framework for equivalence transformation of programs. Program inversion is one of the more advanced applications of supercompilation which we will outline in this section.

We refer to any process of simulating, analyzing or transforming programs by means of programs as *metacomputation*; the term stresses the fact that this activity is one level higher than ordinary computation ("programs as data objects"). Program specialization, composition, and inversion are different metacomputation tasks; programs that carry out these tasks, are *metaprograms*. The step from a program to the application of a metaprogram to the encoded form of the program is a *metasystem transition*; repeated use of metasystem transition leads to a *multi-level metasystem hierarchy*. In the remainder of this paper we adopt the language-independent formalization of [30] based on [27, 35, 84, 97].

Metasystem transition is a key ingredient of Turchin's approach: the construction of hierarchies of metasystems (*e.g.* supercompilers) was taken as the basis for program analysis and transformation [83]. The book [96] defined all three Futamura projections in terms of metasystem transition.

Section 5.1 introduces a formalism for metacomputation, in Sect. 5.2 discusses supercompilation and program inversion, and Sect. 5.3 presents metasystem transition.

5.1 Metacomputation Revisited

Computation. We assume a fixed set D containing programs written in different languages, as well as their input and output data. To express the application of programs to data we define an *application language* A by the grammar

$$A ::= D \mid <A\ A^*>$$

where the symbols $<, > \notin D$ denote the application of a program to its inputs. Capitalized names in `typewriter` font denote arbitrary elements of D. They are free variables of the meta-notation in which the paper is written. For instance, the intended meaning of the A-expression `<P X Y>` is the application of program `P` $\in D$ to the input `X, Y` $\in D$. We are not interested in a specific programming language for writing programs. For simplicity, let all source-, target- and metalanguages be identical.

We write $a \Rightarrow$ `D` to denote the *computation* of an expression $a \in A$ to `D` $\in D$. For instance, `<P X Y>` $\Rightarrow$ `OUT` is the computation of program `P` $\in D$ with input `X, Y` $\in D$ and output `OUT` $\in D$. Two A-expressions $a, b \in A$ are computationally equal if they can be reduced to identical D-expressions:

$$a = b \ \ \textit{iff} \ \ \forall \texttt{X} \in D \colon (a \Rightarrow \texttt{X} \ \ \textit{iff} \ \ b \Rightarrow \texttt{X})$$

Abstraction. To represent sets of A-expressions, we define a *metacomputation language* B by the grammar

$$B ::= D \mid M \mid <B\ B^*>$$

where M is a set of *metavariables*. A metavariable `m` $\in M$ is a placeholder that stands for an unspecified data element `D` $\in D$. We use lowercase names in `typewriter` font to denote elements of M. A B-expression b is an abstraction that represents the set of all A-expressions obtained by replacing metavariables $\mathbf{m} \in M$ by elements of D. We write $a \in b$ to denote that $a \in A$ is an element of the set represented by $b \in B$. We refer to a B-expression also as a *configuration*.

Encoding. Expressions in the metacomputation language need to be represented as data in order to manipulate them by means of programs (ordinary computation cannot reduce B-expressions because metavariables are not in A). A *metacoding* [79] is an injective mapping $B \to D$ to encode B-expressions in D. We are not interested in a specific way of metacoding and assume some metacoding $\overline{\bullet} : B \to D$. Repeated metacoding is well-defined because $D \subset B$.

Metacomputation. It follows from our notation that $\texttt{<MC } \overline{b}\texttt{>} \Rightarrow \texttt{D}$ denotes metacomputation on an expression $b \in B$ using a metaprogram $\texttt{MC} \in D$. The application of $\texttt{MC}$ to the metacoded B-expression is an A-expression that can be reduced by ordinary computation. We should stress that this characterization of metacomputation says nothing about its concrete nature, except that it involves a metaprogram $\texttt{MC}$ that operates on a metacoded configuration $\overline{b}$. Different metaprograms may perform different operations on b, such as program specialization, program composition, or program inversion.

Definition 9 (program specializer). A program $\texttt{SPEC} \in D$ is a *specializer* if for every program $\texttt{P} \in D$, every input $\texttt{X}, \texttt{Y} \in D$ and metavariable $\texttt{y} \in M$, there exists a program $\texttt{R} \in D$ such that

$$\texttt{<SPEC } \overline{\texttt{<P X y>}}\texttt{>} \Rightarrow \texttt{R} \quad \text{and} \quad \texttt{<P X Y>} = \texttt{<R Y>}$$

Definition 10 (program composer). A program $\texttt{CPO} \in D$ is a *composer* if for every program $\texttt{P}, \texttt{Q} \in D$, every input $\texttt{X}, \texttt{Y} \in D$ and metavariables $\texttt{x}, \texttt{y} \in M$, there exists a program $\texttt{R} \in D$ such that

$$\texttt{<CPO } \overline{\texttt{<P <Q x> y>}}\texttt{>} \Rightarrow \texttt{R} \quad \text{and} \quad \texttt{<P <Q X> Y>} = \texttt{<R X Y>}$$

Definition 11 (program inverter). A program $\texttt{INV} \in D$ is a *program inverter* if for every program $\texttt{P} \in D$ injective in its first argument,[1] every input $\texttt{X}, \texttt{Y} \in D$ and metavariable $\texttt{x} \in M$, there exists a program $\texttt{P}^{-1} \in D$ such that

$$\texttt{<INV } \overline{\texttt{<P x Y>}}\texttt{>} \Rightarrow \texttt{P}^{-1} \quad \text{and} \quad \texttt{<P}^{-1} \overline{\texttt{<P X Y>}}\texttt{>} \Rightarrow \texttt{X}$$

In general when $\texttt{P}$ is not injective, $\texttt{P}^{-1}$ must return a list of answers.[2]

---

[1] $\texttt{P}$ is injective in its first argument if for all $\texttt{X1}, \texttt{X2}, \texttt{Y} \in D$: $\texttt{<P X1 Y>} = \texttt{<P X2 Y>}$ implies that $\texttt{X1}$ and $\texttt{X2}$ are the same element of D.

[2] There are two types of inversion: either we are interested in an *existential* solution (one of the possible answers), or in a *universal* solution (all possible answers).

5.2 Inverse Computation by Supercompilation

A supercompiler can be used for program specialization and the transformed program in Fig. 13 illustrates a case of program composition. It is less known that supercompilation is capable of *inverse computation* [81, 65, 1] (we show later how metasystem transition can be used to generate an inverse program P^{-1}). The formulation of inverse computation is as follows. Let EQ be a program that tests the equality of two data elements. Given Y, Z find an X such that

$$\text{<EQ <P X Y> Z>} \Rightarrow \text{'True'}$$

where 'True' is some distinct element of D. Supercompilation, more specifically driving, can be used to obtain a program ANSWER with answers for x internalized:

$$\text{<DRIVE } \overline{\text{<EQ <P x Y> Z>}} \text{>} \Rightarrow \text{ANSWER}$$

Example 1. Let numbers be represented by lists of length n. Then program append a (Fig. 2) implements the addition of two numbers. Using driving (Sect. 2) we can compute $zs - ys$ by inverse computation of addition. The result of interpretive inversion for $zs = 1$ and $ys = 0$, *i.e.* driving eq $(a$ xs $[])$ $[1]$, appears in Fig. 16. The answer, $xs = 1$, can be extracted mechanically from the program.

$$
\begin{array}{ll}
g_1\,[] \stackrel{\triangle}{=} \textit{False} & g_2\,[] \stackrel{\triangle}{=} \textit{True} \\
g_1\,(x{:}xs) \stackrel{\triangle}{=} g_2\,xs & g_2\,(x{:}xs) \stackrel{\triangle}{=} \textit{False}
\end{array}
$$

Fig. 16. Result of driving eq $(a$ xs $[])$ $[1]$.

Example 2. Using supercompilation instead of driving one may produce a finite program even when the list of possible answers is infinite. This may be used for theorem proving [86, 99]. An example is shown in Fig. 17 where the supercompiler (Sect. 3) is applied to eq $(a$ xs $[])$ xs which represents the proposition $\forall n.(n + 0 = n)$ which can be proven only by using induction. The residual program constructed returns *True* for all lists. This proves the theorem.

$$
\begin{array}{l}
g_1\,[] \stackrel{\triangle}{=} \textit{True} \\
g_1\,(x{:}xs) \stackrel{\triangle}{=} g_1\,xs
\end{array}
$$

Fig. 17. Result of supercompiling eq $(a$ xs $[])$ xs.

An early result for inverse computation by driving were obtained in 1972 by performing subtraction by inverse computation of binary addition [80]. In 1973 S.A. Romanenko and later S.M. Abramov implemented an algorithm, Universal Resolving Algorithm (URA), in which driving was combined with a mechanical extraction of answers [1, 65]. For program inversion see also [39, 41, 66, 93, 60].

In logic programming, one defines a predicate by a program <P x y> and solves the inversion problem for Z = 'True'. Theorem proving and program transformation are indistinguishable in the approach outlined above; they are two applications of the same equivalence transformation. The definition of predicates may be perceived as non-procedural, but their semantics is still defined in terms of computation. The application of supercompilation to problem solving and theorem proving has been discussed in [86, 87], the connection to logic programming in [1, 28, 38].

5.3 Metasystem Transition

Having introduced the basic concepts of metacomputation, we now consider the use of multi-level metasystem hierarchies together with a supercompiler. During the construction of multi-level hierarchies, we will frequently need to replace metacoded subexpressions by metavariables. The correct treatment of metacode is so essential in self-application [27], that we make elevated metavariables [97] an integral part of the MST-language. We define a *metasystem transition language* C by the grammar

$$C ::= D \mid M_{I\!N} \mid <C\ C^*>$$

where $M_{I\!N}$ is a set of *elevated metavariables* $m_H, H \in I\!N$. An elevated metavariable m_H ranges over data metacoded H-times. We will denote by D^H the set of metacode $\overline{D}^H$ of all $D \in D$. A metavariable without elevation has 0 as its elevation index. A C-expression c represents the set of all A-expressions obtained by substituting elevated metavariables m_H by elements of D^H.

Metasystem Transition. The construction of each next level in a metasystem hierarchy, *i.e.* each *metasystem transition* (MST) [96], is done in three steps [36]:

(A) given an initial A-expression a,   ('computation')
(B) define a C-expression c such that $a \in c$,   ('abstraction')
(C) apply a metaprogram MC to the metacode $\bar{c}$.   ('metacomputation')

The expression obtained in the last step is again an A-expression and the same procedure can be repeated. Expressions obtained by MST are called *MST-formulas*. This definition says nothing about the goal of the MST, except that it is an abstraction of an A-expression a to a configuration c, followed by the application of a metaprogram MC to $\bar{c}$.

Generating Inverse Programs. The inverse computation of a program can always be performed using driving, but the performance can be poor whilst often more efficient inverse programs are known to exist. Figure 18 show how MST can be used to produce inverse programs by specialization of the universal resolving algorithm URA [1]; see [66]. For notational convenience let <Q x y z> be defined by <EQ <P x y> z>. A specializer SPEC is used for the sake of generality, but it should be clear that a supercompiler SCP can be used instead.

1st MST Define a C-expression (B0) by replacing X by x_0 in the A-expression (A0), and apply URA to the metacoded C-expression (A1) to perform inverse computation: the 1st MST. Inverse computation of Q is achieved.

2nd MST Define a C-expression (B1) by replacing $\overline{Y}, \overline{Z}$ by y_1, z_1 in the A-expression (A1)[3], and apply SPEC$'$ to the metacoded C-expression (A2) to specialize URA and remove its interpretive overhead: the 2nd MST. The result is an inverted program Q^{-1} that returns ANSWER given Y, Z.

3rd MST Define a C-expression (B2) by replacing $\overline{\overline{Q}}$ by q_2 in the A-expression (A2), and apply SPEC$''$ to the metacoded C-expression (A3): the 3rd MST. The result is an inverter INV that converts a program Q into Q^{-1}.

4th MST Define a C-expression (B3) by replacing $\overline{\overline{\text{URA}}}$ by ura$_2$ in the A-expression (A3), and apply SPEC$'''$ to the metacoded C-expression (A4): the 4th MST. The result is an inverter generator INVGEN.

(A0)	$\langle Q\ X\ Y\ Z\rangle \Rightarrow BOOL$	(computation)
(B0)	$\langle Q\ x_0\ Y\ Z\rangle$	(abstraction)
(A1)	$\langle URA\ \overline{\langle Q\ x_0\ Y\ Z\rangle}\rangle \Rightarrow ANSWER$	(1st MST)
(B1)	$\langle URA\ \overline{\langle Q\ x_0\ y_1\ z_1\rangle}\rangle$	(abstraction)
(A2)	$\langle SPEC'\ \overline{\langle URA\ \overline{\langle Q\ x_0\ y_1\ z_1\rangle}\rangle}\rangle \Rightarrow Q^{-1}$	(2nd MST)
(B2)	$\langle SPEC'\ \overline{\langle URA\ \overline{\overline{\langle q_2\ x_0\ y_1\ z_1\rangle}}\rangle}\rangle$	(abstraction)
(A3)	$\langle SPEC''\ \overline{\langle SPEC'\ \overline{\langle URA\ \overline{\overline{\langle q_2\ x_0\ y_1\ z_1\rangle}}\rangle}\rangle}\rangle \Rightarrow INV$	(3rd MST)
(B3)	$\langle SPEC''\ \overline{\langle SPEC'\ \overline{\langle ura_2\ \overline{\overline{\langle q_2\ x_0\ y_1\ z_1\rangle}}\rangle}\rangle}\rangle$	(abstraction)
(A4)	$\langle SPEC'''\ \overline{\langle SPEC''\ \overline{\langle SPEC'\ \overline{\langle ura_2\ \overline{\overline{\langle q_2\ x_0\ y_1\ z_1\rangle}}\rangle}\rangle}\rangle}\rangle \Rightarrow INVGEN$	(4th MST)

Fig. 18. MST-formulas for program inversion.

A hierarchy of metasystems can be visualized using a *2-dimensional notation*[4]: (i) an expression is moved down one line down for each metacoding; (ii) the elevation of a metavariable m_H is shown by a bullet • located H lines below the metavariable. Consider the two-dimensional version of the 3rd MST (A3) as example:

$$\langle SPEC'' \underline{\hspace{5cm}} \rangle \Rightarrow INV$$
$$\langle SPEC' \underline{\hspace{1cm}} q \underline{\hspace{2cm}} \rangle$$
$$\langle URA\_ \mid \_\ y\ z\_\rangle$$
$$\langle \bullet\ x\ \bullet\ \bullet\rangle$$

The *Futamura projections* [23] are, in all probability, the first example of program transformation beyond a single metasystem level, but MST is not lim-

---

[3] We take the liberty to replace subexpressions of $d \in D$ by metavariables and interrupt the horizontal line above the enclosing expression; defined formally in [30].

[4] Introduced by Turchin; a preliminary form appeared in [27].

ited to this application. Turchin suggested MST to increase the power of theorem proving [86] and it inspired a constructive approach to the foundations of mathematics [88]. The philosophical background of MST was exposed in [82]; see also [91, 92].

The first successful self-application of a partial evaluator was reported in [45] and several self-application partial evaluators have been built since then. The book [44] describes approaches to and systems for partial evaluation, and includes a comprehensive bibliography on this topic. A self-applicable partial evaluator for a functional language with Refal data structures is described in [68]. The generation of an algorithm representing binary subtraction from binary addition by self-application of a simple supercompiler was reported in [39]. A self-applicable supercompiler for Refal is described in [98, 60]. Examples of MST include multiple self-application [27, 32], the generation of program transformers [29, 31], the implementation of non-standard semantics [3], and other related work on metacomputation and MST [1, 2, 28, 36, 37, 42, 49, 48].

Acknowledgments. Thanks to Sergei Abramov, Andrei Klimov, Andrei Nemytykh, Victoria Pinchuk, Alexander Romanenko (†), Sergei Romanenko, and last but not least, Valentin F. Turchin for many stimulating discussions and hospitality during visits in Russia and New York. Special thanks are due to Andrei Klimov for transcription and translation of Russian titles. Thanks to John Hatcliff, Neil D. Jones, Jesper Jørgensen, Bern Martens, Kristian Nielsen, and David Sands for stimulating discussions on various topics of this paper. Finally, we are indebted to all members of the Topps group at DIKU for providing an excellent working environment.

The first author was partially supported by an Erwin-Schrödinger-Fellowship of the Austrian Science Foundation (FWF) under grant J0780 & J0964. Both authors were also supported by the DART project funded by the Danish Natural Sciences Research Council.

References

1. S.M. Abramov. Metavychislenija i logicheskoe programmirovanie (Metacomputation and logic programming). *Programmirovanie*, 3:31–44, 1991. (In Russian).
2. S.M. Abramov. Metacomputation and program testing. In *1st International Workshop on Automated and Algorithmic Debugging*, pp. 121–135, 1993.
3. S.M. Abramov. *Metavychislenija i ikh prilozhenija (Metacomputation and its application)*. Nauka, Moscow, 1995. (In Russian).
4. S.M. Abramov and N.V. Kondratiev. Kompiljator, osnovannyj na metode chastichnykh vychislenij (A compiler based on the method of partial evaluation). In *Nekotorye voprosy prikladnojmatematiki i programmnogo obespechenija EhVB*, pp. 66–69. Moscow State University, Moscow, 1982. (in Russian).
5. M. Alpuente, M. Falaschi, and G. Vidal. Narrowing-driven partial evaluation of functional logic programs. In *European Symposium on Programming—ESOP '96*, LNCS. Springer-Verlag, 1996. To appear.
6. L. Beckman, A. Haraldson, Ö. Oskarsson, and E. Sandewall. A partial evaluator and its use as a programming tool. *Artificial Intelligence*, 7:319–357, 1976.
7. R. Bird and P.L Wadler. *Introduction to Functional Programming*. Prentice-Hall, 1988.

8. D. Bjørner, A.P. Ershov, and N.D. Jones, editors. *Partial Evaluation and Mixed Computation*. North-Holland, Amsterdam, 1988.

9. R. Bol. Loop checking in partial deduction. *Journal of Logic Programming*, 16(1&2):25–46, 1993.

10. M.A. Bulyonkov. Polyvariant mixed computation for analyzer programs. *Acta Informatica*, 21:473–484, 1984.

11. R.M. Burstall and J. Darlington. A transformation system for developing recursive programs. *Journal of the Association for Computing Machines*, 24(1):44–67, 1977.

12. C.-L. Chang and R.C.-T. Lee. *Symbolic Logic and Mechanical Theorem Proving*. Computer Science and Applied Mathematics. Academic Press, 1973.

13. C. Consel and O. Danvy. For a better support of static data flow. In J. Hughes, editor, *Functional Programming and Computer Architecture*, vol. 523 of *LNCS*, pp. 495–519. Springer-Verlag, 1991.

14. C. Consel and O. Danvy. Tutorial notes on partial evaluation. In *ACM Symposium in Principles of Programming Languages*, pages 493–501. ACM Press, 1993.

15. C. Consel and S.C. Khoo. Parameterized partial evaluation. *ACM TOPLAS*, 15(3):463–493, 1993.

16. O. Danvy, R. Glück, and P. Thiemann, editors. *Partial Evaluation. Proceedings.* LNCS. Springer-Verlag, 1996. To appear.

17. N. Dershowitz and J.-P. Jouannaud. Rewrite systems. In J. van Leeuwen, editor, *Handbook of Theoretical Computer Science*, pp. 244–320. Elsevier, 1992.

18. J. Dixon. The specializer, a method of automatically writing computer programs. Technical report, Division of Computer Research and Technology, National Institute of Health, Bethesda, Maryland, 1971.

19. A.P. Ershov. On the partial computation principle. *Information Processing Letters*, 6(2):38–41, 1977.

20. A.P. Ershov. On the essence of compilation. In E.J. Neuhold, editor, *Formal Description of Programming Concepts*, pp. 391–420. North-Holland, 1978.

21. A. Ferguson and P.L. Wadler. When will deforestation stop? In *1988 Glasgow Workshop on Functional Programming*, pages 39–56, 1988.

22. S.N. Florencev, Y.V. Oljunin, and V.F. Turchin. (An efficient interpreter for the language Refal). Preprint, Institute of Applied Mathematics, Academy of Sciences of the USSR, Moscow, 1969. (in Russian).

23. Y. Futamura. Partial evaluation of computing process – an approach to a compiler-compiler. *Systems, Computers, Controls*, 2(5):45–50, 1971.

24. Y. Futamura. Partial computation of programs. In E. Goto, K. Furukawa, R. Nakajima, I. Nakata, and A. Yonezawa, editors, *RIMS Symposia on Software Science and Engineering*, vol. 147 of *LNCS*, pp. 1–35, Kyoto, Japan, 1983. Springer-Verlag.

25. Y. Futamura. Program evaluation and generalized partial computation. In *International Conference on Fifth Generation Computer Systems*, pp. 1–8, 1988.

26. J. Gallagher. Tutorial in specialisation of logic programs. In *Symposium on Partial Evaluation and Semantics-Based Program Manipulation*, pp. 88–98. ACM Press, 1993.

27. R. Glück. Towards multiple self-application. In *Proceedings of the Symposium on Partial Evaluation and Semantics-Based Program Manipulation*, pp. 309–320. ACM Press, 1991.

28. R. Glück. Projections for knowledge based systems. In R. Trappl, editor, *Cybernetics and Systems Research'92*, volume 1, pp. 535–542. World Scientific, 1992.

29. R. Glück. On the generation of specializers. *Journal of Functional Programming*, 4(4):499–514, 1994.

30. R. Glück. On the mechanics of metasystem hierarchies in program transformation. In M. Proietti, editor, *Logic Program Synthesis and Transformation. Proceedings*, vol. 1048 of *LNCS*, pp. 234–251. Springer-Verlag, 1996.

31. R. Glück and J. Jørgensen. Generating transformers for deforestation and supercompilation. In B. Le Charlier, editor, *Static Analysis. Proceedings*, volume 864 of *LNCS*, pp. 432–448, Namur, Belgium, 1994. Springer-Verlag.

32. R. Glück and J. Jørgensen. Efficient multi-level generating extensions for program specialization. In S.D. Swierstra and M. Hermenegildo, editors, *Programming Languages, Implementations, Logics and Programs (PLILP'95)*, vol. 982 of *LNCS*, pp. 259–278. Springer-Verlag, 1995.

33. R. Glück, J. Jørgensen, B. Martens, and M.H. Sørensen. Controlling conjunctive partial deduction of definite logic programs. Technical Report CW 226, Katholieke Universiteit Leuven, 1996.

34. R. Glück and A.V. Klimov. Occam's razor in metacomputation: the notion of a perfect process tree. In P. Cousot, M. Falaschi, G. Filè, and G. Rauzy, editors, *Static Analysis. Proceedings.*, vol. 724 of *LNCS*, pp. 112–123. Springer-Verlag, 1993.

35. R. Glück and A.V. Klimov. Metacomputation as a tool for formal linguistic modeling. In R. Trappl, editor, *Cybernetics and Systems'94*, volume 2, pp. 1563–1570. World Scientific, 1994.

36. R. Glück and A.V. Klimov. Metasystem transition schemes in computer science and mathematics. *World Futures*, 45:213–243, 1995.

37. R. Glück and A.V. Klimov. Reduction of language hierarchies. In *Proceedings of the 14th International Congress on Cybernetics*, page To appear, Namur, Belgium, 1995. International Association for Cybernetics.

38. R. Glück and M.H. Sørensen. Partial deduction and driving are equivalent. In M. Hermenegildo and J. Penjam, editors, *Programming Language Implementation and Logic Programming. Proceedings*, vol. 844 of *LNCS*, pp. 165–181. Springer-Verlag, 1994.

39. R. Glück and V.F. Turchin. Application of metasystem transition to function inversion and transformation. In *Proceedings of the ISSAC'90 (Tokyo, Japan)*, pp. 286–287. ACM Press, 1990.

40. R. Gurin and S.A. Romanenko. *Jazyk programmirovanija Refal Pljus (The Refal Plus programming language)*. Intertech, Moscow, 1991. (in Russian).

41. P.G. Harrison. Function inversion. In Bjørner et al. [8], pp. 153–166.

42. J. Hatcliff and Robert Glück. Reasoning about hierarchies of online program specialization systems. In Danvy et al. [16]. To appear.

43. N.D. Jones. The essence of program transformation by partial evaluation and driving. In N.D. Jones, M. Hagiya, and M. Sato, editors, *Logic, Language, and Computation*, vol. 792 of *LNCS*, pp. 206–224. Springer-Verlag, 1994. Festschrift in honor of S.Takasu.

44. N.D. Jones, C.K. Gomard, and P. Sestoft. *Partial Evaluation and Automatic Program Generation*. Prentice-Hall, 1993.

45. N.D. Jones, P. Sestoft, and H. Søndergaard. An experiment in partial evaluation: the generation of a compiler generator. In J.-P. Jouannaud, editor, *Rewriting Techniques and Applications, Dijon, France.*, vol. 202 of *LNCS*, pp. 124–140. Springer-Verlag, 1985.

46. N.D. Jones, P. Sestoft, and H. Søndergaard. Mix: a self-applicable partial evaluator for experiments in compiler generation. *Lisp and Symbolic Computation*, 2(1):9–50, 1989.
47. S.C. Kleene. *Introduction to Metamathematics*. Van Nostrand, 1952.
48. Andrei V. Klimov. Dynamic specialization in extended functional language with monotone objects. In *Proceedings of the Symposium on Partial Evaluation and Semantics-Based Program Manipulation*, pp. 199–210. ACM Press, 1991.
49. A.V. Klimov and S.A. Romanenko. Metavychislitel' dlja jazyka Refal. Osnovnye ponjatija i primery. (A metaevaluator for the language Refal. Basic concepts and examples). Preprint 71, Keldysh Institute of Applied Mathematics, Academy of Sciences of the USSR, Moscow, 1987. (in Russian).
50. A.V. Klimov and S.A. Romanenko. Sistema programmirovanija Refal-2 dlja ES. Opisanie vkhodnogo jazyka (Programming system Refal-2 for ES computers. The source language description). Technical report, Keldysh Institute of Applied Mathematics, Academy of Sciences of the USSR, Moscow, 1987. (in Russian).
51. A.V. Klimov, S.A. Romanenko, and V.F. Turchin. Teoreticheskie osnovy sintaksicheskogo otozhdestvlenija v jazyke Refal (The theory of pattern matching in Refal). Preprint 13, Keldysh Institute of Applied Mathematics, Academy of Sciences of the USSR, Moscow, 1973. (in Russian).
52. J. Komorowski. An introduction to partial deduction. In A. Pettorossi, editor, *Meta-Programming in Logic*, vol. 649 of *LNCS*, pp. 49–69, 1992.
53. J. Komorowski. Special issue on partial deduction. *Journal of Logic Programming*, 16(1&2):1–189, 1993.
54. M. Leuschel, D. De Schreye, and A. de Waal. A conceptual embedding of folding into partial deduction: Towards a maximal integration. Technical Report CW 225, Katholieke Universiteit Leuven, 1995.
55. M. Leuschel and B. Martens. Global control for partial deduction through characteristic atoms and global trees. In Danvy et al. [16]. To appear.
56. J.W. Lloyd and J.C. Shepherdson. Partial evaluation in logic programming. *Journal of Logic Programming*, 11(3-4):217–242, 1991.
57. L.A. Lombardi. Incremental computation. In F. L. Alt and M. Rubinoff, editors, *Advances in Computers*, volume 8, pp. 247–333. Academic Press, 1967.
58. L.A. Lombardi and B. Raphael. Lisp as the language for an incremental computer. In E.C. Berkeley and D.G. Bobrow, editors, *The Programming Language Lisp: Its Operation and Applications*, pp. 204–219, Cambridge, Massachusetts, 1964. MIT Press.
59. B. Martens and J. Gallagher. Ensuring global termination of partial deduction while allowing flexible polyvariance. In L. Stirling, editor, *International Conference on Logic Programming*, pp. 597–613. MIT Press, 1995.
60. A.P. Nemytykh, V.A. Pinchuk, and V.F. Turchin. A self-applicable supercompiler. In Danvy et al. [16]. To appear.
61. K. Nielsen and M.H. Sørensen. Call-by-name CPS-translation as a binding-time improvement. In A. Mycroft, editor, *Static Analysis*, vol. 983 of *LNCS*, pp. 296–313. Springer-Verlag, 1995.
62. R.M. Nirenberg. A practical turing machine representation. *SIGACT News*, 17(3):35–44, 1986.
63. M. Proietti and A. Pettorossi. Unfolding – definition – folding, in this order for avoiding unnecessary variables in logic programs. In *Programming Language Implementation and Logic Programming*, vol. 528 of *LNCS*, pp. 347–358. Springer-Verlag, 1991.

64. G. Puebla and M. Hermenegildo. Implementation of multiple specialization in logic programs. In *Proceedings of the Symposium on Partial Evaluation and Semantics-Based Program Manipulation*, pp. 77–87. ACM Press, 1995.

65. A.Y. Romanenko. The generation of inverse functions in Refal. In Bjørner et al. [8], pp. 427–444.

66. A.Y. Romanenko. Inversion and metacomputation. In *Proceedings of the Symposium on Partial Evaluation and Semantics-Based Program Manipulation. (Yale University, Connecticut)*, pages 12–22. ACM Press, 1991.

67. S.A. Romanenko. Progonka dlja programm na Refale-4 (Driving for Refal-4 programs). Preprint 211, Keldysh Institute of Applied Mathematics, Academy of Sciences of the USSR, Moscow, 1987. (in Russian).

68. S.A. Romanenko. A compiler generator produced by a self-applicable specializer can have a surprisingly natural and understandable structure. In Bjørner et al. [8], pp. 445–463.

69. S.A. Romanenko. Arity raiser and its use in program specialization. In N.D. Jones, editor, *ESOP'90*, vol. 432 of *LNCS*, pages 341–360. Springer-Verlag, 1990.

70. D. Sands. Proving the correctness of recursion-based automatic program transformation. In P. Mosses, M. Nielsen, and M.I. Schwartzbach, editors, *Theory and Practice of Software Development*, vol. 915 of *LNCS*, pages 681–695. Springer-Verlag, 1995.

71. D. Sands. Total correctness by local improvement in program transformation. In *22nd Symposium on Principles of Programming Languages*, pages 221–232. ACM Press, 1995.

72. D. Smith. Partial evaluation of pattern matching in constraint logic programming. In *Symposium on Partial Evaluation and Semantics-Based Program Manipulation*, pp. 62–71. ACM Press, 1991.

73. M.H. Sørensen. Turchin's supercompiler revisited. Master's thesis, Department of Computer Science, University of Copenhagen, 1994. DIKU-rapport 94/17.

74. M.H. Sørensen and R. Glück. An algorithm of generalization in positive supercompilation. In J.W. Lloyd, editor, *Logic Programming: Proceedings of the 1995 International Symposium*, pp. 465–479. MIT Press, 1995.

75. M.H. Sørensen, R. Glück, and N.D. Jones. Towards unifying deforestation, supercompilation, partial evaluation, and generalized partial computation. In D. Sannella, editor, *Programming Languages and Systems*, vol. 788 of *LNCS*, pp. 485–500. Springer-Verlag, 1994.

76. M.H. Sørensen, R. Glück, and N.D. Jones. A positive supercompiler. *Journal of Functional Programming*, 1996. To appear.

77. A. Takano. Generalized partial computation using disunification to solve constraints. In M. Rusinowitch and J.L. Remy, editors, *Conditional Term Rewriting Systems. Proceedings*, vol. 656 of *LNCS*, pp. 424–428. Springer-Verlag, 1993.

78. V.F. Turchin. Metajazyk dlja formal'nogo opisanija algoritmicheskikh jazykov (A metalanguage for the formal description of algorithmic languages). In *Cifrovaja Vychislitel'naja Tekhnika i Programmirovanie*, pp. 116–124. Sovetskoe Radio, Moscow, 1966. (in Russian).

79. V.F. Turchin. Programmirovanie na jazyke Refal. (Programming in the language Refal). Preprint 41, 43, 44, 48, 49, Institute of Applied Mathematics, Academy of Sciences of the USSR, Moscow, 1971. (in Russian).

80. V.F. Turchin. Ehkvivalentnye preobrazovanija rekursivnykh funkcij na Refale (Equivalent transformations of recursive functions defined in Refal). In *Teorija*

Jazykov i Metody Programmirovanija (Proceedings of the Symposium on the Theory of Languages and Programming Methods), pages 31–42, Kiev-Alushta, USSR, 1972. (In Russian).

81. V.F. Turchin. Ehkvivalentnye preobrazovanija programm na Refale (Equivalent transformations of Refal programs). *Avtomatizirovannaja Sistema upravlenija stroitel'stvom. Trudy CNIPIASS*, 6:36–68, 1974. (In Russian).

82. V.F. Turchin. *The Phenomenon of Science*. Columbia University Press, New York, 1977.

83. V.F. Turchin. A supercompiler system based on the language Refal. *SIGPLAN Notices*, 14(2):46–54, 1979.

84. V.F. Turchin. The language Refal, the theory of compilation and metasystem analysis. Courant Computer Science Report 20, Courant Institute of Mathematical Sciences, New York University, 1980.

85. V.F. Turchin. Semantic definitions in Refal and the automatic production of compilers. In N.D. Jones, editor, *Workshop on Semantics-Directed Compiler Generation, Århus, Denmark*, volume 94 of *LNCS*, pp. 441–474. Springer-Verlag, 1980.

86. V.F. Turchin. The use of metasystem transition in theorem proving and program optimization. In J.W. de Bakker and J. van Leeuwen, editors, *Automata, Languages and Programming*, volume 85 of *LNCS*, pp. 645–657, Noordwijkerhout, Netherlands, 1980. Springer-Verlag.

87. V.F. Turchin. The concept of a supercompiler. *Transactions on Programming Languages and Systems*, 8(3):292–325, 1986.

88. V.F. Turchin. A constructive interpretation of the full set theory. *The Journal of Symbolic Logic*, 52(1):172–201, 1987.

89. V.F. Turchin. The algorithm of generalization. In Bjørner et al. [8], pp. 531–549.

90. V.F. Turchin. *Refal-5, Programming Guide and Reference Manual*. New England Publishing Co., Holyoke, Massachusetts, 1989.

91. V.F. Turchin. The cybernetic ontology of action. *Kybernetes*, 22(2):10–30, 1993.

92. V.F. Turchin. On cybernetic epistemology. *Systems Research*, 10(1):3–28, 1993.

93. V.F. Turchin. Program transformation with metasystem transitions. *Journal of Functional Programming*, 3(3):283–313, 1993.

94. V.F. Turchin. On generalization of lists and strings in supercompilation. Technical report, City College of the City University of New York, 1995.

95. V.F. Turchin. Metacomputation: MST plus SCP. In Danvy et al. [16]. To appear.

96. V.F. Turchin, And.V. Klimov, Ark.V. Klimov, V.F. Khoroshevsky, A.G. Krasovsky, S.A. Romanenko, I.B. Shchenkov, and E.V. Travkina. *Bazisnyj Refal i ego realizacija na vychislitelnykh mashinakh (Basic Refal and its implementation on computers)*. GOSSTROJ SSSR, CNIPIASS, Moscow, 1977. (in Russian).

97. V.F. Turchin and A.P. Nemytykh. Metavariables: their implementation and use in program transformation. Technical Report CSc. TR 95-012, City College of the City University of New York, 1995.

98. V.F. Turchin and A.P. Nemytykh. A self-applicable supercompiler. Technical Report CSc. TR 95-010, City College of the City University of New York, 1995.

99. V.F. Turchin, R. Nirenberg, and D. Turchin. Experiments with a supercompiler. In *Conference Record of the ACM Symposium on Lisp and Functional Programming*, pp. 47–55. ACM Press, 1982.

100. P.L. Wadler. Deforestation: Transforming programs to eliminate intermediate trees. *Theoretical Computer Science*, 73:231–248, 1990. Preliminary version in ESOP'88 LNCS vol. 300.

Reasoning about Hierarchies of Online Program Specialization Systems [*]

John Hatcliff   Robert Glück

DIKU, Department of Computer Science, University of Copenhagen
Universitetsparken 1, DK-2100 Copenhagen Ø, Denmark
E-mail: {hatcliff,glueck}@diku.dk

Abstract. We present the language S-Graph-n — the core of a multi-level metaprogramming environment for exploring foundational issues of self-applicable online program specialization.

We illustrate how special-purpose S-Graph-n primitives can be used to obtain an efficient and conceptually simple encoding of programs as data objects. The key feature of the encoding scheme is the use of numerical indices which indicate the number of times that a program piece has been encoded.

Evaluation of S-Graph-n is formalized *via* an operational semantics. This semantics is used to justify the fundamental operations on metavariables — special-purpose tags for tracking unknown values in self-applicable online specialization systems. We show how metavariables can be used to construct biased generating extensions without relying on a separate binding-time analysis phase.

1 Introduction

Metasystem hierarchies have been used for more than a decade to generate compilers and other program generators. A metasystem hierarchy is any situation where a program p_0 is manipulating (*e.g.*, interpreting, compiling, transforming) another program p_1. Program p_1 may be manipulating another program p_2, and so on. A metasystem hierarchy can be diagrammed using an *Metasystem Transition* (MST) scheme as in Figure 1 [7,9,27].

The best known examples are the *Futamura projections* which were the driving force behind the initial work on self-application of program specialization systems. This work identified *binding-time analysis* as a useful tool for attacking the fundamental problem of tracking unknown values, and regarded associated *offline specialization* as essential for taming self-application [15,16].

On the other hand, more powerful *online specialization* methods, such as supercompilation and partial deduction have not yet given satisfactory results for all Futamura projections (not to mention multiple self-application or the specializer projections). It seems harder to reason about the behavior of hierarchies of online systems for several reasons.

I. Semantics of multi-level specialization: There is no static staging of programs (as binding-time analysis gives in offline systems). This makes it harder to predict the behavior of the specializer.

---

[*] This work has been supported by the Danish Research Academy and by the DART project (Design, Analysis and Reasoning about Tools) of the Danish Research Councils.

Fig. 1. MST Scheme of a metasystem hierarchy

II. Identifying positions in hierarchies: There is no analogue to the typing information given by binding-time analysis — that is, it is harder to determine at which level in the hierarchy a entity resides. This is complicated in cases where the hierarchy contains many layers. Multiple encodings of programs as data objects can cause exponential growth in size and further obscure hierarchical positions of objects.

III. Tracking unknowns: It is unclear how to establish semantic principles for tracking unknown values across multiple levels in the metasystem hierarchy. This makes it more difficult to design *e.g.*, a self-applicable online partial evaluator that can produce "biased" generating extensions and satisfy the "Mix criteria" (*i.e.*, all binding-time tests are reduced at specialization time) [14, Chapter 7].

IV. Experimentation: There are simply fewer existing systems for performing experiments. Moreover, existing systems often lack proper metaprogramming environments.

Our goal is to identify and clarify the foundational issues involved in hierarchies of online specialization systems. We believe the best way to achieve this goal is to develop a very simple online specialization system which focuses tightly on the problematic points of online specialization noted above: (I) semantics of specialization, (II) properties of program encodings and identifying position of entities in a hierarchy, (III) tracking unknown values across levels in metasystem hierarchies. The system should also provide a metaprogramming environment which allows one to easily construct different specialization systems (IV). Moreover, the system should be well-suited for supporting stronger forms of online specialization such as supercompilation.

Outline

In this paper, we report on the initial design and partial implementation of such a system. The system is based on S-Graph — a very simple language which has been used to study the foundations of supercompilation [9] and neighborhood analysis [1]. Section 2 revisits the syntax and semantics of S-Graph.

Section 3 discusses problems of program encodings. Based on this discussion, Section 4 presents a new version of S-Graph called S-Graph-n which contains language primitives especially designed for manipulating *metacode* — data objects representing programs.

Section 5 presents special S-Graph-n primitives for representing *metavariables* — tags for tracking unknown values across multiple levels in the hierarchy.

Programs:
    prog ::= *def**
      def ::= (DEFINE (*fname name*$_1$ ... *name*$_n$) *tree*)

Trees:

    tree ::= (IF *cntr tree tree*) | (LET *name exp tree*) | (CALL (*fname arg**)) | *exp*
    cntr ::= (CONS? *arg name name*) | (EQA? *arg arg*)
    exp ::= (CONS *exp exp*) | *arg*
    arg ::= (ATOM *atom*) | (PV *name*)

Fig. 2. Syntax of S-Graph

Building on previous work [7,27], we formalize semantics of metavariables and illustrate how they can be used to construct a simple self-applicable online partial evaluator which can produce "biased" generating extensions without relying on a separate binding-time analysis phase.

Section 6 discusses related work, and Section 7 concludes.

2 S-Graph

Figure 2 presents the syntax of S-Graph — a first-order, functional programming language restricted to tail-recursion. As the name implies, one can think of S-Graph programs as being textual representations of graphs. The only data objects are well-founded, *i.e.*, non-circular, S-expressions (as known from Lisp). A program is a list of function definitions where each function body is built from a few elements: conditionals IF, local bindings LET, function calls CALL, constructors CONS, program variables (PV *name*), and atomic constants (drawn from an infinite set of symbols).

Note the conditional in S-Graph: the test *cntr* may update the environment. As in supercompilation, we refer to such tests as contractions [23]. Two elementary contractions are sufficient for S-expressions:

- (EQA? *arg*$_1$ *arg*$_2$) — tests the equality of two atoms denoted by *arg*$_1$ and *arg*$_2$. If the arguments are non-atomic then the test is undefined.
- (CONS? *exp h t*) — if the value of *exp* is a pair (CONS *val*$_1$ *val*$_2$), then the test succeeds and the variable *h* is bound to *val*$_1$ and the variable *t* to *val*$_2$; otherwise, the test fails.

The arguments of function calls and contractions are restricted to variables and atomic constants in order to limit the number of places where values may be constructed. Because there are no nested function calls, we describe the language as *flat* (*i.e.*, it corresponds to a flow-chart language). Syntactic sugar: we write *' atom* as shorthand for (ATOM *atom*); lower case identifiers as shorthand for (PV *name*). Figure 3 shows the list reverse written in S-Graph.

3 Programs as Data Objects

Metaprogramming requires facilities for encoding programs as data objects. In general, metaprogramming also requires encoding tags (which we call *metavari-*

```
(DEFINE (REVERSE x)
   (CALL (LOOP x 'NIL)))

(DEFINE (LOOP x bag)
   (IF (CONS? x head tail)
       (LET headbag (CONS head bag)
          (CALL (LOOP tail headbag)))
       bag))
```

Fig. 3. List reverse in S-Graph

ables) for representing unknown entities. The encoding must be injective. This ensures that all objects are encoded uniquely, and that encoded objects can be "recovered" with a decoding. For historical reasons, we refer to the encoding as *metacoding* and to decoding as *demetacoding* [26].

In a metasystem hierarchy such as displayed in Figure 1, programs and metavariables may be metacoded many times. For example, p_n of Figure 1 must be metacoded (directly or indirectly) n times, since n systems lie above it in the hierarchy. The number of encodings is called *degree* [27]. As the discussion of p_n illustrates, an object's degree indicates its vertical position in a hierarchy.

In general, there may be different languages with different metacodings on each level of a hierarchy. For simplicity, we consider only one language and assume that the same metacode is used on all levels.

3.1 Metasystem Hierarchies

Metasystem hierarchies are a corner stone of Turchin's approach: the construction of hierarchies of arbitrary height is taken as the basis for program analysis and transformation [21] (in contrast to logics and mathematics which usually deal with two-level hierarchies). For example, the well-known Futamura projections make use of a three-level hierarchy of metasystems (*i.e.*, program specializers). To make multi-level hierarchies practical, one needs facilities for satisfying the following requirements.

1. *Efficient encoding: low space consumption and minimal overhead for manipulating the encoding.* This is essential because repeated metacodings in a metasystem hierarchy may require a significant amount of space and processing time. A straightforward encoding may lead to growth that is exponential in the number of metacodings.
2. *Efficient computation on all levels of a metasystem hierarchy.* Generally speaking: the higher the hierarchy, the slower the overall transformation. Since most non-trivial self-applicable specializers incorporate a self-interpreter for evaluating static expressions, the run-time of multiple self-application typically grows exponentially with the number of self-application levels.

These problems can dramatically impact usability, *e.g.*, of self-application [6,8]. Various approaches have been employed to improve the performance and the manipulation of representations. For instance, the logic programming language Gödel [13] provides built-in metaprogramming facilities for two-level hierarchies.

$$\mu\{(\text{IF } cntr\ tree_1\ tree_2)\} = (\text{CONS } (\text{ATOM IF})\ (\text{CONS } \mu\{cntr\}\ (\text{CONS } \mu\{tree_1\}\ \mu\{tree_2\})))$$
$$\mu\{(\text{LET } name\ exp\ tree)\} = (\text{CONS } (\text{ATOM LET})\ (\text{CONS } (\text{ATOM } name)\ (\text{CONS } \mu\{exp\}\ \mu\{tree\})))$$
$$\ldots$$
$$\mu\{(\text{CONS } exp_1\ exp_2)\} = (\text{CONS } (\text{ATOM CONS})\ (\text{CONS } \mu\{exp_1\}\ \mu\{exp_2\}))$$
$$\mu\{(\text{ATOM } atom)\} = (\text{CONS } (\text{ATOM ATOM})\ (\text{ATOM } atom))$$

Fig. 4. S-Graph metacoding (excerpts)

Turchin's *freezer* mechanism [24] facilitates a dramatic optimization in run time during multiple self-applications [17]. However, it remains to extend and systematically clarify similar techniques in the context of multi-level hierarchies.

Our goal is to lay the foundation for a multi-level metaprogramming environment that fully addresses requirements (1) and (2) above, and that is not biased towards a particular method for metacomputation (*e.g.* partial evaluation, supercompilation). Meeting each of the above requirements depends on the strategies used to (i) represent programs as data (*i.e.*, metacoding), (ii) represent computed values, and (iii) represent known/unknown entities. These representations should be cheap (wrt space), eliminable (*i.e.*, removable by specialization), and efficient to process at specialization time. In the present work, we concentrate on requirement (1) as a prerequisite for (2).

3.2 Criteria for Metacoding

Low space consumption. To illustrate the space consumption problem, consider the straightforward strategy for metacoding S-Graph programs given in Figure 4. The encoding is simple, but leads to an exponential growth of expressions. Using this strategy, the S-Graph expression (CONS (ATOM a) (ATOM b)) metacoded once is

$$\overline{(\text{CONS}(\text{ATOM a})(\text{ATOM b}))} = (\text{CONS } (\text{ATOM CONS})\ (\text{CONS } (\text{CONS } (\text{ATOM ATOM})\ (\text{ATOM a}))\ (\text{CONS } (\text{ATOM ATOM})\ (\text{ATOM b}))))$$

and metacoded twice is

$$\overline{\overline{(\text{CONS}(\text{ATOM a})(\text{ATOM b}))}} = (\text{CONS } (\text{ATOM CONS})\ (\text{CONS } (\text{CONS } (\text{ATOM ATOM})\ (\text{ATOM CONS}))$$
$$(\text{CONS } (\text{ATOM CONS})\ (\text{CONS } (\text{CONS } (\text{ATOM CONS})\ (\text{CONS } (\text{CONS }$$
$$(\text{ATOM ATOM})\ (\text{ATOM ATOM}))\ (\text{CONS } (\text{ATOM ATOM})\ (\text{ATOM a}))))$$
$$(\text{CONS } (\text{ATOM CONS})\ (\text{CONS } (\text{CONS } (\text{ATOM ATOM})\ (\text{ATOM ATOM}))$$
$$(\text{CONS } (\text{ATOM ATOM})\ (\text{ATOM b}))))))))$$

Each overbar represents an application of the metacoding function.

Efficient to process. The encoding must enable facilities for efficient computation on any level in a metasystem hierarchy. For example, the straightforward encoding shown above is not very efficient to process: the time to access a subcomponent (*e.g.* (ATOM b)) in the metacode grows with each level of encoding. Moreover, the time to metacode expressions grows exponentially with each level of encoding.

Compositional. One often needs to embed data with lower degrees as components of constructs with higher degrees (*e.g.*, in a representation of partially static structures). We describe such structures as *non-monotonic* with respect to degree. In some popular metacoding strategies, changing the degree of a single subcomponent may require a non-local modification of the data structure. A familiar example is the *quote* mechanism *à la* Scheme. Consider using this strategy to metacode the expression (CONS (ATOM a) (ATOM b)) two times.

$$\overline{\overline{(\text{CONS}(\text{ATOMa})(\text{ATOMb}))}} = \text{"(CONS (ATOM a) (ATOM b))}$$

Suppose we wish to replace the subexpression (ATOM a) by a variable (representing an unknown value). This requires a non-local change. We have to modify the enclosing expression by "pushing quotes inside" and using functions (here list) to rebuild the enclosing data structure.

$$\overline{\overline{(\text{CONS}}} \; x \; \overline{\overline{(\text{ATOMb})}} = (\text{LIST "CONS } x \text{ "(ATOM b))}$$

A similar situation occurs using the *backquote/comma* mechanism. Representing multiply encoded structures with several different degrees of "unknowns" is even more cumbersome using this metacoding strategy.

Conceptually simple and easy to reason about. In metasystem hierarchies, one often needs to reason about the degree and position of data in a hierarchy, or simply trace the computation in a metasystem hierarchy. The S-Graph encoding of Figure 4 clearly does not satisfy this criteria. Non-compositional encodings such as the *quote* mechanism are also somewhat unsatisfactory in this regard since it is not possible to reason *locally*. For example, one cannot determine the degree of a subcomponent without consulting the entire enclosing expression. The degree of a subcomponent is *relative* to the degree of the enclosing expression.

We now summarize the advantages and disadvantages of the *quote/backquote* mechanism and motivate our proposed solution.

Quote/Backquote Mechanism: The advantages of using the *quote/backquote* mechanism include low space consumption, and fast encoding and decoding (simply adding/removing a quote around an S-expression). The time to encode/decode is constant and independent of the number of levels. The disadvantage of is that changing the degree of a single subexpression may require a non-local modification of the data structure, as shown above. Moreover, one cannot reason locally about a subexpression because the encoding is relative, that is, the degree of a subexpression depends on the degree of the enclosing expression. The *quote/backquote* mechanism is an appropriate solution if a monotone, relative, and non-compositional encoding is sufficient. However, this is generally not the case in metasystem hierarchies.

Level Indexing: In the following section, we introduce language primitives that rely on numerical indices to indicate the number of program encodings. Using the level-indexed primitives, the above expression metacoded once is

$$\overline{(\text{CONS}(\text{ATOMa})(\text{ATOMb}))} = (\text{CONS-1 (ATOM-1 a) (ATOM-1 b)})$$

and metacoded twice is

$\overline{(\text{CONS}(\text{ATOMa})(\text{ATOMb}))} = (\text{CONS-2 } (\text{ATOM-2 a}) (\text{ATOM-2 b}))$

We believe that level indices are preferable for several reasons. Metacoding using level-indexing is space efficient, compositional and allows non-monotonic structures. Also, the typing intuition given by level indices is preferable from a conceptual standpoint: the degree (and thus the vertical position in a hierarchy) can be determined immediately using only local reasoning. Level-indexing also facilitates *metasystem jumps* [17] where control is transferred between levels in a hierarchy. This technique can drastically reduce the second problem of metasystem hierarchies noted above: computation time.

A disadvantage of level-indexing is that metacoding requires time that is linear in the size of the expression (as opposed to constant time for *quote*). However, this is not a big factor in transformation time since metacoding is usually performed in a pre-processing phase. In situations where metacoding and demetacoding do occur during transformation (*e.g.*, when reifying and reflecting data), this cost can be minimalized by parameterizing primitive operations wrt degree. This will be the essence of our approach to implementing metasystem jumps.

4 S-Graph-n

4.1 Syntax

Figure 5 presents the syntax of S-Graph-n — a language with special-purpose constructs for representing programs as data, and tracking unknowns. S-Graph-n trees are constructed from objects of the set Sgn — level-indexed abstract syntax tree nodes. For example, the following are S-Graph-n components.

$$(\text{IF}^2 \ (\text{CONS}^1 \ (\text{ATOM}^3 \ \text{foo}) \ (\text{ATOM}^1 \ \text{bar})) \ (\text{PV}^3 \ x) \ (\text{PV}^4 \ y)) \tag{1}$$

$$(\text{IF}^2 \ (\text{EQA?}^2 \ (\text{ATOM}^2 \ \text{foo}) \ (\text{ATOM}^2 \ \text{bar})) \ (\text{PV}^3 \ x) \ (\text{PV}^4 \ y)) \tag{2}$$

$$(\text{IF}^3 \ (\text{EQA?}^2 \ (\text{ATOM}^3 \ \text{foo}) \ (\text{ATOM}^3 \ \text{bar})) \ (\text{CONS}^1 \ (\text{ATOM}^2 \ 1) \ (\text{ATOM}^2 \ 1)) \ (\text{PV}^4 \ y)) \tag{3}$$

Intuitively, the S-Graph-n components are indexed building blocks for constructing multiply metacoded program pieces. Components can be composed in a fairly arbitrary manner. This allows non-monotonic encodings (as motivated in the previous section). Line (1) illustrates that one can also build components that do not correspond to well-formed programs pieces. This is a common situation in metaprogramming applications: well-formedness must be enforced by the programmer.[2]

The *index* of an S-Graph-n component *sgn* is the level number attached to the outermost construct of *sgn*. In the components above, the index of (1) and (2) is 2, and the index of (3) is 3.

The *degree* of an S-Graph-n component *sgn* (denoted *degree(sgn)*) is the smallest index occurring in *sgn*. In the components above, (1) and (3) have degree 1; (2) has degree 2. Intuitively, if a component has degree n, then it has been metacoded at most n times (though some parts of the component may have

---

[2] One might imagine enforcing well-formedness with a type system. We do not pursue this option here, since typed languages are notoriously hard to work with in self-applicable program specialization.

Components:

  $sgn \in Sgn$
  $sgn ::= (\text{IF}^n \; sgn \; sgn \; sgn) \mid (\text{LET}^n \; name \; sgn \; sgn) \mid \ldots \mid$
    $(\text{CONS?}^n \; sgn \; name \; name) \mid (\text{EQA?}^n \; sgn \; sgn) \mid$
    $(\text{MC?}^n \; sgn \; name \; name \; name) \mid (\text{MV?}^n \; sgn \; name \; name) \mid \ldots \mid$
    $(\text{CONS}^n \; sgn \; sgn) \mid (\text{ATOM}^n \; atom) \mid (\text{PV}^n \; name) \mid$
    $(\text{MC}^n \; sgn \; sgn \; sgn) \mid (\text{MV}^n \; h \; name) \qquad \text{for any } n, h \geq 0$

Trees at level n:

  $tree^n \in Tree[n]$
  $tree^n ::= (\text{IF}^n \; cntr^n \; tree^n \; tree^n) \mid (\text{LET}^n \; name \; exp^n \; tree^n) \mid$
    $(\text{CALL}^n \; (fname \; arg^*)) \mid exp^n$

  $cntr^n \in Cntr[n]$
  $cntr^n ::= (\text{CONS?}^n \; arg^n \; name \; name) \mid (\text{EQA?}^n \; arg^n \; arg^n) \mid$
    $(\text{MC?}^n \; arg^n \; name \; name \; name) \mid (\text{MV?}^n \; arg^n \; name \; name)$

  $exp^n \in Exp[n]$
  $exp^n ::= (\text{CONS}^n \; exp^n \; exp^n) \mid (\text{MC}^n \; arg^n \; arg^n \; arg^n) \mid arg^n \mid mc^n$

  $arg^n \in Arg[n]$
  $arg^n ::= (\text{ATOM}^n \; atom) \mid (\text{PV}^n \; name) \mid (\text{MV}^n \; h \; name) \qquad \text{for any } h \geq 0$

Metacode at level n:

  $mc^n \in Metacode[n]$
  $mc^n ::= (\text{IF}^{n+m} \; exp^n \; exp^n \; exp^n) \mid (\text{LET}^{n+m} \; name \; exp^n \; exp^n) \mid \ldots \mid$
    $(\text{CONS}^{n+m} \; exp^n \; exp^n) \mid (\text{ATOM}^{n+m} \; atom) \mid (\text{PV}^{n+m} \; name) \mid$
    $(\text{MC}^{n+m} \; exp^n \; exp^n \; exp^n) \mid (\text{MV}^{n+m} \; h \; name) \qquad \text{for any } m \geq 1, h \geq 0$

Fig. 5. Syntax of S-Graph-n (excerpts)

been metacoded more times). As motivated in Section 3, degree indicates to which level of a hierarchy a component belongs.

A S-Graph-n component *sgn* is *monotone* if the indices of subcomponents are the same or are increasing as one descends down the abstract syntax tree of *sgn*. Formally, all leaf components are monotone; a non-leaf component *sgn* is monotone if all its immediate subcomponents are monotone, and all indices of immediate subcomponents are greater than or equal to the index of *sgn*. In the components above, (2) is monotone; (1) and (3) are not. Given a set $S \subseteq Sgn$, *monotone*(S) denotes the subset of monotone components of S.

Elements of $Tree[n] \subset Sgn$ are well-formed trees at level n. In the components above, (2) is a well-formed tree at level 2; (1) and (3) are not. A similar intuition lies behind the other syntactic categories of Figure 5.

Elements of $Metacode[n] \subset Tree[n]$ represent encoded program components at level n. Intuitively, these are pieces of abstract syntax trees (encoded m times) manipulated by the program (*e.g.*, interpreter, specializer) running at level n. In the components above, (1),(2), and (3) are all elements of $Metacode[0]$. However, only (2) is an element of $Metacode[1]$ since $(\text{ATOM}^1 \; \textbf{bar})$ in (1) and

$$val^r \in Values[n]$$
$$val^r ::= (\texttt{ATOM}^n\ atom)\ |\ (\texttt{MV}^n\ h\ name)\ |\ (\texttt{CONS}^n\ val^r\ val^r)\ |$$
$$(\texttt{IF}^{n+m}\ val^r\ val^r\ val^r)\ |\ (\texttt{LET}^{n+m}\ name\ val^r\ val^r)\ |\ ...\ |$$
$$(\texttt{MC}^{n+m}\ val^r\ val^r\ val^r)\ |\ (\texttt{MV}^{n+m}\ h\ name) \qquad for\ any\ h \geq 0,\ m \geq 1$$

Fig. 6. S-Graph-n values (excerpts)

$(\texttt{CONS}^1\ (\texttt{ATOM}^2\ 1)\ (\texttt{ATOM}^2\ 1))$ in (3) represent an atom and a CONS instruction in the program running at level 1 (*i.e.*, they are not encoded program pieces relative to level 1).[3]

The constructs $(\texttt{MC}^n\ arg^n\ arg^n\ arg^n)$, $(\texttt{MC?}^n\ arg^n\ name\ name\ name)$ are added to construct and destruct metacode. Metavariables $(\texttt{MV}^n\ h\ name)$ are added to track unknown through a hierarchy of specialization systems. The numerical index h is the *elevation* of the metavariable. The semantics of these constructs will be given in Section 4.3.

Although the semantics is given later, we can present the canonical terms (*i.e.*, results) of evaluation $Values[n] \subset Exp[n]$ (Figure 6). Intuitively, values at level n are either atoms, metavariables, or CONS-cells at level n, or metacode at level n (representing encoded programs from higher levels).

The S-Graph-n machine is implemented in Scheme and is parameterized by a *reference level* n. Given a reference level n, the machine will run programs which are well-formed at level n. S-Graph-n components are represented using Scheme vectors. All data structures (*e.g.*, environment, definition list, *etc.*) in the implementation are built using S-Graph-n components. This makes it trivial to *reify* and *reflect* data (*i.e.*, to move objects up and down the hierarchy) — one need only adjust index values. Furthermore, since the machine runs relative to a certain level n, passing control between various levels is trivial — one need only adjust the reference level. We do not take full advantage of this functionality in the present work; it is the foundation for a future investigation of *metasystem jumps* [27].

When programming in S-Graph-n, one usually takes 0 as the reference level. In the programming examples that we give later, components where indices are omitted are at level 0.

4.2 Metacoding

Figure 7 gives the metacoding function μ for S-Graph-n. There is no increase in the size of the encoded program with each level of encoding — only indices are incremented.[4]

---

[3] We have omitted metacode components for DEFINE constructs for efficiency reasons. A list of definitions is represented instead by a list of function names and a list of function bodies. We have included metacode components for all other constructs because this gives a uniform representation of program trees independent of level. This facilitates an implementation of metasystem jumps.

[4] The increase is logarithmic if one considers the number of bits needed to represent level indices. We ignore this since in practice, the number of encodings never exceeds standard word capacities.

$$\mu\{(\text{IF}^n \ sgn_1 \ sgn_2 \ sgn_3)\} = (\text{IF}^{n+1} \ \mu\{sgn_1\} \ \mu\{sgn_2\} \ \mu\{sgn_3\})$$
$$\mu\{(\text{LET}^n \ name \ sgn_1 \ sgn_2)\} = (\text{LET}^{n+1} \ name \ \mu\{sgn_1\} \ \mu\{sgn_2\})$$
$$\cdots$$
$$\mu\{(\text{CONS}^n \ sgn_1 \ sgn_2)\} = (\text{CONS}^{n+1} \ \mu\{sgn_1\} \ \mu\{sgn_2\})$$
$$\mu\{(\text{ATOM}^n \ atom)\} = (\text{ATOM}^{n+1} \ atom)$$
$$\mu\{(\text{MV}^n \ h \ name)\} = (\text{MV}^{n+1} \ h \ name)$$

Fig. 7. Metacoding function for S-Graph-n (excerpts)

The following property gives characteristics of μ. μ^n denotes the iterated application of μ (*i.e.*, $\mu^n\{sgn\}$ is sgn metacoded n times). For any $S \subseteq Sgn$, $\mu\{S\}$ denotes the set obtained by element-wise application of μ.

Property 1 (Properties of μ)

1. **injectivity:** $\forall sgn_1, sgn_2 \in Sgn$. $sgn_1 \neq sgn_2 \ \Rightarrow \ \mu\{sgn_1\} \neq \mu\{sgn_2\}$

2. **left inverse μ_{-1}:** $\forall sgn \in Sgn$. $sgn = \mu_{-1}\{\mu\{sgn\}\}$

3. **embedding:** $\forall n \geq 0$. $\mu^n\{Sgn\} \supset \mu^{n+1}\{Sgn\}$

4. **canonical representation:**
   $\forall n \geq 0$. $\mu^{n+1}\{Sgn\} \subset (Metacode[n] \cap Values[n])$

5. **preservation of syntactic categories:** $\forall n \geq 0$. $\mu\{\mathcal{C}[n]\} = \mathcal{C}[n+1]$
   where $\mathcal{C} \in \{Tree, Exp, Arg, Cntr, Metacode, Values\}$

6. **preservation of monotonicity:** $\mu\{monotone(Sgn)\} \subset monotone(Sgn)$

7. **correspondence of degree:**
   $\forall sgn \in Sgn$. $degree(sgn) = n \ \Rightarrow \ sgn \in \mu^n\{Sgn\} \ \wedge \ sgn \notin \mu^{n+1}\{Sgn\}$

Property 1.1 states that μ is injective; this implies the existence of a demetacoding function μ_{-1} (Property 1.2).

Property 1.3 reflects the fact that repeated metacoding creates a hierarchy of sets of metacoded components.

Property 1.4 states that programs metacoded at least $n + 1$ times (*i.e.*, programs residing at level $n+1$ or greater) can be adequately represented by values built using the metacode constructs of a program that has been metacoded n times (*i.e.*, by a program residing at level n).

Property 1.5 states that μ preserves syntactic categories (because it only increments indices).

Property 1.6 states that μ preserves monotone components.

Property 1.7 formalizes the earlier intuitive description of *degree* — components of degree n correspond to objects that have been metacoded at most n times.

Trees:

$$\frac{\mathcal{E} \vdash^n_{cntr} cntr^n \implies \langle \mathbf{true}, \mathcal{E}' \rangle \quad \mathcal{P}, \mathcal{E}' \vdash^n_{tree} tree^n_1 \implies val^n}{\mathcal{P}, \mathcal{E} \vdash^n_{tree} (\mathtt{IF}^n \ cntr^n \ tree^n_1 \ tree^n_2) \implies val^n}$$

$$\frac{\mathcal{E} \vdash^n_{cntr} cntr^n \implies \langle \mathbf{false}, \mathcal{E}' \rangle \quad \mathcal{P}, \mathcal{E}' \vdash^n_{tree} tree^n_2 \implies val^n}{\mathcal{P}, \mathcal{E} \vdash^n_{tree} (\mathtt{IF}^n \ cntr^n \ tree^n_1 \ tree^n_2) \implies val^n}$$

$$\frac{\mathcal{E} \vdash^n_{exp} exp^n \implies val^n_1 \quad \mathcal{P}, \mathcal{E}[name \mapsto val^n_1] \vdash^n_{tree} tree^n \implies val^n}{\mathcal{P}, \mathcal{E} \vdash^n_{tree} (\mathtt{LET}^n \ name \ exp^n \ tree^n) \implies val^n}$$

$$\frac{\begin{array}{c} \mathcal{E} \vdash^n_{arg} arg^n_i \implies val^n_i \\ \mathcal{P}(fname) = \langle (name_1, ..., name_m), tree^n \rangle \\ \mathcal{P}, [name_i \mapsto val^n_i] \vdash^n_{tree} tree^n \implies val^n \quad i=1,..,m \end{array}}{\mathcal{P}, \mathcal{E} \vdash^n_{tree} (\mathtt{CALL}^n \ (fname \ arg^n_1, ... arg^n_m)) \implies val^n}$$

Contractions:

$$\frac{\mathcal{E} \vdash^n_{arg} arg^n_1 \implies (\mathtt{ATOM}^n \ atom) \quad \mathcal{E} \vdash^n_{arg} arg^n_2 \implies (\mathtt{ATOM}^n \ atom)}{\mathcal{E} \vdash^n_{cntr} (\mathtt{EQA?}^n \ arg^n_1 \ arg^n_2) \implies \langle \mathbf{true}, \mathcal{E} \rangle}$$

$$\frac{\mathcal{E} \vdash^n_{arg} arg^n_1 \implies (\mathtt{ATOM}^n \ atom_1) \quad \mathcal{E} \vdash^n_{arg} arg^n_2 \implies (\mathtt{ATOM}^n \ atom_2) \quad atom_1 \neq atom_2}{\mathcal{E} \vdash^n_{cntr} (\mathtt{EQA?}^n \ arg^n_1 \ arg^n_2) \implies \langle \mathbf{false}, \mathcal{E} \rangle}$$

$$\frac{\mathcal{E} \vdash^n_{arg} arg^n \implies (\mathtt{CONS}^n \ val^n_1 \ val^n_2)}{\mathcal{E} \vdash^n_{cntr} (\mathtt{CONS?}^n \ arg^n \ name_1 \ name_2) \implies \langle \mathbf{true}, \mathcal{E}[name_i \mapsto val^n_i] \rangle} \quad i = 1, 2$$

$$\frac{\mathcal{E} \vdash^n_{arg} arg^n \implies val^n \quad val^n \neq (\mathtt{CONS}^n \ val^n_1 \ val^n_2)}{\mathcal{E} \vdash^n_{cntr} (\mathtt{CONS?}^n \ arg^n \ name_1 \ name_2) \implies \langle \mathbf{false}, \mathcal{E} \rangle}$$

$$\frac{\mathcal{E} \vdash^n_{arg} arg^n \implies val^n \quad unpack^n(val^n) = \langle val^n_1, val^n_2, val^n_3 \rangle}{\mathcal{E} \vdash^n_{cntr} (\mathtt{MC?}^n \ arg^n \ name_1 \ name_2 \ name_3) \implies \langle \mathbf{true}, \mathcal{E}[name_i \mapsto val^n_i] \rangle} \quad i = 1, 2, 3$$

$$\frac{\mathcal{E} \vdash^n_{arg} arg^n \implies val^n \quad unpack^n(val^n) \ undefined}{\mathcal{E} \vdash^n_{cntr} (\mathtt{MC?}^n \ arg^n \ name_1 \ name_2 \ name_3) \implies \langle \mathbf{false}, \mathcal{E} \rangle}$$

$$\frac{\begin{array}{c} \mathcal{E} \vdash^n_{arg} arg^n \implies (\mathtt{MV}^n \ h \ name) \\ \mathcal{E}' = \mathcal{E}[name_1 \mapsto (\mathtt{ATOM}^n \ h), name_2 \mapsto (\mathtt{ATOM}^n \ name)] \end{array}}{\mathcal{E} \vdash^n_{cntr} (\mathtt{MV?}^n \ arg^n \ name_1 \ name_2) \implies \langle \mathbf{true}, \mathcal{E}' \rangle}$$

$$\frac{\mathcal{E} \vdash^n_{arg} arg^n \implies val^n \quad val^n \neq (\mathtt{MV}^n \ h \ name)}{\mathcal{E} \vdash^n_{cntr} (\mathtt{MV?}^n \ arg^n \ name_1 \ name_2) \implies \langle \mathbf{false}, \mathcal{E} \rangle}$$

Fig. 8. Semantics of S-Graph-n (part 1)

Expressions:

$$\frac{\mathcal{E} \vdash^n_{exp} exp^n_i \implies val^n_i \quad i = 1,2}{\mathcal{E} \vdash^n_{exp} (\text{CONS}^n \, exp^n_1 \, exp^n_2) \implies (\text{CONS}^n \, val^n_1 \, val^n_2)}$$

$$\frac{\mathcal{E} \vdash^n_{exp} exp^n_i \implies val^n_i \quad i = 1,2,3}{\mathcal{E} \vdash^n_{exp} (\text{MC}^n \, exp^n_1 \, exp^n_2 \, exp^n_3) \implies val^n} \quad (\text{if } val^n = \text{pack}^n(val^n_1, val^n_2, val^n_3))$$

$$\frac{\mathcal{E} \vdash^n_{arg} arg^n \implies val^n}{\mathcal{E} \vdash^n_{exp} arg^n \implies val^n} \qquad \frac{\mathcal{E} \vdash^n_{mc} mc^n \implies val^n}{\mathcal{E} \vdash^n_{exp} mc^n \implies val^n}$$

Arguments:

$$\mathcal{E} \vdash^n_{arg} (\text{ATOM}^n \, atom) \implies (\text{ATOM}^n \, atom) \qquad \mathcal{E} \vdash^n_{arg} (\text{MV}^n \, h \, name) \implies (\text{MV}^n \, h \, name)$$

$$\mathcal{E} \vdash^n_{arg} (\text{PV}^n \, name) \implies \mathcal{E}(name)$$

Metacode (excerpts): $(m \geq 1$ in the following rules)

$$\mathcal{E} \vdash^n_{mc} (\text{PV}^{n+m} \, name) \implies (\text{PV}^{n+m} \, name)$$

$$\frac{\mathcal{E} \vdash^n_{mc} exp^n_i \implies val^n_i \quad i = 1,2,3}{\mathcal{E} \vdash^n_{mc} (\text{IF}^{n+m} \, exp^n_1 \, exp^n_2 \, exp^n_3) \implies (\text{IF}^{n+m} \, val^n_1 \, val^n_2 \, val^n_3)}$$

$$\frac{\mathcal{E} \vdash^n_{mc} exp^n_i \implies val^n_i \quad i = 1,2}{\mathcal{E} \vdash^n_{mc} (\text{LET}^{n+m} \, name \, exp^n_1 \, exp^n_2) \implies (\text{LET}^{n+m} \, name \, val^n_1 \, val^n_2)}$$

$$\frac{\mathcal{E} \vdash^n_{mc} exp^n \implies val^n}{\mathcal{E} \vdash^n_{mc} (\text{MV?}^{n+m} \, exp^n \, name_1 \, name_2) \implies (\text{MV?}^{n+m} \, val^n \, name_1 \, name_2)}$$

Fig. 9. Semantics of S-Graph-n (part 2)

4.3 Semantics

Figures 8 and 9 present an operational semantics for S-Graph-n. Judgments for each syntactic category are parameterized by the reference level n. For example, the derivability of the judgment

$$\mathcal{P}, \mathcal{E} \vdash^n_{tree} tree^n \implies val^n$$

signifies that given definitions $\mathcal{P}$ and environment $\mathcal{E}$, $tree^n \in Tree[n]$ evaluates to $val^n \in Values[n]$. The remaining judgments are similar. Definitions $\mathcal{P}$ are not required in the remaining judgments since function calls can only occur in the syntactic category $Tree[n]$. Evaluation of contractions $cntr^n$ returns **true** or **false** as well as a possibly updated environment.

The manipulation of metacode and metavariables is the most unique aspect of programming in S-Graph-n. We discuss this in detail below.

Metacode construction: Metacode components can be

$$\text{unpack}^n((\text{IF}^m \; sgn_1 \; sgn_2 \; sgn_3)) = \langle(\text{ATOM}^n \; p), (\text{ATOM}^n \; \text{IF}),$$
$$(\text{CONS}^n \; sgn_1 \; (\text{CONS}^n \; sgn_2 \; sgn_3)))\rangle$$
$$\text{unpack}^n((\text{LET}^m \; name \; sgn_1 \; sgn_2)) = \langle(\text{ATOM}^n \; p), (\text{ATOM}^n \; \text{LET}),$$
$$(\text{CONS}^n \; (\text{ATOM}^n \; name) \; (\text{CONS}^n \; sgn_1 \; sgn_2)))\rangle$$

$$\dots$$

$$\text{unpack}^n((\text{CONS}^m \; sgn_1 \; sgn_2)) = \langle(\text{ATOM}^n \; p), (\text{ATOM}^n \; \text{CONS}), (\text{CONS}^n \; sgn_1 \; sgn_2))\rangle$$
$$\text{unpack}^n((\text{MV}^m \; h \; name)) = \langle(\text{ATOM}^n \; p), (\text{ATOM}^n \; \text{MV}),$$
$$(\text{CONS}^n \; (\text{ATOM}^n \; h) \; (\text{ATOM}^n \; name)))\rangle$$
$$\text{unpack}^n((\text{ATOM}^m \; atom)) = \langle(\text{ATOM}^n \; p), (\text{ATOM}^n \; \text{ATOM}), (\text{ATOM}^n \; atom)\rangle$$

$$\text{pack}^n((\text{ATOM}^n \; p), (\text{ATOM}^n \; \text{IF}), (\text{CONS}^n \; sgn_1 \; (\text{CONS}^n \; sgn_2 \; sgn_3)))=(\text{IF}^m \; sgn_1 \; sgn_2 \; sgn_3)$$

$$\dots$$

$$\text{pack}^n((\text{ATOM}^n \; p), (\text{ATOM}^n \; \text{ATOM}), (\text{ATOM}^n \; atom))=(\text{ATOM}^m \; atom)$$

Note: The above definitions hold for all p, m, n such that $p > 0$ and $m = n + p$

Fig. 10. Packing and unpacking of metacode (excerpts)

(i) represented as *literals*,
(ii) created using the MC construct.

With (i), the index of the component (as well as elements of base syntax domains such as *atom* and *name*) is known statically, *i.e.* given as literal in the program. Evaluation of components (formalized by the *Metacode* rules of Figure 9) is similar to that of CONS. For example,[5]

```
> (eval 0 '(let x (atom-1 foo) (if-1 x (atom bar) x)))

(if-1 (atom-1 foo) (atom bar) (atom-1 foo))
```

This gives an effect similar to quasi-quotation: a literal construct contains non-value components that may be further evaluated (this is the case with x in if-1 above).

With (ii), the index of the component (as well as base syntax domains such as *atom* and *name*) can be supplied dynamically, *i.e.* computed at runtime. MC takes three arguments: an atom indicating the index of the expression to be created, an atom indicating the tag of the component, and a tree of subcomponents. This is formalized by the rule for MC in Figure 9 and by the rules for **pack** in Figure 10. The value of the index atom must be greater than 0, and the number of subcomponents must correspond to the given tag — otherwise a runtime error occurs. The constraints on n, p, and m in Figure 10 indicate that the index manipulated in the MC and MC? constructs (the index corresponds to p in Figure 10) is *relative* to the reference level n. Note that the reference level is 0 in the following example.

```
> (eval 0 '(let index (atom 1)
             (let tag (atom if)
               (let comp (cons (atom-1 foo)
                               (cons (atom bar) (atom-1 foo)))
```

---

[5] The S-Graph-*n* system is written is Scheme, so data is supplied to the interpreter as S-expressions.

```
                    (mc index tag comp)))))
```

```
(if-1 (atom-1 foo) (atom bar) (atom-1 foo))
```

One may question including both methods (i) and (ii) in the language. Method (i) is needed because metacoding must embed trees (active components) into values (passive components). Method (ii) is required to construct metacode where indices or tags are not known until run time (the usual situation in self-interpretation).

Metacode destruction: Metacode components are destructed using the `MC?` contraction.

```
> (eval 0 '(let metacode (cons-1 (atom-1 a) (atom-1 b))
             (if (mc? metacode index tag comp)
                 (cons index (cons tag comp))
                 (atom false))))
```

```
(cons (atom 1) (cons (atom cons) (cons (atom-1 a) (atom-1 b))))
```

Metavariables: As reflected in the definition of values (Figure 6), metavariables are canonical so their evaluation is trivial. Metavariables are destructed using the `MV?` contraction.

```
> (eval 0 '(if (mv? (mv 0 x) elev name)
               (cons elev name)
               (atom false)))
```

```
(cons (atom 0) (atom x))
```

`MV?` is the *crucial* predicate used in S-Graph-n self-applicable specializers since it determines whether a data object is known or unknown. Using conventional terminology, the test (`MV?` *arg* $name_1$ $name_2$) succeeds if *arg* represents a *dynamic* object. The use of `MV?` in self-application will be detailed in Section 5.

5   Metavariables

High-level abstract presentations of metavariables have been given elsewhere [7,27]. Here we describe the actual operations on metavariables and illustrate the use of these operations in constructing biased generating extensions. Moreover, we give a semantic justification of these operations based on the formal semantics of S-Graph-n presented in Section 4.

5.1   Metavariable attributes

A specializer written in S-Graph-n uses metavariables as tags for representing unknown values in the program that it specializes. A metavariable has three attributes which determine its semantics: *degree*, *domain*, and *elevation*.[6]

$$degree((\text{MV}^n \ h \ name)) = n$$
$$domain((\text{MV}^n \ h \ name)) = Values[n + h + 1]$$
$$elevation((\text{MV}^n \ h \ name)) = h$$

---

[6] The reader should be warned that our definition of metavariable degree differs slightly from other work [7,27]. In those works, our metavariable of degree n has degree $n + 1$.

Example program:

```
(if (eqa? x 'test-x)
    (if (eqa? y 'test-y)
        'true-x-true-y
        'true-x-false-y)
    'false-x)
```

Initial call to the self-applicable specializer:

```
(let tree (if-1 (eqa?-1 (pv-1 x) (atom-1 test-x))
                (if-1 (eqa?-1 (pv-1 y) (atom-1 test-y))
                      (atom-1 true-x-true-y)
                      (atom-1 true-x-false-y))
                (atom-1 false-x))
  (let env (cons (cons (atom x)     (cons (atom y) (atom nil)))
                 (cons (atom test-x) (cons (mv 0 y) (atom nil))))
    (let defs (cons (atom nil) (atom nil))
      (call (spec-start tree env defs)))))
```

Result of specialization:

```
(if-1 (eqa?-1 (pv-1 y) (atom-1 test-y))
      (atom-1 true-x-true-y)
      (atom-1 true-x-false-y))
```

Fig. 11. Specialization example (analogous to the first Futamura projection)

Degree (as we have seen before) indicates the number of times that a metavariable has been metacoded. *Domain* is the set of values over which a metavariable ranges. *Elevation* restricts the domain of the metavariable to a particular set of values (this is motivated in detail below). Although both *degree* and *elevation* are numerical attributes, *degree* is an absolute characteristic, whereas *elevation* is a relative characteristic (it adjusts the domain relative to degree). Thus, *elevation* is unchanged by metacoding and demetacoding (see Figure 7).

5.2 Metavariable examples

Intuitively, a metavariable of degree n is used by a specializer $spec_n$ running at level n to represent an unknown value in the program $prog_{n+1}$ which it is specializing. Specifically, an unknown input parameter x for $prog_{n+1}$ will be bound to a metavariable in the symbolic environment used by $spec_n$ when specializing $prog_{n+1}$.

Consider the example program of Figure 11 where the free variables x and y represent input parameters. The self-applicable specializer is called with three arguments: a metacoded tree (e.g., the initial call for the program being specialized), an initial environment, and a list of metacoded definitions. Figure 11 presents the initial call used to specialize the example program where x is bound to (atom test-x) and y is unknown. The variable tree is bound to a metacoded version of the example program. The noteworthy point: the environment associates x with (atom test-x) and y with (mv 0 y) (*i.e.*, a metavariable of degree 0 and elevation 0). Our example uses no functions, so the definition list defs is empty. The result of specialization (see Figure 11) is a metacoded tree

```
(DEFINE (eval-val val env defs cont pe-cont)
  (IF (CONS? cont cont-tag cont-rest)
       :
     (IF (EQA? cont-tag 'eqa?l)
        (IF (MV? val elev name)
           (CALL (pe-cont val env defs cont pe-cont))
           (CALL (eval-eqa?-cont val env defs cont-rest pe-cont))))

     (IF (EQA? cont-tag 'eqa?r)
        (IF (MV? val elev name)
           (CALL (pe-cont val env defs cont pe-cont))
           (CALL (do-eqa? val env defs cont-rest pe-cont))))

     (IF (EQA? cont-tag 'cons?)
        (IF (MV? val elev name)
           (CALL (pe-cont val env defs cont pe-cont))
           (CALL (do-cons? val env defs cont-rest pe-cont))))
       :
```

Fig. 12. Specializer fragment that checks for unknowns in contractions

(which requires demetacoding before it can be executed).

Intuitively, *spec* uses MV? on x when interpreting the contraction (EQA? x 'test-x). Since x is bound to (atom test-x), MV? fails (signifying that x is known). *spec* uses MV? on y when interpreting the contraction (EQA? y 'test-y). Since y is bound to (mv 0 y), MV? succeeds (signifying that y is unknown).

Figure 12 presents a specializer code fragment that checks for unknowns in contractions. The specializer is written using first-order continuation-passing. The displayed function eval-val dispatches on the continuation tag. For example, that tags eqa?l and eqa?r indicate that val is the left and right component (respectively), of an eqa? contraction. In the example above, the false branch (CALL (eval-eqa?-cont ...)) associated with the eqa?l continuation is executed when evaluating (EQA? x 'test-x); the true branch (CALL (pe-cont ...)) is executed when evaluating (EQA? y 'test-y). pe-cont performs appropriate residualization.

Second Futamura projection analogy: Now consider a situation analogous to the second Futamura projection where we attempt to produce a generating extension for the example program with inputs x and y.

level 0: $spec_0$: _____

level 1: $spec_1$: _____

level 2: $prog$: _____

There are now two copies of the self-applicable specializer: $spec_0$ and $spec_1$. $spec_0$ is specializing $spec_1$ which is specializing *prog*. $spec_1$ and its associated initial call (see Figure 11) are metacoded once. Thus, the metavariable associated with y now has degree 1 and elevation 0. *prog*'s variable x is no longer bound to data;

it now must be associated to a metavariable. Which metavariable? It should not be a metavariable belonging to $spec_1$ (*i.e.*, a metavariable of degree 1) — this would give x the same semantics as y, *i.e.*, x would represent something unknown to $spec_1$. This is not what we want if we desire to produce a generating extension; we want x to appear as known to $spec_1$ but unknown to $spec_0$. Since x is unknown to $spec_0$, it should be associated with metavariable belonging to $spec_0$, *i.e.*, a metavariable of degree 0.

Second Futamura projection analogy *(failed attempt)*: Figure 13 presents the initial call to $spec_0$. tree is now a metacoding of the initial call of Figure 11. The only change is that the data (atom test-x) supplied for x has been replaced by a program variable (pv-1 x). This adhears to our method of representing input parameters as free variables; the data for x is now a parameter to $spec_1$. env associates x with a metavariable (mv 0 x) following the conclusion of the previous paragraph. defs is the lengthy list of metacoded definitions for the self-applicable specializer.

Now consider what happens when x appears as the argument to the (EQA? x 'test-x) contraction in *prog*. $spec_1$ will use the MV? contraction (as shown under the (EQA? cont-tag 'eqa?1) alternative of Figure 12) to see whether the value denoted by x is known or unknown. When $spec_0$ is interpreting this use of the contraction MV? by $spec_1$, it recognizes one of its metavariables in the argument of MV? and has no choice but to residualize it. Figure 13 shows the resulting program (before post-processing and lifting). Space does not permit an detailed explanation, but one can see the residualized MV? contraction and two branches corresponding to the cases where x is known and unknown. This is an instance of the "overly general compiler" problem [14, Chapter 7], and again is not what we usually want in the second Futamura projection.

From a semantic point of view, $spec_0$ residualizes the contraction MV? as used by $spec_1$ since the domain of its metavariable (MV^0 0 x) is $Values[0 + 0 + 1]$. Note that $Values[1]$ (see Figure 6) includes metavariables of degree 1 (belonging to $spec_1$) as *well as other data* of degree 1. So it is impossible for $spec_0$ to tell whether or not a metavariable of degree 1 will flow into the argument of the contraction MV? as used by $spec_1$.

Examining the domain of metavariable (MV^0 0 x) also reveals a *type mismatch*: (MV^0 0 x) ranges over $Values[1]$ (*i.e.*, over values computed at level 1), but (MV^0 0 x) is (indirectly) associated with the program variable x residing at level 2! Thus, the domain of (MV^0 0 x) is too general compared with the actual set of values that may bind to x.

This mismatch can be corrected using the concept of *elevation*. In this case, changing the elevation of (MV^0 0 x) to 1, *i.e.*, (MV^0 1 x) gives the correct domain: $Values[0 + 1 + 1] = Values[2]$.

Second Futamura projection analogy *(successful attempt)*: So say replace the metavariable (mv 0 x) with (mv 1 x) in the environment structure env of Figure 13. Now consider what happens when x appears as the argument to the contraction (EQA? x 'test-x) in *prog*. $spec_1$ will use the MV? contraction (at level 1) as shown in Figure 12 to see whether the value denoted by x is known or unknown. When $spec_0$ is interpreting this use of the contraction MV? by $spec_1$, it recognizes one of its metavariables in the argument of MV?. *However*, $spec_0$ is able to observe (using MV? at level 0) that (MV^0 1 x) has domain $Values[2]$. Note that $Values[2]$ (see Figure 6) *does not* include metavariables of degree 1 (belong-

Initial call to the self-applicable specializer:

```
(let tree (let-1 tree
                 (if-2 (eqa?-2 (pv-2 x) (atom-2 test-x))
                      (if-2 (eqa?-2 (pv-2 y) (atom-2 test-y))
                           (atom-2 true-x-true-y)
                           (atom-2 true-x-false-y))
                      (atom-2 false-x))
              (let-1 env (cons-1 (cons-1 (atom-1 x)
                                         (cons-1 (atom-1 y)
                                                 (atom-1 nil)))
                                 (cons-1 (pv-1 x)
                                         (cons-1 (mv-1 0 y)
                                                 (atom-1 nil))))
                 (let-1 defs (cons-1 (atom-1 nil) (atom-1 nil))
                    (call-1 (spec-start (pv-1 tree)
                                        (pv-1 env)
                                        (pv-1 defs))))))
  (let env (cons (cons (atom x) (atom nil))
                 (cons (mv 0 x) (atom nil)))   ;;; metavariable for x
    (let defs ...                              ;;; metacoded spec defs
      (call (spec-start tree env defs)))))
```

Resulting program (before post-processing and lifting):

```
(if-1 (mv?-1 (mv-0 0 x) elev name)

      (if-2 (eqa?-2 (mv-0 0 x) (atom test-x))        ;;; case: x unknown
            (if-2 (eqa?-2 (mv-1 0 y) (atom test-y))
                  (atom true-x-true-y)
                  (atom true-x-false-y))
         (atom false-x))

      (if-1 (eqa?-1 (mv-0 0 x) (atom test-x))        ;;; case: x known
            (if-2 (eqa?-2 (mv-1 0 y) (atom test-y))
                  (atom true-x-true-y)
                  (atom true-x-false-y))
            (atom false-x)))
```

Resulting program using appropriate elevation:

```
(if-1 (eqa?-1 (pv-1 x) (atom-1 test-x))
   (if-2 (eqa?-2 (pv-2 y) (atom-2 test-y))
       (atom-2 true-x-true-y)
       (atom-2 true-x-false-y))
   (atom-2 false-x))
```

Fig. 13. Specialization example (analogous to the second Futamura projection)

ing to $spec_1$). So it *is possible* for $spec_0$ to tell that a metavariable of degree 1 will never flow into the argument of the contraction MV? as used by $spec_1$. Thus, $spec_0$ can conclude that the use of the contraction MV? by $spec_1$ should fail, *i.e.*, the "else" branch (CALL (eval-eqa?-cont ...)) of the corresponding IF should be executed. Thus, from the point of view of $spec_1$, (PV x) is not associated with a metavariable, but instead represents a known value. Figure 13 gives the program resulting from this appropriate use of elevation. This *is* the result we want: a "biased" generating extension.

5.3 Metavariable semantics

The example above clarifies the role of the MV? contraction in detecting unknowns. Based on an understanding of metavariable *domain*, a specializer at level n properly interprets an MV? contraction used at level $n + 1$. We now define a predicate ϕ_n which specifies the proper interpretation of an MV? contraction performed at level n. Intuitively, $\phi_n(v) \equiv$ "is v unknown at level n?", or in other words, $\phi_n(v) \equiv$ "is v a metavariable of degree n?".

$$
\begin{array}{lll}
(1) & \phi_n((\text{MV}^n \ h \ name)) = true & \text{for all } h \geq 0 \\
(2) & \phi_n((\text{CONS}^n \ val^n \ val^n)) = false & \\
(3) & \phi_n((\text{ATOM}^n \ atom)) = false & \\
(4) & \phi_n(v) = false & \text{for all } v \in Metacode[n] \\
\\
(5) & \phi_n((\text{MV}^{n'} \ h \ name)) = false & \text{if } n' < n \text{ and } n \leq n' + h \\
(6) & \phi_n((\text{MV}^{n'} \ h \ name)) = \perp & \text{if } n' < n \text{ and } n > n' + h
\end{array}
$$

The first four cases are straightforward since the arguments to ϕ_n are elements of $Values[n]$ — the predicate is only true if a value at level n is a metavariable. Note that the case for $\phi_n((\text{MV}^{n'} \ h \ name))$ where $n' > n$ is covered by case (4) since such metavariables are metacode at level n. From the perspective of level n', $(\text{MV}^{n'} \ h \ name)$ is not a metavariable, but an encoded piece of program at level n'.

The remaining cases are the interesting ones from the point of view of self-application.

Case (5) corresponds to situations where a metavariable appears to be a known value to the program running at level n.
Justification: $domain((\text{MV}^{n'} \ h \ name)) = Values[p]$ for some $p > n$, and $Values[p]$ does not include a metavariable of degree n.

Case (6) corresponds to situations where it cannot be determined if the argument of MV? is known or unknown at level n.
Justification: $domain((\text{MV}^{n'} \ h \ name)) = Values[p]$ for some $p \leq n$, and $Values[p]$ includes both metavariable of degree n (unknowns) and known values. Intuitively, the MV? contraction should be residualized in this case.

6 Related Work

The ideas present in this paper have been heavily influenced by three concepts present in Turchin's work [22,23]: metacoding, metavariables, and metasystem transition. Subsequently, these concepts have been formalized [7] and studied in different contexts, *e.g.* [25]. The correct treatment of metacode was found essential in self-application [6] and this concept was singled out as elevation index [27].

The problem of self-application was the driving force behind the work on partial evaluation in the early eighties. The offline approach was originally introduced to avoid the generation of 'overly-general' compilers by self-application of a partial evaluator [15]; see also [14, Sec. 7.3]. Today off-line partial evaluation is the most developed approach to program specialization. This success lent itself to the hypothesis that self-application requires a binding-time analysis prior to specialization proper [16]. This hypothesis has been falsified where it was demonstrated that successful self-application without binding-time analysis is possible [6]. This insight has been used for the specialization of online partial evaluators [19]. A hybrid approach was used in [20] where off- and online partial evaluation was integrated; see also [4]. However, the power of offline partial evaluation is limited by the approximations made during the binding-time analysis; *e.g.*, off-line partial evaluation does not pass the KMP test. This led to the desire to self-apply stronger, online methods such as supercompilation [10,17] and partial deduction [5,11].

The idea of encoding expressions as data that can be manipulated as objects can be traced back to Gödel who used natural numbers for representing expressions in a first order language as data (to prove the well-known completeness and incompleteness theorems). Since then this methods has been used in logics and meta-mathematics to treat theories and proofs as formal objects and to prove properties about them. In computer science, especially in the area of logic programming, the encoding of programs has been studied under various names, e.g. *naming relation* [28,3]. Representing and reasoning about object level theories is an important field in logic and artificial intelligence (e.g. different encodings have been discussed in [12]) and has led to the development of logic languages that support declarative metaprogramming (*e.g.* the programming language Gödel [13]). A multilevel metalogic programming language has been suggested in [2], an approach similar to our multi-level metaprogramming environment, but directed towards the hierarchical organization of knowledge (e.g. for legal reasoning); it allows deductions on different metalevels.

Level indexing was used in [8] to annotated operations in generating extensions with their binding-times which, together with the cogen approach, provided an efficient solution for multiple self-application of offline partial evaluation. In this paper we used level indexing of data to provide a basis for a multi-level metaprogramming environment which is independent of certain transformation paradigms. Recently, multi-level lambda-calculi were studied in [18].

7 Conclusion

We have attempted to clarify semantic and implementation concepts related to the use of metacoding and metavariables in metaprogramming. Several challenging problems lie ahead:

- implementation of metasystem jumps to increase speed of specialization,
- incorporation of stronger specialization techniques such as supercompilation into our self-applicable specializer,

- formalization of more powerful generalization techniques in our context (with metacode and metavariables), and
- development of a user environment for metaprogramming centered around MST scheme as a specification language.

We believe S-Graph-n is an appropriate vehicle for studying these foundational problems associated with hierarchies of online specialization systems. It seems well-suited as the basis of an simple experimental metaprogramming environment that embraces Turchin's view of computation using metasystem transition.

Acknowledgments

Thanks to Sergei Abramov, Neil Jones, Andrei Klimov, Eric Ruf, Michael Sperber, and last but not least, Valentin Turchin for stimulating discussions on various topics of this paper. Special thanks to Kristian Nielsen for comments on an earlier version of this paper. Finally, we would like to thank the participants of the Dagstuhl Seminar on "'Partial Evaluation" for various useful comments.

References

1. S.M. Abramov. *Metavychislenija i ikh prilozhenija (Metacomputation and its applications)*. Nauka, Moscow, 1995. (In Russian).
2. Jonas Barklund. A basis for a multilevel metalogic programming language. Technical Report 81, Uppsala University, Dept. of Computing Science, 1994.
3. Jonas Barklund. Metaprogramming in logic. Technical Report 80, Uppsala University, Dept. of Computing Science, 1994.
4. Charles Consel and Siau Cheng Khoo. Parameterized partial evaluation. *ACM TOPLAS*, 15(3):463–493, 1993.
5. Hiroshi Fujita and Koichi Furukawa. A self-applicable partial evaluator and its use in incremental compilation. *New Generation Computing*, 6(2-3):91–118, June 1988.
6. Robert Glück. Towards multiple self-application. In *Proceedings of the Symposium on Partial Evaluation and Semantics-Based Program Manipulation*, pages 309–320, New Haven, Connecticut, 1991. ACM Press.
7. Robert Glück. On the mechanics of metasystem hierarchies in program transformation. In M. Proietti, editor, *Logic Program Synthesis and Transformation (LoPSTr'95)*, volume 1048 of *Lecture Notes in Computer Science*, pages 234–251. Springer-Verlag, 1996.
8. Robert Glück and Jesper Jørgensen. Efficient multi-level generating extensions for program specialization. In S.D. Swierstra and M. Hermenegildo, editors, *Programming Languages: Implementations, Logics and Programs (PLILP'95)*, volume 982 of *Lecture Notes in Computer Science*, pages 259–278. Springer-Verlag, 1995.
9. Robert Glück and Andrei V. Klimov. Occam's razor in metacomputation: the notion of a perfect process tree. In P. Cousot, M. Falaschi, G. Filè, and G. Rauzy, editors, *Static Analysis. Proceedings. Lecture Notes in Computer Science, Vol. 724*, pages 112–123. Springer-Verlag, 1993.
10. Robert Glück and Valentin F. Turchin. Application of metasystem transition to function inversion and transformation. In *Proceedings of the ISSAC '90 (Tokyo, Japan)*, pages 286–287. ACM Press, 1990.
11. Corin A. Gurr. *A self-applicable partial evaluator for the logic programming language Gödel*. Ph.d. thesis, University of Bristol, 1994.

12. Patricia Hill and John Gallagher. Meta-programming in logic programming. Technical Report 94.22, School of Computer Studies, University of Leeds, 1994.
13. Patricia Hill and John W. Lloyd. *The Gödel Programming Language*. MIT Press, Cambridge, Massachusetts, 1994.
14. Neil D. Jones, Carsten K. Gomard, and Peter Sestoft. *Partial Evaluation and Automatic Program Generation*. Prentice-Hall, 1993.
15. Neil D. Jones, Peter Sestoft, and Harald Søndergaard. An experiment in partial evaluation: the generation of a compiler generator. In J.-P. Jouannaud, editor, *Rewriting Techniques and Applications, Dijon, France. Lecture Notes in Computer Science 202*, pages 124–140. Springer-Verlag, 1985.
16. Neil D. Jones, Peter Sestoft, and Harald Søndergaard. Mix: a self-applicable partial evaluator for experiments in compiler generation. *LISP and Symbolic Computation*, 2(1):9–50, 1989.
17. Andrei Nemytykh, Victoria Pinchuck, and Valentin F. Turchin. A self-applicable supercompiler. In Olivier Danvy, Robert Glück, and Peter Thiemann, editors, *Partial Evaluation. Proceedings*, Lecture Notes in Computer Science, page to appear. Springer-Verlag, 1996.
18. Flemming Nielson and Hanne R. Nielson. Multi-level lambda-calculi: an algebraic description. In Olivier Danvy, Robert Glück, and Peter Thiemann, editors, *Partial Evaluation. Proceedings*, Lecture Notes in Computer Science, page to appear. Springer-Verlag, 1996.
19. Eric Ruf and Daniel Weise. On the specialization of online program specializers. *Journal of Functional Programming*, 3(3):251–281, 1993.
20. Michael Sperber. Self-applicable online partial evaluation. In Olivier Danvy, Robert Glück, and Peter Thiemann, editors, *Partial Evaluation. Proceedings*, Lecture Notes in Computer Science, page to appear. Springer-Verlag, 1996.
21. Valentin F. Turchin. A supercompiler system based on the language Refal. *SIGPLAN Notices*, 14(2):46–54, 1979.
22. Valentin F. Turchin. The language Refal, the theory of compilation and metasystem analysis. Courant Computer Science Report 20, Courant Institute of Mathematical Sciences, New York University, Feb. 1980 1980.
23. Valentin F. Turchin. The concept of a supercompiler. *Transactions on Programming Languages and Systems*, 8(3):292–325, 1986.
24. Valentin F. Turchin. *Refal-5, Programming Guide and Reference Manual*. New England Publishing Co., Holyoke, Massachusetts, 1989.
25. Valentin F. Turchin. Program transformation with metasystem transitions. *Journal of Functional Programming*, 3(3):283–313, 1993.
26. V.F. Turchin. Programmirovanie na jazyke Refal: I. Neformal'noe vvedenie v programmirovanie na jazyke Refal. (Programming in the language Refal: I. Informal introduction to programming in the language Refal). Preprint 41, Institute of Applied Mathematics, Academy of Sciences of the USSR, Moscow, 1971. (In Russian).
27. V.F. Turchin and A.P. Nemytykh. Metavariables: their implementation and use in program transformation. Technical Report CSc. TR 95-012, City College of the City University of New York, 1995.
28. Frank van Harmelen. Definable naming relations in meta-level systems. In A. Pettorossi, editor, *Meta-Programming in Logic. Proceedings*, volume 649 of *Lecture Notes in Computer Science*, pages 89–104, Uppsala, Sweden, 1992. Springer-Verlag.

Type Specialisation for the λ-Calculus; or, A New Paradigm for Partial Evaluation Based on Type Inference

John Hughes

Department of Computer Science, Chalmers Technical University, S-41296 Göteborg, Sweden. URL: http://www.cs.chalmers.se/~rjmh.

1 Introduction

Partial evaluation is a powerful automated strategy for transforming programs, some of whose inputs are known. The classic simple example is the *power* function,

$$power\ n\ x = \text{if } n = 1 \text{ then } x \text{ else } x \times power\ (n-1)\ x$$

which, given that n is known to be 3, can be transformed into the *specialised* version

$$power_3\ x = x \times (x \times x)$$

The computations on known data (*static* computations) are performed by the partial evaluator once and for all, and in general the resulting *residual program* is considerably more efficient than the original.

Over the last decade partial evaluators have developed from experimental toys into well-engineered tools. But the problem of specialising *typed programs* has never been satisfactorily solved. Straightforward methods produce residual programs that operate on the same types of data as the original program, but this may not be appropriate. For example, where the original program needs a sum type, the residual program may actually only use data lying in one summand. The tagging and untagging operations are then an unnecessary overhead; it would be better to simplify the type to the summand actually used. Such *type specialisation* was identified as a 'challenging problem in partial evaluation' by Neil Jones in 1987, but there are still no really satisfactory methods for doing it.

The problem is particularly acute when the program to be specialised is an interpreter. Interpreters are universal programs which can simulate the behaviour of any other; when an interpreter is specialised to the program P, the residual program is equivalent to P, but is expressed in the language that the partial evaluator processes. It can be considered to be *compiled code* for P. But suppose the interpreter is written in a typed language: then values of every type must be represented by injecting them into one *universal type*, a tagged sum of all the types that can occur. When such an interpreter is specialised, the 'compiled code' produced still operates on tagged values of the universal type, and the performance benefits of compiling a typed language are lost.

Jones calls a partial evaluator *optimal* if the result of specialising a self-interpreter for the language the partial evaluator processes to any program P is not only *equivalent* to P, it is *essentially the same* as P. An optimal partial evaluator can 'remove a complete layer of interpretation'. Most partial evaluators for typed languages have not been optimal hitherto, because residual programs contain tagging and untagging operations not present in the programs being compiled.

Removing these tags carries a risk: there is a possibility that residual programs may become ill typed, in the case where a tag check would have failed. Residual programs therefore need to be type-checked. Rather than leaving this for a post-processor, we have taken it as inspiration for a new kind of partial evaluator: whereas previous ones have been, in a sense, generalised evaluators, ours is a kind of generalised type-checker. In this sense our work introduces a new paradigm for partial evaluation.

The partial evaluator we describe is the first optimal partial evaluator for the simply typed λ-calculus. It can specialise types, and can remove all unnecessary tagging and untagging operations. In particular, one universal type in a self-interpreter can be specialised to an arbitrary type in the residual program.

In the next section we informally introduce the basic ideas underlying our partial evaluator. Then we specify its behaviour formally via a set of inference rules. We go on to briefly describe the binding-time checker we use before specialisation, and a post-processor that removes trivial residual computations. Next we describe how the specialiser's inference system has been implemented, and discuss an interesting example: specialisation of an interpreter for the typed λ-calculus. Finally we discuss future improvements, describe related work, and conclude.

2   An Informal Introduction

We shall begin in this section by introducing some of the basic concepts underlying our partial evaluator, and explaining why partial evaluation by type inference is interesting.

Like many other partial evaluators, ours processes a *two-level* language; that is, each construct in the source program is labelled either *static* or *dynamic*, and the partial evaluator performs static computations and builds dynamic ones into the residual program. For example, the number three can appear either statically (3) or dynamically ($\underline{3}$) — we will consistently mark dynamic constructs by underlining, as in this case. Binding times (static *vs.* dynamic) are reflected in the types: 3 is of type **int** while $\underline{3}$ is of type $\underline{\text{int}}$.

Every expression gives rise to a *residual expression* in the specialised program. The residual expression of $\underline{3}$ is of course 3, while the residual expression of 3 is •, which is how we write the unique element of the one-point type[1]. Intuitively, since 3 is known during partial evaluation we can replace it by a dummy value in the specialised program.

We shall use the notation $a \hookrightarrow b$ to mean that source expression a is specialised to residual expression b, for example $\underline{3} \hookrightarrow 3$ and $3 \hookrightarrow$ •. But since we are actually

---

[1] The only element of the one-point type is of course $\bot$, the undefined element, but we prefer to write • to make clear that we mean the dummy value, not the bottom element of some other type. We assume a lazy semantics so that • can be freely passed as a parameter, and so on. If one prefers a strict semantics one must take • to be the defined element of a two-point type instead.

interested in specialising typed programs, we will annotate both source and residual expressions with their types, thus:

$$a : \sigma \hookrightarrow b : \tau$$

We will call σ the *source type* and τ the *residual type*.

The fundamental new idea in this paper is to *propagate static information via residual types*. For example, when we specialise a static integer the residual expression is a dummy value, but the residual type tells us which static value it represents:

$$3 : \text{int} \hookrightarrow \bullet : 3$$

Here '3' is a type with only one element, namely $\bullet$, and which therefore has just the same elements as 4, 5, 6 *etc.* — but which carries different static information.

All expressions, even 'dynamic' ones, carry static information in the form of a residual type. For purely dynamic expressions this is just an ordinary type, for example

$$\underline{3} : \underline{\text{int}} \hookrightarrow 3 : \text{int}$$

But we can often express useful 'partially static' information via a residual type. For example:

- $2 \times \text{int}$, the type of pairs whose first component is statically 2,
- $\text{int} \to (2 \times \text{int})$, the type of functions whose result is a pair with first component statically 2.

This static information is then propagated by type inference.

Our ability to associate static information with dynamic values can lead to very strong specialisation. For example, consider the expression

$$(\lambda f.\text{lift}(f \,@\, 3)) \,@\, (\lambda x.x + 1)$$

Here expressions of the form $\lambda x.e$ are dynamic λ-expressions, which are transformed into residual λ-expressions in the specialised program. The '@' operator is dynamic function application, and the **lift** operator converts a static integer into a dynamic one.

To specialise this expression, we infer the residual type of each subexpression. Note that f is applied to an argument with residual type 3, and so must have residual type $3 \to \tau$ for some τ. But then x must have residual type 3, and so $x + 1$ has residual type 4, and $\lambda x.x + 1$ has residual type $3 \to 4$. This must also be the type of f, and so $f \,@\, 3$ has residual type 4: The **lift** operation can now be specialised to 4. The final result is

$$(\lambda f.4)(\lambda x.\bullet) : \text{int}$$

in which the static computations have been removed, and only the dynamic operations and the result of **lift** remain.

Traditional partial evaluators propagate static information in a different way: static expressions are reduced to values, which are then bound to static variables and so on. There is thus a tight connection between unfolding and staticness. For example, Gomard and Jones λ-MIX (the first partial evaluator for the λ-calculus) insists that since dynamic λ-expressions are not unfolded, both their argument and result must also be dynamic. In our example that would force x to be dynamic, and consequently the addition could not be performed by the specialiser. To specialise this example using λ-MIX, one must annotate the λ-expressions static so that the specialiser can unfold them.

In contrast, there is no need to unfold a λ-expression in order to infer its residual type, and our partial evaluator can therefore specialise the example as it stands. But does this really matter — surely unfolding is desirable in its own right? Our answer is: yes it does matter! No realistic partial evaluator can unfold *all* function calls, and it is the calls that are not unfolded that lead to loss of static information. Type inference gives better static information flow than unfolding, which leads to stronger specialisation. In particular, it is the key to optimal specialisation of typed programming languages.

We can also see from this simple example that the residual programs that our specialiser produces tend to manipulate dummy values — they are the spoor left by purely static computations. To achieve optimal specialisation, there must be *no* trace of static computations in residual programs. But fortunately, such useless expressions are easily identified. We remove them in a post-processing phase we call *void erasure*. The residual expression we derived above was

$$(\lambda f.4)(\lambda x.\bullet)$$

Here the entire second λ-expression is useless, and so void erasure removes both it and the variable (f) it is bound to, resulting in just the expression 4.

3   Specifying the Partial Evaluator

Just as a type checker can be concisely specified by a set of type inference rules, so our partial evaluator can be specified by a set of *specialisation rules*. These rules prescribe how to infer *specialisation judgements*, which are just like typing judgements except that, since we are specifying a program transformation, each judgement contains *two* terms and *two* types. The form of a specialisation judgement is

$$\Gamma \vdash e : \tau \hookrightarrow e' : \tau'$$

Γ is a context containing assumptions on variables, which have a similar form:

$$x : \tau \hookrightarrow e : \tau'$$

where x is the variable and e an expression to substitute for it.

A nice consequence of this approach is that we can specify the partial evaluator in a very modular way. A simple version can be specified with relatively few rules, and each new feature can then be expressed via a new type along with its introduction and elimination rules.

Constructing an implementation of the rules requires a certain amount of cleverness, because they are not all syntax-directed. But we will return to this in a later section: for now, we are just concerned with specifying how the partial evaluator should behave.

3.1 Base Types

We have already seen examples of how base types are specialised. Static and dynamic integer constants are specialised via the rules

$$(SINT) \quad \Gamma \vdash m : \mathbf{int} \hookrightarrow \bullet : m \quad (DINT) \quad \Gamma \vdash \underline{m} : \underline{\mathbf{int}} \hookrightarrow m : \mathbf{int}$$

Primitive operators come in static and dynamic variants, with rules for each operator $\oplus$ of the form

$$(S\oplus) \quad \frac{\Gamma \vdash e_1 : \mathbf{int} \hookrightarrow e_1' : m_1 \quad \Gamma \vdash e_2 : \mathbf{int} \hookrightarrow e_2' : m_2 \quad m_1 \oplus m_2 = n}{\Gamma \vdash e_1 \oplus e_2 : \mathbf{int} \hookrightarrow \bullet : n}$$

$$(D\oplus) \quad \frac{\Gamma \vdash e_1 : \underline{\mathbf{int}} \hookrightarrow e_1' : \mathbf{int} \quad \Gamma \vdash e_2 : \underline{\mathbf{int}} \hookrightarrow e_2' : \mathbf{int}}{\Gamma \vdash e_1 \underline{\oplus} e_2 : \underline{\mathbf{int}} \hookrightarrow e_1' \oplus e_2' : \mathbf{int}}$$

The **lift** operation just introduces a suitable constant in the residual program:

$$(LIFT) \quad \frac{\Gamma \vdash e : \mathbf{int} \hookrightarrow e' : m}{\Gamma \vdash \mathbf{lift}\ e : \underline{\mathbf{int}} \hookrightarrow m : \mathbf{int}}$$

Clearly, other base types could be added with similar rules. We will just remark that it is often useful to have a **void** type, with one element — namely $\bullet$.

$$(VOID) \quad \Gamma \vdash \bullet : \mathbf{void} \hookrightarrow \bullet : \mathbf{void}$$

3.2 Variables and Lets

The context Γ binds variables to a residual expression to be substituted for them: this is how unfolding is implemented. The rule for variables just does the substitution.

$$(VAR) \quad \Gamma, x : \tau \hookrightarrow e : \tau' \vdash x : \tau \hookrightarrow e : \tau'$$

Variables can be bound by **let** expressions, which come in two variants, static and dynamic. Static **let** expressions are unfolded by the partial evaluator, whereas dynamic ones create a **let** in the residual program.

$$(SLET) \quad \frac{\Gamma \vdash e_1 : \sigma \hookrightarrow e_1' : \sigma' \quad \Gamma, x : \sigma \hookrightarrow e_1' : \sigma' \vdash e_2 : \tau \hookrightarrow e_2' : \tau'}{\Gamma \vdash \mathbf{let}\ x = e_1\ \mathbf{in}\ e_2 : \tau \hookrightarrow e_2' : \tau'}$$

$$(DLET) \quad \frac{\Gamma \vdash e_1 : \sigma \hookrightarrow e_1' : \sigma' \quad \Gamma, x : \sigma \hookrightarrow x' : \sigma' \vdash e_2 : \tau \hookrightarrow e_2' : \tau'}{\Gamma \vdash \underline{\mathbf{let}}\ x = e_1\ \underline{\mathbf{in}}\ e_2 : \tau \hookrightarrow \mathbf{let}\ x' = e_1'\ \mathbf{in}\ e_2' : \tau'} \quad x'\ \text{fresh}$$

Notice that the *only* difference between these two rules is the degree of unfolding in the residual program. In particular, there is no need for a variable bound by a dynamic **let** to itself be dynamic. We have exactly the same 'static information' about x in each case, expressed as its residual type σ'. Only the expression to substitute for x varies.

Traditional partial evaluators bind variables to replacement expressions, but have no concept of residual type. A static variable is bound to an expression which is constant. It follows that a variable bound in a dynamic **let**, which will be replaced by a fresh variable in the residual program, cannot be static. This case shows clearly how a type-inference-based partial evaluator can achieve stronger results than an unfolding-based one. [2]

3.3 Product Types

We introduce a dynamic product type, which generates pairs in the residual program. For the time being, we will ignore the possibility of static products, and so for type-setting reasons we refrain from underlining the brackets and comma of a pair.

$$(DPAIR) \quad \frac{\Gamma \vdash e_1 : \sigma \hookrightarrow e_1' : \sigma' \quad \Gamma \vdash e_2 : \tau \hookrightarrow e_2' : \tau'}{\Gamma \vdash (e_1, e_2) : \sigma \underline{\times} \tau \hookrightarrow (e_1', e_2') : \sigma' \times \tau'}$$

$$(DFST) \quad \frac{\Gamma \vdash e : \sigma \underline{\times} \tau \hookrightarrow e' : \sigma' \times \tau'}{\Gamma \vdash \underline{\pi}_1 e : \sigma \hookrightarrow \pi_1 e' : \sigma'} \qquad (DSND) \quad \frac{\Gamma \vdash e : \sigma \underline{\times} \tau \hookrightarrow e' : \sigma' \times \tau'}{\Gamma \vdash \underline{\pi}_2 e : \tau \hookrightarrow \pi_2 e' : \tau'}$$

Note that even though pairs are dynamic, they can very well have static components. For example,

$$\vdash \underline{\text{let }} p = (2, \underline{4}) \underline{\text{ in }} (\text{lift } (\underline{\pi}_1 \ p + 1), \underline{\pi}_2 \ p) : \underline{\text{int}} \times \text{int}$$
$$\hookrightarrow \text{let } p' = (\bullet, 4) \text{ in } (3, \pi_2 \ p') : \text{int} \times \text{int}$$

The residual type of p in this example is $2 \times \text{int}$, which provides the information necessary to perform the static addition. After void erasure, the result becomes

$$\text{let } p' = 4 \text{ in } (3, p')$$

3.4 Tagged Sum Types

We introduce sum types in the form of tagged, n-ary sums, which we write as

$$C_1 \ \tau_1 \mid C_2 \ \tau_2 \mid \ldots \mid C_n \ \tau_n$$

We call the C_i the *constructors* of the type; the order in which we write them is insignificant. We will distinguish constructors lexically using an initial capital letter. Sometimes we shall write such a sum type as $\Sigma_{i=1}^n C_i \ \tau_i$.

Booleans are of course just a special case of a sum type, namely

$$\textit{True } \mathbf{void} \mid \textit{False } \mathbf{void}$$

We shall write *True* $\bullet$ and *False* $\bullet$ as **true** and **false** as usual, and use the ordinary **if-then-else** syntax as syntactic sugar for a case on this type.

We distinguish static and dynamic sum types. Dynamic sum types are identified by underlining (all of) the constructors.

---

[2] Binding a completely static variable with a dynamic <u>let</u> is not particularly useful, since the residual let will in any case be removed by void erasure. But binding a *partially static* variable with a dynamic <u>let</u> definitely is useful.

Static Sum Types Intuitively, if a value is of a static sum type, then we know at specialisation time which summand it lies in. Static constructor applications are specialised as follows:

$$(SCON) \quad \frac{\Gamma \vdash e : \tau \hookrightarrow e' : \tau'}{\Gamma \vdash C\,e : C\,\tau \mid \phi \hookrightarrow e' : C\,\tau'}$$

where ϕ varies over sum types only. Notice that the constructor is preserved in the residual type, and so it need not appear in the residual expression. The residual type $C\,\tau'$ therefore has the same elements as τ', but carries additional static information.

This information is then exploited in the rule for static **case** expressions:

$$(SCASE) \quad \frac{\Gamma \vdash e : \Sigma_{i=1}^{n} C_i\ \sigma_i \hookrightarrow e' : C_k\ \sigma'_k \qquad \Gamma, x_k : \sigma_k \hookrightarrow e' : \sigma'_k \vdash e_k : \tau \hookrightarrow e'_k : \tau'}{\Gamma \vdash \textbf{case}\ e\ \textbf{of}\ [C_i\ x_i \to e_i]_{i=1}^{n} : \tau \hookrightarrow e'_k : \tau'}$$

Here the residual type of the inspected expression tells us which constructor we have, so we can simply choose the right branch directly: the **case** expression leaves no trace in the residual program.

For example, using a tagged sum of integers and booleans

$$Num\ \underline{\textbf{int}} \mid Bool\ \underline{\textbf{bool}}$$

we could construct the expression

$$\textbf{case}\ Num\ (\underline{2+2})\ \textbf{of}\ Num\ n \to Num\ (n \underline{\times} n)$$
$$Bool\ b\ \to Bool\ b$$

Applying (SCON) to $Num\ (\underline{2+2})$ we obtain the specialisation $2+2 : Num\ \underline{\textbf{int}}$, and now applying (SCASE) we can choose the Num branch and derive the specialisation

$$(2+2) \times (2+2) : Num\ \underline{\textbf{int}}$$

as the result.

The example reveals that since the static case rule involves unfolding, code duplication may occur. But we can always avoid it by introducing a dynamic <u>**let**</u>:

$$\vdash \underline{\textbf{let}}\ m = Num\ (\underline{2+2})$$
$$\underline{\textbf{in}}\ \textbf{case}\ m\ \textbf{of}\ Num\ n \to Num\ (n \underline{\times} n)$$
$$Bool\ b\ \to Bool\ b$$
$$: Num\ \underline{\textbf{int}} \mid Bool\ \underline{\textbf{bool}}$$

$$\hookrightarrow \textbf{let}\ m' = 2 + 2\ \textbf{in}\ m' \times m'$$
$$: Num\ \underline{\textbf{int}}$$

Dynamic Sum Types In contrast, when a value is an element of a dynamic sum type we do *not* know which summand it lies in at specialisation time. The rule for constructor application 'forgets' this information, and inserts a constructor into the residual code:

$$(DCON) \quad \frac{\Gamma \vdash e : \tau \hookrightarrow e' : \tau'}{\Gamma \vdash \underline{C}\, e : \underline{C}\, \tau \mid \phi \hookrightarrow C\, e' : C\, \tau' \mid \phi'}$$

The residual type is a sum of the residual types of the summands. Notice that here we concern ourselves only with the C summand; no relationship is imposed between ϕ and ϕ'. In practice however they must have the same constructors, and for each constructor the summand type in ϕ' must be a residual type obtainable from the corresponding summand in ϕ. This condition is enforced by many (DCON) rules, taken together.

The information in the residual type is then used to specialise the branches of dynamic **case** expressions, via the following rule.

$$\Gamma \vdash e : \Sigma_{i=1}^{n}\underline{C_i}\,\sigma_i \hookrightarrow e' : \Sigma_{i=1}^{n}C_i\,\sigma_i'$$

$$(DCASE) \quad \frac{[\Gamma, x_i : \sigma_i \hookrightarrow x_i' : \sigma_i' \vdash e_i : \tau \hookrightarrow e_i' : \tau']_{i=1}^{n}}{\Gamma \vdash \mathbf{case}\ e\ \mathbf{of}\ [\underline{C_i}\ x_i \to e_i]_{i=1}^{n} : \tau \hookrightarrow} \quad x_i'\ \text{fresh}, i \in 1 \ldots n$$
$$\mathbf{case}\ e'\ \mathbf{of}\ [C_i\ x_i' \to e_i']_{i=1}^{n} : \tau'$$

As an example of a dynamic sum type with static components, consider

$$\underline{Num}\ \text{int} \mid \underline{Bool}\ \text{bool}$$

with typical elements $\underline{Num}\ 42$ and $\underline{Bool}\ \text{true}$. These can for example be specialised as follows:

$$\vdash \underline{Num}\ 42 : \underline{Num}\ \text{int} \mid \underline{Bool}\ \text{bool} \hookrightarrow Num\ \bullet : Num\ 42 \mid Bool\ \text{true}$$
$$\vdash \underline{Bool}\ \text{true} : \underline{Num}\ \text{int} \mid \underline{Bool}\ \text{bool} \hookrightarrow Bool\ \bullet : Num\ 42 \mid Bool\ \text{true}$$

Both can be given the same residual type, which we can interpret as follows: we do not know at specialisation time if we have a *Num* or a *Bool*, but *if* we have a *Num*, then its static component is 42, and if we have a *Bool*, then its static component is **true**. When we specialise a corresponding **case** we can make use of this information, for example

$$b : \underline{\text{bool}} \hookrightarrow b' : \text{bool} \vdash \mathbf{let}\ x = \mathbf{if}\ b\ \mathbf{then}\ \underline{Num}\ 42\ \mathbf{else}\ \underline{Bool}\ \text{true}$$
$$\mathbf{in}\ \mathbf{case}\ x\ \mathbf{of}\ \underline{Num}\ n \to \mathbf{lift}\ (n+1)$$
$$\underline{Bool}\ c\ \to \mathbf{if}\ c\ \mathbf{then}\ \underline{1}\ \mathbf{else}\ \underline{0}$$
$$: \underline{\text{int}}$$

$$\hookrightarrow \mathbf{let}\ x' = \mathbf{if}\ b'\ \mathbf{then}\ Num\ \bullet\ \mathbf{else}\ Bool\ \bullet$$
$$\mathbf{in}\ \mathbf{case}\ x'\ \mathbf{of}\ Num\ n' \to 43$$
$$Bool\ c'\ \to 1$$
$$: \text{int}$$

Here x has the residual type we discussed, and the **case** branches are specialised accordingly. Consequently the actual static components need not be preserved in the residual program.

Notice that a dynamic <u>case</u> expression may have a static or partially static result. For example (remembering that **if-then-else** is syntactic sugar for **case**),

$$\text{if } b \text{ \underline{then} } Num \text{ } \underline{3} \text{ \underline{else} } Num \text{ } \underline{4} : Num \text{ \underline{int}} \mid Bool \text{ \underline{bool}}$$

is well-typed and specialises to

$$\text{if } b \text{ then } 3 \text{ else } 4 : Num \text{ int}$$

As expected, the static tags are eliminated from the program, and the static information about the branches is still available in the residual type of the whole. Such an effect is sometimes achieved in traditional partial evaluators using indirect methods such as continuations; here, it is a natural consequence of using type inference.

But this begs the question: what if the static information in the branches fails to match? For example, the expression

$$\text{if } b \text{ \underline{then} } Num \text{ } \underline{3} \text{ \underline{else} } Bool \text{ \underline{true}} : Num \text{ \underline{int}} \mid Bool \text{ \underline{bool}}$$

is also well-typed, but the two branches have *different* static constructors, and therefore different residual types. No specialisation is possible here: we would not be able to assign the residual program a type. Our specialiser therefore rejects this expression.

Notice that this is not a binding-time error: the input expression is well typed, no static value appears where a dynamic one is expected. The error can only be discovered during specialisation, when two residual types fail to match.

3.5 Function Types

We shall also distinguish static and dynamic function types. Dynamic λ-expressions create λ-expressions in the residual programs, whereas static functions are unfolded.

Dynamic Functions The rules for dynamic λ-expressions and applications are quite straightforward extensions of the usual typing rules.

$$(DLAM) \quad \frac{\Gamma, x : \sigma \hookrightarrow x' : \sigma' \vdash e : \tau \hookrightarrow e' : \tau'}{\Gamma \vdash \lambda x.e : \sigma \xrightarrow{} \tau \hookrightarrow \lambda x'.e' : \sigma' \to \tau'} \quad x' \text{ fresh}$$

$$(DAPP) \quad \frac{\Gamma \vdash e_1 : \sigma \xrightarrow{} \tau \hookrightarrow e_1' : \sigma' \to \tau' \quad \Gamma \vdash e_2 : \sigma \hookrightarrow e_2' : \sigma'}{\Gamma \vdash e_1 @ e_2 : \tau \hookrightarrow e_1' \text{ } e_2' : \tau'}$$

We have already seen examples in section 2 showing that dynamic functions may well have static arguments and results, in contrast to unfolding based partial evaluators.

We also introduce a dynamic fixpoint operator, which generates a residual **fix** in the specialised program.

$$(DFIX) \quad \frac{\Gamma \vdash e : \tau \xrightarrow{} \tau \hookrightarrow e' : \tau' \to \tau'}{\Gamma \vdash \underline{\text{fix}} \text{ } e : \tau \hookrightarrow \text{fix } e' : \tau'}$$

Static Functions Static λ-expressions do not generate a function in the residual program; instead they are unfolded by the partial evaluator. Static functions are therefore represented by 'closures' at specialisation time, containing the function body, bound variable, and the context. But such a closure is a mixture of static and dynamic information: although the names, types, and residual types of the variables in the context are all static, their *values* may be dynamic. We therefore transform a static function into a residual *tuple* of the values of the variables in the context, and assign it a residual type containing the remaining parts of the function closure. The specialisation rule for static λ-expressions is therefore

$$(SLAM) \quad [z_i : \tau_i \hookrightarrow e_i : \tau_i']_{i=1}^n \vdash$$
$$\lambda x.e : \sigma \to \tau \hookrightarrow (e_1, \ldots, e_n) : \mathbf{clos} < [z_i : \tau_i \hookrightarrow \tau_i']_{i=1}^n, x, e >$$

For example, consider the program

$$\text{let } m = 42$$
$$\text{in } \text{let } n = \underline{35}$$
$$\text{in } \underline{\text{let }} f = \lambda x.x \underline{+} n \underline{\text{ in }} (f\ \underline{1}, f\ \underline{2})$$

Here the static λ-expression is in the scope of two variables, and so its residual expression is a pair:

$$m : \text{int} \hookrightarrow \bullet : 42, n : \underline{\text{int}} \hookrightarrow 35 : \text{int} \vdash$$
$$\lambda x.x \underline{+} n : \underline{\text{int}} \to \underline{\text{int}} \hookrightarrow$$
$$(\bullet, 35) : \mathbf{clos} < [m : \text{int} \hookrightarrow 42, n : \underline{\text{int}} \hookrightarrow \text{int}], x, x \underline{+} n >$$

This tuple of values is passed around in the residual program instead of the function value, and when a static function is applied the residual type tells us how to interpret it. We extract the function's body from the closure and specialise it, binding the variables in its context to appropriate components of the tuple:

$$(SAPP) \quad \frac{\Gamma \vdash e_1 : \sigma \to \tau \hookrightarrow e_1' : \mathbf{clos} < [z_i : \tau_i \hookrightarrow \tau_i']_{i=1}^n, x, e > \qquad \Gamma \vdash e_2 : \sigma \hookrightarrow e_2' : \sigma' \qquad [z_i : \tau_i \hookrightarrow \pi_i\ e_1' : \tau_i']_{i=1}^n, x : \sigma \hookrightarrow e_2' : \sigma' \vdash e : \tau \hookrightarrow e' : \tau'}{\Gamma \vdash e_1\ e_2 : \tau \hookrightarrow e' : \tau'}$$

In our example, when f's body is specialised at the calls, the free variable n is replaced by the second component of the pair. The result of specialising the complete program is therefore

$$\text{let } f' = (\bullet, 35)$$
$$\text{in } (1 + \pi_2\ f', 2 + \pi_2\ f')$$

Of course void erasure is applicable, and eliminates the projections altogether in this case:

$$\text{let } f' = 35 \text{ in } (1 + f', 2 + f')$$

Our treatment of static functions is very similar to Similix's [Bon91], which replaces them by their dynamic free variables. We don't distinguish dynamic from static *variables*, and the rule above takes all the variables in the context, not just the free ones, but otherwise the idea is the same. We can achieve an effect closer to Similix by adding a weakening rule to drop unused variables from the context before (SLAM) is applied:

$$(WEAK) \quad \frac{\Gamma_1, \Gamma_2 \vdash e : \tau \hookrightarrow e' : \tau'}{\Gamma_1, x : \sigma \hookrightarrow u' : \sigma', \Gamma_2 \vdash e : \tau \hookrightarrow e' : \tau'} \; x \notin FV(e)$$

In our implementation we use weakening to remove all but the free variables before building a static closure. So in the example, the value of f is actually specialised as

$$m : \text{int} \hookrightarrow \bullet : 42, n : \underline{\text{int}} \hookrightarrow 35 : \text{int} \vdash$$
$$\lambda x. x \underline{+} n : \underline{\text{int}} \rightarrow \underline{\text{int}} \hookrightarrow$$
$$35 : \text{clos} < [n : \underline{\text{int}} \hookrightarrow \text{int}], x, x \underline{+} n >$$

in which the unused variable m is dropped.

Static Recursion We express static recursion, which is unfolded at specialisation time, via a fixpoint operator on static functions. But we cannot allow an unrestricted **fix**, because expressions such as **fix** $(\lambda x.\underline{Cons}\,(\underline{1}, x))$ would lead to infinite unfolding at specialisation time. Instead we restrict ourselves to recursive *functions*, and we delay unfolding until a recursive call is actually made. Of course, this is the same solution adopted in strict programming languages.

We cannot conveniently represent recursive functions using the kind of closure we have discussed so far. The difficulty is that the body of a recursive function has the function name itself as a free variable. In the residual program it would have to be represented by a tuple with one component representing the function itself — in other words, equal to the whole tuple. To avoid the need for cyclic structures in the residual program, we introduce a new kind of static closure:

$$\text{rec} < f, \Gamma', x, e >$$

Here f is the recursive function name, and is implicitly bound to the entire closure. The corresponding value in the residual program is just a tuple of the *other* free variables.

Recursive closures are created by the static **fix** rule. The argument of **fix** must be a static function from a static function type $\sigma \rightarrow \tau$ to itself. The (SFIX) rule unfolds that function, thereby specialising the body of the recursive definition, *without* a binding for its parameter, the recursively defined name f. Of course in principle f is in scope in the body, *but* if the body cannot be specialised without reference to it, then the recursion is ill-defined — it would lead to infinite unfolding. In practice we expect the body to be another static λ-expression, which we can specialise just by constructing a static closure. This closure will probably refer to f in its body, but will not contain a binding for f because of the way it is constructed. We convert it into a rec closure, thus binding f, and obtain the final result. Here is the specialisation rule, followed by an example:

$$\Gamma \vdash e_1 : (\sigma \rightarrow \tau) \rightarrow (\sigma \rightarrow \tau) \hookrightarrow$$
$$e_1' : \text{clos} < [z_i : \alpha_i \hookrightarrow \alpha_i']_{i=1}^m, f, e_2 >$$

$$(SFIX) \qquad \frac{[z_i : \alpha_i \hookrightarrow \pi_i \; e_1' : \alpha_i']_{i=1}^m \vdash}{\Gamma \vdash \textbf{fix } e_1 : \sigma \rightarrow \tau \hookrightarrow e_2' : \text{rec} < f, [w_i : \beta_i \hookrightarrow \beta_i']_{i=1}^n, x, e_3 >}{\Gamma \vdash \textbf{fix } e_1 : \sigma \rightarrow \tau \hookrightarrow e_2' : \text{rec} < f, [w_i : \beta_i \hookrightarrow \beta_i']_{i=1}^n, x, e_3 >}$$

As an example, consider the program

> let $n = \underline{35}$
> in $\underline{\text{let}}$ $f = \text{fix}$ $(\lambda g.\lambda x.\text{if } x = 0 \text{ then } n \text{ else } g\ (x - 1)\underline{+1})$
> $\underline{\text{in}}\ f\ 2$

Here the argument of **fix** specialises as follows:

$n : \underline{\text{int}} \hookrightarrow 35 : \text{int} \vdash$
$\quad \lambda g.\lambda x.\text{if } x = 0 \text{ then } n \text{ else } g\ (x - 1)\underline{+1} : (\text{int} \to \underline{\text{int}}) \to (\text{int} \to \underline{\text{int}}) \hookrightarrow$
$\quad\quad 35 : \text{clos} < [n : \underline{\text{int}} \hookrightarrow \text{int}], g, \lambda x.\text{if } x = 0 \text{ then } n \text{ else } g\ (x - 1)\underline{+1} >$

When we unfold this closure without a binding for g, we obtain

$n : \underline{\text{int}} \hookrightarrow 35 : \text{int} \vdash$
$\quad \lambda x.\text{if } x = 0 \text{ then } n \text{ else } g\ (x - 1)\underline{+1} : \text{int} \to \underline{\text{int}} \hookrightarrow$
$\quad\quad 35 : \text{clos} < [n : \underline{\text{int}} \hookrightarrow \text{int}], x, \text{if } x = 0 \text{ then } n \text{ else } g\ (x - 1)\underline{+1} >$

in which g is a free variable. Applying (SFIX), the final result of specialising the **fix** is

$$35 : \text{rec} < g, [n : \underline{\text{int}} \hookrightarrow \text{int}], x, \text{if } x = 0 \text{ then } n \text{ else } g\ (x - 1)\underline{+1} >$$

which is the recursive function we want.

We also need a rule to apply recursive functions: it is just the same as (SAPP), except that it additionally binds the recursive function name to the very function being applied.

$$\Gamma \vdash e_1 : \sigma \to \tau \hookrightarrow e_1' : \text{rec} < f, [z_i : \tau_i \hookrightarrow \tau_i']_{i=1}^n, x, e >$$

$$\Gamma \vdash e_2 : \sigma \hookrightarrow e_2' : \sigma'$$

$$\text{(RSAPP)} \quad \frac{\left\{ \begin{array}{l} [z_i : \tau_i \hookrightarrow \pi_i\ e_1' : \tau_i']_{i=1}^n, \\ f : \sigma \to \tau \hookrightarrow e_1' : \text{rec} < f, [z_i : \tau_i \hookrightarrow \tau_i']_{i=1}^n, x, e >, \\ x : \sigma \hookrightarrow e_2' : \sigma' \end{array} \right\} \vdash e : \tau \hookrightarrow e' : \tau'}{\Gamma \vdash e_1\ e_2 : \tau \hookrightarrow e' : \tau'}$$

Using this rule we can complete the specialisation of our example. The residual program is:

$$\text{let } f = 35 \text{ in } (f + 1) + 1 : \text{int}$$

The static recursion has been unfolded twice, while the function name is bound to a (one-)tuple of its free variables, which is used to interpret the reference to n in the unfolded code.

3.6 Recursive Types

We use no special notation for recursive types, instead we simply allow both source and residual types to be regular trees. For example, the type of static lists is

$$List\ \tau \equiv Nil\ \textbf{void} \mid Cons\ (\tau \underline{\times} List\ \tau)$$

Since the list constructors are static, they do not appear in residual programs. For example,

$$\vdash Cons\,(\underline{1},\,Cons\,(\underline{2},\,Nil\,\bullet)) : List\,\underline{int}\,\hookrightarrow$$
$$(1,\,(2,\,\bullet)) : Cons\,(\mathbf{int}\times Cons\,(\mathbf{int}\times Nil\,\mathbf{void}))$$

The residual type tells us the length of the list, while the residual term is just a (nested) tuple of the list elements.

For an example of a recursive residual type, consider the term $\underline{\mathbf{fix}}\,(\underline{\lambda}l.\,Cons\,(\underline{1},l))$, which evaluates to an infinite list of ones. It specialises as follows:

$$\vdash \underline{\mathbf{fix}}\,(\underline{\lambda}l.\,Cons\,(\underline{1},l)) : List\,\underline{int}\,\hookrightarrow \mathbf{fix}\,(\lambda l'.(1,l')) : \tau$$

where

$$\tau \equiv Cons\,(\mathbf{int}\times\tau)$$

3.7 Polyvariance

So far, we have actually described a form of *monovariant* specialisation — that is, one in which static variables can take only *one* static value. For example, the expression

$$\underline{\mathbf{let}}\,f = \underline{\lambda}x.\mathbf{lift}\,(x+1)\,\underline{\mathbf{in}}\,f\,@\,3 : \mathbf{int}$$

can be specialised to

$$\mathbf{let}\,f = \lambda x.4\,\mathbf{in}\,f\,\bullet : \mathbf{int}$$

But the similar expression

$$\underline{\mathbf{let}}\,f = \underline{\lambda}x.\mathbf{lift}\,(x+1)\,\underline{\mathbf{in}}\,(f\,@\,3,\,f\,@\,4) : \underline{\mathbf{int}\times\mathbf{int}}$$

cannot be specialised at all, because f cannot be assigned both residual types $3 \to \mathbf{int}$ and $4 \to \mathbf{int}$. All useful partial evaluators use polyvariant specialisation, and in this case would create two versions of f, one specialised to each static argument.

Fortunately, our partial evaluator can be extended by adding a new type whose specialisation rules are polyvariant. It is introduced by the operator **poly**:

$$(POLY)\qquad \frac{[\Gamma \vdash e : \tau \hookrightarrow e_i : \tau'_i]_{i=1}^{n}}{\Gamma \vdash \mathbf{poly}\,e : \mathbf{poly}\,\tau \hookrightarrow (e_1,\ldots,e_n) : (\tau'_1,\ldots,\tau'_n)}$$

An expression enclosed by **poly** can be specialised many times, with different residual types in each case. In our example, we will enclose the value of f by **poly** so that it can be specialised to two different arguments.

When we do so, however, we change the type of f to **poly** $(\mathbf{int} \to \mathbf{int})$, which is not a function and so cannot be applied directly. We need another operator, **spec**, to extract a τ from a **poly** τ. The corresponding residual expression selects an element from the tuple of specialisations that **poly** produces.

$$(SPEC)\qquad \frac{\Gamma \vdash e : \mathbf{poly}\,\tau \hookrightarrow e' : (\tau'_1,\ldots,\tau'_n)}{\Gamma \vdash \mathbf{spec}\,e : \tau \hookrightarrow \pi_k\,e' : \tau'_k}$$

In our example, we apply **spec** at the two uses of f, giving

$$\underline{let}\ f = \text{poly}\ \lambda x.\text{lift}\ (x+1)\ \underline{in}\ (\text{spec}\ f\ @\ 3, \text{spec}\ f\ @\ 4)$$

Now f can be given the residual type $(3 \to \text{int}, 4 \to \text{int})$, resulting in the specialisation

$$\text{let}\ f' = (\lambda x'.4, \lambda x'.5)\ \text{in}\ (\pi_1\ f'\ \bullet, \pi_2\ f'\ \bullet)$$

or after void erasure,

$$\text{let}\ f' = (4,5)\ \text{in}\ (\pi_1\ f', \pi_2\ f')$$

3.8 Polyvariant Sums

The polyvariance just introduced creates an n-ary *product* in the residual program; it is natural to ask whether there is a corresponding form which creates an n-ary *sum*. Indeed there is, and moreover, its rules can be derived just by 'reversing the arrows' in the rules above! Of course this would be clearer if we used a categorical notation rather than the λ-calculus, but even so, the rules below are simply the duals of those in the previous section.

We introduce a polyvariant sum type **sum** τ, with constructor $\underline{In}$, which we take apart using a **case** expression. Expressions of type **sum** τ yield residual expressions with an n-ary sum type of the form $\Sigma_{i=1}^{n} In_i\ \tau_i'$. Applications of $\underline{In}$ are specialised to applications of an appropriate In_i. Compare the rule below to (SPEC):

$$(SPECCON)\qquad \frac{\Gamma \vdash e : \tau \hookrightarrow e' : \tau_k'}{\Gamma \vdash \underline{In}\ e : \textbf{sum}\ \tau \hookrightarrow In_k\ e' : \Sigma_{i=1}^{n} In_i\ \tau_i'}$$

$\underline{In}$ can be applied to expressions with *different* residual types to produce expressions with the *same* one, thus providing another way to pass different static arguments to the same function. The example of the previous section can instead be rewritten as

$$\underline{let}\ f = \lambda x.\underline{case}\ x\ \underline{of}\ \underline{In}\ y \to \text{lift}\ (y+1)$$
$$\underline{in}\ (f\ @(\underline{In}\ 3), f\ @(\underline{In}\ 4))$$

Here f can be given the residual type $(In_1\ 3\ |\ In_2\ 4) \to \text{int}$ and the two actual parameters specialised as

$$\vdash \underline{In}\ 3 : \textbf{sum}\ \textbf{int} \hookrightarrow In_1\ \bullet : In_1\ 3\ |\ In_2\ 4$$
$$\vdash \underline{In}\ 4 : \textbf{sum}\ \textbf{int} \hookrightarrow In_2\ \bullet : In_1\ 3\ |\ In_2\ 4$$

When a **case** expression on **sum** τ is specialised, then the residual type of the inspected expression tells us which specialised branches the residual case should contain. The following rule is dual to (POLY):

$$(POLYCASE)\qquad \frac{\Gamma \vdash e_1 : \textbf{sum}\ \sigma \hookrightarrow e_1' : \Sigma_{i=1}^{n} In_i\ \sigma_i' \qquad [\Gamma, x : \sigma \hookrightarrow x' : \sigma_i' \vdash e_2 : \tau \hookrightarrow e_{2,i}' : \tau']_{i=1}^{n}}{\Gamma \vdash \underline{case}\ e_1\ \underline{of}\ \underline{In}\ x \to e_2 : \tau \hookrightarrow}\quad x'\ \text{fresh}$$
$$\text{case}\ e_1'\ \text{of}\ [In_i\ x' \to e_{2,i}']_{i=1}^{n} : \tau'$$

Applied to the example above, we obtain

$$\text{let } f' = \lambda x'.\text{case } x' \text{ of } In_1 \ y' \to 4$$
$$In_2 \ y' \to 5$$
$$\textbf{in } (f \ (In_1 \ \bullet), f \ (In_2 \ \bullet))$$

This completes our specification of the specialiser itself. In the following sections we shall describe the phases that precede and follow the actual specialisation.

4 Type-Checking the Source Language

One way to think of the specialisation rules we have given is that they type-check the source and residual expressions simultaneously. For the source language, well-typing guarantees among other things that dynamic values are not treated as static, and vice versa. But we do not wish to delay type-checking source programs until during specialisation: partly because specialisation may not visit every part of the source program, and therefore might fail to discover some type-errors, and partly because specialisation can be time-consuming and we want to report type errors fast.

We therefore type-check source terms before specialisation. Type correctness guarantees that when we do apply the specialisation rules, any failures to match will involve residual types, not source types.

The typing rules are straightforward, and will not be presented in detail. Most of them can be obtained from the corresponding specialisation rules by erasing the residual terms and types. Occasionally this does not suffice: for example, the rule for static **case** expressions

$$(SCASE) \quad \frac{\Gamma \vdash e : \Sigma_{i=1}^{n} C_i \ \sigma_i \hookrightarrow e' : C_k \ \sigma'_k \qquad \Gamma, x_k : \sigma_k \hookrightarrow e' : \sigma'_k \vdash e_k : \tau \hookrightarrow e'_k : \tau'}{\Gamma \vdash \textbf{case } e \text{ of } [C_i \ x_i \to e_i]_{i=1}^{n} : \tau \hookrightarrow e'_k : \tau'}$$

specialises only *one* branch of the case, corresponding to the residual type of the inspected expression. The typing rule, in contrast, checks *all* branches, and so verifies that every invocation of the specialisation rule will match.

$$(T\text{-}SCASE) \quad \frac{\Gamma \vdash e : \Sigma_{i=1}^{n} C_i \ \sigma_i \qquad [\Gamma, x_i : \sigma_i \vdash e_i : \tau]_{i=1}^{n}}{\Gamma \vdash \textbf{case } e \text{ of } [C_i \ x_i \to e_i]_{i=1}^{n} : \tau}$$

Similarly the specialisation rule for **poly** specialises the enclosed expression many times, while the typing rule only types it once. The specialisation rules for static λ-expressions arrange to unfold them at the point of application, whereas the typing rule is just the usual rule for λ, which verifies that *all* unfoldings will be well-typed. There are no surprises here.

Indeed, the only surprising thing is that the typing rules are so unsurprising. Other authors using two-level languages restrict the ways in which static and dynamic type formers are mixed — for example Nielson and Nielson do so by distinguishing *compile-time* from *run-time* types[NN92]. In contrast we can allow completely free type formation. Type-based binding-time analyses (such as Henglein

[Hen91]) must usually handle 'dependency constraints' which force the result type of a conditional expression to be dynamic if the condition is. In contrast we can allow a dynamic conditional to be of any type whatsoever — even a static integer! Our 'binding-time checker' is simply an ordinary type-checker.

Note that we use a binding-time *checker*, not a binding-time *analyser*: all binding-times are explicitly given by the programmer. We will discuss prospects for binding-time analysis in a later section.

5   Void Erasure

We have seen that residual programs contain many trivial values without computational content. Most of these can be removed by a post-processing phase we call *void erasure*.

We define a predicate τ triv, which holds of 'trivial' types such as 3, void, and $3 \to 4$. Whenever τ triv holds, then $\tau \simeq$ void. We define τ triv as follows:

$$\text{void triv}$$
$$m \text{ triv[m an integer]}$$
$$\sigma \to \tau \text{ triv} \mathrel{\hat{=}} \tau \text{ triv}$$
$$\sigma \times \tau \text{ triv} \mathrel{\hat{=}} \sigma \text{ triv} \wedge \tau \text{ triv}$$
$$\textstyle\sum_{i=1}^{n}\tau_i \text{ triv} \mathrel{\hat{=}} n = 0$$

We treat n-ary products as nested pairs, and the empty product as **void** for the purposes of void erasure.

The triv predicate is the *largest* predicate with these properties, which means that recursive types such as

$$Str\ \tau \equiv \tau \times Str\ \tau$$

can be trivial (in this case provided τ is).

Void erasure consists of removing trivial components from pairs, trivial parameters from functions, and variables bound to trivial values. We are in fact exploiting the isomorphisms

$$\text{void} \times \tau \simeq \tau$$
$$\tau \times \text{void} \simeq \tau$$
$$\text{void} \to \tau \simeq \tau$$

by transforming terms of the more complex types on the left into the corresponding terms of the simpler types on the right. The fact that these are isomorphisms guarantees that void erasure does not change the behaviour of residual programs.

We transform terms depending on their types, which we write as superscripts here. Let ν by a trivial type. The following transformations are applied wherever they are applicable:

$$e^\nu \longrightarrow \bullet$$
$$\text{let } x^\nu = e^\nu \text{ in } e'^\tau \longrightarrow e'$$

It is safe to remove the binding for x, because after applying the first rule no references to x can remain.

$$\lambda x^\nu.e \longrightarrow e$$
$$e^{\nu \rightarrow \tau}\ e'^\nu \longrightarrow e$$

We erase trivial parameters, both formal and actual.

$$(e^\nu, e'^\tau) \longrightarrow e' \qquad \pi_1\ e^{\tau \times \nu} \longrightarrow e$$
$$(e^\tau, e'^\nu) \longrightarrow e \qquad \pi_2\ e^{\nu \times \tau} \longrightarrow e$$

We erase trivial components from pairs, and we must obviously remove the corresponding selector applications also.

These transformations cannot be applied during specialisation, because they depend on knowing residual types. Just as a type-checker may discover the type of an expression some time after it has been visited, so our specialiser may discover a residual type some time after constructing the corresponding residual expression. Hence void erasure must be done in a later pass.

The specialiser also has a tendency to produce terms of the form $\pi_i\ (e_1, \ldots, e_n)$, especially from programs involving static functions. We simplify these terms also during void erasure, although we view this as a hack. The correct solution to this problem would be to introduce a form of static product, whose projections are removed by the specialiser. Doing so, however, is not completely straightforward (see section 8.1).

After void erasure some occurrences of $\bullet$ may remain, but only in contexts where the rules above cannot remove them, such as the argument of a constructor. Our insistence on unary constructors means that such occurrences are really necessary: sometimes void types really are useful!

We note in passing that our assumption of a lazy language is helpful here. Indeed, the void erasure transformation is not safe for a strict language, since it transforms λ-expressions which always terminate into other expressions which may not. A more careful transformation, and more complicated justification, would be needed to apply void erasure in a strict context.

6   Implementing the Specialisation Rules

We have constructed an implementation of the partial evaluator which applies the specialisation rules in much the same way that a type checker applies type inference rules. Since the source expressions are checked for type correctness in advance, our specialiser does not infer source types, only residual expressions and types.

Just as type inference often produces types containing uninstantiated type variables, so our specialiser often produces residual types containing uninstantiated variables. For example, if we specialise $\underline{Num}\ \underline{3}$ then the result is

$$\vdash \underline{Num}\ \underline{3} : \underline{Num}\ \underline{\textbf{int}} \mid \phi \hookrightarrow Num\ 3 : Num\ \textbf{int} \mid \phi'$$

where ϕ' is an uninstantiated residual type variable. Our specialiser maintains a state containing the next free variable and the variable instantiations known so far, just as a type checker does. Residual types are derived using unification, as usual. In order to support cyclic residual types we use a graph unification algorithm.

However, the specialisation rules are not as simple to implement as Hindley-Milner type inference rules, because they are not all syntax-directed. In particular, static case expressions are specialised using the rule

$$(SCASE) \quad \frac{\Gamma \vdash e : \Sigma_{i=1}^{n} C_i \; \sigma_i \hookrightarrow e' : C_k \; \sigma'_k \qquad \Gamma, x_k : \sigma_k \hookrightarrow e' : \sigma'_k \vdash e_k : \tau \hookrightarrow e'_k : \tau'}{\Gamma \vdash \mathbf{case} \; e \; \mathbf{of} \; [C_i \; x_i \to e_i]_{i=1}^{n} : \tau \hookrightarrow e'_k : \tau'}$$

which specialises only *one* of the branches, depending on which summand the residual type of the expression inspected lies in. The implementation specialises this expression first, and if its residual type is $C_k \sigma'_k$ it chooses the kth branch. But unfortunately it is quite possible that the residual type is only an uninstantiated variable! In this case we cannot choose the branch to specialise until later, when the variable becomes instantiated. We have implemented a 'demon' mechanism, which allows a computation to be suspended until a particular variable is instantiated. This mechanism is used in this case.

When the specialisation of an expression must be delayed like this, we do not know its residual expression at the time that enclosing residual expressions are built. We have solved this problem by introducing a kind of 'forward reference' in the residual code: whenever a specialisation is delayed and a demon created we also create a forward reference label which replaces the unknown residual expression. When the demon eventually runs it creates a binding for the label. Thus the residual program is really constructed in two stages: first specialise, producing a program with forward references, then resolve those references, replacing them with the expressions the demons created. Note that labels cannot be considered as ordinary bound variables, because they do not respect scope: the variables in scope in the expression bound to a label are those in scope at its use.

It is possible that some references are never resolved, if the corresponding demon is waiting for a variable that is never instantiated. For example, if we try to specialise

$$\lambda x.\mathbf{case} \; x \; \mathbf{of} \; \begin{array}{l} Num \; a \to \underline{3} \\ Bool \; b \to \underline{4} \end{array}$$

the residual expression will be $\lambda x.\nu_1$ where ν_1 is an unresolved forward reference — a demon is created to wait for the static value of x, but it is never run. We consider such inputs to be erroneous: after all, partial evaluation presupposes that all static inputs are given, and that is not true in this case.

Demons are used in many other cases where rule application depends on residual types that might not be known when the specialiser reaches the term in question. For example, to wait for the arguments of primitive static operations, to wait for the value of a lift, or to wait for the static closure at a static function application.

The most problematic rules to implement are those for polyvariant products and sums. The problems are the same in both cases: in rules (POLY) and (POLYCASE) we do not know which variants to create, and in rules (SPEC) and (SPECCON) we do not know which variant to choose.

We have solved these problems by introducing *indexed sets*, of the form

$$\{(i, \tau_i), (j, \tau_j), \ldots\}$$

to collect the residual types of the variants. Residual n-ary sum and product types are represented as **sum** Φ and **poly** Φ respectively, where Φ is such a set with indexes from 1 to n. The rule we use for (SPEC) becomes

$$(SPEC) \quad \frac{\Gamma \vdash e : \textbf{poly } \tau \hookrightarrow e' : \textbf{poly } (\{(k, \tau')\} \cup \Phi)}{\Gamma \vdash \textbf{spec } e : \tau \hookrightarrow \pi_k \, e' : \tau'}$$

When we apply this rule we leave k uninstantiated, thus deferring the choice of index until later. Φ, the rest of the set, is also uninstantiated at this stage.

When the same polyvariant value is specialised several times, we have to unify sets of the form $\{(i, \tau_i)\} \cup \Phi_1$ and $\{(j, \tau_j)\} \cup \Phi_2$. This is achieved by instantiating Φ_1 and Φ_2: the result is $\{(i, \tau_i), (j, \tau_j)\} \cup \Phi$, where Φ is a new set variable. It is always possible to unify two sets of this form.

The rule for (POLY) becomes

$$(POLY) \quad \frac{[\Gamma \vdash e : \tau \hookrightarrow e_i : \tau'_i]_{(i, \tau') \in \Phi}}{\Gamma \vdash \textbf{poly } e : \textbf{poly } \tau \hookrightarrow (e_1, \ldots, e_n) : \textbf{poly } \Phi}$$

In the implementation, we create a demon which waits for Φ to be instantiated, and then takes each element as it becomes available and constructs an appropriate specialisation of e.

One can compare the behaviour of (SPEC) to adding a new entry to the pending list in a traditional partial evaluator, and (POLY) to scanning the pending list and constructing appropriate specialisations. Of course, we also want to avoid constructing multiple specialisations with the same residual type. But we cannot simply compare two elements τ'_i and τ'_j of a set, because they might both be partially unknown. Instead, we *unify* each new set element with the previously seen ones: if unification succeeds, then we proceed on the assumption that those two elements are equal and only one specialisation is required. But if unification fails, or if we later encounter an error, then we backtrack to this point and try the next element, or construct a new specialisation instead.

The efficiency of the specialiser depends critically on how quickly the wrong alternatives in this process lead to failure. This in turn depends on which order the rules are applied in. An early version specialised applications by first specialising the function, and then specialising the argument. As a result the argument's residual type was not known at the time the function itself was specialised, and most of the real work had to be delayed via a demon until after the argument was specialised. When the function itself was a **spec** expression, this meant adding an element to the set that was almost completely uninstantiated; all pairs of set elements matched at first, leading to very poor performance. Reversing the order to specialise the argument first meant that functions were usually specialised to *known* static arguments, and in the case of a **spec** expression the function types added to the set had different, known arguments so that the wrong alternatives could usually be eliminated at once. This change in the order cut the specialisation time for one simple example from over 27 seconds to around a half a second: it is important!

For the same reason, we delay unifying set elements with one another until *after* one of them has been used to generate a specialisation in the (POLY) rule. Generating such a specialisation tends to run demons which are waiting to instantiate the residual type further, and thus helps avoid initially successful unifications which will only lead to failure when specialisations are actually generated.

Finally, once all other specialisation is complete, we assign indexes 1 to n to the elements of each set. This cannot be done earlier since it is always possible that any two sets Φ_1 and Φ_2 will be unified; if one has begun assigning indexes already in each set, then the assignments may be inconsistent.

The implementation is written in Haskell, and uses a *monad*[Wad92] to provide the mechanisms discussed here, namely a state, demons, and backtracking.

7 Optimal Specialisation of Interpreters

The acid test for our partial evaluator is whether it can remove an entire layer of interpretation, including eliminating type tags. To demonstrate that it can, we specialise a very simple interpreter for the simply typed λ-calculus with constants.

7.1 The Universal Type

In the interpreter, we represent values by elements of the following universal type:

$$Univ \equiv Num\ \underline{\textbf{int}}\ |\ Fun\ (Univ \underset{\sim}{\rightarrow} Univ)$$

We expect integer and function values to appear in residual programs, hence these types are dynamic, but we expect the *type tags* themselves to disappear. Hence we use static constructors.

An example of an expression of this type is

$$Fun\ \left(\underline{\lambda}x.\text{case}\ x\ \text{of}\ \begin{matrix} Num\ y \rightarrow & Num\ (y\underline{+}1) \\ Fun\ z \rightarrow & \dots \end{matrix} \right) : Univ$$

It can be specialised to

$$\lambda x'.x' + 1 : Fun\ (Num\ \textbf{int} \rightarrow Num\ \textbf{int})$$

as follows:

- The outer *Fun* constructor becomes part of the residual type.
- The dynamic $\underline{\lambda}$ creates a residual λ-expression.
- Assume we know from the context that x has residual type *Num* **int**. Then the static **case** chooses the first branch.
- The *Num* constructor becomes part of the residual type.
- The dynamic addition creates a residual addition.

The residual code here contains no tagging and untagging operations. Moreover, the type of the residual expression is essentially **int** $\rightarrow$ **int**, since the *Fun* and *Num* constructors do not change the elements of a residual type. Type specialisation has been achieved. And indeed, it is clear that any type at all built from **int** and function arrow can be obtained as a residual type from *Univ*.

7.2 Expressions

The expressions the interpreter evaluates are of course purely static: we represent them by the type

$$E \equiv Cn \text{ int} \mid Vr \text{ int} \mid Lm \text{ (int} \times E) \mid Ap \text{ } (E \times E) \mid Fx \text{ } E$$

Because our partial evaluator does not handle strings, we represents variable names by integers — but these are just used as distinct names, not de Bruijn numbers.

7.3 The Environment

The environment in the interpreter is represented as a function mapping variable names to values. It may of course be applied to many different (static) variable names. We have a choice between using a *static* function, which is unfolded at each use, and a *polyvariant dynamic* function, which can be specialised to look up many different names. That is, we can choose between the types

$$Env \equiv \text{int} \rightarrow Univ$$
$$Env \equiv \text{poly (int} \xrightarrow{} Univ)$$

Which choice we make affects the representation of residual environments in the specialised program. With a static function type, residual environments will be tuples of values of the variables in scope, and with a polyvariant type they will be tuples of functions specialised to looking up the variables used. But in the latter case, since the arguments of these functions are completely static, they will be removed by void erasure. So in both cases a residual environment is just a tuple of variable values. The difference is that in the former case all variables in scope appear, and in the latter case only those variables which are actually looked up.

However, in the interpreter below residual environments only appear at variable lookups, where selection from the tuple is simplified to a single element in any case, so the difference is not significant.

7.4 An Optimal Interpreter

The interpreter itself appears below.

```
(fix (λeval.λenv.λe.
   case e of
       Cn n      → Num (lift n),
       Vr i      → env i,
       Lm (i, e) → Fun (λv. let env' = λj.if i = j then v else env j
                            in  eval env' e),
       Ap (e₁, e₂) → case eval env e₁ of Fun f → f @(eval env e₂),
       Fx e      → case eval env e of Fun f → fix f))
   (λi. Wrong •)
```

It is a partial application of the *eval* function to the initial environment, that is, a function from closed expressions to their values. We have taken the liberty of pattern matching on pairs, rather than using explicit selectors: this is purely syntactic sugar.

We have chosen to unfold applications of *eval*, and of the environment. The case dispatch on the expression to evaluate is static and disappears of course, as do the type tags *Num* and *Fun*. Indeed, the only dynamic operations in this interpreter are **lift**, used to create constants, the dynamic λ used to create function values, the dynamic application used to interpret *Ap*, and the dynamic **fix** used to interpret *Fx*.

It is clear that this interpreter can be specialised optimally. Just to take one or two examples, if we specialise it to

$$Ap\ (Lm\ (1,\ Vr\ 1),\ Cn\ 3)$$

we obtain

$$(\lambda v.v)\ 3 : Num\ \textbf{int}$$

If we specialise it to

$$Ap\ (Lm\ (1,\ Ap\ (Vr\ 1,\ Cn\ 3)))\ (Lm\ (2,\ Vr\ 2))$$

we obtain

$$(\lambda v.v\ 3)\ (\lambda v.v) : Num\ \textbf{int}$$

If we specialise it to

$$Ap\ (Lm\ (1,\ Ap\ (Ap\ (Vr\ 1,\ Vr\ 1),\ Cn\ 3)),\ Lm\ (2,\ Vr\ 2))$$

which binds variable 1 to the identity function and then applies it both to itself and a number, then we obtain a specialisation time error:

$$\text{Cannot unify } Num\ \alpha \text{ with } Fun\ \beta.$$

Of course this is quite right: the program is not type correct because variable 1 is applied to both a number and a function.

7.5 A Firstifying Interpreter

It is interesting to consider variations on the little interpreter above. For example, suppose we choose to make function values static also, so that we take the universal type to be

$$Univ = Num\ \underline{\textbf{int}}\ |\ Fun\ (Univ \rightarrow Univ)$$

The effect will be to unfold user function applications also, and to replace function values in the residual program by tuples of their free variables. In other words, the result is a first-order program, and the specialiser is doing firstification.

However, this choice for the universal type is very restrictive. It requires that all functions that can reach the same point be closures of the same λ-expression, otherwise the residual types will not match. We can relax this requirement using a polyvariant sum:

$$Univ = Num\ \underline{\textbf{int}}\ |\ Fun\ (\textbf{sum}\ (Univ \rightarrow Univ))$$

Now functions are replaced by elements of a sum type, where the constructor identifies the function, and the component is a tuple of free variables. In other words, an efficient representation of a closure. With this choice of universal type, residual type inference discovers which functions might appear at each point — that is, it does a form of type-based closure analysis.

Rather than unfold user functions at each call, which would lead to code duplication, we introduce a dynamic function *app* which we use to apply function values:

$$app \equiv \lambda f.\lambda x.\text{case } f \text{ of } Fun\ g \to \underline{\text{case } g} \text{ of } In\ h \to h\ x$$

In residual programs, the specialisations of *app* will contain a case for applying each possible closure.

We have given user functions a polyvariant sum type, so that one specialisation of *app* can be used to apply many different functions. But we still have to make *app* itself polyvariant, because its *second* parameter x may take different residual types. The firstifying interpreter is therefore:

> $\underline{\text{let }} app = \text{poly}\lambda f.\lambda x.\text{case } f \text{ of } Fun\ g \to \underline{\text{case } g} \underline{\text{ of }} In\ h \to h\ x$
> $\underline{\text{in }} (\textbf{fix } (\lambda eval.\lambda env.\lambda e.$
>
> $\qquad \text{case } e \text{ of}$
> $\qquad\qquad Cn\ n \qquad \to Num\ (\textbf{lift } n),$
> $\qquad\qquad Vr\ i \qquad \to env\ i,$
> $\qquad\qquad Lm\ (i, e) \quad \to Fun\ (\underline{In}\ (\lambda v.\text{let } env' = \lambda j.\text{if } i = j \text{ then } v \text{ else } env\ j$
> $\qquad\qquad\qquad\qquad\qquad\qquad\qquad \text{in } eval\ env'\ e)),$
> $\qquad\qquad Ap\ (e_1, e_2) \to \text{spec } app\ @(eval\ env\ e_1)\ @(eval\ env\ e_2),$
> $\qquad\qquad Fx\ e \qquad \to \underline{\textbf{fix}}\ (\text{spec } app\ @(eval\ env\ e))$
> $\qquad (\lambda i.\ Wrong\ \bullet)$

We interpret λ-expressions using a static λ, injected into a polyvariant sum type, and we interpret application (and **fix**) using the *app* function we discussed.

When this interpreter is specialised to, for example,

$$Ap\ (\ Lm\ (1, Ap\ (\ Lm\ (2, Ap\ (Vr\ 1, Vr\ 2)),$$
$$Ap\ (Vr\ 1, Cn\ 3))),$$
$$Lm\ (3, Vr\ 3))$$

the residual program is

> $\text{let } app = (\ \lambda f.\lambda x.\text{case } f \text{ of } In_1\ h \to \pi_2\ h\ (In_2\ (x, h))\ (\pi_2\ h\ x\ 3),$
> $\qquad\qquad\qquad \lambda f.\lambda x.\text{case } f \text{ of } In_1\ h \to x,$
> $\qquad\qquad\qquad\qquad\qquad\qquad\qquad In_2\ h \to \pi_2\ (\pi_2\ h)\ (\pi_1\ h)\ x)$
> $\text{in } \pi_1\ app\ (In_1\ app)\ (In_1\ app)$

In this example there are two types of function, and hence two specialisations of *app*. The first can apply $Lm\ (1, \ldots)$, and the second can apply both $Lm\ (2, \ldots)$ and $Lm\ (3, Vr\ 3)$, represented as $In_2\ h$ and $In_1\ h$ respectively.

Notice that every closure contains a reference to *app*. This is not surprising since *app* is indeed a free variable of *eval*, and therefore of each function denotation, but since it is a global variable we might want to avoid building it into every closure. We can do so by passing *app* as an explicit parameter to *eval*, and to each function denotation. We need to make the definition of *app* recursive:

let $app = $ **fix** $\lambda app.\text{poly}\lambda f.\lambda x.$
    $\quad\quad\quad$ case f of $Fun\ g \to$ case g of $In\ h \to h\ app\ x$
in (**fix** $(\lambda eval.\lambda app.\lambda env.\lambda e.$
    $\quad$ case e of
        $\quad\quad Cn\ n \quad\quad \to Num\ (\textbf{lift}\ n),$
        $\quad\quad Vr\ i \quad\quad\ \to env\ i,$
        $\quad\quad Lm\ (i, e) \quad \to Fun\ (In\ (\lambda app'.\lambda v.$
            $\quad\quad\quad\quad\quad\quad\quad$ let $env' = \lambda j.\text{if}\ i = j\ \text{then}\ v\ \text{else}\ env\ j$
            $\quad\quad\quad\quad\quad\quad\quad$ in $\ eval\ app'\ env'\ e)),$
        $\quad\quad Ap\ (e_1, e_2) \to \textbf{spec}\ app\ @(eval\ app\ env\ e_1)\ @(eval\ app\ env\ e_2),$
        $\quad\quad Fx\ e \quad\quad \to \textbf{fix}\ (\textbf{spec}\ app\ @(eval\ app\ env\ e))$
    $\quad app$
    $\quad (\lambda i. Wrong\ \bullet)$

Notice that we interpret λ-expressions as functions of app', so that app is no longer a free variable of the static closures we build. When we specialise this interpreter to the previous example, we obtain

let $app = \text{fix}\lambda app.(\lambda f.\lambda x.\text{case}\ f\ \text{of}\ In_1\ h \to \pi_2\ app\ (In_2\ x)\ (\pi_2\ app\ x\ 3),$
    $\quad\quad\quad\quad\quad\quad \lambda f.\lambda x.\text{case}\ f\ \text{of}\ In_1\ h \to x,$
    $\quad\quad\quad\quad\quad\quad\quad\quad\quad\quad\quad\quad In_2\ h \to \pi_2\ app\ h\ x))$
in $\pi_1\ app\ (In_1\ \bullet)\ (In_1\ \bullet)$

in which the closures now contain only the variables we would expect.

8 Discussion

The partial evaluator we have presented represents a first attempt to base specialisation on type inference. There are certainly a number of areas where improvements or extensions are desirable. In this section we shall discuss further work, and also the pros and cons of inference-based specialisation as a whole.

8.1 Static Products and Arity Raising

Just as we have static sum types whose constructors and cases are removed by the specialiser, so it would be natural to add a static product type whose constructor and selectors are removed. We shall write static pairs as $<x, y>$ in this section.

Static products have a natural connection to *arity raising* [Rom90]; when a static pair is passed to a function, the pair structure can be removed by currying the function:

$$f\ @<x, y> \hookrightarrow f\ x\ y$$

Similarly constructors applied to static pairs can be curried, although this does oblige us to introduce n-ary constructors in residual programs. **let** bindings of static pairs can be transformed into n-ary lets in residual programs:

$$\text{let}\ x = <y, z>\ \text{in}\ e \hookrightarrow \text{let}\ x_1 = y$$
$$x_2 = z$$
$$\text{in}\ e$$

But in other contexts the static pair structure can be more awkward to eliminate. For example, when the result of a dynamic conditional is a static pair, the best we can do is to move the pair structure outward where it can hopefully be removed by one of the transformations above.

$$\textbf{if } b \textbf{ \underline{then} } <x, y> \textbf{ \underline{else} } <u, v> \hookrightarrow <\textbf{if } b \textbf{ then } x \textbf{ else } u, \textbf{if } b \textbf{ then } y \textbf{ else } v>$$

This transformation leads to code duplication, as do several others involving static pairs.

Adding static pairs requires the addition of a large number of transformation rules to move them outwards and eliminate them, and it is not clear that they fit nicely into the specialisation rule framework we have presented. We have therefore left them for future work.

8.2 Polymorphism

Both the source and residual languages of our specialiser are simply typed. Allowing polymorphism in source programs seems reasonably easy, with the caveat that for a polymorphic function to be useful it must be applicable at different source types, and therefore at different residual types, which requires that it also be polyvariant. But generating polymorphic residual programs seems much more difficult.

The standard Milner polymorphic type inference algorithm relies on generalising type variables which remain uninstantiated after an expression's type is inferred. The corresponding strategy in our specialiser would be to generalise residual type variables which remain uninstantiated after an expression's specialisation is complete. But because of the demon mechanism, we do not know when specialisation of an expression *is* complete! The standard strategy is therefore inapplicable here.

Our inability to produce polymorphic residual programs is a serious deficiency. Clearly, optimal specialisation of polymorphic programs cannot be achieved until this restriction is lifted.

8.3 Controlling Polyvariance

Our **poly** construct gives us only crude control over polyvariance. For example, in an interpreter for a simply typed language we might make the *eval* function polyvariant so that it can be specialised to many different expressions. But our specialiser will then be happy to generate *many* specialisations of *eval* to the *same* expression with different static environments! In particular, the body of a λ-expression might thus be compiled several times, with different types for its free variables. This is firstly not the intention if the object language is simply-typed, and secondly may lead to non-termination on ill-typed inputs. We would like to specify that *eval* is polyvariant in its first argument, but that for each value of the first argument there should be only one specialisation to the others! There is a dual problem for polyvariant sums.

One idea would be to introduce a *polyvariant function* type, whose residual type would be a tuple of pairs with *different* first components. But it is unclear at present how to extend our implementation to handle these.

8.4 Non-termination

A related problem with our treatment of polyvariance is that it can cause the specialiser to loop on erroneous inputs, rather than report an error. For example, consider the program

$$\text{let } f = \underline{\text{fix}} \; (\lambda f.\text{poly} \; \underline{\lambda} n.(\text{lift } n, \text{spec } f \; n)) \; \underline{\text{in}} \; \text{spec } f \; 2$$

which specialises to

$$\text{let } f = \text{fix} \; (\lambda f.(2, f)) \; \text{in } f$$

Here both occurrences of **spec** f refer to the same specialisation; our implementation succeeds in unifying their residual types, and in producing the result shown. *But*, if a specialisation error is encountered later, we assume that it may be caused by this unification! We therefore backtrack and try constructing two specialisations of f instead. But of course, in this case this doesn't help. Our specialiser falls into a loop, constructing more and more identical specialisations of f, rather than reporting the error.

To avoid this we would need to use some kind of dependency-directed backtracking, where we only undo a unification if it actually contributed to the detected error. It is not clear how to do this either.

8.5 Dead Code and Subtyping

Our specialiser sometimes generates residual programs containing dead code. For example, consider the program

$$\begin{aligned}
&\underline{\text{let }} f = \lambda x.\underline{\text{case}} \; x \; \underline{\text{of}} \; \underline{In} \; y \to \text{lift } (y+1) \\
&\underline{\text{in}} \; \underline{\text{let }} g = \lambda x.\underline{\text{case}} \; x \; \underline{\text{of}} \; \underline{In} \; y \to \text{lift } (y+2) \\
&\quad \underline{\text{in}} \; \underline{\text{let }} x = \underline{In} \; 3 \\
&\quad\quad \underline{\text{in}} \; f \; x \underline{+} g \; x \underline{+} g \; (\underline{In} \; 4)
\end{aligned}$$

which is specialised to

$$\begin{aligned}
&\text{let } f = \lambda x.\text{case } x \text{ of } In_1 \; y \to 4 \\
&\quad\quad\quad\quad\quad\quad\quad\quad\quad In_2 \; y \to 5 \\
&\text{in } \; \text{let } g = \lambda x.\text{case } x \text{ of } In_1 \; y \to 5 \\
&\quad\quad\quad\quad\quad\quad\quad\quad\quad\quad In_2 \; y \to 6 \\
&\quad \text{in } \; \text{let } x = In_1 \; \bullet \\
&\quad\quad \text{in } \; f \; x + g \; x + g \; (In_2 \; \bullet)
\end{aligned}$$

Here f contains a case for $In_2 \; y$, even though it is never applied to such an argument. This case branch is therefore dead code.

The reason the dead code is generated is that g is applied to both x and $\underline{In} \; 4$, and therefore its residual type must be $(In_1 \; 3 \mid In_2 \; 4) \to \text{int}$, which forces the residual type of x to be $In_1 \; 3 \mid In_2 \; 4$. Now since f is also applied to x, it must have the same residual type as g, and so must contain cases for the same arguments.

Dead code is a problem in partial evaluation, because it is possible that generating the dead branch might lead to a specialisation time error, and so to failure of the whole specialisation. In this particular case it may be possible to avoid it by introducing *subtyping* on residual types. One would then give x the residual type In_1 3, which would be a subtype of In_1 3 | In_2 4, thus permitting x to be passed to g without forcing it to have the larger type, and in turn forcing dead code to be generated in f.

We have explained this problem in terms of polyvariant sums, but a dual example can be constructed using polyvariant products, and a similar approach using subtyping offers hope of a solution here too.

8.6 Self-application

Self-application of our partial evaluator is still some way off. To achieve it, we will need to redesign our monad carefully in order to separate the static and meta-static information held as the values of residual type variables. When the partial evaluator is specialised, residual programs will of course use a similar monad, with all the mechanism of demons, uninstantiated variables, and backtracking. Generated compilers will pass all data around via unification: reasonable enough for types, but a little curious for the program being compiled! It is interesting to wonder whether we could replace unification by a simpler, more functional mechanism in some cases.

8.7 Correctness of Partial Evaluation

We have specified a program specialiser, but we have not proved that there is any relation at all between the *semantics* of source programs, and the semantics of their specialisations! We will need to define an interpretation for specialisation judgements, and prove the inference rules sound. We leave this proof for future work.

8.8 Specialisation-Time Errors

Our specialiser is unusual in that well-typed source programs may give rise to specialisation time errors (when residual types fail to match). One referee considered that this revealed a weakness in the two-level type system:

> "It is the very definition of well-annotated two-levelness that specialisation cannot go wrong. The fact that your specialiser can reject some of its input just shows an inadequacy between your specialiser and the binding-time annotations of its source programs."

We argue that, on the contrary, the possibility of specialisation time errors is inherent in optimal specialisation of typed languages.

When a partial evaluator is used for compiling by specialising an interpreter, we can distinguish three interesting times:

- *run-time*, when the compiled code (specialised interpreter) is run,
- *compile-time*, when the interpreter is specialised to a particular program,
- *compiler-generation time*, when the interpreter is pre-processed to prepare it for specialisation.

Binding-time analysis, and any other checking of the interpreter in the absence of a particular program to specialise it to, is done at compiler-generation time. Is it reasonable to apply any criterion at compiler-generation time, which guarantees that no errors can occur at compile-time?

We claim the answer is no: it is an inherent property of compilers for typed programming languages that they refuse to compile ill-typed programs. Indeed, it is precisely *because* they reject ill-typed programs that they are able to generate code for well-typed ones that does not manipulate type tags. No analysis at compiler generation time can guarantee that all programs to be compiled will be well-typed; type errors cannot be detected earlier than compile-time.

Analogously, an optimal specialiser for typed programs must reject some inputs at specialisation time. No binding-time analysis can guarantee that specialisation time errors will not occur.

8.9 Binding-time Analysis

Our specialiser processes completely annotated programs; the programmer decides whether each value will be static or dynamic. Certainly we find a binding-time *checker* very useful, which ensures that the programmer's annotations are consistent. But most other partial evaluators use a binding-time *analyser* to decide automatically which expressions are dynamic, given a division of the program's inputs into dynamic and static. What are the prospects for coupling a binding-time analysis to our partial evaluator?

Unfortunately, we believe they are not very good. Our partial evaluator is of a different nature to other offline ones, and is less well suited to an automatic choice of binding times. Every partial evaluator admits a certain amount of freedom in this choice — there may be different ways to annotate the same program consistently. Thus one may be able to choose whether a particular expression should be static or dynamic. With a conventional partial evaluator, it is always better to choose static[3]. Binding-time analysers therefore choose the 'most static' consistent annotation. But in our case, although making types more static certainly improves the results of specialisation, it can also lead to specialisation-time errors.

For example, in the λ-calculus interpreter in section 7.4 we chose to make the universal type *Univ* a *static* sum type. As a consequence type tags are eliminated from residual programs, but at the cost of restricting the λ-terms that can be compiled by specialising this interpreter to be well-typed. If we had instead chosen to use a *dynamic* sum type, then we could have compiled all λ-terms, but type tags and checks would have remained in the residual code. In other words, the choice of binding-time here determines whether we compile a statically or dynamically typed λ-calculus. It is hard to see that such a choice can be made automatically.

On the other hand, a less ambitious form of binding-time analysis may be possible. For example, if λ-expressions are annotated static or dynamic, then perhaps applications need not be, since one can infer from the type of the function which

---

[3] Unless this leads to large or unbounded static variation — see Jones' article in this volume.

kind of application is intended. In general, if the programmer provides enough annotations that there is only one consistent way to complete them, then that completion can safely be constructed automatically.

8.10 Is Unification Desirable in a Partial Evaluator?

One may ask whether the mechanisms in our partial evaluator are overkill: maybe optimal specialisation of typed programs could be achieved in a simpler way? We think not.

Suppose we generate a compiler for a typed language by specialising a partial evaluator to a particular interpreter. If the generated compiler is not to insert type checks in the code that it generates, then it must perform type inference. To do so, it must propagate type information via unification. But type information in the generated compiler is of course just static information in the partial evaluator. It follows that the partial evaluator must propagate static information at least as effectively as unification does. We consider it very natural that a partial evaluator that can be specialised to obtain a compiler that performs type inference, should itself be based on the mechanisms of type inference.

9 Related Work

The first partial evaluator for the λ-calculus, Gomard and Jones' λMIX, also processes a two-level typed language[GJ91]. But in contrast to ours, there is only one dynamic type: **code**. Consequently residual programs are untyped. One benefit is that interpreters to be specialised by λMIX need not inject dynamic values into a universal type: no explicit type tags appear in either source or residual programs. On the other hand, the type tags are actually present in the implementation of the dynamically typed language, and there is no way to get rid of them.

Restricted forms of type specialisation have been used in the past. Romanenko's *arity raising* replaces a list whose length is known statically by a tuple[Rom90]. Launchbury generalised the idea using *projections* to divide data into a static structure containing dynamic components[Lau91]. Such a partially static structure can be replaced in the residual program by a tuple of its dynamic components. However, Launchbury's partial evaluator cannot remove type tags in general because the result of a dynamic conditional is forced to be purely dynamic, and so type tags become unknown at that point. Similarly the dynamic components cannot contain nested static parts, so their types cannot be specialised. Finally, this technique is limited to first-order programs.

Weise and Ruf describe an online method for computing the static parts of dynamic values in an untyped language [WR90]. They can even compute static parts of dynamic conditionals, by 'generalising' the static parts of the two branches. In the case that they match, the dynamic conditional has an informative static value, and in the case that they do not, it doesn't. They can handle function values by treating them as closures. However, they cannot represent disjunctive static information as we do using dynamic sums, and they do not use the information obtained to change the representation of dynamic values.

Continuation-based specialisation (invented by Consel and Danvy [CD91], and further developed by Bondorf [Bon92]) also enables dynamic conditionals to yield static results, by moving the context (represented as a continuation) into the branches. A dynamic conditional in a context C

$$C[\underline{\text{if}}\ b\ \underline{\text{then}}\ e_1\ \underline{\text{else}}\ e_2]$$

is specialised instead as

$$\underline{\text{if}}\ b\ \underline{\text{then}}\ C[e_1]\ \underline{\text{else}}\ C[e_2]$$

Obviously, if e_1 and e_2 are static, then they can be used statically in C. But in contrast to our case, it is not an error for e_1 and e_2 to have different static values — the context is simply specialised twice.

However, a continuation-based specialiser cannot be used to remove type tags. The trouble is that the context C can only be specialised to e_1 or e_2 if it is itself static: if the context simply applies a dynamic continuation then no specialisation is possible, and e_1 and e_2 are themselves forced to be dynamic. Because unboundedly many continuations may arise during an execution of most programs, making all continuations static would lead to non-termination at specialisation time. So some continuations must be dynamic, and so must their arguments therefore — including any type tags. This is enough to force type tags to be dynamic everywhere.

Mogensen has proposed a form of type specialisation which he calls *constructor specialisation*[Mog93]. Here some components of a user-defined algebraic type may be classified as static. For example, consider the type of integer lists

$$\textbf{data intlist} = Nil\,|\,Cons\ \textbf{int intlist}$$

Suppose that the integer elements are static. Then applications of *Cons* are *specialised* to their integer parameters; if *Cons* is applied to 1, 2 and 3, then specialised constructors $Cons_1$, $Cons_2$ and $Cons_3$ are defined. The residual program will then contain a specialised type

$$\textbf{data intlist}_0 = Nil\,|\,Cons_1\ \textbf{intlist}_0\,|\,Cons_2\ \textbf{intlist}_0\,|\,Cons_3\ \textbf{intlist}_0$$

instead of the original. All case expressions matching on *Cons* must also be specialised, to have a case for each new constructor. In each such case, the value of the static component is known, and so a static value has in effect been extracted from dynamic data.

However, constructor specialisation cannot remove type tags from residual programs — only specialise them. The specialisation of types is monovariant: each type in the source yields one type in the residual program. The method is limited to first order programs. But like us, Mogensen uses 'forward references' to generate the residual program out-of-order.

Mogensen's constructor specialisation was the inspiration for our polyvariant sums (section 3.8), which provide essentially the same mechanism.

Constructor specialisation has been generalised by Dussart et al. [DBV95] to be polyvariant: one data type in the source program may give rise to arbitrarily many in the residual program. Like ours, their partial evaluator collects static information about dynamic expressions which is used to decide their residual type. In this case the static information is expressed as a grammar, which should be compared to our potentially cyclic residual types. There is clearly a close relationship to our own work — but also significant differences. The static information associated with dynamic expressions is determined by abstract interpretation, not by inference as in our case. This analysis precedes specialisation, rather than being an integral part of it. Perhaps this is why it requires approximations to ensure termination, such as a restriction to so-called 'flat grammars'. In the residual programs, datatypes with constructors are transformed into datatypes with (other) constructors: in other words, tags are never eliminated altogether[4]. This is not surprising since the partial evaluator never rejects inputs as ours does; ill-typed programs can be compiled by the generated compilers. Finally, the method described is for first-order programs only, and a planned extension to higher-order requires a control-flow analysis with attendant approximations. In contrast our inference based approach handles full λ-calculus simply and naturally.

Danvy's recent work on *type-directed partial evaluation* may perhaps be related [Dan96]. Danvy 'residualises' two-level λ-terms given their type. His residual programs are typed, and it is possible to derive different terms from the same source term by residualising it at different types. But it does not seem as though his method solves the problem of type tags in residual programs.

Both λMIX and Danvy's recent work are monovariant specialisers. Both use unfolding, and can duplicate expressions in the process, but neither can duplicate expressions without unfolding. So for example, a single recursive function cannot be specialised to two mutually recursive residual functions (unfolding would be dangerous in this case). Polyvariant specialisation can be awkward in a higher-order language because recognising that two specialisations are the same may require comparing static function values. In our work, we need only compare residual function *types*, not functions themselves, and so polyvariant specialisation is unproblematic.

10 Conclusions

We have presented a new paradigm for partial evaluation, inspired by type inference. Our partial evaluator is specified in terms of *specialisation rules* that prescribe how a source expression and type should be transformed into a residual expression and type. Static information is represented in the residual types, in contrast to traditional partial evaluators which effectively represent it in the transformed expression. Thus we break the link between staticness and unfolding: a variable can be static even if the specialiser does not substitute a value for it; static information is propagated by unification, not by substitution. As a result we obtain better static information flow, and consequently stronger specialisation, than traditional partial evaluators.

We can describe our specialiser in a very modular way: each specialisation feature is tied to a particular type in the source language, with associated introduction and elimination rules. Each feature is specified independently, and features can be

---

[4] This specialiser is however optimal for a language with *only* constructor types — because then all values have some kind of tag, which need not be eliminated. See Mogensen's paper in this volume.

combined in arbitrary ways. In contrast to earlier two-level languages, we can allow free formation of types. This has led to a number of new results.

Our partial evaluator performs type specialisation: this fits naturally into the framework, since there is no reason to expect source and residual types to be the same. Ours is the first specialiser which can obtain an *arbitrary* type in the residual program by specialising one universal type in the source program.

We can allow dynamic functions to take partially static arguments and return partially static results; this is the key to optimal specialisation of typed programs, where the static information represents type information. Ours is the first optimal specialiser for a typed, higher-order language.

Ours is also the first specialiser to support both higher-order functions and constructor specialisation. This combination is powerful: we can obtain closure analysis and firstification as a simple application.

We conclude that inference-based specialisation is a very promising new approach. But our prototype specialiser suffers from a number of drawbacks, and we are already aware of several desirable extensions. There is much more work to be done.

Finally, although we have described our approach in terms of the λ-calculus, the basic idea is quite general. We see no reason why similar results should not be obtainable for other typed languages, including imperative ones.

Acknowledgements

This is an appropriate place to thank Neil Jones: not only has his pioneering work inspired myself and many others over the years, but one of his talks on a very different approach to type specialisation was the direct stimulus to the work described here. Neil, Olivier Danvy, and the anonymous referees provided exceptionally good comments on the draft of this paper, and Dirk Dussart and Peter Thiemann offered useful insights that have improved the final version. I am grateful to them all.

References

[Bon91] Anders Bondorf. Automatic autoprojection of higher order recursive equations. *Science of Computer Programming*, 17(1-3):3–34, December 1991. Selected papers of ESOP '90, the 3rd European Symposium on Programming.

[Bon92] Anders Bondorf. Improving binding times without explicit cps-conversion. In *1992 ACM Conference on Lisp and Functional Programming. San Francisco, California*, pages 1–10, June 1992.

[CD91] Charles Consel and Olivier Danvy. For a Better Support of Static Data Flow. In John Hughes, editor, *Functional Programming and Computer Architecture*, LNCS, pages 496–519. Springer-Verlag, 1991.

[Dan96] Olivier Danvy. Type-directed partial evaluation. In *Symposium on Principles of Programming Languages*. ACM, jan 1996.

[DBV95] Dirk Dussart, Eddy Bevers, and Karel De Vlaminck. Polyvariant Constructor Specialisation. In *Proc. ACM Conference on Partial Evaluation and Program Manipulation*, La Jolla, California, 1995.

[GJ91]   C. K. Gomard and N. D. Jones. A partial evaluator for the untyped lambda-calculus. *Journal of Functional Programming*, 1(1):21–70, January 1991.

[Hen91] Fritz Henglein. Efficient type inference for higher-order binding-time analysis. In J. Hughes, editor, *FPCA*, pages 448–472. 5th ACM Conference, Cambridge, MA, USA, Springer-Verlag, August 1991. Lecture Notes in Computer Science, Vol. 523.

[Lau91] J. Launchbury. *Projection Factorisations in Partial Evaluation (PhD thesis)*, volume 1 of *Distinguished Dissertations in Computer Science*. Cambridge University Press, 1991.

[Mog93] Torben Æ. Mogensen. Constructor specialization. In David Schmidt, editor, *ACM Symposium on Partial Evaluation and Semantics-Based Program Manipulation*, pages 22–32, June 1993.

[NN92]   F. Nielson and H. R. Nielson. *Two-Level Functional Languages*. Cambridge Tracts in Theoretical Computer Science. Cambridge University Press, 1992.

[Rom90] S. A. Romanenko. Arity raiser and its use in program specialisation. In *Proc. 3rd European Symposium on Programming, Lecture Notes in Computer Science Vol. 432*, pages 341–360. Springer-Verlag, May 1990.

[Wad92] P. Wadler. The essence of functional programming. In *Proceedings 1992 Symposium on principles of Programming Languages*, pages 1–14, Albuquerque, New Mexico, 1992.

[WR90]   Daniel Weise and Erik Ruf. Computing types during program specialization. Technical Report CSL-TR-90-441, Stanford Computer Science Laboratory, October 1990.

What *Not* to Do When Writing an Interpreter for Specialisation

Neil D. Jones*

DIKU, University of Copenhagen
e-mail: `neil@diku.dk`

Abstract. A partial evaluator, given a program and a known "static" part of its input data, outputs a *specialised* or *residual* program in which computations depending only on the static data have been performed in advance.

Ideally the partial evaluator would be a "black box" able to extract nontrivial static computations whenever possible; which never fails to terminate; and which always produces residual programs of reasonable size and maximal efficiency, so all possible static computations have been done. *Practically* speaking, partial evaluators often fall short of this goal; they sometimes loop, sometimes pessimise, and can explode code size.

A partial evaluator is analogous to a spirited horse: while impressive results can be obtained when used well, the user must know what he/she is doing. Our thesis is that *this knowledge can be communicated* to new users of these tools.

This paper presents a series of examples, concentrating on a quite broad and on the whole quite successful application area: using specialisation to remove interpretational overhead. It presents both positive and negative examples, to illustrate the effects of program style on the efficiency and size of the of target programs obtained by specialising an interpreter with respect to a known source program. It concludes with a checklist summarising what was learned from the examples, discussions, and problem analyses.

1 Introduction

1.1 The phenomena

In my opinion (and, I hope, in yours too after looking at the following examples), there exist a number of *real phenomena* in specialisation, i.e. frequently occurring specialisation problems that are nontrivial to solve; there exist styles of programming that can be expected to give *any* partial evaluator difficulties; and one can *learn and communicate* programming style that leads to good specialisation, i.e. high speedups without explosion of code size.

---

* This research was partially supported by the Danish *DART* project, and the Esprit BRA *Atlantique*.

1.2 Making implicit knowledge explicit

Some of the following examples will make the experienced reader grit his or her teeth, saying "I would never dream of programming my interpreter in such an absurd way!" This is indeed true — but inexperienced users often commit just these errors of thought or of programming style (I speak from experience with students.) A major point of this article is to make manifest some of the *implicit knowledge* we have acquired in our field, so newcomers can avoid encountering and having to figure out how to solve the same problems in "the school of hard knocks."

1.3 Dependence on particular specialisation algorithms

The advice alluded to in this paper's title would seem, at least to some extent, relative to which *class of specialisation algorithms* is used. I have carefully written to avoid having to take account of remarks of the form "yes, but I can solve that problem using feature XXX of my partial evaluator."

Accounting for such possible remarks, followed by responses ("even so, ..."), etc. could easily tend to lead to an infinite regress, or to a protracted discussion whose line would be hard to follow. Even worse, it would make it hard at the end to say what really had been accomplished by the discussion.

2 Concepts and notations

We use familiar notations, for example D is a data set that contains all first-order values, including *all program texts*. Inputs may be paired, e.g. "d.e" is in D if both d and e are in D. We may also write (d.e) or (d,e). For concreteness the reader may think of D as Lisp/Scheme lists, and programs as written in Scheme. However the points below are not language-dependent, and some example interpreters will be written in imperative languages.

The *semantic function* of program p is a partial function $[\![p]\!] : D \to D \cup \{\bot\}$, so $[\![p]\!](d) = d' \in D$ is the result of running p on input $d \in D$ (and is $\bot$ if p fails to terminate on d.)

We will assume the underlying implementation language is defined by an (unspecified) operational semantics. Computations are given by *sequences* (for imperative languages) or, more generally, by *computation trees*.

Further, program run time is assumed roughly proportional to the size of the computation tree deducing $[\![p]\!](d) = d'$. (This will become relevant in the discussion of linear speedup.) Notation: $time_p(d) \in I\!N$ is the time taken to compute $[\![p]\!](d)$ (and is ∞ if p fails to terminate on d.)

Given program p and "static" input $s \in D$, program p_s is the *result of specialising* p *to* s if $[\![p]\!](s.d) = [\![p_s]\!](d)$ for every "dynamic" input $d \in D$. Well-known terms are to call p_s a *residual program* for p with respect to s, or a version of p *specialised to* s[2].

A *partial evaluator* (or *specialiser*) is a program mix such that for every program p and "static" input s $\in D$, program $[\![mix]\!](p.s)$ is a version of p specialised to s.

Clearly a trivial mix is easy to build (e.g. by Kleene's *s-m-n* Theorem of the 1930s.) The practical goal is to make $p_s = [\![mix]\!](p.s)$ *as efficient as possible*, by performing many of p's computations — ideally, all those that depend on s alone. The *speedup* realised by mix on program p and static input s is the following ratio:

$$\text{speedup}_s(d) = \frac{time_p(s, d)}{time_{p_s}(d)}$$

(Note that for each static input s it is a function of d.)

Some programs are well-suited to specialisation, yielding substantial speedups, and others are not. Given a specialiser mix, a *binding-time improvement* is the transformation of program p into an equivalent program q such that $[\![p]\!] = [\![q]\!]$, but specialisation of q to various s gives larger speedups than specialisation of p to the same s.

Other languages. If unspecified, as above, we assume a standard implementation language L is intended. Otherwise, if another language S is used, we make this explicit as follows. The *semantic function* of a program p is a partial function $[\![p]\!]^S : D \to D \cup \{\perp\}$, so $[\![p]\!]^S(d)$ is the result of running p on input $d \in D$ ($\perp$ if p fails to terminate on d.) Further, $time_p^S(d)$ is the time taken to compute $[\![p]\!]^S(d)$ (and is ∞ if p fails to terminate on d.)

Interpreters. Program int is an *interpreter for language* S if for all S-programs s and data $d \in D$

$$[\![int]\!](s.d) = [\![s]\!]^S(d)$$

3 Assumptions in this paper

For definiteness and to avoid having to "hit a moving target," I now list the assumptions of this paper. Readers are welcome to reply by describing how other techniques can solve some or all of these problems; but should be honest enough to admit it if their techniques introduce yet other problems.

---

[2] This definition concerns only correctness of specialisation, and takes no account of how specialisation is done. It is thus a purely *extensional* definition, ignoring "intensional" features of p such as efficiency or size; these are treated for concrete examples in the following text. A more intensional view is often taken in logic programming [7], and sometimes by other authors in functional and imperative programming.

3.1 Restrictions in this discussion

1. The programs to be specialised are assumed expressed in an *untyped first-order functional* language, using an informal syntax. Consequently all our interpreter texts, etc. are in this form; however the *languages they interpret* may be functional, imperative, higher-order, logic, etc.

2. Offline specialisation is assumed: before actual specialisation begins, all of program p's operations and calls or other control transfers are *annotated* as either **static**: do at specialisation time; or as **dynamic**: generate code to be executed at run time.

3. Every function parameter (in the program to be specialised) is either *totally static* or *totally dynamic*. Thus there is no *partially static data* in these examples.

4. We assume that a BTA (*binding-time analysis*) does the annotations, e.g. separately as in Schism, or integrated into the text as in Similix:

   ```
   append(X_S,Y_D) = if_S  X =_S 'nil then Y
                     else cons_S(hd_S(X), append_S(tl_S X, Y))
   ```

5. No *distributivity rules* are used, e.g. to transform from 1 to 2 below:

   ```
   1: static1  + (if dynamic_test then static2 else static3)
   2: if dynamic_test then (static1+static2) else (static1+static3)
   ```

   This has been called "CPS specialisation" — a rather unfortunate name in my opinion since the concept makes perfect sense without continuations, or even without higher-order functions. For instance, distributivity or "CPS specialisation" can even be done in logic programming:

   ```
   p(D, Result) :- test(D, S), Result is S1 + S.
   test([],     S2).
   test([X|Xs], S3).
   ```

   is equivalent to

   ```
   p([], Result)      :- Result is S1 + S2.
   p([X|Xs], Result) :- Result is S1 + S3.
   ```

6. *The Trick* or η-conversion will not be used unless explicitly stated. This is a programming device (described in [6]) to make static otherwise dynamic values, provided they are known to be of bounded static variation (this term is defined below.)

7. No global optimisations are done, e.g.

   dead code elimination (a logic programming analog is removing code that is certain to fail); or

   common subexpression elimination, especially ones containing function calls (a logic programming analog is removing duplicated goals.)

3.2 Remarks on the restrictions

The lack of partially static data can be overcome in more than one way; for
instance it is of less significance for online specialisers such as Fuse [13], supercompilation [12], or most logic programming specialisers [10, 4]; but then new
problems arise concerning control, termination, etc.

An offline specialiser such as Similix [1] or Schism [2] usually does analyses,
often involving some form of tree grammar [8], to statically describe all possible
runtime data shapes and to exploit this. Alternatively, a *bifurcation* transformation [9, 3] splits a program with partially static data into one part with
completely static data, and another part with both static and dynamic data.

Online and offline specialisation. I maintain that many of specialisation *problems*
are essentially independent of which type of specialisation *algorithm* one uses,
or of whether one is specialising functional, logic, or imperative programs. This
holds even though a particular problem might manifest itself in different ways,
e.g. in an offline functional specialiser as a *nontermination problem*, or in logic
programming as causing an *unnecessarily conservative* specialisation, leading to
little or no speedup. Further, I claim that:

– Several of the "binding-time improvements" exemplified below to avoid non-
  termination or code size explosion would improve specialisation of logic programs as well as functional programs.
– Binding-time improvements done to improve offline specialiser results often
  improve online specialisation results too. This can either be by causing more
  to be statically computable, or by reducing the size of the residual program.

4 Bounded static variation: the key to termination of the specialiser

Nontermination at specialisation time can occur for one of two reasons: an

– Attempt to build an *infinitely large* command, expression or literal; or an
– Attempt to build a residual program containing *infinitely many* program
  points (labels, defined function, or procedures.)

The basic cause is the same: the specialiser's *unfolding strategy* is the main cause
of the one or the other misbehaviour. In either case nontermination makes a
specialiser less suitable for use by nonexperts, and *quite unsuitable for automatic
use*. Further, failure to terminate gives the user very little to go on to discover
the problem's cause, in order to repair it.

Two attitudes to nontermination have been seen: in functional programming,
infinite static loops are often seen as the user's fault, so there is no need for the
specialiser to account for them. Logic programming most often requires that
the specialiser *always terminate*. One reason is the Prolog "negation as finite
failure" semantics, which means that changing termination properties can change

semantics, and even answer sets. Each view can be (and has been) both defended and attacked.

Current work on functional program specialisation concerns a BTA conservative enough to guarantee that specialisation always terminates, and still gives good results when specialising interpreters [5].

4.1 Pachinko, execution, and specialisation

Normal execution follows only one sequential control thread. Specialisation, however, must account for *all possible control threads* the subject program could enter into, for all possible dynamic inputs.

An analogy: the popular Japanese "Pachinko" entertainment involves steel balls that fall through a lattice of pins. Sequential execution corresponds to dropping only one ball, which thus traverses only one trajectory. On the other hand, specialisation to static input s corresponds to dropping an infinite set of balls at once — all those which share s as given static input, but have *all possible* dynamic input values. Reasoning about specialisation, e.g. residual program finiteness or efficiency, requires reasoning about such a (most often infinite) set of trajectories.

Reachable states. Let function[3] f defined in program p have number of parameters denoted by "arity(f)" and let parameter values range over the set V. The ith parameter of f will be writen as f_i.

A *state* is a pair $(f, \overline{\alpha})$ where $\overline{\alpha} \in V^{\text{arity}(f)}$. Notation: $\overline{\alpha}_i$ is the ith component of parameter tuple $\overline{\alpha} \in V^{\text{arity}(f)}$. Thus $\overline{\alpha}_i$ is the value of f_i in state $(f, \overline{\alpha})$.

State $(f, \overline{\alpha})$ can *reach* state $(g, \overline{\beta})$, written $(f, \overline{\alpha}) \rightarrow^* (g, \overline{\beta})$, if computation of f on parameter values $\overline{\alpha}$ directly requires the value of g on parameter values $\overline{\beta}$. (Formal definition of this is straightforward.)

4.2 Definition of bounded static variation

Let ';' be the parameter *tuple concatenation operator*, suppose $f1$ is the initial (entry) function[3] of program p, and let $s, d \in I\!N$, where $s + d = \text{arity}(f1)$. We assume (for simplicity) that the first s parameters of $f1$ are static, and the remaining d parameters are dynamic. The set of *statically reachable states* $S\mathcal{R}(\overline{\sigma})$ consists of all states $(f, \overline{\alpha})$ reachable in 0, 1, or more steps from some initial call with $\overline{\sigma} \in V^s$ as static program input, and an arbitrary dynamic input $\overline{\delta}$:

$$S\mathcal{R}(\overline{\sigma}) = \{(f, \overline{\alpha}) \mid \exists \delta \in V^d : (f1, \overline{\sigma}; \overline{\delta}) \rightarrow^* (f, \overline{\alpha})\}$$

The ith parameter f_i of f is of *bounded static variation*, written BSV(f_i), iff for all $\overline{\sigma} \in V^s$, the following set is finite:

$$\{\overline{\alpha}_i \mid (f, \overline{\alpha}) \in S\mathcal{R}(\overline{\sigma})\}$$

---

[3] These definitions are easy to extend to imperative languages, and are not difficult to extend to logic programming.

This captures the intuitive notion that f's ith parameter only varies finitely during all computations in which the static program input is fixed to some $\bar{\sigma}$, and dynamic program input varies freely.

Such a parameter may, in principle, be classified as "static." Most such parameters are directly computable from the static program inputs. Exceptions do occur, for example the following expression is of BSV even if x is dynamic:

```
if x mod 2 = 0 then 'EVEN else 'ODD
```

5   Compositionality and semicompositionality of interpreters

Suppose each of an interpreter's function parameters has been classified as either nonsyntactic, or as *syntactic*, in which case its values range only over phrases from the source language — perhaps or perhaps not extracted from the interpreted source program, henceforth called src.

The interpreter is defined to be **compositional** if for any definition of a function with syntactic parameters, the syntactic parameters of any subcall involving recursion are always *proper substructures of the calling function's* syntactic parameters. Clearly in any computation by a compositional interpreter, the syntactic parameters of any functions called are necessarily substructures of the source program src being interpreted. Thus they are quite obviously of BSV.

The compositionality requirement ensures that the interpreter can be specialised with respect to its static input src by simple unfolding — a process *guaranteed to terminate* (though perhaps not fully satisfactory, unless additional specialisation-time computations are done.)

A weaker requirement, also guaranteeing BSV, is for the interpreter to be **semicompositional**, meaning that called parameters must be *substructures of the original source program* src, but need not decrease locally in every call.

Semicompositionality can even allow syntactic parameters to grow; the only requirement is that the set of their values is limited to range over the set of all substructures of src (perhaps including the whole of src itself.) Consequently, **while**'s meaning can be defined in terms of itself, and procedure calls may be elaborated by applying an execution funtion to the body of the called procedure (both of which violate strict compositionality.)

Semicompositionality does not guarantee termination at run time; but it does guarantee finiteness of the set of specialised program points — so *termination of specialisation* can be ensured by a natural unfolding strategy (unfold, unless this function has been seen before with just these static parameter values.)

6   Where do interpreters come from?

An interpreter is just a program. It can be used to define a new language (so a source program meaning is whatever the interpreter yields when given it and *its* input); or to implement a language already defined by other means, e.g. by an operational or denotational semantics.

Rules for Expressions

Constant :	$\langle S, M, c \cdot C \rangle$	$\Rightarrow \langle c \cdot S, M, C \rangle$
Variable :	$\langle S, M, \mathbf{x}i \cdot C \rangle$	$\Rightarrow \langle M(\mathbf{x}i) \cdot S, M, C \rangle$
Composite :	$\langle S, M, (e_1 \, op \, e_2) \cdot C \rangle$	$\Rightarrow \langle S, M, e_1 \cdot e_2 \cdot op \cdot C \rangle$
Operator :	$\langle \underline{n_2} \cdot \underline{n_1} \cdot S, M, op \cdot C \rangle$	$\Rightarrow \langle \underline{n_1 \, op \, n_2} \cdot S, M, C \rangle$

Rules for Programs

Null :	$\langle S, M, \mathtt{null} \cdot C \rangle$	$\Rightarrow \langle S, M, C \rangle$
Assign :	$\langle S, M, (\mathbf{x}i\text{:=}e) \cdot C \rangle$	$\Rightarrow \langle i \cdot S, M, e \cdot \mathbf{assign} \cdot C \rangle$
Sequence :	$\langle S, M, (p_1 \,;\, p_2) \cdot C \rangle$	$\Rightarrow \langle S, M, p_1 \cdot p_2 \cdot C \rangle$
Test :	$\langle S, M, (\mathtt{if}\, b\, \mathtt{then}\, p_1\, \mathtt{else}\, p_2) \cdot C \rangle$	$\Rightarrow \langle p_1 \cdot p_2 \cdot S, M, b \cdot \mathbf{if} \cdot C \rangle$
Loop :	$\langle S, M, (\mathtt{while}\, b\, \mathtt{do}\, p_1) \cdot C \rangle$	$\Rightarrow \langle b \cdot p_1 \cdot S, M, b \cdot \mathbf{while} \cdot C \rangle$

Rules for assign, if and while

$$\langle \underline{n} \cdot i \cdot S, M, \mathbf{assign} \cdot C \rangle \quad \Rightarrow \langle S, M[\mathbf{x}i \mapsto \underline{n}], C \rangle$$

$$\langle \mathbf{true} \cdot p_1 \cdot p_2 \cdot S, M, \mathbf{if} \cdot C \rangle \quad \Rightarrow \langle S, M, p_1 \cdot C \rangle$$

$$\langle \mathbf{false} \cdot p_1 \cdot p_2 \cdot S, M, \mathbf{if} \cdot C \rangle \quad \Rightarrow \langle S, M, p_2 \cdot C \rangle$$

$$\langle \mathbf{true} \cdot b \cdot p_1 \cdot S, M, \mathbf{while} \cdot C \rangle \Rightarrow \langle S, M, p_1 \cdot (\mathtt{while}\, b\, \mathtt{do}\, p_1) \cdot C \rangle$$

$$\langle \mathbf{false} \cdot b \cdot p_1 \cdot S, M, \mathbf{while} \cdot C \rangle \Rightarrow \langle S, M, C \rangle$$

Figure 6.1: Instructional interpreter.

6.1 Interpreters derived from execution models

Many interpreters simply embody some model of runtime execution, e.g. Pascal's "stack of activation records" or Algol 60's "thunk" mechanism. Following is a simple example.

An interpreter used for instruction at DIKU.

Computation is by a linear sequence

$$(S_1, M_1, C_1) \to (S_2, M_2, C_2) \to \ldots$$

of states of form (S, M, C). S is a *computation* stack, $M : \{\mathbf{x}0, \mathbf{x}1, \ldots\} \to Value$ is a *memory* containing the values of variables $\mathbf{x}i$, and C is a *control* stack, containing bits of commands and expressions that remain to be evaluated/executed. (Remark: C is in essence a materialisation in the form of data of the program's *continuation* from the current point of execution.)

For readability we describe this interpreter (call it `int-instruct`) by a set of transition rules in Figure 6.1. Note that the C component is neither compositional nor semicompositional. The underlines, e.g. $\underline{n}$, indicate numeric runtime values, and $M[\mathbf{x}i \mapsto \underline{n}]$ is a memory M' identical to M, except that $M'(\mathbf{x}i) = \underline{n}$.

6.2   Interpreters derived from denotational semantics

A *denotational semantics* [11] consists of

- a collection of *domain equations* specifying the partially ordered value sets
  to which the meanings (denotations) of program pieces and auxiliaries such
  as environments will belong, and
- a collection of *semantic functions* mapping program pieces to their meanings
  in a compositional way (as defined in Section 5.)

In practice a denotational semantics resembles a program in a modern functional
language such as ML, Haskell, or Scheme. Indeed the designers of such languages
have to a certain extent built denotational concepts into them. One instance
is syntax and implementation techniques to make programs with higher-order
functions easy to write and not too expensive to use. Another notable instance
is *continuations*, which have come from the metalevel of language descriptions
(an invention devised to formalise **goto**) down to the subject language level.

   A difference from operational definitions is that fixpoints are conceptually
evaluated "all at once" in denotational semantics, and only unfolded "upon demand" in functional languages. Still, the net effect is that many denotational
language definitions can simply be transliterated into functional programs.

   One problem with a denotational semantics is that it necessarily uses a "universal domain," capable of expressing *all possible run-time values* of all programs
that can be given meaning. This, combined with the requirement of compositionality, often leads to an (over-)abundance of higher-order functions. These two
together imply that domain definitions very often must be both *recursive and
higher-order*, creating both mathematical and implementational complications
(e.g. reflexive domains and contravariance in a function space functor.)

   Examples are familiar, and omitted for brevity.

6.3   Interpreters derived from operational semantics

Operational semantics seems more manageable, since emphasis is on judgements
formed from first-order objects (although finite functions are allowed.) They
come in two flavours: *big-step* in which a judgement is of form

   $\ldots \vdash Exp \Rightarrow$ Final answer

and *small-step* in which a judgement is of form

   $\ldots \vdash Exp \Rightarrow Exp'$

which describes expression evaluation by reducing one expression repeatedly to
another, until a final answer is obtained. In both cases a language definition is
a set of *inference rules*. A judgement is proven to hold by constructing a proof
tree with it as root, and where each local subtree is an instance of an inference
rule. Examples are omitted for brevity, but the approaches should be clear from
the following program implementation examples.

```
; Type is: Program x Program_value -> Output_value

Run(pgm, input) = Eval(e1, ns1, cons(input, 'nil), pgm) where
                        e1  = lookbody(first_fcn(pgm), pgm)
                        ns1 = lookfcns(first_fcn(pgm), pgm)

; Type is: Expression x Namelist x Valuelist x Program ->
Value

Eval(e, ns, vs, pgm) =    case e of
  constant             : constant
  'X                   : lookparams(X, ns, vs)

  '(e1 binop e2)       : apply(binop, v1, v2) where
                              v1 = Eval(e1, ns, vs, pgm)
                              v2 = Eval(e2, ns, vs, pgm)

  '(if e0 e1 e2)       : if  Eval(e0, ns, vs, pgm)
                              then  Eval(e1, ns, vs, pgm)
                              else  Eval(e2, ns, vs, pgm)

  '(call f es)  : Eval(e1, ns1, vs1, pgm) where
                              e1  = lookbody(f, pgm)
                              ns1 = lookfcns(f, pgm)
                              vs1 = Evlist(es, ns, vs, pgm)

Evlist(es, ns, vs, pgm) =    case es of
                'nil          : nil
                'cons(e1 es1) : cons(Eval(e1, ns, vs, pgm),
                                     Evlist(es1, ns, vs, pgm))
```

Figure 6.2: Big-step semantics in program form.

Transliterating these two types of operational semantics into program form gives interpreters of rather different characteristics. Big-step semantics are conceptually nearer denotational semantics than small-step semantics, since source syntax and program meanings are clearly separated. Small-step semantics work by symbolic source-to-source code reduction, and so are nearer equational or rewrite theories, for example traditional treatments of the λ-calculus.

An interpreter derived from a big-step operational semantics. The interpreter int-big-step of Figure 6.2 implements a "big-step" semantics. The program has only one input, but its internal functions may have any number of parameters. This may be seen in the interpretation of (call f es).

Interpreters derived from small-step operational semantics.

At first sight, a small-step operational semantics seems quite unsuitable for specialisation. A familiar example is the usual definition of reducibility in the lambda calculus. This consists of a few rules for reduction, e.g. α, β, η, and *context rules* stating that these can be applied when occuring inside other syntactic constructs. Problems with direct implementation include:

- *Nondeterminism*: many redexes may be reducible within the same λ-expression;
- *Nondirectionality of computation*: rewriting may occur either from left to right or vice versa (conversion versus reduction); and
- *Syntax rewriting*: the subject program's syntax is continually changed, in ways impossible statically to predict while specialising an interpreter.

These are also problems for implementations, often resolved as follows:

- Nondeterminism: reduction is sometimes restricted to occur only from the outermost syntactic operator, using call-by-value or some other fixed strategy;
- Nondirectionality: rewriting occurs only from left to right, until a normal form is obtained.

More generally, nondeterminism is often resolved by defining explicit *evaluation contexts* $C[]$. Each is an "expression with a hole in it" indicated by the $[]$. Determinism may be achieved by defining evaluation contexts so the *unique decomposition property* holds: any expression E has exactly one decomposition of form $E = C[E']$ where $C[]$ is an evaluation context. Given this, computation proceeds through a series of rewritings of such configurations.

The problem of syntax rewriting causes particular problems for specialisation. The reason is that rewriting often leads to an infinity of different specialisation-time values. For example, this can occur in the λ-calculus if β-reduction is implemented by substitution in an expression with recursion, either implicitly by the Y compinator or explicitly by a `fix` construct.

One solution is to use *closures* instead of rewriting, essentially a "lazy" form of β-reduction. This easily allows building a semicompositional big-step interpreter, but problems still remain for small-step interpreters, for example dealing with so-called "delta rules.".

Some small-step semantics have a property that can be thought of as *dual to semicompositionality*: every decomposition $E = C[E']$ that occurs in a given computation is such that $C[]$ consists of *the original program with a hole in it*, and E' is a normal form value, e.g. a number or a closure.

Such a dual semicompositional semantics can usually be specialised well. The condition is violated, however (for an example,) if the semantics implements function or procedure calls by substituting the body of the called function or procedure in place of the call itself (a similar example is seen in Section 7.2 below.)

Rules for Expressions

Constant : $\langle S, M, c \cdot C \rangle$ $\Rightarrow \langle c \cdot S, M, C \rangle$

Variable : $\langle S, M, \mathbf{x}i \cdot C \rangle$ $\Rightarrow \langle M(\mathbf{x}i) \cdot S, M, C \rangle$

Composite : $\langle S, M, (e_1 \, op \, e_2) \cdot C \rangle$ $\Rightarrow \langle S, M, e_1 \cdot e_2 \cdot op \cdot C \rangle$

Operator : $\langle \underline{n_2} \cdot \underline{n_1} \cdot S, M, op \cdot C \rangle \Rightarrow \langle \underline{n_1 \, op \, n_2} \cdot S, M, C \rangle$

Rules for Programs

Null : $\langle S, M, \mathtt{null} \cdot C \rangle$ $\Rightarrow \langle S, M, C \rangle$

Assign : $\langle S, M, (\mathbf{x}i{:=}e) \cdot C \rangle$ $\Rightarrow \langle S, M, e \cdot \mathbf{assign} \cdot i \cdot C \rangle$

Seq. : $\langle S, M, (p_1 \, ; p_2) \cdot C \rangle$ $\Rightarrow \langle S, M, p_1 \cdot p_2 \cdot C \rangle$

Test : $\langle S, M, (\mathtt{if} \, b \, \mathtt{then} \, p_1 \, \mathtt{else} \, p_2) \cdot C \rangle$ $\Rightarrow \langle S, M, b \cdot \mathbf{if} \cdot p_1 \cdot p_2 \cdot C \rangle$

Loop : $\langle S, M, \ p \cdot C \rangle$ if $p = (\mathtt{while} \, b \, \mathtt{do} \, p_1) \Rightarrow \langle S, M, b \cdot \mathbf{while} \cdot p_1 \cdot p \cdot C \rangle$

Rules for assign, if and while

$\langle \underline{n} \cdot S, M, \mathbf{assign} \cdot i \cdot C \rangle$ $\Rightarrow \langle S, M[\mathbf{x}i \mapsto \underline{n}], C \rangle$

$\langle \mathbf{true} \cdot S, M, \mathbf{if} \cdot p_1 \cdot p_2 \cdot C \rangle$ $\Rightarrow \langle S, M, p_1 \cdot C \rangle$

$\langle \mathbf{false} \cdot S, M, \mathbf{if} \cdot p_1 \cdot p_2 \cdot C \rangle$ $\Rightarrow \langle S, M, p_2 \cdot C \rangle$

$\langle \mathbf{true} \cdot S, M, \mathbf{while} \cdot p_1 \cdot p \cdot C \rangle$ $\Rightarrow \langle S, M, p_1 \cdot p \cdot C \rangle$

$\langle \mathbf{false} \cdot S, M, \mathbf{while} \cdot p_1 \cdot p \cdot C \rangle \Rightarrow \langle S, M, C \rangle$

Figure 7.1: Modified instructional interpreter.

7 Bounded or unbounded static variation?

7.1 Analysis of the instructional interpreter

The interpreter `int-instruct` of Figure 6.1 works quite well for computation and proof, and has been used for many exercises and proofs of program properties in the course "Introduction to Semantics." On the other hand, it does not specialise at all well! The source of the problem: suppose one is given the source program p, i.e. the initial control stack contents are $C = \mathrm{p} \cdot ()$, but that the memory M is unknown, i.e. dynamic.

Clearly the value stack S must also be dynamic, since it receives values from M as in the second transition rule. But this implies that *anything* put into S and then retrieved from it again must also be dynamic. In particular this includes: the index i of a variable to be assigned; the **then** and **else** branches of an **if** statement; and the test of a **while** statement. Consequently *all of these* become dynamic, and so essentially no specialisation at all occurs.

A better version for specialisation.

The problem is easy to fix: just place the above-mentioned syntactic entities on the *control stack*: the index i of a variable to be assigned; the **then** and **else** branches of an **if** statement; and the test of a **while** statement. This leads to the interpreter of Figure 7.1, again as a set of transition rules.

Bounded static variation of the control stack. In this version stack C is built up only from pieces of the original program. Further, given any one source program C takes on only finitely many different possible values. Even though C can grow when a **while** command is processed, it is easy to see that it cannot grow unboundely for any one, fixed, source program. Thus C may safely be annotated as "static."

This version specialises much better. The effect is to yield a target program consisting of labeled transitions from one (S, M) pair to another — in essence with one transition (more or less) for each point in the original program, and no source code at all. Many of these transitions involve no change to either S or M, and so are removable by a trivial "transition compression."

7.2 A small but problematic extension: procedures

Procedures are easily added by adding a fourth component $(S, M, C, Pdefs)$ where $Pdefs$ is a list of mutually recursive procedure definitions. A procedure call is handled by looking up the procedure's name in $Pdefs$, and replacing the call by the body of the called procedure.

Rule for Procedure declarations
$\langle S, M, (\textbf{procedure } P : p) \cdot C, \; Pdefs \rangle \Rightarrow \langle S, M, C, \; P : p \cdot Pdefs \rangle$

Rule for Procedure calls
$\langle S, M, (\textbf{call } P) \cdot C, \ldots P : p \ldots \rangle \qquad \Rightarrow \langle S, M, \; p \cdot C, \ldots P : p \ldots \rangle$

Even though this looks quite innocent, it causes control stack C *no longer to be of bounded static variation.* To see why, consider say the factorial function defined recursively:

```
Procedure Fac :
if N = 0 then Result := 1
else {N := N-1; call Fac; N := N+1; Result:= N * Result}
```

The control stack's depth will be proportional to the initial value of N, which is dynamic! The result: an unpleasant choice between infinite specialisation on the one hand (for any recursive procedure); or, on the other hand, classifying C as dynamic, which will result in the existence of source code at run time, and very little speedup.

Can this problem be solved? Yes, by using "the trick." The point is that even though $Pdefs$ is a dynamic data structure, each of its components comes from the source program p. This fact can be exploited to modify the interpreter so as gain better specialisation.

A sketch: add another procedure call rule, to make the procedure "return" explicit:

Rules for Procedure calls

$$\langle S, M, (\textbf{call } P) \cdot C, \ldots P : p \ldots \rangle \Rightarrow \langle S, M, \ p \cdot \textbf{return} \cdot C, \ldots P : p \ldots \rangle$$
$$\langle S, M, \textbf{return} \ \cdot C, \ldots P : p \ldots \rangle \Rightarrow \langle S, M, C, \ldots P : p \ldots \rangle$$

Interestingly, use of "the trick" leads to something close to the target code "return address," widely used in pragmatic compiler construction. *Claim* (easy to verify): any possible C stack top entry below **return** can only be a command appearing in the source program.

A list **Tops** of all such can thus be precomputed from the source program, and so is of BSV. Now program the **return** transition as follows: pop the top of C off, and compare it with the elements of **Tops**. Once an equality with $\textbf{Tops}_i$ is found (as it must be,) apply the transitions of Figure 7.1, doing the pattern matching against $\textbf{Tops}_i$.

The comparison with **Tops** entries will specialise into a series of tests and branches, which realise the procedure return. (Ideally this could be done even faster, by an indirect jump.) In this way all pattern matching will become static, and source text will be used at run time only to implement the return.

The exact form of the source text as used in these comparisons is in fact irrelevant, since its only function is to determine where in the target program control is to be transferred — and so it can be replaced by a *token*, one for each command in **Tops**. Such tokens are in effect return addresses.

7.3 Analysis of the "big-step" interpreter

Interpreter `int-big-step` from Figure 6.2 specialises well. Even though not compositional (as defined in Section 6.2), it is *semicompositional* since the parameters e, ns, and pgm of Eval are always substructures of the original source program (not necessarily proper.)

In this case recursion causes no problems; there is no stack, and nothing can grow unboundedly as in the extended instructional interpreter, or as in many small-step semantics.

A non-semicompositional variant.

Now consider the interpreter of Figure 6.2, extended by a "LET" construction. This is easy to modify by adding an extra CASE:

```
Eval(e, ns, vs, pgm) =    case e of ...

    '(let X = e1 in e2) : Eval(e2, cons('X, ns), cons(v1, vs), pgm)
                    where   v1 = Eval(e1, ns, vs, pgm)
```

With this change, parameter ns can take on values that are *not substructures of* pgm. Now ns can grow (and without limit) since more deeply nested levels of let expressions will give rise to longer lists ns. Nonetheless, ns *only grows when* e *shrinks*. Further, it can be reset by a function call, but only to values that are part of pgm. Consequently, for any fixed source program, parameter ns *cannot grow unboundedly as a function of the size* of `int-big-step`'s static input `pgm`, and so is of bounded static variation.

7.4 Dynamic binding

Suppose in this interpreter the "function call" construction were implemented differently, as follows:

```
Eval(e, ns, vs, pgm) =    case e of   ...

'(call f es): Eval(e1, append(ns1,ns), append(vs1,vs), pgm) where
                       e1  = lookbody(f, pgm)
                       ns1 = lookfcns(f, pgm)
                       vs1 = Evlist(es, ns, vs, pgm)
```

This can easily be seen to cause ns to become of *unbounded static variation*. Interestingly, the dynamic name binding in the call has an indirect effect on `Eval`. In order to avoid nontermination od specialisation, we must classify the interpreter parameter ns as dynamic. Intuitively, the reason is that the length of ns is no longer tied to any syntactic property of `pgm`. For more technical details, see [5].

The consequence is (as in Lisp) that target programs obtained by specialising `int-big-step` will contain parameter *names* as well as their values, and function `lookparams` will become a run-time procedure rather than a specialisation-time one, substantially increasing target program running times and space usage.

8 On code explosion

Big problems can arise even when everything not classified as dynamic is of bounded static variation!!

8.1 Dead static parameters

A parameter is *semantically dead* at a program point if changes to its value cannot affect the output of the current program. Syntactic approximations to this property are widely used in optimising compilers, especially to minimise register usage.

Now the size of specialised program p_s critically depends on the number of its *specialised program points*, each of form $\ell_{(s_1,...,s_k)}$ where ℓ is one of p's program points, and $(s_1, \ldots, s_k)$ are the values of static parameters whose scope includes point ℓ.

Clearly dead static parameters will merely increase the size of specialised program p_s, without changing its computation in any way – so removal of dead static parameters can reduce its size. Our first experience with this problem, for a simple imperative language (see [6],) was that not acounting for dead static variables led to a residual program 500 times larger!

8.2 Synchronicity in static parameter variation

A good example: binary search. The following imperative program p performs binary search in an ordered (increasing) table $T_0, \ldots, T_n$ where $n = 2^m - 1$ and with initial call Find(T, 0, 2^{m-1}, x). Parameter x is the target to be found, i points to a position in the table, and delta is the size of the portion i...i + delta of the table currently being searched.

```
Find(T, i, delta, x) =
  Loop: if delta = 0 then
              if x = T[i] then return(i) else return(NOTFOUND);
          if x >= T[i+delta] then i := i + delta;
          delta := delta/2;
          goto Loop
```

We begin by assuming that delta is classified as static and that i is dynamic Using a term from [6], the program is *weakly oblivious*, since the comparison with x does not affect the value assigned to delta.

Specialising with respect to static initial delta $= 2^{3-1} = 4$ and dynamic i gives program p_8:

```
        if x >= T[i+4] then i := i+4;
        if x >= T[i+2] then i := i+2;
        if x >= T[i+1] then i := i+1;
        if  x = T[i]   then return(i) else return(NOTFOUND)
```

In general p_n runs in time $O(\log(n))$, and with a better constant coefficient than the original general program. Moreover, it has size $O(\log(n))$ — acceptable for all but extremely large tables.

A bad example: binary search. To illustrate the problems that can occur, consider the same binary search program above with n static. One may certainly classify both parameters delta and i as static, since both range over $0, 1, \ldots, n - 1$. The resulting program is, however, not oblivious since the test on x affects the value of static i. Said differently, parameters i and delta are *independently varying static parameters*.

Specialisation with respect to static initial delta $= 4$ and i $= 0$ now gives the program in Figure 8.1.

The specialised program again runs in time $O(\log(n))$, and with a slightly better constant coefficient than above. On the other hand it has size $O(n)$ — exponentially larger than the weakly oblivious version! This is unacceptably large, except for rather small tables.

8.3 Some consequences of binding-time improvements

Binding-time improvements can lead to unexpectedly slow target code. Two typical examples follow.

Interpretation of a program with procedure calls is straightforward if no regard is taken of static-dynamic separation, e.g. a stack containing both source

```
   if x >= T[4] then
    if x >= T[6] then
     if x >= T[7] then
       [if x = T[7] then return(7) else return(NOTFOUND)] else
       [if x = T[6] then return(6) else return(NOTFOUND)] else
     if x >= T[5] then
       [if x = T[5] then return(5) else return(NOTFOUND)]
       [if x = T[4] then return(4) else return(NOTFOUND)] else
    if x >= T[2] then
     if x >= T[3] then
       [if x = T[3] then return(3) else return(NOTFOUND)] else
       [if x = T[2] then return(2) else return(NOTFOUND)] else
    if x >= T[1] then
       [if x = T[1] then return(1) else return(NOTFOUND)]
       [if x = T[0] then return(0) else return(NOTFOUND)]
```

Figure 8.1: A large program yielded by specialising binary search.

program text fragments and runtime values may be used. A binding-time improvement can, with some work, split this stack into separated static and dynamic parts. A complication is that the stack depth is dynamic, but "the trick" referred to in [6] can be used to keep the topmost (current) name part of the stack frame static.

Target programs produced by specialising such an interpreter may be slower than expected when doing procedure *returns*. The point is that a procedure return is traditionally compiled into an indirect goto. If this is not available, or if the partial evaluator cannot handle it (and few can!), the one-instruction "return jump" will be translated into a series of tests and control transfers, one to each possible return point.

An exactly analogous problem occurs for the lambda calculus: semicompositionality can be ensured by using closures and "the trick." But the consequence is that every function call will be translated into a series of tests and calls.

8.4 An unfortunate programming style

The interpreter sketch of Figure 8.2 essentially implements a "big-step" semantics for a tiny imperative language. Nonetheless it does not specialise at all well (though specialisation does in fact terminate.)

This uses a quite natural idea: if a variable has not already been bound in the store, then it is in effect added, with initial value zero. While it creates no problems for execution, this apparently quite innocent trick can cause catastrophically large target programs to be generated when specialising the interpreter to a source program. The reason is that mix must take account of *all execution possibilities*.

For an example, consider a source program of the following form:

```
    Run(pgm, input) = Exec(Cmd1, ns1, cons(input, 'nil), pgm) where
                Cmd1 = lookbody(first_fcn(pgm), pgm)
                ns1  = lookfcns(first_fcn(pgm), pgm)

    ; Exec : Command x Names x Values x Program -> Names x Values

    Exec(Cmd, ns, vs, pgm) = case Cmd of

      '(C1 ; C2)     :  Exec(C2, ns, ns1, vs1, pgm)  where
          (ns1, vs1) = Exec(C1, ns, vs, pgm),

      '(X := X + 1) : if member(X, ns)
          then (ns, update(X, 1+lookparams(X,ns,vs), ns, vs))
          else (cons(X, ns), cons(1,vs))

      '(IF e THEN C1 ELSE C2) :
          if  eval(e0, ns, vs, pgm) then  Exec(C1, ns, vs, pgm)
                                    else  Exec(C2, ns, vs, pgm)

    Eval(Cmd, ns, vs, pgm) = ...
```

Figure 8.2: Interpreter for a simple imperative language.

```
    IF test1 THEN X1 := X1 + 1;
    IF test2 THEN X2 := X2 + 1;
    ...
    IF testn THEN Xn := Xn + 1;
```

After test1 is processed at specialisation time, mix will have to allow for either branch to have been taken, so the resulting store = (ns, vs) could either have X1 present or absent. After the second test, 4 possibilities must be accounted for. As a consequence, specialisation will generate a target program whose size is exponential in n.

The problem is easily fixed, by revising the interpreter to first scan the entire source program, collecting an initial store in which every variable is bound to zero. The result will yield a target program whose size is proportional to that of the source program. A further optimisation is that the type of Exec can be merely

```
    Exec: Command x Names x Values x Program -> Values
```

with correspondingly smaller target code.

9   On speedup

Assuming that the specialiser terminates, it is natural to ask: how much speedup can be obtained; how does the amount of speedup relate to the way the subject program is written; and how can one avoid code size explosion?

We begin with a resume (and improvement) of the argument [6] that one can (usually) expect at most speedup by a linear multiplicative factor. We will see, however, that the size of the factor can depend on the static inputs, e.g. one often observes, for instance in pattern matching, that larger static data leads to larger speedups as a function of the size of d. The argument below also applies to *deforestation* and *supercompilation*.

9.1   Embedding computations into original computations

In most partial evaluators the residual computations can be described more simply than those of the specialiser. Consider a given program p, and static and dynamic inputs s, d. Let p_s be the result of specialising p to s.

A **first observation** (on all functional or imperative partial evaluators I have seen): there exists an order-preserving *injective mapping* ψ

– *from* the operations done in the computation of $[\![p_s]\!](d)$
– *to* the operations done in the original computation of $[\![p]\!](s, d)$.

The reason is that specialisers normally just sort computations by p into *static operations*: those done during specialisation, and *dynamic operations*: those done by the residual program, for which code is generated. Most specialisers do not rearrange the order in which computation is performed, or invent new operations not in p, so residual computations can be embedded 1-1 into original ones.

A **second observation, in the opposite direction**: some operations done in the computation of $[\![p]\!](s, d)$ can be forced to be residual, because they use parts of d, which is unavailable at specialisation time. Call such an operation in the $[\![p]\!](s, d)$ computation *forced dynamic*. Since it cannot be done by mix, residual code must be executed to realise its effect.

It holds for most partial evaluators (but not all) that there exists an order-preserving *surjective order-preserving mapping* ϕ from

– the forced dynamic operations in the computation of $[\![p]\!](s, d)$, onto
– corresponding operations in the computation of $[\![p_s]\!](d.)$

Why most specialisers give at most linear speedup. Let $time\text{-}force_p(s, d)$ be the number of forced dynamic operations done while computing $[\![p]\!](s, d)$. Assuming that all of these *must* be performed by the specialised program, we get a lower bound on its running time: $time\text{-}force_p(s, d) \leq time_{p_s}(d)$.

All other p operations can be performed without knowing d: they depend only on s. The maximum length of any sequence of such operations (assuming of course that specialisation terminates) is thus some function $f(s)$ of the static

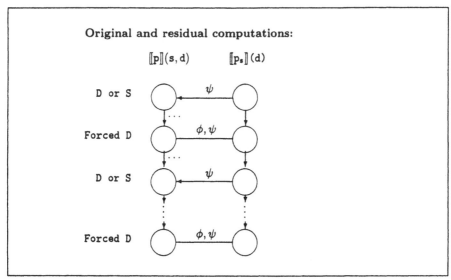

Figure 9.1: Correspondences between original and residual computations.

program input. Thus at most $f(\mathbf{s})$ static operations occur between any two forced dynamic operations, yielding $time_{\mathrm{p}}(\mathbf{s}, \mathbf{d}) \leq (1 + f(\mathbf{s})) \cdot time\text{-}force_{\mathrm{p}}(\mathbf{s}, \mathbf{d})$.

Combining these, we see that $time_{\mathrm{p}}(\mathbf{s}, \mathbf{d}) \leq (1 + f(\mathbf{s})) \cdot time_{\mathrm{p}_\mathbf{s}}(\mathbf{d})$, so

$$\text{speedup}_\mathbf{s}(\mathbf{d}) = \frac{time_{\mathrm{p}}(\mathbf{s}, \mathbf{d})}{time_{\mathrm{p}_\mathbf{s}}(\mathbf{d})} \leq 1 + f(\mathbf{s})$$

This second observation explains the fact that, in general, partial evaluators yield at most linear speedup independent of d, as illustrated in Figure 9.1.

9.2 Ways to break the linear speedup barrier

The argument just given rests on the existence of an order-preserving "onto" mapping of forced operations in original computations to residual ones. This is not always the case, and specialisers working differently can obtain superlinear speedup. Three cases follow:

Dead code elimination: if mix can examine its residual program and discover "semantically dead" code whose execution does not influence the program's final results, such code can be removed. If it contains dynamic operations, then there will be dynamic $[\![\mathbf{p}]\!](\mathbf{s}, \mathbf{d})$ operations not corresponding to any $[\![\mathbf{p}_\mathbf{s}]\!](\mathbf{d})$ operations at all. In this situation, between the two p operations corresponding to two $\mathbf{p}_\mathbf{s}$ operations there can occur a number of p operations *depending on dynamic input*, which were removed by the dead code elimination technique.

A logic programming analogy is the specialiser-time detection of branches in the Prolog's *SLD computation tree* which are guaranteed to fail (and may depend on dynamic data.) This is much more significant than in functional programming, in which time-consuming sequences of useless operations are most likely a sign of bad programming — whereas the ability to prune useless branches of search trees is part of the essence of logic programming.

Removing repeated subcomputations is another way to achieve super-linear speedup, and somehow seems less trivial than just eliding useless computations. The program transformation literature abounds with large speedups achieved by using memoisation to avoid recomputation of results, the standard one being to go from the exponential-time Fibonacci function to a linear-time (or even logarithmic-time) one. Integrating such more powerful transformations into fully automated partial evaluators remains a challenging problem, and in my opinion one well worth attempting.

10   Summary: what to do and not to do ...

By hook or by crook, ensure that *every* static parameter is of BSV. To do this, recall from Section 4.1 the "Pachinko principle:" that specialisation must account for *all possible computation paths* on any one set of static inputs, given *all possible dynamic inputs* coupled with them. More concretely:

1. Write your interpreter compositionally if possible, or at least semicompositionally (Section 5.)
2. If practical, write it by transliterating a big-step operational (Section 6.3) or a denotational semantics (Section 6.2.) This usually gives at least semicompositionality.
3. If your interpreter is based on a runtime execution model, you will have to do your own analyses concerning which parameters are of BSV. Beware of data structures that contain static data but can *grow unboundedly under dynamic control.* An example: the control stack C of Section 6.1.
4. If your interpreter is based on a small-step operational semantics (Section 6.3), first ensure *determinism* and *uniqueness of redexes.*
   (Here I'm assuming the implementation language is deterministic; if your specialiser handles nondeterministic languages, it is ahead of the state of the art as I know it.)
   Once determinism and redex uniqueness are established, ensure that the set of evaluation contexts is finite for any one source program. One way is by introducing closures or similar devices to ensure "dual semicompositionality."
5. In order to avoid *code explosion,* ensure that at any program point:
   - There are no *dead static variables* (Section 8.1.)
   - There are no (or as few as possible) *independent static parameters* (Section 8.2.)
6. Don't expect *superlinear speedup* (as a function of the dynamic input size), unless the specialiser used is rather sophisticated (Section 9.1.)
7. If you wish to achieve superlinear speedup on an insufficiently sophisticated specialiser, then *write your interpreter* to incorporate techniques such as those seen in Section 9.2 (memoisation, static detection of semantically dead code.)

Acknowledgements Warm thanks are due to many in the Topps group at DIKU, especially Arne Glenstrup; and to participants in the 1996 Partial Evaluation Dagstuhl meeting, in particular Peter Thiemann, Olivier Danvy, and Robert Glück.

References

1. A. Bondorf and O. Danvy, 'Automatic autoprojection of recursive equations with global variables and abstract data types,' *Science of Computer Programming*, 16:151–195, 1991.
2. C. Consel, 'New insights into partial evaluation: The Schism experiment,' in H. Ganzinger (ed.), *ESOP '88, 2nd European Symposium on Programming, Nancy, France, March 1988 (Lecture Notes in Computer Science, vol. 300)*, pp. 236–246, Berlin: Springer-Verlag, 1988.
3. A. De Niel, E. Bevers, and K. De Vlaminck, 'Partial evaluation of polymorphically typed functional languages: The representation problem,' in M. Billaud *et al.* (eds.), *Analyse Statique en Programmation Équationnelle, Fonctionnelle, et Logique, Bordeaux, France, Octobre 1991 (Bigre, vol. 74)*, pp. 90–97, Rennes: IRISA, 1991.
4. J. Gallagher: Specialization of logic programs. PEPM 93 (Partial Evaluation and Semantics-based Program Manipulation), pp. 88-98. ACM Press, 1993.
5. N.D. Jones, A.G. Genstrup 'BTA Algorithms to ensure termination of offline partial evaluation,' submitted to *Second Andrei Ershov Memorial Conference, Akademgorodok, Russia*, June 1996.
6. Neil D. Jones, C.K. Gomard, P. Sestoft, *Partial Evaluation and Automatic Program Generation*, Prentice Hall International Series in Computer Science, 1993.
7. J.W. Lloyd, J.C. Shepherdson, 'Partial evaluation in logic programming,' *Journal of Logic Programming* 11(3-4), pp. 217–242, 1991.
8. T. Mogensen, 'Partially static structures in a self-applicable partial evaluator,' in D. Bjørner, A.P. Ershov, and N.D. Jones (eds.), *Partial Evaluation and Mixed Computation*, pp. 325–347, Amsterdam: North-Holland, 1988.
9. T. Mogensen, 'Separating binding times in language specifications,' in *Fourth International Conference on Functional Programming Languages and Computer Architecture, London, England, September 1989*, pp. 14–25, Reading, MA: Addison-Wesley, 1989.
10. D. Sahlin, 'The Mixtus approach to automatic partial evaluation of full Prolog,' in S. Debray and M. Hermenegildo (eds.), *Logic Programming: Proceedings of the 1990 North American Conference, Austin, Texas, October 1990*, pp. 377–398, Cambridge, MA: MIT Press, 1990.
11. D.A. Schmidt, *Denotational Semantics*, Boston, MA: Allyn and Bacon, 1986.
12. V.F. Turchin, 'The concept of a supercompiler,' *ACM Transactions on Programming Languages and Systems*, 8(3):292–325, July 1986.
13. D. Weise, R. Conybeare, E. Ruf, and S. Seligman, 'Automatic online partial evaluation,' in J. Hughes (ed.), *Functional Programming Languages and Computer Architecture, Cambridge, Massachusetts, August 1991 (Lecture Notes in Computer Science, vol. 523)*, pp. 165–191, Berlin: Springer-Verlag, 1991.

Efficiently Generating Efficient Generating Extensions in Prolog

Jesper Jørgensen* and Michael Leuschel**

K.U. Leuven, Department of Computer Science
Celestijnenlaan 200A, B-3001 Heverlee, Belgium
e-mail: {jesper,michael}@cs.kuleuven.ac.be

Abstract. The so called "cogen approach" to program specialisation, writing a compiler generator instead of a specialiser, has been used with considerable success in partial evaluation of both functional and imperative languages.

This paper demonstrates that this approach is also applicable to partial evaluation of logic programming languages, also called partial deduction. Self-application has not been as much in focus in partial deduction as in partial evaluation of functional and imperative languages, and the attempts to self-apply partial deduction systems have, of yet, not been altogether that successful. So, especially for partial deduction, the cogen approach could prove to have a considerable importance when it comes to practical applications.

It is demonstrated that using the cogen approach one gets very efficient compiler generators which generate very efficient generating extensions which in turn yield (for some examples at least) very good and non-trivial specialisation.

1 Introduction

Partial evaluation has over the past decade received considerable attention both in functional (e.g. [23]), imperative (e.g. [1]) and logic programming (e.g. [13, 26, 42]). In the context of pure logic programs, partial evaluation is often referred to as *partial deduction*, the term partial evaluation being reserved for the treatment of impure logic programs. A convention we will also adhere to in this paper.

Guided by the *Futamura projections* (see e.g. [23]) a lot of effort, specially in the functional partial evaluation community, has been put into making systems self-applicable. A partial evaluation or deduction system is called *self-applicable* if it is able to effectively[1] specialise itself. In that case one may, according to the second Futamura projection, obtain *compilers* from interpreters and, according to the third Futamura projection, a *compiler generator* (cogen for short).

---

* Supported by HCM Network "Logic Program Synthesis and Transformation".
** Supported by the Belgian GOA "Non-Standard Applications of Abstract Interpretation"

[1] This implies some efficiency considerations, e.g. the system has to terminate within reasonable time constrains, using an appropriate amount of memory.

However writing an effectively self-applicable specialiser is a non-trivial task — the more features one uses in writing the specialiser the more complex the specialisation process becomes, because the specialiser then has to handle these features as well. This is why so far no partial evaluator for full Prolog (like MIXTUS [45], or PADDY [43]) has been made effectively self-applicable. On the other hand a partial deducer which specialises only purely declarative logic programs (like SAGE in [18] or the system in [7]) has itself to be written purely declaratively leading to slow systems and impractical compilers and compiler generators.

So far the only practical compilers and compiler generators have been obtained by striking a delicate balance between the expressivity of the underlying language and the ease with which it can be specialised. Two approaches for logic programming languages along this line are [11] and [39]. However the specialisation in [11] is incorrect with respect to some of the extra-logical built-ins, leading to incorrect compilers and compiler generators when attempting self-application (a problem mentioned in [7], see also [39, 28]). LOGIMIX [39] does not share this problem, but gives only modest speedups (when compared to results for functional programming languages, see [39]) when self-applied.

The actual creation of the cogen according to the third Futamura projection is not of much interest to users since cogen can be generated once and for all once a specialiser is given. Therefore, from a users point of view, whether a cogen is produced by self-application or not is of little importance, what is important is that it exists and that it has an improved performance over direct self-application. This is the background behind the approach to program specialisation called the *cogen approach*: instead of trying to write a partial evaluation system which is neither too inefficient nor too difficult to self-apply one simply writes a compiler generator directly. This is not as difficult as one might imagine at first sight: basically cogen turns out to be just a simple extension of a "binding-time analysis" for logic programs (something first discovered for functional languages in [21]).

In this paper we will describe the first cogen written in this way for a logic programming language: a small subset of Prolog.

The most noticeable advantages of the cogen approach is that the cogen and the compilers it generates can use all features of the implementation language. Therefore, no restrictions due to self-application have to be imposed (the compiler and the compiler generator don't have to be self-applied)! As we will see, this leads to extremely efficient compilers and compiler generators. So, in this case, having extra-logical features at our disposal makes the generation of compilers easier and less burdensome.

Some general advantages of the cogen approach are: the cogen manipulates only syntax trees and there is no need to implement a self-interpreter (meta-interpreter for the underlying language); values in the compilers are represented directly (there is no encoding overhead); and it becomes easier to demonstrate correctness for non-trivial languages (due to the simplicity of the transformation). In addition, the compilers are stand-alone programs that can be distributed without the cogen.

A further advantage of the cogen approach for logic languages is that the compilers and compiler generators can use the non-ground representation (and even a compiled version of it). This is in contrast to self-applicable partial deducers which *must* use the ground representation in order to be declarative (see [20, 34, 18]). In fact the non-ground representation executes several orders of magnitude faster than the ground representation (even after specialising, see [8]) and, as shown in [34], can be impossible to specialise satisfactorily by partial deduction alone. (Note that even [39] uses a "mixed" representation approach [31, 20]).

Although the Futamura projections focus on how to generate a compiler from an interpreter, the projections of course also apply when we replace the interpreter by some other program. In that case the program produced by the second Futamura projection is not called a compiler, but a *generating extension*. The program produced by the third Futamura projection could rightly be called a *generating extension generator* or gengen, but we will stick to the more conventional cogen.

The main contributions of this work are:

- the first description of a handwritten compiler generator (cogen) for a logic programming language which shows that such a program has quite an elegant and natural structure.
- a formal specification of the concept of *binding-time analysis* (*BTA*) in a (pure) logic programming setting and a description of how to obtain a generic algorithm for partial deduction from such a *BTA* (by describing how to obtain an unfolding and a generalisation strategy from the result of a *BTA*).
- benchmark results showing the efficiency of the cogen, the generating extensions and the specialised programs.

The paper is organised as follows: In Sect. 2 we formalise the concept of off-line partial deduction and the associated binding-time analysis. In Sect. 3 we present and explain our cogen approach in a pure logic programming setting. In Sect. 4 we present some examples and results underlining the efficiency of the cogen. We conclude with some discussions in Sect. 5.

2 Off-Line Partial Deduction

Throughout this paper, we suppose familiarity with basic notions in logic programming ([35]). Notational conventions are standard and self-evident. In particular, in programs, we denote variables through strings starting with (or usually just consisting of) an upper-case symbol, while the notations of constants, functions and predicates begin with a lower-case character.

We will also use the following not so common notations. Given a function $f : A \mapsto B$ we often use the *natural extension* of f, $f^* : 2^A \mapsto 2^B$, defined by $f^*(S) = \{f(s) \mid s \in S\}$. Similarly, given a function $f : A \mapsto 2^B$ we also define the function $f_\cup : 2^A \mapsto 2^B$, by $f_\cup(S) = \cup_{s \in S} f(s)$. Both f^* and $f_\cup$ are homomorphisms[2] from 2^A to 2^B. Given a function $f : A \times B \mapsto C$ and an element $a \in A$ we define the curried version of f, $f_a : B \mapsto C$, by $f_a(X) = f(a, X)$. Finally, we will denote by $A_{\text{if}} \to A_{\text{then}}$; A_{else} the Prolog conditional.

2.1 A Generic Partial Deduction Method

Given a logic program P and a goal G, *partial deduction* produces a new program P' which is P "specialised" to the goal G; the aim being that the specialised program P' is more efficient than the original program P for all goals which are instances of G.

The underlying technique of partial deduction is to construct "incomplete" SLDNF-trees and then extract the specialised program P' from these incomplete search trees (by taking resultants, see below). An *incomplete* SLDNF-tree is a SLDNF-tree which, in addition to success and failure leaves, may also contain leaves where no literal has been selected for a further derivation step. Leaves of the latter kind will be called *dangling* ([37]). In the context of partial deduction these incomplete SLDNF-trees are obtained by applying an unfolding rule, defined as follows.

Definition 1. (Unfolding rule) An *unfolding rule U* is a function which, given a program P and a goal G, returns a finite, (possibly) incomplete and non-trivial[3] SLDNF-tree for $P \cup \{G\}$.

Given an incomplete SLDNF-tree, partial deduction will generate a set of clauses by taking resultants. Resultants are defined as follows.

Definition 2. (*resultants*(τ), *leaves*(τ)) Let P be a normal program and A an atom. Let τ be a finite, incomplete SLDNF-tree for $P \cup \{\leftarrow A\}$ in which A has been selected in the root node. Let $\leftarrow G_1, \ldots, \leftarrow G_n$ be the goals in the (non-root) leaves of the non-failing branches of τ. Let $\theta_1, \ldots, \theta_n$ be the computed answers of the derivations from $\leftarrow A$ to $\leftarrow G_1, \ldots, \leftarrow G_n$ respectively. Then the set of resultants, *resultants*(τ), is defined to be the set of clauses $\{A\theta_1 \leftarrow G_1, \ldots, A\theta_n \leftarrow G_n\}$. We also define the set of leaves, *leaves*(τ), to be the atoms occurring in the goals $G_1, \ldots, G_n$.

Partial deduction, as defined for instance in [36] or [4], uses the resultants for a given set of atoms A to construct the specialised program (and for each atom in A a different specialised predicate definition will be generated). Under the conditions stated in [36], namely closedness and independence, correctness of the specialised program is guaranteed.

In a lot of practical approaches (e.g. [12, 13, 15, 31, 28, 29]) independence is ensured by using a *renaming* transformation which maps dependent atoms

---

[2] The function $h : 2^A$ to 2^B is a homomorphism iff $h(\emptyset) = \emptyset$ and $h(S \cup S') = h(S) \cup h(S')$.

[3] A trivial SLDNF-tree is one whose root is a dangling leaf. This restriction is necessary to obtain correct partial deductions. See also Definition 2 below.

to new predicate symbols. Adapted correctness results can be found in [3] (see also [32]). Renaming is often combined with argument *filtering* to improve the efficiency of the specialised program (see e.g. [14]).

Closedness can be ensured by using the following outline of a partial deduction algorithm (similar to the ones used in e.g. [12, 13, 29, 30]).

Algorithm 3. (Partial deduction)

1. Let S_0 be the set of atoms to be specialised and let $i = 0$.
2. Apply the unfolding rule U to each element of S_i: $\Gamma_i = U_P^*(S_i)$.
3. $S_{i+1} = abstract(S_i \cup leaves_U(\Gamma_i))$
4. If $S_{i+1} \neq S_i$ (modulo variable renaming) increment i and restart at step 2, otherwise generate the specialised program by applying a renaming (and filtering) transformation to $resultants_U(\Gamma_i)$.

The abstraction operation is usually used to ensure termination and can be formally defined as follows ([12, 13]).

Definition 4. An operation $abstract(S)$ is any operation satisfying the following conditions. Let S be a finite set of atoms; then $abstract(S)$ is a finite set of atoms S' with the same predicates as those in S, such that every atom in S is an instance of an atom in S'.

If the above algorithm terminates then the closedness condition is satisfied. Finally note that in the above algorithm the atoms in $leaves_U(\Gamma_i)$ are all added and abstracted simultaneously, i.e. the algorithm progresses in a breadth-first manner. In general this will yield a different result from a depth-first progression (i.e. adding one atom at a time). If however *abstract* is a homomorphism[4] then both progressions will yield exactly the same set of atoms and thus the same specialisation.

2.2 Off-Line Partial Deduction and Binding-Time Analysis

In Algorithm 3 one can distinguish between two different levels of control. The unfolding rule U controls the construction of the incomplete SLDNF-trees. This is called the *local control* (we will use the terminology of [13, 38]). The abstraction operation controls the construction of the set of atoms for which local SLDNF-trees are built. We will refer to this aspect as the *global control*.

The control problems have been tackled from two different angles: the so-called *off-line* versus *on-line* approaches. The *on-line* approach performs all the control decisions *during* the actual specialisation phase (in our case the one depicted in Algorithm 3). The *off-line* approach on the other hand performs an analysis phase *prior* to the actual specialisation phase, based on some rough descriptions of what kinds of specialisations will have to be performed. The analysis phase provides annotations which then guide the control aspect of the proper specialisation phase, often to the point of making it completely trivial.

---

[4] I.e. $abstract(\emptyset) = \emptyset$ and $abstract(S \cup S') = abstract(S) \cup abstract(S')$.

Partial evaluation of functional programs ([10, 23]) has mainly stressed off-line approaches, while supercompilation of functional ([47, 46]) and partial deduction of logic programs ([15, 45, 6, 9, 37, 38, 29, 33]) have concentrated on on-line control. (Some exceptions are [39, 31, 28].)

The main reason for using the off-line approach is to achieve effective self-application ([24]). But the off-line approach is in general also more efficient, since many decisions concerning control are made before and not during specialisation. For the cogen approach to be efficient it is vital to use the off-line approach, since then the (local) control can be hard-wired into the generating extension.

Most off-line approaches perform a so called *binding-time analysis (BTA)* prior to the specialisation phase. This phase classifies arguments to predicate calls as either *static* or *dynamic*. The value of a static argument is definitely known (bound) at specialisation time whereas a dynamic argument is not definitely known (it might only be known at the actual run-time of the program). In the context of partial deduction, a static argument can be seen as being a term which is guaranteed not to be more instantiated at run-time (it can never be less instantiated at run-time). For example if we specialise a program for all instances of $p(a, X)$ then the first argument to p is static while the second one is dynamic — actual run-time instances might be $p(a, b), p(a, Z), p(a, X)$ but not $p(b, c)$. We will also say that an atom is static if all its arguments are static and likewise that a goal is static if it consist only of static (literals) atoms.

We will now formalise the concept of a binding-time analysis. For that we first define the concept of divisions which classify arguments into static and dynamic ones.

Definition 5. (Division) A *division of arity* n is a couple (S, D) of sets of integers such that $S \cup D = \{1, \ldots, n\}$ and $S \cap D = \emptyset$.

We also define the function *divide* which, given a division and a tuple of arguments, divides the arguments into the static and the dynamic ones:
$divide_{(S,D)}((t_1, \ldots, t_n)) = ((t_{i_1}, \ldots, t_{i_k}), (t_{j_1}, \ldots, t_{j_l}))$ where $(i_1, \ldots, i_k)$ (resp. $(j_1, \ldots, j_k)$) are the elements of S (resp. D) in ascending order.

As a notational convenience we will use $(\delta_1, \ldots, \delta_n)$ to denote a division (S, D) of arity n, where $\delta_i = s$ if $i \in S$ and $\delta_i = d$ if $i \in D$. For example (s, d) denotes the division $(\{1\}, \{2\})$ of arity 2. From now on we will also use the notation $Pred(P)$ to denote the predicate symbols occurring inside a program P. We now define a division for a program P which divides the arguments of every predicate $p \in Pred(P)$ into the static and the dynamic ones:

Definition 6. (Division for a program) A *division Δ for a program P* is a mapping from $Pred(P)$ to divisions having the arity of the corresponding predicates. In accordance with the notations outlined at the beginning of this section, we will often write Δ_p for $\Delta(p)$. We also define the function Δ_p^s by $\Delta_p^s(\overline{x}) = \overline{y}$ iff $divide_{\Delta_p}(\overline{x}) = (\overline{y}, \overline{z})$. Similarly we define the function Δ_p^d by $\Delta_p^d(\overline{x}) = \overline{z}$ iff $divide_{\Delta_p}(\overline{x}) = (\overline{y}, \overline{z})$.

Example 1. $(\{1\}, \{2\})$ is a division of arity 2 and $(\{2, 3\}, \{1\})$ a division of arity 3 and we have for instance $divide_{(\{2,3\},\{1\})}((a, b, c)) = ((b, c), (a))$. Let P be a program containing the predicate symbols $p/2$ and $q/3$. Then $\Delta = \{p/2 \mapsto (\{1\}, \{2\}), q/3 \mapsto (\{2, 3\}, \{1\})\}$ is a division for P (using the notational convenience introduced above we can also write $\Delta = \{p/2 \mapsto (s, d), q/3 \mapsto (d, s, s)\}$). We then have for example $\Delta_q^s((a, b, c)) = (b, c)$ and $\Delta_q^d((a, b, c)) = (a)$.

Divisions can be ordered. A division is more general than another one if it classifies more arguments as dynamic. This is captured by the following definition.

Definition 7. *(Partial order of divisions)* Divisions of the same arity are partially ordered: $(S, D) \sqsubseteq (S', D')$ iff $D \subseteq D'$.

We also define the notation $\bot_n = (\{1, \ldots, n\}, \emptyset)$ and $\top_n = (\emptyset, \{1, \ldots, n\})$.

This order can be extended to divisions for some program P. We say that Δ' is *more general* than Δ, denoted by $\Delta \sqsubseteq \Delta'$, iff for all predicates $p \in Pred(P)$: $\Delta_p \sqsubseteq \Delta'_p$.

As already mentioned, a binding-time analysis will, given a program P (and some description of how P will be specialised), perform a pre-processing analysis and return a *division* for P describing when values will be bound (i.e. known). It will also return an *annotation* which will then guide the local unfolding process of the actual partial deduction. From a theoretical viewpoint an annotation restricts the possible unfolding rules that can be used (e.g. the annotation could state that predicate calls to p should never be unfolded whereas calls to q should always be unfolded). We therefore define annotations as follows:

Definition 8. *(Annotation)* An *annotation* $\mathcal{A}$ is a set of unfolding rules (i.e. it is a subset of the set of all possible unfolding rules).

In order to be really off-line, the unfolding rules in the annotation should not take the unfolding history into account and should not depend "too much" on the actual values of the static (nor dynamic) arguments. In the following subsection we will come back on what annotations can look like from a practical viewpoint. We are now in a position to formally define a binding-time analysis in the context of (pure) logic programs:

Definition 9. *(BTA,BTC)* A *binding-time analysis (BTA)* yields, given a program P and an initial division Δ_0 for P, a couple $(\mathcal{A}, \Delta)$ consisting of an annotation $\mathcal{A}$ and a division Δ for P more general than Δ_0. We will call the result of a binding-time analysis a *binding-time classification (BTC)*.

The initial division Δ_0 gives information about how the program will be specialised. In fact Δ_0 specifies what the initial atom(s) to be specialised (i.e. the ones in S_0 of Algorithm 3) will look like (if p' does not occur in S_0 we simply set $\Delta_0(p') = \bot_n$). The role of Δ is to give information about what the atoms in Algorithm 3 will look like at the global level. In that light, not all *BTC* as specified above are correct and we now develop a safety criterion for a BTC wrt a given program. Basically a BTC is safe iff every atom that can potentially appear in one of the sets S_i of Algorithm 3 (given the restrictions imposed by the annotation of the BTA) corresponds to the patterns described by Δ. Note that if a predicate p is always unfolded by the unfolding rule used in Algorithm 3 then it is irrelevant what the value of Δ_p is.

For simplicity, we will from now on impose that a *static* argument must be *ground.*[5] In particular this guarantees our earlier requirement that the argument will not be more instantiated at run-time.

Definition 10. (*safe wrt Δ*) Let P be a program and let Δ be a division for P and let $p(\bar{t})$ be an atom with $p \in Pred(P)$. Then $p(\bar{t})$ is *safe wrt Δ* iff $\Delta_p^s(\bar{t})$ is a tuple of ground terms. A set of atoms S is *safe wrt Δ* iff every atom in S is safe wrt Δ. Also a goal G is *safe wrt Δ* iff all the atoms occurring in G are safe wrt Δ.

For example $p(a, X)$ is safe wrt $\Delta = \{p/2 \mapsto (s, d)\}$ while $p(X, a)$ is not.

Definition 11. (safe BTC, safe BTA) Let $\beta = (\mathcal{A}, \Delta)$ be a BTC for a program P and let $U \in \mathcal{A}$ be an unfolding rule. Then β is a *safe BTC for P and U* iff for every goal G, which is safe wrt Δ, U returns an incomplete SLDNF-tree whose leaf goals are safe wrt Δ. Also β is a *safe BTC for P* iff it is a safe BTC for P and for every unfolding rule $U \in \mathcal{A}$. A BTA is *safe* if for any program P it produces a safe BTC for P.

So, the above definition requires atoms to be safe in the leaves of incomplete SLDNF-trees, i.e. at the point where the atoms get abstracted and then lifted to the *global* level.[6] So, in order for the above condition to ensure safety at all stages of Algorithm 3, the particular abstraction operation should not abstract atoms which are safe wrt Δ into atoms which are no longer safe wrt Δ. This motivates the following definition:

Definition 12. An abstraction operation *abstract* is *safe wrt a division Δ* iff for every finite set of atoms S, which is safe wrt Δ, *abstract(S)* is also safe wrt Δ.

2.3 A Particular Off-Line Partial Deduction Method

In this subsection we define a specific off-line partial deduction method which will serve as the basis for the cogen developed in the remainder of this paper. For simplicity, we will from now on restrict ourselves to definite programs. Negation will in practice be treated in the cogen either as a built-in or via the *if-then-else* construct (see Appendix A).

Let us first define a particular unfolding rule.

---

[5] This simplifies stating the safety criterion of a BTA because one does not have to reason about "freeness". In a similar vein this also makes the BTA itself easier.

[6] Also, when leaving the pure logic programming context and allowing extra-logical built-ins (like =../2) a *local* safety condition will also be required.

Definition 13. $(U_{\mathcal{L}})$ Let $\mathcal{L} \subseteq Pred(P)$. We will call $\mathcal{L}$ the set of *reducible* predicates. Also an atom will be called reducible iff its predicate symbol is in $\mathcal{L}$. We then define the unfolding rule $U_{\mathcal{L}}$ to be the unfolding rule which selects the leftmost reducible atom in each goal (and of course, for atomic goals $\leftarrow A$ in the root, it always selects A).

We will use such unfolding rules in Algorithm 3 and we will restrict ourselves (to avoid distracting from the essential points) to safe BTA's which return results of the form $\beta = (\{U_{\mathcal{L}}\}, \Delta)$. In the actual implementation of the cogen (Appendix B) we use a slightly more liberal approach in the sense that specific program points (calls to predicates) are annotated as either reducible or non-reducible. Also note that nothing prevents a BTA from having a pre-processing phase which splits the predicates according to their different uses.

Example 2. Let P be the following program

(1) $p(X) \leftarrow q(X, Y), q(Y, Z)$
(2) $q(a, b) \leftarrow$
(3) $q(b, a) \leftarrow$

Let $\Delta = \{p \mapsto (s), q \mapsto (s, d)\}$. Then $\beta = (\{U_{\{q\}}\}, \Delta)$ is a safe BTC for P. For example the goal $\leftarrow p(a)$ is safe wrt Δ and unfolding it according to $U_{\{q\}}$ will lead (via the intermediate goals $\leftarrow q(a, Y), q(Y, Z)$ and $\leftarrow q(b, Z)$) to the empty goal $\square$ which is safe wrt Δ. Note that every selected atom is safe wrt Δ.[7] Also note that $\beta' = (\{U_{\{\}}\}, \Delta)$ is a *not* a safe BTC for P. For instance, for the goal $\leftarrow p(a)$ the unfolding rule $U_{\{\}}$ just performs one unfolding step and thus stops at the goal $\leftarrow q(a, Y), q(Y, Z)$ which contains the unsafe atom $q(Y, Z)$.

The only thing that is missing in order to arrive at a concrete instance of Algorithm 3 is a (safe) abstraction operation, which we define in the following.

Definition 14. $(gen_{\Delta}, abstract_{\Delta})$ Let P be a program and Δ be a division for P. Let $A = p(\bar{t})$ with $p \in Pred(P)$. We then denote by $gen_{\Delta}(A)$ an atom obtained from A by replacing all dynamic arguments of A (according to Δ_p) by distinct variables.
We also define the abstraction operation $abstract_{\Delta}$ to be the natural extension of the function gen_{Δ}: $abstract_{\Delta} = gen_{\Delta}^{*}$.

For example, if $\Delta = \{p/2 \mapsto (s, d), q/3 \mapsto (d, s, s)\}$ then $gen_{\Delta}(p(a, b)) = p(a, X)$ and $gen_{\Delta}(q(a, b, c)) = q(X, b, c)$. Then $abstract_{\Delta}(\{p(a, b), q(a, b, c)\}) = \{p(a, X), q(X, b, c)\}$. Note that, trivially, $abstract_{\Delta}$ is safe wrt Δ.

Note that $abstract_{\Delta}$ is a homomorphism and hence, as already noted, we can use a depth-first progression in Algorithm 3 and still get the same specialisation. This is something which we will actually do in the practical implementation.

In the remainder of this paper we will use the following off-line partial deduction method:

---

[7] As already mentioned, this is not required in definition 11 but (among others) such a condition will have to be incorporated for the selection of extra-logical built-in's.

Algorithm 15. (off-line partial deduction)

1. Perform a *BTA* (possibly by hand) returning results of the form $(\{U_{\mathcal{L}}\}, \Delta)$
2. Perform Algorithm 3 with $U_{\mathcal{L}}$ as unfolding rule and *abstract$_\Delta$* as abstraction operation. The initial set of atoms S_0 should only contain atoms which are safe wrt Δ.

Proposition 16. *Let $(\{U_{\mathcal{L}}\}, \Delta)$ be a safe BTC for a program P. Let S_0 be a set of atoms safe wrt Δ. If Algorithm 15 terminates then the final set S_i only contains atoms safe wrt Δ.*

We will explain how this particular partial deduction method works by looking at an example.

Example 3. We use a small generic parser for a set of languages which are defined by grammars of the form $S ::= aS|X$ (where X is a placeholder for a terminal symbol). The example is adapted from [26] and the parser P is depicted in Fig. 1.

Given the initial division $\Delta_0 = \{nont/3 \mapsto (s, d, d), t/3 \mapsto \perp_3\}$ a *BTA* might return the following result $\beta = (\{U_{\{t/3\}}\}, \Delta)$ where $\Delta = \{nont/3 \mapsto (s, d, d), t/3 \mapsto (s, d, d)\}$. It can be seen that β is a safe *BTC* for P.

Let us now perform the proper partial deduction for $S_0 = \{nont(c, R, T)\}$. Note that the atom $nont(c, R, T)$ is safe wrt Δ_0 (and hence also wrt Δ). Unfolding the atom in S_0 yields the SLD-tree in Fig. 2. We see that the atoms in the leaves are $\{nont(c, V, T)\}$ and we obtain $S_1 = S_0$. The specialised program after renaming and filtering looks like:

$$nont_c([a|V], R) \leftarrow nont_c(V, R)$$
$$nont_c([c|R], R) \leftarrow$$

---

(1) $nont(X, T, R) \leftarrow t(a, T, V), nont(X, V, R)$
(2) $nont(X, T, R) \leftarrow t(X, T, R)$

(3) $t(X, [X|ES], ES) \leftarrow$

Fig. 1. A parser

3 The cogen approach for logic programming languages

For presentation purposes we from now on suppose that in Algorithm 15 the initial set S_0 consists of just a single atom A_0 (a convention adhered to by a lot of practical partial deduction systems).

A *generating extension* of a program P with respect to a given safe *BTC* $(\{U_{\mathcal{L}}\}, \Delta)$ for P, is a program that performs specialisation (using part 2 of

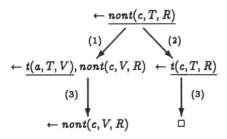

Fig. 2. Unfolding the parser of Fig. 1

Algorithm 15) of any atom A_0 which is safe wrt Δ. So in the case of the parser from Ex. 3 a generating extension is a program that, when given the safe call $nont(c, R, T)$, produces the residual program shown in the example.

A *compiler generator*, *cogen*, is a program that given a program P and a safe *BTC* β for P produces a generating extension of P wrt β.

We will first consider what the generating extensions wrt a program P and a safe *BTC* β should look like. Once this is clear we will consider what *cogen* should look like.

As already stated, a generating extension should specialise safe calls to predicates. Let us first consider the unfolding aspect of specialisation. The partial deduction algorithm first unfolds the initial top-level atom (to ensure a non-trivial tree). It then proceeds with the unfolding until no more reducible atoms can be selected and collects the atoms in the leaves of the unfolded SLDNF-tree. This process is repeated for all the new (generalised) atoms which have not yet been unfolded, until no more new non-reducible atoms are found. Notice that all predicates may potentially have to be unfolded.

The crucial idea for simplicity and efficiency of the generating extension is to incorporate a specific predicate p_u for each predicate p/n. This predicate has $n + 1$ arguments and is tailored towards unfolding calls to p/n. The first n arguments correspond to the arguments of the call to p/n which has to be unfolded. The last argument collects the result of the unfolding process. More precisely, $p_u(t_1, ..., t_n, B)$ will succeed for each branch of the incomplete SLDNF-tree obtained by applying the unfolding $U_{\mathcal{L}}$ to $p(t_1, ..., t_n)$ whereby it will return in B the atoms in the leaf of the branch[8] and also instantiate $t_1, ..., t_n$ via the composition of *mgu*'s of the branch. For complete SLDNF-trees (i.e. for atoms which get fully unfolded) the above can be obtained very *efficiently* by simply executing the original predicate definition of p for the goal $\leftarrow p(t_1, ..., t_n)$ (no atoms in the leaves have to be returned because there are none). To handle the case of incomplete SLDNF-trees we just have to adapt the definition of p so that unfolding can be stopped (for non-reducible predicates according to $U_{\mathcal{L}}$) and so that in that case the atoms in the leaves are collected.

---

[8] For reasons of clarity and simplicity in unflattened form.

This can be obtained very easily by transforming every clause defining the predicate p/n into a clause for $p_u/(n+1)$, as done in the following definition. The following could actually be called a *compiled* non-ground representation, and contributes much to the final efficiency of the generating extensions.

Definition 17. Let P be a program and $C = p(\bar{t}) \leftarrow A_1, ..., A_k$ a clause of P defining a predicate symbol p/n. Let $\mathcal{L} \subseteq Pred(P)$ be a set of reducible predicate symbols. We then define the clause $C_u^{\mathcal{L}}$ for the predicate p_u to be:

$$p_u(\bar{t}, [\mathcal{R}_1, ..., \mathcal{R}_k]) \leftarrow \mathcal{S}_1, ..., \mathcal{S}_k$$

where

1. $\mathcal{S}_i = q_u(\bar{s}, \mathcal{R}_i)$ and $\mathcal{R}_i$ is a fresh unused variable, if $A_i = q(\bar{s})$ is reducible
2. $\mathcal{S}_i = true$ and $\mathcal{R}_i = A_i$, if A_i is not reducible

We will denote by $P_u^{\mathcal{L}}$ the program obtained by applying the above transformation to every clause in P and removing all *true* atoms from the bodies.

In the above definition inserting a literal of the form $q_u(\bar{s}, \mathcal{R}_i)$ corresponds to further unfolding whereas inserting *true* corresponds to stopping the unfolding process. In the case of Ex. 3 with $\mathcal{L} = \{t/3\}$, applying the above to the program P of Fig. 1 gives rise to the following program $P_u^{\mathcal{L}}$:

```
nont_u(X,T,R,[V1,nont(X,V,R)]) :- t_u(a,T,V,V1).
nont_u(X,T,R,[V1]) :- t_u(X,T,R,V1).
t_u(X,[X|R],R,[]).
```

Evaluating the above code for the call nont_u(c,T,R,Leaves) yields two computed answers which correspond to the two branches in Fig. 1:

```
> ?-nont_u(c,T,R,Leaves).
  T = [a | _52]
  Leaves = [[],nont(c,_52,R)]
Yes ;
  T = [c | R]
  Leaves = [[]]
Yes
```

The above code is of course still incomplete as it only handles the unfolding process and we have to extend it to treat the global level as well. Firstly, calling p_u only returns the atoms of one leaf of the SLDNF-tree, so we need to add some code that collects the information from all the leaves. This can be done very efficiently using Prolog's findall predicate. So in the following call findall(B,nont_u(c,R,T,B),Bs) the Bs will be instantiated to the following list q[[[],nont(c,_48,_49)],[[]]] which essentially corresponds to the leaves of the SLDNF-tree in Fig. 2, since by flattening out we obtain: [nont(c,_48,_49)]. Furthermore, if we call

```
findall(clause(nont(c,T,R),Bdy),nont_u(c,T,R,Bdy),Cs)
```

we will even get in Cs a representation of the two resultants of Ex. 3.

Once all the resultants have been generated, the body atoms have to be generalised (using gen_Δ) and unfolded if they have not been encountered yet. The easiest way to achieve this is to add a function p_m for each non-reducible predicate such that, p_m implements the global control aspect of the specialisation. That is, for every atom $p(\bar{t})$, if one calls $p_m(\bar{t}, R)$ then R will be instantiated to the residual call of $p(\bar{t})$ (i.e. the call after filtering and renaming, for instance the residual call of $p(a, b, X)$ might be $p_1(X)$). At the same time p_m also generalises this call, checks if it has been encountered before and if not, unfolds the atom, generates code and prints the resultants (residual code) of the atom. We have the following definition of p_m:

Definition 18. Let P be a program and p/n be a predicate defined in P. Let $\mathcal{L} \subseteq Pred(P)$ be a set of reducible predicate symbols. For $p \in Pred(P)$ we define the clause C_m^p, defining the predicate p_m, to be:

$$p_m(\bar{t}, R) \leftarrow$$
$$(find\_pattern(p(\bar{t}), R) \rightarrow true$$
$$; \ (insert\_pattern(p(\bar{s}), H),$$
$$findall(C, (p_u(\bar{s}, B), treat\_clause(H, B, C)), Cs),$$
$$pp(Cs),$$
$$find\_pattern(p(\bar{t}), R))).$$

where $p(\bar{s}) = gen_\Delta(p(\bar{t}))$. Finally we define $P_m^{\mathcal{L}} = \{C_m^p \mid p \in Pred(P) \setminus \mathcal{L}\}$.[9]

In the above, the predicate *find_pattern* checks whether its first argument is a call that has been encountered before and its second argument is the residual call to this (with renaming and filtering performed). This is achieved by keeping a list of the predicates that have been encountered before along with their renamed and filtered calls. So, if the call to *find_pattern* succeeds, then R has been instantiated to the residual call of $p(\bar{t})$, if not, then the other branch of the conditional is tried.

The predicate *insert_pattern* will add a new atom (its first argument) to the list of atoms encountered before and return (in its second argument H) the generalised, renamed and filtered version of the atom. The atom H will provide (maybe further instantiated) the head of the resultants to be constructed. This call to *insert_pattern* is put first to ensure that an atom is not specialised over and over again at the global level.

The call to $findall(C, (p_u(\bar{s}, B), treat\_clause(H, B, C)), Cs)$ unfolds the generalised atom $p(\bar{s})$ and returns a list of residual clauses for $p(\bar{s})$ (in Cs). The call to $p_u(\bar{s}, B)$ inside *findall* returns a leaf goal of the SLDNF-tree for $p(\bar{s})$. This goal is going to be the body of a residual clause with head H. For each of the atoms in the body of this clause two things have to be done. First, for each atom a

---

[9] This corresponds to saying that only reducible atoms can occur at the global level, and hence only reducible atoms can be put into the initial set of atoms S_0 of Algorithm 3. If this is not what you want then just change the above definition to "$p \in Pred(P)$" or to "$p \in (Pred(P) \setminus \mathcal{L}) \cup \{p_0\}$".

specialised residual version has to be generated if necessary. Second, each atom has to be replaced by a call to a corresponding residual version. Both of these tasks can be performed by calling the corresponding "m" function of the atoms, so if a body contains an atom $p(\bar{t})$ then $p_m(\bar{t}, R)$ is called and the atom is replaced by the value of R. The task of treating the body in this way is done by the predicate *treat_clause* and the third argument of this is the new clauses.

The predicate *pp* pretty-prints the clauses of the residual program. The last call to *find_pattern* will instantiate R to the residual call of the atom $p(\bar{t})$.

We can now define what a generating extension of a program is:

Definition 19. Let P be a program, $\mathcal{L} \in Pred(P)$ a set of predicates and $(\{U_{\mathcal{L}}\}, \Delta)$ a safe BTC for P, then the *generating extension* of P with respect to $(\{U_{\mathcal{L}}\}, \Delta)$ is the program $P_g = P_u^{\mathcal{L}} \cup P_m^{\mathcal{L}}$.

The complete generating extension for Ex. 3 is shown in Fig. 3.

```
nont_m(B,C,D,E) :-
   (find_pattern(nont(B,C,D),E) -> true
   ; (insert_pattern(nont(B,F,G),H),
       findall(I,(nont_u(B,F,G,J),treat_clause(H,J,I)),K),
       pp(K),
       find_pattern(nont(B,C,D),E)
       )).
nont_u(B,C,D,[E,memo(nont(B,G,D))]) :- t_u(a,C,G,E).
nont_u(H,I,J,[K]) :- t_u(H,I,J,K).
t_u(L,[L|M],M,[]).
```

Fig. 3. The generating extension for the parser

The generating extension is called as follows: if one wants to specialise an atom $p(\bar{t})$, where p is one of the non-reducible predicates of the subject program P then one calls the predicate p_m of the generating extension in the following way $p_m(\bar{t}, \_)$.

The job of the cogen is now quite simple: given a program P and a safe BTC β for P, generate a generating extension for P consisting of the two parts described above. The code of the essential parts of our cogen is shown in Appendix B. The predicate predicate generates the definition of the global control m-predicates for each non-reducible predicate of the program whereas the predicates clause, bodys and body take care of translating clauses of the original predicate into clauses of the local control u-predicates. Note how the second argument of bodys and body corresponds to code of the generating extension whereas the third argument corresponds to code produced at the next level, i.e. at the level of the specialised program. Further details on extending the *cogen* to handle built-ins and the if-then-else can be found in Appendix A.

4   Examples and Results

In this section we present some experiments with our *cogen* system as well as with some other specialisation systems. We will use three example programs to that effect.

The first program is the parser from Ex. 3. We will use the same annotation as in the previous sections: $nont \mapsto (s, d, d)$.

The second example program is the "mixed" meta-interpreter (sometimes called *InstanceDemo*) for the ground representation of [12, 13, 31] in which the goals are "lifted" to the non-ground representation for resolution. We will specialise this program given the annotation $solve \mapsto (s, d)$, i.e. we suppose that the object program is given and the query to the object program is dynamic.

Finally we also experimented with a regular expression parser, which tests whether a given string can be generated by a given regular expression. The example is taken from [39]. In the experiment we used $dgenerate \mapsto (s, d)$ for the initial division, i.e. the regular expression is fully known whereas the string is dynamic.

4.1   Experiments with COGEN

The Tables 1, 2 and 3 summarise our benchmarks of the COGEN system. The timings were by using Prolog by BIM on a Sparc Classic running Solaris (timings, at least for Table 1, were almost identical for a Sun 4).

Program	Time	Annotation
parser	0.02 s	$nont \mapsto (s, d, d)$
solve	0.06 s	$solve \mapsto (s, d)$
regexp	0.02 s	$dgenerate \mapsto (s, d)$

Table 1. Running COGEN

Program	Time	Query
parser	0.01 s	$nont(c, T, R)$
solve	0.01 s	$solve("\{q(X) \leftarrow p(X), p(a) \leftarrow\}", Q)$
regexp	0.03 s	$dgenerate("(a + b) * .a.a.b", S)$

Table 2. Running the generating extension

Program	Speedup Factor	Runtime Query
parser	2.35	$nont(c, [\overbrace{a, \ldots, a}^{18}, c, b], [b])$
solve	7.23	$solve("\{q(X) \leftarrow p(X), p(a) \leftarrow\}", " \leftarrow q(a)")$
regexp	101.1	$dgenerate("(a + b) * .a.a.b", "abaaaabbaab")$

Table 3. Running the specialised program

The results depicted in Tables 1, 2 and 3 are very satisfactory. The generating extensions are generated very efficiently and also run very efficiently. Furthermore the specialised programs are also very efficient and the speedups are very satisfactory. The specialisation for the *parser* example corresponds to the one obtained in Ex. 3. By specialising *solve* our system COGEN was able to remove almost all the overhead of the ground representation, something which has been achieved for the first time in [12]. In fact, the specialised program looks like this:

```
solve__0([]).
solve__0([struct(q,[B])|C]) :- solve__0([struct(p,[B])]), solve__0(C).
solve__0([struct(p,[struct(a,[])])|D]) :- solve__0([]), solve__0(D).
```

The specialised program obtained for the *regexp* example actually corresponds to a deterministic automaton, a feat that has also been achieved by the system LOGIMIX in [39]. For further details about these examples, as well as the experiments, see [25].

4.2 Experiments with other Systems

We also performed the experiments using some other specialisation systems. All systems were able to satisfactorily handle the *parser* example and came up with (almost) the same specialised program as COGEN. More specific information is presented in the following paragraphs.

MIXTUS ([45]) is a partial evaluator for full Prolog which is not (effectively) self-applicable. We experimented with version 0.3.3 of MIXTUS. MIXTUS came up with exactly the same specialisation as our COGEN for the *parser* and *solve* examples. MIXTUS was also able to specialise the *regexp* program, but not to the extent of generating a deterministic automaton.

We experimented with the SP system (see [12]), a specialiser for a subset of Prolog (not including the *if-then-else*). For the *solve* example SP was able to obtain the same specialisation as COGEN, but only after re-specialising the specialised program a second time. Due to the heavy usage of the *if-then-else* the *regexp* example could not be handled directly by SP.

LOGIMIX ([39]) is a self-applicable partial evaluator for a subset of Prolog, containing *if-then-else*, side-effects and some built-in's. This system falls within the off-line setting and requires a binding time annotation. It is not (yet) fully automatic, in the sense that the program has to be hand-annotated. For the *parser* and *regexp* examples, LOGIMIX came up with almost the same programs than COGEN. We were not able to annotate *solve* properly. It might be that this example cannot be handled by LOGIMIX because the restrictions on the annotations are more severe than ours (in COGEN the unfoldable predicates do not require a division and COGEN allows non-deterministic unfolding — the latter seems to be crucial for the *solve* example).

LEUPEL ([28, 31]) is a (not yet effectively self-applicable) partial evaluator for a subset of Prolog, very similar to the one treated by LOGIMIX. The system is guided by an annotation phase which is unfortunately also not automatic. The annotations are "semi-online", in the sense that conditions (tested in an on-line manner) can be given on when to make a call reducible or non-reducible. For the *parser* and *regexp* examples the system performed the same specialisation as COGEN. For the *solve* example LEUPEL even came up with a better specialisation than COGEN, in the sense that unfolding has also been performed at the object level:

```
solve__1([]).
solve__1([struct(q,[struct(a,[])])|A]) :- solve__1(A).
solve__1([struct(p,[struct(a,[])])|A]) :- solve__1(A).
```

Such optimisations depend on the particular object program and are therefore outside the reach of purely off-line methods.

CHTREE is a fully automatic system for a declarative subset of Prolog (similar to the language handled by SP) based on the work in [29, 33]. It is an on-line system which has a very precise abstraction operation, minimising specialisation losses. We used a local unfolding rule based on the homeomorphic embedding relation (see e.g. [33, 46]). For the *solve* example the CHTREE came up with a better specialisation than COGEN, almost identical to the one obtained by LEUPEL (but this time fully automatically). Due to the heavy usage of the *if-then-else* the *regexp* example could, similarly to SP, not be handled directly by CHTREE.

We also did some experiments with the PADDY system (see [43]) written for full Eclipse (a variant of Prolog). PADDY basically performed the same specialisation of *solve* as CHTREE or LEUPEL, but left some useless tests and clauses inside. PADDY was also able to specialise the *regexp* program, but again not to the extent of generating a deterministic automaton.

Finally we tried out the self-applicable partial deducer SAGE (see [18]) for the logic programming language Gödel. SAGE came up with (almost) the same specialised program for the *parser* example as COGEN. SAGE performed little specialisation on the *solve* example, returning almost the unspecialised program back. Due to the heavy usage of the *if-then-else* the *regexp* example could not be handled by SAGE.

4.3 Comparing Transformation Times

The systems which gave us access to the transformation times were PADDY, MIX-TUS, LEUPEL, CHTREE and LOGIMIX. The results can be found in Table 4. The columns marked by *spec* contain the times needed to produce the specialised program (i.e. the time to perform the first Futamura projection), whereas the columns marked by *genex* contain the times needed to produce the generating extensions (i.e. performing the second Futamura projection). The latter columns only make sense for COGEN, for the self-applicable system LOGIMIX as well as for COGEN$_{logimix}$ obtained via the third Futamura projection of LOGIMIX. As can be seen in Table 4, COGEN is by far the fastest system overall, as well for specialisation as for compiler generation, while producing almost the best specialised code.

More details about the experiments can be found in [25]. Note however that the timings of CHTREE include the printing of tracing information and that a rather naive implementation of the homeomorphic embedding relation was used.

Finally the figures in Tables 1 and 2 really shine when compared to the compiler generator and the generating extensions produced by the self-applicable SAGE system. Unfortunately self-applying SAGE is currently not possible for normal users, so we had to take the timings from [18]: generating the compiler generator takes about 100 hours (including garbage collection), generating a generating extension took for the examples (which are probably more complex than the ones treated in this section) in [18] at least 11.8 hours (with garbage collection). The speedups by using the generating extension instead of the partial evaluator range from 2.7 to 3.6 but the execution times for the system (including pre- and post-processing) still range from 113*s* to 447*s*.

Specialiser	Prolog System	Architecture	*parser genex*	*parser spec*	*solve genex*	*solve spec*	*regexp genex*	*regexp spec*
COGEN	BIM	Sparc Classic	0.02 s	0.01 s	0.06 s	0.01 s	0.02 s	0.03 s
MIXTUS	SICStus	Sparc Classic	-	0.14 s	-	1.36 s	-	13.63 s
PADDY	Eclipse	Sun4	-	0.05 s	-	0.80 s	-	3.17 s
CHTREE	BIM	Sparc Classic	-	0.21 s	-	9.07 s	-	-
LEUPEL	BIM	Sparc Classic	-	0.11 s	-	0.64 s	-	4.00 s
LOGIMIX	SICStus	Sparc Classic	1.47 s	0.02 s	-	-	1.28 s	0.09 s
COGEN$_{logimix}$	SICStus	Sparc Classic	1.10 s	0.02 s	-	-	0.98 s	0.08 s

Table 4. Comparative Table of Specialisation Times

5 Discussion and Future Work

In comparison to other partial deduction methods the cogen approach may, at least from the examples given in this paper, seem to do quite well with respect to speedup and quality of residual code, and outperform any other system with respect to transformation speed. But this efficiency has a price. Since our approach is off-line it will of course suffer from the same deficiencies than other off-line systems when compared to on-line systems. Also, no partially static structures were needed in the above examples and our system cannot handle these, so it will probably have difficulties with something like the *transpose* program (see [12]) or with a non-ground meta-interpreter. However, our notion of *BTA* and *BTC* is quite a coarse one and corresponds roughly to that used in early work on self-applicability of partial evaluators for functional programming languages, so one might expect that this could be refined considerably.

Although our approach is closely related to the one for functional programming languages there are still some important differences. Since computation in our cogen is based on unification, a variable is not forced to have a fixed binding time assigned to it. In fact the binding-time analysis is only required to be safe, and this does not enforce this restriction. Consider the following program:

```
g(X) :- p(X),q(X)
p(a).
q(a).
```

If the initial division Δ_0 states that the argument to g is dynamic, then Δ_0 is safe for the program and the unfolding rule that unfolds predicates p and q. The residual program that one gets by running the generating extensions is:

```
g__0(a).
```

In contrast to this any cogen for a functional language known to us will classify the variable X in the following analogue functional program (here exemplified in Scheme) as dynamic:

```
(define (g X) (and (equal? X a) (equal? X a)))
```

and the residual program would be identical to the original program.

One could say that our system allows divisions that are not uniformly congruent in the sense of Launchbury [27] and essentially, our system performs specialisation that a partial evaluation system for a functional language would need some form of *driving* to be able to do.

Whether application of the cogen approach is feasible for specialisation of other logical programming languages than Prolog is hard to say, but it seems essential that such languages have some metalevel built-in predicates, like Prolog's findall and call predicates, for the method to be efficient. This means that it is probably not possible to use the approach (efficiently) for Gödel. Further work will be needed to establish this.

Related Work in Partial Evaluation

The first hand-written compiler generator based on partial evaluation principles was, in all probability, the system *RedCompile* for a dialect of Lisp [2]. Since then successful compiler generators have been written for many different languages and language paradigms [44, 21, 22, 5, 1, 16].

In the context of definite clause grammars and parsers based on them, the idea of hand writing the compiler generator has also been used in [40, 41].[10] However it is not based on (off-line) partial deduction. The exact relationship to our work is currently being investigated.

---

[10] Thanks to Ulrich Neumerkel for pointing this out.

Future Work

The most obvious goal of the near future is to see if a complete and precise binding-time analysis can be developed. Since we imposed that a *static* term must be ground, one might think that the *BTA* corresponds exactly to groundness analysis. This is however not entirely true because a standard groundness analysis gives information about the arguments at the point where a call is selected (and often imposing left-to-right selection). In other words, it gives groundness information at the local level when using some standard execution. A *BTA* however requires groundness information about the arguments of calls in the leaves, i.e. at the point where these atoms are lifted to the global level. So what we actually need is a groundness analysis adapted for unfolding rules and not for standard execution of logic programs. However, by re-using and running a standard groundness analysis on a transformed version of the program to be specialised, we can come up with a reasonable *BTA*. More details, along with some initial experiments using the PLAI system [19], can be found in [25].

On a slightly longer term one might try to extend the cogen and the binding-time analysis to handle partially static structures. It also seems natural to investigate to what extent more powerful control and specialisation techniques (like the unfold/fold transformations, [42]) can be incorporated into the cogen in the context of conjunctive partial deduction ([32, 17]).

Acknowledgements

We thank Maurice Bruynooghe, Bart Demoen, Danny De Schreye, André De Waal, Robert Glück, Gerda Janssens, Bern Martens, Torben Mogensen and Ulrich Neumerkel for interesting discussions on this work. We also thank André De Waal for helping us with some partial evaluation experiments, Gerda Janssens for providing us with valuable information about abstract interpretation and Bern Martens for finding the title of the paper and for providing us with formulations for the text of the paper. Bern Martens also provided valuable feedback on a draft of this paper. Finally we are grateful to Danny De Schreye for his stimulating support and to anonymous referees for their helpful comments.

References

1. L. O. Andersen. *Program Analysis and Specialization for the C Programming Language*. PhD thesis, DIKU, University of Copenhagen, May 1994. (DIKU report 94/19).
2. L. Beckman, A. Haraldson, Ö. Oskarsson, and E. Sandewall. A partial evaluator and its use as a programming tool. *Artificial Intelligence*, 7:319–357, 1976.
3. K. Benkerimi and P. M. Hill. Supporting transformations for the partial evaluation of logic programs. *Journal of Logic and Computation*, 3(5):469–486, October 1993.
4. K. Benkerimi and J. W. Lloyd. A partial evaluation procedure for logic programs. In S. Debray and M. Hermenegildo, editors, *Proceedings of the North American Conference on Logic Programming*, pages 343–358. MIT Press, 1990.

5. L. Birkedal and M. Welinder. Hand-writing program generator generators. In M. Hermenegildo and J. Penjam, editors, *Programming Language Implementation and Logic Programming. Proceedings*, volume 844 of *LNCS*, pages 198–214, Madrid, Spain, 1994. Springer-Verlag.

6. R. Bol. Loop checking in partial deduction. *Journal of Logic Programming*, 16(1&2):25–46, 1993.

7. A. Bondorf, F. Frauendorf, and M. Richter. An experiment in automatic self-applicable partial evaluation of prolog. Technical Report 335, Lehrstuhl Informatik V, University of Dortmund, 1990.

8. A. F. Bowers and C. A. Gurr. Towards fast and declarative meta-programming. In K. R. Apt and F. Turini, editors, *Meta-logics and Logic Programming*, pages 137–166. MIT Press, 1995.

9. M. Bruynooghe, D. De Schreye, and B. Martens. A general criterion for avoiding infinite unfolding during partial deduction. *New Generation Computing*, 11(1):47–79, 1992.

10. C. Consel and O. Danvy. Tutorial notes on partial evaluation. In *Proceedings of POPL'93*, Charleston, South Carolina, January 1993. ACM Press.

11. H. Fujita and K. Furukawa. A self-applicable partial evaluator and its use in incremental compilation. *New Generation Computing*, 6(2 & 3):91–118, 1988.

12. J. Gallagher. A system for specialising logic programs. Technical Report TR-91-32, University of Bristol, November 1991.

13. J. Gallagher. Tutorial on specialisation of logic programs. In *Proceedings of PEPM'93, the ACM Sigplan Symposium on Partial Evaluation and Semantics-Based Program Manipulation*, pages 88–98. ACM Press, 1993.

14. J. Gallagher and M. Bruynooghe. Some low-level transformations for logic programs. In M. Bruynooghe, editor, *Proceedings of Meta90 Workshop on Meta Programming in Logic*, pages 229–244, Leuven, Belgium, 1990.

15. J. Gallagher and M. Bruynooghe. The derivation of an algorithm for program specialisation. *New Generation Computing*, 9(3 & 4):305–333, 1991.

16. R. Glück and J. Jørgensen. Efficient multi-level generating extensions for program specialization. In *Programming Languages, Implementations, Logics and Programs (PLILP'95)*, LNCS 982, pages 259–278. Springer-Verlag, 1995.

17. R. Glück, J. Jørgensen, B. Martens, and M. Sørensen. Controlling conjunctive partial deduction of definite logic programs. Technical Report CW 226, Departement Computerwetenschappen, K.U. Leuven, Belgium, February 1996. Submitted.

18. C. A. Gurr. *A Self-Applicable Partial Evaluator for the Logic Programming Language Gödel.* PhD thesis, Department of Computer Science, University of Bristol, January 1994.

19. M. Hermenegildo, R. Warren, and S. K. Debray. Global flow analysis as a practical compilation tool. *The Journal of Logic Programming*, 13(4):349–366, 1992.

20. P. Hill and J. Gallagher. Meta-programming in logic programming. Technical Report 94.22, School of Computer Studies, University of Leeds, 1994. To be published in *Handbook of Logic in Artificial Intelligence and Logic Programming, Vol. 5.* Oxford Science Publications, Oxford University Press.

21. C. K. Holst. Syntactic currying: yet another approach to partial evaluation. Technical report, DIKU, Department of Computer Science, University of Copenhagen, 1989.

22. C. K. Holst and J. Launchbury. Handwriting cogen to avoid problems with static typing. Working paper, 1992.

23. N. D. Jones, C. K. Gomard, and P. Sestoft. *Partial Evaluation and Automatic Program Generation.* Prentice Hall, 1993.

24. N. D. Jones, P. Sestoft, and H. Søndergaard. Mix: a self-applicable partial evaluator for experiments in compiler generation. *LISP and Symbolic Computation,* 2(1):9–50, 1989.

25. J. Jørgensen and M. Leuschel. Efficiently generating efficient generating extensions in Prolog. Technical Report CW 221, K.U. Leuven, Belgium, February 1996. Accessible via http://www.cs.kuleuven.ac.be/~lpai.

26. J. Komorowski. An introduction to partial deduction. In A. Pettorossi, editor, *Proceedings Meta'92,* pages 49–69. Springer-Verlag, LNCS 649, 1992.

27. J. Launchbury. *Projection Factorisations in Partial Evaluation.* Distinguished Dissertations in Computer Science. Cambridge University Press, 1991.

28. M. Leuschel. Partial evaluation of the "real thing". In L. Fribourg and F. Turini, editors, Logic Program Synthesis and Transformation — Meta-Programming in Logic. *Proceedings of LOPSTR'94 and META'94,* LNCS 883, pages 122–137, Pisa, Italy, June 1994. Springer-Verlag.

29. M. Leuschel. Ecological partial deduction: Preserving characteristic trees without constraints. In M. Proietti, editor, Logic Program Synthesis and Transformation. *Proceedings of LOPSTR'95,* LNCS 1048, pages 1–16, Utrecht, Netherlands, September 1995. Springer-Verlag.

30. M. Leuschel and D. De Schreye. An almost perfect abstraction operation for partial deduction using characteristic trees. Technical Report CW 215, K.U. Leuven, Belgium, October 1995. Submitted for Publication. Accessible via http://www.cs.kuleuven.ac.be/~lpai.

31. M. Leuschel and D. De Schreye. Towards creating specialised integrity checks through partial evaluation of meta-interpreters. In *Proceedings of PEPM'95, the ACM Sigplan Symposium on Partial Evaluation and Semantics-Based Program Manipulation,* pages 253–263, La Jolla, California, June 1995. ACM Press.

32. M. Leuschel, D. De Schreye, and A. de Waal. A conceptual embedding of folding into partial deduction: Towards a maximal integration. Technical Report CW 225, Departement Computerwetenschappen, K.U. Leuven, Belgium, February 1996. Submitted.

33. M. Leuschel and B. Martens. Global control for partial deduction through characteristic atoms and global trees. In *this volume.*

34. M. Leuschel and B. Martens. Partial deduction of the ground representation and its application to integrity checking. In J. Lloyd, editor, *Proceedings of ILPS'95, the International Logic Programming Symposium,* pages 495–509, Portland, USA, December 1995. MIT Press. Extended version as Technical Report CW 210, K.U. Leuven. Accessible via http://www.cs.kuleuven.ac.be/~lpai.

35. J. Lloyd. *Foundations of Logic Programming.* Springer Verlag, 1987.

36. J. W. Lloyd and J. C. Shepherdson. Partial evaluation in logic programming. *The Journal of Logic Programming,* 11:217–242, 1991.

37. B. Martens and D. De Schreye. Automatic finite unfolding using well-founded measures. *Journal of Logic Programming,* 1995. To Appear.

38. B. Martens and J. Gallagher. Ensuring global termination of partial deduction while allowing flexible polyvariance. In L. Sterling, editor, *Proceedings ICLP'95,* pages 597–613, Kanagawa, Japan, June 1995. MIT Press.

39. T. Mogensen and A. Bondorf. Logimix: A self-applicable partial evaluator for Prolog. In K.-K. Lau and T. Clement, editors, Logic Program Synthesis and Transformation. *Proceedings of LOPSTR'92,* pages 214–227. Springer-Verlag, 1992.

40. G. Neumann. Transforming interpreters into compilers by goal classification. In M. Bruynooghe, editor, *Proceedings of Meta90 Workshop on Meta Programming in Logic*, pages 205–217, Leuven, Belgium, 1990.

41. G. Neumann. A simple transformation from Prolog-written metalevel interpreters into compilers and its implementation. In A. Voronkov, editor, Logic Programming. *Proceedings of the First and Second Russian Conference on Logic Programming*, LNCS 592, pages 349–360. Springer-Verlag, 1991.

42. A. Pettorossi and M. Proietti. Transformation of logic programs: Foundations and techniques. *The Journal of Logic Programming*, 19 & 20:261–320, May 1994.

43. S. Prestwich. The PADDY partial deduction system. Technical Report ECRC-92-6, ECRC, Munich, Germany, 1992.

44. S. A. Romanenko. A compiler generator produced by a self-applicable specializer can have a surprisingly natural and understandable structure. In D. Bjørner, A. P. Ershov, and N. D. Jones, editors, *Partial Evaluation and Mixed Computation*, pages 445–463. North-Holland, 1988.

45. D. Sahlin. Mixtus: An automatic partial evaluator for full Prolog. *New Generation Computing*, 12(1):7–51, 1993.

46. M. Sørensen and R. Glück. An algorithm of generalization in positive supercompilation. In J. Lloyd, editor, *Proceedings of ILPS'95, the International Logic Programming Symposium*, pages 465–479, Portland, USA, December 1995. MIT Press.

47. V. Turchin. The concept of a supercompiler. *ACM Transactions on Programming Languages and Systems*, 8(3):292–325, 1986.

A Extending the cogen

It is straightforward to extend the cogen to handle primitives, i.e. built-ins (=/2, not/1, =../2, call/1,...) or externally defined user predicates. The code of these predicates will not be available and therefore no predicates to unfold them can be generated. The generating extension can either contain code that completely evaluates calls to primitives in which case the call will then be marked reducible or code that produces residual calls to such predicates in which case the call is marked non-reducible. So we extend the transformation of Def. 17 with the following two rules:

3. $S_i = A_i$ and $R_i = []$ if A_i is a reducible built-in
4. $S_i = true$ and $R_i = A_i$ if A_i is a non-reducible built-in

As a last example of how to extend the method we will show how to handle the Prolog version of the conditional: $A_{if} \rightarrow A_{then}; A_{else}$. For this we will introduce the notation G^R where $G = A_1, ..., A_k$ to mean the following:

$$G^R = S_1, ..., S_k$$

where S_i, R_i are defined as in Def. 17 and $R = [R_1, ..., R_k]$ (i.e. this allows us perform the transformations recursively on the sub-components of a conditional).

If the test of a conditional is marked as reducible then the generating extension will simply contain a conditional with the test unchanged and where the two "branches" contain code for unfolding the two branches (similar to the body of a function indexed by "u"), i.e. Def. 17 is extended with the following rule:

5. $S_i = (G_1 \rightarrow (G_2^{\mathcal{R}}, \mathcal{R}_i = \mathcal{R}); (G_3^{\mathcal{R}'}, \mathcal{R}_i = \mathcal{R}'))$ and $\mathcal{R}_i$ is a fresh variable, if $A_i = (G_1 \rightarrow G_2 ; G_3)$ is reducible.

If the test goal of the conditional is non-reducible then we assume that the three subgoals are either a call to a non-reducible predicate, a call to a non-reducible (dynamic) primitive or another dynamic conditional. This restriction is not severe, since if a program contains conditionals that get classified as dynamic by the *BTA* and these contain arbitrary subgoals then the program may by a simple source language transformation be transformed into a program which satisfies the restriction. Def. 17 is extended with the following rule:

6. $S_i = (A_1', A_2', A_3')^{[\mathcal{R}, \mathcal{R}', \mathcal{R}'']}$ and $\mathcal{R}_i = (\mathcal{R} \rightarrow \mathcal{R}'; \mathcal{R}'')$, if $A_i = (A_1' \rightarrow A_2'; A_3')$ is non-reducible.

where A_1', A_2' and A_3' are goals that satisfy the restriction above. This restriction ensures that the three goals $\{A_i' \mid i = 1, 2, 3\}$ compute their residual code independently of each other and the residual code for the conditional is then a conditional composed from this code.

B   A Prolog cogen

This appendix contains the listing of the cogen. The system is available via http://www.cs.kuleuven.ac.be/~lpai.

```
/* ----------- */
/* C O G E N */
/* ----------- */

cogen :-
  findall(C,predicate(C),Clauses1),
  findall(C,clause(C),Clauses2),
  pp(Clauses1),
  pp(Clauses2).

flush_cogen :- print_header,flush_pp.

predicate(clause(Head,[if([find_pattern(Call,V)],[true],
                          [insert_pattern(GCall,H),
                           findall(NClause,
                                   (RCall,treat_clause(H,Body,NClause)),
                                   NClauses),
                           pp(NClauses),
                           find_pattern(Call,V)])])) :-
  generalise(Call,GCall),
  add_extra_argument("_u",GCall,Body,RCall),
  add_extra_argument("_m",Call,V,Head).
```

```
clause(clause(ResCall,ResBody)) :-
  ann_clause(Call,Body),
  add_extra_argument("_u",Call,Vars,ResCall),
  bodys(Body,ResBody,Vars).

bodys([],[],[]).
bodys([G|GS],GRes,VRes) :-
  body(G,G1,V),
  filter_cons(G1,GS1,GRes,true),
  filter_cons(V,VS,VRes,[]),
  bodys(GS,GS1,VS).

filter_cons(H,T,HT,FVal) :-
        ((nonvar(H),H = FVal) -> (HT = T) ; (HT = [H|T])).

body(unfold(Call),ResCall,V) :-
  add_extra_argument("_u",Call,V,ResCall).
body(memo(Call),true,memo(Call)).
body(call(Call),Call,[]).
body(rescall(Call),true,rescall(Call)).
body(if(G1,G2,G3),     /* Static if: */
    if(RG1,[RG2,(V=VS2)],[RG3,(V=VS3)]),V) :-
  bodys(G1,RG1,VS1), bodys(G2,RG2,VS2), bodys(G3,RG3,VS3).
body(resif(G1,G2,G3), /* Dynamic if: */
    [RG1,RG2,RG3],if(VS1,VS2,VS3)) :-
  body(G1,RG1,VS1), body(G2,RG2,VS2), body(G3,RG3,VS3).

generalise(Call,GCall) :-
  delta(Call,STerms,_), Call =.. [Pred|_],
  delta(GCall,STerms,_), GCall =.. [Pred|_].

add_extra_argument(T,Call,V,ResCall) :-
  Call =.. [Pred|Args],res_name(T,Pred,ResPred),
  append(Args,[V],NewArgs),ResCall =.. [ResPred|NewArgs].

res_name(T,Pred,ResPred) :-
  name(PE_Sep,T),string_concatenate(Pred,PE_Sep,ResPred).

print_header :-
  print('/'),print('* --------------------- *'),print('/'),nl,
  print('/'),print('* GENERATING EXTENSION *'),print('/'),nl,
  print('/'),print('* --------------------- *'),print('/'),nl,
  print(':'),print('- reconsult(memo).'),nl,
  print(':'),print('- reconsult(pp).'),nl,
  (static_consult(List) -> pp_consults(List) ; true),nl.
```

Global Control for Partial Deduction through Characteristic Atoms and Global Trees

Michael Leuschel* and Bern Martens**

Department of Computer Science
Katholieke Universiteit Leuven
Celestijnenlaan 200A, B-3001 Heverlee, Belgium
e-mail : {michael,bern}@cs.kuleuven.ac.be

Abstract. Recently, considerable advances have been made in the (on-line) control of logic program specialisation. A clear conceptual distinction has been established between local and global control and on both levels concrete strategies as well as general frameworks have been proposed. For global control in particular, recent work has developed concrete techniques based on the preservation of characteristic trees (limited, however, by a given, arbitrary depth bound) to obtain a very precise control of polyvariance. On the other hand, the concept of an m-tree has been introduced as a refined way to trace "relationships" of partially deduced atoms, thus serving as the basis for a general framework within which global termination of partial deduction can be ensured in a non ad hoc way.

Blending both, formerly separate, contributions, in this paper, we present an elegant and sophisticated technique to globally control partial deduction of normal logic programs. Leaving unspecified the specific local control one may wish to plug in, we develop a concrete global control strategy combining the use of characteristic atoms and trees with global (m-)trees. We thus obtain partial deduction that always terminates in an elegant, non ad hoc way, while providing excellent specialisation as well as fine-grained (but reasonable) polyvariance.

We conjecture that a similar approach may contribute to improve upon current (on-line) control strategies for functional program transformation methods such as (positive) supercompilation.

1 Introduction

A major concern in the specialisation of functional ([4, 14, 32]) as well as logic programs ([23, 16, 8, 29, 5]) has been the issue of control: How can the transformation process be guided in such a way that termination is guaranteed and results are satisfactory?

This problem has been tackled from two (until now) largely separate angles: the so-called *off-line* versus *on-line* approaches. Partial evaluation of functional

---

* Supported by the Belgian GOA "Non-Standard Applications of Abstract Interpretation".
** Postdoctoral Fellow of the K.U.Leuven Research Council.

programs ([4, 14]) has mainly stressed the former, while supercompilation of functional ([32, 33, 31]) and partial deduction of logic programs ([10, 30, 2, 3, 24, 27, 18]) have concentrated on on-line control. (Some exceptions are [34, 28, 17, 15].) It is within this on-line control tradition that the present work provides a novel and important contribution.

In partial deduction of logic programs, one distinguishes two levels of control ([8, 27]): the local and the global level. In a nutshell, the local level decides on how SLD(NF)-trees for individual atoms should be built. The (leaves of the) resulting trees allow to construct specialised clauses for the given atoms ([23, 1]). At the global level on the other hand, one typically attends to the overall correctness of the resulting program (satisfying the closedness condition in [23]) and strives to achieve the "right" amount of polyvariance, producing sufficiently many (but not too much) specialised versions for each predicate definition in the original program.

Gallagher in [8] writes that providing adequate global control seems much harder than handling the local level. So, in this paper, it is to the latter, global, level that we (again) turn our attention. In recent work, both authors of the present paper have already, separately, investigated issues in global control of partial deduction. [27] and its extended and slightly revised version [26] focus on termination and provide a quite general, refined framework for global control, different instances of which can be taken as the core of practical systems. [18] on the other hand starts from the central role of characteristic trees in preserving specialisation and determining polyvariance (as first proposed in [10]). It shows how partial deduction can be governed through the use of *characteristic atoms*, combining the usual atoms to be partially deduced with the characteristic trees to be enforced upon them. Global termination, however, is guaranteed at the cost of imposing an arbitrary, ad hoc depth bound on characteristic trees (as in all earlier partial deduction based on characteristic trees, see e.g. [10, 7, 19]).

In the present paper, we endeavour to obtain the best of both worlds, blending (a slightly adapted version of) the general framework in [27, 26] with the use of characteristic atoms and trees as in [18]. We thus obtain a very elegant, sophisticated and precise apparatus for on-line global control of partial deduction.

Below, we first recapitulate some necessary background material and provide motivating examples for our approach in Sect. 2. Subsequently, Sect. 3 contains the formal elaboration of our method, including a partial deduction algorithm, parameterised by its local control, the particular choice of which is left open in this paper. Next, in Sect. 4, we return to the examples in Sect. 2, showing how indeed the method developed in Sect. 3 deals properly with them and leads to greatly improved practical specialisation results. Finally, a possible drawback of the presented approach as well as some connections with related work in supercompilation are briefly discussed. We conclude the paper in Sect. 5.

In order to remain within reasonable space limits, we have not included any proofs. These can be found in [21], which also contains a section on post-processing the output of Algorithm 28 as well as a more extensive discussion of experimental results, connections to other work, and assorted topics.

2 Ecological Partial Deduction and the Depth Bound Problem

In what follows, we assume the reader to be familiar with the basic concepts of logic programming and partial deduction, as they are presented in e.g. [22, 23]. Throughout, unless stated explicitly otherwise, the terms "(logic) program" and "goal" will refer to a *normal* logic program and goal, respectively.

Given a program P and a goal G, partial deduction produces a new program P' which is P "specialised" to the goal G. The underlying technique is to construct "incomplete" SLDNF-trees for a set of atoms $\mathcal{A}$ to be specialised and extract the program P' from these incomplete search trees by taking resultants (for each atom in $\mathcal{A}$ a different specialised predicate definition will thus be generated). An *incomplete* SLDNF-tree is an SLDNF-tree which, in addition to success and failure leaves, may also contain leaves where no literal has been selected for a further derivation step. Leaves of the latter kind will be called *dangling*. Under the conditions stated in [23], namely closedness and independence, correctness of the specialised program is guaranteed.

In the context of partial deduction, incomplete SLDNF-trees are obtained by applying an unfolding rule, defined as follows:

Definition 1. An *unfolding rule* U is a function which given a program P and a goal G returns a finite (possibly incomplete) SLDNF-tree[3] for $P \cup \{G\}$.

2.1 Ecological Partial Deduction

The problem of *controlling polyvariance* in partial deduction boils down to finding a *terminating* procedure to produce a *finite* set of atoms $\mathcal{A}$ which satisfies the *correctness* conditions of [23] while at the same time being as *precise* as possible (usually the more fine-grained and instantiated the set $\mathcal{A}$ is, the better the potential for specialisation is). Most approaches in the literature so far are based on the syntactic structure of the atoms to be specialised, but it can be shown (see e.g. [19, 18]) that this provides insufficient detail.

[10, 7] therefore introduced the notion of a *characteristic tree*, capturing how atoms are specialised and as such constituting a more refined basis for polyvariance. The following definitions are adapted from [7, 18, 19].

Definition 2. Let G_1 be a goal and let P be a program the clauses of which are numbered. Let $G_1, \ldots, G_n$ be a finite, incomplete SLDNF-derivation of $P \cup \{G_1\}$. The *characteristic path* of the derivation is the sequence $(l_1, c_1), \ldots, (l_{n-1}, c_{n-1})$, where l_i is the position of the selected literal in G_i, and c_i is defined as:
 - if the selected literal is an atom, then c_i is the number of the clause chosen to resolve with G_i.
 - if the selected literal is $\neg p(\bar{t})$, then c_i is the predicate p.

The set of all characteristic paths for a given goal G and program P will be denoted by $chpaths(G, P)$.

---

[3] We even allow a trivial SLDNF-tree, i.e. one whose root is a dangling leaf.

Definition 3. Let G be a goal, P a program and U an unfolding rule. Then *the characteristic tree τ of G (in P) via U* is the set of characteristic paths of the non-failing derivations of the incomplete SLDNF-tree obtained by applying U to G (in P). We introduce the notation $chtree(G, P, U) = \tau$. We also say that τ is *a characteristic tree of G (in P)* if it is *the* characteristic tree for some unfolding rule U. Also τ is *a characteristic tree* if it is a characteristic tree of some G in some P.

Example 1. Let P be the following program:

(1) $member(X, [X|T]) \leftarrow$
(2) $member(X, [Y|T]) \leftarrow member(X, T)$

Let $A_1 = member(a, [a, b])$ and $A_2 = member(a, [a])\}$. Suppose that A_1, A_2 are unfolded as depicted in Fig. 1. Then both these atoms have the same characteristic tree $\tau = \{((1,1))\}$.

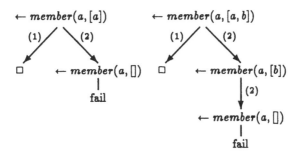

Fig. 1. Incomplete SLDNF-trees for example 1

Note that the characteristic path of an empty derivation is the empty path $()$, and the characteristic tree of a trivial SLDNF-tree is $\{()\}$. Characteristic trees are an interesting abstraction of SLDNF-trees because they capture the specialisation performed locally by partial deduction. If two atomic goals have the same characteristic tree then the same branches have been pruned by partial deduction and the atoms have been unfolded in the same way (i.e. to the same depth and the same clauses have been resolved with literals in the same position). Furthermore the goals in the bodies of the resultants have the same structure, varying only by the actual call patterns, meaning that in principle a single predicate definition can be used. As such, a characteristic tree is an almost perfect characterisation of the partial deduction of an atom and of the specialisation that has been performed.[4] For more details about the interest and relevance of characteristic trees, we refer to [10, 7, 19, 18].

---

[4] Sometimes atoms with different characteristic trees have (almost) identical resultants (due to independence of the computation rule) and could therefore also be replaced by a single predicate definition. Normalising characteristic trees (after unfolding) by imposing e.g. a left-to-right ordering of selected literals and delaying the selection of negative literals to the end solves this problem (see also [19]). Thanks to Maurice Bruynooghe for pointing this out. A similar effect can also be obtained by using the trace terms of [12].

When using characteristic trees to control polyvariance, the atoms to be specialised are classified according to their characteristic tree. The basic idea is to *have only one specialised version for each characteristic tree*. If several atoms have the same characteristic tree, then they are *abstracted by a single more general atom*. Earlier approaches to partial deduction using characteristic trees [7, 10] have been limited by not being able to *preserve characteristic trees* in that abstraction process (implying that the generalisation has a different local specialisation behaviour). As shown in [18, 19], this can lead to important precision losses as well as non-termination.

The problem has been solved in [18] by simply *imposing* characteristic trees on the generalised atoms. [5] This amounts to associating characteristic trees with the atoms to be specialised, thus allowing the preservation of characteristic trees without having to construct intricate generalisations. The rest of this subsection recapitulates and adapts the necessary material from [18].

From now on, throughout the rest of this paper, we implicitly assume the existence of some given finite underlying language $\mathcal{L}$ in which atoms and terms, goals and programs are expressed.

We first introduce the crucial notion of a *characteristic atom*.

Definition 4. A *P-characteristic atom*, for a given program P, is a couple (A, τ) consisting of an atom A and a characteristic tree τ with $\tau \subseteq chpaths(\leftarrow A, P)$.

Often, when the context allows it, we will drop the P annotation and simply refer to *characteristic* atoms. Also note that τ is not necessarily a characteristic tree of $\leftarrow A$ in P.

Example 2. Let $CA_1 = (member(a, [a, b]), \tau)$, $CA_2 = (member(a, [a]), \tau)$ with $\tau = \{((1, 1))\}$, and let P be the program from Example 1. CA_1 and CA_2 are both P-characteristic atoms with the same characteristic tree component. The method of [18] will abstract CA_1, CA_2 by $CA_3 = (member(a, [a|T]), \{((1, 1))\})$, i.e. it *imposes* the characteristic tree $\{((1, 1))\}$ on the *msg* of the atom components. CA_3 is also a P-characteristic atom, but this time $\{((1, 1))\}$ is not a characteristic tree of $member(a, [a|T])$ (depending on the unfolding rule the characteristic tree of $member(a, [a|T])$ is: $\{((1, 1)), ((1, 2))\}$ or $\{((1, 1)), ((1, 2), (1, 1)), ((1, 2), (1, 2))\}$ or something even deeper).

The following definition associates a set of concretisations with each characteristic atom.

---

[5] Another solution is presented in [19], which is however limited to definite programs and certain unfolding rules, but enjoys a better overall precision. The core ideas of the present paper can also be used to enhance the [19] method in order to eliminate a similar depth bound problem.

Definition 5. An atom A is a *precise concretisation* of a P-characteristic atom (A', τ') iff A is an instance of A' and for some unfolding rule U we have that $chtree(\leftarrow A, P, U) = \tau'$. An atom B is a *concretisation* of (A', τ') iff it is an instance of a precise concretisation of (A', τ').

A P-characteristic atom can thus be seen as standing for a (possibly infinite) set of atoms, namely the concretisations according to the above definition.

Example 3. Take the P-characteristic atom $CA_3 = (member(a, [a|T]), \{((1, 1))\})$ from Example 2. The atoms $member(a, [a])$ and $member(a, [a, b])$ are precise concretisations of CA_3 (given the unfolding rule of Fig. 1). Also, note that neither $member(a, [a|T])$ nor $member(a, [a, a])$ are concretisations of CA_3.

A characteristic atom (A, τ) uniquely determines a set of resultants:

Definition 6. Let (A, τ) be a P-characteristic atom. If $\tau \neq \{()\}$ then $\delta(P, (A, \tau))$ is the set of all (necessarily non-failing) SLDNF-derivations for $P \cup \{\leftarrow A\}$ such that their characteristic paths are in τ. If $\tau = \{()\}$ then $\delta(P, (A, \tau))$ is the set of all non-failing SLD-derivations for $P \cup \{\leftarrow A\}$ of length 1.[6]

Definition 7. Let (A, τ) be a P-characteristic atom. Let $\{\delta_1, \ldots, \delta_n\}$ be the SLDNF-derivations in $\delta(P, (A, \tau))$ and let $\leftarrow G_1, \ldots, \leftarrow G_n$ be the goals in the leaves of these derivations. Let $\theta_1, \ldots, \theta_n$ be the computed answers of the derivations from $\leftarrow A$ to $\leftarrow G_1, \ldots, \leftarrow G_n$ respectively. Then the set of resultants $\{A\theta_1 \leftarrow G_1, \ldots, A\theta_n \leftarrow G_n\}$ is called the *partial deduction of* (A, τ) *in* P. Every atom occurring in some of the G_i will be called a *body atom (in P)* of (A, τ). We will denote the set of such body atoms by $BA_P(A, \tau)$.

For example the partial deduction of $(member(a, [a|T]), \{((1, 1))\})$ in the program P of Example 1 will be $\{member(a, [a|T]) \leftarrow\}$. Note that it is different from any set of resultants that can be obtained for incomplete SLDNF-trees of the ordinary atom $member(a, [a|T])$. However the partial deduction is valid for any concretisation (as defined in Definition 5) of $(member(a, [a|T]), \{((1, 1))\})$.

The approach in [18] generates a partial deduction not for a set of atoms but for a set of *characteristic* atoms. Algorithm 28 below (also) computes exactly such a set of characteristic atoms. The actual code of the specialised program is then produced by unfolding the atoms according to their associated characteristic trees, as described in Definitions 6 and 7.

Of course, the same atom A might occur in several characteristic atoms with entirely different characteristic trees. In order to guarantee correctness of the specialised program, renaming (as well as filtering, see also [9]) is added in [18]. Then, given the following coveredness condition, correctness of the specialised program is established in [18].

Definition 8. Let P be a program and $\mathcal{A}$ a set of characteristic atoms. Then $\mathcal{A}$ is called P-*covered* iff for every characteristic atom in $\mathcal{A}$ each of its body atoms in P is a concretisation of a characteristic atom in $\mathcal{A}$.

---

[6] The reason behind the special treatment of the case $\tau = \{()\}$ is that at least one unfolding step is needed to avoid the problematic resultant $A \leftarrow A$ in Definition 7.

2.2 The Depth Bound Problem

When, for the given program, query and unfolding rule, the above sketched method generates a *finite number of different characteristic trees*, its global control regime guarantees termination and correctness of the specialised program as well as "perfect"[7] polyvariance: *For every predicate, exactly one specialised version is produced for each of its different associated*[8] *characteristic trees.* Now, [18], as well as all earlier approaches based on characteristic trees ([10, 7, 19]), achieves the mentioned finiteness condition at the cost of imposing an ad hoc (typically very large) depth bound on characteristic trees. However, for a fairly *large class of realistic programs* (and unfolding rules), *the number of different characteristic trees generated, is not naturally bounded.* In those cases, the underlying depth bound will have to ensure termination, meanwhile propagating its ugly, ad hoc nature into the resulting specialised program. We illustrate this problem through some examples, setting out with a slightly artificial, but very simple one.

Example 4. The following is the well known reverse with accumulating parameter where a list type check on the accumulator has been added.

(1) $rev([], Acc, Acc) \leftarrow$
(2) $rev([H|T], Acc, Res) \leftarrow ls(Acc), rev(T, [H|Acc], Res)$
(3) $ls([]) \leftarrow$
(4) $ls([H|T]) \leftarrow ls(T)$

As can be noticed in Fig. 2, (determinate ([10, 7, 19]) and well-founded ([3, 25, 24]), among others) unfolding produces an infinite number of different characteristic atoms, all with a different characteristic tree. Imposing a depth bound of say 100, we obtain termination, but the algorithm produces 100 different *reverse* versions and the specialised program looks like:

(1') $rev([], [], []) \leftarrow$
(2') $rev([H|T], [], Res) \leftarrow rev_2(T, [H], Res)$
(3') $rev_2([], [A], [A]) \leftarrow$
(4') $rev_2([H|T], [A], Res) \leftarrow rev_3(T, [H, A], Res)$

$\vdots$

(197') $rev_{99}([], [A_1, \ldots, A_{98}], [A_1, \ldots, A_{98}]) \leftarrow$
(198') $rev_{99}([H|T], [A_1, \ldots, A_{98}], Res) \leftarrow rev_{100}(T, [H, A_1, \ldots, A_{98}], Res)$
(199') $rev_{100}([], [A_1, \ldots, A_{99}|AT], [A_1, \ldots, A_{99}|AT]) \leftarrow$
(200') $rev_{100}([H|T], [A_1, \ldots, A_{99}|AT], Res) \leftarrow$
$$ls(AT), rev_{99}(T, [H, A_1, \ldots, A_{99}|AT], Res)$$
(201') $ls([]) \leftarrow$
(202') $ls([H|T]) \leftarrow ls(T)$

This program is certainly far from optimal and clearly exhibits the ad hoc nature of the depth bound.

---

[7] W.r.t. local precision, see [19, 18].
[8] I.e. a characteristic tree associated to an atom with this predicate symbol.

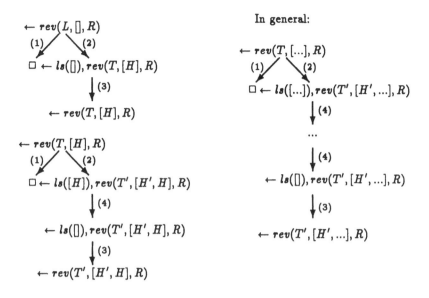

Fig. 2. SLD-trees for Example 4

Situations like the above typically arise when an accumulating parameter influences the computation, because then the growing of the accumulator causes a corresponding growing of the characteristic trees. To be fair, it must be admitted that with most simple programs, this is not the case. For instance, in the standard reverse with accumulating parameter, the accumulator is only copied in the end, but never influences the computation. As illustrated by Example 4 above, this state of affairs will often already be changed when one adds type checking in the style of [11] to even the simplest logic programs.

Among larger and more sophisticated programs, cases like the above become more and more frequent, even in the absence of type checking.[9] For instance, in an explicit unification algorithm, one accumulating parameter is the substitution built so far. It heavily influences the computation because new bindings have to be added and checked for compatibility with the current substitution. Another example is the "mixed" meta-interpreter of [13, 20] (sometimes called *InstanceDemo*; part of it is depicted in Fig. 3) for the ground representation in which the goals are "lifted" to the non-ground representation for resolution. To perform the lifting, an accumulating parameter is used to keep track of the variables that have already been encountered. This accumulator influences the computation: Upon encountering a new variable, the program inspects the accumulator.

---

[9] Especially since efficiently written programs often use accumulating parameters.

```
Program:
(1)  make_non_ground(GrTerm, NgTerm) ←
         mng(GrTerm, NgTerm, [], Sub)
(2)  mng(var(N), X, [], [sub(N, X)]) ←
(3)  mng(var(N), X, [sub(N, X)|T], [sub(N, X)|T]) ←
(4)  mng(var(N), X, [sub(M, Y)|T], [sub(M, Y)|T1]) ←
         not(N = M), mng(var(N), X, T, T1)
(5)  mng(struct(F, GrArgs), struct(F, NgArgs), InSub, OutSub) ←
         l_mng(GrArgs, NgArgs, InSub, OutSub)
(6)  l_mng([], [], Sub, Sub) ←
(7)  l_mng([GrH|GrT], [NgH|NgT], InSub, OutSub) ←
         mng(GrH, NgH, InSub, InSub1),
         l_mng(GrT, NgT, InSub1, OutSub)

Example query:
         ← make_non_ground(struct(f, [var(1), var(2), var(1)]), F)
          ↝ c.a.s. {F/struct(f, [Z, V, Z])}
```

Fig. 3. Lifting the ground representation

Example 5. Let $A = l\_mng(Lg, Ln, [sub(N, X)], S)$ and P be the program of Fig. 3 (this situation arose in a real-life experiment). As can be seen in Fig. 4, unfolding A (e.g. using well-founded measures) causes the addition of the atom $l\_mng(Tg, Tn, [sub(N, X), sub(J, Hn)], S)$ at the global (control) level. Notice that the third argument has grown (i.e. we have an accumulator).

So, when in turn unfolding $l\_mng(Tg, Tn, [sub(N, X), sub(J, Hn)], S)$, we will obtain a deeper characteristic tree (because mng traverses the third argument and thus needs one more step to reach the end) which will have as one of its leaves the atom $l\_mng(Tg', Tn', [sub(N, X), sub(J, Hn), sub(J', Hn')], S)$. An infinite sequence of ever growing characteristic trees results and again, as in Example 4, we obtain non-termination without a depth bound, and very unsatisfactory (ad hoc) specialisations with it.

Summarising, computations influenced by one or more growing data structures are by no means rare and will, very often, lead to ad hoc behaviour of partial deduction where the global control is founded on characteristic trees with a depth bound. In the next section, we show how this annoying depth bound can be lifted without endangering termination.

3   Partial Deduction using Global Trees

3.1   Introduction

A general framework for global control, not relying on any depth bounds, is proposed in [27, 26]. Marked trees (m-trees) are introduced to register descendency

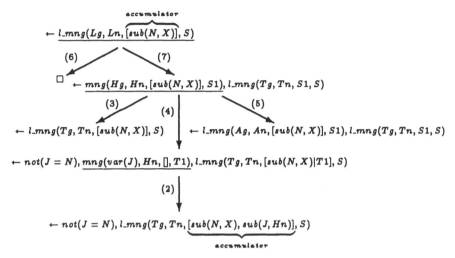

Fig. 4. Accumulator growth in Example 5

relationships among atoms at the global level. The overall tree is then kept finite through ensuring monotonicity of well-founded measure functions and termination of the algorithm follows, provided the generalisation operation (on atoms) is similarly well-founded. It is to this framework that we now turn for inspiration on how to solve the depth bound problem uncovered in Subsect. 2.2.

The basic idea will be to watch over the evolution of characteristic trees associated to atoms along the branches of the global tree. Obviously, just measuring the depth of characteristic trees would be far too crude: Global branches would be cut off prematurely and entirely unrelated atoms could be mopped together through generalisation, resulting in completely unacceptable specialisation losses. No, as can be seen in Fig. 2, we need a more refined measure which would somehow spot when a characteristic tree (piecemeal) "contains" characteristic trees appearing earlier in the same branch of the global tree. If such a situation arises (as it indeed does in Example 4), it seems reasonable to stop expanding the global tree, generalise the offending atoms and produce a specialised procedure for the generalisation instead.

However, a closer look at the following variation of Example 5 shows that also this approach would sometimes overgeneralise and consequently fall short of providing sufficiently detailed polyvariance.

Example 6. Reconsider the program in Fig. 3, and suppose that local control uses determinate unfolding. Let us now start partial deduction for the atom $A = mng(G, struct(cl, [struct(f, [X, Y])|B]), [], S)$ (also this situation arose in a real-life experiment). When unfolding A (see Fig. 5), we obtain an SLDNF-tree containing the atom $mng(H, struct(f, [X, Y]), [], S1)$ in one of its leaves. If we subsequently (determinately) unfold the latter atom, we obtain a tree that is "larger" than its predecessor, also in the more refined sense. Potential non-termination would therefore be detected and a generalisation operation executed.

However, the atoms in the leaves of the second tree are more general than those already met, and simply continuing partial deduction without generalisation will lead to natural termination without any depth bound intervention.

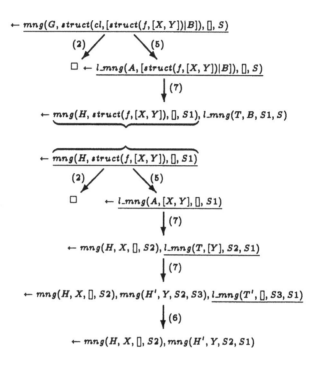

Fig. 5. SLD-trees for Example 6

Example 6 demonstrates that only measuring growth of characteristic trees, even in a refined way, does not always lead to satisfactory specialisation.[10] Luckily, the same example also suggests a solution to this problem: Rather than measuring and comparing characteristic trees, we will *scrutinise entire characteristic atoms, comparing both the syntactic content of the ordinary atoms they contain and the associated characteristic trees.* Accordingly, the global tree nodes will not be labeled by plain atoms as in [27, 26], but by entire characteristic atoms.

The rest of this section, then, contains the formal elaboration of this new approach.

---

[10] In fact, whenever the (local) unfolding rule does not unfold "as deeply as possible" (for whatever reason), then a growing characteristic tree might simply be caused by splitting the "maximally deep tree" in such a way that the second part "contains" the first part.

3.2 More on Characteristic Atoms

Generalising Characteristic Atoms. We extend the notions of variants, instances and generalisations, familiar for ordinary atoms,[11] to characteristic trees and atoms:

Definition 9. A characteristic tree τ_1 is *more general* than another characteristic tree τ_2, denoted by $\tau_1 \preceq \tau_2$, iff τ_2 can be obtained by attaching subtrees to the leaves of τ_1. A characteristic atom (A_1, τ_1) is *more general* than another characteristic atom (A_2, τ_2), denoted by $(A_1, \tau_1) \preceq (A_2, \tau_2)$, iff $A_1 \preceq A_2$ and $\tau_1 \preceq \tau_2$. Also (A_1, τ_1) is a *variant* of (A_2, τ_2), denoted by $(A_1, \tau_1) \equiv (A_2, \tau_2)$, iff $(A_1, \tau_1) \preceq (A_2, \tau_2)$ and $(A_2, \tau_2) \preceq (A_1, \tau_1)$. Finally, $CA_1 \prec CA_2$ holds when $CA_1 \preceq CA_2$ but not $CA_1 \equiv CA_2$.

Note that $\{()\}$, a characteristic tree containing a single, empty path, can be extended into a more specific characteristic tree, while the empty characteristic tree $\emptyset = \{\}$ cannot.

Example 7. Let $\tau_1 = \{((1,3))\}$, $\tau_2 = \{((1,3),(2,4))\}$ and $\tau_3 = \{((1,3)),((1,4))\}$, then we have that $\tau_1 \preceq \tau_2$ and $\tau_1 \prec \tau_2$ but not that $\tau_1 \preceq \tau_3$ nor $\tau_2 \preceq \tau_3$.

The following proposition shows that the above definition makes sense wrt the set of ordinary atoms represented by characteristic atoms.

Proposition 10. Let CA_1, CA_2 be two characteristic atoms such that $CA_1 \preceq CA_2$. Then every atom A which is a concretisation of CA_2 is also a concretisation of CA_1.

Finally, we extend the notion of *most specific generalisation (msg)* to characteristic trees and atoms:

Definition 11. Let τ_1, τ_2 be two P-characteristic trees. Then $msg(\tau_1, \tau_2)$ is the most specific characteristic tree which is more general than both τ_1 and τ_2. Let $(A_1, \tau_1), (A_2, \tau_2)$ be two characteristic atoms. Then $msg((A_1, \tau_1), (A_2, \tau_2)) = (msg(A_1, A_2), msg(\tau_1, \tau_2))$.

Note that the above *msg* for characteristic atoms is still unique up to variable renaming. Its further extension to *sets* of characteristic atoms (rather than just pairs) is straightforward, and will not be included explicitly.

Example 8. Given $\tau_1 = \{((1,3))\}$, $\tau_2 = \{((1,3),(2,4))\}$, $\tau_3 = \{((1,3)),((1,4))\}$, $\tau_4 = \{((1,3),(2,4)),((1,3),(2,5))\}$, we have that $msg(\tau_1, \tau_2) = \tau_1$, $msg(\tau_1, \tau_3) = msg(\tau_2, \tau_3) = \{()\}$ and $msg(\tau_2, \tau_4) = \tau_1$.

---

[11] For ordinary atoms, $A_1 \preceq A_2$ will denote that A_1 is more general than A_2.

Ordering Characteristic Atoms. We now proceed to introduce an order relation on characteristic atoms. It will be instrumental in guaranteeing termination of the partial deduction method to be presented.

Definition 12. A set $V, \leq_V$ is called *well-quasi-ordered (wqo)* iff for any infinite sequence of elements $e_1, e_2, \ldots$ in V there are $i < j$ such that $e_i \leq_V e_j$. We also say that $\leq_V$ is a *well-quasi order (wqo)* on V.

An interesting wqo is the homeomorphic embedding relation $\trianglelefteq$ of [31] (where it is adapted from [6]).

Definition 13. The *homeomorphic embedding* relation $\trianglelefteq$ on atoms and terms[12] is defined inductively as follows:

1. $X \trianglelefteq Y$ for all variables X, Y
2. $s \trianglelefteq f(t_1, \ldots, t_n)$ if $s \trianglelefteq t_i$ for some i
3. $f(s_1, \ldots, s_n) \trianglelefteq f(t_1, \ldots, t_n)$ if $\forall i \in \{1, \ldots, n\} : s_i \trianglelefteq t_i$.

Example 9. We have: $p(a) \trianglelefteq p(f(a))$, $X \trianglelefteq X$, $p(X) \trianglelefteq p(f(Y))$, $p(X, X) \trianglelefteq p(X, Y)$ and $p(X, Y) \trianglelefteq p(X, X)$.

Proposition 14. *The relation $\trianglelefteq$ is a wqo on the set of atoms and terms.*

The intuition behind Definition 13 is that when some structure re-appears within a larger one, it is homeomorphically embedded by the latter. As is argued in [31], this provides a good starting point for detecting growing structures created by (hence) possibly non-terminating processes.

However, as can be observed in Example 9, the homeomorphic embedding relation $\trianglelefteq$ as defined in Definition 13 is rather crude wrt variables. In fact, all variables are treated as if they were the same variable, a practice which is clearly undesirable in a logic programming context. Intuitively, in the above example, $p(X, Y) \trianglelefteq p(X, X)$ is acceptable, while $p(X, X) \trianglelefteq p(X, Y)$ is not.[13]

To remedy the problem, we refine the above introduced homeomorphic embedding as follows:

Definition 15. Let A, B be atoms or terms. Then B *(strictly homeomorphically)* embeds A, written as $A \trianglelefteq^* B$, iff $A \trianglelefteq B$ and A is not a strict instance of B.

Example 10. We now have that $p(X, Y) \trianglelefteq^* p(X, X)$ but not $p(X, X) \trianglelefteq^* p(X, Y)$. Note that still $X \trianglelefteq^* Y$ and $X \trianglelefteq^* X$.

Proposition 16. *The relation $\trianglelefteq^*$ is a wqo on the set of atoms and terms.*

---

[12] Expressed in the language $\mathcal{L}$ which we implicitly assume underlying the programs and queries under consideration. Remember that it contains only finitely many constant, function and predicate symbols ! This property is of crucial importance for the proofs in [21].

[13] $p(X, X)$ can be seen as standing for something like $and(eq(X, Y), p(X, Y))$ which clearly embeds $p(X, Y)$, but the reverse does not hold.

We now extend the embedding relation of Definition 15 to characteristic atoms. One way to obtain a wqo is to first define a term representation of characteristic trees and then use the embedding relation $\trianglelefteq^*$ with this term representation.

Definition 17. By $\lceil . \rceil$ we denote an injective, monotonic[14] mapping from characteristic trees to (ordinary) atoms.

Such a mapping can be easily constructed by representing leaves of the tree by variables. For example we could have $\lceil \{((1,3))\} \rceil = select(1, [match(3, X)])$ and $\lceil \{((1,3),(2,4))\} \rceil = select(1, [match(3, select(2, [match(4, X)]))])$.[15]

Definition 18. Let (A_1, τ_1) and (A_2, τ_2) be two characteristic atoms. We say that (A_2, τ_2) *embeds* (A_1, τ_1), denoted by $(A_1, \tau_1) \trianglelefteq^* (A_2, \tau_2)$, iff $A_1 \trianglelefteq^* A_2$ and $\lceil \tau_1 \rceil \trianglelefteq^* \lceil \tau_2 \rceil$.

Proposition 19. *Let A be a set of P-characteristic atoms. Then $A, \trianglelefteq^*$ is well-quasi-ordered.*

Finally, we consider the relationship between $\trianglelefteq^*$ and $\preceq$ on characteristic atoms.

Proposition 20. *Let CA_1, CA_2, CA_3 be characteristic atoms such that $CA_3 \preceq CA_2$. Then $CA_1 \trianglelefteq^* CA_3 \Rightarrow CA_1 \trianglelefteq^* CA_2$.*

So, a generalisation of a given characteristic atom will only embed characteristic atoms already embedded by the given one.

Proposition 21. *Let CA_1, CA_2 be characteristic atoms such that $CA_2 \preceq CA_1$. Then $CA_1 \trianglelefteq^* CA_2$ iff $CA_1 \equiv CA_2$.*

Proposition 22. *Let $CA_1, \ldots, CA_n$ be characteristic atoms and assume that $M = msg(CA_1, \ldots, CA_n)$.[16] Then the following three statements are equivalent (where $1 \le i \le n$):*

1. $CA_i \trianglelefteq^* M$
2. $CA_i \equiv M$
3. $CA_i \preceq CA_1, \ldots, CA_i \preceq CA_n$

Properties 20 and 22 will be used to prove termination of the partial deduction algorithm in Sect. 3.4. Note that Propositions 21 and 22 do not hold for the $\trianglelefteq$ relation (which makes $\trianglelefteq$ less suitable for ensuring termination of partial deduction).

---

[14] I.e. if $\tau_1 \prec \tau_2$ then $\lceil \tau_1 \rceil \prec \lceil \tau_2 \rceil$.

[15] Note that $\{((1,3))\} \prec \{((1,3),(2,4))\}$ and indeed $\lceil \{((1,3))\} \rceil \prec \lceil \{((1,3),(2,4))\} \rceil$.

[16] As we in fact already did in the pair-wise case, we slightly abuse notation by not writing $msg(\{CA_1, \ldots, CA_n\})$, while that is of course actually what is intended.

3.3 Global Trees

In this subsection, we adapt and instantiate the m-tree concept presented in [27, 26] according to our particular needs in this paper.

Definition 23. A *global tree* γ_P for a program P is a (finitely branching) tree where nodes can be either *marked* or *unmarked* and each node carries a label which is a P-characteristic atom.

In other words, a node in a global tree γ_P will look as follows: $(n, mark, (A, \tau_A))$, where n is the node identifier, *mark* an indicator that can take the values u or m designating whether the node is marked or not, and the P-characteristic atom (A, τ_A) is the node's label. Informally, a marked node corresponds to a characteristic atom which has already been treated by the partial deduction algorithm. We will often omit the P subscript when it is either clear from or not relevant in the particular context we are considering.

In the sequel, we consider a global tree γ partially ordered through the usual *ancestor_node* $>_\gamma$ *descendent_node* relationship. Given a node $n \in \gamma$, we denote by $Anc_\gamma(n)$ the set of its γ ancestor nodes (including itself).

Let γ_P be a global tree. Then we will henceforth denote as L_{γ_P} the set of its labels. And for a given node n in a tree γ, we will refer to its label by l_n.

Definition 24. Let γ be a global tree. Then we define its *associated label mapping* f_γ as the one-to-one mapping $f_\gamma : \gamma, >_\gamma \to L_\gamma, \trianglelefteq^*$ such that $n \mapsto l_n$. f_γ will be called *non-monotonic* iff $\exists n_1, n_2$ such that $n_1 >_\gamma n_2$ and $l_{n_1} \trianglelefteq^* l_{n_2}$.

Definition 25. We call a global tree γ *well-quasi-ordered* if f_γ is not non-monotonic.

Theorem 26. *A global tree γ is finite if it is well-quasi-ordered.*

3.4 An Algorithm for Partial Deduction

In this subsection, we present the actual partial deduction algorithm where global control is imposed through characteristic atoms in a global tree.

We first introduce the following definition:

Definition 27. Let A be an ordinary atom, U an unfolding rule and P a program. Then $chatom(A, P, U) = (A, \tau)$ where $chtree(\leftarrow A, P, U) = \tau$.

A formal description of the algorithm can be found in Fig. 6. Please note that it is parameterised by an unfolding rule U, thus leaving the particulars of local control unspecified. Without loss of generality, we suppose the initial goal to consist of a single atom.

As in e.g. [8, 27, 18], Algorithm 28 does not output a specialised program, but rather a set of (characteristic) atoms from which the actual code can be generated in a straightforward way. Most of the algorithm is self-explanatory, except perhaps the For-loop. In $\mathcal{B}$, all the characteristic atoms are assembled,

Algorithm 28.

Input
  a normal program P and goal $\leftarrow A$
Output
  a set of characteristic atoms $\mathcal{A}$
Initialisation
  $\gamma := \{(1, u, (A, \tau_A))\}$
While γ contains an unmarked leaf **do**
  let n be such an unmarked leaf in γ: $(n, u, (A_n, \tau_{A_n}))$
  mark n
  $\mathcal{B} := \{chatom(B, P, U) | B \in BA_P(A_n, \tau_{A_n})\}$
  For each $(B, \tau_B) \in \mathcal{B}$ **do**
    If $\mathcal{H} = \{(C, \tau_C) \in Anc_\gamma(n) | (C, \tau_C) \trianglelefteq^* (B, \tau_B)\} = \emptyset$
      Then add $(n_B, u, (B, \tau_B))$ to γ as a child of n
      Else If $\{(D, \tau_D) \in Anc_\gamma(n) | (D, \tau_D) \preceq (B, \tau_B)\} = \emptyset$
          Then add $(n_B, u, msg(\mathcal{H} \cup \{(B, \tau_B)\}))$ to γ as a child of n
  Endfor
Endwhile
$\mathcal{A} := L_\gamma$

Fig. 6. Partial deduction with global trees.

corresponding to the atoms occurring in the leaves of the SLDNF-tree built (locally, of course) for A_L according to τ_{A_L}. Elements of $\mathcal{B}$ are subsequently inserted into γ as (unmarked) child nodes of L if they do not embed the label of n or any of its ancestor nodes. If one does, and it is an instance of n's label or that of an ancestor of n, then it is simply not added to γ. Finally, if a characteristic atom $(B, \tau_B) \in \mathcal{B}$ does embed an ancestor label, but there is no more general characteristic atom to be found labelling any of the ancestor nodes, then n receives a child node carrying as label the most specific generalisation of (B, τ_B) and all embedded ancestor labels. The latter case is of course the most interesting: Simply adding a node labelled (B, τ_B) would endanger termination. Adding the msg label instead secures finiteness, while trying to preserve as much information as seems possible.[17] We obtain the following theorems:

Theorem 29. *Algorithm 28 always terminates.*

Theorem 30. *Let P be a program, input to Algorithm 28, and $\mathcal{A}$ the corresponding set of characteristic atoms produced as output. Then $\mathcal{A}$ is P-covered.*

From Theorem 30, correctness of the specialisation follows as in [18].

---

[17] Further enhancing precision through even more cautious generalisation will be a topic of future research.

Finally, we have developed a post-processing phase reducing the polyvariance to some minimal level without removing any of the specialisation performed by the partial deduction described in Algorithm 28 (see Sect. 3.5 of [21]).

4 Experimental Results and Discussion

Creating a fully fledged implementation of Algorithm 28 and the above described post-processing is the subject of ongoing work. However, to preliminarily check whether the developed ideas actually lead to improved practical results, we enhanced the system used for ecological partial deduction in [18] with global control through embedding and generalisation on characteristic atoms. We experimented with the result (denoted by $eco-embed$), comparing its performance with ecological partial deduction as in [18]. In the latter case, various depth bounds were imposed on the (local) SLDNF-trees in order to ensure termination (hence the notation $eco-db\_$). Finally, in the experiments described below, local control is always based on the embedding relation on the atoms in the proof tree structure (i.e. it checks whether selected literals in covering ancestors, see [3], are embedded), possibly cut off by the imposed depth bound.

We report on three experiments. In the first one, we specialised the *reverse* (with type checking) program of Example 4 for the atom $rev(L, [], R)$. The second and third experiment involved the "lifting" *solve* meta-interpreter ([13, 20]). The program depicted in Fig. 3 is actually an excerpt from its code. Experiment 2 consisted in specialising this program for $solve(["c1", "c2", U], [struct(fa, [X, Y])])$, where $"e"$ denotes the ground representation of an expression e, $c1$ denotes the clause $fa(X, Y) \leftarrow p(X, Y), m(X)$ and $c2$ the clause $mo(X, Y) \leftarrow p(X, Y), f(X)$. Finally, in Experiment 3, we specialised the same *solve* for the atom $solve(["c1", "c2", "p(a, b)\leftarrow", "m(a)\leftarrow"], [struct(fa, [X, Y])])$.

The first two experiments illustrate the problems encountered in Examples 4 and 5, and have to rely on a depth-bound for termination when using ecological partial deduction as in [18]. The third experiment does not require a depth bound, but illustrates another (well-known) adverse effect of using depth bounds.

The results are summarised in Tables 1, 2 and 3. The experiments were performed using Prolog by BIM on a Sparc Classic running Solaris. The size of the compiled code is expressed in units, 1 unit corresponding to 4.08 bytes on a Sparc Classic. The (compiled code) run times were obtained by using the $time/2$ predicate of Prolog by BIM on an extensive number of queries.

Experiment 1 shows that the additional polyvariance produced by using a depth bound to ensure termination does not pay off in efficiency but increases the code size unnecessarily. Experiment 2 illustrates this even more poignantly. The amount of polyvariance produced by the method $eco-db50$ was even so big that we could not complete the partial deduction.[18]

In Experiment 3, it is interesting to note that, even with a depth bound of 50 and for this very simple object program, we do not yet get the optimal result ! So,

---

[18] After running for over several hours, producing 134 different predicates and generalising 80 times, $eco-db50$ overflowed the heap limit of 4.5 Megabytes.

for Experiment 2, the depth bound of 50 generates way too much polyvariance, while for Experiment 3, the depth bound of 50 is not sufficient to guarantee optimal specialisation of the same program ! Concluding, it seems very likely that the global control improvements proposed in this paper will indeed pay off in partial deduction practice.

Method	Run Time	#Clauses/#Predicates	Compiled Code Size
original	6.7 s	4/2	203 u
eco–embed	6.7 s	6/3	331 u
eco–db10	6.7 s	23/12	1 955 u
eco–db50	7.1 s	103/52	29 573 u
eco–db100	7.5 s	203/102	122 391 u

Table 1. Experiment 1, *rev* program

Method	Run Time	#Clauses/#Predicates	Compiled Code Size
original	3.07 s	16/8	1 328 u
eco–embed	1.42 s	138/26	26 390 u
eco–db10	1.84 s	328/68	65 863 u
eco–db50	- s	-/ $\geq$134	- u

Table 2. Experiment 2, *solve* program

Method	Run Time	#Clauses/#Predicates	Compiled Code Size
original	2.44 s	16/8	1 328 u
eco–embed	0.04 s	1/1	77 u
eco–db10	1.63 s	34/19	4 164 u
eco–db50	0.06 s	8/4	1 062 u

Table 3. Experiment 3, *solve* program for another query

Note that the current system (*eco–embed*) does not yet structure the characteristic atoms in a global tree, but still just puts them in a set as in [18]. For the above described experiments, this had no influence, but generalisation with non-ancestors may in general severely limit specialisation potential.

A possible drawback of the global control method as laid out in Sect. 3, might be its considerable complexity. Indeed, first, ensuring termination through a well-quasi-ordering is structurally much more costly than the alternative of using a well-founded ordering. The latter only requires comparison with a single "ancestor" object and can be enforced without any search through "ancestor lists" (see [24]). Testing for well-quasi-ordering, however, unavoidably does entail such searching and repeated comparisons with several ancestors. Moreover, in our particular case, checking $\triangleleft^*$ on characteristic atoms is in itself a quite costly operation, adding considerably to the innate complexity of maintaining a well-quasi-ordering. It remains therefore to be seen whether a global control such as the one above can be used (or approximated in an efficient way) in circumstances where speed (or complexity) of the transformation is an important factor.

We conclude this section with a brief discussion on the relation between our global control and what may be termed thus in supercompilation ([32, 33, 31]). We already pointed out that the inspiration for using $\trianglelefteq$ derives from [31]. In that paper, a generalisation strategy for positive supercompilation (no negative information propagation while driving) is proposed. It uses $\trianglelefteq$ to compare nodes in a marked partial process tree (a notion roughly corresponding to marked or global trees in partial deduction). These nodes, however, only contain syntactical information. It is our current understanding that both the addition of something similar to characteristic trees and the use of the refined $\trianglelefteq^*$ embedding can lead to improvements of the method proposed in [31]. Finally, we return to an observation made in [26]: Neighbourhoods of order "n" in (full) supercompilation ([33]), are essentially the same as classes of atoms (or goals) with an identical depth n characteristic tree. Adapting our technique for supercompilation would therefore probably allow to remove the depth bound on neighbourhoods.

5 Conclusion

In this paper, we have developed a sophisticated on-line global control technique for partial deduction of normal logic programs. Importing and adapting m-trees from [27, 26], we have overcome the need for a depth bound on characteristic trees to guarantee termination of partial deduction as proposed in [18]. Plugging in a depth bound free local control strategy (see e.g. [3, 24]), we thus obtain a fully automatic, concrete partial deduction method that always terminates and produces precise and reasonable polyvariance, without resorting to any ad hoc techniques. To the best of our knowledge, this is the very first such method.

Along the way, we have defined generalisation and embedding on characteristic atoms, refining the homeomorphic embedding relation $\trianglelefteq$ from [31] into $\trianglelefteq^*$, and showing that the latter is more suitable in a logic programming setting. Initial experiments with a partial implementation of the method showed its great practical value; A fully fledged implementation and further experimentation are the subjects of ongoing work.

Acknowledgements

We thank the following persons for interesting comments and/or stimulating discussions on this work: Eddy Bevers, Danny De Schreye, André de Waal, Robert Glück, Neil Jones, Jesper Jørgensen, Torben Mogensen, Kristian Nielsen, David Sands and Morten Heine Sørensen. André de Waal, Jesper Jørgensen and an anonymous referee gave useful feedback on a draft version of this paper. Alain Callebaut provided helpful information on benchmarking Prolog by BIM programs. Finally, we gratefully acknowledge Danny De Schreye's (almost) never failing enthusiasm and support.

References

1. K. Benkerimi and J. W. Lloyd. A partial evaluation procedure for logic programs. In S. Debray and M. Hermenegildo, editors, *Proceedings NACLP'90*, pages 343–358, Austin, Texas, October 1990. MIT Press.

2. R. Bol. Loop checking in partial deduction. *Journal of Logic Programming*, 16(1&2):25–46, 1993.

3. M. Bruynooghe, D. De Schreye, and B. Martens. A general criterion for avoiding infinite unfolding during partial deduction. *New Generation Computing*, 11(1):47–79, 1992.

4. C. Consel and O. Danvy. Tutorial notes on partial evaluation. In *Proceedings POPL'93*, Charleston, South Carolina, January 1993. ACM.

5. D. De Schreye, M. Leuschel, and B. Martens. Tutorial on program specialisation (abstract). In J.W. Lloyd, editor, *Proceedings ILPS'95*, pages 615–616, Portland, Oregon, December 1995. MIT Press.

6. N. Dershowitz and J.-P. Jouannaud. Rewrite systems. In J. van Leeuwen, editor, *Handbook of Theoretical Computer Science, Vol. B*, pages 243–320. Elsevier, MIT Press, 1990.

7. J. Gallagher. A system for specialising logic programs. Technical Report TR-91-32, Computer Science Department, University of Bristol, U.K., November 1991.

8. J. Gallagher. Specialisation of logic programs: A tutorial. In *Proceedings PEPM'93, ACM SIGPLAN Symposium on Partial Evaluation and Semantics-Based Program Manipulation*, pages 88–98, Copenhagen, June 1993. ACM Press.

9. J. Gallagher and M. Bruynooghe. Some low-level source transformations for logic programs. In M. Bruynooghe, editor, *Proceedings Meta'90*, pages 229–244, Leuven, April 1990.

10. J. Gallagher and M. Bruynooghe. The derivation of an algorithm for program specialisation. *New Generation Computing*, 9(3&4):305–333, 1991.

11. J. Gallagher and D. A. de Waal. Deletion of redundant unary type predicates from logic programs. In K.-K. Lau and T. Clement, editors, *Proceedings LOPSTR'92*, pages 151–167. Springer-Verlag, Workshops in Computing Series, 1993.

12. J. P. Gallagher and L. Lafave. Regular approximations of computation paths in logic and functional languages. In *this volume*.

13. P. M. Hill and J. Gallagher. Meta-programming in logic programming. Technical Report 94.22, School of Computer Studies, University of Leeds, U.K., August 1994. To appear in Volume V of the Handbook of Logic in Artificial Intelligence and Logic Programming, Oxford University Press.

14. N. D. Jones, C. K. Gomard, and P. Sestoft. *Partial Evaluation and Automatic Program Generation*. Prentice Hall, 1993.

15. J. Jørgensen and M. Leuschel. Efficiently generating efficient generating extensions in Prolog. In *this volume*.

16. J. Komorowski. An introduction to partial deduction. In A. Pettorossi, editor, *Proceedings Meta'92*, pages 49–69. Springer-Verlag, LNCS 649, 1992.

17. M. Leuschel. Partial evaluation of the "real thing". In L. Fribourg and F. Turini, editors, *Proceedings LOPSTR'94 and META'94*, pages 122–137. Springer-Verlag, LNCS 883, 1995.

18. M. Leuschel. Ecological partial deduction: Preserving characteristic trees without constraints. In M. Proietti, editor, *Proceedings of LOPSTR'95*, pages 1–16. Springer-Verlag, LNCS 1048, 1996.

19. M. Leuschel and D. De Schreye. An almost perfect abstraction operation for partial deduction using characteristic trees. Technical Report CW215, Departement Computerwetenschappen, K.U.Leuven, Belgium, October 1995. Submitted for Publication. Accessible via http://www.cs.kuleuven.ac.be/~lpai.

20. M. Leuschel and D. De Schreye. Towards creating specialised integrity checks through partial evaluation of meta-interpreters. In *Proceedings of PEPM'95, the ACM Sigplan Symposium on Partial Evaluation and Semantics-Based Program Manipulation*, pages 253–263, La Jolla, California, June 1995. ACM Press.

21. M. Leuschel and B. Martens. Global control for partial deduction through characteristic atoms and global trees. Technical Report CW220, Departement Computerwetenschappen, K.U.Leuven, Belgium, December 1995. Accessible via http://www.cs.kuleuven.ac.be/~lpai.

22. J. W. Lloyd. *Foundations of Logic Programming*. Springer-Verlag, 1987.

23. J. W. Lloyd and J. C. Shepherdson. Partial evaluation in logic programming. *Journal of Logic Programming*, 11(3&4):217–242, 1991.

24. B. Martens and D. De Schreye. Automatic finite unfolding using well-founded measures. *Journal of Logic Programming*, 1996. To Appear, abridged and revised version of Technical Report CW180, Departement Computerwetenschappen, K.U.Leuven, October 1993, accessible via http://www.cs.kuleuven.ac.be/~lpai.

25. B. Martens, D. De Schreye, and T. Horváth. Sound and complete partial deduction with unfolding based on well-founded measures. *Theoretical Computer Science*, 122(1-2):97–117, 1994.

26. B. Martens and J. Gallagher. Ensuring global termination of partial deduction while allowing flexible polyvariance. Technical Report CSTR-94-16, Computer Science Department, University of Bristol, U.K., December 1994. Accessible via http://www.cs.kuleuven.ac.be/~lpai.

27. B. Martens and J. Gallagher. Ensuring global termination of partial deduction while allowing flexible polyvariance. In L. Sterling, editor, *Proceedings ICLP'95*, pages 597–611, Shonan Village Center, Kanagawa, Japan, June 1995. MIT Press.

28. T. Mogensen and A. Bondorf. Logimix: A self-applicable partial evaluator for Prolog. In K.-K. Lau and T. Clement, editors, *Proceedings LOPSTR'92*, pages 214–227. Springer-Verlag, Workshops in Computing Series, 1993.

29. A. Pettorossi and M. Proietti. Transformation of logic programs: Foundations and techniques. *Journal of Logic Programming*, 19/20:261–320, 1994.

30. D. Sahlin. Mixtus: An automatic partial evaluator for full Prolog. *New Generation Computing*, 12(1):7–51, 1993.

31. M. H. Sørensen and R. Glück. An algorithm of generalization in positive supercompilation. In J.W. Lloyd, editor, *Proceedings ILPS'95*, pages 465–479, Portland, Oregon, December 1995. MIT Press.

32. V. F. Turchin. The concept of a supercompiler. *ACM Transactions on Programming Languages and Systems*, 8(3):292–325, 1986.

33. V. F. Turchin. The algorithm of generalization in the supercompiler. In D. Bjørner, A. P. Ershov, and N. D. Jones, editors, *Partial Evaluation and Mixed Computation*, pages 531–549. North-Holland, 1988.

34. D. Weise, R. Conybeare, E. Ruf, and S. Seligman. Automatic online partial evaluation. In J. Hughes, editor, *Proceedings of the 3rd ACM Conference on Functional Programming Languages and Computer Architecture*, pages 165–191, Cambridge, Massachusets, USA, August 1991. Springer-Verlag, LNCS 523.

Squeezing Intermediate Construction in Equational Programs

Alain Miniussi, David J. Sherman

Laboratoire Bordelais de Recherche en Informatique, Université Bordeaux-1
351, cours de la Libération, 33405 Talence Cedex, FRANCE

Abstract. In this paper we give a general introduction to the particular problems associated with partial evaluation of intermediate code for equational programs, and propose some criteria for deciding whether an unfolding strategy is good enough from a practical standpoint. We then present a new algorithm for driving unfolding of EM code programs, and show that, in addition to terminating, it produces a good result. As we have already implemented the new strategy, this final point is demonstrated with a number of concrete examples.

Keywords: intermediate code, program transformation, equational programming, executable specifications.

1   Introduction

Partial evaluation of equational programs seeks to improve the running time of a program by compressing purely intermediate rewrite steps in the computation. Such transformation removes various kinds of overhead associated with rewriting, such as intermediate rewriting steps, boxing and unboxing of arithmetic values, and intermediate constructions resulting from recursive definitions.

As in related applications of partial evaluation, the problem centers around the search for *unfolding strategies*: algorithms that decide where and how often to unwind recursive invocations of the rewriting engine. As with all such problems, the search is for strategies that *terminate* while at the same time unfolding enough of the program to let the specializer do useful work. While the former property can be proved mathematically, the latter relies on our subjective judgment: is the result *good enough* to justify the added expense incurred by the program transformation?

In this paper, we first present a general introduction to the problem of partial evaluation for equational programs, and establish a number of goals for the partial evaluator. We then present a new strategy for driving unfolding for equational programs, based on what we call "squeezing" of build instructions. After establishing that this new strategy terminates, we show to what extent it reaches the goals we have established, by considering some interesting examples and their transformation by our experimental partial evaluator. We then conclude.

1.1 Equational Programming

An equational program is a set of left-linear, nonambiguous equations on terms, interpreted as an unordered set of left-to-right rewrite rules[O'D87, O'D85]. The resulting rewrite system is used to generate a *pattern-matching automaton*, implemented by an imperative program in *EM code* (see, for example, [She94a]). The job of the EM code program is to *stabilize* a term in its run-time heap, that is, to produce a head-normal form for the term with respect to the given rewrite system. The stabilization of a term usually involves the recursive stabilization of certain of its subterms, as indicated by the *index tree*[HL79, HL91a, HL91b] used to produce the pattern-matching automaton.

The EM code program is subjected to various optimizing transformations, including partial evaluation (as outlined below), before finally being used to generate efficient assembly code.

The resulting executable program accepts a question, in the form of an input term, and produces a correct answer—correct in the sense that the result is a logical consequence of the question and the equational specification; and an answer in the sense that it obeys certain syntactic restrictions, particularly that it is a normal form. The output driver produces a normal form for the input term using repeated calls to the EM code program and recursive descent of the head-normal forms.

As our concern in this paper is the transformation of EM code and not applications of equational program properly speaking, we refer the interested reader to [O'D85, O'D87].

1.2 Expected Benefits

What do we expect to gain by applying partial evaluation techniques to equational programs? In general, partial evaluation seeks to produce a residual program that performs only the part of the computation that depends on the dynamic part of the input. The appropriate notion of "computation" for an equational computation is a rewriting step, and we expect a partial evaluator for equational programs to produce a residual program that does only rewriting steps based on the dynamic part of the input.

There are two inaccuracies in this characterization. First, the identification of a dynamic part of the input is artificial. The static part of the input that we wish to inject into the partial evaluator consists of the right-hand sides of rewrite rules, and as such already exists in the program. We will say more about this in section 1.3.

Second, the notion of rewrite step is too coarse, and does not give us enough room to manoeuvre. A rewrite step consists in fact of a sequence of smaller operations performed by the program: identification of the appropriate rewrite rule and redex, by inspecting symbols in the subject term; construction of the corresponding right-hand side, by allocating nodes in the heap; and actually performing the rewrite, by overwriting the root node of the redex or setting an indirection pointer. All of these operations are performed by instructions in the

EM code program corresponding to the rewrite system, and our partial evaluator works at the level of these instructions rather than at the level of a rewrite step. As a result, the residual program may perform operations that correspond to only part of a rewrite step, or may mix the operations for several rewrite steps if that proved more efficient. The residual program, while still preserving the semantics of the original equation definition, will typically no longer correspond to an equational definition.

What, concretely, do we hope to gain? The intermediate operations that we want to avoid fall roughly into four categories, as outlined below.

Rewriting overhead: in many cases we want simply to compose rewriting rules, avoiding construction of the part of the intermediate term produced by the first rule that serves only to activate the second rule. This is the main goal of the work presented in chapter 6 of [Str88]. Of course, arbitrary composition of rewriting rules would lead to undecidability and termination problems, but many simple cases are easy to detect. Consider, for example, a collection of rules that dispatch on the type of an object, as indicated by a constructor; if these rules are activated by a right-hand side that also creates the object in question, we would prefer to avoid the constructor and simply activate to corresponding rule.

Another way of saying this is that the user should not be penalized for breaking one equation into several intermediate ones, since that can greatly improve the readability of the program. The equations

$$a = g[f[a,b,c]]$$
$$g[x] = d$$

might be clearer than the single equation $a = d$, if g has some special meaning for the reader.

Box/unbox optimizations: the EM code program can manipulate values, such as integers, that can only be stored in the subject term in boxed form. The boxing and subsequent unboxing of these values in the midst of a sequence of arithmetic operations can be avoided in the residual program by treating the boxing operation as a term construction. This improvement was presented in [MMSS94]. The reasoning in this work is that, while the abnormal case of a poorly-formed arithmetic expression can lead to complicated treatment to obey the equational semantics, in normal cases the user should not have to pay a performance penalty.

Loops for recursive definitions: recursive rules designed to traverse recursively-defined structures can be implemented by loops in the EM code program that do not contain any intermediate construction. This improvement was demonstrated in [SS92] and [She94b], and resembles the treeless transformations proposed by Wadler (e.g. [Wad88]). These improvements in particular cannot be represented by source code transformations at the level of the rewrite rules.

Special cases: Consider the equations

$$f[x] = k[x,x]$$
$$k[a,x] = c .$$

The head-normal forms of an f-term have either a c or a k at the root, depending on whether the subterm of f was an a or not. In the former case, we would like to avoid constructing the intermediate k term. This corresponds to the priority rewriting system

$$1 : f[a] = c$$
$$2 : f[x] = k[x,x]$$
$$3 : k[a,x] = c .$$

We cannot express this special treatment of f[a] at the source level, since the resulting rewrite system contains an overlap (and so is not nonambiguous). Of course, we have no trouble representing this treatment in the EM code program: the multi-way choice for the child of an f term is easily performed by a branch instruction, in this case created by unfolding the right-hand side and thus the inspection of the x under the k.

There are other gains possible, but these above provide our main motivation. We will consider these desiderata in section 3, when we evaluate the results of our new partial evaluation strategy.

1.3 Particular Difficulties

Why does the treatment of equational programs present any particular difficulty? The EM code program that we propose to treat is written in an imperative language like any other, with variables, function calls, and the like; one might reasonably wonder why we do not simply use an existing partial evaluator to do the job. In the following we outline a number of points particular to the equational case, which force us to consider its partial evaluation as a distinct problem.

First, the EM code program to be partially evaluated is generated from an equational specification. The programmer is not, and cannot be expected to be, aware of the EM code program, nor qualified to modify it. Our partial evaluator must in consequence be completely automatic. In particular this rules out any possibility for *binding time improvements*, as the results of analyses of EM code programs are quite practically useless for the author of the equational specification. Furthermore, the partial evaluator must terminate in all cases. Nontermination of partial evaluation provides no useful information to the equational programmer, and it is unreasonable to suppose that such a programmer has any power to rewrite his specification in a way that does not lead to nontermination of the partial evaluator. The argument that nontermination of the partial evaluator is acceptable in the case of a nonterminating program does not hold for the equational case, since the use of lazy evaluation makes theoretically infinite computations both useful and easy to manipulate[O'D85, Reb93].

Second, while there are recursive calls in the EM code program, there are no function bodies to be treated *en bloc* as units of unfolding. Before partial evaluation starts, all calls in the program are to the initial instruction of the program, which represents the start state of a pattern-matching automaton (see section 4.1, page 63, of [She94b] for details); as the body of the call is the whole program, it is clearly not reasonable to treat the bodies of calls as indivisible unfolding units. Indeed, the semantics of EM code permits a recursive call to *any* instruction in the program, so long as the callee stack frame is correctly initialized. This is in fact an advantage, as it permits great flexibility in the choice of unfolding strategy, but makes unfolding decisions necessarily more complicated. The notion of *filters*, as proposed by Consel in Schism[Con88, Con92], while an interesting compromise, does not seem to work in our case.Even if we could construct the filters automatically, as required by the preceding paragraph, we would be reduced to putting one on every instruction.

Third, there is no opportunity for binding-time analysis. What we treat as the partial input exists already in the program in the form of right-hand sides; what we want from our partial evaluator is in some sense a sophisticated form of constant propagation. The idea of an expensive BTA performed once, followed by many cheap partial evaluations with regard to different partial inputs, does not correspond to our situation. The partial evaluation will be performed only once, with regard to a partial input known in advance. Furthermore, typical binding-time analyses are relatively expensive (Palsberg claims cubic times for flow-based binding-time analyses in [Pal95]), which unacceptably lengthens the compilation cycle time.

1.4   The Existing Strategy

The existing strategy, as described in [SS92] and [She94b], uses the build instructions directly to drive unfolding and specialization. The build instructions are physically pushed, one step at a time, deeper into the tree structure of the program. A build instruction b, presented with a successor instruction i, can either move over i, specializing i if it uses the result of the b or leaving it untouched if not; remain stuck before i, if i uses b in a way that does not permit specialization (for example if i is another build instruction); or, if i is a call, unfold *one* instruction i' from the target of i. In the last case, the call i is modified to point to the successor instruction of i', and the build b continues with the copy of i' as its new successor. A given build instruction will eventually either get stuck, stop unfolding, or fall off the bottom of the program because it is no longer needed for subsequent computations.

The termination of this strategy depends on the fact that each build does a bounded amount of work, and that the number of builds in the program is fixed at the start. In order to guarantee the latter condition, no build instruction is ever unfolded from the body of a call, since this would increase the number of builds. But it is easy to construct an example for which this strategy is inadequate. Consider the example from page 133 of [She94b], the equations

$a = b$

$f[b,x] = c$

$g[x] = f[a,x].$

The problem is that the result of a reduction participates in a reduction above it. We cannot infer that $g[x] = c$ unless the a constructed by the third rule is unfolded and pushed through the unfolded f branch.

In terms of the two criteria evoked in section 1, this strategy is not good enough.

2 Driving Unfolding with Build Squeezing

We now develop an improved algorithm for unfolding and specialization of EM code programs. Before presenting the new algorithm, in section 2.3, we provide some necessary definitions and terminology in section 2.1, and give (in section 2.2) an intuitive description of how the new algorithm works. Section 2.4 is devoted to a more accurate description of the algorithm and to termination issue.

2.1 Prerequisites and Definitions

Definition 1. Let P be an EM-code program whose root is the branch instruction branch R0. We call the *subprogram SP* of P the instruction tree rooted at i where i is a direct successor instruction of branch R0.

We call the *subprogram marked with f*, where f is a symbol, the subprogram reached from branch R0 if R0 is the address of a term whose root symbol is f.

In the example program shown in figure 1 (page 12), the subprogram marked with k is the tree of seven instructions rooted at the assignment for R4.

Definition 2. A call instruction of a given subprogram is said to be *outermost* iff it has no ancestor of type call in that subprogram.

Definition 3. All the call instructions of a non modified program are tagged as being *stabilizing*. These tags are maintained during unfolding.

Definition 4. We define a topological order on registers as the ordering induced by the build instructions: $R_x = \text{build}(R1, \ldots, Rn) \Rightarrow \forall 1 \leq i \leq n, R_x < R_i$

Definition 5. We call *elementary unfolding* the operation consisting, for a given call c, of:

- unfolding the target instruction of c
- specializing if possible the generated instruction,
- shallow unfolding of the generated call.

Note that elementary unfolding always terminates and that does not introduce nonstabilizing calls.

Definition 6. We call *shallow unfolding* of a call c w.r.t. a predicate p, the recursively defined operation consisting, as long as p is true, in:

1. elementary unfolding of c,
2. shallow unfolding any remaining `call` corresponding to c.

When the predicate p is the constant function $p = true$, we call this simply "shallow unfolding".

2.2 A Intuitive Description

The main intuition is that we want to remove `build` instructions, representing their intended effect in the program counter of the running program rather than in the contents of the heap memory. We can remove a `build` instruction when we are sure that any subsequent use of the memory cell it would have created can be adequately taken into account by the modified program. We use the information in the `build` instruction to specialize other instructions, so that these other instructions no longer make use of the memory cell in question. In some sense, then, we want the specialization of other instructions to "use up" all of the information in the `build` instruction, so that we can throw it away.

Consider, for example, the instruction

```
R₁ = build f (R₂,R₃) .
```

The program can use the result of this `build` in three ways:

1. it might inspect the symbol f;
2. it might use one of the children R_2 or R_3;
3. it might need to output R_1 for use in another invocation of the program.

In the third case, we cannot avoid allocating a node for R_1, but in the first two we only need some information that would be stored in the node.

Of course, it is entirely possible that the information in a `build` instruction escapes from the nearby context, and we must leave it in the program. Such is trivially the case for `build` whose result is part of the output of the program. More interestingly, it is also the case for `build` that do not participate in the current reduction to head-normal form; we cannot let the specializer go so far as to interfere with the laziness of the evaluation, which could change not only the running time but the termination properties of the compiled program.

Other instructions in the program use the information provided by a `build` instruction by inspecting the contents of the memory cell it creates. These inspections, performed by `branch` and `down` instructions, occur chiefly in the stabilizing calls for the `build` instruction. The context in which the information from a `build` instruction is likely to be used up can therefore often be restricted to a particular subprogram, in particular the one that follows the same symbol as the `build` instruction in question.

The main idea, then, is that we unfold the stabilizing call for a `build` instruction until the specializer has either squeezed all of the useful information out of it, or realizes that the `build` will escape from the nearby context and can be squeezed no further.

2.3 Formal Description

The partial evaluator treats each subprogram only once:

```
procedure peval(program P)
begin
    W = list of subprograms of P
    under-modification = ∅
    for each A in W
        treat(A)
end
```

To treat a subprogram A, we squeeze each of its builds. Note that we need to be careful about the moment at which we squeeze a build since we do not allow a second chance.

```
procedure treat(subprogram A)
begin
    if A not in W return
    remove A from W
    R = list of build instructions of A
        in topological order (suborder: by
        outermost stabilizing call)
    lock(A)
    for each B in R
        squeeze(B)
    unlock(A)
end
```

The particular order between the build instructions is justified in section 2.4 and does not affect the termination of the strategy.

Now, we are going to exploit all the information we have about the build. Note that if the subject program does not contain any recursive definition, squeeze will not encounter any locked subprograms, and one can easily verify that the goals one and four mentioned in section 1.2 are reached.

```
procedure squeeze(build B)
begin
    S = list of stabilizing calls for B,
        in flow-path order
    buffer = under-modification
    under-modification = under-modif-
            ication ∪{path of i |i ∈ S}
    A = the subprogram marked with the
```

```
            symbol of B
      if A not locked
            treat(A)
            for each C ∈ S
                  shallow unfold C
      else /* treatment of recursion: */
            for each C in S
                  shallow unfold C up to the frontier,
                  defined by under-modification.
         under-modification = buffer
end
```

2.4   Explanation of the Algorithm and Termination

What order among build do we use, and indeed which build have stabilizing calls that we can unfold? Consider the sequence of build that construct, bottom-up, the right-hand side of an equation. The last build in the sequence builds the root of the right-hand side, and is therefore the first build whose result will be inspected by the top-down inspection of the term performed by the recursive invocation of the automaton. This recursive invocation, after inspecting the root node of the term, will then proceed to recursively stabilize certain child nodes. Thus we see that these recursive stabilizations, when unfolded after the original build sequence, become stabilizing calls for build instructions earlier in the sequence.

So, what we are reduced to, is this: we pick a build near the top of the right-hand side it participates in, for which we can find a stabilizing call, and we unfold (while specializing) the body of this call to expose the stabilizing calls for the rest of the build in the right-hand side.

The preceding answers the question of what order to use between the build in a given right-hand side, or more broadly a given subprogram, but not the question of what order to use between the subprograms themselves. The choice is not completely arbitrary, since, when we unfold the body of a stabilizing call, we would prefer that the instructions that we unfold are already as specialized as possible. By choosing a good order between subprograms, we can take advantage specialization work in other places in the program. The simplest thing is to let the treatment of stabilizing calls determine the treatment of subprograms: before unfolding the subprogram that corresponds to a stabilizing call, we make sure we have already treated that subprogram. If the subprogram has not already been treated, we suspend the treatment under way while we treat the other one. The recursive treatment of subprograms mimics the recursive stabilization of the subject term.

Termination follows from the fact that there are a fixed number of subprograms, and that each subprogram is treated only once. Before continuing our description, let us look at a simple nonrecursive example to see how the treatment of subprograms is ordered and how this guarantees termination. We consider the system:

$$a = g[a]$$
$$g[x] = d \ ,$$

For which the corresponding initial program is:

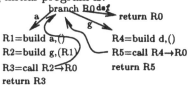

```
                         branch R0 def        return R0
                      a                   g
              R1=build a,()          R4=build d,()
              R2=build g,(R1)        R5=call R4→R0
              R3=call R2→R0          return R5
              return R3
```

Let us say that we start with the a subprogram. The first `build` we try to squeeze is `R2=build g,(R1)` since R2 is the only stabilized built register of the subprogram. The symbol associated with this build is g; since the corresponding subprogram is not treated, we treat it. We apply the same procedure which leads to treatment of the subprogram corresponding to d, that is to say the `def` branch, for which there is no treatment to do. After unfolding and automatic clean-up, we obtain the EM code program:

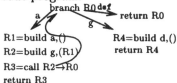

```
                         branch R0 def        return R0
                      a                   g
              R1=build a,()          R4=build d,()
              R2=build g,(R1)        return R4
              R3=call R2→R0
              return R3
```

We then come back to the treatment of the first build (i.e. `R2=build g,(R1)`) and unfold the g subprogram, which leads to:

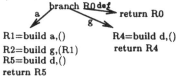

```
                         branch R0 def        return R0
                      a                   g
              R1=build a,()          R4=build d,()
              R2=build g,(R1)        return R4
              R5=build d,()
              return R5
```

We must then treat the remaining two builds, `R1=build a, ()` and `R2=build g,(R1)`; as they are not associated with a stabilizing call, we have no work to do. Note that we do not treat `R5=build d,()`, which was not in the subprogram at the begining of the whole treatment. After removal of useless `build`s, we obtain:

```
                         branch R0 def        return R0
                      a                   g
              R5=build d,()          R4=build d,()
              return R5              return R4
```

The intuitive argument for termination depends on treating each subprogram only once, and we can see that we run into trouble in the presence of recursive definitions. Consider:

$$f[x] = g[x];$$
$$g[x] = f[x];$$

and its associated EM code:

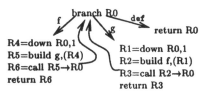

We see that the treatment of a subprogram leads to the treatment of the other and so on.

When we start treating a subprogram, then, we have to mark it as *locked* so that a recursive attempt to treat this same subprogram realizes that the treatment is already under way. The treatment of a subprogram locked in another context can be anything legal, as long as it terminates. A recursive attempt could simply stop right away—this would certainly guarantee termination—but such a strategy is not sophisticated enough. Consider the following EM code, which illustrates a typical situation when one use arithmetic:

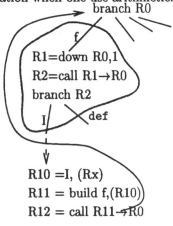

(I is a meta symbol used to box integers). The dotted part is very interesting for us since it corresponds to the type checking and unboxing of an integer that has just been boxed. If we can unfold that part of the program, we are sure to avoid the type checking and unboxing operation and, more importantly, we have good opportunity to remove the boxing operation performed by R10 = build I,(Rx) and then to work directly on the integer. Such a situation is also illustrated in the last example of section 3. More generally, refusing unfolding in such a situation takes away the possibility to use all the information stored in the subterm rooted at the node inducing the recursive reference.

Recall the main intuition from earlier: we want to squeeze all of the information out of a build and use it for specialization. The more we unfold from the stabilizing call, the more opportunities we have to use up the information in the build that is driving the unfolding. Recall further that the choice of a good order between subprogram treatments lets the specializer take advantage of work done elsewhere. As long as the unfolding does not overrun the specialization work driven by other build, we can unfold as much as we like (as long as such unfolding terminates, of course) without worrying about lost opportunities. Since all of the further specialization work that we want to take advantage of happens below stabilizing calls, it suffices to restrict unfolding to a frontier defined by the stabilizing calls undergoing unfolding in suspended contexts.

The techniques can produce efficient programs like the last two shown in section 3.

3 Results

In this section, we show the results of our partial evaluator on some interesting examples, in order to show that the results of our new strategy are good enough with respect to the criteria evoked in section 1.

Our first example is from categories one and four, namely, rewriting overhead and special cases. Figure 1 shows the initial EM code program corresponding to the equations

$$f[x] = k[x,x]$$
$$k[a,x] = c ,$$

and figure 2 shows the code after our partial evaluator has finished with it. Note that no useless build instructions are performed, especially in the case of the input term f[a].

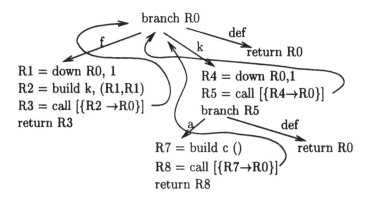

Fig. 1. Initial code for f[x] = k[x,x]; k[a,x] = c.

The second example shows the third category of expected gains, the treatment of recursive definitions—in fact, mutually-recursive definitions in this example. The equations are

$$even[zero] = True$$
$$even[S[x]] = odd[x]$$
$$odd[zero] = False$$
$$odd[S[x]] = even[x] ,$$

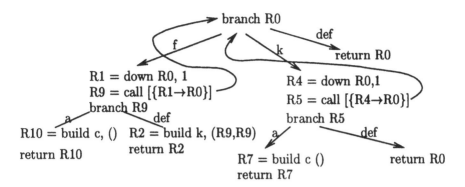

Fig. 2. Optimized code for f[x] = k[x,x]; k[a,x] = c.

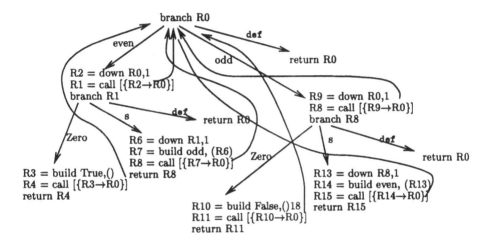

Fig. 3. Initial code for even system

which calculates the parity of numbers written in successor-notation. The original program is shown in figure 3, and the result after partial evaluation can be seen in figure 4. With a reasonable[1] input term, such as even[S[S[S[S[S[zero]]]]]], the program recursively calculates the correct result without any useless build instructions. Inspecting the program in figure 4, we can in fact see that the recursive definitions have given rise to recursive loops in the optimized program.

Our final example shows how our techniques treat arithmetic computations, which is both an example of treatment of special cases and box/unbox optimizations. The interesting part of the input equations are

---

[1] Much of the program is in fact devoted to correct treatment of unreasonable terms, as required by the semantics.

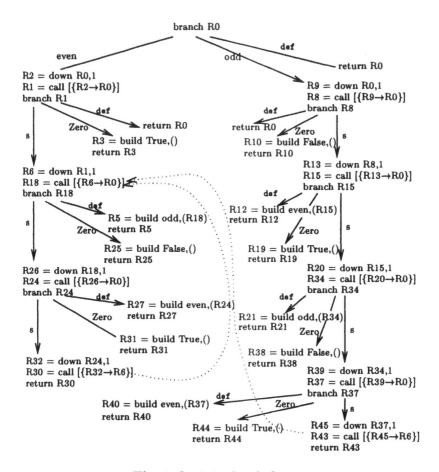

Fig. 4. Optimized code for even system

$$f[x] = if[null[x], 0, inc[f[dec[x]]]]$$
$$if[True, x, y] = x$$
$$if[False, x, y] = y$$

(here, we do not clutter the presentation with the equations that define incrementation, decrementation, and the test null). The original EM code program is shown in figure 5. After unfolding and specialization, taking advantage of the if equations, the resulting program is as shown in figure 6. The important improvement is that the type of the argument is not checked twice in the inner loop of the program.

Further improvements to this last example are possible to make its speed comparable with the corresponding recursive C program, but as these further improvements involve the assembly-code generator of the compiler, we instead refer the interested reader to [MMSS94].

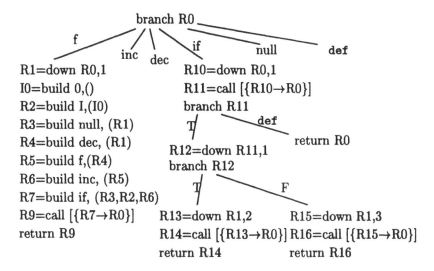

Fig. 5. Initial code for f[x]=if[null[x],0,inc[f[dec[x]]]]; if[True,x,y]=x; if[False,x,y]=y.

4 Related Work

The use of program transformation of equational programs to fuse intermediate constructions ([Str87, Str88]), is predated by the corresponding work for functional programs. Such fusing is an important characteristic of Turchin's supercompiler[Tur86], the main goal of Wadler's deforestation algorithm[Wad88], and can be traced back to Burstall and Darlington[BD77]. Recent work by Chin[Chi94] provides an interesting framework for this idea, classifying functions and their parameters as *producers* and *consumers* of symbols, as a way to decide when intermediate structures can be safely eliminated. This classification, as well as the recent extension by Sørensen[Sør94] using tree grammars, would be interesting as an analysis technique for driving unfolding and specialization of equational programs. The use of a grammar resembles, in fact, to the work currently in progress by Thierry Aimé at Bordeaux.

The idea of pushing information around in the program as a way to drive transformation has recently seen new developments. In [GK93], Glück and Klimov propose the notion of a *perfect process tree* for representing computations and the propagation of information; the development of such a graph can be used to ensure that all information about known values is propagated along specialized branches of the program. In [SGJ94], Sørensen, Glück, and Jones compare four transformation methodologies on the basis of their information propagation properties, and show that a *positive supercompiler* makes enough information available to directly produce the famous Knuth-Morris-Pratt example. An important task is to see whether this kind of comparison can show any fundamental differences between evaluation strategies used for partial evaluation that are ap-

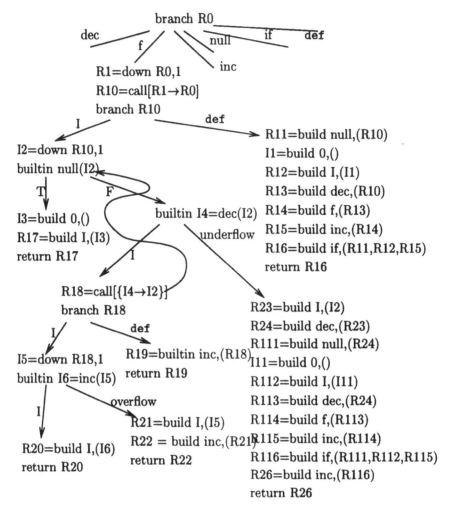

Fig. 6. Optimized code for f[x]=if[null[x],0,inc[f[dec[x]]]]; if[True,x,y]=x; if[False,x,y]=y.

propriate for functional programs and the evaluation strategies induced by the needs of term rewriting.

Henglein and Jørgensen[HJ94], as well as Leroy[Ler92], Peyton Jones and Launchbury [JL91], and Poulsen[Pou93] have recently treated the particular case of box/unbox improvements for polymorphically-typed languages such as Standard ML. The former, in particular, propose an optimality criterion for a marking (called a *completion*) of a program with explicit box/unbox operations. While the box/unbox operations in EM code programs are certainly explicit, this optimality criterion seems uninteresting in the equational case, for two reasons. First, their criterion applies to different completions of the same, otherwise unchanged, program; while our partial evaluator may modify the program in a way that permits further box/unbox improvements. Second, their criterion assumes an equal cost for the two types of operations, which is wildly inaccurate for EM code programs: a boxing operation is 3-15 times more expensive than an unbox operation. As a result, an EM code program considered optimal by [HJ94] may in fact be more costly.

5 Conclusion

Equational programs have a number of constraints that *a priori* lead to difficulties when we ask for an efficient implementation. The choice of term-rewriting, while natural and appropriate for preserving the semantic purity of the language, leads to costly run-time overhead. By representing the rewriting system in the form of a program in the right intermediate language and by performing partial evaluation on this program, though, we can recognize and remove much of the purely intermediate work.

We can expect to avoid several kinds of overhead associated with rewriting. Intermediate rewriting steps can be removed, giving the same effect as a straightforward composition of rewriting steps. Box/unbox operations and basic type checking, necessitated by the treatment of numeric and atomic values, can be improved by treating the box operation as a construction and using constant propagation. And finally, intermediate term constructions used to drive recursive definitions can be removed in many cases.

Intuitively, these improvements come about by moving information about the contents of run-time terms *out* of the run-time heap and *into* the program counter. In general, the partial evaluator unfolds part of a recursive invocation of the pattern-matcher into a context where build instructions provide more information, and specializes the unfolded instructions with respect to this information. The additional information about the run-time term is encoded in the text of the program.

Unfolding strategies must give subjectively good results, such as those described in the second paragraph above, and they must terminate. Realizing that the results produced by the strategy described in [SS92] are not good enough, we developed a new strategy based on what we call "squeezing" of build instructions. This strategy tries to identify what parts of the recursive invocation will use the information in a build instruction, and unfold enough of these instructions to use up all of the information in the build. By identifying a finite number of potential treatment contexts, the termination of this strategy follows directly. The new strategy also treats these unfolded parts of the program in an order that mimics the recursive stabilization order of the pattern-matcher, so as to (as much as possible) take advantage of unfolding and specialization work in other parts of the program.

The results of our implementation of this strategy show that we get good experimental results on typical examples. Particularly, we see the improvements described above: avoidance of intermediate rewrites, box/unbox overhead, and constructions that drive recursion.

Nevertheless, a fair amount of related work remains to be done. We need first of all to integrate the new partial evaluator in the equation compiler, which would permit systematic use of these program transformations as well as a quantitative evaluation of their value. Improvements to this strategy might also be made by the inclusion of Thierry Aimé's (yet unpublished) thesis work on typing equational systems. It would furthermore be interesting to define a formal description of the kinds of practical gains we see, that is, to formalize a guarantee of the results of these transformations. The idea of *improvement*, as defined by Sands[San95], might be an interesting way to attack the question of guarantees while providing the means to show total correctness of the transformations. Finally, the interaction between the partial evaluator and various backend optimizations used by our compiler remains an open question, particularly as regards instruction and data cache locality. All four of these questions are the subjects of ongoing research.

References

[BD77]   R. M. Burstall and John Darlington. A transformation system for developing recursive programs. *Journal of the ACM*, 24(1), 1977.

[Chi94]   Wei-Ngan Chin. Safe fusion of functional expressions II: Further improvements. *Journal of Functional Programming*, 4(4):515–555, 1994.

[Con88]   Charles Consel. New insights into partial evaluation: the Schism experiment. In *ESOP'88, Second European Symposium on Programming*, volume LLNCS 300. Springer-Verlag, 1988.

[Con92]   Charles Consel. Report on Schism '92. Technical Report , Pacific Software Research Center, Oregon Graduate Institute of Science and Technology, 1992.

[GK93]   Robert Glück and Andrei Klimov. Occam's razor in metacomputation: the notion of a perfect process tree. In *Static Analysis, LNCS 724*, Padova, Italy, September 1993. Springer-Verlag.

[HJ94]   Fritz Henglein and Jesper Jorgensen. Formally optimal boxing. In *Principles of Programming Languages*, Portland, Oregon, January 1994. ACM Press.

[HL79]   Gèrard Huet and Jean-Jacques Lévy. Computations in non-ambiguous linear term rewriting systems. Technical Report 359, INRIA, 1979.

[HL91a]   Gérard Huet and Jean-Jacques Lévy. Computations in orthogonal rewriting systems, I. In *Computational Logic: Essays in Honor of Alan Robinson*, chapter 11, pages 395–414. The MIT Press, 1991.

[HL91b]   Gérard Huet and Jean-Jacques Lévy. Computations in orthogonal rewriting systems, II. In *Computational Logic: Essays in Honor of Alan Robinson*, chapter 12, pages 415–443. The MIT Press, 1991.

[JL91]   Simon Peyton Jones and John Launchbury. Unboxed values as first-class citizens. In *Proceedings of Conference on FUnctional Programming Languages and Computer Architecture (FPCA)*, volume LNCS 523. Springer-Verlag, August 1991.

[Ler92]   Xavier Leroy. Unboxed objects and polymorphic typing. In *Proceedings of the 19th Annual ACM SIGPLAN-SIGACT Symposium on Principles of Programming Languages (POPL)*. ACM Press, January 1992.

[MMSS94]   Timo Metzemakers, Alain Miniussi, David J. Sherman, and Robert I. Strandh. Improving arithmetic performance using fine-grain unfolding. In Manuel Hermenegildo and Jaan Penjam, editors, *International Conference on Programming Language Implementation and Logic Programming (LNCS 844)*, pages 324–339. Springer-Verlag, September 1994.

[O'D85]   Michael J. O'Donnell. *Equational Logic as a Programming Language*. MIT Press, 1985.

[O'D87]   Michael J. O'Donnell. Survey of the equational logic programming project. In *Colloquium on Resolution of Equations in Algebraic Structures*, 1987.

[Pal95]   Jens Palsberg. Comparing flow-based binding-time analyses. In *International Joint Conference on the Theory and Practice of Software Development (TAPSOFT)*, volume LLNCS 915. Springer-Verlag, 1995.

[Pou93]   Eigil Poulsen. Representation analysis for efficient implementation of polymorphism. Master's Thesis, DIKU, University of Copenhagen, 1993.

[Reb93]   Samuel Alexander Rebelsky. *Tours, A System for Lazy Term-based Communication*. PhD thesis, University of Chicago, Chicago, Illinois, 1993.

[San95]   David Sands. Proving the correctness of recursion-based automatic program transformations. In *Proceedings of TAPSOFT '95, the Sixth International Joint Conference on the Theory and Practice of Software Development*, 1995.

[SGJ94]   Morten Heine Sørensen, Robert Glück, and Neil Jones. Towards unifying partial evaluation, deforestation, supercompilation, and gpc. In *Proceedings of the European Symposium on Programming, ESOP'94*, January 1994.

[She94a]   David J. Sherman. EM code semantics, analysis, and optimization. Technical Report 827-94, LaBRI, Université Bordeaux–1, 1994. (Revised August 1993).

[She94b]   David J. Sherman. *Run-time and Compile-time Improvements to Equational Programs*. PhD thesis, University of Chicago, Chicago, Illinois, 1994.

[Sør94]   Morten Heine Sørensen. A grammar-based data-flow analysis to stop deforestation. In *Proceedings of CAAP'94, Colloquium on Trees in Algebra and Programming*. Springer-Verlag, 1994.

[SS92]   David J. Sherman and Robert I. Strandh. Call unfolding strategies for equational logic programs. In *Proceedings of the ACM SIGPLAN Workshop on Partial Evaluation and Semantics-Based Program Manipulation*, San Francisco, California, 1992.

[Str87]   Robert I. Strandh. Optimizing equational programs. In *Proceedings of the Second International Conference on Rewrite Techniques and Applications*, 1987.

[Str88]   Robert I. Strandh. *Compiling Equational Programs into Efficient Machine Code*. PhD thesis, Johns Hopkins University, Baltimore, Maryland, 1988.

[Tur86]   Valentin Turchin. The concept of a supercompiler. *ACM Transactions on Programming Languages*, 8(3):292–325, 1986.

[Wad88]   Philip Wadler. Deforestation: Transforming programs to eliminate trees. In *Second European Symposium on Programming*. Springer-Verlag, 1988.

Evolution of Partial Evaluators:
Removing Inherited Limits

Torben Æ. Mogensen

DIKU, University of Copenhagen, Denmark

Abstract. We show the evolution of partial evaluators over the past ten years from a particular perspective: the attempt to remove limits on the structure of residual programs that are inherited from structural bounds in the original programs. It will often be the case that a language allows an unbounded number or size of a particular features, but each program (being finite) will only have a finite number or size of these features. If the residual programs cannot overcome the bounds given in the original program, that can be seen as a weakness in the partial evaluator, as it potentially limits the effectiveness of residual programs. The inherited limits are best observed through specializing a self-interpreter and examining the object programs produced by specialisation of this. We show how historical developments in partial evaluators gradually remove inherited limits, and suggest how this principle can be used as a guideline for further development.

1 Introduction

Much has happened in the field of partial evaluation in the past ten years. The evolution has taken many different paths, focusing on different problems. We will show below that many seemingly unrelated developments serve similar purposes: removal of *inherited limits*. More often than not, the developments have been introduced for solving immediate practical problems observed through experiments, without explicit awareness of the general underlying principle.

In this paper we first introduce the concept of inherited limits, and discuss why we think it may be a problem. We then, as a case study, define a small first-order functional language and show how successive refinements of an initially very simple specialisation method each remove an inherited limit, until our final version can be seen to have none. We then round up by discussing how to use the principle of inherited limits to suggest further studies in partial evaluation methods, and noting some important developments in partial evaluation that can not be related to removal of inherited limits.

2 Inherited Limits

It has been stated (I forget by whom) that in computer science (as well as many other areas) there are only three reasonable limits: zero, one and infinity.

This principle has often been used in language design, such that there typically is no arbitrary bounds on nesting depth, size of program, number of variables etc, unless that bound is uniformly set to one, as e.g. the nesting depth of function definitions in C.

But while the language as a whole imposes no such bounds, each program (being finite) will normally be limited to a finite depth, size or number of these features. For example, all Pascal programs will have a finite nesting depth of functions, a finite number of variables and a finite dimension of arrays, even though the language definition imposes no bound on these features.

The fact that any single program only uses a bounded number or size of a feature does not usually cause any problem, and there really is no natural way to avoid it, even if it did.

It is when new programs are derived by specialisation or other transformations from a single original programs that we may encounter a problem: the derived programs may not be able to exceed the limits imposed by the original program. Why is this a problem? Philosophically speaking, we can see that the derived programs can not use the full potential of the programming language: a better result may be obtained by using one more level of nesting, one more variable or one more dimension in an array. It is less clear to what extent this is a practical problem, though. I will argue that if partial evaluators are to be used for compiling by specialising interpreters, then it is indeed a problem.

When compiling by partial evaluation, each object program is a specialised version of the interpreter. The interpreter, being a single program, will have finite bounds on features that the language itself has no limitation for. If the residual programs can not exceed these bounds, only a subset of the target language is exploited. If the source language has uniform limits for these features, it is no problem. But if not, in particular if the source language is an extended version of the target language, this is a problem.

In the "challenging problems" collection from the '87 PEMC workshop, (Neil Jones 1987) suggested that a partial evaluator is "strong enough" (later the term *optimal* is used) if it is possible to completely remove the interpretation overhead of a self-interpreter by specialisation. The case of self-interpretation is interesting, as it is easy to judge to what extent the interpretation overhead has been removed by comparing the source and target programs, as these are in the same language. If the target program is identical to the source program (modulo renaming and reordering) it is safe to conclude that all interpretation overhead has been removed.

Note that for the test above to be a test on the quality of the partial evaluator, not the self-interpreter, we must not insist on a particular self-interpreter. We must argue that no matter how a self-interpreter is written, we can not obtain optimality. This is where considering inherited limits becomes a useful yardstick: if the partial evaluator inherits a bound from the original program relating to a feature that the language has no limit for, then we can argue that optimality can not be achieved.

Inherited limits are only interesting for features where it costs something to

$$Program \rightarrow TypeDecl^* \ FunDecl^+$$

$$TypeDecl \rightarrow \textbf{data} \ TypeId \ = \ ConDecl$$

$$
\begin{aligned}
ConDecl \ \rightarrow \ & ConId \ TypeId^* \\
| \ & ConId \ TypeId^* \ | \ ConDecl
\end{aligned}
$$

$$FunDecl \rightarrow FunId \ VarId^* \ = \ Expr$$

$$
\begin{aligned}
Expr \quad \rightarrow \ & VarId \\
| \ & FunId \ Expr^* \\
| \ & ConId \ Expr^* \\
| \ & \textbf{case} \ Expr \ \textbf{of} \ Branch^+
\end{aligned}
$$

$$Branch \ \rightarrow \ ConId \ VarId^* \ => \ Expr$$

Fig. 1. Syntax of a small functional language

```
data int  = Zero | Succ int
data list = Nil | Cons int list

f a b = case a of
          Nil      => b
          Cons n l => Cons (g n) (f b l)

g n = case n of
        Zero   => Zero
        Succ m => m
```

Fig. 2. A small program.

simulate an unbounded number/size with a bounded number/size. This is the usual case, but one can argue that one-dimensional arrays can simulate multi-dimensional arrays at no cost, since the code generated for the explicit index calculation using one-dimensional arrays is the same as the code generated by a compiler for index calculation in multi-dimensional arrays. Such arguments are, however, often implementation-specific and not always convincing.

As a case study we will successively refine a partial evaluator, removing inherited limits as we go along. To do so, we define a small first-order functional language and a self-interpreter for this language. We will test how well the partial evaluator can compile a small test program by specialising the self-interpreter to this program, and suggest changes to the partial evaluator from observed deficiencies.

```
data num   = Z | S num
data univ  = Con num ulist
data ulist = Un | Uc univ ulist
data funs  = Fn | Fun exp funs
data exp   = Var num | Fap num elist | Cap num elist | Case exp elist
data elist = En | Ec exp elist

append a b = case a of
               Un      => b
               Uc v a => Uc v (append a b)

hd vs = case vs of
          Un     => Con Z Un
          Uc v vs => v

tl vs = case vs of
          Un     => Un
          Uc v vs => vs
```

Fig. 3. Type declarations and utility functions used by self-interpreter.

3 A Small Language

We have chosen a very simple language as our test-bed. We must not be too simple, however, as we must have some limits to remove. An example of too simple a language is the pure lambda calculus, where a five-line partial evaluator is able to remove all interpretation overhead when specialising a three-line self-interpreter as seen in (Mogensen 1992). A suitable compromise is the language whose syntax is described in Fig. 1. A small program in the language is shown in Fig. 2.

We have non-nested function definitions working over simple algebraic data types. Programs are assumed to be type-correct (monomorphically). Case-expressions are exhaustive. A self-interpreter for the language is shown in Fig. 4. The self-interpreter uses some type declarations and utility functions shown in Fig. 3. We will not show these in the programs below unless they are changed.

The type univ is a universal data type, used to represent values of any type. Elements of univ consists of a constructor number and a list of values. The types funs, and exp represent syntax of functions, expressions. The types ulist, funs and elist represent lists of values, function definitions and expressions. Due to the monomorphic restriction, separate types are required for these. Variables are referred to by their expected position in the environment, and functions by their position in the program. The type declarations of the source program are not represented in the self-interpreter, as they have no operational significance. The function apply takes as arguments a function index (f), a list of function definitions (fs), a list of arguments to the function (args) and the representation (p) of the entire program. apply uses the index to find the corresponding function definition and passes the body expression, the arguments and the program to

```
run p args = apply Z p args p

apply f fs args p =
  case fs of
    Fn        => Con Z Un
    Fun e fs => case f of
                  Z   => eval e args p
                  S f => apply f fs args p

eval e vs p =
  case e of
    Var n    => lookup n vs
    Fap n es => apply n p (evallist es vs p) p
    Cap n es => Con n (evallist es vs p)
    Case e es => case (eval e vs p) of
                   Con n vs1 => eval (select n es) (append vs1 vs) p

evallist es vs p =
  case es of
    En       => Un
    Ec e es => Uc (eval e vs p) (evallist es vs p)

lookup n vs =
  case n of
    Z   => hd vs
    S n => lookup n (tl vs)

select n es =
  case es of
    En       => Cap Z En
    Ec e es => case n of
                 Z   => e
                 S n => select n es
```

Fig. 4. Self-interpreter for a small functional language.

```
Fun (Case (Var Z)
          (Ec (Var (S Z))
          (Ec (Cap (S Z) (Ec (Fap (S Z) (Ec (Var Z) En))
                          (Ec (Fap Z (Ec (Var (S (S (S Z))))
                                      (Ec (Var (S Z)) En)))
                          En)))
          En)))
    (Fun (Case (Var Z)
              (Ec (Cap Z En)
              (Ec (Var Z)
               En)))
     Fn)
```

Fig. 5. Representation of the test program as data.

eval. eval evaluates the expression in the environment defined by vs. It uses the program representation p when interpreting function applications.

4 Specialisation Methods

We now study a number of specialisation methods for the small language introduced above. We will deliberately avoid details about the implementation of these methods, we will describe *what* is to be done rather than *how*. In particular, we will try not to make the description specific to online or offline specialisation, nor will we consider self-application.

Since we want to state properties about the partial evaluators independently of a particular self-interpreter, we will allow ourselves to rewrite the self-interpreter to get maximum benefit from each partial evaluator. In essence, we will perform binding time improvements (Jones *et al.* 1993, chapter 12) as we see fit.

4.1 Method 1: Constant Folding

Our first simple algorithm for partial evaluation is *constant folding*, essentially as found in many optimising compilers. While the language is different, the method closely resembles "global" constant propagation as described e.g. in (Kildall 1973).

The essence is: if a formal parameter to a function is given the same known value in all calls to a function, the parameter is eliminated from the definition and all calls and all further references to it are replaced by the value. Local reductions are performed.

This is a very primitive method, and indeed little reduction is done when specialising an interpreter. The result of specialising the self-interpreter in Fig. 4 to the test program in Fig. 2 is shown in Fig. 6.

The two occurrences of "(Fun ...)" actually refer to the entire representation of the test program, as shown in Fig. 5. Note that we have been able to remove the p parameter from both apply and eval. This is likely to give a small speedup, but nothing dramatic. The source program is still essentially interpreted in the residual program.

If we do not count the size of in-lined constants, the residual programs produced by constant folding are never larger than the original program. This is a very severe inherited limit, which we remove in method 2.

4.2 Method 2: Adding Unfolding

In order to remove the inherited limit of program size, we introduce unfolding of function calls. This resembles loop-unrolling and inlining as done by optimising compilers.

In our extended specialisation method, we essentially apply constant folding *after* call unfolding and local reduction of case-expressions. This means that we

```
run args = apply Z (Fun ...) args

apply f fs args =
  case fs of
    Fn        => Con Z Un
    Fun e fs => case f of
                  Z   => eval e args
                  S f => apply f fs args

eval e vs =
  case e of
    Var n    => lookup n vs
    Fap n es => apply n (Fun ...) (evallist es vs)
    Cap n es => Con n (evallist es vs)
    Case e es => case (eval e vs) of
                   Con n vs1 => eval (select n es) (append vs1 vs)

evallist es vs =
  case es of
    En        => Un
    Ec e es => Uc (eval e vs) (evallist es vs)

lookup n vs =
  case n of
    Z   => hd vs
    S n => lookup n (tl vs)

select n es =
  case es of
    En        => Cap Z En
    Ec e es => case n of
                 Z   => e
                 S n => select n es
```

Fig. 6. Residual program made by method 1.

can eliminate a parameter if it is identical in all *non-unfolded* calls, even if it is non-constant in unfolded calls.

The decision of which function calls to unfold can be made off-line by program annotation, inserted manually as in (Jones *et al.* 1985) or automatically as in (Bondorf 1993), or it can be done on-line by studying the computation history as in e.g. (Berlin and Weise 1990). For simplicity of presentation, we have chosen the manual off-line approach.

We choose to unfold all calls to eval, evallist, lookup and select and all directly recursive calls to apply. It is safe also to unfold hd and tl, but doing so will make the residual program much larger and less readable (though a bit faster, since we eliminate some calls). The reason for not unfolding these is hence mostly expository.

Unfortunately, our present interpreter doesn't yield good results with this method. The reason is that we do not know which case-branch is selected (the result of select is unknown) when interpreting a case-expression. This means

Before:

```
... eval (select n es) (append vs1 vs) p

select n es =
  case es of
    En      => Cap Z En
    Ec e es => case n of
                 Z   => e
                 S n => select n vs
```

After:

```
... eselect n es (append vs1 vs) p

eselect n es vs p =
  case es of
    En      => Con Z Un
    Ec e es => case n of
                 Z   => eval e vs p
                 S n => eselect n es vs p
```

Fig. 7. Applying "The Trick" to selection of case-branches.

that the expression to evaluate is not always known, even with full unfolding of `eval`. We do, however, know that the expression must be one of the case-branches, so we can apply "The Trick", a commonly used binding time improvement described in (Bondorf 1993). We just move the recursive call to `eval` into the `select` function, obtaining a new function `eselect`. In the new version, all calls to `eval` will have known expression arguments. The transformation is shown in Fig. 7.

The result of specialising the modified self-interpreter with respect to the test program is shown in Fig. 8.

The resulting target program is about the same size as the original interpreter[1], so this in itself doesn't show that the inherited limit has been removed. However, it is easily seen that the size of the residual program grows with the size of the source program. Closer inspection shows that the dispatch on syntax of expressions has been eliminated, removing a large part of the interpretation overhead.

The result is, however, still a far cry from being identical to the source program. Looking at inherited limits we quickly note that any target program will have exactly 3 functions: `run`, `apply` and `append`. This is less than the number of functions in the interpreter, and this is indeed the case regardless of which interpreter is chosen, as the specialiser can only eliminate functions and parameters, not invent new functions.

---

[1] It would have been larger, had we unfolded `hd` and `tl`.

4.3 Method 3: Polyvariant Specialisation

```
run args = apply Z args

apply f args =
 case f of
   Z   =>
    case (hd args) of
      Con n vs1 =>
       case n of
         Z   => hd (tl args)
         S n =>
          case n of
            Z   =>
             Con (S Z)
                (Uc (apply (S Z)
                          (Uc (hd (append vs1 args)) Un))
                (Uc (apply Z
                          (Uc (hd (tl (tl (tl (append vs1 args))))) Un)
                          (Uc (hd (tl (append vs1 args))) Un)))
                Un))
            S n => Con Z Un
   S f =>
    case f of
      Z   =>
       case (hd args) of
         Con n vs1 =>
          case n of
            Z   => Con Z
            S n =>
             case n of
               Z   => hd (append vs1 args)
               S n => Con Z Un
      S f => Con Z Un
```

Fig. 8. Residual program made by method 2.

As most readers will have guessed by now, the limit on the number of functions can be removed by using *polyvariant specialisation*, allowing each original function to be specialised to several different versions, depending on the known input. This idea was essential for the success of the MIX-project described in (Jones *et al.* 1985), but had earlier been applied to imperative languages e.g. by Itkin (1983) and Bulyonkov (1988).

Stated shortly, our third method is:

Unfoldable calls are unfolded, and local reductions are made. In non-unfoldable calls, the values of the known arguments are used to create specialised variants of the function (one for each value of the known arguments). Each specialised variant has a unique name, and the known parameters are eliminated.

Since the number of variants of a function depends on the number of different known arguments to it (which may be unbounded), we have removed the inherited limit. The residual program obtained by applying polyvariant specialisation to the interpreter with respect to our test program is shown in Fig. 9.

```
run args = apply_0 args

apply_0 args =
 case (hd args) of
   Con n vs1 =>
     case n of
       Z   => hd (tl args)
       S n =>
         case n of
           Z   =>
             Con (S Z)
                 (Uc (apply_1
                             (Uc (hd (append vs1 args)) Un))
                 (Uc (apply_0
                             (Uc (hd (tl (tl (tl (append vs1 args)))))) Un)
                             (Uc (hd (tl (append vs1 args))) Un)))
                 Un))
         S n => Con Z Un

apply_1 args =
  case (hd args) of
    Con n vs1 =>
      case n of
        Z   => Con Z
        S n =>
          case n of
            Z   => hd (append vs1 args)
            S n => Con Z Un
```

Fig. 9. Residual program made by method 3.

We note that there now is a specialised version of apply for each function in
the source program. We have, however, not significantly reduced the interpretation overhead compared to the previous version. For some applications, though,
polyvariant specialisation is essential to obtaining good results.

Looking at Fig. 9 we note that all specialised versions of apply have exactly
one argument: args. It is easy to see that a specialised variant of a function
can have no more parameters than the original, since a parameter is either
eliminated (if known) or retained (if unknown). This is the next inherited limit
we will remove.

4.4 Method 4: Partially Static Values

There are several ways to remove the limitation on the number of parameters.
In the MIX project (Jones *et al.* 1985), a post process was at one stage used,
which guided by user annotations would split a residual parameter into several.
This was automated by Romanenko (1990). We will, instead, use the approach
from (Mogensen 1988), where we keep track of known parts of values that may
contain unknown components. When specialising a function it is specialised with
respect to the known parts of the partially known arguments, and each unknown

Before:
```
data exp     = Var num | Fap num elist | Cap num elist | Case exp elist

... eselect n es (append vs1 vs) p

eselect n es vs p =
  case es of
    En       => Con Z Un
    Ec e es => case n of
                 Z  => eval e vs p
                 S n => eselect n es vs p
```

After:
```
data exp     = Var num | Fap num elist | Cap num elist | Case exp blist
data blist = Bn | Bc num exp blist

... bselect n bs vs1 vs p

bselect n bs vs1 vs p =
  case bs of
    Bn          => Con Z Un
    Bc m e bs => case n of
                   Z   => append_eval m vs1 Un vs e p
                   S n => bselect n bs vs p

append_eval m vs1 vs2 vs e p =
  case m of
    Z   => b
    S m => case vs1 of
             Un      => eval e (rev vs2 vs) p
             Uc v vs1 => append_eval m vs1 (Uc v vs2) vs e p

rev vs2 vs =
  case vs2 of
    Un        => vs
    Uc v vs2 => rev vs2 (Uc v vs)
```

Fig. 10. Binding time improvements for partially static values.

part becomes a separate argument. The number of parameters to a specialised function hence depends on the number of unknown components of a partially known value. Since this can be unbounded, we have removed the limit.

The prime targets for partially known values in our interpreter are the parameter args in apply and the parameter vs in eval, evallist and lookup.

While the elements of the arg are unknown at specialisation time, the structure (length) is known (assuming it is known in the initial call to run, which is not unreasonable), since it is built by evallist, and hence gets the same length as the list of expressions es.

We might expect the same to be true for vs, but unfortunately this is not so. The reason is that the contents of a constructed value is appended to vs when

```
run args_0 args_1 = apply_0 args_0 args_1

apply_0 args_0 args_1 =
 case args_0 of
   Con n vs1 =>
     case n of
       Z   => args_1
       S n =>
        case n of
          Z   =>
           case vs1 of
              Un        => Con Z Un
              Uc v0 vs1 =>
                 case vs1 of
                    Un        => Con Z Un
                    Uc v1 vs1 =>
                      Con (S Z)
                       (Uc (apply_1 v0)
                       (Uc (apply_0 args_1 v1)
                       Un))
          S n => Con Z Un

apply_1 args_0 =
  case args_0 of
    Con n vs1 =>
      case n of
        Z   => Con Z
        S n =>
         case n of
           Z   => case vs1 of
                   Un        => Con Z Un
                   Uc v vs1 => v
          S n => Con Z Un
```

Fig. 11. Residual program made by method 4.

interpreting a case-expression. Following the idea from our previous binding time improvement, we will move the appending into the **eselect** function, so we know which constructor was applied when we do the appending. Unfortunately, we do not with our present program representation have sufficient information to know the length of the list we append to vs, even when we know the constructor. So we need yet another binding time improvement, this time affecting our program representation: we must explicitly indicate the arity of constructors in case expressions. The required changes are shown in Fig. 10. All the shown functions are unfolded during specialisation.

The binding time improvement could be simplified somewhat if we could return a partially static value across a dynamic conditional (which is possible with CPS-based specialisation as described in (Bondorf 1992)), as we then just would have needed to add an extra controlling argument to append.

Now we will also unfold append, hd and tl, as we can eliminate these now the structure (spine) of the environment is static.

Applying specialisation with partially static values to the new version of the interpreter and the test program, we get the target program shown in Fig. 11.

We can see that the two specialised versions of `apply` have different numbers of parameters, corresponding to the parameters of the functions in the source program. While neither of these are larger than the original number of parameters to `apply`, other source programs can cause that. The target program is also both smaller and faster than the previous, having replaced the nested case-expressions used for variable lookup by direct references to new variable names. The case switching on `vs1` comes from `append_eval`.

The goal function `run` now has two parameters, which are of a different type to the `args` argument of the original `run` function. Strictly speaking, this means that the residual program is not correct with respect to the usual mix-equation (Jones *et al.* 1993). But there is a well-defined correspondence between the two new arguments and the single old argument, so this is not a problem in practice.

While our target program now fits a page, it is still far larger than the test program, and a good bit slower. A source of inefficiency is that all values in the interpreted program are represented using a single uniform representation. More specifically, the constructors in the residual program are always a subset of the constructors in the original program. Since the language as a whole puts no limit on the number of different constructors, we clearly have an inherited limit.

4.5   Method 5: Constructor Specialisation

We removed the inherited limit on functions by introducing polyvariant specialisation of functions. We will use a similar solution to the constructor problem: polyvariant specialisation of constructors as introduced in (Mogensen 1993).

The observation is that we sometimes lose information during specialisation. This is for example when a partially static value is returned from a non-unfolded function. Instead of converting such partially static values to (completely dynamic) residual expressions, we can specialise the topmost constructor with respect to the static parts of its arguments, leaving the dynamic parts as separate arguments to the new constructor, exactly as we did for function calls in method 4. In addition to noting the new name and the types of the residual arguments in the type declaration, all case expressions that branch on the original constructors must now branch on the specialised constructors. The branches of these case expressions can use the known parts of the arguments to the constructor, just like residual functions can use the known parts of the arguments to the function.

In our interpreter, the `Con` constructor of the `univ` type is our target for constructor specialisation. We can specialise this with respect to its tag value and the structure of the list of arguments. Hence, each specialised version of `Con` will have the same number of parameters as the source-program constructor it represents.

An interesting consequence of using constructor specialisation in our interpreter is that the binding time improvements we introduced along the way are no longer necessary: the original version from Fig. 4 yields exactly the same residual programs as the binding-time improved one.

The target program obtained by constructor specialisation is shown in Fig. 12.

```
data univ  = Con_0 | Con_1 univ | Con_2 univ univ

run args_0 args_1 = apply_0 args_0 args_1

apply_0 args_0 args_1 =
 case args_0 of
   Con_0        => args_1
   Con_1 v0     => Con_0           /* unreachable */
   Con_2 v0 v1 => Con_2 (apply_1 v0) (apply_0 args_1 v1)

apply_1 args_0 =
  case args_0 of
    Con_0        => Con_0
    Con_1 v0     => v0
    Con_2 v0 v1 => v0              /* unreachable */
```

Fig. 12. Residual program made by method 5.

Zero and Succ are represented by the specialised constructors Con_0 and Con_1, and Nil and Cons by Con_0 and Con_2. The specialised constructors have the same number of arguments as those that they represent, so we have not only removed the limit on the number of different constructors, but also on the number of arguments to these. There is a similar problem with respect to the mix-equation, as the one noted in Sect. 4.4, but again this is not a problem in practice.

The number of operations performed by the residual program when running is the same as for the source program, except for a single call from run to apply_0. But the target program is not just a renaming of the source program: there are "dead" branches in both case-expressions and there is only a single type definition. Both of these problems are caused by having a single residual type for all specialised constructors from a single source type.

In our example the dead branches are relatively harmless, but it is conceivable that dead branches can be a sizable fraction of the target program or cause errors/looping during specialization. Also, only if we assume constant time branch selection, regardless of the number of branches, have we eliminated all interpretation overhead.

4.6 Method 6: Type Specialisation

In order to remove the inherited limit of the number of types in the residual program, we allow different specialised versions of the same original constructor to be in different residual types. The system described by Dussart (1995)

```
data univ_0 = Con_0 | Con_1 univ_0
data univ_1 = Con_2 | Con_3 univ_0 univ_1

run args_0 args_1 = apply_0 args_0 args_1

apply_0 args_0 args_1 =
 case args_0 of
   Con_2       => args_1
   Con_3 v0 v1 => Con_2 (apply_1 v0) (apply_0 args_1 v1)

apply_1 args_0 =
  case args_0 of
   Con_0       => Con_0
   Con_1 v0    => v0
```

Fig. 13. Residual program made by method 6.

does this, as does the type specializer described in (Hughes 1996). The following method is not exactly the same, but shows the essential idea:

When a constructor is specialised, a new type is created for the specialised instance. Only when necessary (e.g. when occurring in different branches of the same case-expression) are types joined. The same constructor applied to the same static arguments may occur in several types, if the uses are independent. Hence, the residual name of a specialized constructor depends not only on the static arguments, but also on the type it will eventually be part of.

The residual program obtained by type specialisation is shown in Fig. 13.

Now we have two specialised versions of the univ type. univ_0 corresponds to the int type of the source program, and univ_1 corresponds to list. Con_0 and Con_2 both correspond to Con Z Un, but are given different names because the residual types are different.

With the sole exception of the superfluous run function, the residual program is just a renaming of the source program. We can see that (after removing run and with some simple assumptions about how types are joined) the target program will *always* be a renaming of the source program. Hence, we can reasonably conclude that all interpretation overhead has been removed. Similarly, we can conclude that all inherited limits have been removed.

5 Other Evolution and Natural Selection

Our focus on a single aspect of the evolution of partial evaluation is in some way similar to the way palaeontologists may focus on the evolution of the thigh bone from early salamanders to humans. While it shows an important aspect of the adaptation to land-based life, it is not the whole story.

One may choose to focus on entirely different aspects to show how the field has developed. Indeed, Olivier Danvy (1993) has suggested that reducing the need for manual binding time improvement is a driving force behind much of the developments of partial evaluators – something we have explicitly chosen to ignore in this study.

There may also be different ways to remove inherited limits than the ones shown above. We noted that the limit on number of parameters has been handled differently, by a post-process, e.g. in (Romanenko 1990). Similarly, it is possible that limits on types and constructors can be handled by post processing. When several methods exist, a form of "natural selection" may determine which method survives. By all appearances, the use of partially static structures has ousted post-processing as a means of removing the bound on parameters. It is too early yet to tell for the later developments. Also, some inherited limits may be considered unimportant (as they have little significance for effectivity), so no method for removing them will be widely used.

As we saw in Sect. 4.5, some methods for removing inherited limits may also reduce the need for binding time improvements. This is true also for partially static structures, and was indeed one of the original motivations for introducing these. This may have been a major reason for the success of this approach over arity raising (Romanenko 1990), which only solves the variable splitting problem, and bifurcation (Mogensen 1989), (De Neil *et al.* 1990), which only solves the binding time improvement aspect.

6 Further Work

By removing all inherited limits in our example language, we may have given the impression that the problem is now solved. This is far from the case. Our language is very simple, and has few features. Every time a new feature is added to a language, a new inherited limit may potentially be added to a partial evaluator, even when it has been extended to handle the new feature. Below, we list a number of common features of programming languages, and discuss the principle of removing inherited limits that these features may introduce.

Nesting of Scopes. Our simple language has flat scoping, but it is common to have unbounded nesting of functions or procedures in programming languages (a notable exception being C). It turns out to be simple to allow arbitrary nesting in the residual program, just by unfolding calls to non-locally defined functions/procedures. This has been done in lambda-mix (Gomard and Jones 1991) and ML-mix (Birkedal and Welinder 1993). Some non-trivial interactions between nested scoping and higher-order functions have been studied by Malmkjær and Ørbæk (1995).

Array Dimensions. I doubt any existing partial evaluator can take a source program using (at most) two-dimensional arrays and produce a residual program using three-dimensional arrays. Nor is it easy to see how to do this in a natural fashion. A post-process may detect that access patterns corresponds to higher-dimensional arrays, but it is hard to see how "dimension raising" may be done as an integral part of the specialisation process.

Modules. When specialising a modular language, it should, by our principle, be desirable to create residual programs with more modules than the original program. The work by Heldal & Hughes (1996) presents a possible solution to this, where the modularization of the residual program reflects modularization of the static data.

Classes. In object oriented languages, it is natural to generate specialised instances of objects within a class. But our principle extends to creating entirely new class hierarchies in residual programs, which is less clear how to achieve.

Patterns. Languages with pattern matching usually allow arbitrarily complex patterns. If a partial evaluator can not generate patterns that are more complex than those found in the original program, this is an inherited limit. A solution to this problem is to combine several residual patterns into fewer, but larger patterns. It might be argued that a compiler will separate the pattern matching into nested tests anyway, so the limit may have no significance for the speed of residual programs. This argument is, however, implementation dependent.

Other. Similar problems may occur for features like exceptions, constraints, processes, streams etc. It is not clear to the author if moving to a polymorphic language will introduce new potentially inherited limits.

7 Conclusion

What we have tried to impart to the reader is an awareness of the idea that a partial evaluator may cause residual programs to inherit limits from the original programs, and that this may be a problem.

The intention is to inspire developers of partial evaluators to consider if their partial evaluators exhibit such inherited limits, and decide if they think these important enough to deal with. In other words, the awareness of the problem may be used as a guideline for refining specialisation technology.

Identifying the problem is, however, only the first step. Knowing that a limit is inherited does not always suggest a solution. A good example of this is the array dimension limit, which has no obvious solution.

It may not be obvious which limits, if any, are inherited. A test for this may be done by attempting to write a self-interpreter and specialise this. If the residual programs are renamings of the original, it is evidence that no inherited limits exist. Otherwise, the problem may be in the interpreter or the specialiser, and the experiment may suggest which. In general, if a problem with residual programs can be solved by rewriting the original program (no matter how extensively), then the problem is not due to an inherited limit.

Note that we have only required that a self-interpreter exists which allows the residual programs to be identical to the source programs. Hence, we have not out-ruled the possibility of writing self-interpreters where partial evaluation would inject the residual programs into some sub-language, e.g. CPS style. This ability is important, and we should aim to keep this.

Not all improvements of partial evaluators are instances of removing inherited limits. Important subjects such as improved binding time analysis, control of termination, automatic binding time improvements, speed of specialisation, self-application, addition of language features etc. are all important developments that are orthogonal to the removal of inherited limits.

References

Berlin, A., Weise, D.: Compiling scientific code using partial evaluation. IEEE Computer vol. 23, no. 5, (1990), 25–37.

Birkedal, L. Welinder, M.: Partial evaluation of Standard ML. Masters Thesis, DIKU, University of Copenhagen, Denmark, (1993).

Bondorf, A.: Improving binding times without explicit CPS-conversion. LFP '92, Lisp Pointers, vol. V, no. 1, ACM Press (1992), 1–10.

Bondorf, A.: Similix manual, system version 5.0. Tech. Report, DIKU, University of Copenhagen, Denmark, (1993).

Bulyonkov, M. A.: A theoretical approach to polyvariant mixed computation. Proceedings of the IFIP TC2 Workshop on Partial Evaluation and Mixed Computation, Gammel Avernæs, Denmark, 18-24 October, 1987, North-Holland (1988), 51–64.

Danvy, O.: On the evolution of partial evaluators. DART technical report, University of Aarhus, Denmark (1993).

De Niel, A., Bevers, E., De Vlaminck, K.: Program bifurcation for a polymorphically typed functional language. PEPM '91, ACM Press (1991), 142–153.

Dussart, D., Bevers, E., De Vlaminck, K.: Polyvariant constructor specialisation. PEPM '95, ACM Press (1995), 54–65.

Gomard, C. K., Jones, N. D.: A partial evaluator for the untyped lambda-calculus. Journal of Functional Programming, vol. 1, no. 1, January 1991, 21–69.

Heldal, R., Hughes, J.: Partial evaluation and separate compilation. Proceedings of the Partial Evaluation Workshop, Dagstuhl 1996, O. Danvy, R. Glück, P. Thiemann (eds.), Springer-Verlag Lecture Notes in Computer Science 1996.

Hughes, J.: Type specialistion for the λ-calculus. Proceedings of the Partial Evaluation Workshop, Dagstuhl 1996, O. Danvy, R. Glück, P. Thiemann (eds.), Springer-Verlag Lecture Notes in Computer Science 1996.

Itkin, V.E.: On partial and mixed program execution. Program optimization and transformation, Novosibirsk Computing Center, (1983), 17–30.

Jones, N. D., Sestoft, P., Søndergaard, H.: An experiment in partial evaluation: the generation of a compiler generator. Rewriting Techniques and Applications, Springer LNCS 202, Springer-Verlag, (1985), 124–140.

Jones, N. D. (collector): Challenging problems in partial evaluation and mixed computation. Proceedings of the IFIP TC2 Workshop on Partial Evaluation and Mixed Computation, Gammel Avernæs, Denmark, 18-24 October, 1987, North-Holland (1988), 1–14.

Jones, N. D., Gomard, C. K., Sestoft, P.: Partial evaluation and automatic program generation. Prentice-Hall, 1993

Kildall, G. A.: A unified approach to global program optimization. POPL'73, ACM Press (1973), 194–206.

Malmkjær, K., Ørbæk, P.: Polyvariant specialisation for higher-order, block-structured languages. PEPM '95, ACM Press (1995), 66–76.

Mogensen, T. Æ.: Partially static structures in a self-applicable partial evaluator. Proceedings of the IFIP TC2 Workshop on Partial Evaluation and Mixed Computation, Gammel Avernæs, Denmark, 18-24 October, 1987, North-Holland (1988), 325–347.

Mogensen, T. Æ.: Separating Binding Times in Language Specifications. FPCA '89, Addison-Wesley (1989), 14–25.

Mogensen, T. Æ.: Self-applicable partial evaluation for pure lambda calculus. PEPM'92, Yale tech. report YALEU/DCS/RR-909 (1992), 116–121.

Mogensen, T. Æ.: Constructor specialization. PEPM '93, ACM Press (1993), 22–32.

Romanenko, S. A.: Arity raiser and its use in program specialization. ESOP '90, LNCS 432, Springer-Verlag (1990), 341–360.

A Self-Applicable Supercompiler

Andrei P. Nemytykh
Victoria A. Pinchuk
Programming Systems Institute, Pereslavl-Zalesski, Russia
Valentin F. Turchin
The City College of New York

Abstract

A *supercompiler* is a program which can perform a deep transformation of programs using a principle which is similar to *partial evaluation*, and can be referred to as *metacomputation*. Supercompilers that have been in existence up to now (see [12], [13]) were not self-applicable: this is a more difficult problem than self-application of a partial evaluator, because of the more intricate logic of supercompilation. In the present paper we describe the first self-applicable model of a supercompiler and present some tests. Three features distinguish it from the previous models and make self-application possible: (1) The input language is a subset of Refal which we refer to as *flat* Refal. (2) The process of *driving* is performed as a transformation of *pattern-matching graphs*. (3) *Metasystem jumps* are implemented, which allows the supercompiler to avoid interpretation whenever direct computation is possible.

Keywords: program transformation, supercompilation, metacomputation, self-application, metasystem transition, MST-schemes, metacode, pattern-matching graphs, Refal.

1 Introduction

Self-applicability of a program transformer is well known to lead to new possibilities, such as automatic creation of compilers from interpreters (see [2], [10], [1], [3]). Self-applicability of a partial evaluator was first achieved in [3]. A *supercompiler* is a program which can perform a deep transformation of programs using a principle which is similar to *partial evaluation*, and is referred to as *metacomputation*. Supercompilers that have been in existence up to now (see [12], [13]) were not self-applicable: this is a more difficult problem than self-application of a partial eveluator, because of the more intricate logic of supercompilation. [1]

In the present paper we describe the first fully self-applicable model of a supercompiler. We concentrate on the three features of this model which distinguish it from the previous models and make self-application possible.

---

[1]Some steps in this direction, though, were reported in [8].

- The input language is simplified to a subset of Refal which we refer to as *flat* Refal (Sec.2).

- The process of *driving* (see [11],[13]), which plays the key role in the construction of the transformed program, is performed as a transformation of *flat pattern-matching graphs* which preserves their functional meaning.

- *Metasystem jumps*, as described in [15], are implemented (Sec.4). This feature allows the supercompiler to avoid interpretation whenever a direct computation is possible.

In Sec.5 the results of the testing of the new supercompiler are discussed.

2   Flat Refal

For the purpose of program transformation, it makes sense to have object programs written in a maximally simplified programming language, into which programs written in a more convenient language can be automatically translated. The supercompiler described here uses *flat Refal* as the language of object programs. Flat Refal is used in two forms different in syntax: the *sentential* form, which is convenient for the human user, and the *pattern-matching graph* form, which is actually transformed in the supercompiler.

Flat Refal is the lowest level in the hierarchy of the existing versions of Refal which, historically, started from the *basic* version and was then extended up as *extended Refal* and down as *strict* and now *flat* Refal. We wrote the programs constituting the supercompiler in extended Refal. For self-application we first translate the supercompiler from extended Refal into strict Refal; this translation can be fully automatic, but in our tests it was partly manual. Then the text in strict Refal is automatically converted into flat Refal: first in the sentential form (for debugging), and then, finally, in the graph form, in which it becomes an object program for the higher level supercompiler.

Definition of basic, strict and extended Refal can be found in [11], [13], [14]. A brief description of flat Refal follows.

The syntax of flat Refal is given in Table 1. The fundamental data structure of Refal, the *expression*, is more general than the list, or s-expression, used in Lisp, Prolog, and many functional languages. It allows concatenation as one of the two basic constructions; the other construction is enclosure in parentheses, which makes it possible to represent trees. An expression may be empty, in which case it is represented either by the metasymbol [], or just by an empty space. A string of characters can be represented using only one pair of quotes: 'abc'.

The two types of variables in Refal correspond to the two basic syntactic types: *s-variables*, such as s.1 or s.x, take exactly one symbol as its value; *e-variables*, as e.2, can have any expression as its value.

Definition: (1) An *object expression* is an expression which includes no variables.

symbol	::=	symbolic-name ‖ number ‖ ' character '
expression	::=	[] ‖ term expression
term	::=	symbol ‖ variable ‖ (expression)
variable	::=	s.index ‖ e.index
index	::=	number ‖ symbolic-name
function-def	::=	fn-name { sentences }
fn-name	::=	symbolic-name
sentences	::=	sentence ‖ sentence sentences
sentence	::=	left-side = right-side ;
left-side	::=	rigid-pattern
rigid-pattern	::=	*see below*
right-side	::=	expression ‖ function-call
function-call	::=	< fn-name expression >
program	::=	function-def ‖ function-def program

Table 1: The syntax of flat Refal

(2) A *rigid pattern* is an expression such that (a) none of its subexpressions has the form $E_1\mathbf{e}.i_1 E_2\mathbf{e}.i_2 E_3$, where E_1 etc. are arbitrary expressions, and (b) no e-variable appears in the pattern twice. □

The semantics of Refal is based on pattern-matching. We denote the matching of an object expression E_o, the *argument* of the matching, to a rigid pattern P as $E_o : P$. This is an operation the result of which is either a substitution for the variables in P which transforms P into E_o, in which case matching succeeds and the substitution is referred to as its *resolution*, or a statement that there is no such substitution (matching fails). A pattern can be seen as a set of object expressions. Therefore, we write $E_o \in P$ if the matching $E_o : P$ is successful.

It can be easily proved (see [11]) that a matching $E : P$, where P is a rigid pattern, has no more than one resolution.

Refal sentences are rewrite rules. The sentences are tried in the order they are written, and the first applicable sentence is used. The right-hand side of every Refal rule in the flat version of the language is either an expression or a single function call; nested function calls are not allowed. (Strict Refal, like flat Refal, requires that the left-hand sides be rigid patterns, but it allows any combinations of expressions and function calls in the right-hand sides.) In flat Refal, information exchange takes place only through variables, not through the values taken by function calls. This is an iterative, not recursive, style of programming.

We do not require, though, that the user writes programs in flat Refal; as mentioned above, programs can be written in strict Refal and automatically converted into a flat form. The idea of the translation algorithm is to add to each function one more argument which maintains a representation of the stack of deferred function calls. When the right side of a sentence in the original (not flat) program contains nested calls, the function call which is to be evaluated first is left in the right side of the sentence; all other calls are reworked into stack elements and added to the first argument in the required order. If the right side is passive, a special function Pop is called, which pops the stack appropriately. There is no need to go into the details of the algorithm.

From the view-point of supercompilation, the difference between strict and flat Refal is not so salient as when we compare the respective programming styles. With strict Refal, configurations of the Refal machine include deferred function calls, which are, in the previous supercompilers, represented by a stack. With flat Refal, configurations are flat, but the first argument may represent the same stack with which the strict-Refal supercompiler is working. The advantage of our present approach is that the stack is not a separate structure, but just one of the parameters. It can be treated as other parameters, which is causes considerable simplification. On the other hand, if we want to treat the stack as a separate structure, we still can do it in the flat setting, by giving a special treatment to the first argument.

3   Pattern-matching graphs

Below we briefly describe the most important features of a form of flat Refal programs which we refer to as (flat) *pattern-matching graphs*, or *Refal graphs*. A program in flat Refal is automatically converted into a pattern-matching graph.

A pattern-matching graph can be seen as sum of products of three varieties of the pattern-matching operation: *contractions, assignments* and *restrictions*. Product represents sequential execution of operations, sum – parallel execution. Common beginnings of products can be factorized (left-distributive law), hence a pattern-matching graph can be seen as a tree where nodes are the points at which the common part of two or more products – to be referred as *paths* – ends, and the sum of various continuations – *branches* – starts. In the following we describe the operations in Refal graphs.

In our definition of the pattern matching $E_o : P$ the left side E_o was supposed to be an object expression (no variables). Now we generalize this concept by allowing pattern-matching pairs where the left side E is, an arbitrary expression. The variables in E are supposed to be *bound*, i.e. have definite values (object expressions). The execution of generalized pattern-matching consists of two steps: first we substitute for the bound variables in E their values, which results in some object expression E_o; then we execute the matching $E_o : P$, where the left side is now an object expression. As a result of a successful matching, the free variables in the pattern P get certain values (object expressions again). If there are no variables in the pattern and the matching is successful, as in $a : a$, the result is denoted as $\mathbf{I}$(the identity operation); if matching fails, the result is denoted as $\mathbf{Z}$(impossible operation).

Definition: (1) A *contraction* is a pattern matching $v : P$, where v is a variable and P is a rigid pattern; we shall denote this contraction as $v \xrightarrow{c} P$.
(2) An *assignment* is a pattern matching $E : v$, where E is an expression and v a variable; we shall denote this assignment as $E \xleftarrow{a} v$.

(3) The *list* of n Refal expressions $E_1, E_2, \ldots, E_n$ is the expression:

$$(E_1)(E_2) \ldots (E_n)$$

(4) A *varlist* is a list of free variables where no variable appears twice. One varlist, V_1, is a *subset* of another, V_2, if every variable from V_1 is also in V_2. Two varlists are *equal* (but not necessarily *identical*) if each is a subset of the other. The list of all variables that enter a pattern E is denoted as $\mathbf{var}(E)$.

(5) A *list contraction* is a pattern matching $V : P$, where V is a varlist of n variables and P is a rigid list of the same number of pattern expressions. We shall denote this contraction as $V \xrightarrow{c} P$.

(6) A *list assignment* is a pattern matching $E : V$, where V is a varlist of n variables and E is an arbitrary list of the same number of pattern expressions. We shall denote this assignment as $E \xleftarrow{a} V$. $\square$

We shall often skip the word "list" referring to contractions and assignments when it is clear from the context whether the operation involves one variable or a list of variables.

Our notation of contractions and assignments may seem unusual, but it is quite logical and convenient. It is derived from the following two principles. (1) On the left side we have bound (old, defined) variables; on the right side free (new, to be defined) variables. (2) When the operation is understood as a substitution, the arrow is directed from the variable to its replacement.

An example. $\mathbf{x} \xrightarrow{c} \mathbf{s.1} \; \mathbf{x'a'}$ is a contraction for $\mathbf{x}$. If the value of $\mathbf{x}$ is 'myshka', after the execution of this contraction $\mathbf{x}$ becomes 'yshk', and a new variable $\mathbf{s.1}$ becomes defined with the parentheses which enclose the ready part of the stringthe value 'm', which is written down as the assignment 'm' $\xleftarrow{a} \mathbf{s.1}$. If $\mathbf{x}$ is 'kot' the result is the impossible operation $\mathbf{Z}$(failure of matching).

Decisions as to which of the paths is to be taken are governed by contractions and *restrictions*, which is one more operation used in pattern-matching graphs. A contraction is, essentially, *negation* of contraction. It has the form: $(\# \; G)$, where G is a tree of contractions. It is evaluated to $\mathbf{Z}$if one of the paths (contraction products) succeed; and to $\mathbf{I}$otherwise. Due to the use of restrictions, different branches starting at the same node can be processed independently. This is not so in the case of the sentential form of Refal, where only those cases come to each given sentence which failed at all preceding sentences.

To discuss the tests reported in the present paper, we only need to understand contractions and assignments, and have a general idea of the syntax of graphs.

The programming of the supercompiler was based on a set of relations of equivalency for the algebra of pattern-matching operations. The most important equation is the *clash* between an assignment and a contraction for the same variable, which is *resolved* in a matching:

$$(e \xleftarrow{a} v)(v \xrightarrow{c} p) = e : p$$

Thus the example above can be seen as the equation:

$$(\text{'myshka'} \overset{a}{\leftarrow} x) \ (x \overset{c}{\rightarrow} s.1 \times \text{'a'}) = (\text{'yshk'} \overset{a}{\leftarrow} x) \ (\text{'m'} \overset{a}{\leftarrow} s.1)$$

Here is an example of resolution which includes the contraction of a bound variable:

$$(\text{'kot's.2} \overset{a}{\leftarrow} x) \ (x \overset{c}{\rightarrow} x \text{'a'}) = (s.2 \overset{c}{\rightarrow} \text{'a'}) \ (\text{'kot'} \overset{a}{\leftarrow} x)$$

With Refal graphs, driving is an application of the commutation relations for pattern-matching operations. A path in the normal form, in which it appears in function definitions and represents one step of the Refal machine, has the structure CRA, where the letters stand for Contraction, Restriction and Assignment, respectively. A sequence (walk) of two paths representing two steps is $C_1 R_1 A_1 C_2 R_2 A_2$. Resolving the clash $A_1 C_2$ and then adjusting contractions and restrictions according to commutation relations, we return the walk to the normal form: we have made one step of driving.

The function call to be computed is given as a graph of the form:

$$value\text{-}list \overset{a}{\leftarrow} var\text{-}list; \mathbf{fn}(F)$$

where $\mathbf{fn}(F)$ stands for the graph defining the function F; $var\text{-}list$ is the list of input variables in the graph of F; $value\text{-}list$ is the list of the values assigned to the input variables. The values normally include *configuration variables*. Clashes between these assignments and contractions for input variables with which $\mathbf{fn}(F)$ normally starts make the beginning of driving. In the end of supercompilation we have a program with configuration variables as the new input variables. The final result of computation on every exit of the graph is assigned to the special "external world" variable e.out: $e \overset{a}{\leftarrow} \text{e.out}$.

4   Metasystem jumps

In self-application of the supercompiler we have a three-level hierarchy of functions: f_0, f_1, f_2 where f_0 is some function, f_1 and f_2 the supercompiler. In this hierarchy a function f_n at the level n is transformed by a function f_{n+1} at the level $n+1$, which is, thereby, a metasystem with respect to f_n. Creation of each new level is a *metasystem transition*, or MST for short.

In [15] a system was developed which makes it possible to automatically change the level at which the computation is done: we call this *metasystem jumps*. Thus, whenever f_{n+1} is to evaluate (partially) f_n, control is first passed to f_n for a direct evaluation, as far as possible. When no step can be made because of unknown values of variables, control is passed back to f_{n+1} for driving. Examples in [15] show that metasystem jumping may result in a speed-up factor of more than 20.

The system developed in [15] was used in the present work. We refer the reader to that paper for details, introducing only the notation used there, since we need it for discussion of tests.

E	$\mu\{E\}$
[]	[]
S	S
s.i	('s'i)
e.i	('e'i)
(E)	('*'$\mu\{E\}$)
$<E>$	('!'$\mu\{E\}$)
E_1E_2	$\mu\{E_1\}\mu\{E_2\}$

Table 2: The metacode

The domain of a function defined in Refal is a set of *object expressions*. Refal programs, however, may use most general Refal expressions, including evaluation brackets < and > and free variables. Hence we cannot directly write Refal programs which manipulate Refal programs. To do this we must map the set of general Refal expressions on the set of object expressions and use the images of "hot" objects, i.e. free variables and evaluation brackets, instead of these objects themselves.

We call this mapping a *metacode*, and denote the metacode transformation of E as $\mu\{E\}$; if E is, syntactically, one Refal term, the curly brackets can be dropped. Obviously, metacoding must have a unique inverse transformation, *demetacoding*, so it must be injective.

We used, in the terminology of [15] an *internal* metacode defined by Table 2, where S is any symbol, and i the index of a variable.

In the hierarchy f_0, f_1, f_2 the function f_1 has a metacoded call of f_0 as its argument; f_2 has the metacoded call of f_1 as its argument. We use *MST schemes* for a clear representation of such hierarchies. An MST scheme is built according to the rule: whenever a subexpression has the form $E_1\mu\{E_2\}E_3$, the metacoded part is moved one level down and replaced by dots on the main level:

$$E_1\mu\{E_2\}E_3 \quad \Longleftrightarrow \quad \begin{array}{ccc} E_1 & \dots & E_3 \\ & E_2 & \end{array}$$

The parts of the overall Refal expression which belong to different metasystem levels are put on different lines. Refal expressions on the bottom level are written the same way as if they were on the top level; metacoding is implicit and is indicated by putting them one line down. To convert an MST scheme into an executable function call, we must metacode each level as many times as long is its distance from the top.

In addition, we can move up some variables in an MST scheme, leaving in the old place a *bullet* •. If a variable $t.i$ (type t, index i) is raised by h levels – the number referred to as its *elevation* — then the meaning of the bullet-variable pair is $\mu^{n-h}\{<\text{Dn}^h t.i>\}$, where Dn (read 'Down') is a Refal function which performs the metacode transformation on object expressions. Thus a bullet-variable pair can be seen as a variable metacoded $n - h$ times, but the possible values of such a variable are only such that they could result from metacoding an object expression h times. In particular, if an input variable is of an elevation h, its desired value must be metacoded h times before the beginning of computation. (See more about elevated variables in [15]).

Moving variables up radically changes the way the expression represented by the scheme will be executed. To read an MST scheme correctly, the following *rule of two levels* can be used:

The variables on the top level are free. They are the arguments of the function represented by the MST scheme as a whole; some specific values must be substituted for them before computation. The variables on the next level down are the variables of the function whose definition (the program for it) results from the computation on the top level.

As an example, consider the well-known problem of compilation.

Let <L e.program,e.data> be a Refal interpreter of some language L. Let P be a program in L. Using the supercompiler we can translate P into an efficient program in Refal by partial evaluation according to the MST scheme:

```
<Scp ................>
    <L  P  ,e.data>
```

Now suppose we want a *function* which would accept any arbitrary program, not just P. If we simply put the variable e.program instead of P:

```
<Scp .....................>
    <L e.program, e.data>
```

we will not get what we want. Here the variables for data and for program are on the same level and are treated in the same way. Using the rule of two levels we see that the result will be a function of two variables: this is, again, an interpreter. No partial evaluation takes place, because the value of e.program remains unknown. If we want partial evaluation, we must raise the variable e.program to the level of Scp:

```
<Scp ...e.program..........>
    <L    •    , e.data>
```

Now the rule of two levels tells us that a specific program will be asked by this function as the value of the argument e.program. Then partial evaluation will take place, returning a program for a function of the variable e.data. It is, of course, a translation of e.program. The function defined by this MST scheme may further be subject to a transformation by another partial evaluator. It will then produce an efficient compiler for L.

It should be noted that in the calls of function transformers such as Scp there is, implicitly, one more argument, which is not shown in our MST schemes: the definition (program for) all function calls on the object level.

5 Testing

Our system is still under debugging, but we can, already, show a few interesting tests. We have tested our supercompiler on several "classical" for partial evaluation problems, such as string pattern-matching and compilation, but here we are concerned only with self-application and similar problems.

5.1 Test 1

Before attempting self-application, we ran a few tests which demonstrate "almost self-application": a three-level scheme where Scp transforms a metainterpreter applied to some program. One of the simplest tests is:

```
<Scp ........... >
   <Int ... e.x  >
      <Fab • >
```

Here Fab is a simple function which changes every 'a' to 'b'. Its definition in flat Refal is:

```
Fab { e.1 = <Fab1 () e.1> }
Fab1 {
   (e.1) 'a'e.2 = <Fab1 (e.1'b') e.2>;
   (e.1) s.3 e.2 = <Fab1 (e.1 s.3) e.2>;
   (e.1) = e.1; }
```

Function Int is an interpreter of flat Refal. The argument x of Fab is *elevated* by one level to become free for Int and bound for Scp. The call of Int, by its definition, computes <Fab x> with an arbitrary x by interpretation of the program for Fab. This function is equivalent to Fab but works much slower. Transforming it by Scp returns an equivalent program, which is, as it should be expected, an exact copy of the original program for Fab, except for the names of variables.

5.2 Test 2

The supercompiler Scp at the top level of MST schemes in self-application is denoted as Scp2. It was written in extended Refal; its size: 302 sentences. It was manually translated into strict Refal; the size became 347 sentences. Then it was automatically translated into a flat form (499 sentences), which then was used as Scp1, to which Scp was applied. Thus, Scp1 and Scp2 represent the same algorithm written in two versions of Refal. We could use Scp1 in the place of Scp2 to have "very strict" self-application, but we used Scp2 for the convenience of testing.

In Test 2 the scheme of self-application was:

```
<Scp2 ............ >
   <Scp1 ....... >
      <Fab e.1>
```

We see from the rule of two levels that Scp1 is a function of no variables (a constant) whose value is the definition of a function of e.1 which is equivalent to Fab. The supercompiler on the level 2, Scp2, has no variables on either top, or the next level; it transforms a function (namely, Scp1), which is a constant. To sum up: Scp2 outputs a program which outputs a program which is equivalent to the original program for Fab and, in fact, identical to it (except the names of variables), because it cannot be improved.

The actual output of the supercompiler is a bit more complex. The program produced by the supercompiler can be seen as the expression:

$$(\text{Define } def(f_1)\dots def(f_n))(\text{Call } G_{in})$$

which combines a list of the definitions of new functions f_i and the initial function call to compute G_{in}. The function definition $def(f_i)$ is of the form:

$$\mu{<}Config{>} = \text{Fn}i : \mu\{Prog_i\}$$

where $<Config>$ is a recurrent configuration in terms of the initial program, Fni is the symbolic name of the corresponding new function f_i, and $Prog_i$ the program for it.

The output of the 2nd-level supercompiler Scp2 is a metacoded program which we shall denote as $\mu\{Prog2\}$. In Test 2 it is this:

$$\mu\{Prog2\} = (\text{Define })\ (\text{Call } \mu\{\mu\{Prog1\} \overset{a}{\leftarrow} \text{e.out}\})$$

This program simply outputs the metacoded program $Prog1$:

$$\mu\{Prog1\} = (\text{Define } \mu{<}\text{Fab1(e.23)e.24}{>}=\text{Fn1}:\mu\{Prog0\})$$
$$(\text{Call } \mu\{()(\text{e.1})\overset{a}{\leftarrow}(\text{e.23})(\text{e.24})\text{fn(Fn1)}\})$$

Program $Prog1$ is the result of supercompilation by Scp1 of the call <Fab e.1>; therefore it must be equivalent to it. $Prog1$ defines one recursive function Fn1 which is the supercompiled function call <Fab1(e.23)e.24>. The variables of this configuration become the variables of the definition of $Prog0$. Therefore, the initial call is a call of Fn1 after the necessary assignments to the variables (e.23)(e.24). The program $Prog0$ is the program for Fn1; it results from supercompilation of Fab1, and it is identical to it, except for the different names of variables. This is exactly what one should have expected.

5.3 Test 3

The MST scheme in this test is:

```
<Scp2 ................ >
    <Scp1 ... s.2 .... >
        <Fab  •  e.1 >
```

Here the argument of Fab is s.2 e.1, i.e. it starts with some symbol s.2. We have raised s.2 to become a free variable in the call of Scp1. According to the Rule of two levels, the result of Scp2 is a function of s.2. This function outputs a program to compute <Fab s.2 e.1 for two cases of s.2: 'a' and not 'a'.

The actual output of Scp2 is:

$$Prog2 = (\texttt{Define }) (\texttt{Call } \mu\{Prog1\})$$

where $Prog1$ is the initial graph, which we present in the sentential form for readability:

```
Prog1 {
    'a' =  (Define μ<Fab1 ('b')e.1>=Fn1: μProg01)
           (Call μ{()(e.1)←ᵃ(e.23)(e.24); fn(Fn1)});
    s.2 =  (Define μ<Fab1 (s.2)e.1>=Fn2: μProg02)
           (Call μ{()(e.1)←ᵃ(e.23)(e.24); fn(Fn2)});
         }
```

We see that Prog1, indeed, depends on s.2 and includes two cases where its value is 'a', or any value distinct from 'a'. In both cases the structure of the value is similar to that in the preceding test. The difference is that *partial evaluation* took place with respect to s.2. Look at the recurrent calls of Fab1 under Define. Within the parentheses which enclose the ready part of the string we see the already processed first symbol of the string: either 'b', if it was 'a' originally, or the unchanged s.2 otherwise. The programs $Prog01$ and $Prog02$ for Fn1 and Fn2, respectively, are:

```
Fn1 {
    (e.23) 'a'e.24 = <Fn1 (e.23'b') e.24>;
    (e.23) s.25 e.24 = <Fn1 (e.23 s.25) e.24>;
    (e.23) = 'b'e.23; }


Fn2 {
    (e.37) 'a'e.38 = <Fn2 (e.37'b') e.38>;
    (e.37) s.39 e.38 = <Fn2 (e.37 s.39) e.38>;
    (e.37) = μ⁻¹{s.2} e.37; }
```

These programs are, basically, the same as the initial program for Fab1, except that they are modified because of the partial evaluation which took place. Functions Fn1 and Fn2 depend on e.1 alone; s.2 has already been processed and is kept within the parentheses in Fab1 calls. When the string is exhausted and the output is done, s.2 must be added at the beginning of the string resulting from processing e.1, converted to 'b' in Fn1, or left unchanged in Fn2.

The variable s.2 enters the program P_2 in the *negative* degree of metacode. This is the result of the variable s.2 being *elevated*. Recall that the meaning of a variable elevated by h levels and metacoded $n - h$ times is $\mu^{n-h}\{<D n^h s.2>\}$. In our case $h = 1$, and $n = 2$. When $\mu\{Prog1\}$ which is yielded by $Prog2$ is demetacoded, the metacode level from 1 becomes 0, but the elevation h remains 1, which means that the value of s.2 is a metacoded (once) symbol. When it is substituted by $Prog1$ in $\mu\{Prog01\}$ and $\mu\{Prog02\}$, we have a correct – all on the level 1 – program. When it is demetacoded as a whole the result will be a correct working program (level 0); the value of $s.2$ will be demetacoded together with the rest of the program. However, if we want to write down the demetacoded program for Fn2 for an arbitrary **s.2**, we must insert in the proper place the demetacoded symbol which is the value of **s.2**. This is exactly what $\mu^{-1}\{s.2\}$ means.

It should be noted that with our metacode, symbols do not change under metacoding or demetacoding. Yet it would be an error to put **s.2** instead of $\mu^{-1}\{s.2\}$, because **s.2** is not a free variable in the definition of Fn2. The sentence which results from such a replacement would be syntactically faulty: the right side of the sentence would include a variable which does not enter the left side.

5.4 Test 4

The MST scheme is:

```
<Scp2 ...............>
    <Scp1 ... e.1...>
        <Fab ..•..>
```

Here we have elevated the whole argument **e.1**. Because of this, Scp1 is *not* transforming the program for Fab. It has no bound variables, therefore the call of Fab is a *constant* for it. What is going on is this. Scp1 gets a value e of **e.1** at input, computes the value $e' =$<Fab E>, and then outputs a program which outputs the constant e'. As for Scp2, it outputs a program which is equivalent to Scp1, i.e. it does the same thing, but much more efficiently; ideally, as efficient as the function Fab itself outputs is value.

The actual result of supercompilation is:

$Prog2 =$(Define μ<$Conf$>=Fn1: $\mu\{Prog1\}$)
(Call $\mu\{()(e.1)\overset{a}{\leftarrow}(e.59)(e.60);$ fn(Fn1)$\}$)

Here $Conf$ is one of the configurations in the supercompilation of Scp1 by Scp2. It is big and hardly manageable by a human user. When Scp2 works on Scp1 it finds recurrent configurations, which become new recursive functions. $Conf$ is such (and the only) configuration. The only thing about it that is easy to establish is that it includes two free variables: **e.59** and **e.60**.

The program $Prog1$ is:

```
Fn1 {
    (e.59) 'a'e.60 = <Fn1 (e.59'b') e.60>;
    (e.59) s.72 e.60 = <Fn1 (e.59 s.72) e.60>;
    (e.59) = (Define )(Call e.59 ⤆ μ{e.out});
    e.59 = (Define ) (Call Z); }
```

Since the variable **e.1** has elevation 1, its intended value must be metacoded before the computation by Scp1. This remains true also for Scp2, because it produces a program which faithfully follows the input-output requirements for Scp1.

At the first glance it may seem that the assignment in the third sentence of Fn1 has an error: the output variable e.out is metacoded, while e.59 is not. But e.59 is, like e.1 elevated; indeed, it is the result of processing e.60, and the initial value assigned to e.60 is e.1. Function Fn1 outputs a metacoded program. When it is demetacoded, $\mu\{e.out\}$ becomes e.out, and *the value of* e.59 is demetacoded. So, the result is as it should be.

Function Fn1 mimics the recursive function Fab1, except that it has one more sentence: the fourth. This also is a consequence of the fact that Scp1 works in metacode. Fab1 is defined in expectation that its second subargument is always a string of symbols. If it starts with a parenthesis, the Refal machine fails (comes to an abnormal stop); the value of the function in this case is not defined. But when Scp1 works in metacode and discovers a parenthesis it *does not fail*. In our language of graphs there is a special operation for this situation: Z. This is our way to say in metacode that the original function causes failure (abnormal stop). So, if none of the first three sentences of Fn1 works, then the fourth sentence assigns Z as the output value.

It is interesting to compare Tests 3 and 4 with regard to the level at which recursion loops are closing. The Define part of the output consists of those configurations which were found recurrent. In Test 3 the function transformed by Scp2 depends on a symbol variable only; there is no recursion on this argument (see the MST scheme). Therefore, the Define part of the output is empty. The function transformed by Scp1, on the contrary, depends on an e-variable, thus on this level we have two recurrent configurations Fn1 and Fn2, in the Define part. In Test 4 Scp2 works on a recursive function of an e-variable, hence the appearance of recurrent configurations is inevitable.

5.5 Test 5

The next two tests demonstrate another use of a supercompiler: in a combination with non-standard interpreters of the object language. Our language, flat Refal, does not allow us to perform lazy evaluation. To amend this, we have written in flat Refal a *lazy* interpreter Lazy-Int of a full functional language (strict Refal). Given a program in strict Refal, we interpret it by Lazy-Int and supercompile this process by Scp according to the following MST-scheme:

```
<Scp ..................... >
   <Lazy-Int .. (e.1)... >
      <Fbc <Fab • >>
```

The program which is implicit in the call of Lazy-Int defines two functions: Fab and Fbc. Function Fab is a non-flat recursive function:

```
Fab {
  'a'e.1 = 'b'<Fab e.1>;
  s.2 e.1 = s.2 <Fab e.1>;
    = ; }
```

It replaces every 'a' by 'b'. Function Fbc is defined analogously and replaces every 'b' by 'c'. The lazy interpreter works on the composition of these two functions. The expectation was that after supercompilation we should have a flat one-loop program which converts both 'a' and 'b' into 'c'.

And indeed, the resulting program is exactly as expected:

```
Fac {
    () = ;
    (e.1 ) = <F1C1 ()(e.1 )> ; }
F1C1 {
    (e.25 )('a'e.26 ) = <F1C1 (e.25 'c')(e.26 )> ;
    (e.25 )('b'e.26 ) = <F1C1 (e.25 'c')(e.26 )> ;
    (e.25 )(s.29 e.26 ) = <F1C1 (e.25 s.29 )(e.26 )> ;
    (e.25 )() = e.25 ; }
```

It transforms a two-pass program into an equivalent one-pass program.

5.6 Test 6

In this test we use the supercompiler in a combination with an even less standard interpreter: an inverse interpreter Inv-Int which executes a function definition (in a form of a graph) from its ends to its beginnings, and computes the value of the input when an output is given. Inv-Int stops after finding the first solution and is relatively simple, because we have put rather strong constraints on its input – a program to invert. They are:

- The program must be in flat Refal.

- The right side of each sentence, or the argument of a function call in the right side, must be a rigid pattern.

- All variables of the left side of a sentence must be met also in the right side.

The MST-scheme in Test 6 was:

```
<Scp ............................. >
    <Inv-Int .......... (e.1)... >
        <Rev e.x >
```

The interpreter Inv-Int expects a configuration which depends on the input variable e.x, and the output value assigned to the free variable e.1. Implicit in the call is the program which defines the function Rev:

```
Rev { e.x = <Rev1 (e.x) ()>; }

Rev1 { (s.1 e.x) (e.y) = <Rev1 (e.x) (s.1 e.y)>;
() (e.y) =  e.y; }
```

The interpreter finds a value of e.x such that

$$\text{<Rev e.x>} = \text{e.1}$$

and gives it out as its value.

Function Rev reverses its argument. Since its reversal is itself, the best we can expect from the supercompiler is that it returns a function definition identical to the above program for Rev. And it does so.

We can see this result as a proof that $Rev^{-1} = Rev$, and therefore, a proof that <Rev<Rev<e.1>> is the identity function. It shoud be noted that this double reverse configuration cannot be reduced by direct supercompilation to the identity function – even such a function that passes through the string symbol by symbol, without changing them.

5.7 Conclusion

What we have shown in these tests is the hard core of the supercompiler system. For specific applications, special front and back ends can be added. For instance, the system requires that the value of an elevated variable be metacoded at input and demetacoded at output. Clearly, this can be included into the system, and the end user need not know anything about this. MST-schemes can also be formed for a wide class of problems without bothering the user with such details.

Our tests show that a supercompiler can be self-applicable. The important thing here is not, of course, just to apply it to itself and obtain *some* target program; this program must be a good, efficient program. We gave examples of such non-trivial transformations. A big program (Scp) is applied to a big program (Scp itself or a non-standard interpreter) and produces a small residue, which is the desired solution to the problem. Sure enough, the zero-level programs in these tests are still small, not big, but we believe that this is a matter of some technical details: eliminating bugs and fine-tuning some of the algorithms, such as generalization. Writing supercompilers, like writing compilers, is a *technology*. It develops slowly by accumulating small discoveries and improvements.

Acknowlegements. First tests of the present supercompiler were discussed in the summer of 1994 in Copenhagen, Moscow and Pereslavl (Russia). The authors thanks the participants – especially Sergei Abramov, Sergei Chmutov, Robert Glück, Neil Jones, Andrei Klimov, Arkadi Klimov, Torben Mogensen, Sergei Romanenko, Morten Sørensen – for useful comments.

References

[1] Ershov, A.P. On the essence of compilation, In: E.J.Neuhold(ed) *Formal Description of Programming Concepts*, pp.391-420, North-Holland, 1978.

[2] Futamura, Y., Partial evaluation of computation process – an approach to compiler compiler. *Systems, Computers, Controls*, 2,5 (1971) pp.45-50.

[3] Jones N., Sestoft P., Sondergaard H., An experiment in partial evaluation: the generation of a compiler generator. In: Jouannaud J.-P. (Ed.) *Rewriting Techniques and Applications*, Dijon, France, LNCS 202, Springer, 1985.

[4] Jones, Neil. The essence of program transformation by partial evaluation and driving. In: *Proc. of The Atlantique Worlshop on Semantics Based Program Manipulation*, N.Jones and C.Talcott Ed. Copenhagen University, pp.134-147, 1994.

[5] Glück, R., Towards multiple self-application, *Proceedings of the Symposium on Partial Evaluation and Semantics-Based Program Manipulation (Yale University)*, ACM Press, 1991, pp.309-320.

[6] Glück, R. and Klimov, And., Occam's razor in metacomputation: the notion of a perfect process tree. In: *Static Analysis*, COusot et.al (Eds), LNCS Vol 724, pp.112-123, Springer-Verlag 1993.

[7] Glück R. and Sørensen, M.H. Partial deduction and driving are equivalent. In: *Symposium on Programming Language Implementation and Logic Programming (PLILP'94)*, LNCS, Springer-Verlag, 1994.

[8] Glück R. and Turchin V., Experiments with a Self-applicable Supercompiler, CCNY Technical Report, 1989.

[9] Turchin, V.F., Equivalent transformations of recursive functions defined in Refal. In: Teoriya Yazykov I Metody Postroeniya Sistem Programmirovaniya (Proceedings of the Symposium), Kiev-Alushta (USSR), pp.31-42, 1972 (in Russian).

[10] Turchin V.F.,Klimov A.V. et al, *Bazisnyi Refal i yego realizatsiya na vychislitel'nykh mashinakh* (Basic Refal and its implementation on computers) GOSSTROY SSSR, TsNIPIASS, Moscow, 1977 (in Russian).

[11] Turchin, V.F. *The Language Refal, the Theory of Compilation and Metasystem Analysis*, Courant Computer Science Report #20, New York University, 1980.

[12] Turchin, V.F., Nirenberg, R.M., Turchin, D.V. Experiments with a supercompiler. In: *ACM Symposium on Lisp and Functional Programming* (1982), ACM, New York, pp. 47-55.

[13] Turchin, V.F. The concept of a supercompiler, *ACM Transactions on Programming Languages and Systems*, **8**, pp.292-325, 1986.

[14] Turchin V., *Refal-5, Programming Guide and Reference Manual*, New England Publishing Co., 1989.

[15] Turchin V., Nemytykh, A. Metavariables: Their implementation and use in Program Transformation, CCNY Technical Report CSc TR-95-012, 1995.

Multi-Level Lambda-Calculi: An Algebraic Description

Flemming Nielson and Hanne Riis Nielson

DAIMI, Aarhus University, Denmark.

Abstract. Two-level λ-calculi have been heavily utilised for applications such as partial evaluation, abstract interpretation and code generation. Each of these applications pose different demands on the exact details of the two-level structure and the corresponding inference rules. We therefore formulate a number of existing systems in a common framework. This is done in such a way as to conceal those differences between the systems that are not essential for the multi-level ideas (like whether or not one restricts the domain of the type environment to the free identifiers of the expression) and thereby to reveal the deeper similarities and differences. In their most general guise the multi-level λ-calculi defined here allow multi-level structures that are not restricted to (possibly finite) linear orders and thereby generalise previous treatments in the literature.

1 Introduction

The concept of two-level languages is at least a decade old [7, 4] and the concept of multi-level languages at least four years old [11]. In particular two-level languages have been used extensively in the development of partial evaluation [1, 3] and abstract interpretation [5, 8] but also in areas such as code generation [9] and processor placement [12].

Our goal is to cast further light on the two-level λ-calculi that may be found in the literature. We will show that there is a high degree of *commonality* in the approach taken: there are a number of levels (e.g. binding-times) and relations between them. Also we will stress that there are major *differences* that to a large extent are *forced* by the characteristics of the application domains (be it partial evaluation, code generation, abstract interpretation, or processor placement). In our view it is important to understand this point, that the application domains place different demands on the formalisation, before it makes sense to compare formalisations with a view to identifying their relative virtues.

We proceed by synthesising these considerations into a general description of multi-level languages. We thereby solve the problem of generalising from a (possibly finite) linearly ordered structure to a much less restrictive structure of levels. We thus pave the way for future work on further making the notions independent of the λ-calculus and on defining parameterised classes of multi-level λ-calculi.

Remark about the choice of levels. Perhaps the most obvious generalisation of a notion of two levels is a (possibly finite) interval in $\mathbf{Z} \cup \{-\infty, \infty\}$ (with the elements corresponding to the levels [11, 1]). A somewhat more abstract possibility is to use a general partially ordered set (with the elements corresponding to the levels as is briefly discussed in [11]) although a Kripke-structure [6] (with the worlds corresponding to the levels) would fit just as well. This might suggest that the ultimate choice is to let the levels be given by a category because a partial order can indeed be viewed as a particularly simple category. We shall find it more appropriate[1] to use a many-sorted algebra with sorts corresponding to the levels and operators corresponding to the relationships between the levels; one reason is that it avoids the need for coding many-argument concepts as one-argument concepts using cartesian products, another is that it naturally allows different relationships between the levels for different syntactic categories, and yet a third reason is that it allows finer control over the relationship between the levels in that it does not necessarily impose transitivity.

2 Preliminaries

Programming languages are characterised by a number of syntactic categories and by a number of constructs for combining syntactic entities to new ones. Using the terminology of many-sorted algebras we shall represent the set of names of syntactic categories as a set of sorts and the methods as operators. To this end we begin by reviewing some concepts from many-sorted algebras [14, 2].

A many-sorted signature Σ over a set S of sorts consists of a set (also denoted Σ) of operators; each operator $\sigma \in \Sigma$ is assigned a rank, denoted $\mathsf{rank}(\sigma) \in S^* \times S$, designating the sequence of sorts of the arguments and the sort of the result; if $\mathsf{rank}(\sigma) = (s_1 \cdots s_n; s)$ we shall say that σ is an n-ary operator.

A Σ-algebra M consists of a (usually non-empty) set M_s (called the carrier) for each sort $s \in S$ and a total function $\sigma_M : M_{s_1} \times \cdots \times M_{s_n} \to M_s$ for each operator $\sigma \in \Sigma$ of rank $(s_1 \cdots s_n; s)$.

The free Σ-algebra $T(\Sigma)$ has as carrier $T(\Sigma)_s$ the set of terms of sort s that can be built using the operators of Σ; as operators it has the constructions of

---

[1] These approaches are not too dissimilar in their descriptive power and thus to some extent a matter of taste: a many-sorted algebra can be regarded as a cartesian category (with objects corresponding to sequences of sorts and operators corresponding to morphisms), and a cartesian category can be regarded as a many-sorted algebra (with sequences of sorts corresponding to objects and morphisms corresponding to operators).

new terms. In a similar way the free Σ-algebra $T(\Sigma, X)$ over X has as carrier $T(\Sigma, X)_s$ the set of terms of sort s that can be built using the operators of Σ and the identifiers in X where each identifier $x \in X$ has an associated sort, denoted $\mathsf{sort}(x)$; as operators it has the constructions of new terms. Another way to present this is to say that $T(\Sigma, X) = T(\Sigma \cup X)$ where the rank of x is given by $\mathsf{rank}(x) = (; \mathsf{sort}(x))$.

A homomorphism h from a Σ-algebra M_1 to a Σ-algebra M_2 consists of a sort-preserving mapping from the carriers of M_1 to those of M_2 such that for each operator $\sigma \in \Sigma$ and for all values $v_1, \cdots, v_n$ in M_1 of the required sorts, the equation $h(\sigma_{M_1}(v_1, \cdots, v_n)) = \sigma_{M_2}(h(v_1), \cdots, h(v_n))$ holds in M_2.

A derivor d from a signature Σ_1 over S to a signature Σ_2 over S is a mapping that sends an operator $\sigma \in \Sigma_1$ of rank $(s_1 \cdots s_n; s)$ to a term $d(\sigma) \in T(\Sigma_2, \{x_1, \cdots, x_n\})_s$ constructed from the operators of Σ_2 together with the identifiers $\{x_1, \cdots, x_n\}$ such that if each x_i has sort $\mathsf{sort}(x_i) = s_i$ then $d(\sigma)$ obeys the sorting rules and gives a term of sort s.

We shall define a *uniform derivor* from a signature Σ_1 over S to a signature Σ_2 over S to be a rank-preserving partial mapping δ from Σ_1 to Σ_2 that is only allowed to be undefined on unary operators of Σ_1; it extends to a derivor (also denoted δ) by mapping $\sigma \in \Sigma_1$ of rank $(s_1 \cdots s_n; s)$ to $(\delta(\sigma))(x_1, \cdots, x_n)$ if $\delta(\sigma)$ is defined and to x_1 otherwise; note that for this derivor all $\delta(\sigma)$ contains at most one operator symbol.

3 A descriptive approach to multi-level lambda-calculi

In this section we shall define the syntax of the lambda-calculus and some common features of multi-level structures. The aim is to provide a small universe in which some of the different formalisations of multi-level languages found in the litterature can be explained as necessary variations over a theme.

λ-*calculus.* The simply typed λ-calculus λ is the programming language specified by the following data. The sorts (or syntactic categories) are Typ and Exp. The signature (or the set of type and expression forming constructs) Σ is given by:

$\to: (\mathsf{Typ}^2; \mathsf{Typ})$	$\mathtt{int} : (; \mathsf{Typ})$	$\mathtt{bool} : (; \mathsf{Typ})$
$c_i : (; \mathsf{Exp})$	$x_i : (; \mathsf{Exp})$	$\lambda x_i. : (\mathsf{Exp}; \mathsf{Exp})$
$@ : (\mathsf{Exp}^2; \mathsf{Exp})$	$\mathtt{if} : (\mathsf{Exp}^3; \mathsf{Exp})$	$\mathtt{fix} : (\mathsf{Exp}; \mathsf{Exp})$

for i ranging over some index set. There are two well-formedness judgements: $\vdash^{\mathsf{T}} t$ for the well-formedness of the type t and $A \vdash^{\mathsf{E}} e : t$ for the well-formedness of the expression e (yielding type t assuming free identifiers are typed according to the type environment A). The inductive definition of these well-formedness judgements is given by the following inference rule for $\vdash^\mathsf{T}$:

$$[\text{ok}] \ \frac{}{\vdash^\mathsf{T} t}$$

(stating that all types are well-formed and where we regard an axiom as an inference rule with no premises) and for $\vdash^\mathsf{E}$:

$$[c_i] \ \frac{}{A \vdash^\mathsf{E} c_i : t} \ \text{if } t = \mathsf{Type}(c_i) \qquad [x_i] \ \frac{}{A \vdash^\mathsf{E} x_i : t} \ \text{if } t = A(x_i)$$

$$[\lambda x_i] \ \frac{A[x_i : t_i] \vdash^\mathsf{E} e : t}{A \vdash^\mathsf{E} \lambda x_i.e : t_i \to t} \qquad [\mathbb{Q}] \ \frac{A \vdash^\mathsf{E} e_0 : t_1 \to t_2 \qquad A \vdash^\mathsf{E} e_1 : t_1}{A \vdash^\mathsf{E} e_0 \mathbb{Q} e_1 : t_2}$$

$$[\texttt{fix}] \ \frac{A \vdash^\mathsf{E} e : t \to t}{A \vdash^\mathsf{E} \texttt{fix } e : t} \qquad [\texttt{if}] \ \frac{A \vdash^\mathsf{E} e_0 : \texttt{bool} \qquad A \vdash^\mathsf{E} e_1 : t \qquad A \vdash^\mathsf{E} e_2 : t}{A \vdash^\mathsf{E} \texttt{if } e_0 \ e_1 \ e_2 : t}$$

for some unspecified table Type giving the type of constants.

Note that this is just the algebraic presentation of the well-known simply typed λ-calculus: we have the two syntactic categories (represented by the sorts), we have the abstract syntax (represented by the signature), and we have the well-formedness judgements and the inference rules for their definition. We are stepping slightly outside the algebraic framework in allowing type environments, and operations upon these, even though there is no sort corresponding to type environments; this could very easily be rectified but at the price of a more cumbersome formalisation.

Remark about the choice of λ-calculus. An alternative presentation λ' of the simply typed λ-calculus has the same sorts, the same signature, the same well-formedness judgements but other rules of inference. For $\vdash^\mathsf{T}$ it has:

$$[\texttt{int}] \ \frac{}{\vdash^\mathsf{T} \texttt{int}} \qquad [\texttt{bool}] \ \frac{}{\vdash^\mathsf{T} \texttt{bool}} \qquad [\to] \ \frac{\vdash^\mathsf{T} t_1 \qquad \vdash^\mathsf{T} t_2}{\vdash^\mathsf{T} t_1 \to t_2}$$

and for $\vdash^\mathsf{E}$ the rule $[\lambda x_i]$ is changed to:

$$[\lambda x_i] \ \frac{A[x_i : t_i] \vdash^\mathsf{E} e : t}{A \vdash^\mathsf{E} \lambda x_i.e : t_i \to t} \ \text{if } \vdash^\mathsf{T} t_i$$

where it is natural to include as an explicit condition that the argument type is well-formed. Since actually all types in λ' are well-formed, just as in λ, the two presentations are for all practical purposes equivalent. Consequently our development below must be sufficiently flexible that it does not matter whether we base ourselves on λ or on λ'.

Multi-level structure. A multi-level structure B (for λ) is characterised by the sorts Typ and Exp, a non-empty set W^B (also denoted B) of levels, and a $(W^B \times \{\mathsf{Typ}, \mathsf{Exp}\})$-sorted signature $\Omega^B = \Omega^B_e \cup \Omega^B_i$. Here

- Ω^B_e contains those operators that must be explicitly given,

whereas $\Omega^B_i = \{\iota^b_{s_1 \cdots s_n;s} \mid b \in B \land s_i, s \in \{\mathsf{Typ}, \mathsf{Exp}\}\}$ contains those operators $\iota^b_{s_1 \cdots s_n;s}$ of rank $((b, s_1) \cdots (b, s_n); (b, s))$ that we shall regard as implicitly present. We shall write $|B|$ for the cardinality of W^B.

As we shall see the intention is that the implicit operators ι allow arbitrary inference rules as long as we stay at the same level but that whenever we change levels there must be an explicitly given operator that supports (or permits) this. We shall illustrate this with examples below.

Multi-level λ-calculus. A multi-level λ-calculus L over B (and λ) is characterised by the sorts Typ and Exp, the multi-level structure B, the well-formedness judgements $\vdash^{\mathsf{T}}_b t$ and $A \vdash^{\mathsf{E}}_b e : t$ (where b ranges over B), and the following information:

- a $\{\mathsf{Typ}, \mathsf{Exp}\}$-sorted signature Σ^L (defining the syntax of L); and
- a set R^L of labelled inference rules for the well-formedness judgements, where for simplicity of notation we allow distinct rules to share the same label; and
- a uniform derivor $\delta : \Sigma^L \to \Sigma$ that is extended to map $\vdash^s_b$ to $\vdash^s$ and thereby may be used to map judgements and inferences of L to judgements and inferences of λ in a mostly compositional manner; and

such that each inference rule $\Delta \in R^L$ satisfies:

(i) its label identifies an operator $\omega \in \Omega^B$ of rank $((b_1, s_1) \cdots (b_n, s_n); (b, s))$ such that the premises of Δ concern the well-formedness judgements $\vdash^{s_i}_{b_i}$ and the conclusion concerns the well-formedness judgement $\vdash^s_b$ and the only judgements $\vdash^{s'}_{b'}$ allowed in the side condition have $b' = b$; and

(ii) the rule $\delta(\Delta)$ is a permissible[2] rule in λ.

We should point out that since the set R^L of rules usually is finite and the set Ω^B_i of implicitly given operators is infinite, the set Ω^B_i contains many operators for which there is no need; however, this presents no complications for our development.

---

[2] We say that a rule Δ is a permissible rule for a rule set R whenever the set of provable judgements using R equals the set of provable judgements using $R \cup \{\Delta\}$. More restrictive demands on a rule might be that it is a derived rule or even that it is an existing rule in R. If we were to adopt one of the more restrictive possibilities then the choice between λ and λ' would be of importance.

3.1 Example: code generation [11]

We shall now show that the restriction of the two-level λ-calculus of [11] to λ (summarised in Appendix A.1) is an instance of the present framework. To this end we define the two-level language $L = L_{cg}$.

Two-level structure. Let B contain the two levels c (for compile-time) and r (for run-time). The signature Ω^B then has the following explicitly given operators:

- UP: $((r, \mathsf{Typ}); (c, \mathsf{Typ}))$
- up: $((r, \mathsf{Exp}); (c, \mathsf{Exp}))$
- dn: $((c, \mathsf{Exp}); (r, \mathsf{Exp}))$

The operator UP indicates that run-time types can be embedded in compile-time types thereby imposing the ordering that r is "less than" c. The operator up indicates that values of run-time expressions (i.e. code) can be manipulated at compile-time and the operator dn that values of compile-time expressions can be used at run-time.

Two-level λ-calculus. The signature Σ^L is given by:

$$\to^c, \to^r : (\mathsf{Typ}^2; \mathsf{Typ}) \qquad \mathsf{int}^c, \mathsf{int}^r : (; \mathsf{Typ}) \qquad \mathsf{bool}^c, \mathsf{bool}^r : (; \mathsf{Typ})$$

$$c_i^c, c_i^r : (; \mathsf{Exp}) \qquad x_i : (; \mathsf{Exp}) \qquad \lambda^c x_i., \lambda^r x_i. : (\mathsf{Exp}; \mathsf{Exp})$$

$$@^c, @^r : (\mathsf{Exp}^2; \mathsf{Exp}) \qquad \mathsf{if}^c, \mathsf{if}^r : (\mathsf{Exp}^3; \mathsf{Exp}) \qquad \mathsf{fix}^c, \mathsf{fix}^r : (\mathsf{Exp}; \mathsf{Exp})$$

Note that we have two copies of every operator of Σ (except identifiers that can be viewed as place-holders). Annotations with r corresponds to the underlining notation used in [11] and annotations with c to the absence of underlinings.

For *types* the well-formedness rules include two copies of the well-formedness rules of λ' (one for $b = c$ and one for $b = r$):

$$[\iota^b] \; \frac{}{\vdash_b^\mathsf{T} \mathsf{int}^b} \qquad\qquad [\iota^b] \; \frac{}{\vdash_b^\mathsf{T} \mathsf{bool}^b} \qquad\qquad [\iota^b] \; \frac{\vdash_b^\mathsf{T} t_1 \quad \vdash_b^\mathsf{T} t_2}{\vdash_b^\mathsf{T} t_1 \to^b t_2}$$

On top of this we have a bridging rule corresponding to the operator UP of the two-level structure:

$$[UP] \; \frac{\vdash_r^\mathsf{T} t_1 \to^r t_2}{\vdash_c^\mathsf{T} t_1 \to^r t_2}$$

allowing us to transfer run-time function spaces to compile-time. It is trivial to verify that we have given the correct treatment of types:

Fact 1. $\vdash^{\mathsf{T}}_b t$ *if and only if* $\vdash t : b$ *(in Appendix A.1).*

For *expressions* we have two slightly modified copies of the well-formedness rules of λ' (one for $b = c$ and one for $b = r$). To capture the formulation of [11] we shall let the type environment A associate a level b and a type t with each identifier x_i:

$$[\iota^b] \quad \frac{}{A\vdash^{\mathsf{E}}_b c^b_i : t} \text{ if } t = \mathsf{Type}(c^b_i) \wedge \vdash^{\mathsf{T}}_b t \qquad [\iota^b] \quad \frac{}{A\vdash^{\mathsf{E}}_b x_i : t} \text{ if } t = A(x^b_i) \wedge \vdash^{\mathsf{T}}_b t$$

$$[\iota^b] \quad \frac{A[x^b_i : t_i]\vdash^{\mathsf{E}}_b e : t}{A\vdash^{\mathsf{E}}_b \lambda^b x_i.e : t_i \rightarrow^b t} \text{ if } \vdash^{\mathsf{T}}_b t_i \qquad [\iota^b] \quad \frac{A\vdash^{\mathsf{E}}_b e_0 : t_1\rightarrow^b t_2 \quad A\vdash^{\mathsf{E}}_b e_1 : t_1}{A\vdash^{\mathsf{E}}_b e_0 @^b e_1 : t_2}$$

$$[\iota^b] \quad \frac{A\vdash^{\mathsf{E}}_b e : t\rightarrow^b t}{A\vdash^{\mathsf{E}}_b \mathtt{fix}^b e : t} \qquad [\iota^b] \quad \frac{A\vdash^{\mathsf{E}}_b e_0 : \mathtt{bool}^b \quad A\vdash^{\mathsf{E}}_b e_1 : t \quad A\vdash^{\mathsf{E}}_b e_2 : t}{A\vdash^{\mathsf{E}}_b \mathtt{if}^b e_0 \ e_1 \ e_2 : t}$$

where as before[3] we leave the table Type unspecified. On top of this we have two bridging rules corresponding to the operators *up* and *dn* of the two-level structure:

$$[dn] \quad \frac{A'\vdash^{\mathsf{E}}_c e : t}{A\vdash^{\mathsf{E}}_r e : t} \text{ if } \vdash^{\mathsf{T}}_r t \wedge \mathbf{gr}(A') \subseteq \mathbf{gr}(A)$$

$$[up] \quad \frac{A'\vdash^{\mathsf{E}}_r e : t}{A\vdash^{\mathsf{E}}_c e : t} \text{ if } \vdash^{\mathsf{T}}_c t \wedge \mathbf{gr}(A') \subseteq \mathbf{gr}(A) \wedge \forall(x^{b'}_i : t') \in \mathbf{gr}(A') : (b' = c \wedge \vdash^{\mathsf{T}}_c t')$$

where $\mathbf{gr}(A) = \{(x^b_i : t) \mid A(x^b_i) = t\}$ is the *graph* of A. It is trivial to establish the following relationship between the typing judgements:

Fact 2. $A\vdash^{\mathsf{E}}_b e : t$ *implies* $\vdash^{\mathsf{T}}_b t$.

To show that we have given the correct treatment for expressions we define a mapping $\langle \cdots \rangle$ into the type environments of Appendix A.1:

$$\langle \cdots [x^b_i : t] \cdots \rangle = \langle \cdots \rangle [x_i : t : b]\langle \cdots \rangle$$

and we then prove:

Lemma 3. $A\vdash^{\mathsf{E}}_b e : t$ *if and only if* $\langle A \rangle \vdash e : t : b$ *(in Appendix A.1).*

---

[3] Actually there is a small subtlety here concerning the $A[x^b_i : t_i]$ notation: if A already contains $[x^{b'}_i : t'_i]$ for $b' \neq b$, will the update then remove the entry for $x^{b'}_i$ or not? In line with [11] we shall assume that the entry *is* removed, although it would be feasible to take the other approach and then perhaps replace the operators $x_i \in \Sigma$ with $x^b_i \in \Sigma$.

To show that we have defined a multi-level λ-calculus we define a *uniform derivor* δ from L_{cg} into λ: it simply removes all annotations. It is then fairly straightforward to prove:

Fact 4. L_{cg} *is a multi-level* λ*-calculus.*

The same story goes for letting the uniform derivor map into λ'. It is instructive to point out that although we modelled the two-level λ-calculus after λ' our notion of two-level language is flexible enough that it is of no importance whether the derivor maps back to λ or λ'.

3.2 Example: partial evaluation [3]

We shall now show that the restriction of the binding time analysis of [3] to λ (summarised in Appendix A.2) is an instance of the present framework. To this end we define the two-level language $L = L_{pe}$.

Two-level structure. Let B contain the two levels D (for dynamic) and S (for static). The signature Ω^B then has the following explicitly given operators:

- DN: $((D, \mathsf{Typ}); (S, \mathsf{Typ}))$
- dn: $((D, \mathsf{Exp}); (S, \mathsf{Exp}))$
- $up, coer$: $((S, \mathsf{Exp}); (D, \mathsf{Exp}))$

The operator DN indicates that dynamic types can be embedded in static types; usually this is reflected by imposing an ordering $S \leq D$ saying that S computations take place "before" D computations[4]. The operators dn and up reflect that expressions at the two levels can be mixed much as in Subsection 3.1 and the presence of *coer* reflects that some form of coercion of static values to dynamic values can take place.

Two-level λ-calculus. We use the following signature Σ^L:

$$\to^D, \to^S : (\mathsf{Typ}^2; \mathsf{Typ}) \quad \mathsf{int}^D, \mathsf{int}^S : (; \mathsf{Typ}) \quad \mathsf{bool}^D, \mathsf{bool}^S : (; \mathsf{Typ})$$

$$c_i^D, c_i^S : (; \mathsf{Exp}) \qquad x_i : (; \mathsf{Exp}) \qquad \lambda^D x_i., \lambda^S x_i. : (\mathsf{Exp}; \mathsf{Exp})$$

$$@^D, @^S : (\mathsf{Exp}^2; \mathsf{Exp}) \quad \mathsf{if}^D, \mathsf{if}^S : (\mathsf{Exp}^3; \mathsf{Exp}) \quad \mathsf{fix}^S : (\mathsf{Exp}; \mathsf{Exp})$$

---

[4] Intuitively, the level D corresponds to the level r of Subsection 3.1 and similarly the level S corresponds to the level c. The ordering imposed on D and S above will then be the dual of the ordering imposed on c and r in Subsection 3.1. This is analogous to the dual orderings used in data flow analysis and in abstract interpretation. By the duality principle of lattice theory these differenes are only cosmetic.

This is very similar to Subsection 3.1 except that (adhering to the design decisions of [3]) there is no $\mathtt{fix}^D$, i.e. all fix point computations must be static.

For *types* we first introduce the following well-formedness rules:

$$[\iota^b] \ \frac{}{\vdash_b^\mathsf{T} \mathtt{int}^b} \qquad [\iota^b] \ \frac{}{\vdash_b^\mathsf{T} \mathtt{bool}^b} \qquad [\iota^b] \ \frac{}{\vdash_b^\mathsf{T} t_1 \to^b t_2}$$

(where b ranges over $\{S, D\}$). Note that the rule for $t_1 \to^b t_2$ has no premises! Then we have the following bridging rule corresponding to the operator *DN*:

$$[DN] \ \frac{\vdash_D^\mathsf{T} t}{\vdash_S^\mathsf{T} t}$$

allowing us to use any dynamic type as a static type. One can then prove that we have given the correct treatment of types:

Fact 5. $\vdash_b^\mathsf{T} t$ *if and only if* $b \leq \mathsf{top}(t)$ *(in Appendix A.2).*

For *expressions* we first introduce the following slightly modified copies of rules from λ':

$$[\iota^b] \ \frac{}{A \vdash_b^\mathsf{E} c_i^b : t} \text{ if } t = \mathsf{Type}(c_i^b) \wedge \vdash_b^\mathsf{T} t \qquad [\iota^b] \ \frac{}{A \vdash_b^\mathsf{E} x_i : t} \text{ if } t = A(x_i) \wedge \vdash_b^\mathsf{T} t$$

$$[\iota^b] \ \frac{A[x_i : t_i] \vdash_b^\mathsf{E} e : t}{A \vdash_b^\mathsf{E} \lambda^b x_i.e : t_i \to^b t} \text{ if } \vdash_b^\mathsf{T} t_i \qquad [\iota^b] \ \frac{A \vdash_b^\mathsf{E} e_0 : t_1 \to^b t_2 \quad A \vdash_b^\mathsf{E} e_1 : t_1}{A \vdash_b^\mathsf{E} e_0 @^b e_1 : t_2} \text{ if } \vdash_b^\mathsf{T} t_2$$

$$[\iota^b] \ \frac{A \vdash_S^\mathsf{E} e : t \to^b t}{A \vdash_S^\mathsf{E} \mathtt{fix}^S e : t} \qquad [\iota^b] \ \frac{A \vdash_b^\mathsf{E} e_0 : \mathtt{bool}^b \quad A \vdash_b^\mathsf{E} e_1 : t \quad A \vdash_b^\mathsf{E} e_2 : t}{A \vdash_b^\mathsf{E} \mathtt{if}^b \ e_0 \ e_1 \ e_2 : t}$$

(where b ranges over $\{S, D\}$). Note that compared with Subsection 3.1 we have not extended the entries in A with information about the level. In addition we have the following bridging rules corresponding to the operators *up*, *dn* and *coer*:

$$[up] \ \frac{A \vdash_S^\mathsf{E} e : t}{A \vdash_D^\mathsf{E} e : t} \text{ if } \vdash_D^\mathsf{T} t \qquad [dn] \ \frac{A \vdash_D^\mathsf{E} e : t}{A \vdash_S^\mathsf{E} e : t}$$

$$[coer] \ \frac{A \vdash_S^\mathsf{E} e : \mathtt{int}^S}{A \vdash_D^\mathsf{E} e : \mathtt{int}^D} \qquad [coer] \ \frac{A \vdash_S^\mathsf{E} e : \mathtt{bool}^S}{A \vdash_D^\mathsf{E} e : \mathtt{bool}^D}$$

Note that the rule [*coer*] has no counterpart in Subsection 3.1. It is trivial to establish the following relationship between the typing judgements:

Fact 6. $A \vdash_b^\mathsf{E} e : t$ *implies* $\vdash_b^\mathsf{T} t$.

To show that we have given the correct treatment for expressions we prove:

Lemma 7. $A \vdash^{\mathsf{E}}_b e : t$ *if and only if* $A \vdash e : t \ \land \ b \leq \mathsf{top}(t)$ *(in Appendix A.2).*

To show that we have defined a multi-level λ-calculus we define a uniform derivor δ from L_{pe} into λ: it simply removes all annotations. It is then fairly straight-forward to prove:

Fact 8. L_{pe} *is a multi-level λ-calculus.*

Remark about the design decisions of [3]. In the above rule for $t_1 \to^b t_2$ it is *not* required that the subtypes t_1 and t_2 are well-formed. So using the system of [3] one can in fact prove

$$\emptyset \vdash \lambda^D x.x : (\mathtt{int}^S \to^D \mathtt{int}^S) \to^D (\mathtt{int}^S \to^D \mathtt{int}^S) \tag{*}$$

One may argue that this is unfortunate since traditional partial evaluators cannot exploit this information. However, we can easily rectify this in our setting: replace the above rule for $t_1 \to^b t_2$ with

$$\frac{\vdash^{\mathsf{T}}_b t_1 \quad \vdash^{\mathsf{T}}_b t_2}{\vdash^{\mathsf{T}}_b t_1 \to^b t_2}$$

thus bringing the system closer to that of Subsection 3.1. As a consequence we can remove the side condition $\vdash^{\mathsf{T}}_b t_2$ from the rule for application since well-formedness of t_2 now can be deduced from the well-formedness of $t_1 \to^b t_2$. Note that with these changes (*) is no longer derivable. We call this new system L'_{pe} and would expect it to be more useful than L_{pe}.

3.3 Example: multi-level partial evaluation [1]

We shall now show that the restriction of the multi-level binding time analysis of [1] to λ (summarised in Appendix A.3) is an instance of the present framework. To this end we define the two-level language $L = L_{mp}$.

Multi-level structure. Let B contain the levels $0, 1, \cdots, \mathsf{max}$ where intuitively 0 stands for static and $1, \cdots, \mathsf{max}$ for different levels of dynamic. The signature Ω^B then has the following explicitly given operators:

- $DN^{b'}_b : ((b + b', \mathsf{Typ}); (b, \mathsf{Typ}))$ for $0 \leq b < b + b' \leq \mathsf{max}$
- $dn^{b'}_b : ((b + b', \mathsf{Exp}); (b, \mathsf{Exp}))$ for $0 \leq b < b + b' \leq \mathsf{max}$
- $up^{b'}_b, lift^{b'}_b : ((b, \mathsf{Exp}); (b + b', \mathsf{Exp}))$ for $0 \leq b < b + b' \leq \mathsf{max}$

Thus $DN_b^{b'}$ allows us to embed types at level $b + b'$ at the lower level b; this imposes the ordering that $b < b + b'$ much as in Subsection 3.2. The operators $dn_b^{b'}$ and $up_b^{b'}$ reflect that expressions on the various levels can be mixed and the presence of $lift_b^{b'}$ reflects that some form of lifting of values at level b to level $b + b'$ can be performed.

Multi-level λ-calculus. We use the following signature Σ^L where $b \in \{0, 1, \cdots, \mathrm{max}\}$:

$$\rightarrow^b : (\mathsf{Typ}^2; \mathsf{Typ}) \quad \mathsf{int}^b : (; \mathsf{Typ}) \qquad \mathsf{bool}^b : (; \mathsf{Typ})$$

$$c_i^b : (; \mathsf{Exp}) \qquad x_i : (; \mathsf{Exp}) \qquad \lambda^b x_i. : (\mathsf{Exp}; \mathsf{Exp})$$

$$\mathbb{Q}^b : (\mathsf{Exp}^2; \mathsf{Exp}) \quad \mathsf{if}^b : (\mathsf{Exp}^3; \mathsf{Exp}) \qquad \mathsf{fix}^0 : (\mathsf{Exp}; \mathsf{Exp})$$

$$\mathsf{lift}_b^{b'} : (\mathsf{Exp}; \mathsf{Exp}) \text{ for } 0 \leq b < b + b' \leq \mathsf{max}$$

As in Subsection 3.2 (adhering to the design decisions of [1]) all fix point computations are required to be static[5], i.e. at level 0. Note that in addition to the annotations on the operators of λ we also have the new operators $\mathsf{lift}_b^{b'}$.

For *types* we first introduce the following well-formedness rules:

$$[\iota^b] \; \frac{}{\vdash_b^\mathsf{T} \mathsf{int}^b} \qquad [\iota^b] \; \frac{}{\vdash_b^\mathsf{T} \mathsf{bool}^b} \qquad [\iota^b] \; \frac{\vdash_b^\mathsf{T} t_1 \quad \vdash_b^\mathsf{T} t_2}{\vdash_b^\mathsf{T} t_1 \rightarrow^b t_2}$$

(where b ranges over $\{0, 1, \cdots, \mathsf{max}\}$). Then we have the following bridging rules corresponding to the operator $DN_b^{b'}$:

$$[DN_b^{b'}] \; \frac{\vdash_{b+b'}^\mathsf{T} t}{\vdash_b^\mathsf{T} t}$$

allowing us to use any type at level $b + b'$ at the lower level b. One can then prove that we have given the correct treatment of types:

Fact 9. $\vdash_b^\mathsf{T} t$ *if and only if* $\| t \| \geq b$ *(in Appendix A.3).*

For *expressions* we first introduce the following slightly modified copies of λ':

$$[\iota^b] \; \frac{}{A \vdash_b^\mathsf{E} c_i^b : t} \text{ if } t = \mathsf{Type}(c_i^b) \wedge \vdash_b^\mathsf{T} t \quad [\iota^b] \; \frac{}{A \vdash_b^\mathsf{E} x_i : t} \text{ if } t = A(x_i) \wedge \vdash_b^\mathsf{T} t$$

$$[\iota^b] \; \frac{A[x_i : t_i] \vdash_b^\mathsf{E} e : t}{A \vdash_b^\mathsf{E} \lambda^b x_i.e : t_i \rightarrow^b t} \text{ if } \vdash_b^\mathsf{T} t_i \qquad [\iota^b] \; \frac{A \vdash_b^\mathsf{E} e_0 : t_1 \rightarrow^b t_2 \quad A \vdash_b^\mathsf{E} e_1 : t_1}{A \vdash_b^\mathsf{E} e_0 \mathbb{Q}^b e_1 : t_2}$$

$$[\iota^b] \; \frac{A \vdash_0^\mathsf{E} e : t \rightarrow^b t}{A \vdash_0^\mathsf{E} \mathsf{fix}^0 e : t} \qquad [\iota^b] \; \frac{A \vdash_b^\mathsf{E} e_0 : \mathsf{bool}^b \quad A \vdash_b^\mathsf{E} e_1 : t \quad A \vdash_b^\mathsf{E} e_2 : t}{A \vdash_b^\mathsf{E} \mathsf{if}^b e_0 e_1 e_2 : t}$$

---

[5] In [1] recursive computations are specified implicitly.

(where b ranges over $\{0, 1, \cdots, \mathsf{max}\}$). In addition we have the following bridging rules corresponding to the operators $up_b^{b'}$, $dn_b^{b'}$ and $lift_b^{b'}$:

$$[up_b^{b'}] \ \frac{A \vdash_b^{\mathsf{E}} e : t}{A \vdash_{b+b'}^{\mathsf{E}} e : t} \ \text{ if } \vdash_{b+b'}^{\mathsf{T}} t \qquad [dn_b^{b'}] \ \frac{A \vdash_{b+b'}^{\mathsf{E}} e : t}{A \vdash_b^{\mathsf{E}} e : t}$$

$$[lift_b^{b'}] \ \frac{A \vdash_b^{\mathsf{E}} e : \mathsf{int}^b}{A \vdash_{b+b'}^{\mathsf{E}} \mathtt{lift}_b^{b'} \ e : \mathsf{int}^{b+b'}} \qquad [lift_b^{b'}] \ \frac{A \vdash_b^{\mathsf{E}} e : \mathsf{bool}^b}{A \vdash_{b+b'}^{\mathsf{E}} \mathtt{lift}_b^{b'} \ e : \mathsf{bool}^{b+b'}}$$

It is trivial to establish the following relationship between the typing judgements:

Fact 10. $A \vdash_b^{\mathsf{E}} e : t$ *implies* $\vdash_b^{\mathsf{T}} t$.

To show that we have given the correct treatment for expressions we prove:

Lemma 11. $A \vdash_b^{\mathsf{E}} e : t$ *if and only if* $A \vdash e : t \ \wedge \ \| t \| \geq b$ *(in Appendix A.3).*

To show that we have defined a multi-level λ-calculus we define a uniform derivor δ from L_{mp} into λ: it simply removes all annotations and all occurrences of $\mathtt{lift}_b^{b'}$. It is then fairly straightforward to prove:

Fact 12. L_{mp} *is a multi-level λ-calculus.*

3.4   Example: abstract interpretation [5]

We shall now show that the two-level language TML[dt,dt] of [5] can be seen as an instance of the present framework. However, as our current framework does not directly support combinator introduction we shall prefer to consider a version of [5] where the combinators are replaced by λ-expressions; consequently it will be instructive to think only of forward program analyses. Given these considerations we can define the two-level language $L = L_{ai}$ as follows.

Two-level structure. The two-level structure B has the two levels d (for domain) and l (for lattice). The signature Ω^B has the following explicitly given operators:

- *UP*: $((l, \mathsf{Typ}); (d, \mathsf{Typ}))$
- *DN*: $((d, \mathsf{Typ}), (l, \mathsf{Typ}); (l, \mathsf{Typ}))$
- *up*: $((l, \mathsf{Exp}); (d, \mathsf{Exp}))$
- *dn*: $((d, \mathsf{Exp}); (l, \mathsf{Exp}))$

Here *UP* reflects that a lattice is a domain, and *DN* reflects that a domain and a lattice in certain cases can be put together and produce a lattice. The operations *up* and *dn* reflect that expressions denoting elements of domains and lattices can be mixed much as compile-time/run-time and static/dynamic expressions could in Subsections 3.1 and 3.2.

Two-level λ-calculus. We shall basically use the same signature Σ^L as in Subsection 3.1:

$$\to^d, \to^l : (\mathsf{Typ}^2; \mathsf{Typ}) \quad \mathtt{int}^d, \mathtt{int}^l : (; \mathsf{Typ}) \quad \mathtt{bool}^d, \mathtt{bool}^l : (; \mathsf{Typ})$$

$$c_i^d, c_i^l : (; \mathsf{Exp}) \qquad x_i : (; \mathsf{Exp}) \qquad \lambda^d x_i., \lambda^l x_i. : (\mathsf{Exp}; \mathsf{Exp})$$

$$@^d, @^l : (\mathsf{Exp}^2; \mathsf{Exp}) \quad \mathtt{if}^d, \mathtt{if}^l : (\mathsf{Exp}^3; \mathsf{Exp}) \quad \mathtt{fix}^d, \mathtt{fix}^l : (\mathsf{Exp}; \mathsf{Exp})$$

For *types* the well-formedness rules include two copies of the well-formedness rules of λ' as was the case in Subsection 3.1:

$$[\iota^b] \ \frac{}{\vdash_b^\mathsf{T} \mathtt{int}^b} \qquad [\iota^b] \ \frac{}{\vdash_b^\mathsf{T} \mathtt{bool}^b} \qquad [\iota^b] \ \frac{\vdash_b^\mathsf{T} t_1 \quad \vdash_b^\mathsf{T} t_2}{\vdash_b^\mathsf{T} t_1 \to^b t_2}$$

(where b ranges over $\{l, d\}$). On top of this we have the bridging rule

$$[UP] \ \frac{\vdash_l^\mathsf{T} t}{\vdash_d^\mathsf{T} t}$$

which corresponds to the one in Subsection 3.2 and is somewhat more general than the one in Subsection 3.1; also we have an additional bridging rule

$$[DN] \ \frac{\vdash_d^\mathsf{T} t_1 \quad \vdash_l^\mathsf{T} t_2}{\vdash_l^\mathsf{T} t_1 \to^d t_2}$$

that has no counterpart in Subsections 3.1 and 3.2. It is straightforward to show that $\vdash_d^\mathsf{T} t'$ holds if and only if $\mathbf{dt}(t')$ holds in [5], and that $\vdash_l^\mathsf{T} t'$ holds if and only if $\mathbf{lt}(t')$ holds in [5].

For *expressions* we have two slightly modified copies of the well-formedness rules of λ':

$$[\iota^b] \ \frac{}{A \vdash_b^\mathsf{E} c_i^b : t} \ \text{if } t = \mathsf{Type}(c_i^b) \wedge \vdash_b^\mathsf{T} t \quad [\iota^b] \ \frac{}{A \vdash_b^\mathsf{E} x_i : t} \ \text{if } t = A(x_i^b) \wedge \vdash_b^\mathsf{T} t$$

$$[\iota^b] \ \frac{A[x_i^b : t_i] \vdash_b^\mathsf{E} e : t}{A \vdash_b^\mathsf{E} \lambda^b x_i.e : t_i \to^b t} \ \text{if } \vdash_b^\mathsf{T} t_i \qquad [\iota^b] \ \frac{A \vdash_b^\mathsf{E} e_0 : t_1 \to^b t_2 \quad A \vdash_b^\mathsf{E} e_1 : t_1}{A \vdash_b^\mathsf{E} e_0 @^b e_1 : t_2}$$

$$[\iota^b] \ \frac{A \vdash_b^\mathsf{E} e : t \to^b t}{A \vdash_b^\mathsf{E} \mathtt{fix}^b e : t} \qquad [\iota^b] \ \frac{A \vdash_b^\mathsf{E} e_0 : \mathtt{bool}^b \quad A \vdash_b^\mathsf{E} e_1 : t \quad A \vdash_b^\mathsf{E} e_2 : t}{A \vdash_b^\mathsf{E} \mathtt{if}^b \ e_0 \ e_1 \ e_2 : t}$$

(where b ranges over $\{l, d\}$). On top of this we have the two bridging rules

$$[dn] \ \frac{A \vdash^{\mathsf{E}}_{d} e : t}{A \vdash^{\mathsf{E}}_{l} e : t} \ \text{if} \ \vdash^{\mathsf{T}}_{l} t$$

$$[up] \ \frac{A \vdash^{\mathsf{E}}_{l} e : t}{A \vdash^{\mathsf{E}}_{d} e : t}$$

It is trivial to establish the following relationship between the typing judgements:

Fact 13. $A \vdash^{\mathsf{E}}_{b} e : t$ *implies* $\vdash^{\mathsf{T}}_{b} t$.

To show that we have defined a two-level λ-calculus we define a uniform derivor δ: as in the previous examples it simply removes all annotations. It is then fairly straightforward to prove:

Fact 14. L_{ai} *is a multi-level λ-calculus.*

4 Conclusion

In this paper we have cast further light on some of the multi-level languages reported in the literature. This has had the effect of highlighting the essential differences and similarities and to pinpoint design decisions in existing calculi that should perhaps be reconsidered; examples include the restriction on fix^{b} in L_{pe} and L_{ml} and the "peculiar" well-typing in L_{pe} as opposed to L'_{pe}.

Generalisations of this work (already begun) would include dealing with arbitrary programming languages that need not be based on the λ-calculus and that need not be typed. Indeed they may have many more syntactic categories (for example declarations and statements) and more advanced typing constructs (polymorphism of one kind or the other).

In another direction the descriptive approach of the present paper should be complemented with a prescriptive approach as in [11]. This prescriptive approach should be more flexible than the one of [11], but is unlikely ever to be as flexible as a descriptive approach: it is like approximating a property from the below as well as the above (using a maxim from abstract interpretation). This work (already begun) is likely to focus on the λ-calculus and seems hard to achieve for arbitrary programming languages.

Acknowledgements. Thanks to Martin Berger, Dirk Dussart, Jesper Jørgensen, and the referees for valuable feedback. This work was supported in part by the DART project (The Danish Research Councils) and the LOMAPS project (ESPRIT Basic Research).

References

1. R. Glück and J. Jørgensen: Efficient Multi-level Generating Extensions for Program Specialization. *PLILP'95*, Springer Lecture Notes in Computer Science, vol. 982: pp. 259–278, 1995.
2. J. A. Goguen and J. W. Thatcher and E. G. Wagner: An Initial Algebra Approach to the Specification, Correctness and Implementation of Abstract Data Types. *Current Trends in Programming Methodology*, vol. 4, (R. T. Yeh, editor), Prentice-Hall, 1978.
3. F. Henglein and C. Mossin: Polymorphic Binding-Time Analysis. *ESOP'94*, Springer Lecture Notes in Computer Science, vol. 788: pp. 287–301, 1994.
4. N. D. Jones and P. Sestoft and H. Søndergaard: An Experiment in Partial Evaluation: the Generation of a Compiler Generator. *Rewriting Techniques and Applications*, Springer Lecture Notes in Computer Science, vol. 202: pp. 124–140, 1985.
5. N. D. Jones and F. Nielson: Abstract Interpretation: a Semantics-Based Tool for Program Analysis. *Handbook of Logic in Computer Science*, vol. 4: pp. 527–636, Oxford University Press, 1995.
6. J. C. Mitchell: Type Systems for Programming Languages. *Handbook of Theoretical Computer Science: Formal Models and Semantics*, vol. B: pp. 365–458, Elsevier Science Publishers (and MIT Press), 1990.
7. F. Nielson: *Abstract Interpretation using Domain Theory*. PhD thesis, University of Edinburgh, Scotland, 1984.
8. F. Nielson: Two-Level Semantics and Abstract Interpretation. *Theoretical Computer Science — Fundamental Studies*, vol. 69: pp. 117–242, 1989.
9. F. Nielson and H. R. Nielson: Two-level semantics and code generation. *Theoretical Computer Science*, vol. 56(1): pp. 59–133, 1988.
10. H. R. Nielson and F. Nielson: Automatic Binding Time Analysis for a Typed λ-calculus. *Science of Computer Programming*, vol. 10: pp. 139–176, 1988.
11. F. Nielson and H. R. Nielson: *Two-Level Functional Languages*. Vol. 34 of *Cambridge Tracts in Theoretical Computer Science*, Cambridge University Press, 1992.
12. F. Nielson and H. R. Nielson: Forced Transformations of Occam Programs. *Information and Software Technology*, vol. 34(2): pp. 91–96, 1992.
13. C. Strachey: The Varieties of Programming Languages. Technical Monograph PRG-10, Programming Research Group, University of Oxford, 1973.
14. M. Wirsing: Algebraic Specification. *Handbook of Theoretical Computer Science: Formal Models and Semantics*, vol. B: pp. 675–788, Elsevier (and MIT Press), 1990.

A   Subsets of existing systems

A.1   Code generation: [11]

In this subsection we summarise the binding time analysis of [11] (excluding product types and list types) as it pertains to the lambda calculus of the present paper.

For types [11] defines a predicate $\vdash t : b$:

$$\overline{\vdash \texttt{int}^b : b} \qquad \overline{\vdash \texttt{bool}^b : b} \qquad \frac{\vdash t_1 : b \quad \vdash t_2 : b}{\vdash t_1 \rightarrow^b t_2 : b} \qquad \frac{\vdash t_1 \rightarrow^r t_2 : r}{\vdash t_1 \rightarrow^r t_2 : c}$$

For expressions the typing rules have the form $A \vdash e : t : b$ and are defined by:

$$\frac{}{A \vdash c_i^b : t : b} \text{ if } t = \mathsf{Type}(c_i^b) \wedge \vdash t : b \qquad \frac{}{A \vdash x_i : t : b} \text{ if } (t : b) = A(x_i) \wedge \vdash t : b$$

$$\frac{A[x_i : (t_i : b)] \vdash e : t : b}{A \vdash \lambda^b x_i.e : t_i \to^b t : b} \text{ if } \vdash t_i : b \qquad \frac{A \vdash e_0 : t_1 \to^b t_2 : b \qquad A \vdash e_1 : t_1 : b}{A \vdash e_0 @^b e_1 : t_2 : b}$$

$$\frac{A \vdash e : t \to^b t : b}{A \vdash \mathtt{fix}^b\, e : t : b} \qquad \frac{A \vdash e_0 : \mathtt{bool}^b : b \qquad A \vdash e_1 : t : b \qquad A \vdash e_2 : t : b}{A \vdash \mathtt{if}^b\, e_0\, e_1\, e_2 : t : b}$$

$$\frac{A \vdash e : t : c}{A \vdash e : t : r} \text{ if } \vdash t : r$$

$$\frac{A' \vdash e : t : r}{A \vdash e : t : c} \text{ if } \vdash t : c \wedge \mathsf{gr}(A') = \{(x_i : t' : b') \in \mathsf{gr}(A) \mid b' = c \wedge \vdash t' : c\}$$

A.2 Partial evaluation: [3]

In this subsection we present a restriction of the binding time analysis of [3] to the lambda calculus of the present paper. Compared with [3] we do not incorporate the qualified types (including polymorphism and constraints on binding times).

First define $\mathsf{top}(t)$ to be the annotation at the top level of t, i.e. $\mathsf{top}(\mathtt{int}^b) = b$, $\mathsf{top}(\mathtt{bool}^b) = b$, and $\mathsf{top}(t_1 \to^b t_2) = b$; in [3] one writes t^b to indicate that $\mathsf{top}(t) = b$. Then the inference system for expressions is:

$$\frac{}{A \vdash c_i^b : t} \text{ if } t = \mathsf{Type}(c_i^b) \qquad \frac{}{A \vdash x_i : t} \text{ if } t = A(x_i)$$

$$\frac{A[x_i : t_i] \vdash e : t}{A \vdash \lambda^b x_i.e : t_i \to^b t} \text{ if } b \leq \mathsf{top}(t_i) \wedge b \leq \mathsf{top}(t)$$

$$\frac{A \vdash e_0 : t_1 \to^b t_2 \qquad A \vdash e_1 : t_1}{A \vdash e_0 @^b e_1 : t_2} \text{ if } b \leq \mathsf{top}(t_1) \wedge b \leq \mathsf{top}(t_2)$$

$$\frac{A \vdash e : t \to^b t}{A \vdash \mathtt{fix}^S\, e : t}$$

$$\frac{A \vdash e_0 : \mathtt{bool}^b \qquad A \vdash e_1 : t \qquad A \vdash e_2 : t}{A \vdash \mathtt{if}^b\, e_0\, e_1\, e_2 : t} \text{ if } b \leq \mathsf{top}(t)$$

$$\frac{A \vdash e : \mathtt{int}^S}{A \vdash e : \mathtt{int}^D} \qquad \frac{A \vdash e : \mathtt{bool}^S}{A \vdash e : \mathtt{bool}^D}$$

A.3 Multi-level partial evaluation: [1]

In this subsection we present a restriction of the binding time analysis of [1] (expressed using Scheme) to the lambda calculus of the present paper.

For types [1] defines a predicate $\vdash t : b$:

$$\frac{}{\vdash \mathtt{int}^b : b} \text{ if } 0 \le b \le \mathsf{max} \qquad\qquad \frac{}{\vdash \mathtt{bool}^b : b} \text{ if } 0 \le b \le \mathsf{max}$$

$$\frac{\vdash t_1 : b_1 \qquad \vdash t_2 : b_2}{\vdash t_1 \to^b t_2 : b} \text{ if } b_1 \ge b \wedge b_2 \ge b$$

Based on this define $\| t \| = b$ if and only if $\vdash t : b$.

For expressions the typing rules are:

$$\frac{}{A \vdash c_i^b : t} \text{ if } t = \mathsf{Type}(c_i^b) \qquad\qquad \frac{}{A \vdash x_i : t} \text{ if } t = A(x_i)$$

$$\frac{A[x_i : t_i] \vdash e : t}{A \vdash \lambda^b x_i.e : t_i \to^b t} \text{ if } \| t_i \| \ge b \qquad\qquad \frac{A \vdash e_0 : t_1 \to^b t_2 \qquad A \vdash e_1 : t_1}{A \vdash e_0 @^b e_1 : t_2}$$

$$\frac{A \vdash e_0 : \mathtt{bool}^b \qquad A \vdash e_1 : t \qquad A \vdash e_2 : t}{A \vdash \mathtt{if}^b \ e_0 \ e_1 \ e_2 : t} \qquad \frac{A \vdash e : t \to^b t}{A \vdash \mathtt{fix}^0 \ e : t}$$

$$\text{if } \| t \| \ge b$$

$$\frac{A \vdash e : \mathtt{int}^b}{A \vdash \mathtt{lift}_b^{b'} \ e : \mathtt{int}^{b+b'}} \text{ if } b < b+b' \le \mathsf{max} \qquad \frac{A \vdash e : \mathtt{bool}^b}{A \vdash \mathtt{lift}_b^{b'} \ e : \mathtt{bool}^{b+b'}} \text{ if } b < b+b' \le \mathsf{max}$$

Compared with [1] we have added an obvious side condition to the rules for abstraction and lifting so as to ensure that the types derivable for the expressions are well-formed.

A Comparative Revisitation of Some Program Transformation Techniques

Alberto Pettorossi[1] and Maurizio Proietti[2]

[1] Department of Informatics, Systems, and Production,
University of Roma Tor Vergata, 00133 Roma, Italy. adp@iasi.rm.cnr.it
[2] IASI-CNR, Viale Manzoni 30, 00185 Roma, Italy. proietti@iasi.rm.cnr.it

Abstract. We revisit the main techniques of program transformation which are used in partial evaluation, mixed computation, supercompilation, generalized partial computation, rule-based program derivation, program specialization, compiling control, and the like. We present a methodology which underlines these techniques as a 'common pattern of reasoning' and explains the various correspondences which can be established among them. This methodology consists of three steps: i) symbolic computation, ii) search for regularities, and iii) program extraction. We also discuss some control issues which occur when performing these steps.

1 Introduction

During the past years researchers working in various areas of program transformation, such as partial evaluation, mixed computation, supercompilation, generalized partial computation, rule-based program derivation, program specialization, and compiling control, have been using very similar techniques for the development and derivation of programs.

Unfortunately, that similarity has not always been given enough attention because of some lack of interaction among the various groups of researchers involved in these areas. This was motivated by the fact that the objectives of these groups were somewhat different, as for instance, program derivation, compiler generation, and program optimization. Another reason for the lack of interaction was the fact that the programming languages used, whether imperative, functional, or logic, often made a significant difference in the way the various techniques were actually implemented and applied.

In recent years comparisons have been made and correspondences have been established among the different techniques in some particular cases [25,44,48]. For some time already, the scientific community has been aware that many such correspondences exist in general, and they are based on the fact that those techniques all share the same underlining methodology which we want to describe in this paper. This general methodology shows that correspondence results may have somewhat complex formalizations, but they are not accidental.

We know from various papers, conferences, and discussions with people working in the area of program transformation that the methodology we will describe here is indeed 'common knowledge'. Thus, the aim of this work is mainly to clarify some issues related to this common knowledge and, as a side-effect, to indicate why the correspondence results do hold and also to present the main features of a general framework where different transformation techniques could be combined together.

2 A Preliminary Example

In this section we revisit a familiar example of program derivation using a functional language based on first-order recursive equations and the *unfold/fold* transformation system with rules and strategies [10,40]. This revisitation allows us to present in a concrete case the three steps of the general methodology for program transformation we want to introduce, namely, i) symbolic computation, ii) search for regularities, and iii) program extraction. Various instances of this methodology were developed in the seventies independently by many people in several research fields such as partial evaluation, mixed computation, unfold/fold transformation, and supercompilation.

Suppose we are given the following initial program for computing the Fibonacci function:

1. $fib(0) = 1$
2. $fib(1) = 1$
3. $fib(n + 2) = fib(n + 1) + fib(n)$ for $n \geq 0$

The computation of $fib(k)$ for any natural number $k \geq 0$, requires an exponential number of sums. We want to derive a more efficient program so that the number of the required sums is at most linear for *all* $k \geq 0$. This universal quantification of the variable k over the set of natural numbers, motivates the first step of the general methodology which consists in considering a single *symbolic computation* depending on k (or possibly a finite set of symbolic computations), instead of the infinite set of concrete computations, one for each value of k.

Various models of symbolic computations have been proposed in the literature within various program transformation systems. We will consider here the m-dag model [3] which given a recursive program, uses a directed acyclic graph to represent the father-son relationship among the function calls evoked by the given program.

Thus, in our case, starting from the root-node $fib(k)$ we generate, using Equation 3, the two son nodes $fib(k-1)$ and $fib(k-2)$. The arguments $k-1$ and $k-2$ are computed by *matching* in the algebra of integers. Thus, for instance, $fib(k)$ which matches the left-hand-side $fib(n+2)$ of Equation 3 for $n = k-2$ evokes the two recursive calls $fib(k-1)$ and $fib(k-2)$, corresponding to $fib(n+1)$ and $fib(n)$, respectively, in the right-hand-side of that equation. From the node $fib(k-1)$ we then generate the son nodes $fib(k-2)$ and $fib(k-3)$, and we identify the two distinct nodes for $fib(k-2)$. We then continue the node generation and the node identification process in a breadth-first manner. Obviously, this process is potentially infinite in the sense that from $fib(k)$ we can generate the son node $fib(k-i)$ for any $i \geq 0$.

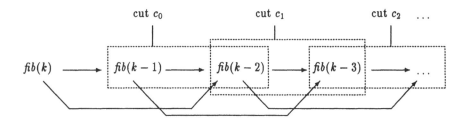

Fig. 1. An initial portion of the m-dag for the *fib* function with the first three cuts of a progressive sequence of cuts.

In Figure 1 we have represented an initial portion of the m-dag for the *fib* function. In constructing this m-dag it is assumed that the argument of every call of the function *fib* is greater than 1, and thus, Equation 3 is used for generating two new nodes from any given node.

Now the general methodology we want to present, requires in its second step, the *search for a suitable regularity* valid in the whole m-dag, and fortunately, as we will see, there is no need for the complete representation of the infinite m-dag.

In our case, a suitable regularity is the existence of a 'progressive sequence of cuts' [38]. Informally, this means that in the m-dag with initial node $fib(k)$ there is a sequence $\langle c_0, c_1, \ldots \rangle$ of sets of nodes with the following properties: i) all sets, also called *cuts*, have equal cardinality, say C, ii) after removing a set of that sequence the resulting m-dag has two disconnected parts (this is why each set of the sequence is called a cut), iii) for any two successive cuts, say c_i and c_{i+1}, we have that: $c_i \neq c_{i+1}$, $\forall n \in c_{i+1} \exists m \in c_i$ such that if $n \neq m$ then $m > n$, and $\forall m \in c_i \exists n \in c_{i+1}$ such that if $n \neq m$ then $m > n$, where $>$ denotes the transitive closure of the father-son relationship among nodes, iv) there are $1 + C$ functions, say $p_0, p_1, \ldots, p_C$, which all have arity C and are defined in terms of basic functions only, such that: (*a*) $fib(k)$ can be computed from the C function calls in the cut c_0 using p_0, and (*b*) $\forall i \geq 0, \forall j$, with $1 \leq j \leq C$, the j-th function call in the cut c_i can be computed from the function calls in the cut c_{i+1} using p_j, and v) for every value of k, with $k \geq 0$, in the sequence of cuts there exists a cut whose function calls, instantiated to that value of k, can be computed using basic functions only, without requiring the computation of the son calls.

A progressive sequence of cuts in the m-dag with initial node $fib(k)$ is: $\sigma = \langle \{fib(k-1), fib(k-2)\}, \{fib(k-2), fib(k-3)\}, \ldots \rangle$.

A different progressive sequence whose cuts have cardinality three, is: $\langle \{fib(k-1), fib(k-2), fib(k-4)\}, \{fib(k-5), fib(k-6), fib(k-8)\}, \ldots \rangle$.

Then the third step of the general methodology is the *extraction of the new program* from the symbolic computation and the discovered regularity. In our case, given the progressive sequence of cuts σ, we apply the tupling strategy [10,38] and we introduce the function $t(n) = \langle fib(n+1), fib(n) \rangle$ which for any sequence of values of the variable n, gives us the corresponding sequence of values of the function calls in the cuts of σ. Using the unfold/fold technique [10] we then get the following program:

1. $fib(0) = 1$
2. $fib(1) = 1$
4. $fib(n + 2) = u + v$ where $\langle u, v \rangle = t(n)$ for $n \geq 0$
5. $t(0) = \langle 1, 1 \rangle$
6. $t(n + 1) = \langle u + v, u \rangle$ where $\langle u, v \rangle = t(n)$ for $n \geq 0$

As expected, this program uses only $O(n)$ sums to compute the value of $fib(n)$. The reader should notice that Equations 5 and 6 are obtained in the unfold/fold technique by looking for the explicit recursive definition of the new tuple function $t(n)$. In particular, Equation 6 is derived as follows:

$$t(n+1) = \langle fib(n+2), fib(n+1) \rangle = \{\text{unfolding}\} =$$
$$= \langle fib(n+1) + fib(n), fib(n+1) \rangle = \{\text{where-abstraction and tupling}\} =$$
$$= \langle u+v, u \rangle \text{ where } \langle u, v \rangle = \langle fib(n+1), fib(n) \rangle = \{\text{folding}\} =$$
$$= \langle u+v, u \rangle \text{ where } \langle u, v \rangle = t(n)$$

The where-abstraction step avoids the double evaluation of $fib(n+1)$ while computing $t(n+1)$, and the last folding step avoids the double evaluations of the fib calls 'at every level of recursion', thus, it makes the efficiency gains of the where-abstraction step computationally significant. This is why in the unfold/fold technique one looks for final folding steps to be made at the end of the derivation. The same occurs, for instance, in the supercompilation technique where one looks for 'self-sufficient models' of the computation [52].

In the following sections we illustrate in some detail the general methodology for program transformation we have seen in action in this preliminary example. We also indicate the way in which various techniques for program transformation proposed in the literature fit into this general methodology. In Section 3 we consider the symbolic computation model called the symbolic trace tree used in compiling control, and we briefly compare it with the models used in other program transformation systems. In Section 4 we illustrate the idea of finding suitable regularities in the symbolic computations, and in particular, we consider the case of partial evaluation in logic programming. In Section 5 we address the problem of extracting new programs from symbolic computations. Since the application of the general methodology is highly nondeterministic and may also lead to infinite constructions, we need some techniques for its control. Those techniques are analyzed in Section 6. In Sections 7 we relate the general methodology to program specialization, deforestation, and finite differencing, and finally, in Section 8 we briefly present some correspondences among various program transformation techniques.

3 Symbolic Computation Models

A method for transforming a given initial program into a new program which behaves efficiently for every input value, is to look for suitable properties which hold for every computation performed by the initial program. These properties can often be discovered by applying the general technique, called *abstract interpretation* [13], by which we represent a possibly infinite set of concrete computations, one for every input value, by a single symbolic computation, and then by reasoning on that symbolic computation.

Various models of symbolic computations have been proposed in the literature, and we briefly discuss them at the end of this section. Now we consider in some detail a particular symbolic computation model, called *symbolic trace tree*, which has its relevance in the transformation technique for logic programs called compiling control [7].

The Symbolic Trace Tree for Compiling Control

A logic program can be viewed as the union of some 'logic definitions' (that is, the axioms of a theory) and a 'control strategy' (that is, a theorem prover) [29]. The efficiency of a logic program very often depends on the control strategy. Thus, in order to achieve high performances, the programmer, instead of relying on the evaluation strategy provided by the system, may define his own control strategy. This can be done, for instance, via *modes* or *delay declarations* [33] based on the instantiation patterns of the goals during execution. However, one may avoid the difficulty of dealing with those declarations at run-time by using the *compiling control* technique as we now indicate.

Let S_{left} be the familiar Prolog control strategy, which selects the literals in the goal at hand in a sequential order from left to right. Given a logic program P_1 and an efficient control strategy S_{eff} for P_1, we want to derive a new program P_2 such that, for a given class of goals, P_1 with control strategy S_{eff} and P_2 with control strategy S_{left} have equivalent computational behaviour. According to the general methodology we have presented in Section 2, compiling control works in three steps as follows.

1. Starting from a symbolic input goal, in the first step compiling control generates a *symbolic trace tree* using the control strategy S_{eff}. The symbolic trace tree represents the class of concrete computations, each of which corresponds to a concrete goal in the class of goals represented by the symbolic input goal.

2. We then look for a *finite* description of the symbolic trace tree which is potentially infinite. This is done by identifying *similar* nodes and thus, generating a finite graph, possibly cyclic, called *symbolic trace graph*. The notion of similarity may vary according to the particular instances of the compiling control technique one uses.

3. In the final third step a new program P_2 is extracted from the symbolic trace graph. By construction, the behaviour of P_2 with the control strategy S_{left} is equivalent to that of P_1 with control strategy S_{eff}.

   This equivalence establishes the correctness of the transformation and it is based on the relationship between the concrete and the symbolic computations which is formalized, as we will see in the example below, by using the abstract interpretation technique.

Ideas related to compiling control have also been investigated in the area of functional programming within the so called *filter promotion* strategy [4, 14], whereby function evaluations can be anticipated for avoiding unnecessary computations and improving program behaviour.

In the following example we will see in action the compiling control technique. The final program can also be derived by using unfold/fold program transformations as shown in [50].

Example 1. [*Common Subsequences*] Let us consider the following logic program *Csub*, which generates all common subsequences X of not necessarily consecutive elements of two sequences Y and Z. Sequences are represented as lists.

1. $csub(X, Y, Z) \leftarrow subseq(X, Y), subseq(X, Z)$
2. $subseq([\,], X) \leftarrow$
3. $subseq([A|X], [A|Y]) \leftarrow subseq(X, Y)$
4. $subseq(X, [B|Y]) \leftarrow subseq(X, Y)$

Let us consider the set I of input goals of the form $csub(x, y, z)$, where x is a free variable and y and z are ground lists. For these goals the control strategy S_{left} is, in general, inefficient because it first evaluates $subseq(x, y)$ and generates a binding, say $\bar{x}$, for x and then it tests whether or not $subseq(\bar{x}, z)$ holds.

The following *producer-consumer* coroutining strategy, called S_{pc}, allows for a more efficient execution of the above program. This strategy assumes that an atomic goal A is said to be a *consumer* (of bindings) iff all its arguments are instances of the arguments of every clause head which is unifiable with A itself, and otherwise the atom A is said to be a *producer* (of bindings). The strategy S_{pc} can be defined as follows: in the goal at hand S_{pc} chooses for execution the leftmost consumer, if any, and otherwise it chooses the leftmost producer.

In order to represent a set of concrete goals as a single symbolic goal, we consider the set G of all ground terms and the set F of all free variables. These two sets, together with the empty set of terms and the set of all (ground and nonground) terms, form the domain of an abstract interpretation which is a lattice. (The reader unfamiliar with abstract interpretations in logic programming may refer to [2,6,32].)

A finite portion of the symbolic trace tree for a goal in I, generated by using the program *Csub* and the control strategy S_{pc}, is depicted in Figure 2 (where for the time being, the upgoing arrows are to be ignored). The root is labeled by the symbolic input goal $csub(X^F, Y^G, Z^G)$, meaning that in every concrete computation the input goal is of the form $csub(X, Y, Z)$ where X is a free variable and Y and Z are bound to ground terms. In the goals labeling the non-root nodes of that tree, a variable with superscript F means that in every concrete computation that variable is bound to a (possibly different) free variable, whereas a variable with superscript G means that in every concrete computation that variable is bound to a ground term.

In the node M we have unfolded the atom $subseq(X^F, Y^G)$ because it unifies either with clause 2 (if $Y^G = [\,]$) or with clauses 3 and 4 (if Y^G is a non-empty ground list). In both cases $subseq(X^F, Y^G)$ is a producer, and for the same reasons, also $subseq(X^F, Z^G)$ is a producer. In the node N we have unfolded the atom $subseq([A^F|X1^F], Z^G)$ because it is a consumer and $subseq(X1^F, Y1^G)$ is a producer.

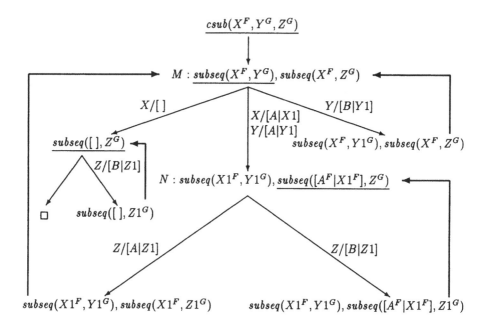

Fig. 2. An initial portion of the symbolic trace tree for *Csub*. The atoms selected for unfolding by the strategy S_{pc} are underlined. Upgoing arrows relate symbolic goals which are variants of each other. These arrows do *not* denote arcs of the tree.

The goal labeling any non-root node of the symbolic trace tree is obtained from the goal of the corresponding father node according to the following unfolding process: i) we select an atom of the goal in the father node following the strategy S_{pc}, ii) we unify the selected atom with the heads of all clauses in *Csub*, iii) we replace the selected atom by the bodies of the unifying clauses, whereby getting the son nodes, and iv) we apply to the son nodes the bindings computed by unification. In the symbolic trace tree the arc from a father node to a son node is labeled by the bindings for the variables of the father node that are computed during the corresponding unfolding step by the unification process.

The variable superscripts in any son node are obtained from the superscripts in the corresponding father node by taking into account that: i) the unification of a ground term with a term containing variables binds all variables to ground terms, and ii) the unification of a variable with a term containing variables does not bind any variable in that term. We leave to the reader the task of formalizing the process of computing the variable superscripts. This can be done by using the notion of *abstract unification*, that is, unification among terms in the domain of the abstract interpretation [2,6,32].

Now, as in the second step of the general methodology, compiling control searches for regularities in the symbolic trace tree with the aim of deriving a finite representation of that tree. In our case this finite representation can be obtained by identifying goals which are variants of each other and have the same superscripts. By doing so we get the finite cyclic graph, called *symbolic trace graph*, depicted in Figure 2 where nodes related by upgoing arrows are to be identified.

The theory of abstract interpretation can be used for proving various correctness properties of the symbolic trace graph and in particular, the fact that it indeed represents the set of all concrete computations generated by the given set of input goals, in the sense that every concrete computation follows a sequence of arcs in that graph and at each computation step the concrete goals are instances of the symbolic goals in the corresponding nodes and they agree with the superscripts.

As we will discuss in the next section, this finite representation property has a fundamental importance and it allows us to perform the third step of the general methodology, that is, the derivation of a new program from the initial one.

Finiteness of the symbolic trace graphs is related to analogous properties which are required in other transformation techniques, such as *self-sufficiency* of the graphs of states and transitions in supercompilation [52], *foldability* of the unfolding trees in unfold/fold program transformation [43], and *closedness* in partial deduction [31].

The extraction of the derived program is performed as we now indicate (see also Figure 3).

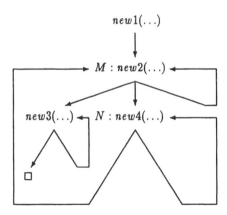

Fig. 3. The symbolic trace graph derived from the symbolic trace tree of Figure 2 after the introduction of the new predicate names: $new1$, $new2$, $new3$, and $new4$.

We introduce new predicate names, say $new1, new2, \ldots$, one for each set of non-empty variant goals, and for each arc $U \xrightarrow{\theta} V$ of the symbolic trace tree, with $V \neq \square$, we introduce the new clause $newh(U)\theta \leftarrow newk(V)$, where the predicate names occurring in U and V are to be considered as function names, because they now occur in argument positions. For the arc $subseq([\,], Z) \rightarrow \square$ we introduce the new clause $new3(subseq([\,], Z)) \leftarrow$.

Thus, we get the following new program:

$$new1(csub(X, Y, Z)) \leftarrow new2(subseq(X, Y), subseq(X, Z))$$
$$new2(subseq([\,], Y), subseq([\,], Z)) \leftarrow new3(subseq([\,], Z))$$
$$new2(subseq([A|X1], [A|Y1]), subseq([A|X1], Z)) \leftarrow$$
$$new4(subseq(X1, Y1), subseq([A|X1], Z))$$
$$new2(subseq(X, [B|Y1]), subseq(X, Z)) \leftarrow$$
$$new2(subseq(X, Y1), subseq(X, Z))$$
$$new3(subseq([\,], Z)) \leftarrow$$
$$new3(subseq([\,], [B|Z1])) \leftarrow new3(subseq([\,], Z1))$$
$$new4(subseq(X1, Y1), subseq([A|X1], [A|Z1])) \leftarrow$$
$$new2(subseq(X1, Y1), subseq(X1, Z1))$$
$$new4(subseq(X1, Y1), subseq([A|X1], [B|Z1])) \leftarrow$$
$$new4(subseq(X1, Y1), subseq([A|X1], Z1))$$

For goals of the form $new1(csub(X, Y, Z))$, this program computes the same answers as the ones computed by $Csub$ for goals of the form $csub(X, Y, Z)$ where X is a free variable and Y and Z and ground terms. The derived program, however, is more efficient than the initial one because it is more deterministic.

In order to avoid the presence of nested terms, intermediate predicates, and subsumed clauses, we then perform some final simple transformations which are similar to 'post-unfolding' in the supercompilation technique. Thus, we get the following program [50]:

$$new5([\,], Y, Z) \leftarrow$$
$$new5([A|X], [A|Y], Z) \leftarrow new6(A, X, Y, Z)$$
$$new5(X, [B|Y], Z) \leftarrow new5(X, Y, Z)$$
$$new6(A, X, Y, [A|Z]) \leftarrow new5(X, Y, Z)$$
$$new6(A, X, Y, [B|Z]) \leftarrow new6(A, X, Y, Z)$$

where the predicates $new5$ and $new6$ correspond in Figure 2 (and 3) to node M and N, respectively. $\square$

Other Symbolic Computation Models

Now we would like to consider some other symbolic computation models which have been proposed in the literature both for functional and logic languages. They differ for the information which is recorded during the symbolic computation steps. However, all of them use a basic operation similar to unfolding, which may be viewed as an abstraction of a computation step. The specific form of this basic operation varies in accordance with the language and the semantics considered.

Burstall and Darlington [10] have the *execution tree* model which is used to discover the new function definitions, the so called *eureka definitions*, to be introduced during the derivation of new programs via *folding/unfolding* transformations. The execution tree may be viewed as an abstraction of the concrete computation and consists of a tree of recursive calls constructed by unfolding a symbolic input term. The *m-dags* of recursive calls [3,38], which have been presented in our preliminary example, are further developments of this approach. A symbolic computation model based on unfolding, the so called *unfolding tree*, that is, a tree of clauses obtained by unfolding, has been proposed for logic programming in [43,41].

In Turchin's supercompilation technique [52], the symbolic computation process is performed by *driving*, which is analogous to unfolding. The driving process generates a tree of configurations, or a graph if we identify nodes with *similar* configurations. This graph is called *graph of states and transitions*. A similar model is the *partial process tree* used in the *positive supercompilation* technique [47,48]. There is, however, a difference between unfolding à la Burstall and Darlington and driving à la Turchin: by unfolding we replace an expression which matches the left-hand side of an equation by the corresponding instance of the right-hand side, whereas by driving a sort of unification process, rather than matching, takes place. This makes driving very similar to the unfolding mechanism we have seen in action in the compiling control example above. A formal correspondence between driving and unfolding in logic programming can be found in [25].

More similarities between supercompilation and other techniques used for transforming logic programs are based on the idea of performing symbolic computations by *meta-programs* or, in Turchin's terminology, *metasystem transitions* [24,54]. For instance, the transformation technique presented by Gallagher in [20] works by specializing a *meta-interpreter*, that is, a logic program which works as an interpreter for logic programs, w.r.t. a particular input program. Also the symbolic trace tree for compiling control may be generated using a meta-interpreter.

More complex operations may be performed during symbolic computation. For instance, in supercompilation one is allowed to use any 'clever trick' [52, page 293], in GPC-trees [19] one may use theorem provers to partially evaluate conditionals, and when constructing unfolding trees of logic programs one may perform, together with unfolding and folding steps, also goal replacement steps [41]. By these goal replacement steps we replace old goals by new equivalent goals using lemmas whose proofs are done off-line.

A special model of symbolic computation is the *SLDNF-tree* which is the basis for the partial evaluation technique in logic programming [31]. In this model the symbolic computation coincides with the concrete one (which can also be represented as an SLDNF-tree), because in logic programming one is allowed to run programs with input goals which contain free variables. Further refinements of partial evaluation, such as the techniques based on *characteristic trees* [22,30], use notions which are abstractions of SLDNF-trees.

4 Searching for Regularities in Symbolic Computations

In this section we consider the problem of searching for regularities in a symbolic computation model of the program at hand. These regularities may be used for extracting a new program.

It is hard to devise a general notion of regularity which ensures that the derived programs are in all cases more efficient than the initial ones. Thus, different notions of regularity have been considered in the various program transformation techniques. Those notions, however, are not unrelated, and indeed most of them refer to *similarity* relations which hold between nodes of symbolic computation models. In particular, let us consider again the compiling control example of the previous section. In that example we have seen that an efficient program which embodies an enhanced control strategy, can be extracted from the symbolic trace tree when each leaf goal is a variant of an ancestor goal and the corresponding renaming substitution preserves the instantiation of the variables (that is, the superscripts G and F). This correspondence between nodes of the symbolic trace tree is the similarity used in compiling control.

In other symbolic computation models one may find other similarity relations (not necessarily symmetric) which formalize the fact that a configuration (or a set of configurations) of the symbolic computation can be expressed in terms of a previously generated configuration (or set of configurations). For instance, in the case of the m-dag model described in the Fibonacci example, a cut may be considered to be similar to the next cut in a progressive sequence [38], because we can get the function calls in a cut from those of the next cut by substituting an expression for a variable (in our case, $k-1$ for k).

Since we should be able to derive a new program from the symbolic computation of a given initial program, it is important that we find a *finite* representation of the potentially infinite symbolic computation, because as we will see in the next section, the structure of the derived program is closely related to that of the symbolic computation. This explains why several notions of regularity require that one should find a finite set of configurations such that every configuration in the symbolic computation is similar to a configuration in that set.

Now we look at the partial evaluation technique in logic programming and we indicate the particular notions of similarity and regularity which are used there. We will then mention how these concepts are used in other transformation techniques.

Regularities in Partial Evaluation of Logic Programs

Partial evaluation is a well-known program transformation technique which allows us to derive a new program from an old one when part of the input data is known before evaluation. The reader may refer to [12,21,26] for introductions and surveys on this topic.

In the case of logic programming, where partial evaluation is also called *partial deduction*, it is usually assumed that we are given an initial program P and a set A of possibly non-ground atoms, and by partial deduction of P w.r.t.

A, we want to derive a new program P' such that P and P' compute the same answers for every input goal which is an instance of an atom in A.

One of the most popular techniques for partial deduction has been formalized by Lloyd and Shepherdson [31]. In that technique the program P' is obtained by collecting together the clauses, called *resultants*, which are constructed as follows: for each element A_i of A, i) we first construct a finite portion, containing more than one node, of an SLDNF-tree, say T_i, for the program P and the atom A_i, then ii) we consider the non-failing branches of T_i and the goals at their leaves, say $B_{i1}, \ldots, B_{ir}$, and the computed substitutions along these branches, say $\theta_{i1}, \ldots, \theta_{ir}$, and finally, iii) we construct the clauses: $A_i\theta_{i1} \leftarrow B_{i1}, \ldots, A_i\theta_{ir} \leftarrow B_{ir}$.

The SLDNF-trees constructed for partial deduction can be viewed as symbolic computations starting from the atoms in A and representing all SLDNF-trees starting from atoms which are instances of the atoms in A.

If we now assume that: i) every atom in P' is an instance of an atom in A, that is, P' is *A-closed*, and ii) no two atoms in A have a common instance, that is, A is an *independent* set of atoms, then P' is a *correct* partial deduction of P w.r.t. A, in the sense that for every input goal G which is an instance of an atom in A, we have that $P \cup \{\leftarrow G\}$ has a computed answer substitution θ iff $P' \cup \{\leftarrow G\}$ has the computed answer substitution θ, and $P \cup \{\leftarrow G\}$ finitely fails iff $P' \cup \{\leftarrow G\}$ finitely fails [31]. The following example shows that partial deduction can be viewed as a particular case of our general program transformation methodology made out of three steps.

Example 2. [*Partial Deduction of a Parser*] Let us consider the following *Parse* program, adapted from [49, page 381], for parsing words of context free languages.

$$parse(Grammar, [Symb], [Symb|X]\backslash X) \leftarrow terminal(Symb)$$
$$parse(Grammar, [Symb], Word) \leftarrow nonterminal(Symb),$$
$$member(Symb \rightarrow Symbs, Grammar),$$
$$parse(Grammar, Symbs, Word)$$
$$parse(Grammar, [Symb1, Symb2|Symbs], WordX\backslash X) \leftarrow$$
$$parse(Grammar, [Symb1], WordX\backslash Y),$$
$$parse(Grammar, [Symb2|Symbs], Y\backslash X)$$
$$terminal(0) \leftarrow$$
$$terminal(1) \leftarrow$$
$$nonterminal(s) \leftarrow$$
$$nonterminal(u) \leftarrow$$

The first argument of *parse* is a grammar represented as a list of productions of the form $Symb \rightarrow Symbs$, where $Symb$ is a nonterminal symbol and $Symbs$ is a sequence of terminal or nonterminal symbols. The second argument of *parse* is a list representing the sentential form at hand. The third argument is the word W to parse which is represented as a difference-list, that is, $X\backslash Y$ is the difference list representing W iff W concatenated with Y is X. This representation allows for an efficient word decomposition, which is needed in the third clause of *parse*.

Suppose that we want to specialize our parser w.r.t. the grammar

$$\{s \rightarrow 0\ u, \quad u \rightarrow 1, \quad u \rightarrow 0\ u\ u, \quad u \rightarrow 1\ s\}$$

where s is the start symbol. In other words, we want to partially evaluate *Parse* w.r.t. the input goal $parse(\Gamma, [s], X \backslash [\ ])$ where Γ is the term $[s \rightarrow [0, u], u \rightarrow [1],$ $u \rightarrow [0, u, u], \quad u \rightarrow [1, s]]$ representing the given grammar. To this aim, we consider the following independent set A of two atoms:

$$A = \{parse(\Gamma, [s], X \backslash Y),\ parse(\Gamma, [u], X \backslash Y)\}$$

which will allow us to partially evaluate the given program w.r.t. the input goal $parse(\Gamma, [s], X \backslash [\ ])$ because this goal is an instance of the atom $parse(\Gamma, [s], X \backslash Y)$ in that set [31].

We then construct the two finite initial portions T_1 and T_2 of SLDNF-trees (in this case no negation as failure steps are needed, because the program is positive) depicted in Figure 4. In this figure: i) an arc stands for one or more SLDNF-resolution steps, ii) underlined atoms are the ones which are unfolded, iii) when not indicated the substitution corresponding to a successful arc is the identity substitution, iv) × denotes failure, v) □ denotes success, and vi) upgoing arrows relate leaf goals to root goals of which they are instances (these arrows are not arcs of the SLDNF-trees).

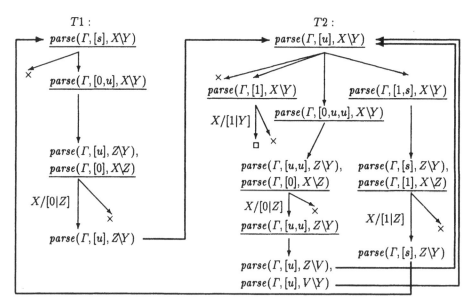

Fig. 4. Two finite portions T_1 and T_2 of SLDNF-trees for the *Parse* program.

The resultants of the non-failing branches of these two SLDNF-trees are the following clauses:

$$parse(\Gamma, [s], [0|Z] \backslash Y) \leftarrow parse(\Gamma, [u], Z \backslash Y)$$
$$parse(\Gamma, [u], [1|Y] \backslash Y) \leftarrow$$

$$parse(\Gamma, [u], [0|Z]\backslash Y) \leftarrow parse(\Gamma, [u], Z\backslash V), parse(\Gamma, [u], V\backslash Y)$$
$$parse(\Gamma, [u], [1|Z]\backslash Y) \leftarrow parse(\Gamma, [s], Z\backslash Y)$$

These resultants form an A-closed set of clauses and therefore they constitute a correct partial deduction of *Parse* w.r.t. A.

Similarly to the compiling control example, the above program may be further improved by introducing, using the *renaming* transformation [21], new predicate names corresponding to the different instances of the predicate *parse*. By doing so (and also by renaming some variables), we get the following final program *PdParse*:

$$pd\_parse(X) \leftarrow parse\_s(X, [\,])$$
$$parse\_s([0|X], Y) \leftarrow parse\_u(X, Y)$$
$$parse\_u([1|X], X) \leftarrow$$
$$parse\_u([0|X], Y) \leftarrow parse\_u(X, Z), parse\_u(Z, Y)$$
$$parse\_u([1|X], Y) \leftarrow parse\_s(X, Y)$$

The correctness results for partial deduction can easily be extended to the case where we consider the above renaming transformation. In this example we have that, for every term w, $Parse \cup \{\leftarrow parse(\Gamma, [s], w\backslash[\,])\}$ has a computed answer substitution θ iff $PdParse \cup \{\leftarrow pd\_parse(w)\}$ has the computed answer substitution θ, and $Parse \cup \{\leftarrow parse(\Gamma, [s], w\backslash[\,])\}$ finitely fails iff $PdParse \cup \{\leftarrow pd\_parse(w)\}$ finitely fails. □

One may notice that the A-closedness property of the program derived by partial deduction from a program P w.r.t. A, is equivalent to the following property of the set of SLDNF-trees constructed for the partial deduction of P w.r.t. A: each atom occurring in a non-failing leaf of an SLDNF-tree in this set of trees is an instance of an atom occurring in a root (not necessarily within the same tree). If a set of SLDNF-trees enjoys this property we will say that it is *closed* (see Figure 4 for an example where this property holds).

The notion of a closed set of SLDNF-trees nicely illustrates the idea of regularity of a symbolic computation. Indeed, that notion is based on the similarity relation whereby a leaf node is similar to a set of root nodes iff every atom in the goal of that leaf is an instance of the atom in a root of the given set. We also have that a closed SLDNF-tree T, that is, a closed set of SLDNF-trees with one tree only, represents an infinite SLDNF-tree where all goals may be expressed in terms (more precisely, are conjunctions of instances) of the finite set of goals occurring in T. Moreover, given a closed set of SLDNF-trees we may derive a program which is equivalent to, and hopefully more efficient than the initial program, by extracting clauses from their non-failing root-to-leaf paths.

Other Notions of Regularity

We have mentioned at the beginning of this section the notions of regularity used in compiling control and in some unfold/fold techniques for functional programs. Now we will briefly discuss some other forms of regularities in symbolic computation models.

One of the earliest transformation techniques which uses concepts analogous to 'similarity' and 'regularity', is Turchin's supercompilation. As already mentioned in Section 1, the symbolic computation model for supercompilation is the directed graph of states and transitions constructed by driving and generalization steps (In Section 6 we will give more details on the generalization operation). In this directed graph a configuration C_j is similar to a previously generated one C_i iff C_j is a *specialization* of C_i, that is, the set of concrete computation states represented by C_j is a subset of that of C_i. The notion of regularity corresponds to that of *self-sufficiency*: a finite graph of states and transitions is said to be self-sufficient when every configuration is either *passive* (that is, an expression made out of basic operators) or similar to a previously generated one.

Related concepts of similarity and regularity are also present in various versions of the supercompilation technique, such as *positive supercompilation* [48].

Also in the unfold/fold technique for the transformation of logic programs, we encounter a similarity notion and a regularity notion. They are related to the construction of unfolding trees [43] which are used for guiding the application of the unfold/fold rules. The similarity notion is the *foldability of a clause* and we say that a clause is foldable when its body (except for some basic predicates) is an instance of the body of an ancestor clause in the tree. The regularity notion is the *foldability of the unfolding tree* and we say that an unfolding tree is foldable when it has a finite upper portion whose leaves are foldable clauses or clauses whose bodies either are made out of basic predicates or contain failures. The reader will realize the very close relationship between the notions of foldable unfolding trees and closed SLDNF-trees we have presented above.

In the generalized partial computation technique the similarity notion between nodes in a GPC-tree is determined by the absence of the so called P-redexes [19]. In particular, in a GPC-tree a node N is similar to an ancestor node M if i) $\lambda x. f(x)$ is the function computed at node M with domain dom_M, ii) $\lambda x. A[f(B[x])]$ is the function computed at node N where $A[\ldots]$ and $B[\ldots]$ are suitable contexts and $B[x]$ ranges over dom_N, and iii) $dom_M \subseteq dom_N$. The regularity notion of a GPC-tree is, as usual, based on the fact that every leaf node is either a basic value or similar to an ancestor node. We cannot go into more details here. However, we want to stress that, in sharp contrast to supercompilation, in generalized partial computation one performs an unfolding step when a node represents a subset of the set of the concrete computation states represented by a previously generated node. The underlying assumption is that with more information on the input data one may get more specialized and hopefully, more efficient programs. We will return on this issue of specialization versus generalization in Section 6.

5 Program Extraction

In this section we consider the third step of the general methodology, that is, the process of extracting a new program from the symbolic computation of the given initial program and also the suitable regularities which have been discovered.

We have already remarked that it is important that the regularities are 'suitable', that is, they indeed allow for program extraction. We are not interested here in the formalization of this suitability notion. It will be enough to consider the particular case, which is the most frequent in practice, where the symbolic computation is described by means of a directed graph whose arcs correspond to concrete computation steps. There are basically two approaches to program extraction in this case: either the *direct extraction* or the *extraction via transformation rules*.

An example of the first approach can be taken from partial deduction, where there is a simple way of deriving the clauses of the final program directly from the closed set of SLDNF-trees which have been constructed by applying, for instance, the procedure described in [21]. Indeed, every path from the root to a non-failing leaf in those trees, generates a clause of the program to be extracted. Also in generalized partial computation we directly extract programs from the corresponding GPC-trees by looking at their paths, but we may also allow for the use of some recursion removal techniques [19].

An example of program extraction via transformation rules may be given using the transformation of the Fibonacci program presented in Section 2. We start from the known regularity, that is, the existence of a progressive sequence of cuts, and we perform the extraction by exploiting the properties of that sequence as follows: i) we first introduce by the definition rule the new function $t(n)$ which tuples together the function calls in a generic cut, ii) we apply the unfolding rule and the where-abstraction rule to express the initial function call in terms of the calls in the first cut whereby extracting Equation 4, that is, $fib(n + 2) = u + v$ where $\langle u, v \rangle = t(n)$, iii) by applying the unfolding rule we compute the value of the function calls in the cut for which there is no need to compute the calls of their son nodes whereby extracting Equation 5, that is, $t(0) = \langle 1, 1 \rangle$, and finally, iv) we apply the unfolding, where-abstraction, and folding rules to compute the values of the function calls in a cut from those in the next cut whereby extracting Equation 6, that is, $t(n + 1) = \langle u + v, u \rangle$ where $\langle u, v \rangle = t(n)$.

This program extraction shows that for the *fib* function the existence of a progressive sequence of cuts is a suitable regularity, and indeed the various properties of that sequence suggest the actions to be performed during the extraction itself.

For the extraction of the new program of the *fib* function we can also use the direct approach, but it is necessary to construct a symbolic computation model which is more informative than the one based on the m-dags used in Section 2. This more informative model is based on the construction of a set of trees which can be obtained by an extension of the positive supercompilation technique described in [47]. The extension is motivated by the fact that in positive supercompilation it is not possible to directly exploit the interactions among different function calls because they belong to different branches of the process trees. We will not give here the formal rules for the construction of this more informative model of computation. It will be enough to say that we follow closely the positive supercompilation and partial deduction techniques. There are, however, some differences. In particular, the differences w.r.t. positive supercompilation include the rules that: i) when folding can be performed we do not expand the process tree and we initialize a new tree, instead, and ii) when constructing trees we perform together with unfolding and lemma application steps, also where-abstraction steps and tupling steps. Tupling consists in the introduction of new functions defined in terms of tuples of some old functions. These tuples of functions are those which allow us to take advantage of the interaction among different function calls. Differences w.r.t. partial deduction include: i) a new notion of the similarity relation among nodes: a node N_1 with label $expr_1$ is similar to a node N_2 with label $C[expr_2]$ iff the expressions $expr_1$ and $expr_2$ are variants of each other, and $C[\ldots]$ is a context made out of basic functions only, and ii) a new notion of closedness: a set of trees is said to be closed iff every leaf of every tree has a similar root (according to the new notion we have now introduced).

A possible criterium for terminating the construction of a tree is as follows: a node of a tree is a leaf if either i) it cannot be subject to any unfolding or ii) it is similar to a root or iii) it has been produced by a tupling step. In this last case we initialize a new tree whose root is the tuple which has been introduced by the tupling step.

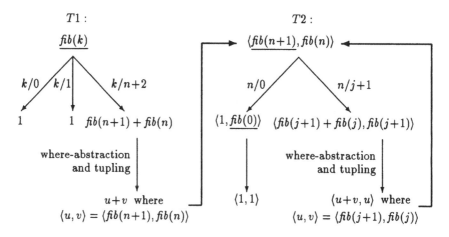

Fig. 5. Two trees which represent a symbolic computation of the *fib* function. Underlined expressions are the unfolded ones. Leaves are related to their similar roots by upgoing arrows. Those arcs are *not* arcs of the trees.

In Figure 5 we have depicted a set of trees which represent the symbolic computation of the *fib* function from which we can get the new program for *fib* by direct extraction. Given the trees of Figure 5 the extraction of the new program is performed as follows. Analogously to what we have seen in the previous section for partial deduction, we first give a new name to the new roots we have introduced ($\langle fib(n+1), fib(n) \rangle$ only in our case). This operation in the unfold/fold technique corresponds to the definition of 'eureka predicates' [10], and in the partial deduction technique corresponds to renaming [21]. We then perform some folding steps corresponding to the nodes which have similar roots, and we finally extract an equation for each root-to-leaf path in the trees obtained after folding, by taking into account also the substitutions along the paths.

6 Control Issues

The various steps of the general methodology for program transformation and in particular, the symbolic computation process must be controlled in some way if one wants to derive very efficient programs. Now we briefly consider these control issues which can be classified into two different categories: *local* and *global* control issues.

6.1 Local Control Issues

When the symbolic computation is performed via unfolding steps (or driving), we may get into *non-deterministic* situations, whereby the symbolic computation steps may allow for more than one successor expression (or configuration). For instance, during the symbolic execution of a logic program often we may choose in more than one way the atom to unfold, and analogously, during the symbolic execution of a functional program often there is a choice of the expression to be evaluated in the following execution step. Different choices may drastically affect the following step of the general methodology, that is, the search for suitable regularities. These choices may be subject to constraints, like for instance, the fact that the symbolic computation should preserve the semantics of the concrete computations it represents. For example, in functional programs if we consider the call-by-value semantics, the innermost function calls should be evaluated before the outermost ones.

Many techniques for controlling unfolding and driving have been proposed in the various models of symbolic computations (see for instance, [11,43,55] and the preceding compiling control example). In particular, several authors have studied the problem of when to stop unfolding, and for instance, one may decide to do so when unfolding is no longer deterministic [21] or when the expression in the node at hand can be 'embedded' in the expression in one of its ancestors [47]. A general technique for ensuring the termination of the unfolding process is described in [8].

During the construction of a symbolic computation model, in order to derive programs with high performances it is often important, in practice, to perform *lemma application* steps, that is, to substitute subexpressions by equivalent new subexpressions. The reader familiar with program derivation techniques knows that these lemma applications, also called *law applications* in functional programming or *goal replacements* in logic programming, may allow for a great improvement of program performances which is otherwise impossible (see [26,56] for some upper bounds on the program speedups which can be obtained without the use of lemmas). Typical lemmas one wishes to apply are: associativity of concatenation, existence of a neutral element for *plus* and *times*, etc. Actually, these lemmas should preserve equivalence of the whole expressions where the substitutions take place, and therefore, they should determine congruences, not simply equivalences.

The control issue related to these lemma applications concerns the problem that while generating the symbolic computation model, one has to decide which lemma should be applied and where it should be applied. This is an important issue which does not have a general solution, because unfortunately, there is no theory by which in all cases we may guide the search and the application of lemmas so that a suitable regularity will eventually be discovered.

The ability to perform lemma application steps makes program transformation very closely related to theorem proving, and indeed some people have looked at techniques which allow for an easy integration of the two areas, by for instance, making derivations and proofs in the same transformational style. Among other techniques we want to mention the *unfold/fold proof method*, which can be used both for program transformation à la Burstall-Darlington and for equivalence proofs. This unfold/fold method can be traced back to Scott (see [10]) and Kott [28] in the case of functional programs, and in the case of logic programs it has been recently presented in [45]. Also Turchin in [52, page 293] explicitly refers to the interaction of theorem proving and program transformation. He advocates the use of theorem provers for the discovery of 'clever properties' when deriving new configurations from old configurations, and he shows how one can, in principle, use supercompilation for proving theorems (see also [51]). In [19] the interaction between theorem proving and program derivation is used for generalized partial computation which is an enhanced partial evaluation technique.

Local control issues also include the decision of when and where to apply the composition strategy and the tupling strategy during program transformation (although for some aspects one may also consider that these strategies do refer to global control issues). We consider the composition strategy in the next section when presenting the deforestation technique, while we have already seen the tupling strategy in action in the *fib* example in the previous section. The composition strategy may generate efficient programs because it may avoid the construction of unnecessary intermediate data structures, while the tupling strategy may avoid repeated subcomputations because it groups together function calls which share the same variables.

6.2   Global Control Issues

In this category of control issues we consider those which are related to the problem of generating a *finite* symbolic computation model with suitable regularities.

We first consider the *generalization* issue, whereby instead of generating the computation model for the function (or predicate) at hand, we generate the model for a generalization of that function (or predicate). The advantage of this technique is that, for the notions of similarity one uses in practice, the generalized function generates configurations which are similar to already constructed ones more often than the non generalized function. Thus, it may be the case that functions with infinite computation models have generalizations with finite models. This situation is analogous to the one often encountered in theorem proving, whereby if a given lemma cannot be proved by induction, one may look for a suitable generalization with the hope of successfully performing an inductive proof of the generalized lemma. Indeed, the new variables introduced by generalization may allow new matches among expressions, and thus, one may perform the proof of the generalized lemma by applying the stronger inductive hypothesis. An application of the generalization technique occurred, in particular, in the partial deduction of the *Parse* program (see Section 4), where the atom $parse(\Gamma, [s], X \backslash [\,])$ has been generalized to $parse(\Gamma, [s], X \backslash Y)$.

In program transformation, generalization is often motivated by the need for folding [14], that is, the need of considering an expression as an instance of another. Thus, generalization is realized by promoting some subexpressions to variables, and usually one considers the most specific common generalization of the two expressions at hand. Sometimes, however, one has to allow for *higher order generalizations* (also called *lambda abstractions* [42]), by which an expression, say $C[e]$, is replaced by the function application $(\lambda x.C[x])e$ where the subexpression e has been promoted to the bound variable x. Here is a simple example of program derivation using higher order generalization.

Example 3. [*Palindrome*] The following program tests whether or not a given list l is a palindrome:

1. $palin(l) = eqlist(l, rev(l))$
2. $eqlist([\,], l) = null(l)$
3. $eqlist(a : l_1, l) = (a = hd(l))$ *and* $eqlist(l_1, tl(l))$
4. $rev([\,]) = [\,]$
5. $rev(a : l) = rev(l) :: [a]$

where : and :: stand for the operators *cons* and *append*, respectively, $null(l) =$ *true* iff $l = [\,]$, and hd and tl are the *head* and *tail* selectors. This program visits the given list twice, a first time for its reversal (using rev) and a second time for testing equality (using $eqlist$). We look for an improved program which does not make these two visits. By unfolding we get:

6. $palin([\,]) = $ *true*
7. $palin(a : l) = (a = hd(rev(a : l)))$ *and* $eqlist(l, tl(rev(a : l)))$

When trying to fold the r.h.s. of Equation 7 using Equation 1 we have a mismatch between the two expressions $eqlist(l, rev(l))$ and $eqlist(l, tl(rev(a : l)))$. We apply higher order generalization to Equation 7 and we have:

8. $palin(a : l) = eqlist(a : l, rev(a : l)) = \{\text{higher order generalization}\} =$
   $= (\lambda x. eqlist(a : l, x)) \; rev(a : l)$

where the mismatching subexpression has been promoted to the bound variable x. Now, both $\lambda x. eqlist(a : l, x)$ and $rev(a : l)$ visit the same data structure $a : l$. We perform a tupling step as suggested by the tupling strategy, and we define:

9. $Q(l) = \langle \lambda x.\, eqlist(l, x), rev(l) \rangle$

whose recursive equations are as follows:

10. $Q([\,]) = \langle \lambda x.\, eqlist([\,], x), rev([\,]) \rangle = \{unfolding\} = \langle \lambda x.\, null(x), [\,] \rangle$

11. $Q(a : l) = \langle \lambda x.\, eqlist(a : l, x), rev(a : l) \rangle = \{unfolding\} =$
$= \langle \lambda x.\, (a = hd(x))\ and\ eqlist(l, tl(x)), rev(l) :: [a]) \rangle = \{folding\} =$
$= \langle \lambda x.\, (a = hd(x))\ and\ u(tl(x)), v :: [a]) \rangle$ where $\langle u, v \rangle = Q(l)$

Now we can fold Equation 1 using Equation 9 and we get:

12. $palin(l) = u(v)$ where $\langle u, v \rangle = Q(l)$

The final program made out of Equations 12, 10, and 11, visits the input list only once in the sense that $Q(a : l)$ is defined in terms of $Q(l)$ only.   □

However, there may be some drawbacks in applying generalization steps and one should use generalization with parsimony. Indeed, when an expression is generalized to a variable, we loose information about the structure of the generalized expression and that loss may prevent some further improvements. Consider, for instance, Equation 7 of Example 3. The most specific common generalization of the two mismatching expressions in Equation 7 and Equation 1 which did not allow us to perform a folding step, leads to the introduction of the new function d defined as follows: $d(l_1, l_2) = eqlist(l_1, l_2)$. But, unfortunately, in this definition we have now lost the important information that the second argument of d is the reversal of the first argument, while we will use the function d only for arguments satisfying this constraint. Obviously, for computing the function d we cannot hope for a better program than the one provided by Equations 2 and 3, and thus, by using d there is no hope of deriving an efficient program for $palin$. This example also shows the superiority of the higher order generalization over the familiar generalization from expressions to variables. Indeed, as the reader may verify, if one introduces the function

9'. $Q'(l, x) = \langle eqlist(l, x), rev(l) \rangle$

then the final program one derives, visits the input list twice in the call-by-value mode of evaluation.

Other generalizations may require some form of 'reflection' on the symbolic computation constructed so far. For instance, in the supercompilation approach during the construction of the symbolic computation model, the generalization steps can be suggested by an analysis of the part of the computation model already constructed. This analysis makes use of so called *walk grammars* and *meta-transition systems* to reason about *computation histories* in a given model [54]. The analysis may be used, in particular, for avoiding the risk of generalizing 'too early' (see, for instance, [53]). Related works are the ones concerned with program improvement based on the analysis of computation histories for which the reader may refer to [1] where a recursion removal technique is described.

Among other forms of reflection on symbolic computations, let us now mention the one related to the *introduction of new operators*. This technique consists in the promotion of a sequence of computations to an independent procedure.

For instance, as shown in the following example, a sequence of additions can be promoted to a single multiplication.

Example 4. [*Introducing New Operators*] Let us consider the Fibonacci program of Section 2 and let us consider the *transformation tree* model [25]. From Equation 3 we get:

7. $fib(k) = fib(k-1) + fib(k-2) = \{\text{unfolding}\} =$
   $= fib(k-2) + fib(k-3) + fib(k-2) = \{\text{introducing multiplication}\} =$
   $= 2\ fib(k-2) + fib(k-3) = \{\text{unfolding}\} =$
   $= 3\ fib(k-3) + 2\ fib(k-4) = \ldots$

Let us now assume that we have discovered the following regularity valid for any $n, k \geq 0$:

8. $fib(k + n + 2) = fib(n + 1)\ fib(k + 1) + fib(n)\ fib(k)$

This regularity comes from the observation, which may be hard to make in a mechanical way, that when constructing the transformation tree for $fib(k)$, the multiplicative constants in the two summands are values of the *fib* function itself (see also [39]). By the unfold/fold technique we are now able to derive the program made out of the following equations, together with Equations 1 and 2 [39]:

9. $fib(2k + 2) = fib(k + 1)^2 + fib(k)^2$
10. $fib(2k + 3) = fib(k + 1)\ fib(k + 2) + fib(k)\ fib(k + 1) = \{\text{unfolding}\} =$
    $= fib(k + 1)\ (fib(k + 1) + fib(k)) + fib(k)\ fib(k + 1)$

and they hold for any $k \geq 0$. Now we may discover one more regularity, namely, the fact that in the m-dag of this last program there is a progressive sequence of cuts, each of them being made out of two consecutive calls of *fib*. Thus, we apply the tupling strategy and we introduce the following function, defined for any $k \geq 0$:

11. $p(k) = \langle fib(k + 1), fib(k) \rangle$

By applying the unfold/fold technique we can then derive the explicit definition of the function $p(k)$ and the following final program:

1. $fib(0) = 1$
2. $fib(1) = 1$
12. $fib(k + 2) = a + b$ where $\langle a, b \rangle = p(k)$
13. $p(0) = \langle 1, 1 \rangle$
14. $p(1) = \langle 2, 1 \rangle$
15. $p(2k + 2) = \langle a^2 + 2ab, a^2 + b^2 \rangle$ where $\langle a, b \rangle = p(k)$
16. $p(2k + 3) = \langle a^2 + (a + b)^2, a^2 + 2ab \rangle$ where $\langle a, b \rangle = p(k)$

where Equations 12, 15, and 16 hold for any $k \geq 0$. This program is very efficient and takes only $O(\log(n))$ arithmetic operations for computing $fib(n)$ (see also [39]). $\square$

In the partial evaluation field, researchers have studied a method for improving program efficiency which we may classify under the global control issues. This method, called *polyvariant specialization* [9], specializes programs, instead of generalizing them. Indeed, it allows for the generation of various different versions of the same program with the objective of achieving higher performances. The improvement of performances comes from the fact that having more information about the inputs to the program (or function call) one can make some more simplifications at compile time. This method can be viewed as the opposite to generalization, by which one constructs a general program to compute several distinct, but similar functions. Unfortunately, there is no general theory which for any given program tells us when it is better to specialize or to generalize.

There is an inherent limitation in looking for an optimal strategy of when and where to perform specialization and/or generalization steps. Indeed, one cannot hope to construct a universal technique for finding a suitable regularity whenever there is one, which allows us to improve any given program, because the equivalence of two functions can be expressed as a regularity of their symbolic computation models, and yet equivalence of functions is undecidable. However, in practice, regularities which are useful for program transformation, are often decidable properties, and they can also be found by means of efficient algorithms.

7   Relating the Three Step Program Transformation Methodology to Program Specialization, Deforestation, and Finite Differencing

The three steps of the general program transformation methodology we have presented in the previous sections do not always refer to a definite sequence of actions performed when applying a particular program transformation technique. For supercompilation, unfold/fold transformation, generalized partial computation, compiling control, and partial deduction, one may easily identify those three steps of the methododlogy. However, for some other techniques, like partial evaluation of functional and imperative programs, program specialization, mixed-computation [15], or deforestation [55], it is not always easy to do the same. Nevertheless, we think that the concepts of symbolic computation, search for regularities, and extraction of final programs, are to some extent present in those techniques as well.

To see this, we would like to report the following phrases taken from [26, pages 68–69]:

"Our main thesis is that program specialization can be done in three steps.

1. Given the value of part of the program's input, obtain a description of all computational states reachable when running the program on all possible input values.

2. Redefine the program's control by incorporating parts of the data state into the control state, yielding perhaps several specialized versions of each of the program's control points (0, 1, or more; hence the term *polyvariant* specialization).

3. The resulting program usually contains many trivial transitions. Optimize it by traditional techniques, yielding the specialized (or *residual*) program."

This description of the three steps which underline most program specialization techniques, including partial evaluation and mixed computation, matches quite closely the three steps of the methodology we have presented in this paper.

The first step of the program specialization methodology corresponds to our first two steps, that is, the generation of a symbolic computation process and the search for regularities of this symbolic computation. More precisely, as we have shown in Section 3, symbolic computation can be used to 'obtain the description of all computational states reachable when running the program on all possible input values'. By finding suitable regularities we may make sure that this description is *finite*.

In practice, however, many specialization techniques use symbolic computation models based on abstract interpretation which, unlike the models considered in this paper, cannot always be described in terms of an unfolding process. Among these abstract interpretation-based techniques we would like to mention the techniques for *binding time analysis* [27,34] and the *regular approximation* techniques for approximating the least Herbrand model of a logic program [23].

The second and third steps of the program specialization methodology correspond to what we have called here 'extraction of the new program'. In this paper we have only pointed out the derivation techniques which substantially change the program's control and we have not given much attention to various post-processing techniques (see, for instance, the renaming techniques in the compiling control example and in the partial deduction example presented in the previous sections). These post-processing techniques can be considered to be part of Step 3 of program specialization.

The reader may notice that program specialization is a particular instance of the general program methodology we presented in this paper, because it is idempotent [54], in the sense that when specializing a program which has been already specialized, we get the same program we derived after the first specialization. Other transformation methods, such as supercompilation and rule-based program transformation are not idempotent. This fact can be illustrated by Example 4 where after deriving the program made out of Equations 1, 2, 9, and 10, by discovering a new regularity we were able to derive a new and more efficient program.

Some elements of the general methodology based on symbolic computation, search for regularities, and extraction of final programs are also present in the deforestation technique.

Deforestation is designed to eliminate intermediate data structures from functional programs by introducing new function definitions which are equivalent to the composition of already available functions. In this sense deforestation can be viewed as an instance of the *composition strategy* (also called *fusion*) introduced in the field of unfold/fold transformation [10,18] and it is also closely related to Scherlis' *internal specialization* [46] and supercompilation [48].

Deforestation works via generating, by an unfolding process, from an initial term containing nested function calls other (possibly infinitely many) terms. Although deforestation does not explicitly construct any symbolic computation model, the unfolding steps it requires can be viewed as a symbolic computation. The idea of finding regularities by identifying similar configurations is also present. In particular, the deforestation algorithm terminates only if a finite number of terms modulo variants, is generated during unfolding. If this is the case then it is possible to avoid intermediate data structures by introducing a finite number of new function definitions which correspond to (a subset of) the terms generated by unfolding.

Finally, among other techniques for program derivation we want to consider also *finite differencing* [35,36]. The revisitation of this technique as an instance of our general methodology is not very straightforward. However, the three steps of finite differencing, which are:

> "i) syntactic recognition of computational bottlenecks appearing within a program P, ii) choosing invariants whose maintenance inside P allows these bottlenecks to be removed, and iii) scheduling how collections of invariants can be maintained in P" [35, page 40]

correspond, respectively, to: i) the symbolic computation model which allows for the detection of the bottlenecks, ii) the search for regularities which are the invariants to be maintained, and iii) the program extraction by which new sequences of operations are generated with the objective of maintaining those invariants. The reader may find more information about finite differencing in the cited papers.

8 Correspondences Among Some Program Transformation Techniques

We will not present in details the formal relationships and correspondences among the many program transformation techniques mentioned in this paper, because as we already said, these correspondences can be considered as 'common knowledge' of the people working in the field. Let us simply mention among some other similar results, the following ones: i) the unfold/fold view of the mixed computation technique described in [16], ii) the equivalence of driving in supercompilation and partial deduction shown in [25] for a particular class of programs, and iii) the straightforward way of using the unfold/fold transformation technique to simulate partial deduction [44]. We now present this simulation in a simple example.

Example 5. Suppose we want to partially evaluate the following program:

$$p([\,],Y) \leftarrow$$
$$p([H|T],Y) \leftarrow q(T,Y)$$
$$q(T,Y) \leftarrow Y = b$$

$$q(T, Y) \leftarrow p(T, Y)$$

with respect to the set $\{p(X, a)\}$. We follow the partial deduction technique as proposed in [31] and we get the initial portion of the SLDNF-tree $T1$ depicted in Figure 6. By considering the non-failing branches of that tree and taking the corresponding resultants, we get the program $P1$:

$$p([\,], a) \leftarrow$$
$$p([H|T], a) \leftarrow p(T, a)$$

which is a correct partial deduction because the requirements for independence and closedness are satisfied. Indeed, i) independence is a trivial consequence of the fact that in the set $\{p(X, a)\}$ there is one atom only, and ii) closedness is a consequence of the fact that the atoms $p([\,], a)$, $p([H|T], a)$, and $p(T, a)$ are all instances of $p(X, a)$.

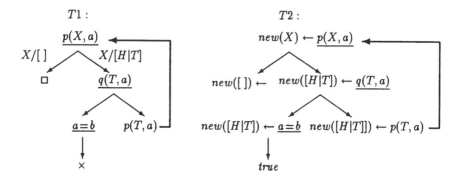

Fig. 6. An SLDNF-tree for partial deduction ($T1$) and the corresponding unfolding tree ($T2$). Underlined goals are the unfolded ones. Upgoing arrows relate similar nodes.

Using the unfold/fold method we first introduce a clause whose body is made out of the goal $p(X, a)$ and whose head has a fresh predicate symbol, say $newp$. The arguments of the head are the variables occurring in the body. Thus, we introduce the clause:

$$newp(X) \leftarrow p(X, a)$$

Then, by using the unfold/fold method, we derive a program which can be used for evaluating queries of the form: $\leftarrow newp(X)$, instead of $\leftarrow p(X, a)$. The derivation process takes the form of the unfolding tree $T2$ depicted in Figure 6. From that tree we can extract the following program $P2$ by performing, as we have indicated in Section 5, a final folding step (whereby the body $p(T, a)$ is replaced by $newp(T)$):

$$newp([\,]) \leftarrow$$
$$newp([H|T]) \leftarrow newp(T)$$

which has performances similar (actually, higher, because $newp$ has one argument only) to those of $P1$. □

The reader should notice the perfect correspondence between partial deduction and the unfold/fold technique we have now illustrated. In particular, we want to stress that the condition which allowed us to perform the final folding step during program extraction, that is, the fact that $p(T, a)$ is an instance of the body of the clause $newp(X) \leftarrow p(X, a)$, is exactly the same condition, that is, closedness, which ensures the correctness of the partial deduction process [31].

9 Conclusions

We have presented a general methodology for the derivation of programs which underlines some familiar program transformation techniques like, for instance, partial evaluation, supercompilation, rule-based program derivation, program specialization, and compiling control. This methodology can often be mechanized, although the extent to which this mechanization is possible, very much depends on the technique under consideration.

This methodology is made out of three steps. They are: i) the construction of the symbolic computation model, ii) the search for regularities in that model, and iii) the extraction of the new program. Through the presentation of these steps and some examples, we have illustrated in an informal way the correspondences among the above-mentioned program transformation techniques. They are all based on the construction of some sort of finite directed graphs whose arcs represent either the steps of the computations or the similarity relations among computation states (or configurations). We have also briefly considered the so called control issue. It is related to the problem of guiding the actions to be performed during the three steps of the methodology, and in particular we have looked at various forms of the generalization strategy.

In this paper we have stressed the similarities among the various techniques for program transformation. There are, however, also many differences among them. They are due, besides other reasons, to the different languages and the different semantics which are considered, and to the degree of automation which is required for their implementation. For instance, in the case of partial evaluation one strives for a completely automated process, whereas in supercompilation and rule-based program derivation, one also allows for interactive theorem proving capabilities.

Acknowledgements

We have profited from many conversations with several people over the past years. In particular, we would like to mention R. S. Bird, M. Bruynooghe, R. M. Burstall, W.-N. Chin, J. Darlington, D. De Schreye, A. P. Ershov, M. S. Feather, Y. Futamura, J. Gallagher, R. Glück, N. D. Jones, T. Mogensen, B. Möller, H. Partsch, R. Paige, P. Pepper, W. L. Scherlis, V. Turchin, P. Wadler, and our colleagues of the IFIP W.G. 2.1, the Italian Progetto Finalizzato Sistemi Informatici e Calcolo Parallelo, and Compulog II Esprit Project. We thank S. Renault and M. H. Sørensen for comments on a draft of this paper.

References

1. J. Arsac and Y. Kodratoff. Some techniques for recursion removal from recursive functions. *ACM Transactions on Programming Languages and Systems*, 4(2):295–322, 1982.

2. R. Barbuti, R. Giacobazzi, and G. Levi. A general framework for semantics-based bottom-up abstract interpretation of logic programs. *ACM Transactions on Programming Languages and Systems*, 15(1):133–181, 1993.

3. R. S. Bird. Tabulation techniques for recursive programs. *ACM Computing Surveys*, 12(4):403–418, 1980.

4. R. S. Bird. The promotion and accumulation strategies in transformational programming. *ACM Toplas*, 6(4):487–504, 1984.

5. D. Bjørner, A. P. Ershov, and N. D. Jones, editors. *Partial Evaluation and Mixed Computation*. North-Holland, 1988. IFIP TC2 Workshop on Partial and Mixed Computation, Gammel Avernæs, Denmark, 1987.

6. M. Bruynooghe and D. Boulanger. Abstract interpretation for (constraint) logic programming. In B. Mayoh, E. Tyugu, and J. Penjam, editors, *Constraint Programming*, NATO ASI Series F, Vol. 131, pages 228–260. Springer-Verlag, 1994.

7. M. Bruynooghe, D. De Schreye, and B. Krekels. Compiling control. *Journal of Logic Programming*, 6:135–162, 1989.

8. M. Bruynooghe, D. De Schreye, and B. Martens. A general criterion for avoiding infinite unfolding during partial deduction of logic programs. *New Generation Computing*, 11:47–79, 1992.

9. M. A. Bulyonkov. Polyvariant mixed computation for analyzer programs. *Acta Informatica*, 21:473–484, 1984.

10. R. M. Burstall and J. Darlington. A transformation system for developing recursive programs. *Journal of the ACM*, 24(1):44–67, January 1977.

11. W.-N. Chin. Safe fusion of functional expressions. In *Proceedings of ACM SIGPLAN Symposium on Lisp and Functional Programming, San Francisco, Calif., U.S.A.*, pages 11–20. ACM Press, 1992.

12. C. Consel and O. Danvy. Tutorial notes on partial evaluation. In *Proceedings 20th ACM SIGPLAN-SIGACT Symposium on Princples of Programming Languages (POPL '93)*, pages 493–501. ACM Press, 1993.

13. P. Cousot and R. Cousot. Abstract interpretation: A unified lattice model for static analysis of programs by construction of approximation of fixpoints. In *Proceedings 4th ACM-SIGPLAN Symposium on Princples of Programming Languages (POPL '77)*, pages 238–252. ACM Press, 1977.

14. J. Darlington. An experimental program transformation system. *Artificial Intelligence*, 16:1–46, 1981.

15. A. P. Ershov. On the partial computation principle. *Information Processing Letters*, 6(2):38–41, 1977.

16. A. P. Ershov. Mixed computation: Potential applications and problems for study. *Theoretical Computer Science*, 18(1):41–67, 1982.

17. A.P. Ershov, D. Bjørner, Y. Futamura, K. Furukawa, A. Haraldson, and W. Scherlis, editors. *Special Issue of New Generation Computing: Workshop on Partial Evaluation and Mixed Computation*, volume 6, Nos. 2&3. Ohmsha Ltd. and Springer-Verlag, 1988.

18. M. S. Feather. A survey and classification of some program transformation techniques. In L. G. L. T. Meertens, editor, *Proceedings IFIP TC2 Working Conference*

on Program Specification and Transformation, Bad Tölz, Germany, pages 165–195. North-Holland, 1987.

19. Y. Futamura, K. Nogi, and A. Takano. Essence of generalized partial computation. *Theoretical Computer Science*, 90:61–79, 1991.

20. J. P. Gallagher. Transforming programs by specializing interpreters. In *Proceedings Seventh European Conference on Artificial Intelligence, ECAI '86*, pages 109–122, 1986.

21. J. P. Gallagher. Tutorial on specialization of logic programs. In *Proceedings of ACM SIGPLAN Symposium on Partial Evaluation and Semantics Based Program Manipulation, PEPM '93, Copenhagen, Denmark*, pages 88–98. ACM Press, 1993.

22. J. P. Gallagher and M. Bruynooghe. The derivation of an algorithm for program specialisation. *New Generation Computing*, 6(2):305–333, 1991.

23. J. P. Gallagher and D.A. de Waal. Fast and precise regular approximation of logic programs and their uses. In *Proceedings of the 11th International Conference on Logic Programming, ICLP'94*, pages 599–613. MIT Press, 1994.

24. R. Glück. On the mechanics of metasystem hierarchies in program transformation. In M. Proietti, editor, *Proceedings of LOPSTR '95, Utrecht, The Netherlands*, Lecture Notes in Computer Science 1048, pages 234–251. Springer-Verlag, 1996.

25. R. Glück and M. H. Sørensen. Partial deduction and driving are equivalent. In M. Hermenegildo and J. Penjam, editors, *International Symposium on Programming Language Implementation and Logic Programming, PLILP '94*, Lecture Notes in Computer Science 844, pages 165–181. Springer-Verlag, 1994.

26. N. D. Jones, C. K. Gomard, and P. Sestoft. *Partial Evaluation and Automatic Program Generation*. Prentice Hall, 1993.

27. N. D. Jones, P. Sestoft, and H. Søndergaard. Mix: A self-applicable partial evaluator for experiments in compiler generation. *LISP and Symbolic Computation*, 2(1):9–50, 1989.

28. L. Kott. The McCarthy's induction principle: 'oldy' but 'goody'. *Calcolo*, 19(1):59–69, 1982.

29. R. A. Kowalski. Algorithm = Logic + Control. *Communications of the ACM*, 22(7):424–436, 1979.

30. M. Leuschel. Ecological partial deduction: Preserving characteristic trees without constraints. In *Proceedings of LOPSTR '95, Utrecht, The Netherlands*, Lecture Notes in Computer Science, pages 1–16. Springer-Verlag, 1996.

31. J. W. Lloyd and J. C. Shepherdson. Partial evaluation in logic programming. *Journal of Logic Programming*, 11:217–242, 1991.

32. K. Marriott, H. Søndergaard, and N. D. Jones. Denotational abstract interpretation of logic programs. *ACM Transactions on Programming Languages and Systems*, 16(1):35–101, 1994.

33. L. Naish. *Negation and Control in Prolog*. Lecture Notes in Computer Science 238. Springer-Verlag, 1985.

34. H. R. Nielson and F. Nielson. Automatic binding time analysis for a typed λ-calculus. In *Proceedings of the ACM Symposium on Principles of Programming Languages*, pages 98–106, 1988.

35. R. Paige. Symbolic finite differencing - Part I. In N. D. Jones, editor, *Third European Symposium on Programming, ESOP '90*, Lecture Notes in Computer Science 432, pages 36–56. Springer-Verlag, 1990.

36. R. Paige and S. Koenig. Finite differencing of computable expressions. *ACM Transactions on Programming Languages and Systems*, 4(3):402–454, 1982.

37. R. Paige, J. Reif, and R. Wachter, editors. *Parallel Algorithm Derivation and Program Transformation, Proc. Workshop at Courant Institute of Mathematical Sciences, New York, USA, 1991*. Kluwer Academic Publishers, 1993.

38. A. Pettorossi. A powerful strategy for deriving efficient programs by transformation. In *ACM Symposium on Lisp and Functional Programming*, pages 273–281. ACM Press, 1984.

39. A. Pettorossi and R. M. Burstall. Deriving very efficient algorithms for evaluating linear recurrence relations using the program transformation technique. *Acta Informatica*, 18:181–206, 1982.

40. A. Pettorossi and M. Proietti. Rules and strategies for program transformation. In B. Möller, H. Partsch, and S. Schuman, editors, *Formal Program Development, IFIP TC2/W.G. 2.1 State-of-the-Art Report*, Lecture Notes in Computer Science 755, pages 263–304. Springer-Verlag, 1993.

41. A. Pettorossi and M. Proietti. Transformation of logic programs: Foundations and techniques. *Journal of Logic Programming*, 19,20:261–320, 1994.

42. A. Pettorossi and A. Skowron. The lambda abstraction strategy for program derivation. *Fundamenta Informaticae*, XII(4):541–561, 1989.

43. M. Proietti and A. Pettorossi. Synthesis of eureka predicates for developing logic programs. In N. D. Jones, editor, *Third European Symposium on Programming, ESOP '90*, Lecture Notes in Computer Science 432, pages 306–325. Springer-Verlag, 1990.

44. M. Proietti and A. Pettorossi. The loop absorption and the generalization strategies for the development of logic programs and partial deduction. *Journal of Logic Programming*, 16(1–2):123–161, 1993.

45. M. Proietti and A. Pettorossi. Synthesis of programs from unfold/fold proofs. In Y. Deville, editor, *Logic Program Synthesis and Transformation, Proceedings of LOPSTR '93, Louvain-la-Neuve, Belgium*, Workshops in Computing, pages 141–158. Springer-Verlag, 1994.

46. W. L. Scherlis. Program improvement by internal specialization. In *Proc. 8th ACM Symposium on Principles of Programming Languages, Williamsburgh, Va*, pages 41–49. ACM Press, 1981.

47. M. H. Sørensen and R. Glück. An algorithm of generalization in positive supercompilation. In J. W. Lloyd, editor, *Proceedings of the 1995 International Logic Programming Symposium (ILPS '95)*, pages 465–479. MIT Press, 1995.

48. M. H. Sørensen, R. Glück, and N. D. Jones. Towards unifying partial evaluation, deforestation, supercompilation, and GPC. In D. Sannella, editor, *Fifth European Symposium on Programming Languages and Systems, ESOP '94*, Lecture Notes in Computer Science 788, pages 485–500. Springer-Verlag, 1994.

49. L. S. Sterling and E. Shapiro. *The Art of Prolog*. The MIT Press, Cambridge, Massachusetts, 1994. Second Edition.

50. H. Tamaki and T. Sato. Unfold/fold transformation of logic programs. In S.-Å. Tärnlund, editor, *Proceedings Second International Conference on Logic Programming, Uppsala, Sweden*, pages 127–138. Uppsala University, 1984.

51. V. F. Turchin. The use of metasystem transition in theorem proving and program optimization. In *Proceedings of 7th Colloquium on Automata, Languages and Programming*, Lecture Notes in Computer Science 85, pages 645–657. Springer-Verlag, 1980.

52. V. F. Turchin. The concept of a supercompiler. *ACM TOPLAS*, 8(3):292–325, 1986.

53. V. F. Turchin. The algorithm of generalization in the supercompiler. In D. Bjørner, A. P. Ershov, and N. D. Jones, editors, *Partial Evaluation and Mixed Computation*,

Proc. of the IFIP TC2 Working Conference, Gammel Avernæs, Denmark, 1987. North-Holland, 1988.

54. V. F. Turchin. Program transformation with metasystem transitions. *Journal of Functional Programming*, 3(3):283–313, 1993.

55. P. L. Wadler. Deforestation: Transforming programs to eliminate trees. In *Proceedings of ESOP '88*, Lecture Notes in Computer Science 300, pages 344–358. Springer-Verlag, 1988.

56. H. Zhu. How powerful are folding / unfolding transformations? *Journal of Functional Programming*, 4(1):89–112, 1994.

A Theory of Logic Program Specialization and Generalization for Dealing with Input Data Properties

Alberto Pettorossi[1] and Maurizio Proietti[2]

[1] Department of Informatics, Systems, and Production,
University of Roma Tor Vergata, 00133 Roma, Italy. adp@iasi.rm.cnr.it
[2] IASI-CNR, Viale Manzoni 30, 00185 Roma, Italy. proietti@iasi.rm.cnr.it

Abstract. We address the problem of specializing logic programs w.r.t. the contexts where they are used. We assume that these contexts are specified by means of computable properties of the input data. We describe a general method by which, given a program P, we can derive a specialized program P^1 such that P and P^1 are equivalent w.r.t. every input data satisfying a given property. Our method extends the techniques for partial evaluation of logic programs based on Lloyd and Shepherdson's approach, where a context can only be specified by means of a finite set of bindings for the variables of the input goal. In contrast to most program specialization techniques based on partial evaluation, our method may achieve superlinear speedups, and it does so by using a novel generalization technique.

1 Introduction

Program specialization is a technique which can be used for deriving from a given program, a new and hopefully more efficient program, by exploiting the knowledge of the context in which the given program is used. This knowledge can be expressed as a property which is satisfied by the input data. Thus the specialization of a program P w.r.t. a set of input data satisfying a property φ, called *static property*, consists in the derivation of a new program P^1 such that

for each value of x in the domain of the input data,

$$\text{if} \quad \varphi(x) \quad \text{then} \quad P(x) \equiv P^1(x) \tag{1}$$

where $\equiv$ is a chosen equivalence relation w.r.t. a given semantics.

This concept of program specialization includes that of *partial evaluation* where one assumes that x is a pair (s, d) of a *static* variable s and a *dynamic* variable d, and $\varphi(x)$ is of the form: $s = v$, where v is a value in the domain of the input data. However, since most of the work on program specialization deals with the special case of partial evaluation, often these two concepts are identified (see, for instance, [7]).

In this paper we consider the problem of specializing logic programs without negation, that is, *definite* logic programs [9]. We assume that the semantics of a program P is its least Herbrand model $M(P)$, that is, $M(P) = \{A \mid A \text{ is a}$

ground atom and $P \models A$}. We also assume that the static property $\varphi(X)$ is specified by a predicate $q(X)$ defined by the logic program to be specialized.

Thus, in our case, program specialization can be reformulated as follows: given a logic program P, a goal $q(X)$, called the *static* goal, and an input goal $p(X)$, called the *dynamic* goal, we want to derive a new program P^1, called *specialized* (or *residual*) program, and a new input goal $p^1(X)$ such that

for every ground substitution θ for X,

$$\text{if} \quad M(P) \models q(X)\theta \quad \text{then} \quad \left(M(P) \models p(X)\theta \text{ iff } M(P^1) \models p^1(X)\theta\right) \quad (2)$$

If this condition holds we say that *program P^1 with input goal $p^1(X)$ is a specialization of program P with input goal $p(X)$ w.r.t. the static goal $q(X)$*, and we also write $\langle P^1, p^1(X) \rangle$ *is a specialization of* $\langle P, p(X) \rangle$ *w.r.t.* $q(X)$.

The partial evaluation technique for logic programs as presented by Lloyd and Shepherdson [10], may be viewed as performing program specialization w.r.t. a static goal of the form $X = t$ where t is a possibly non-ground term.

Some extensions of partial evaluation, both of functional and logic programs, have been proposed to deal with static properties of input data, instead of static values. These extensions incorporate complex forms of reasoning based on abstract interpretation [3,4] and theorem proving [1,5].

By contrast, we propose a new technique which is based on the unfolding rule and a very limited form of goal replacement. On the one hand, this technique allows us to specify static properties in a precise way (unlike abstract interpretation) and, on the other hand, we avoid the use of very general theorem provers which may require complex heuristics for their effective use.

We now briefly describe our extension of Lloyd and Shepherdson's technique. Assume that the programs P and P^1 do not share any predicate symbol (this hypothesis will be relaxed in the sequel) and let Q be the subset of clauses in P on which the evaluation of $q(X)$ may depend. We observe that Condition (2) is equivalent to the following condition:

for every ground substitution θ for X,

$$M(P) \models \left(\{q(X)\}\, p(X)\right)\theta \quad \text{iff} \quad M(Q \cup P^1) \models \left(\{q(X)\}\, p^1(X)\right)\theta \quad (3)$$

where $\{S\}\, D$ is an alternative notation (borrowed from [1]) for the conjunction (S, D) which explicitly indicates that S is a property that holds when the evaluation of D is performed. If Condition (3) holds we say that $\langle P^1, p^1(X) \rangle$ *is a specialization of P w.r.t. the static part of the goal $\{q(X)\}\, p(X)$*. Condition (3) is equivalent to

$$M(P \cup P^1) \models \forall X \left(\{q(X)\}\, p(X) \leftrightarrow \{q(X)\}\, p^1(X)\right) \quad (4)$$

which makes it clear that the correctness of program specialization is proved by showing the equivalence of two goals.

Notice that after program specialization, the specialized predicate $p^1(X)$ defined by the specialized program P^1, is equivalent to $p(X)$ when $q(X)$ holds, but it need not be equivalent to the conjunction $\{q(X)\}\, p(X)$.

We will provide a proof method which allows us to conclude that Condition (4) holds by constructing, via unfolding and goal replacement steps, two finite trees T and T^1 such that: i) goal $\{q(X)\}\ p(X)$ is at the root of T, ii) goal $\{q(X)\}\ p^1(X)$ is at the root of T^1, iii) T and T^1 are *closed* trees (see Section 4), and iv) T and T^1 are *isomorphic* (see Section 5).

This proof method justifies our specialization technique described in Section 4, which, in fact, from a closed tree T with goal $\{q(X)\}\ p(X)$ at its root, derives the clauses for a new atom $p^1(X)$ such that there exists a closed tree T^1 with goal $\{q(X)\}\ p^1(X)$ at its root, such that T and T^1 are isomorphic.

It is straightforward to extend our techniques to the general case where: i) the predicates p, p^1, and q have any arity, ii) the static goal is any conjunction of atoms, instead of $q(X)$ only, and iii) the static and dynamic goals share any number of variables. Indeed, the formal presentation of our technique in Section 4 and its correctness proof in Section 5, are done for this general case.

In Section 6 we present a generalization technique which allows us to derive very efficient specialized programs. In particular, we give some examples where program specialization achieves superlinear speedups. Finally, in Section 7 we briefly compare our techniques with related specialization techniques both for logic and functional programs.

2 Preliminary Notions

In this section we introduce some definitions which are used in the sequel. By $hd(C)$ and $bd(C)$ we denote the head and the body, respectively, of a clause C. Goals are conjunctions of zero or more atoms. The empty goal is denoted by $\square$ and a clause with head A and empty body is written as $A \leftarrow$. The conjunction operator denoted by "," is commutative, and thus the order of the atoms in a goal is not significant. By contrast, when performing specializations we use a specific rule to eliminate duplicate occurrences of an atom in a goal. This is motivated by the fact that two distinct occurrences of the same atom may have different static/dynamic classifications (see Section 4). By $vars(G)$ we denote the set of variables occurring in a goal G.

Given a predicate p occurring in a definite program P, the *definition* of p in P is the set of all clauses in P whose head predicate is p. We say that a predicate p *depends on* a predicate q in a program P iff *either* there exists in P a clause of the form $p(\ldots) \leftarrow B$ such that q occurs in the goal B *or* there exists in P a predicate r such that p depends on r in P and r depends on q in P. The *relevant part* of program P for predicate p, denoted by $Rel(P, p)$, is the union of the following definitions in P: i) the definition of p and (ii) the definitions of all the predicates on which p depends in P.

We now give two rules which are used to derive new goals from old goals during program specialization.

Definition 1 (Unfolding Rule). Let C be a clause and G be the goal (H, A, K), where H and K are (possibly empty) goals and A is an atom. Suppose that A and $hd(C)$ are unifiable via the most general unifier θ. By *unfolding G* w.r.t. A using C we derive the goal $(H, bd(C), K)\theta$.

Thus, an application of the unfolding rule essentially is an application of the SLD-resolution rule.

Definition 2 (Goal Replacement Rule). Let P be a program and G be a goal of the form (H, U, K), where H, U, and K are (possibly empty) goals. Let V be a goal such that the following equivalence holds:

$$M(P) \models \forall X_1, \ldots, X_n \, (U \leftrightarrow V) \tag{5}$$

where $X_1, \ldots, X_n$ are the variables occurring in $U \leftrightarrow V$. By *goal replacement* (or simply, *replacement*) of U by V in G we derive the goal (H, V, K).

The process of deriving new goals from old ones by applying the unfolding and the goal replacement rules, is represented as a tree of goals as follows.

Definition 3 (Unfolding-Replacement Tree and Forest). Given a program P and a goal G, an *unfolding-replacement tree* (or *UR-tree*) for $\langle P, G \rangle$ is a non-empty, finite, directed tree with nodes labeled by goals and arcs labeled by substitutions such that:

- the goal labeling the root, also called root-goal, is G,
- if M is a node labeled by a goal G_M then exactly one of the following three cases occurs:
  1. M has no sons, and G_M is called a leaf-goal,
  2. G_M is of the form (H, A, K) and A is unifiable with the heads of the (standardized apart) clauses $C_1, \ldots, C_n$, with $n \geq 1$, in P via the most general unifiers $\theta_1, \ldots, \theta_n$, respectively. In this case M has n sons, say $N_1, \ldots, N_n$, and for $i = 1, \ldots, n$, the node N_i is labeled by the goal derived by unfolding G_M w.r.t. A using C_i and the arc from M to N_i is labeled by θ_i,
  3. G_M is of the form (H, U, K) and Equivalence (5) holds. In this case M has exactly one son N labeled by the goal (H, V, K) derived by the replacement of U by V in G_M, and the arc from M to N is labeled by the identity substitution which we denote by ε.

A node N is said to be a *failing node* iff it is labeled by a goal G_N, called a *failing goal*, such that $M(P) \models \forall X_1, \ldots, X_n \, (\neg G_N)$, where $X_1, \ldots, X_n$ are the variables occurring in G_N. In particular, if G_N is of the form (H, A, K) and A is an atom which is not unifiable with the head of any clause in P, then N is a failing node. A path from a node to a leaf is called a *branch*, and a branch ending with a failing leaf-node is called a *failing branch*.

A finite, non-empty set of UR-trees is called a *UR-forest*.

The reader will notice that the unfolding-replacement trees introduced here are similar to the SLD-trees considered in [10], where, however, no goal replacements are allowed.

3   An Introductory Example

This example was given in [8] to show that the usual partial evaluation techniques as described by Lloyd and Shepherdson [10], are not adequate. Let us consider the following logic program, call it *Append-Last*:

1. $append([\,], Ys, Ys) \leftarrow$
2. $append([X|Xs], Ys, [X|Zs]) \leftarrow append(Xs, Ys, Zs)$
3. $last([X], X) \leftarrow$
4. $last([X|Xs], Y) \leftarrow last(Xs, Y).$

Let us suppose that we want to specialize *Append-Last* w.r.t. the static part of the goal:

$$\{append(Xs, [a], Ys)\}\ last(Ys, Z) \tag{6}$$

that is, we look for the specialization of *Append-Last* with input goal $last(Ys, Z)$ w.r.t. the static goal $append(Xs, [a], Ys)$, which indeed expresses the fact that the last element of the list Ys is a. Partial evaluation techniques like those in [10] are not applicable in this case, because there is no input goal of the form $last(t, Z)$ such that for some choice of the term t the set of all instances of t is the set of all lists whose last element is a.

Let us now consider the UR-tree T depicted in Figure 1 with root-goal $\{append(Xs, [a], Ys)\}\ last(Ys, Z)$. In this figure and in the subsequent ones the static goals are written between curly brackets, unfolded atoms are underlined, and an upgoing arrow from goal H to goal K indicates that H is an instance of K, but that arrow itself is *not* an arc of the UR-tree.

Notice that in the non-failing leaves of T the only occurrence of the predicate *last* is in the goal $\{append(Xs1, [a], Ys1)\}\ last(Ys1, Z)$ which is an instance (actually, a variant) of the root-goal. In Section 4 this property of a UR-tree is generalized to the notion of *closed specialization tree*.

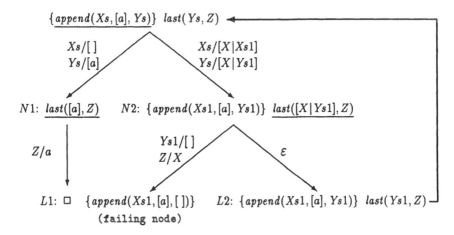

Fig. 1. The UR-tree T with root-goal $\{append(Xs, [a], Ys)\}\ last(Ys, Z)$.

Now we look for a new definition of the predicate *last*, by which we can construct, starting from a root-goal equal to the one of T, a UR-tree T^1 which has the same set of $\langle G, \theta \rangle$ pairs, where G is a non failing leaf-goal and θ is the composition of the substitutions along the branch from the root to G, restricted to the variables occurring in the root-goal.

In order to find such new clauses for *last* we apply the following technique which is a generalization of that considered in [10] for computing the *resultants* of a given SLD-tree.

Let us first consider in the tree T the non-failing branches together with their substitutions, which have been produced by performing an unfolding step w.r.t. an atom with predicate *last*. They are: i) branch $b1$ from node $N1$ to leaf $L1$, and ii) branch $b2$ from node $N2$ to leaf $L2$, that is:

$b1.$ $last([a], Z) \xrightarrow{\{Z/a\}} \square$

$b2.$ $\{append(Xs1, [a], Ys1)\}\, last([X|Ys1], Z) \xrightarrow{\varepsilon} \{append(Xs1, [a], Ys1)\}$
$\qquad\qquad last(Ys1, Z).$

Given these branches we consider the corresponding resultants

$B1.$ $last([a], a) \leftarrow$
$B2.$ $last([X|Ys1], Z) \leftarrow last(Ys1, Z).$

(In Definition 7 we introduce the formal notion of resultant we use in this paper.)

We have that the leaf-goals and the substitutions associated with the two branches $b1$ and $b2$, can be derived by using clauses $B1$ and $B2$, instead of clauses 3 and 4. In this situation we say that clauses $B1$ and $B2$ *validate* branches $b1$ and $b2$ (see Definition 14 for this concept).

Notice that branch $b1$ is also validated by either one of the following two clauses, which are *generalizations* of clause $B1$:

5. $last([Z], Z) \leftarrow$
6. $last(Ys, a) \leftarrow$

because, by unfolding $last([a], Z)$ using either clause 5 or clause 6 we get the empty leaf-goal and the substitution $\{Z/a\}$ associated with branch $b1$.

Furthermore, by using clause 6 one may validate not only branch $b1$ but also branch $b2$. In fact, the leaf-goal of $b2$ can be derived by a goal replacement step, if we assume that clause 6 is the only clause defining the predicate *last*. Condition (5) for goal replacement is fulfilled because by unfolding $\{append(Xs1, [a], Ys1)\}\, last([X|Ys1], Z)$ w.r.t. $last([X|Ys1], Z)$ using clause 6 we get the result we also get by unfolding $\{append(Xs1, [a], Ys1)\}\, last(Ys1, Z)$ w.r.t. $last(Ys1, Z)$ using again clause 6, and the unfolding rule preserves equivalence w.r.t. the least Herbrand model semantics.

As a consequence of what we have said so far, by using the program made out of clauses 1, 2, and 6, we may construct a UR-tree T^1 (see Figure 2) which has the same non-failing branches of T and the same associated substitutions. Branch $b1$ from node $N1$ to node $L1$ of T^1 is generated by an unfolding step, whereas branch $b2$ from node $N2$ to node $L2$ is generated by a goal replacement step justified by the fact that $\{append(Xs1, [a], Ys1)\}$ $last([X|Ys1], Z)$ and $\{append(Xs1, [a], Ys1)\}$ $last(Ys1, Z)$ are equivalent in the least Herbrand model of clauses 1, 2, and 6.

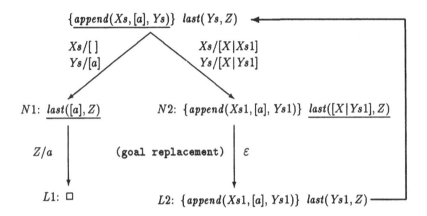

Fig. 2. The UR-tree T^1 with root-goal $\{append(Xs, [a], Ys)\}$ $last(Ys, Z)$.

As indicated later in Sections 5 and 6 (see Theorems 12 and 15), the existence of tree T^1 ensures that the following property holds for all ground terms x, y, and z:

if $\quad M(Append\text{-}Last) \models append(x, [a], y)$

then $\quad M(Append\text{-}Last) \models last(y, z)$ iff $M(\{\text{clause } 6\}) \models last(y, z)$. (7)

Thus, according to Condition (2), $\langle \{\text{clause } 6\}, \ last(Ys, Z) \rangle$ is a specialization of *Append-Last* w.r.t. the static part of $\{append(Xs, [a], Ys)\}$ $last(Ys, Z)$.

The reader should notice that, as already mentioned in the Introduction, the goal $\{append(Xs, [a], Ys)\}$ $last(Ys, Z)$, where $last(Ys, Z)$ is defined by clauses 3 and 4, is *not* equivalent to the specialized predicate $last(Ys, Z)$ defined by clause 6. Indeed, there are ground terms x, y, and z such that

$$M(Append\text{-}Last) \models \{append(x, [a], y)\} \ last(y, z) \ \text{ iff}$$
$$M(\{\text{clause } 6\}) \models last(y, z)$$

does *not* hold. However, Condition (7) shows that if $append(Xs, [a], Ys)$ holds then the two definitions of $last(Ys, Z)$ are equivalent.

In the next sections we present a general theory of program specialization which justifies the various steps performed during the development of this *Append-Last* example. In the general case where the specialized program is derived from more than one tree, we will see that one also needs to perform some predicate renaming steps for avoiding undesired interactions among specialized clauses.

4 Deriving Specialized Programs from Unfolding Trees

In this section we describe our technique for deriving specialized programs from UR-trees. Actually, we need to construct UR-trees of a particular kind, called *specialization trees*, which we introduce in the sequel.

We first need some preliminary notions. We assume that the predicates occurring in a program P are partitioned into two disjoint sets: the *basic predicates* and the *defined predicates*. We require that basic predicates do not depend on defined predicates. Also the atoms that we consider during program specialization are assumed to be either *basic atoms* or *defined atoms*, depending on whether their predicates are basic or defined.

The distinction between basic and defined predicates is introduced for ensuring the correctness of our specialization technique. Indeed, it is well known (see, for instance, [13]), that the unrestricted use of the goal replacement rule may lead to incorrect programs. However, goal replacement steps which replace basic atoms by new basic atoms are always correct (see Section 5). A more general way of stratifying program predicates to ensure the correctness of program transformations based on unfolding, folding, and goal replacement, is proposed in [15].

We have seen in our introductory example, that the atoms of a given goal may be classified as either static or dynamic. This classification of the atoms is taken into account for the extraction of the specialized program from a set of specialization trees (see Definition 8). Indeed, each clause of the specialized program is obtained from the dynamic atoms of a non-failing branch of a specialization tree. We assume that *all* atoms occurring in a UR-tree are classified as either static or dynamic (thereby determining a partition of those atoms), and in order to derive that classification for every atom, we will give rules which are based on the classification of the atoms in the root-goal and on the way in which the UR-tree is constructed.

The goals made out of static atoms only are called *static goals* and the goals made out of dynamic atoms only are called *dynamic goals*. A goal which is written as $\{S\}\,D$, is the conjunction of a static goal S and a dynamic goal D.

Based on the static/dynamic classification of goals, we can also partition the non-leaf nodes of a UR-tree as indicated in the following definition.

Definition 4 (s-Nodes, d-Nodes, Branching Nodes). A non-leaf node N in a UR-tree is said to be an *s-node* iff either its k (≥ 1) sons are derived by unfolding w.r.t. a static atom, or its son is derived by a goal replacement step which replaces an old static goal by a new static goal. The definition of a *d-node* is obtained from that of an s-node by replacing every occurrence of 'static' by 'dynamic'.

A node (either an s-node or a d-node) is said to be a *branching* node iff its sons are more than one, that is, they are derived by unfolding a goal w.r.t. an atom which unifies with the head of more than one program clause.

Definition 5 (Specialization Tree). A *specialization tree* for a program P, a static goal S, and a dynamic defined atom D, is a UR-tree for $\langle P, \{S\}\,D\rangle$, where each atom is classified as either static or dynamic. We now list the restrictions on the use of the unfolding and replacement rules during the construction of a specialization tree for $\langle P, \{S\}\, D\rangle$, and we also indicate how to classify as either static or dynamic every atom in that tree.

1. If $(H\theta, bd(C)\theta, K\theta)$ is the goal derived by unfolding a goal of the form (H, A, K) w.r.t. A using clause C, then i) the atoms occurring in the goals $H\theta$ and $K\theta$ have the same static/dynamic classification of the corresponding atoms in H and K, and ii) the atoms occurring in $bd(C)\theta$, if any, have the same static/dynamic classification of A.
2. If a goal replacement is performed, whereby an old goal U is replaced by a new goal V, then at least one of the following four cases applies (where S_1 and D_1 denote goals and, as usual, the order of the atoms is not significant):
    i) U is of the form $\{X, S_1\}\, D_1$ and V is of the form $\{Y, S_1\}\, D_1$, where X and Y are static goals made out of basic atoms only;
    ii) U is of the form $\{S_1\}\, X, D_1$ and V is of the form $\{S_1\}\, Y, D_1$, where X and Y are dynamic goals made out of basic atoms only;
    iii) U is of the form $\{G\}\, G$ and V is of the form $\{G\}$ for some goal G (deletion of a duplicate dynamic goal);
    iv) U is of the form $\{G\}\, A$ and V is of the form $\{G\}\, A^1$, where A^1 is an atom derived in a previous process of program specialization w.r.t. the static goal G. More precisely, P is of the form $Q \cup Q^1$ and $\langle Q^1, A^1\rangle$ is a specialization of $\langle Q, A\rangle$ w.r.t. G (see Definition 8).
3. Every branch from the root to a non-failing leaf contains at least one goal derived by performing an unfolding step w.r.t. a dynamic defined atom.
4. Every ancestor of a branching s-node is an s-node.

Notice that, in all goal replacements which can take place during the construction of a specialization tree, we replace a goal U by a new goal which differs from U either in the static part only or in the dynamic part only. Thus, the static/dynamic classification of the atoms occurring in son-goals can be inferred in the obviuos way from the static/dynamic classifications of the father-nodes.

Notice also that case 2.iv) may indeed be viewed as a goal replacement step, because if $\langle Q^1, A^1\rangle$ is a specialization of $\langle Q, A\rangle$ w.r.t. the static goal G, then (by Property (4) or, more formally, by Property (10) of the following Theorem 12) we have that Condition (5) of the goal replacement rule is satisfied, that is, the following property holds:

$$M(Q \cup Q^1) \models \forall X_1, \ldots, X_n\, (\{G\}\, A \leftrightarrow \{G\}\, A^1) \tag{8}$$

where $X_1, \ldots, X_n$ are the variables occurring in (G, A, A^1).

Definition 6 (Closed Specialization Forest). A *specialization forest* for a program P, a static goal S, and a dynamic defined atom D, is a finite, non-empty set of specialization trees such that every tree is constructed by using program P and $\{S\}\, D$ is one of the root-goals.

A specialization forest is said to be *closed* iff for each leaf-goal L one of the following three cases applies: 1) L is a failing goal, or 2) L contains no occurrences of defined dynamic atoms, or 3) for every dynamic defined atom A occurring in L, there exist a static, possibly empty (sub)goal G of L, a root-goal $\{H\}\, B$ of a tree in the forest, and a substitution σ such that $G = H\sigma$ and $A = B\sigma$.

A specialization tree T is said to be closed iff the specialization forest $\{T\}$ is closed.

Examples of closed specialization trees and forests may be found in Figures 1, 4, and 6. As already mentioned, in those figures an upgoing arrow from a leaf-goal L to a root-goal R, indicates that L contains a subgoal (possibly L itself) which is an instance of R.

Our notion of closed specialization tree is strongly related to the notion of closedness considered by Lloyd and Shepherdson [10], which, however, refers to resultants, and not to trees. Indeed, the reader may verify that a set of resultants of a set F of SLDNF-trees enjoys the closedness property defined in [10] iff for each leaf-goal L of a tree in F, one of the following three cases applies: 1) L is a failing goal, or 2) L is the empty goal, or 3) each atom occurring in L is an instance of an atom occurring in a root (not necessarily of the same tree) of F.

Notice that in Lloyd and Shepherdson's technique the root-goal of an SLDNF-tree can only be an atom, there is no distinction between static and dynamic goals, and there is no distinction between basic and defined atoms. Notice also that Definition 6 does not require that *all* static atoms occurring in a leaf-goal of a closed specialization forest are instances of static atoms occurring in the roots. Indeed, we do not want to derive new clauses to evaluate static goals. Likewise, we do not want to derive new clauses for the dynamic basic atoms, and this is why in Definition 6 (Case 3), in the leaves of a closed specialization forest we consider dynamic defined atoms only.

In the following definition we indicate how to derive from a specialization forest new, specialized clauses, called *resultants*, to evaluate dynamic defined atoms.

Definition 7 (Resultants). Given a specialization tree T, a d-node N of T is said to be *topmost* in T iff no ancestor of N is a d-node.

Let $\{S\}\, D$ be the label of a topmost d-node N in T (thus, D is a dynamic defined atom). Let us consider a branch from N to a *non-failing* leaf L, whose goal is $\{Ss\}\, Ds$, where Ds is a possibly empty, possibly non-atomic goal. Let θ be the composition of the substitutions along that branch. Then the clause $D\theta \leftarrow Ds$ is a *resultant* of that branch from N to L.

The set of the resultants of a specialization tree T is $\{r \mid r$ is a resultant of a branch from a topmost d-node of T to a non-failing leaf of $T\}$.

The following Definition 8 introduces the notion of program specialization based on specialization trees. Thus Definition 5 and Definition 8 depend on each other, because during the construction of a specialization tree one may consider the result of a previous program specialization (see case 2.iv in Definition 5).

A program specialization is derived from a specialization forest by first collecting all resultants of that forest, then renaming the predicates so that two resultants have the same head predicate iff they come from the same specialization tree, and finally adding the clauses defining the basic predicates occurring in the resultants.

Definition 8 (Program Specialization). Let P be a program, S_1 be a static goal, and D_1 be a dynamic defined atom. Let $\{T_i \mid i = 1, \ldots, n\}$ be a closed specialization forest for $\langle P, \{S_1\} D_1\rangle$ such that $\{S_1\} D_1$ is the root-goal of T_1. A *specialization* of $\langle P, D_1\rangle$ w.r.t. the static goal S_1 *via* the closed specialization forest $\{T_i \mid i = 1, \ldots, n\}$, is the pair $\langle P^1, D^1\rangle$ where P^1 is a program and D^1 is an atom which are obtained as follows:

1. Let R be the union of the sets R_i of the resultants of T_i, for $i = 1, \ldots, n$; rename *all* occurrences of the defined predicates in R, whereby deriving a new set $\overline{R}$ of clauses, as follows:
   1.1 for $i = 1, \ldots, n$, the predicate symbol in the head of every resultant of T_i is renamed by decorating it with the superscript i, and
   1.2 an atom A of the form $p(\ldots)$ in the body of the resultant of a branch with leaf-goal L is renamed to $p^i(\ldots)$ if there exist a static, possibly empty (sub)goal G of L and a substitution σ such that $G = S_i \sigma$ and $A = D_i \sigma$, where $\{S_i\} D_i$ is the root-goal of T_i.
2. P^1 is obtained as the set $\overline{R} \cup Rel(P, q_1) \cup \ldots \cup Rel(P, q_k)$ of clauses, where $q_1, \ldots, q_k$ are the basic predicates occurring in $\overline{R}$.
3. If D_1 is the atom $p(\ldots)$ then D^1 is the atom $p^1(\ldots)$ (thus, as a consequence of the predicate renaming performed at Point 1, D^1 is unifiable only with the heads of the renamed resultants derived from T_1).

Notice that, in general, for any given specialization forest more than one program specialization can be constructed (because Point 1.2 of Definition 8 allows for nondeterminism).

Our introductory example in Section 3 includes an example of program specialization according to Definition 8. In particular, the reader may notice that nodes $N1$ and $N2$ are the topmost d-nodes of the closed specialization tree for $\langle Append\text{-}Last, \{append(Xs, [a], Ys)\} last(Ys, Z)\rangle$ depicted in Figure 1. In our example we have already shown how to compute the resultants of the branches from $N1$ and $N2$ to the non-failing leaves $L1$ and $L2$, respectively. The resultants of those branches are clauses $B1$ and $B2$. The predicate renaming indicated at Point 1 of Definition 8, in this case consists of replacing in clauses $B1$ and $B2$ the predicate symbol *last* by the new symbol $last^1$ because the specialization forest is made out of one tree only.

5 Correctness of Program Specialization

We first notice that the specialization process described in the previous section may sometimes give incorrect programs. We present in this section a result which ensures correctness if the specialization forest satisfies an extra condition which generalizes that of *independence of a set of atoms* considered in [10].

We now show an example where the program specialization defined in Section 4 gives an incorrect result. Let us consider the program P:

1. $p(X) \leftarrow X = 0$
2. $q(X) \leftarrow X = 0$
3. $q(X) \leftarrow X = 1$
4. $X = X \leftarrow$

In order to derive a specialization of $\langle P, p(X) \rangle$ w.r.t. the static goal $q(X)$ we first construct the closed specialization tree shown in Figure 3.

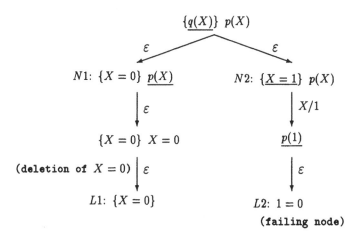

Fig. 3. A closed specialization tree with renamed resultant $p^1(X) \leftarrow$.

Then, according to Definition 8, from that tree we get the following program P^1 (due to the resultant of the non-failing branch from $N1$ to $L1$):

5. $p^1(X) \leftarrow$

We have that $M(P) \not\models \{q(1)\} p(1)$ whereas $M(\{\text{clause 2, clause 3}\} \cup P^1) \models \{q(1)\} p^1(1)$, and therefore, by Condition (3), $\langle P^1, p^1(X) \rangle$ is *not* a specialization of $\langle P, p(X) \rangle$ w.r.t. $q(X)$. We get this undesired result because the resultant '$p(X) \leftarrow$' of the branch from $N1$ to $L1$ where $X = 0$ holds, can also be used in the case where $X = 1$ holds. Indeed, $p(X)$ also occurs in the branch from $N2$ to $L2$ where $X = 1$ holds. Thus, unlike the case of partial evaluation based on Lloyd and Shepherdson's approach, the renaming of the predicates which occur in the resultants of a closed specialization forest, does not ensure the correctness of the specialization.

For avoiding problems of the kind we have now mentioned, it suffices that the dynamic atoms labeling the roots of the branches from which we compute the resultants (that is, the topmost d-nodes) do not have common instances. This remark motivates the introduction of the following notion of independent nodes.

Definition 9 (Independent Nodes). Let $N1$ and $N2$ be two nodes in a specialization tree labeled by two goals of the form $\{G\}\, A$ and $\{H\}\, B$, respectively. $N1$ and $N2$ are *independent* iff A and B have no common instances.

Our correctness result stated in the following Theorem 12, holds in the case where the topmost d-nodes in each tree of the specialization forest for $\langle P, \{S\}\, D\rangle$ are pairwise independent.

For the proof of Theorem 12 we also need to show that, if we construct, according to Definition 8, a specialized program P^1 with input goal D^1 from a program P with input goal D w.r.t. a static goal S, then (the universal closure of) the goal equivalence $\{S\}\, D \leftrightarrow \{S\}\, D^1$ holds in the least Herbrand model of $P \cup P^1$. This goal equivalence is proved by showing that $\langle P \cup P^1, \{S\}\, D\rangle$ and $\langle P \cup P^1, \{S\}\, D^1\rangle$ generate *isomorphic* closed specialization forests as indicated in the following Lemma 11. We now introduce the notion of isomorphism between forests which will also apply to specialization forests.

Definition 10 (Forest Isomorphism). Let us consider the two forests (with the same number of trees) $T = \{T_i \mid i = 1, \ldots, m\}$ and $U = \{U_i \mid i = 1, \ldots, m\}$ whose nodes are labeled by goals and whose arcs are labeled by substitutions. For $i = 1, \ldots, m$, let TR_i and UR_i be the root-goals of the trees T_i and U_i, respectively. We assume that for $i = 1, \ldots, m$, $vars(TR_i) = vars(UR_i)$. Let $\{TL_{ij} \mid j = 1, \ldots, n_i\}$ and $\{UL_{ij} \mid j = 1, \ldots, n_i\}$ be the multiset of non-failing leaf-goals of T_i and U_i, respectively. For $i = 1, \ldots, m$ and $j = 1, \ldots, n_i$, let θ_{ij} be the composition of all substitutions along the branch from the root of T_i to TL_{ij}, and similarly, let μ_{ij} be the composition of all substitutions along the branch from the root of U_i to the leaf labeled by UL_{ij}. We say that T is *isomorphic* to U iff for $i = 1, \ldots, m$ and $j = 1, \ldots, n_i$, we have that:

1. the leaf-goal UL_{ij} can be obtained from the leaf-goal TL_{ij} by simultaneously replacing in TL_{ij} zero or more occurrences of instances of root-goals of T by the corresponding instances of root-goals of U, that is, by simultaneously replacing in TL_{ij} the occurrences $TR_{k1}\sigma_{k1}, \ldots, TR_{ks}\sigma_{ks}$, for some substitutions $\sigma_{k1}, \ldots, \sigma_{ks}$ with $\{k1, \ldots, ks\} \subseteq \{1, \ldots, m\}$, by $UR_{k1}\sigma_{k1}, \ldots, UR_{ks}\sigma_{ks}$, respectively, and
2. $X\theta_{ij} = X\mu_{ij}$ for every X in $vars(TR_i)$.

Lemma 11. *Let us consider two specialization forests, say* $T = \{T_i \mid i = 1, \ldots, m\}$ *and* $U = \{U_i \mid i = 1, \ldots, m\}$, *constructed for the same program* P *and possibly distinct root-goals. For* $i = 1, \ldots, m$, *let* TR_i *and* UR_i *be the root-goals of* T_i *and* U_i, *respectively, with* $vars(TR_i) = vars(UR_i)$. *If* T *and* U *are isomorphic, then for* $i = 1, \ldots, m$,

$$M(P) \models \forall X_1, \ldots, X_k\, (TR_i \leftrightarrow UR_i)$$

where $\{X_1, \ldots, X_k\} = vars(TR_i)$.

Theorem 12 (Correctness of Specialization). *Let* P *be a program,* S_1 *be a static goal, and* D_1 *be a dynamic defined atom. Let* $\langle P^1, D^1\rangle$ *be a specialization* *of $\langle P, D_1 \rangle$ w.r.t. S_1 via the closed specialization forest $\{T_i \mid i = 1, \ldots, n\}$ such that the root of T_1 is $\{S_1\} D_1$. Suppose that $vars(\{S_1\} D_1) = \{X_1, \ldots, X_k\}$, and for $i = 1, \ldots, n$, any two distinct topmost d-nodes of T_i are independent. Then, we have that:*

for each ground substitution θ for $X_1, \ldots, X_k$,

$$\text{if} \quad M(P) \models S_1\theta \quad \text{then} \quad M(P) \models D_1\theta \quad \text{iff} \quad M(P^1) \models D^1\theta \tag{9}$$

or, equivalently,

$$M(P \cup P^1) \models \forall X_1, \ldots, X_k (\{S_1\} D_1 \leftrightarrow \{S_1\} D^1). \tag{10}$$

Proof. (Sketch) Let us consider the program $P \cup P^1$. Due to the renaming process during program specialization, P and P^1 may share occurrences of basic predicates only. The basic predicates which are common to P and P^1, have identical definitions (modulo renaming of variables) in these two programs, and thus after performing the union of the two programs, we can delete the duplicate definitions of these predicates without affecting the least Herbrand model semantics.

Our notion of resultant together with the closedness and independence conditions, ensures that, by using the clauses in $P \cup P^1$, we can construct a specialization forest $\{U_i \mid i = 1, \ldots, n\}$ which is isomorphic to $\{T_i \mid i = 1, \ldots, n\}$, being $\{S_1\} D^1$ and the root-goal of U_1. Thus, Property (10) follows from Lemma 11.

We now show that (9) and (10) are equivalent. By definition of Herbrand model, Property (10) is equivalent to

for each ground substitution θ for $X_1, \ldots, X_k$,

$$M(P \cup P^1) \models \{S_1\}\theta \quad \text{and} \quad M(P \cup P^1) \models D_1\theta \quad \text{iff} \tag{11}$$
$$M(P \cup P^1) \models \{S_1\}\theta \quad \text{and} \quad M(P \cup P^1) \models D^1\theta$$

Since the basic predicates which are common to P and P^1, have the same definitions in P, P^1, and $P \cup P^1$, and no other predicate is common to P and P^1, we have that (11) is equivalent to

for each ground substitution θ for $X_1, \ldots, X_k$,

$$M(P) \models \{S_1\}\theta \quad \text{and} \quad M(P) \models D_1\theta \quad \text{iff} \tag{12}$$
$$M(P) \models \{S_1\}\theta \quad \text{and} \quad M(P^1) \models D^1\theta$$

which is logically equivalent to (9). $\qquad \square$

6 Program Specialization via Generalized Resultants

In this section we introduce a program generalization technique which, when combined with the specialization techniques described in Section 4, allows us to derive very efficient specialized programs.

Our generalization technique consists in replacing the set $\{R_1, \ldots, R_n\}$ of resultants of a specialization tree T by a set $\{G_1, \ldots, G_m\}$ of clauses such that, for $i = 1, \ldots, m$, G_i is a generalization of a clause in $\{R_1, \ldots, R_n\}$. In the case of the *Append-Last* program presented in Section 3, by applying our technique we replace the clauses

B1. $last([a], a) \leftarrow$
B2. $last([X \mid Ys1], Z) \leftarrow last(Ys1, Z)$

which are the resultants of the specialization tree of Figure 1, by the clause:

6. $last(Ys, a) \leftarrow$

which is a generalization of clause B1.

Later in this section we present a result (see Theorem 15) which ensures that the specialized program constructed via the generalized clauses $G_1, \ldots, G_m$, instead of the resultants $R_1, \ldots, R_n$, is correct if by using $G_1, \ldots, G_m$ we can construct a suitable UR-tree which is isomorphic to T.

In the following definition we present the concept of *generalized resultants* of a specialization tree T, and indeed, by using a set of generalized resultants, we can construct the UR-tree isomorphic to T which is needed for ensuring the correctness of the program specialization.

Definition 13 (Generalized Resultants). Let T be a specialization tree for $\langle P, \{S\}\, D \rangle$. Let $\{R_1, \ldots, R_n\}$ be the set of resultants of all branches of T from topmost d-nodes to non-failing leaves. A set $\{G_1, \ldots, G_m\}$ of clauses, with $m \leq n$, is called a set of *generalized resultants* of T iff

α. for $i = 1, \ldots, m$, there exists a substitution θ_i such that $G_i\theta_i = R_i$ (we assume that the order of the clauses is not significant), and

β. the set $\{G_1, \ldots, G_m\}$ *validates* each subtree rooted in a topmost d-node of T in the sense specified by the next definition.

Definition 14 (Tree Validation). Let P be a program, S be a static goal, D be a dynamic defined atom, and $\{G_1, \ldots, G_m\}$ be a set of clauses, possibly not in P. Let T be a specialization tree for $\langle P, \{S\}\, D \rangle$. Let U be the specialization tree with root-goal $\{S\}\, D$ which is obtained by unfolding once $\{S\}\, D$ w.r.t. D using $\{G_1, \ldots, G_m\}$.
We say that $\{G_1, \ldots, G_m\}$ *validates* the tree T iff there exists a tree V which is isomorphic to U and it is obtained from T by first choosing in the leaves of T *zero or more* occurrences of dynamic defined atoms, and then performing *one* unfolding step w.r.t. each one of these occurrences using $\{G_1, \ldots, G_m\}$. (Thus, in particular, $\{G_1, \ldots, G_m\}$ *validates* T if T is isomorphic to U.)

The reader may check that in our introductory example, {clause 6} validates both branches $b1$ and $b2$ of the specialization tree of Figure 1 and, therefore, it is a set of generalized resultants of that tree.

Let us now briefly explain why program specialization based on generalized resultants is correct.

Let T be a specialization tree for a program $\langle P, \{S\}\, D \rangle$. Let us assume that the predicates occurring in the static goals of T do not depend (in program P) on the predicate of D (this assumption is not actually a restriction because we may use predicate renaming to make it always true). Let Q be the set of definitions in P of the predicates different from the predicate of D.

We now show that if $\{G_1, \ldots, G_m\}$ is a set of generalized resultants of T, then we can construct a UR-tree isomorphic to T by using $Q \cup \{G_1, \ldots, G_m\}$ and also some extra clauses, say $New_1, \ldots, New_k$, which however, will not be part of the specialized program.

Since the upper portion of T made out of s-nodes can be constructed by using clauses in Q, we have only to show that for each subtree $\overline{T}$ rooted in a topmost d-node of T, we can construct, by using $Q \cup \{G_1, \ldots, G_m\}$, a tree $\overline{T}^1$ isomorphic to $\overline{T}$. The root-goal of $\overline{T}^1$ is equal to the root-goal, say $\{\overline{S}\}\,\overline{D}$, of $\overline{T}$. The construction of $\overline{T}^1$ is done in two steps: (Step 1) we first show that Condition (β) of Definition 13 allows for the replacement of the root-goal $\{\overline{S}\}\,\overline{D}$ of $\overline{T}^1$ by an equivalent goal $\{\overline{S}\}\,NewD$, where $NewD$ is an atom with a new predicate suitably defined, and (Step 2) we then get the desired tree $\overline{T}^1$ isomorphic to $\overline{T}$ by unfolding $\{\overline{S}\}\,NewD$ w.r.t. $NewD$.

Let us now look at these steps in more detail.

(Step 1) Let $NewD$ be an atom obtained from $\overline{D}$ by renaming the predicate symbol occurring in $\overline{D}$ to a fresh new symbol. Let $\{S_1\}\,D_1, \ldots, \{S_k\}\,D_k$ be the non-failing leaf-goals of $\overline{T}$. For $i = 1, \ldots, k$, let θ_i be the composition of the substitutions computed along the branch of $\overline{T}$ from the root to the leaf containing $\{S_i\}\,D_i$, and let New_i be the clause $NewD\,\theta_i \leftarrow D_i$. We have that:

$$M(Q \cup \{G_1, \ldots, G_m, New_1, \ldots, New_k\}) \models \forall X_1, \ldots, X_r\,(\{\overline{S}\}\,\overline{D} \leftrightarrow \{\overline{S}\}\,NewD) \quad (13)$$

where $X_1, \ldots, X_r$ are the variables occurring in $\{\overline{S}\}\,\overline{D}$ (or $\{\overline{S}\}\,\overline{NewD}$), because by hypothesis, $\{G_1, \ldots, G_m\}$ validates $\overline{T}$ and therefore, by unfolding the two goals $\{\overline{S}\}\,\overline{D}$ and $\{\overline{S}\}\,NewD$ using clauses in $\{G_1, \ldots, G_m, New_1, \ldots, New_k\}$ we get two isomorphic trees. Thus Equivalence (13) is a consequence of Lemma 11.

Now, by making use of (13), we may apply the goal replacement rule to the root-goal $\{\overline{S}\}\,\overline{D}$ of $\overline{T}$ and we derive the new goal $\{\overline{S}\}\,NewD$.

(Step 2) We unfold $\{\overline{S}\}\,NewD$ w.r.t. $NewD$ using clauses $New_1, \ldots, New_k$, and the construction of these clauses ensures that we get exactly the same substitutions and the same non-failing leaf-goals of $\overline{T}$. Thus, the UR-tree $\overline{T}^1$ we have obtained is isomorphic to $\overline{T}$.

Notice that the UR-tree $\overline{T}^1$ constructed using $\{G_1, \ldots, G_m\}$ together with the set $\{New_1, \ldots, New_k\}$ of clauses, is not a specialization tree, because the goal replacement performed at Step 1 does not respect the restrictions of Definition 5, Point 2.

Notice also that the clauses in $\{New_1, \ldots, New_k\}$ are needed only for proving Equivalence (13), and not for the run-time evaluation of (instances of) D because the predicate of D does not depend on the predicate of $NewD$. Thus, $New_1, \ldots, New_k$ need not be included in the specialized program.

Now, the existence of an isomorphism between the specialization tree T and the UR-tree T^1 constructed by using the generalized resultants $\{G_1, \ldots, G_m\}$ of

T, allows us to prove a fact analogous to Lemma 11. The rest of the proof of correctness of our specialization technique is similar to the proof of Theorem 12. In particular, if we can construct a *closed* specialization forest, we have that, except for the basic predicates, no predicate occurring in the initial program is needed in the specialized program. Thus, the specialized program is made out of all (possibly renamed) generalized resultants together with the clauses defining the basic predicates.

The procedure for extracting specialized programs from closed specialization forests by using generalized resultants, is a modification of the construction presented in Definition 8 obtained by using 'generalized resultants', instead of 'resultants'. In the following theorem we refer to program specializations performed according to this modified construction.

Theorem 15 (Correctness of Specialization via Generalized Resultants).
Let P be a program, S_1 be a static goal, and D_1 be a dynamic atom. Let $\langle P^1, D^1 \rangle$ be a specialization of $\langle P, D_1 \rangle$ w.r.t. S_1 constructed from a closed specialization forest for $\langle P, \{S_1\} D_1 \rangle$ by using generalized resultants. Assuming that $\{X_1, \ldots, X_k\} = vars(\{S_1\} D_1)$, we have that:

for each ground substitution θ for $X_1, \ldots, X_k$,
$$\text{if} \quad M(P) \models S_1\theta \quad \text{then} \quad M(P) \models D_1\theta \quad \text{iff} \quad M(P^1) \models D^1\theta \qquad (14)$$

or, equivalently,
$$M(P \cup P^1) \models \forall X_1, \ldots, X_k \left(\{S_1\} D_1 \leftrightarrow \{S_1\} D^1 \right). \qquad (15)$$

The reader may notice that when we use generalized resultants, instead of resultants, the independence condition is no longer necessary to ensure that we can construct suitable isomorphic trees (or, more generally, forests) which are needed to prove the correctness of program specialization. This explains why the independence condition does not appear in the hypotheses of Theorem 15. One can also show that, if the independence condition holds for a given specialization tree, then the resultants of that tree are also generalized resultants.

It may be the case that no set of generalized resultants exists for a given specialization forest. When this happens, to apply our technique one has to construct a different specialization forest. The study of the strategies for obtaining specialization forests for which generalized resultants exist, is beyond the scope of this paper.

The following example, taken from [1], shows a complete derivation by program specialization with generalized resultants. It is important to notice that the derivation in [1] is supported by the discovery and the proof of crucial lemmas, whereas we perform unfolding and generalization steps only.

Example 1 (Quicksort of Decreasing Lists). Let us consider the following program *Quicksort*, where $\geq$ and $<$ may be regarded as basic predicates:

1. $quicksort([\,], Ls, Ls) \leftarrow$

2. $quicksort([X|Xs], Ts, Ys) \leftarrow partition(Xs, X, Ss, Bs),$
$\qquad quicksort(Bs, Ts, Ys1),$
$\qquad quicksort(Ss, [X|Ys1], Ys)$

3. $partition([\,], X, [\,], [\,]) \leftarrow$

4. $partition([B|Vs], A, [B|Ss], Bs) \leftarrow A \geq B, partition(Vs, A, Ss, Bs)$

5. $partition([B|Vs], A, Ss, [B|Bs]) \leftarrow A < B, partition(Vs, A, Ss, Bs)$

6. $decr([\,]) \leftarrow$

7. $decr([X]) \leftarrow$

8. $decr([X1, X2|Xs]) \leftarrow X1 \geq X2, decr([X2|Xs]).$

Suppose that we want to specialize *Quicksort* w.r.t. the static part of the goal $\{decr(Xs)\} \, quicksort(Xs, Ys, Zs)$.

We will see that, for this program specialization we first need to specialize *Quicksort* w.r.t. the static part of $\{decr([X1|Xs1])\} \, partition(Xs1, X1, S, B)$.

To perform this auxiliary specialization, we construct the closed specialization tree, say T_1, for the pair:

$$\langle \, Quicksort, \quad \{decr([X1|Xs1])\} \, partition(Xs1, X1, S, B) \rangle$$

which is depicted in Figure 4. The resultants of that tree are:

9. $partition([\,], X, [\,], [\,]) \leftarrow$

10. $partition([X2|Xs2], X1, [X2|S1], B) \leftarrow partition(Xs2, X1, S1, B).$

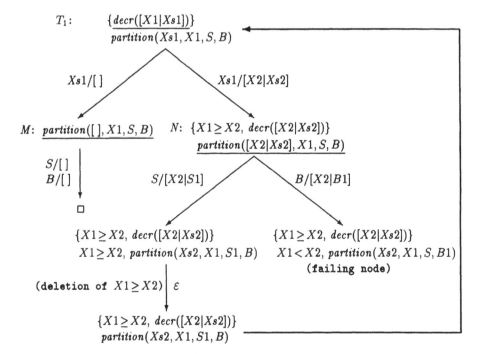

Fig. 4. The closed specialization tree T_1 for *Quicksort* with root-goal $\{decr([X1|Xs1])\}$ $partition(Xs1, X1, S, B)$.

Now we consider the following clause:

11. $partition(Xs, X, Xs, [\,]) \leftarrow$

which is a generalization of clause 9. We have that {clause 11} is a set of generalized resultants of T_1. To show this, we have to verify that {clause 11} validates
all subtrees of T_1 rooted in the topmost d-nodes of T_1, which are node M labeled
by the goal

$partition([\,], X1, S, B)$

and node N labeled by the goal

$\{X1 \geq X2, decr([X2|Xs2])\}\ partition([X2|Xs2], X1, S, B).$

The following facts i) and ii) hold.

i) By unfolding the goal in M using clause 11 we get a specialization tree,
   say U_M, with root-goal $partition([\,], X1, S, B)$, a unique arc labeled by the
   substitution $\{S/[\,], B/[\,]\}$, and leaf-goal $\square$. U_M is isomorphic to the subtree
   of T_1 rooted in M. Thus, {clause 11} validates this subtree.
ii) By unfolding the goal in N using clause 11 we get the specialization tree
   U_N depicted in Figure 5. By unfolding the non-failing leaf-goal $\{X1 \geq
   X2, decr([X2|Xs2])\}\ partition(Xs2, X1, S1, B)$ of the subtree of T_1 rooted
   in N, we get the tree V_N depicted in Figure 5. U_N and V_N are isomorphic
   and thus {clause 11} also validates the subtree of T_1 rooted in N.

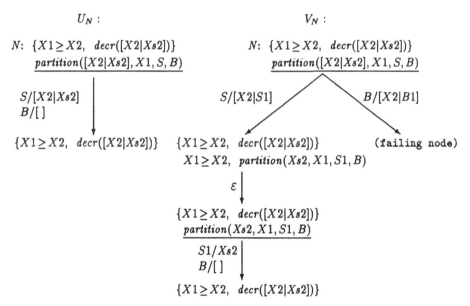

Fig. 5. The isomorphic trees U_N and V_N for the validation of the subtree rooted of T_1 in
N.

Thus, the program made out of the renamed clause:

11.r $partition^1(Xs, X, Xs, [\,]) \leftarrow$

with input goal $partition^1(Xs1, X1, S, B)$ is a specialization of *Quicksort* with input goal $partition(Xs1, X1, S, B)$ w.r.t. the static goal $decr([X1|Xs1])$. The correctness of the derivation is ensured by Theorem 15 because T_1 is closed (recall that the independence property is not needed when we use generalized resultants).

Now, we are ready to address the main problem of specializing *Quicksort* w.r.t. the static part of the goal $\{decr(Xs)\}\ quicksort(Xs, Ys, Zs)$. This problem can be solved by adding clause 11.r to *Quicksort* and by looking for the specialization of the program *Quicksort* $\cup \{$clause11.r$\}$ w.r.t. the static part of the goal $\{decr(Xs)\}\ quicksort(Xs, Ys, Zs)$.

Therefore, we construct the closed specialization forest F for $\langle$*Quicksort* $\cup$ $\{$clause11.r$\}$, $\{decr(Xs)\}\ quicksort(Xs, Ys, Zs)\rangle$ made out of the trees R_1 and R_2 depicted in Figure 6. During the construction of F we use the result of the auxiliary program specialization we have performed, that is, we use the fact that $\langle\{$clause 11.r$\}$, $partition^1(Xs1, X1, S, B)\rangle$ is a specialization of $\langle$*Quicksort*, $partition(Xs1, X1, S, B)\rangle$ w.r.t. $decr([X1|Xs1])$ (see Point 2.iv of Definition 5 where it is indicated how to use previous program specializations during the construction of specialization trees).

The resultants of R_1 are:

12. $quicksort([\,], Ys, Ys) \leftarrow$
13. $quicksort([X1|S], Ys1, Zs) \leftarrow quicksort(S, [X1|Ys1], Zs)$

and the resultants of R_2 are:

14. $quicksort([\,], [X1|Ys1], [X1|Ys1]) \leftarrow$
15. $quicksort([Y1|S1], [X1|Ys1], Zs) \leftarrow quicksort(S1, [Y1, X1|Ys1], Zs)$.

After predicate renaming we get our final specialized program which reverses a list in linear time:

12.r $quicksort^1([\,], Ys, Ys) \leftarrow$
13.r $quicksort^1([X1|S], Ys1, Zs) \leftarrow quicksort^2(S, [X1|Ys1], Zs)$
14.r $quicksort^2([\,], [X1|Ys1], [X1|Ys1]) \leftarrow$
15.r $quicksort^2([Y1|S1], [X1|Ys1], Zs) \leftarrow quicksort^2(S1, [Y1, X1|Ys1], Zs)$.

The correctness of the derivation of our final program is a consequence of Theorem 12 because the specialization forest F is closed and the independence property holds. To see this, notice that in R_1 there is one topmost d-node only, that is, the root, and thus the independence property trivially holds. In R_2 we have precisely two topmost d-nodes, labeled by the goals

$quicksort([\,], [X1|Ys1], Zs)$ and

$\{X1 \geq Y1, decr([Y1|S1])\}\ quicksort([Y1|S1], [X1|Ys1], Zs)$,

respectively, and the atoms with predicate *quicksort* have no common instances. Therefore the two nodes are independent.

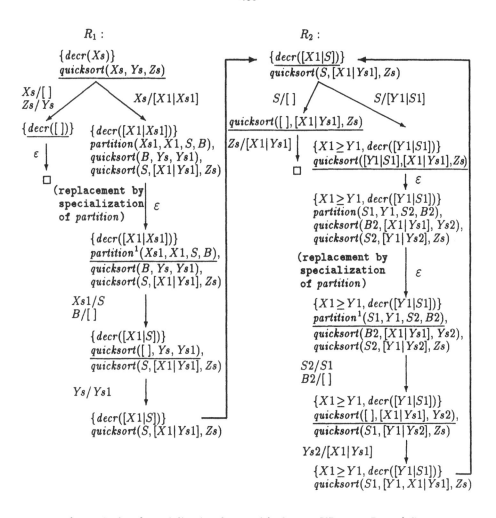

Fig. 6. A closed specialization forest with the two UR-trees R_1 and R_2.

7 Related Work and Concluding Remarks

We have proposed some program specialization techniques which extend the techniques for the partial evaluation of logic programs based on [10]. As in [10] we specialize a program w.r.t. the context where it is used. However, in [10] this context can be defined in terms of bindings of the form $X = t$, where t is a possibly non-ground term, whereas we allow for the definition of more complex contexts, such as those definable by means of any predicate computed by a logic program.

We believe that most of the automated tools and systems developed for partial evaluation methods based on [10], can easily be adapted to take into account our extended techniques, because they are based on similar concepts. Our techniques can be implemented in an efficient way and, in particular, the generalization step proposed in Section 6 requires in practice only a very limited search.

The idea of specializing logic programs w.r.t. complex contexts is strongly related to the techniques of *internal specialization* [14] and *finite differencing* [12], in the case of functional and set-based imperative languages, respectively. However, it is hard to establish a formal relationship among these techniques, because of the different formalisms used.

In the field of functional programming various extensions of the partial evaluation technique have been proposed to deal with properties of the input data. *Parametrized Partial Evaluation* [3] allows for the specialization of programs w.r.t. properties of the input data which are described by means of approximated representations based on abstract interpretations. *Generalized Partial Computation* [5] allows for the use of theorem provers for dealing with properties which restrict the domains of the functional programs to be specialized.

In our approach, we avoid the use of abstract interpretations and we specify properties of the input data in a precise way. We also avoid the need for very sophisticated theorem provers by using only the unfolding rule together a limited form of the goal replacement rule.

Also in the area of logic programs there are various papers which extend partial evaluation with objectives similar to ours. Bossi et al. [1] introduce a method based on unfolding and folding rules à la Burstall and Darlington [2], with some extra rules to deal with contexts (or *constraining* predicates). However, as in [5], most of the power of this method relies on the proof of properties of the program to be specialized, which makes its automation very hard. Moreover, we believe that by using the unfolding and folding rules according to the method of [1], without proving extra program properties, it is impossible to work out the examples we have presented in this paper.

The method presented in [11] is an adaptation of [1] to the case of Prolog programs with the left-to-right, depth-first control strategy. No theorem proving capabilities are allowed in this method, which as a result, is strictly less powerful than the one described in [1].

Finally, de Waal and Gallagher [4,6] have proposed various techniques to extend partial evaluation. In particular, the notion of *partial evaluation with conditions* is strongly related to our specialization tree. However, similarly to [3], de Waal and Gallagher's approach makes use of a number of abstract interpretation techniques, whereas as already mentioned, our techniques are based on syntactic transformation rules only.

Acknowledgements

We would like to thank the organizers of the Dagstuhl Seminar on "Partial Evaluation" for their kind invitation and the anonymous referees for comments and suggestions. We acknowledge some very fruitful conversations with J. Gallagher and M. H. Sørensen. Our thanks also go to M. Leuschel and B. Martens for pointing out to us the example shown in Section 3.

References

1. A. Bossi, N. Cocco, and S. Dulli. A method for specializing logic programs. *ACM Transactions on Programming Languages and Systems*, 12(2):253–302, April 1990.

2. R. M. Burstall and J. Darlington. A transformation system for developing recursive programs. *Journal of the ACM*, 24(1):44–67, January 1977.

3. C. Consel and S.C. Khoo. Parameterized partial evaluation. *ACM Transactions on Programming Languages and Systems*, 15(3):463–493, 1993.

4. D. A. de Waal and J. P. Gallagher. Specialization of a unification algorithm. In T. Clement and K.-K. Lau, editors, *Logic Program Synthesis and Transformation, Proceedings LOPSTR '91, Manchester, U.K.*, Workshops in Computing, pages 205–221. Springer-Verlag, 1992.

5. Y. Futamura and K. Nogi. Generalized partial computation. In D. Bjørner, A. P. Ershov, and N. D. Jones, editors, *Partial Evaluation and Mixed Computation*, pages 133–151. North-Holland, 1988.

6. J. P. Gallagher and D.A. de Waal. Deletion of redundant unary type predicates from logic programs. In *Proceedings of LoPSTr'92, Manchester, U.K.*, pages 151–167. Springer-Verlag, 1993.

7. N. D. Jones, C. K. Gomard, and P. Sestoft. *Partial Evaluation and Automatic Program Generation*. Prentice Hall, 1993.

8. M. Leuschel and B. Martens. Partial deduction of the ground representation and its application to integrity checking. In J. W. Lloyd, editor, *Proceedings of the 1995 International Logic Programming Symposium (ILPS'95)*, pages 495–509. MIT Press, 1995.

9. J. W. Lloyd. *Foundations of Logic Programming*. Springer-Verlag, Berlin, 1987. Second Edition.

10. J. W. Lloyd and J. C. Shepherdson. Partial evaluation in logic programming. *Journal of Logic Programming*, 11:217–242, 1991.

11. U. W. Neumerkel. *Specialization of Prolog Programs with Partially Static Goals and Binarization*. PhD thesis, Technical University Wien, Austria, 1992.

12. R. Paige and S. Koenig. Finite differencing of computable expressions. *ACM Transactions on Programming Languages and Systems*, 4(3):402–454, 1982.

13. A. Pettorossi and M. Proietti. Transformation of logic programs: Foundations and techniques. *Journal of Logic Programming*, 19,20:261–320, 1994.

14. W. L. Scherlis. Program improvement by internal specialization. In *Proc. 8th ACM Symposium on Principles of Programming Languages, Williamsburgh, Va*, pages 41–49. ACM Press, 1981.

15. H. Tamaki and T. Sato. A generalized correctness proof of the unfold/fold logic program transformation. Technical Report 86-4, Ibaraki University, Japan, 1986.

Program Specialization via Program Slicing

Thomas Reps and Todd Turnidge
Computer Sciences Department, University of Wisconsin–Madison
1210 West Dayton Street, Madison, WI 53706 USA
e-mail: {reps,turnidge}@cs.wisc.edu

Abstract. This paper concerns the use of program slicing to perform a certain kind of program-specialization operation. We show that the specialization operation that slicing performs is different from the specialization operations performed by algorithms for partial evaluation, supercompilation, bifurcation, and deforestation. To study the relationship between slicing and these operations in a simplified setting, we consider the problem of slicing functional programs. We identify two different goals for what we mean by "slicing a functional program" and give algorithms that correspond to each of them.

1. Introduction

Program slicing is an operation that identifies semantically meaningful decompositions of programs, where the decompositions consist of elements that are not textually contiguous [43, 28, 13]. Program slicing has been studied primarily in the context of imperative programming languages [37]. In such languages, slicing is typically carried out using *program dependence graphs* [19, 28, 6, 13]. There are two kinds of slices of imperative programs: (i) a *backward slice* of a program with respect to a set of program elements S consists of all program elements that might affect (either directly or transitively) the values of the variables used at members of S; (ii) a *forward slice* with respect to S consists of all program elements that might be affected by the computations performed at members of S [13]. For example, a C program and one of its backward slices is shown in Figure 1. Slicing—and subsequent manipulation of slices—shows great promise for helping with many software-engineering problems: It has applications in program understanding, maintenance [9, 10], debugging [23], testing [3, 2], differencing [12,14], reuse [27], and merging [12].

This paper concerns the use of slicing to perform program specialization, and how slicing-based specialization relates to partial evaluation and other specialization operations. The contributions of the paper can be summarized as follows:

- We show that the specialization operation that slicing performs is *different from the specialization operations performed by partial evaluation, supercompilation, bifurcation, and deforestation*. In particular, there are situations in which the specialized programs that we create via slicing could not be created as the result of applying partial evaluation, supercompilation, bifurcation, or deforestation to the original unspecialized program.
- To study the relationship between slicing and partial evaluation in a simplified setting, we consider the problem of *slicing functional programs*. We identify two different goals for what we mean by "slicing a functional program" and give algorithms that correspond to each of them.
- We adapt techniques from shape analysis [16], strictness analysis [39], and program bifurcation [26] so that *our slicing algorithms can handle certain kinds of heap-allocated data structures* (*e.g.*, lists, trees, and dags). This represents a contribution to the slicing literature: By permitting programs to be sliced with respect to "partially needed structures", our techniques create non-trivial slices of programs that make use of heap-allocated data structures.

```
static int add(a, b)              static int add(a, b)
int a, b;                         int a, b;
{                                 {
  return(a + b);                    return(a + b);
}                                 }
void main()                       void main()
{                                 {
  int sum, i;                       int [    ] i;
  sum = 0;                          [            ]
  i = 1;                          i = 1;
  while (i < 11) {                while (i < 11) {
    sum = add(sum, i);             [                  ]
    i = add(i, 1);                 i = add(i, 1);
  }                               }
  printf("sum = %d\n", sum);       [                  ]
  printf("i = %d\n", i);          printf("i = %d\n", i);
}                                 }
```

Figure 1. A C program and the backward slice of the program with respect to the statement *printf("i = %d\n", i)*. In the slice, the starting point for the slice is shown in italics, and the empty boxes indicate where program elements have been removed from the original program.

- We present *a re-examination of certain aspects of program bifurcation* in terms of the machinery developed for slicing functional programs.

The remainder of the paper is organized as follows: Section 2 demonstrates specialization via slicing, and shows that slicing performs a different kind of specialization operation from those performed by partial evaluation, supercompilation, bifurcation, and deforestation. Section 3 presents our methods for slicing functional programs. Section 4 compares the semantic issues that arise in specialization via partial evaluation versus specialization via slicing. Section 5 describes how our techniques relate to work on program bifurcation. Section 6 discusses related work. Section 7 presents some concluding remarks.

2. Program Specialization: Slicing Versus Partial Evaluation

In some circles, the terms "program specialization" and "partial evaluation" are treated almost as synonyms, although sometimes "program specialization" carries the nuance of expressing a broader perspective that encompasses a number of kindred techniques, such as "generalized partial evaluation" [8], "supercompilation" [38], "bifurcation" [26], and "deforestation" [40]. However, this overlooks an often unappreciated fact, namely that program slicing can also be used to perform a kind of program specialization—and one that is different from the kinds of specializations that partial evaluation and its close relatives are capable of performing.

Example. In the context of imperative programs, this phenomenon is illustrated by the C program shown in the first column of Figure 2 and the two slices shown in the second and third columns. The program in the first column is a scaled-down version of the UNIX word-count utility. It scans a file, counts the number of lines and characters in the file, and prints the results. Thus, this program implements the same action that would be obtained by invoking the UNIX word-count utility with the *–lc* flag (*i.e.*, *wc –lc*). However, unlike the actual UNIX word-count utility, procedure line_char_count is *not* parameterized by a second argument to allow the caller to choose which of the output quantities are to be printed.

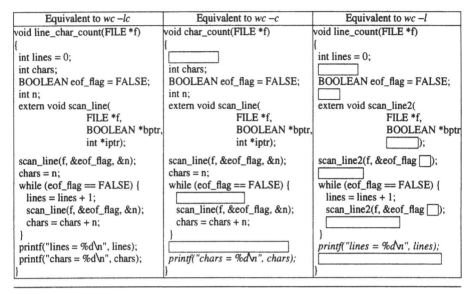

Figure 2. A scaled-down version of the UNIX word-count utility and two of its backward slices.

The procedure char_count shown in column two of Figure 2 is the (backward) slice of line_char_count with respect to the statement *printf("chars = %d\n", chars)*. This slice implements the same action that would be obtained by invoking *wc −c*: it scans a file and counts only characters. The procedure line_count shown in column three is the slice of line_char_count with respect to the statement *printf("lines = %d\n", lines)*. Line_count implements the same action that would be obtained by invoking *wc −l*: it scans a file and counts only lines.

Had the implementor of line_char_count foreseen the need to parameterize the procedure with a second parameter to allow the caller to vary the procedure's output behavior (call this hypothetical procedure "line_char_count+"), then char_count and line_count could have been obtained by partially evaluating line_char_count+ with respect to −c and −l, respectively. However, **given the unparameterized line_char_count of Figure 2, partial evaluation does not provide a way to obtain procedures char_count and line_count**. Procedure line_char_count has only the *single* parameter f, and thus there is no opportunity for partial evaluation with respect to a full parameter value. We can perform *full evaluation* (if f's value is provided) or *no evaluation* (if f's value is withheld). Furthermore, none of the information in parameter f controls whether the output consists of just the character count, just the line count, or both the character count and line count together. Thus, even if a partially static value were supplied for f, it would not provide the right kind of information that a partial evaluator would need to create char_count and line_count. □

This example shows that slicing performs a different program-specialization operation than that obtained via partial evaluation (or the other forwards-oriented specialization operations). The two approaches are actually *complementary*: Partial evaluation and its forwards-oriented relatives take information known at the *beginning* of a program and push it *forward*; backward slicing takes a demand for information at the *end* of a program and pushes it *backward*.

In addition, slicing-based specialization has another characteristic that sets it apart from the forwards-oriented specialization operations. The parameters to functions and procedures define the range of usage patterns that the designer of a piece of software has anticipated. This imposes some limitations on partial evaluation, super-compilation, and bifurcation in the sense that they support tailoring of existing software only in ways that have already been "foreseen" by the software's author. In contrast, slicing-based specialization permits programs to be specialized in ways that do not have to be anticipated—via parameterization—by the writer of the original program.

3. Slicing Functional Programs

To elucidate further the relationship between partial evaluation and program slicing, in this section of the paper we study the problem of how to slice functional programs. By considering slicing in a simplified context—and in particular one in which the majority of work on partial evaluation has been carried out—we can better understand the relationship between partial evaluation and slicing, including both common and complementary aspects.

There are other benefits as well: Past work on shape analysis [16], strictness analysis [39], and program bifurcation [26] for functional programs has developed techniques to handle certain kinds of heap-allocated data structures (*e.g.*, lists, trees, and dags); we use similar techniques to formulate a slicing algorithm that can handle programs that use (heap-allocated) lists, trees, and dags. The slicing algorithm can create non-trivial slices, where the goal is to satisfy a demand for a "partially needed structure".

The slicing algorithm will be formulated for a first-order LISP-like functional language that has the constructor and selector operations NIL, CONS, CAR, and CDR for manipulating heap-allocated data (*i.e.*, lists and dotted pairs), together with appropriate predicates (EQUAL, ATOM, and NULL), but no operations for destructive updating (*e.g.*, RPLACA and RPLACD). The constructs of the language are

x_i	(ATOM e_1)	(CONS e_1 e_2)	(OP $op\ e_1\ e_2$)
(QUOTE c)	(NULL e_1)	(IF $e_1\ e_2\ e_3$)	(DEFINE ($main\ x_1\ \cdots\ x_k$) e_{main})
(CAR e_1)	(EQUAL $e_1\ e_2$)	(CALL $f\ e_1\ \cdots\ e_k$)	(DEFINE ($f\ x_1\ \cdots\ x_k$) e_f)
(CDR e_1)			

A program is a list of function definitions, with a distinguished top-level goal function, named *main*, that cannot be called by any of the other functions. We assume that the distinguished atom "NIL" is used for terminating lists, and that there is also a special empty-tree value (different from NIL), denoted by "?".

3.1. Projection Functions and Regular Tree Grammars

Our approach to slicing functional programs involves formulating the problem as one of symbolically composing the program to be sliced with an appropriate *projection function* π_{main}. A projection function π is an idempotent function (*i.e.*, $\pi \circ \pi = \pi$) that approximates the identity function (*i.e.*, $\pi \sqsubseteq id$). A projection function can be used to characterize what information should be "discarded" and what information should be "retained" from the value that a function computes. Thus, projection function π_{main} represents a demand for a "partially needed structure". In the nomenclature used in the slicing literature, π_{main} is called the *slicing criterion*.

Example. Let ID be the identity function $\lambda x.x$ and let Ω be $\lambda x.?$, the function that always returns the empty-tree value. If f and g are two projection functions, let $\langle f.g \rangle$ denote the projection function on pairs such that $\langle f.g \rangle (x.y) = (f(x).g(y))$. Suppose we want to slice a functional version of the line_char_count program from Figure 2, say LineCharCount, where LineCharCount takes a string and returns a pair consisting of the line count and the character count. Then a program LineCount that only counts lines can be defined by LineCount $=_{df}$ $\langle$ID.$\Omega\rangle \circ$ LineCharCount. That is, program LineCount can be created by slicing LineCharCount with respect to the slicing criterion $\langle$ID.$\Omega\rangle$. $\square$

The challenge is to devise a slicing algorithm that, given a program p and a projection function π, creates a program that behaves like $\pi \circ p$. The slicing algorithm will create the composed program by symbolically pushing π backwards through the body of p and simplifying the function body in appropriate ways.

There are a number of techniques developed for partial evaluation that are related to this goal. For example, projection functions have been used in binding-time analysis for partial evaluation in the presence of partially static structures [20,25]. However, for slicing, we need to propagate projection functions backwards—from function outputs to function arguments. Thus, the slicing problem has similarities with algorithms that propagate projection functions backwards to perform strictness analysis of lazy functional languages [15,39].

Instead of the fixed, finite domain of projection functions used in [15] and [39], we will use regular tree grammars (see below), which can be viewed as (representations of) projection functions. Specifically, we will use the variant of regular tree grammars that Mogensen used in his work on program bifurcation [26].[1]

A finite tree (or dag) T can be treated formally as a finite prefix-closed set of strings $L(T)$, where $L(T)$ consists of the set of access paths in T. Strings in $L(T)$ are either ε (the empty string), or of the form $s_1.s_2. \cdots .s_k$, where the s_i are selectors, or of the form $s_1.s_2. \cdots .s_k.a$, where a is an atom. There is a further "tree constraint" on $L(T)$, which is that if $s_1.s_2. \cdots .s_k.a \in L(T)$, then $L(T)$ cannot contain any string of the form $s_1.s_2. \cdots .s_k.x$, where x is either a selector or an atom different from a. The special empty-tree value "?" corresponds to the empty set of access paths (i.e., $L(?) = \varnothing$).

A projection function π on tree- (or dag-)structured data can also be treated formally as a prefix-closed set of strings $L(\pi)$. However, we do not insist that $L(\pi)$ have the "tree constraint", nor must $L(\pi)$ necessarily be finite. Given a tree T and projection function π, the application of π to T, denoted by $\pi(T)$, yields a tree T' such that $L(T') = L(\pi) \cap L(T)$. In other words, $\pi(T)$ prunes tree T, producing tree T'.

For our purposes, we need projection functions that correspond to *infinite* sets of paths. To represent each projection function in a *finite* way, we use a certain kind of regular tree grammar. Regular tree grammars are a formalism for defining a (possibly infinite) collection of trees that share certain structural properties in common. In this paper, we use a limited class of regular tree grammars, which has two main restrictions: (i) each nonterminal appears on the left-hand side of exactly one production; (ii) each production has one of the following five forms, where A and B stand for either $\top$, $\bot$, or a set of nonterminal names:

$$N \rightarrow \top \qquad N \rightarrow \bot \qquad N \rightarrow \bullet \qquad N \rightarrow \langle A.B \rangle \qquad N \rightarrow \bullet \mid \langle A.B \rangle$$

The symbol "$\bullet$" is a special symbol that denotes any atom; "$\top$" denotes the set of all trees; "$\bot$" denotes the set consisting of the empty tree; the symbols "$\langle$" and "$\rangle$" denote the pairing of trees.

---

[1] In Mogensen's work, regular tree grammars are used as "shape descriptors", to summarize the possible "shapes" that heap-allocated structures in a program can take on, as well as (representations of) projection functions. We will also use regular tree grammars in both of these ways; they are used as shape descriptors in Section 3.4.

Example. In the following regular tree grammar, nonterminal *OddList* denotes the collection of all odd-length finite lists in which all elements in odd positions along the list are atoms:

$$Atom \rightarrow \bullet \qquad OddList \rightarrow \langle\{Atom\}.\{EvenList\}\rangle \qquad EvenList \rightarrow \bullet \mid \langle\top.\{OddList\}\rangle$$

(Because we do not distinguish NIL from the other atoms, *OddList* actually denotes lists terminated by any atom. This is only a matter of convenience; it would be possible to extend the class of grammars introduced above to treat NIL separately from the other atoms.) □

Given a regular tree grammar G, each nonterminal of G can be viewed as denoting (*i.e.*, generating) a set of trees. However, we have no direct use for this view, and instead view each nonterminal as denoting a (possibly infinite) prefix-closed set of access paths. (Actually, this set of paths is the union of the sets of access paths in the aforementioned set of trees.)

To define the access paths V_N denoted by a nonterminal N, we treat the grammar as a collection of equations on prefix-closed sets of strings. For example, if the right-hand side for nonterminal N is $\top$, then we have the equation $V_N = Paths$, where *Paths* is the universe of finite access paths. If the right-hand side for nonterminal N is $\bot$, then we have the equation $V_N = \varnothing$. If the right-hand side for nonterminal N is

$$\bullet \mid \langle\{A_1, \cdots, A_a\}.\{B_1, \cdots, B_b\}\rangle,$$

the equation for N is

$$V_N = \text{ATOM} \cup \textbf{cons}(V_{A_1} \cup \cdots \cup V_{A_a}, V_{B_1} \cup \cdots \cup B_{A_b}).$$

In this equation, ATOM is the set of atoms, and **cons** is a set-valued function defined as follows:

$$\textbf{cons} =_{df} \lambda S_1.\lambda S_2.\{\varepsilon, \text{hd}, \text{tl}\} \cup \{\text{hd}.p_1 \mid p_1 \in S_1\} \cup \{\text{tl}.p_2 \mid p_2 \in S_2\}.$$

The language of access paths denoted by a nonterminal N is the value of V_N in the least solution to the grammar's equations.

Because a regular tree grammar has a finite number of productions, it provides a way to give a finite presentation of a collection of projection functions: Every nonterminal N corresponds to an associated projection function π_N, where $L(\pi_N) = V_N$.

During context analysis (see Section 3.2), we create an appropriate projection function for each point in the program. This requires us to be able to perform certain operations on projection functions. However, during context analysis all "manipulations of projection functions" are done indirectly, by performing (syntactic) manipulations on right-hand sides of regular-tree-grammar productions. In particular, Figure 3 defines the operator "join", denoted by $\sqcup$, which combines two regular-tree-grammar right-hand sides. It follows from Figure 3 and the equations for V_N given above that if A and B are two regular-tree-grammar right-hand sides, $A \sqcup B$ denotes the union of the languages that A and B denote. (Note that "$\mid$" is a "syntactic" symbol that appears in regular-tree-grammar right-hand sides. It should not be confused with $\sqcup$, which is an operation for combining two right-hand sides (to yield a third right-hand side).)

For any given regular tree grammar, we will occasionally use a nonterminal as a synonym for its right-hand side. In addition, we allow $\top$ to be replaced with $\bullet \mid \langle\top.\top\rangle$ whenever convenient or necessary.

Remark. The regular tree grammars defined above are not the only form of regular tree grammars that have been defined. For example, one alternative definition has only singleton nonterminals in each branch of each pair that occurs on the right-hand

$$\begin{aligned}
\bot \sqcup x &= x \\
\top \sqcup x &= \top \\
\bullet \sqcup \bullet \mid \langle A.B \rangle &= \bullet \mid \langle A.B \rangle \\
\bullet \sqcup \langle A.B \rangle &= \bullet \mid \langle A.B \rangle \\
\langle A.B \rangle \sqcup \langle C.D \rangle &= \langle A \otimes C.B \otimes D \rangle \\
\bullet \mid \langle A.B \rangle \sqcup \langle C.D \rangle &= \bullet \mid \langle A \otimes C.B \otimes D \rangle \\
\bullet \mid \langle A.B \rangle \sqcup \bullet \mid \langle C.D \rangle &= \bullet \mid \langle A \otimes C.B \otimes D \rangle
\end{aligned}$$

$$X \otimes Y = \begin{cases} \top & \text{if } X = \top \text{ or } Y = \top \\ X & \text{if } Y = \bot \\ Y & \text{if } X = \bot \\ X \cup Y & \text{otherwise} \end{cases}$$

Figure 3. Definition of the join operator $\sqcup$ for combining two regular-tree-grammar right-hand sides. (Join is also commutative; *i.e.*, $x \sqcup y = y \sqcup x$.)

side of a grammar rule, but allows there to be more than one such pair in each right-hand side [16]. This yields a more powerful tree-definition formalism. A feeling for the kind of information that is lost by using sets of nonterminals can be obtained by considering how the join of two right-hand sides is handled under the two approaches:

$$\langle N_1.N_2 \rangle \sqcup \langle N_3.N_4 \rangle = \langle N_1.N_2 \rangle \mid \langle N_3.N_4 \rangle \qquad \langle \{N_1\}.\{N_2\} \rangle \sqcup \langle \{N_3\}.\{N_4\} \rangle = \langle \{N_1, N_3\}.\{N_2, N_4\} \rangle$$

(a) Jones and Muchnick [16]   (b) Mogensen [26]

Approach (a) forms a right-hand side with multiple alternatives; this preserves the links between N_1 and N_2 and between N_3 and N_4. In approach (b), a single right-hand-side pair is formed that has a set of nonterminals in each arm; this breaks the links between N_1 and N_2 and between N_3 and N_4. The tree descriptions are sharper with regular tree grammars of type (a): With type-(a) grammars, nonterminals N_1 and N_4 can never occur simultaneously, whereas type-(b) grammars permit N_1-trees to be paired with N_4-trees.

However, the way we have defined the correspondence between a nonterminal and its projection function is based on the set of *access paths* of a set of trees (and not on the set of trees *per se*). That is, our intention is to use type-(b) grammars as a way to define sets of access paths, one set per nonterminal. For this purpose, type-(a) grammars are no sharper than type-(b) grammars. In addition, it is computationally more expensive to use and manipulate type-(a) grammars [26]. (It should be noted that type-(b) grammars can be thought of as simply a formalism for defining prefix-closed regular *string* languages. Our use of the term "regular tree grammars" for them follows Mogensen's usage [26].) □

3.2. Context Analysis via Regular Tree Grammars

For slicing, we are concerned with information that *might be needed* to compute some portion of the *desired part* of function *main*'s return value, where the "desired part" of the return value is characterized by the "slicing criterion", namely projection function π_{main}. Projection function π_{main} represents a "contract" to limit attention to the portions—if any—of *main*'s return value that lie on the access paths in $L(\pi_{main})$. Thus, in the slice we need only retain the parts of the original program that could contribute to a portion of *main*'s return value that lies on an access path in $L(\pi_{main})$. To identify these parts of the program, the slicing algorithm will propagate π_{main} backwards through the body of the program and simplify the program's subexpressions in appropriate ways.

The goal of slicing is to create a program q such that, on all inputs, q returns the same value as $\pi_{main} \circ p$ applied to the same input. That is,

$$[\![q]\!] = \pi_{main} \circ [\![p]\!] \qquad (\dagger)$$

where $[\![\cdot]\!]$ represents the meaning function of the language. Because projection function π_{main} is idempotent, we have

$$\pi_{main} \circ [\![q]\!] = \pi_{main} \circ (\pi_{main} \circ [\![p]\!]) = (\pi_{main} \circ \pi_{main}) \circ [\![p]\!] = \pi_{main} \circ [\![p]\!] = [\![q]\!].$$

Thus, strictly speaking, the return value of q's *main* function should contain *no* portions that lie outside of the access paths in $L(\pi_{main})$. In certain situations, we will relax condition ($\dagger$) to $[\![q]\!] \sqsupseteq \pi_{main} \circ [\![p]\!]$ and (safely) let q's *main* function return a value that *does* have portions that lie outside of the access paths in $L(\pi_{main})$.

Slicing criterion π_{main} is specified by giving a regular tree grammar. For example, the *Atom/OddList/EvenList* grammar given earlier is an example of the kind of description that could be furnished as input to the slicing procedure.

The process of propagating π_{main} backwards through the program is carried out by a *context-analysis* phase. Context analysis is concerned with describing, for each subexpression n of the program, what parts of the values computed by n are possibly needed in *main*'s return value [15,39]. In our case, context analysis creates a regular tree grammar whose nonterminals correspond to the interior points in the program's expression tree, thereby associating each subexpression of the program with (a representation of) a projection function.

The context analysis is specified in Figure 4, which gives schemas for generating one or more equations at each node of the program's expression tree. In general, these schemas generate a collection of mutually recursive equations over two sets of variables: variables of the form Context(n), where n is an interior point in the program's expression tree, and variables of the form ContextEnv(m), where m is the name of a function or a formal parameter.[2] These variables take on right-hand sides of regular-tree-grammar productions as their values. For example, ContextEnv(f), ContextEnv(x_i), and Context(n) are "right-hand-side-valued" variables that correspond to a function named f, a parameter named x_i, and a subexpression labeled n, respectively. We then find the least solution of these equations in the (syntactic) domain of right-hand sides of regular-tree-grammar productions. The solution to the Context equations is then interpreted as a regular tree grammar whose productions are of the form "$n \to$ value of Context(n)". This grammar associates each nonterminal (*i.e.*, program point) n with a prefix-closed set of access paths V_n. Thus, the grammar represents (in a finite way) a projection function for each interior point in the program's expression tree.

Example. We illustrate context analysis for a functional version of the line_char_count program from Figure 2. Function LineCharCountAux uses two accumulating parameters, lc and cc, to build up the line and character counts as it travels down the list-valued parameter str.

```
(DEFINE (main str) (CALL LineCharCountAux str '0 '0)) -- LineCharCount

(DEFINE (LineCharCountAux str lc cc)
   (IF (NULL str)
      (CONS lc cc)
      (IF (EQUAL (CAR str) 'nl)
         (CALL LineCharCountAux (CDR str) (OP + lc '1) (OP + cc '1))
         (CALL LineCharCountAux (CDR str) lc (OP + cc '1)))))
```

The annotated version of the program is

---

[2]We assume that all formal parameters have unique names (*e.g.*, by qualifying them with the name of the function to which they belong).

Form of expression	Equations associated with expression
$n : x_i$	$\text{Context}(x_i) = \text{Context}(n)$
$n : (\text{QUOTE } c)$	---
$n : (\text{CAR } n_1 : e_1)$	$\text{Context}(n_1) = \text{if Context}(n) = \perp \text{ then } \perp \text{ else } \langle \{n\}.\perp \rangle$
$n : (\text{CDR } n_1 : e_1)$	$\text{Context}(n_1) = \text{if Context}(n) = \perp \text{ then } \perp \text{ else } \langle \perp.\{n\} \rangle$
$n : (\text{ATOM } n_1 : e_1)$	$\text{Context}(n_1) = \text{if Context}(n) = \perp \text{ then } \perp \text{ else } \bullet \mid \langle \perp.\perp \rangle$
$n : (\text{NULL } n_1 : e_1)$	$\text{Context}(n_1) = \text{if Context}(n) = \perp \text{ then } \perp \text{ else } \bullet \mid \langle \perp.\perp \rangle$
$n : (\text{EQUAL } n_1 : e_1 \; n_2 : e_2)$	$\text{Context}(n_1) = \text{if Context}(n) = \perp \text{ then } \perp \text{ else } \top$
	$\text{Context}(n_2) = \text{if Context}(n) = \perp \text{ then } \perp \text{ else } \top$

$n : (\text{CONS } n_1 : e_1 \; n_2 : e_2)$

$$\text{Context}(n_1) = \begin{cases} \top & \text{if Context}(n) = \top \text{ or } \bullet \mid \langle \top.B \rangle \text{ or } \langle \top.B \rangle \\ \perp & \text{if Context}(n) = \perp \text{ or } \bullet \text{ or } \bullet \mid \langle \perp.B \rangle \text{ or } \langle \perp.B \rangle \\ \bigsqcup_{a \in A} \text{Context}(a) & \text{if Context}(n) = \bullet \mid \langle A.B \rangle \text{ or } \langle A.B \rangle \end{cases}$$

$$\text{Context}(n_2) = \begin{cases} \top & \text{if Context}(n) = \top \text{ or } \bullet \mid \langle B.\top \rangle \text{ or } \langle B.\top \rangle \\ \perp & \text{if Context}(n) = \perp \text{ or } \bullet \text{ or } \bullet \mid \langle B.\perp \rangle \text{ or } \langle B.\perp \rangle \\ \bigsqcup_{a \in A} \text{Context}(a) & \text{if Context}(n) = \bullet \mid \langle B.A \rangle \text{ or } \langle B.A \rangle \end{cases}$$

$n : (\text{IF } n_1 : e_1 \; n_2 : e_2 \; n_3 : e_3)$	$\text{Context}(n_1) = \text{if Context}(n) = \perp \text{ then } \perp \text{ else } \bullet \mid \langle \perp.\perp \rangle$
	$\text{Context}(n_2) = \text{Context}(n)$
	$\text{Context}(n_3) = \text{Context}(n)$
$n : (\text{CALL } f n_1 : e_1 \cdots$	$\text{Context}(n_i) = \text{if Context}(n) = \perp \text{ then } \perp \text{ else ContextEnv}(x_i),$
$\quad n_k : e_k)$	where f is defined by $(\text{DEFINE } (f x_1 \cdots x_k) \; e_f)$
$n : (\text{OP } op \; n_1 : e_1 \; n_2 : e_2)$	$\text{Context}(n_1) = \text{if Context}(n) = \perp \text{ then } \perp \text{ else } \bullet$
	$\text{Context}(n_2) = \text{if Context}(n) = \perp \text{ then } \perp \text{ else } \bullet$
$(\text{DEFINE } (\textit{main } x_1 \cdots x_k)$	$\text{ContextEnv}(\textit{main}) = \pi_{\textit{main}}$
$\quad n_0 : e_{\textit{main}})$	$\text{ContextEnv}(x_i) = \bigsqcup_{m : x_i \in e_{\textit{main}}} \text{Context}(x_i)$
	$\text{Context}(n_0) = \text{ContextEnv}(\textit{main})$
$(\text{DEFINE } (f x_1 \cdots x_k)$	$\text{ContextEnv}(f) = \bigsqcup_{m : (\text{CALL } f a_1 \cdots a_s) \in \text{CallsTo}(f)} \text{Context}(m)$
$\quad n_0 : e_f)$	$\text{ContextEnv}(x_i) = \bigsqcup_{m : x_i \in e_f} \text{Context}(x_i)$
	$\text{Context}(n_0) = \text{ContextEnv}(f)$

Figure 4. Equations for context analysis.

$(\text{DEFINE } (\text{main str}) \; n_0 : (\text{CALL LineCharCountAux } n_1 : \text{str } n_2 : '0 \; n_3 : '0))$

$(\text{DEFINE } (\text{LineCharCountAux str lc cc})$
$\quad n_4 : (\text{IF } n_5 : (\text{NULL } n_6 : \text{str})$
$\quad\quad n_7 : (\text{CONS } n_8 : \text{lc } n_9 : \text{cc})$
$\quad\quad n_{10} : (\text{IF } n_{11} : (\text{EQUAL } n_{12} : (\text{CAR } n_{13} : \text{str}) \; n_{14} : '\text{nl})$
$\quad\quad\quad n_{15} : (\text{CALL LineCharCountAux } n_{16} : (\text{CDR } n_{17} : \text{str})$
$\quad\quad\quad\quad n_{18} : (\text{OP} + n_{19} : \text{lc } n_{20} : '1)$
$\quad\quad\quad\quad n_{21} : (\text{OP} + n_{22} : \text{cc } n_{23} : '1))$
$\quad\quad\quad n_{24} : (\text{CALL LineCharCountAux } n_{25} : (\text{CDR } n_{26} : \text{str})$
$\quad\quad\quad\quad n_{27} : \text{lc}$
$\quad\quad\quad\quad n_{28} : (\text{OP} + n_{29} : \text{cc } n_{30} : '1)))))$

Suppose we want to slice LineCharCount with respect to slicing criterion $\langle \top.\perp \rangle$. The value of $\pi_{\textit{main}}$ is $\langle \top.\perp \rangle$; the initial value of Context for all program points and of ContextEnv for all functions and parameters is $\perp$. The values for the Context and ContextEnv variables in the least-fixed-point solution of the equations are:

$$\text{ContextEnv(main)} = \langle \top.\bot \rangle$$
$$\text{ContextEnv(main:str)} = \bullet \mid \langle \top.\{n_{16}, n_{25}\} \rangle$$
$$\text{ContextEnv(LineCharCountAux)} = \langle \top.\bot \rangle$$
$$\text{ContextEnv(LineCharCountAux:str)} = \bullet \mid \langle \top.\{n_{16}, n_{25}\} \rangle$$
$$\text{ContextEnv(LineCharCountAux:lc)} = \top$$
$$\text{ContextEnv(LineCharCountAux:cc)} = \bot$$

$\text{Context}(n_0) = \langle \top.\bot \rangle$	$\text{Context}(n_1) = \bullet \mid \langle \top.\{n_{16}, n_{25}\} \rangle$	$\text{Context}(n_2) = \top$
$\text{Context}(n_3) = \bot$	$\text{Context}(n_4) = \langle \top.\bot \rangle$	$\text{Context}(n_5) = \bullet \mid \langle \bot.\bot \rangle$
$\text{Context}(n_6) = \bullet \mid \langle \bot.\bot \rangle$	$\text{Context}(n_7) = \langle \top.\bot \rangle$	$\text{Context}(n_8) = \top$
$\text{Context}(n_9) = \bot$	$\text{Context}(n_{10}) = \langle \top.\bot \rangle$	$\text{Context}(n_{11}) = \bullet \mid \langle \bot.\bot \rangle$
$\text{Context}(n_{12}) = \top$	$\text{Context}(n_{13}) = \langle\{n_{12}\}.\bot \rangle$	$\text{Context}(n_{14}) = \top$
$\text{Context}(n_{15}) = \langle \top.\bot \rangle$	$\text{Context}(n_{16}) = \bullet \mid \langle \top.\{n_{16}, n_{25}\} \rangle$	$\text{Context}(n_{17}) = \langle \bot.\{n_{16}\} \rangle$
$\text{Context}(n_{18}) = \top$	$\text{Context}(n_{19}) = \bullet$	$\text{Context}(n_{20}) = \bullet$
$\text{Context}(n_{21}) = \bot$	$\text{Context}(n_{22}) = \bot$	$\text{Context}(n_{23}) = \bot$
$\text{Context}(n_{24}) = \langle \top.\bot \rangle$	$\text{Context}(n_{25}) = \bullet \mid \langle \top.\{n_{16}, n_{25}\} \rangle$	$\text{Context}(n_{26}) = \langle \bot.\{n_{25}\} \rangle$
$\text{Context}(n_{27}) = \top$	$\text{Context}(n_{28}) = \bot$	$\text{Context}(n_{29}) = \bot$
$\text{Context}(n_{30}) = \bot$		

These values agree with our intuition. Slicing criterion $\langle \top.\bot \rangle$ means: "The line count is of interest, but not the character count." As we would hope, the arithmetic expressions concerned with computing the line count (program points n_2, n_{18}, and n_{27}) are all associated with $\top$ (*i.e.*, "needed"), but the arithmetic expressions that compute the character count (n_3, n_{21}, and n_{28}) are all associated with $\bot$.

We can trace the flow of these context values through the program as follows: The call to LineCharCountAux in main causes the context π_{main} to be propagated to n_4, the body of LineCharCountAux. This context then passes through the IF expression at n_4 to the CONS expression at n_7. Here the context $\langle \top.\bot \rangle$ is split up, generating context $\top$ for variable lc and context $\bot$ for cc. Because lc is one of the formal parameters of LineCharCountAux, its context is collected and propagated to the appropriate expressions at all of LineCharCountAux's call sites, which causes expressions n_2, n_{18}, and n_{27} to have the context $\top$. $\square$

```
SliceExp(n : e) =
    if Context(n) = ⊥ then (QUOTE ?)
    else case e of
        n : xi:                         xi
        n : (QUOTE c):                  (QUOTE πContext(n)(c))
        n : (CAR n1 : e1):              (CAR SliceExp(n1 : e1))
        n : (CDR n1 : e1):              (CDR SliceExp(n1 : e1))
        n : (ATOM n1 : e1):             (ATOM SliceExp(n1 : e1))
        n : (NULL n1 : e1):             (NULL SliceExp(n1 : e1))
        n : (EQUAL n1 : e1 n2 : e2):    (EQUAL SliceExp(n1 : e1) SliceExp(n2 : e2))
        n : (CONS n1 : e1 n2 : e2):     (CONS SliceExp(n1 : e1) SliceExp(n2 : e2))
        n : (IF n1 : e1 n2 : e2 n3 : e3): (IF SliceExp(n1 : e1) SliceExp(n2 : e2) SliceExp(n3 : e3))
        n : (CALL f n1 : e1 ··· nk : ek): (CALL f SliceExp(n1 : e1) ··· SliceExp(nk ek))
        n : (OP op n1 : e1 n2 : e2):    (OP op SliceExp(n1 : e1) SliceExp(n2 : e2))
    endcase fi
```

Figure 5. Type I slicing: Given the results of context analysis, function SliceExp is applied to each function body to create the sliced program.

3.3. Creating the Slice

For slicing, we also need to create a simplified version of the program (*i.e.*, the slice itself). We can actually identify two different goals for what we mean by "slicing a functional program", which we call Type I and Type II slices.

In Weiser's original definition of slicing for imperative programs, a slice is obtained from the original program by deleting zero or more statements [43, pp. 353]. Type I slicing is the analogue for functional programs of Weiser's slicing operation: subexpressions of the program, rather than statements, are deleted. A *Type I slice* prunes the program as follows: For every subexpression whose context is ⊥, the result of evaluating the expression will not be used, as long as the client of the sliced program abides by the access "contract" given by π_{main}. Consequently, it is safe to replace every such subexpression by the expression '?. In other words, as long as the client of the sliced program abides by the access "contract" given by π_{main}, the values that can be inspected will be the same as those generated by the original main program. The Type I slicing operation is shown in Figure 5.

Example. The final program that results from slicing LineCharCount is as follows:

(DEFINE (main str) (CALL LineCharCountAux str '0 '?))

(DEFINE (LineCharCountAux str lc cc)
  (IF (NULL str)
    (CONS lc '?)
    (IF (EQUAL (CAR str) 'nl)
      (CALL LineCharCountAux (CDR str) (OP + lc '1) '?)
      (CALL LineCharCountAux (CDR str) lc '?))))

In this program, all expressions associated solely with the computation of the character count have been replaced by '?.

A simple clean-up step removes formal parameter cc from LineCharCountAux and the corresponding actual parameters at the three calls on LineCharCountAux: A formal parameter and its corresponding actual parameters can be removed whenever the context of the formal parameter is ⊥. □

In SliceExp, the case for a subexpression n of the form (QUOTE c) is handled by applying a projection function $\pi_{\text{Context}(n)}$ to c. This function is constructed from the value of Context(n) as follows:

(i)   We first normalize the regular tree grammar so that each branch of each pair consists of a single symbol: ⊤, ⊥, or a (single) nonterminal. Normalization of the grammar is carried out by the following method (which we will call *join-normalization*):

    • A set of nonterminals $\{N_1, N_2, \cdots, N_k\}$ is replaced by a new nonterminal N and a production for N is added to the grammar; the right-hand side of the new production is the join of the right-hand sides of the productions for N_1, N_2, $\cdots$, and N_k. This process is repeated until each branch of each pair on the right-hand side of a production (including the newly introduced productions) consists of a single symbol.

    • During this process, a table is kept of which new nonterminals correspond to which sets of old nonterminals, and this table is consulted to reuse new nonterminals whenever possible. Because there is a finite number of such nonterminal sets, the process must terminate.

(ii) Given such a normalized grammar, $\pi_{\text{Context}(n)}$ is defined as follows:

$$\pi_\top = \lambda t.t \quad \pi_\bullet = \lambda t.\text{if atom}(t) \text{ then } t \text{ else ? fi}$$
$$\pi_\bot = \lambda t.? \quad \pi_{\langle A.B\rangle} = \lambda t.\text{if atom}(t) \text{ then ? else cons}(\pi_A(t), \pi_B(t)) \text{ fi}$$
$$\pi_{\bullet \mid \langle A.B\rangle} = \lambda t.\text{if atom}(t) \text{ then } t \text{ else cons}(\pi_A(t), \pi_B(t)) \text{ fi}$$

(For the sake of uniformity, in these rules we assume that A and B stand for either $\top$, $\bot$, or a nonterminal symbol.)

A *Type II* slice differs from a Type I slice because it is allowed to introduce *additional* material into the sliced program. A Type II slice prunes out "extra" information that is found in the values returned by programs created by Type I slicing. The reason that such extra information exists is that the context analysis of Section 3.2 is a monovariant analysis. Because different portions of the result of a function may be needed at different call sites, with a Type I slice a function may return more information than is needed at a specific call site. In addition, more information may be present in a variable than is needed at all uses of that variable. For this reason, a sliced program generated by a Type I slice may occasionally return more information than is actually needed. This does not present a problem as long as all accesses are confined to the "contract" implicit in π_{main}. However, there may be times when we want the slice to be "stingy"; we want it to remove unneeded information when it arises. For this purpose, we define the method for Type II slicing shown in Figure 6. In places where it can detect that unneeded information might be introduced, the Type II slicing procedure inserts an explicit call to an appropriate projection function to trim down the return value.

(In the LineCharCount example, the Type I and Type II slices are identical; no projection functions would be inserted by the Type II slicing method.)

3.4. An Improved Slicing Algorithm

A further improvement of the slicing algorithm can be obtained by combining *shape information* with context information. To describe this extension, it is convenient to give a formulation of the shape-analysis problem in a way that is similar in style to

---

```
SliceExp(n : e) =
    if Context(n) = ⊥ then (QUOTE ?)
    else case e of
        n : xᵢ:                          if Context(n) = ContextEnv(xᵢ) then xᵢ
                                         else (CALL π_Context(n) xᵢ) fi
        n : (QUOTE c):                   (QUOTE π_Context(n)(c))
        n : (CAR n₁ : e₁):               (CAR SliceExp(n₁ : e₁))
        n : (CDR n₁ : e₁):               (CDR SliceExp(n₁ : e₁))
        n : (ATOM n₁ : e₁):              (ATOM SliceExp(n₁ : e₁))
        n : (NULL n₁ : e₁):              (NULL SliceExp(n₁ : e₁))
        n : (EQUAL n₁ : e₁ n₂ : e₂):     (EQUAL SliceExp(n₁ : e₁) SliceExp(n₂ : e₂))
        n : (CONS n₁ : e₁ n₂ : e₂):      (CONS SliceExp(n₁ : e₁) SliceExp(n₂ : e₂))
        n : (IF n₁ : e₁ n₂ : e₂ n₃ : e₃): (IF SliceExp(n₁ : e₁) SliceExp(n₂ : e₂) SliceExp(n₃ : e₃))
        n : (CALL f n₁ : e₁ ··· nₖ : eₖ): if Context(n) = ContextEnv(f) then
                                                (CALL f SliceExp(n₁ : e₁) ··· SliceExp(nₖ eₖ))
                                         else (CALL π_Context(n)
                                                (CALL f SliceExp(n₁ : e₁) ··· SliceExp(nₖ eₖ)))
                                         fi
        n : (OP op n₁ : e₁ n₂ : e₂):      (OP op SliceExp(n₁ : e₁) SliceExp(n₂ : e₂))
    endcase fi
```

Figure 6. Type II slicing: A second method for slicing a functional program.

the context-analysis equation schemas of Figure 4. The equation schemas for shape analysis are presented in Figure 7. In shape analysis, regular tree grammars are used as shape descriptors to summarize the possible shapes of values (as characterized by a set of access paths) that may be returned by a subexpression.

To be able to combine shape information with context information, we also need the operation on right-hand sides of regular-tree-grammar productions that is defined as follows:

$$M \oplus N =_{df} ((M = \bot) \text{ or } (N = \bot) \text{ or } (M = \bullet \text{ and } N = \langle A.B \rangle) \text{ or } (N = \bullet \text{ and } M = \langle A.B \rangle)).$$

The improvement to the slicing algorithm consists of replacing the first line of (either version of) SliceExp with

$$\text{if Shape}(n) \oplus \text{Context}(n) \text{ then } (\text{QUOTE ?})$$

The reason this is safe is that if $\text{Shape}(n) \oplus \text{Context}(n)$ is true at subexpression n, then the value created at n can never contain any of the access paths in $L(\text{Context}(n))$. Because we are limiting attention to the portions of n's possible return values that lie on the access paths in $L(\text{Context}(n))$—of which there are none—we can replace subexpression n with '?.

Example. Suppose we use slicing criterion $\bullet$ to slice the following program:

Form of expression	Equations associated with expression
$n : x_i$	$\text{Shape}(n) = \text{ShapeEnv}(x_i)$
$n : (\text{QUOTE } c)$	$\text{Shape}(n) = \text{ConstShape}(c)$
$n : (\text{CAR } n_1 : e_1)$	$\text{Shape}(n) = \begin{cases} \top & \text{if Shape}(n_1) = \top \text{ or } \bullet \mid \langle \top.B \rangle \text{ or } \langle \top.B \rangle \\ \bot & \text{if Shape}(n_1) = \bot \text{ or } \bullet \text{ or } \bullet \mid \langle \bot.B \rangle \text{ or } \langle \bot.B \rangle \\ \bigsqcup_{a \in A} \text{Shape}(a) & \text{if Shape}(n_1) = \bullet \mid \langle A.B \rangle \text{ or } \langle A.B \rangle \end{cases}$
$n : (\text{CDR } n_1 : e_1)$	$\text{Shape}(n) = \begin{cases} \top & \text{if Shape}(n_1) = \top \text{ or } \bullet \mid \langle B.\top \rangle \text{ or } \langle B.\top \rangle \\ \bot & \text{if Shape}(n_1) = \bot \text{ or } \bullet \text{ or } \bullet \mid \langle B.\bot \rangle \text{ or } \langle B.\bot \rangle \\ \bigsqcup_{a \in A} \text{Shape}(a) & \text{if Shape}(n_1) = \bullet \mid \langle B.A \rangle \text{ or } \langle B.A \rangle \end{cases}$
$n : (\text{ATOM } n_1 : e_1)$	$\text{Shape}(n) = \text{if Shape}(n_1) = \bot \text{ then } \bot \text{ else } \bullet$
$n : (\text{NULL } n_1 : e_1)$	$\text{Shape}(n) = \text{if Shape}(n_1) = \bot \text{ then } \bot \text{ else } \bullet$
$n : (\text{EQUAL } n_1 : e_1 \ n_2 : e_2)$	$\text{Shape}(n) = \text{if Shape}(n_1) = \bot \text{ or Shape}(n_2) = \bot \text{ then } \bot \text{ else } \bullet$
$n : (\text{CONS } n_1 : e_1 \ n_2 : e_2)$	$\text{Shape}(n) = \langle \{n_1\} . \{n_2\} \rangle$
$n : (\text{IF } n_1 : e_1 \ n_2 : e_2 \ n_3 : e_3)$	$\text{Shape}(n) = \begin{cases} \bot & \text{if Shape}(n_1) = \bot \\ \text{Shape}(n_2) \sqcup \text{Shape}(n_3) & \text{otherwise} \end{cases}$
$n : (\text{CALL } f e_1 \cdots e_k)$	$\text{Shape}(n) = \text{ShapeEnv}(f)$
$n : (\text{OP } op \ n_1 : e_1 \ n_2 : e_2)$	$\text{Shape}(n) = \text{if } (\bullet \sqsubseteq \text{Shape}(n_1)) \text{ and } (\bullet \sqsubseteq \text{Shape}(n_2)) \text{ then } \bullet \text{ else } \bot$
$(\text{DEFINE } (main \ x_1 \cdots x_k)$	$\text{ShapeEnv}(main) = \text{Shape}(n_0)$
$\quad n_0 : e_{main})$	$\text{ShapeEnv}(x_i) = \text{InitialShapeEnv}(x_i)$
$(\text{DEFINE } (f \ x_1 \cdots x_k)$	$\text{ShapeEnv}(f) = \text{Shape}(n_0)$
$\quad n_0 : e_f)$	$\text{ShapeEnv}(x_i) = \bigsqcup_{m : (\text{CALL } f n_1 : a_1 \cdots n_i : a_i) \in \text{CallsTo}(f)} \text{Shape}(n_i)$

Figure 7. Equations for shape analysis. The desired solution of these equations is the least-fixed-point solution. The notation "$\bullet \sqsubseteq \text{Shape}(n)$" means that $\bullet$ is in $\text{Shape}(n)$. Auxiliary function $\text{ConstShape}(c)$ returns a shape descriptor for a constant c. InitialShapeEnv is a map from $main$'s formal parameters to their (known) initial shape descriptors.

(DEFINE (main) (CALL mycons '1 '2))
(DEFINE (mycons x y) (CONS x y)).

Without the suggested improvement, both versions of SliceExp create the program

(DEFINE (main) (CALL mycons '? '?))
(DEFINE (mycons x y) (CONS '? '?)),

which contains a wasted function call and also returns a value that contains extra information. With the improvement, both versions of SliceExp create

(DEFINE (main) '?)
(DEFINE (mycons x y) '?).

□

4. Semantic Issues

We do not have space in this paper for an in-depth treatment of the issue of how the semantics of a slice relates to the semantics of the original program. In fact, our techniques do not guarantee that equation (†) of Section 3.2 holds (*i.e.*, $[\![q]\!] = \pi_{main} \circ [\![p]\!]$) when the programming language has a call-by-value semantics. The reason is that, for a call-by-value language, slicing may change the termination behavior; that is, a slice may terminate on inputs on which the original program diverges. Slicing can never introduce *divergence*; it can only introduce *termination*, which, from a pragmatic standpoint, is a quite reasonable situation.

Example. For (single-procedure) programs in imperative languages, the need for a lazy semantics can be illustrated by means of the following example: Consider the three programs P_1, P_2, and P_3:

P_1	P_2	P_3
x = 0;	x = 0;	x = 0;
for (i = 1; ; i++) { }	w = 1;	☐
y = x;	y = x;	y = x;

P_3 is the slice of P_1 with respect to y = x; P_3 is also the slice of P_2 with respect to y = x. Let $\sqsubseteq_{sl}$ denote the "is-a-slice-of" relation, and let $\sqsubseteq_{sem}$ denote the semantic approximation relation.

In a standard direct denotational semantics for an imperative language (denoted by $\mathbf{M}[\![\,\cdot\,]\!]$), commands are (strict) store-to-store transformers. Because program P_1 contains an infinite loop, we have $\mathbf{M}[\![P_1]\!] = \lambda s. \perp_{store}$. Consequently, even though $P_3 \sqsubseteq_{sl} P_1$ and $P_3 \sqsubseteq_{sl} P_2$, we have $\mathbf{M}[\![P_1]\!] \sqsubseteq_{sem} \mathbf{M}[\![P_3]\!] \sqsubseteq_{sem} \mathbf{M}[\![P_2]\!]$. In other words, with the standard treatment of the semantics of imperative languages, the relation "is-a-slice-of" is not consistent with the semantic approximation relation.

However, there is a non-standard setting in which the hoped-for relationships *do* hold. Ramalingam and Reps have defined an equational *value-sequence*-oriented semantics (as opposed to a conventional *state-oriented* semantics) for a variant of the program dependence graph [30] (see also [5]). Rather than treating each program point as a state-to-state transformer, the value-sequence semantics treats each program point as a *value-sequence transformer* that takes (possibly infinite) argument sequences from dependence predecessors to a (possibly infinite) output sequence. The latter sequence represents the *sequence of values* computed at that point during program execution. Because dependence edges can bypass infinite loops, the value-sequence semantics is *more defined than* a standard operational or denotational semantics. For example, the vertex for statement y = x in program P_1 has the singleton sequence "[0]" rather than, for example, the uncompleted sequence "$\perp$". (This agrees with the sequence for y = x in program P_3, which is also "[0]".)

With the value-sequence semantics, it is trivial to show that $\sqsubseteq_{sl}$ and $\sqsubseteq_{sem}$ are consistent: A slice is the subgraph of the dependence graph found by following edges of the dependence graph backwards from the vertex v of interest; this subgraph corresponds exactly to the subset S_v of the equations that can affect the value-sequence at v. Because we followed *all* paths backwards from v to identify S_v, the solutions to equation system S_v and to the full equation system must be identical for all vertices that occur in both the program and the slice. Consequently, in this framework the semantics of a slice approximates the semantics of the full program.

(Other approaches to lazy semantics for program dependence graphs include [35], [4], and [1].) □

For readers who are uncomfortable with the "semantic anomaly" that a slice does not preserve the termination behavior of the original program, we would like to point out that this situation is far more acceptable than the semantic anomaly exhibited by partial evaluation, where, due to the well-known problems with non-termination of partial evaluators in the presence of static-infinite computations ([17, pp. 265-266], [36, pp. 501-502], [25, pp. 337], [18, pp. 299], and [5]), partial evaluation can introduce *divergence*. That is, the specializer *itself* can diverge on programs that would not diverge on all dynamic inputs if executed in their unspecialized form.

- Partial evaluation is faithful to the termination properties of the original program only under the assumption that the operators in the language—including the conditional operator—have call-by-value semantics.
- Similarly, but with less potential for disruptive behavior, program slicing is faithful to the termination properties of the original program only under the assumption that the operators in the language have call-by-name semantics.

While no reasonable programming languages have call-by-value conditionals, there do exist programming languages with call-by-name semantics.

5. A Re-Examination of Program Bifurcation

In [26], Mogensen describes a method to perform program bifurcation. Briefly stated, bifurcation is a way to transform a program that takes partially static structures as arguments into two programs: one in which all of the parameters are totally static, and a second in which all of the parameters are either totally static or totally dynamic. This section outlines how some of the steps used in program bifurcation can be redefined in terms of program slicing.

Mogensen defines operations that split a function f into a function f_S, which computes the purely static part of f's result, and a function f_D, which computes the dynamic part of f's result. We will refer to these operations as BifS and BifD, respectively. BifS identifies and removes all possibly dynamic expressions; BifD identifies and removes static expressions whose values are not needed for the dynamic result. In Mogensen's formulation of them, BifS and BifD do not incorporate a true neededness analysis; instead, they use binding-time information (which is computed by propagating information through the program in the forward direction) as a sort of "pseudo-neededness" information.

Mogensen begins by performing binding-time analysis. He uses a domain of regular tree grammars that is much like the domain we use: his symbol S corresponds to our symbol $\top$; his D, to our $\bot$; and his *atomS*, to our •. The binding-time analysis can be defined as the fixed point of a set of equations that are similar to our shape-analysis and context-analysis equations. (We have omitted this reformulation for reasons of space.) The binding-time analysis produces, for pertinent expressions in the program, a regular tree grammar describing "how static" each expression is guaranteed to be. Specifically, when interpreted as a prefix-closed set of strings, the regular-tree-grammar production associated with a subexpression n describes (a subset of) the set of all access paths that are guaranteed not to lead to data that is dynamic in any value returned by *n*. (This is not to say that all access paths described by the grammar rule for *n* necessarily exist in each of *n*'s possible return values.) The final step of bifurcation is to apply BifS and BifD to each function of the program.

BifS and BifD are similar to, but not precisely, Type II slices. This motivates us to formulate revised bifurcation operations, called BifS' and BifD', that are based on program slicing (and hence *do* perform a true neededness analysis). Some of the advantages of using a "true" over a "pseudo" neededness analysis are as follows:

- For BifS', static expressions whose values are not needed for the static result can now be identified and removed.
- For BifD', dead dynamic code can now be identified and removed.

Below, we will only illustrate bifurcation procedure BifS'. (Because BifD' uses BifS' as a subroutine, some, but not all, of the differences between BifD' and BifD are inherited from the differences between BifS' and BifS.) The BifS' procedure is as follows:

(i) Binding-time analysis is performed, using the given (possibly partially static) binding times for *main*'s variables.
(ii) A "meet-normalization" procedure is applied to the resulting regular tree grammar. (The grammars used in Mogensen's binding-time analysis are of a kind that is dual to the kind we use, and hence the results of binding-time analysis must be normalized by a process dual to the join-normalization operation defined in Section 3.3. This converts the productions of the grammar obtained from binding-time analysis to ones in which each branch of each right-hand-side pair is a singleton set. The normalized grammar can then be interpreted as a grammar of the kind we are using for slicing.)
(iii) The nonterminals in the normalized grammar are systematically renamed to remove all uses of the names of the program's functions, formal parameters, and subexpressions.
(iv) A Type II slice of the program is then performed, using the (renamed) binding-time descriptor for function *main* as the slicing criterion π_{main}.

Example. Consider the program

(DEFINE (main a b c d) (IF c (CONS a b) (CONS a d)))

with the following binding times for the inputs: a:S, b:S, c:S, d:D.[3] The value of π_{main} generated by the binding-time analysis is $\langle S.D \rangle$. The program generated by BifS is

(DEFINE (main a b c d) (IF c (CALL $\pi_{\langle S.D \rangle}$ (CONS a b)) (CONS a '?))),

whereas BifS' yields

(DEFINE (main a b c d) (IF c (CONS a '?) (CONS a '?)))).

The expression b is retained by BifS because it is static, whereas BifS' classifies the expression as unneeded ($\perp$) and prunes it from the sliced program. □

While the differences between what the two versions of BifS produce are not earthshaking, they provide another viewpoint for understanding the results presented in this paper:

- The essence of the rewriting step used in program bifurcation is the analogue for functional programs of program slicing (which had been defined earlier for imperative programs).

---

[3]In this example, we are using binding times in which none of the parameters are partially static. This is done merely to give the simplest possible example of the differences between BifS and BifS'.

- Slicing of functional programs is a program-specialization operation of interest in its own right and can be isolated from the rest of the machinery that is part of bifurcation.

6. Relation to Previous Work

In the slicing community, slicing has long been recognized as a way to specialize programs. Many of the proposed applications of slicing are based on its properties as a specialization operation. For example,

- Weiser proposed using slicing to decompose programs into separate threads that can be run in parallel [42]. Each thread computes a portion of what is computed by the original program.
- Horwitz, Reps, and Prins proposed an algorithm for merging two variants A and B of a program $Base$ [12]. The algorithm breaks down $Base$, A, and B into their constituent slices and chooses among them to create the merged program. By selecting appropriate slices, the algorithm guarantees that the merged program exhibits all changed behavior of A with respect to $Base$, all changed behavior of B with respect to $Base$, and all behavior that is common to all three [31].
- Bates and Horwitz proposed to use slicing to avoid redoing the part of a test suite that is unaffected by a change to a program [2].
- Andersen Consulting's interactive Cobol System Renovation Environment (Cobol/SRE) is a system for re-engineering legacy systems written in Cobol [27]. It uses slicing as the fundamental operation that users employ to select program fragments of interest. Operations are provided for combining slices (*i.e.*, union, intersection, and difference). These fragments are then used to reorganize the program by extracting the code fragments and repackaging them into independent modules.

Most work on slicing has concerned imperative programming languages. In the context of functional languages, a slicing-like operation is used by Liu and Teitelbaum as a cleanup step in their transformational methodology for deriving incremental versions of functional programs from non-incremental functional programs [21]. In their work, slices can be taken only with respect to projection functions that express finite-depth access patterns in a tree. A similar technique also appears in Romanenko's work on "arity raising" [34] (a method for handling partially static structures in a partial evaluator). In contrast, the slicing method we have presented uses regular-tree grammars to express projection functions that have arbitrary-depth (but regular) access patterns.

This paper concerns the complementary relationship between slicing and partial evaluation when *backward* slicing is considered as a specialization operation. Another kind of relationship between slicing and partial evaluation has been established by Das, Reps, and Van Hentenryck who showed how three variants of *forward* slicing can be used to carry out binding-time analysis for imperative programs [5].

This paper has been greatly influenced by the literature on partial evaluation and related operations, particularly by Mogensen's paper on program bifurcation [26]. In particular, the variant of regular tree grammars that we have used is based on Mogensen's work (as opposed to the version of regular tree grammars used by Jones and Muchnick [16] and the normalized set equations used by Reynolds [33]).

The context analysis that we have used to define the slicing algorithm is related to the "neededness" analysis defined by Hughes [15] and also to the "strictness analysis" of Wadler and Hughes, which is also capable of identifying whether the value of a subexpression is ignored [39, pp. 392]. Our analysis is somewhat different from these two and, in general, incomparable to them. For instance, the latter analyses are both formulated in terms of a fixed, finite set of projection functions for characterizing "neededness patterns" of list-manipulation programs. The use of a fixed set of projection functions makes the analysis efficient, but it also introduces some limitations on the class of neededness patterns that can be identified. (This is not to say that only uninteresting neededness information can be discovered. On the contrary, Hughes's analysis is able to determine that in the length function the spine of the argument list is needed, but the elements of the list are not needed.) Because our work is based on regular tree grammars, our analysis is capable of handling a broader class of neededness patterns: The advantage of the regular-tree grammar approach is that it "adapts" to the patterns that are used in a particular program.

Another issue concerns the monovariant versus polyvariant treatment of functions. In the work of Hughes, Wadler and Hughes, and Liu and Teitelbaum, the context analyses that are used create projection-function transformers for each source-program function, which are then employed at each call site to determine how the call site's local context is transformed. This is only feasible when the domain of projection functions is small (*e.g.* Wadler and Hughes work with a 10-point domain of projection functions). Because our domain of projection functions—regular-tree grammars—is large, our work follows Mogensen and uses a monovariant analysis (*i.e.*, the contexts of all calls to a function f are combined to determine the context of f's body). This monovariant analysis loses precision, but the alternative polyvariant analysis would involve tabulating a collection of functions of type "regular-tree-grammar $\rightarrow$ regular-tree-grammar".

7. Concluding Remarks

This paper has shown how program slicing can be used to carry out a certain kind of program-specialization operation. Because the paper extends existing slicing techniques by making use of techniques that are closely related to ones that have been used in both partial evaluation and program bifurcation, the paper serves to bridge the gap between two communities—the partial-evaluation community and the program-slicing community—that are both working on semantics-based program manipulation but that (to date) have had relatively limited contact. For these two communities, the salient connections to the material presented in the paper are as follows:

- Our results should be of interest to the partial-evaluation community because we have demonstrated a new way of specializing programs that is different from the specialization operations carried out by partial evaluation, supercompilation, bifurcation, and deforestation. In addition, the slicing-based specialization operation has another characteristic that sets it apart from partial evaluation (and other forwards-oriented specialization operations): Slicing-based specialization permits programs to be specialized in ways that do not have to be anticipated by the author of the original program (in the sense that specialization is not linked to the parameters to functions and procedures provided in the original program).
- Our results should also be of interest to the program-slicing community. Although several previous papers have studied the impact of dependences carried through heap-allocated data structures [11,29,7,22,41,24,32], our work sheds new light on the problem of creating non-trivial slices of programs that make use of heap-allocated data structures.

Acknowledgements

This work was supported by the National Science Foundation under grant CCR-9100424 and by the Advanced Research Projects Agency under ARPA Order 8856 (monitored by the Office of Naval Research under contract N00014-92-J-1937).

References

1. Ballance, R.A., Maccabe, A.B., and Ottenstein, K.J., "The program dependence web: A representation supporting control-, data-, and demand-driven interpretation of imperative languages," *Proceedings of the ACM SIGPLAN 90 Conference on Programming Language Design and Implementation*, (White Plains, NY, June 20-22, 1990), *ACM SIGPLAN Notices* **25**(6) pp. 257-271 (June 1990).

2. Bates, S. and Horwitz, S., "Incremental program testing using program dependence graphs," pp. 384-396 in *Conference Record of the Twentieth ACM Symposium on Principles of Programming Languages*, (Charleston, SC, January 10-13, 1993), ACM, New York, NY (1993).

3. Binkley, D., "Using semantic differencing to reduce the cost of regression testing," *Proceedings of the 1992 Conference on Software Maintenance* (Orlando, FL, November 9-12, 1992), pp. 41-50 (1992).

4. Cartwright, R. and Felleisen, M., "The semantics of program dependence," *Proceedings of the ACM SIGPLAN 89 Conference on Programming Language Design and Implementation*, (Portland, OR, June 21-23, 1989), *ACM SIGPLAN Notices* **24**(7) pp. 13-27 (July 1989).

5. Das, M., Reps, T., and Van Hentenryck, P., "Semantic foundations of binding-time analysis for imperative programs," pp. 100-110 in *Proceedings of the ACM SIGPLAN Symposium on Partial Evaluation and Semantics-Based Program Manipulation (PEPM 95)*, (La Jolla, California, June 21-23, 1995), ACM, New York, NY (1995).

6. Ferrante, J., Ottenstein, K., and Warren, J., "The program dependence graph and its use in optimization," *ACM Trans. Program. Lang. Syst.* **9**(3) pp. 319-349 (July 1987).

7. Field, J., "A simple rewriting semantics for realistic imperative programs and its application to program analysis," Proceedings of the SIGPLAN Workshop on Partial Evaluation and Semantics-Based Program Manipulation, (San Francisco, CA, June 1992), Technical Report YALEU/DCS/RR-909, Department of Computer Science, Yale University, New Haven, CT (1992).

8. Futamura, Y. and Nogi, K., "Generalized partial computation," pp. 133-152 in *Partial Evaluation and Mixed Computation: Proceedings of the IFIP TC2 Workshop on Partial Evaluation and Mixed Computation*, (Gammel Avernaes, Denmark, October 18-24, 1987), ed. D. Bjørner, A.P. Ershov, and N.D. Jones,North-Holland, New York, NY (1988).

9. Gallagher, K.B., "Using program slicing in software maintenance," Ph.D. dissertation and Tech. Rep. CS-90-05, Computer Science Department, University of Maryland, Baltimore Campus, Baltimore, MD (January 1990).

10. Gallagher, K.B. and Lyle, J.R., "Using program slicing in software maintenance," *IEEE Transactions on Software Engineering* **SE-17**(8) pp. 751-761 (August 1991).

11. Horwitz, S., Pfeiffer, P., and Reps, T., "Dependence analysis for pointer variables," *Proceedings of the ACM SIGPLAN 89 Conference on Programming Language Design and Implementation*, (Portland, OR, June 21-23, 1989), *ACM SIGPLAN Notices* **24**(7) pp. 28-40 (July 1989).

12. Horwitz, S., Prins, J., and Reps, T., "Integrating non-interfering versions of programs," *ACM Trans. Program. Lang. Syst.* **11**(3) pp. 345-387 (July 1989).

13. Horwitz, S., Reps, T., and Binkley, D., "Interprocedural slicing using dependence graphs," *ACM Trans. Program. Lang. Syst.* **12**(1) pp. 26-60 (January 1990).

14. Horwitz, S., "Identifying the semantic and textual differences between two versions of a program," *Proceedings of the ACM SIGPLAN 90 Conference on Programming Language Design and Implementation*, (White Plains, NY, June 20-22, 1990), *ACM SIGPLAN Notices* **25**(6) pp. 234-245 (June 1990).

15. Hughes, J., "Backwards analysis of functional programs," pp. 187-208 in *Partial Evaluation and Mixed Computation: Proceedings of the IFIP TC2 Workshop on Partial Evaluation and Mixed Computation*, (Gammel Avernaes, Denmark, October 18-24, 1987), ed. D. Bjørner, A.P. Ershov, and N.D. Jones,North-Holland, New York, NY (1988).

16. Jones, N.D. and Muchnick, S.S., "Flow analysis and optimization of Lisp-like structures," pp. 102-131 in *Program Flow Analysis: Theory and Applications*, ed. S.S. Muchnick and N.D. Jones,Prentice-Hall, Englewood Cliffs, NJ (1981).

17. Jones, N.D., "Automatic program specialization: A reexamination from basic principles," pp. 225-282 in *Partial Evaluation and Mixed Computation: Proceedings of the IFIP TC2 Workshop on Partial Evaluation and Mixed Computation*, (Gammel Avernaes, Denmark, October 18-24, 1987), ed. D. Bjørner, A.P. Ershov, and N.D. Jones,North-Holland, New York, NY (1988).

18. Jones, N.D., Gomard, C.K., and Sestoft, P., *Partial Evaluation and Automatic Program Generation*, Prentice-Hall International, Englewood Cliffs, NJ (1993).

19. Kuck, D.J., Kuhn, R.H., Leasure, B., Padua, D.A., and Wolfe, M., "Dependence graphs and compiler optimizations," pp. 207-218 in *Conference Record of the Eighth ACM Symposium on Principles of Programming Languages*, (Williamsburg, VA, January 26-28, 1981), ACM, New York, NY (1981).

20. Launchbury, J., *Projection Factorizations in Partial Evaluation*, Cambridge University Press, Cambridge, UK (1991).

21. Liu, Y.A. and Teitelbaum, T., "Caching intermediate results for program improvement," in *Proceedings of the ACM SIGPLAN Symposium on Partial Evaluation and Semantics-Based Program Manipulation (PEPM 95)*, (La Jolla, California, June 21-23, 1995), ACM, New York, NY (1995).

22. Livadas, P.E. and Rosenstein, A., "Slicing in the presence of pointer variables," Technical Report SERC-TR-74-F, Software Engineering Research Center, University of Florida, Gainesville, FL (June 1994).

23. Lyle, J. and Weiser, M., "Experiments on slicing-based debugging tools," in *Proceedings of the First Conference on Empirical Studies of Programming*, (June 1986), Ablex Publishing Co. (1986).

24. Lyle, J.R., Wallace, D.R., Graham, J.R., Gallagher, K.B., Poole, J.P., and Binkley, D.W., "Unravel: A CASE tool to assist evaluation of high integrity software," Report NISTIR 5691, National Institute for Standards and Technology, Gaithersburg, MD (August 1995).

25. Mogensen, T., "Partially static structures in a self-applicable partial evaluator," pp. 325-347 in *Partial Evaluation and Mixed Computation: Proceedings of the IFIP TC2 Workshop on Partial Evaluation and Mixed Computation*, (Gammel Avernaes, Denmark, October 18-24, 1987), ed. D. Bjørner, A.P. Ershov, and N.D. Jones,North-Holland, New York, NY (1988).

26. Mogensen, T., "Separating binding times in language specifications," pp. 12-25 in *Fourth International Conference on Functional Programming and Computer Architecture*, (London, UK, Sept. 11-13, 1989), ACM Press, New York, NY (1989).

27. Ning, J.Q., Engberts, A., and Kozaczynski, W., "Automated support for legacy code understanding," *Commun. of the ACM* **37**(5) pp. 50-57 (May 1994).

28. Ottenstein, K.J. and Ottenstein, L.M., "The program dependence graph in a software development environment," *Proceedings of the ACM SIGSOFT/SIGPLAN Software Engineering Symposium on Practical Software Development Environments*, (Pittsburgh, PA, Apr. 23-25, 1984), *ACM SIGPLAN Notices* **19**(5) pp. 177-184 (May 1984).

29. Pfeiffer, P. and Selke, R.P, "On the adequacy of dependence-based representations for programs with heaps," in *Proceedings of the International Conference on Theoretical Aspects of Computer Software (TACS '91)*, (Sendai, Japan, September 1991), *Lecture Notes in Computer Science*, Vol. 526, ed. T. Ito and A.R. Meyer,Springer-Verlag, New York, NY (1991).

30. Ramalingam, G. and Reps, T., "Semantics of program representation graphs," TR-900, Computer Sciences Department, University of Wisconsin, Madison, WI (December 1989).

31. Reps, T. and Yang, W., "The semantics of program slicing and program integration," pp. 360-374 in *Proceedings of the Colloquium on Current Issues in Programming Languages*, (Barcelona, Spain, March 13-17, 1989), *Lecture Notes in Computer Science*, Vol. 352, Springer-Verlag, New York, NY (1989).

32. Reps, T., "Shape analysis as a generalized path problem," pp. 1-11 in *Proceedings of the ACM SIGPLAN Symposium on Partial Evaluation and Semantics-Based Program Manipulation (PEPM 95)*, (La Jolla, California, June 21-23, 1995), ACM, New York, NY (1995).

33. Reynolds, J.C., "Automatic computation of data set definitions," pp. 456-461 in *Information Processing 68: Proceedings of the IFIP Congress 68*, North-Holland, New York, NY (1968).

34. Romanenko, S., "Arity raiser and its use in program specialization," pp. 341-360 in *Proceedings of the Third European Symposium on Programming*, (Copenhagen, Denmark, May 15-18, 1990), *Lecture Notes in Computer Science*, Vol. 432, ed. N. Jones,Springer-Verlag, New York, NY (1990).

35. Selke, R.P, "A rewriting semantics for program dependence graphs," pp. 12-24 in *Conference Record of the Sixteenth ACM Symposium on Principles of Programming Languages,* (Austin, TX, Jan. 11-13, 1989), ACM, New York, NY (1989).
36. Sestoft, P., "Automatic call unfolding in a partial evaluator," pp. 485-506 in *Partial Evaluation and Mixed Computation: Proceedings of the IFIP TC2 Workshop on Partial Evaluation and Mixed Computation,* (Gammel Avernaes, Denmark, October 18-24, 1987), ed. D. Bjørner, A.P. Ershov, and N.D. Jones,North-Holland, New York, NY (1988).
37. Tip, F., "A survey of program slicing techniques," *Journal of Programming Languages* **3** pp. 121-181 (1995).
38. Turchin, V.F., "The concept of a supercompiler," *ACM Trans. Program. Lang. Syst.* **8**(3) pp. 292-325 (July 1986).
39. Wadler, P. and Hughes, R.J.M., "Projections for strictness analysis," pp. 385-407 in *Third Conference on Functional Programming and Computer Architecture,* (Portland, OR, Sept. 14-16, 1987), *Lecture Notes in Computer Science,* Vol. 274, ed. G. Kahn,Springer-Verlag, New York, NY (1987).
40. Wadler, P., "Deforestation: Transforming programs to eliminate trees," *Theoretical Computer Science* **73** pp. 231-248 (1990).
41. Weise, D., Crew, R.F., Ernst, M., and Steensgaard, B., "Value dependence graphs: Representation without taxation," pp. 297-310 in *Conference Record of the Twenty-First ACM Symposium on Principles of Programming Languages,* (Portland, OR, Jan. 16-19, 1994), ACM, New York, NY (1994).
42. Weiser, M., "Reconstructing sequential behavior from parallel behavior projections," *Information Processing Letters* **17** pp. 129-135 (October 1983).
43. Weiser, M., "Program slicing," *IEEE Transactions on Software Engineering* **SE-10**(4) pp. 352-357 (July 1984).

Specialization of Imperative Programs Through Analysis of Relational Expressions

Alexander Sakharov

Motorola
1501 W. Shure Drive
Arlington Heights, IL 60004, USA
sakharov@cig.mot.com

Abstract

An inter-procedural data flow analysis operating on control flow graphs and collecting information about program expressions is described in this paper. The following relational and other expressions are analyzed: equivalences between program expressions and constants; linear-ordering inequalities between program expressions and constants; equalities originating from some program assignments; atomic constituents of controlling expressions of program branches. Analysis is executed by a worklist-based fixpoint algorithm which interprets conditional branches and incorporates a rule-based inference procedure. Two variants of the polyvariant program point specialization using results of the analysis are presented. The both specializations are done at the level of control flow graphs. The variants differ in terms of the size of residual programs.

1 Introduction

Despite wide usage of procedural languages, only few successful attempts have been made to apply partial evaluation to these languages. One of the reasons of the limited success of partial evaluation in this domain is due to the fact that advanced data flow analysis techniques created for imperative languages have not been used to support specialization.

Partial evaluation is called on-line if analysis is done during specialization. Partial evaluation is called off-line if analysis is done before specialization. Off-line techniques, that are considered more appropriate for procedural languages [3], employ binding time analysis to guide specialization. Binding time analysis annotates each statement as either static or dynamic by dividing variables into static or dynamic [17].

This paper presents an off-line technique. It advocated the use of data flow analysis as an information source for specialization. An original data flow analysis method that collects information for specialization of imperative programs is described in this paper. This analysis annotates each program point with a set of static expressions. The analysis reaches far beyond detection of static variables. Expressions whose variables are not static can be classified as static by this analysis.

The control flow graph [1] is probably the most adequate, useful, and generic model for analysis and optimization of programs in procedural languages. Data flow analyses operate on environments [10, 23] that are associated with nodes or edges of control flow graphs. In our analysis framework, environments represent relational expressions and other propositions. Specialization is done at the level of control flow graphs. Two specializations using the information collected by our analysis are presented. One is a variant of the polyvariant program point specialization [6, 17, 3]. This specialization may generate huge residual programs. The other is an original technique which is a limited polyvariant specialization. It results in smaller residual programs. This paper focuses on the limited variant.

Analysis of relational expressions and other propositions expands partial evaluation horizons: not only static values of variables but also other assertions may serve as pre-conditions for partial evaluation of imperative programs (see also [12,9]). Our analysis and edge-based specialization can also be viewed as general purpose analysis and optimization methods, respectively.

Environments in our analysis are basically conjunctions of certain predicate formulas. These predicate formulas include: atomic constituents of controlling expressions of program branches and their negations; equalities originating from some program assignments and equality negations; equivalences between program expressions and constants of the respective types as well as negations of the equivalences; linear-ordering inequalities between program expressions and constants. Other atomic predicate expressions may serve as additional environment constituents. Note that some environment constituents may represent formulas whose predicate symbols or other operations are missing from the language. Binary relations that express aliasing information are an example [20].

The environments are designed to capture relevant program properties while remaining compact. Note that most predicate symbols in procedural languages are either equivalence relations or linear orderings. Our analysis takes advantage of tracking various properties of all program expressions (and possibly others) simultaneously. Transfer functions [1], which are determined by the constructs of the respective language, are not fixed in the framework. Because of this, this framework is applicable to various languages. For instance, the language may include arrays, pointers, and their relevant operations.

The analysis is done by a worklist-based fixpoint algorithm that interprets conditional branches and involves a simple and fast inference procedure. The analysis algorithm presented here is an advanced version of the algorithm from [24]. The asymptotic time complexity of the analysis algorithm is proportional to the square of program size times the complexity of the transfer functions in use. Thus, the complexity of this analysis is almost the same as that of conventional constant propagation [26].

The inference procedure serves to derive additional assertions. It is repeatedly invoked as propagation progresses. The inference procedure is based on rules. Some rules express properties of equivalence relations and linear orderings. Other rules are determined by language operations and are not fixed in the framework. Through the rules, the inference procedure exploits both positive atomic propositions and their negations. Though the inference is incomplete, this heuristic inference procedure is an analysis core that distinguishes this analysis algorithm from others. The choice of an inference procedure is driven by the goal to derive as much as possible without imposing a burden in terms of analysis time complexity. Of course, this goal is achieved at expense of theoretical soundness.

The complete polyvariant specialization using our analysis will be called *store-based* because program point versions are defined by store sets [16]. Analysis information in the form of environments is used to represent store sets. The limited variant is called *edge-based* because it employes edges of control flow graphs as program point versions. The edge-based specialization is accomplished through the following steps: disjoint subgraphs whose in-links are limited to one node are selected; selected subgraphs are replicated; local propagation of analysis information is done within subgraphs; static expressions are replaced by the respective constants; other optimizations are performed. The edge-based specialization results in smaller residual code because the number of specialization variants for a subgraph is limited by the number of its in-links.

Section 2 of this paper gives motivating examples which are revisited in section 9. Section 3 outlines control flow graphs in use. Section 4 describes environments associated with graph elements. The rules used in analysis are described in section 5. Section 6 gives the analysis algorithm, while section 7 outlines its properties. Program specialization is presented in section 8. Section 10 surveys related work.

2 Motivation

The following example illustrates our partial evaluation technique. The C code fragment below implements a few transitions of a finite state machine.

```
#define TRANS(A,B,C) { if (state==A) { if (event==B) { state=C;
#define END_TR continue; } } }
...
do { TRANS(off,on_off,on) toggle(); END_TR
if ( vol_trg ) { TRANS(off,vol_up,on) toggle(); volume=1; END_TR }
... } ...
```

If no other transition applies to state off, procedure toggle does not affect variables from this fragment, and vol_trg is a static variable (not equal 0), then the edge-based specialization makes it possible to transform this loop into more efficient code:

```
do { if (state==off)
    { if (event==on_off)
        { state=on; toggle(); }
    else if (event==vol_up)
        { state=on; toggle(); volume=1; } }
else ... } ...
```

Here is yet another example (in C) showing the power of our partial evaluation technique:

```
int p(int a[], int n, int b) { int s=0; int i=0; int flag=1; float t; float t0=0.01;
do { if ( flag==1 ) { if ( b>=0 ) t=1+2*t0; else t=1+2*v; }
    else if ( a[i]*u>= b ) { { if ( a[i]*u+b>=2 ) t=1; else t=1+4*v; } t=(t-0.01)*(1-t0); }
    else t=1+2*v;
    s+=a[i]*t; t0*=0.985; flag=0;
} while ( ++i<=n ); return s; }
```

If n=100 and b≥1 are pre-conditions for partial evaluation of procedure p, then the edge-based specialization in combination with dead-store elimination [1] gives residual code that can be represented in C as follows:

```
int p(int a[], int b) { int s=0; int i=0; int flag=1; float t; float t0=0.01;
s+=a[0]*1.02; t0*=0.985; ++i;
do { if ( a[i]*u>= b ) t=0.99*(1-t0); else t=1+2*v;
s+=a[i]*t; t0*=0.985;
} while ( ++i<=100 ); return s; }
```

The store-based specialization followed by dead-store elimination results in the code below:

```
int p(int a[], int b) { int s=0; int i=0; int flag=1; float t; float t0=0.01;
s+=a[0]*1.02;
```

```
if ( a[1]*u>= b ) t=0.980248; else t=1+2*v;
s+=a[1]*t;
...
if ( a[100]*u>= b ) t=0.987849; else t=1+2*v;
s+=a[100]*t;
return s; }
```

3 Program Model

Let us distinguish four types of nodes in the graphs: conditional branches, assignments, calls, and returns. Each conditional branch has two out-edges. The branch node is controlled by a predicate expression. Control is transferred to either the then-branch or the else-branch according to the value of the expression. Assignments embody calculations and variable updates. Each assignment has one out-edge. Each call node also has one out-edge leading to the callee. Return nodes have multiple out-edges leading to all return points. Neither call nor return nodes update any variable values. Calculations of parameter and return values are modeled by assignments in control flow graphs. There are two distinguished dummy nodes: the start node and the end node. The start node has no in-edges and one out-edge. The end node has no out-edges.

We assume that every procedure has one return node. Predicate expressions controlling branches are supposed to be atomic, i.e. they do not contain propositional connectives [8]. Branches whose controlling expressions contain propositional connectives can be reduced to nested branches without propositional connectives by application of so-called short-circuit rules [11]. It is assumed that the size of all expressions from conditional branches and assignments is bounded by a constant. We also assume that assignments do not contain calls and that controlling expressions of conditional branches do not have side effects. Conditional branches with side effects and assignments containing calls can be eliminated through introduction of new variables and inclusion of additional assignments. Note that the above transformations of the program control flow graph can be done in linear time.

We do not fix data types and operations permitted in expressions. They depend on the language. For instance, expressions may include array subscripting, operations on pointers, etc. Equivalence relations and linear orderings are preferable for our analysis. When possible, other predicate symbols should be expressed through these. Major constructs of imperative programming languages fall into this control flow graph model. Note that recursive procedures are allowed. Jump tables and dynamic calls/returns are not included in the model for reducing technicality.

4 Analysis Framework

Let Θ denote a set of non-predicate expressions without side effects. It includes all arithmetic and language-specific expressions originating from the program and all their subexpressions (except constants). The cardinal number of Θ should be proportional to program size. Let Π be a set of atomic predicate expressions without side effects. It includes the set of controlling expressions of program branches and equalities originating from program assignments whose left- and right-hand sides belong to Θ and which do not refer to one object in both states: before and after assignment. The cardinal number of Π should be proportional to program size. Although, the only result of not complying with the limitations on the cardinal numbers of Θ and Π is a higher complexity of the analysis.

For the sake of reducing technicality, we do not allow predicate expressions be subexpressions. We assume that one element of Θ or Π corresponds to all textually identical expressions. Moreover, expressions which differ because of inversion of operands of commutative operations are identified, and a single specimen is kept in Θ or Π. This identification can be done by a recursive algorithm operating on pairs of expressions. A more sophisticated identification of equal expressions could be based on further developments of ideas of Knuth and Bendix [19].

Let us define the domain of environments - Ω. Two special values - undef and none - will be used as values of environment constituents. Every environment V from Ω is triplet (V.s,V.t,V.u). The formulas given by equivalence relations (i.e. reflexive, symmetric, transitive, total relations) connecting expressions from Θ and constants of the respective types are represented by (V.s[1],...,V.s[k]). For every equivalence relation p from the language and every expression e from Θ, one element of array V.s represents assertions $p(e,\_)$, and one element of V.s represents assertions $\neg p(e,\_)$. Here and below, _ stands for a constant of the respective type. Every V.s[i] is a constant that takes underscore's position, undef, or none. At minimum, equality is represented by V.s elements.

The formulas given by linear orderings (i.e. reflexive, antisymmetric, transitive, total relations) connecting expressions from Θ and constants are represented by (V.t[1],...,V.t[h]). For every linear ordering p from the language and every expression e from Θ, one element of array V.t represents assertions $p(e,\_)$, and one element of V.t represents assertions $p(\_,e)$. Every V.t[i] is a constant that takes underscore's position, undef, or none.

The predicate expressions of Π are represented by (V.u[1],...,V.u[m]). One element of V.u corresponds to every predicate expression from Π. Each V.u[i] is undef, none, true, or false.

Environments serve to represent assertions about program points. Every environment V from Ω maps to formula $\Phi(V)$ if V does not contain undef:

$$\Phi(V)=\Phi(V.s[1])\&...\&\Phi(V.s[k])\&\Phi(V.t[1])\&...\&\Phi(V.t[h])\&\Phi(V.u[1])\&...\&\Phi(V.u[m])$$

$\Phi(V.u[i])$ is the respective predicate from Π if V.u[i] is true, its negation if V.u[i] is false, or proposition T if V.u[i] is none [8]. If V.s[i] representing $p(e,\_)$ is constant c, then $\Phi(V.s[i])$ is expression $p(e,c)$. If V.s[i] representing $\neg p(e,\_)$ is constant c, then $\Phi(V.s[i])$ is expression $\neg p(e,c)$. If V.s[i] is none, then $\Phi(V.s[i])$ is proposition T. If V.t[i] representing $p(e,\_)$ $(p(\_,e))$ is constant c, then $\Phi(V.t[i])$ is expression $p(e,c)$ $(p(c,e))$. If V.t[i] is none, $\Phi(V.t[i])$ is T.

Let us define a binary operation called μ on Ω as follows:

$$\mu(V,V')=(V.s[1]^\wedge V'.s[1],...,V.s[k]^\wedge V'.s[k],V.t[1]^\wedge V'.t[1],...,V.t[h]^\wedge V'.t[h],$$
$$V.u[1]^\wedge V'.u[1],...,V.u[m]^\wedge V'.u[m])$$

The following rules define $^\wedge$ for V.s, V.t, and V.u elements:

- For any v: undef $^\wedge$ v = v $^\wedge$ undef = v;   none $^\wedge$ v = v $^\wedge$ none = none;
  v $^\wedge$ v = v;   true $^\wedge$ false = false $^\wedge$ true = none.

- Let V.s[i] and V'.s[i] represent $p(e,\_)$ (or $\neg p(e,\_)$), and
  V.s[i] and V'.s[i] are constants of the respective type:
  If $p(V.s[i],V'.s[i])$ then V.s[i] $^\wedge$ V'.s[i] = V.s[i], otherwise V.s[i] $^\wedge$ V'.s[i] = none.

- Let V.t[i] and V'.t[i] represent $p(\_,e)$, and
  V.t[i] and V'.t[i] are constants of the respective type:
  If $p(V.t[i],V'.t[i])$ then V.t[i] $^\wedge$ V'.t[i] = V.t[i], otherwise V.t[i] $^\wedge$ V'.t[i] = none.

- Let $V.t[i]$ and $V'.t[i]$ represent $p(e,\_)$, and
  $V.t[i]$ and $V'.t[i]$ are constants of the respective type:
  If $p(V'.t[i],V.t[i])$ then $V.t[i] \wedge V'.t[i] = V.t[i]$, otherwise $V.t[i] \wedge V'.t[i] = $ none.

Operation μ plays the role of meet [18,14], but it is not commutative. Non-commutativity is due to $\wedge$ for $V.t$ elements. This operation for $V.t$ elements is similar to widening [10, 5]. We will use notation $x \leq y$ if the formula $x = \mu(x,y)$ holds. The same notation will be also used in application to environment constituents: $a \leq b$ iff $a = a \wedge b$.

Proposition 1. Relation $\leq$ is a pre-ordering, i.e. for any x,y,z:
$$x \leq x$$
$$x \leq y \ \& \ y \leq z \Longrightarrow x \leq z$$

For any x and y:
$$\mu(x,y) \leq x$$
$$\mu(x,y) \leq y$$

Proof. Reflexivity is obvious. If $x \leq y$ and $y \leq z$, then $x.u[i] = x.u[i] \wedge y.u[i]$ and $y.u[i] = y.u[i] \wedge z.u[i]$ for $i = 1,...,m$. Similar equalities hold for .s and .t components of x, y, and z. The fact that the aforementioned equalities imply equalities $x.s[i] = x.s[i] \wedge z.s[i]$, $x.t[i] = x.t[i] \wedge z.t[i]$, $x.u[i] = x.u[i] \wedge z.u[i]$ is proven by considering all possible cases for constituents of x, y, and z: undef, none, true, false for $u[i]$; undef, none, constants for $s[i]$ and $t[i]$ (including cases with differently related constants).

The inequality $\mu(x,y) \leq x$ is proven by checking that the following equalities hold for any x and y: $(x.u[i] \wedge y.u[i]) \wedge x.u[i] = x.u[i] \wedge y.u[i]$; $(x.t[i] \wedge y.t[i]) \wedge x.t[i] = x.t[i] \wedge y.t[i]$; $(x.s[i] \wedge y.s[i]) \wedge x.s[i] = x.s[i] \wedge y.s[i]$. The inequality $\mu(x,y) \leq y$ is proven by the same method. ∎

Proposition 2. If $x \leq y$, neither x nor y contains undef, then $\Phi(y)$ implies $\Phi(x)$.

Proof. Clearly, the inequality $x.s[i] \leq y.s[i]$ implies that $\Phi(y.s[i]) \Longrightarrow \Phi(x.s[i])$. Similar implications hold for pairs $(x.t[i],y.t[i])$ and $(x.u[i],y.u[i])$. Therefore, $\Phi(y.s[1])$ &...& $\Phi(y.s[k])$ & $\Phi(y.t[1])$ &...& $\Phi(y.t[h])$ & $\Phi(y.u[1])$ &...& $\Phi(y.u[m])$ implies $\Phi(x.s[1])$ &...& $\Phi(x.s[k])$ & $\Phi(x.t[1])$ &...& $\Phi(x.t[h])$ & $\Phi(x.u[1])$ &...& $\Phi(x.u[m])$ if $x \leq y$. ∎

It is assumed that transfer function $f_N: \Omega \to \Omega$ is defined for every assignment node N [1, 18, 14]. Transfer functions depend on the language in use. In presence of pointers, transfer functions should subsume approximation of alias effects [1]. Consider a sample transfer function for assignment $v:=e$ where v is an integer variable and e is an arithmetic expression. First, the transfer function sets to none all $V.s$, $V.t$, and $V.u$ elements which contain v. Second, the transfer function sets $V.s$ and $V.t$ elements representing v to the respective elements representing e. Third, if $v=e$ belongs to Π, then the transfer function sets $V.u[i]$ representing $v=e$ to true.

5 Rules

The rules used by the inference procedure have the form of implications. Their consequent is an atomic predicate formula or its negation. The antecedent is conjunction of atomic predicate formulas or their negations. In each rule, there is one selected atomic predicate formula that is called *base*. The base is a pattern for an assertion represented by an environment constituent. All other atomic predicate formulas either express conditions or are patterns for relational expressions represented by .s or .t environment constituents. There are two types of variables in the formulas. Variables of the first type occur in patterns and serve as counterparts of expressions from Θ. All variables of the first type should occur in a base part that is a counterpart of an expression from Θ or Π. Variables of the second type are bound with constants. At least one occurrence of this variable in a rule is a constant counterpart in a formula that is a pattern.

All rules ought to be valid formulas [8]. Rules may vary for different languages. There is a common class of rules, though. It includes the following rules given for all arithmetic (f) and predicate (r) operations:

$$e_1=c_1 \ \& \ ... \ \& \ e_s=c_s ==> f(e_1,...,e_s)=f(c_1,...,c_s)$$
$$e_1=c_1 \ \& \ ... \ \& \ e_s=c_s \ \& \ r(c_1,...,c_s) ==> r(e_1,...,e_s)$$
$$e_1=c_1 \ \& \ ... \ \& \ e_s=c_s \ \& \ \neg r(c_1,...,c_s) ==> \neg r(e_1,...,e_s)$$

Other common rules embody properties of equivalence relations and linear orderings. Here are several sample rules from this class:

$$\neg p(e_1,e_2) \ \& \ p(e_1,c_1) ==> \neg p(e_2,c_1)$$
$$q(e_1,c_1) ==> q(e_1,c_1)$$
$$q(e_1,e_2) \ \& \ q(e_2,c_1) ==> q(e_1,c_1)$$
$$e_1=c_1 ==> q(e_1,c_1)$$
$$p(e_1,c_1) \ \& \ p(e_2,c_2) \ \& \ p(c_1,c_2) ==> p(e_1,e_2)$$
$$p(e_1,c_1) \ \& \ \neg p(e_2,c_2) \ \& \ p(c_1,c_2) ==> \neg p(e_1,e_2)$$
$$q(e_1,c_1) \ \& \ q(c_2,e_2) \ \& \ q(c_1,c_2) ==> q(e_1,e_2)$$
$$q(e_1,c_1) \ \& \ q(c_1,c_2) ==> q(e_1,c_2)$$
$$q(e_1,c_1) \ \& \ q(c_2,e_2) \ \& \ \neg q(c_1,c_2) \ \& \ c_1 \neq c_2 ==> e_1 \neq e_2$$

where p is an equivalence relation, q is a linear ordering, e_i are variables of the first type whereas c_i stand for variables of the second type. Base formulas are shown in italics. The examples below exhibit language-specific rules:

$$e_1 \geq c_1 \ \& \ e_2 \geq c_2 ==> e_1+e_2 \geq c_1+c_2$$
$$q(e_1,c_1,) \ \& \ e_2=1 ==> q(e_1*e_2,c_1)$$
$$e_1-e_2 \leq c_1 \ \& \ e_2 \leq c_2 ==> e_1 \leq c_1+c_2$$

6 Analysis Algorithm

We use a worklist-based fixpoint algorithm (BC) to propagate environments. This algorithm updates the worklist by symbolically interpreting the program. It starts with an optimistic assumption about propagated values and proceeds by changing the values until it reaches a fixed point. BC utilizes algorithm R which does an incomplete inference. R evaluates expressions from both Θ and Π. It also derives assertions including equivalences, their negations, and linear-ordering inequalities from other assertions. Results of this paper apply to any other more advanced inference algorithm while that other algorithm satisfies the statement of Lemma 1 (see below) and while its time complexity is the same, i.e. linear.

Elements of the worklist W employed by the algorithm are pairs: the pair comprises a value from Ω and an edge. Also, nodes are placed on W to serve as marks. The marks enable usage of W as a stack. The value from Ω assigned to node N is denoted AN(N). The value from Ω assigned to edge E is denoted AE(E). AN and AE constitute the output of BC.

D(N) denotes the sole descendant of assignment/start/call node N. If N is a branch node, then $D_t(N)$ and $D_f(N)$ denote the then-descendant and else-descendant of N, respectively. $D_c(N)$ is the callee for node N, and $D_r(N)$ is the return node of the callee. S is the start node.

Let I stand for the entire program input including initial variable values. A(I) will denote an environment whose constituents are none except for constants representing equalities for given static variables or other pre-conditions.

We assume that elements of arrays .s and .t in environments are ordered by the size of expressions of Θ. Loops in R should iterate from smaller expressions to bigger ones. We assume that two tables - one for elements of Θ and one for elements of both Θ and Π - are created before running BC. Each entry of the first table contains indices of .s and .t elements that represent properties of the respective expression from Θ. Each entry of the second table contains references to the first table for all immediate subexpressions of the expression from Θ or Π. These tables make it possible to execute R in linear time.

Algorithm BC

```
set AN(S) <- A(I);
set W <- { ( A(I),(S,D(S)) ) };
for every AN(N) except AN(S) do
    set AN(N) <- (undef,...,undef);
for every AE(N,M) do
    set AE(N,M) <- (undef,...,undef);
while W is not empty do begin
    if there is pair ( B,(M,N) ) in W after the last mark K then begin
        set AE(M,N) <- μ(AE(M,N),B);
        set AN(N) <- μ(AN(N),AE(M,N));
        if N is an assignment and
        μ(AE(N,D(N)),R(f_N(AE(M,N))),(N,D(N))) is different from AE(N,D(N)) then
            add ( R(f_N(AE(M,N))),(N,D(N)) ) to W;
        else if N is a call and
        μ(AE(N,D_c(N)),AN(N)) is different from AE(N,D_c(N)) then begin
            put N on W as a mark;
            add ( AE(M,N),(N,D_c(N)) ) to W end
        else if N is a branch controlled by an expression represented by u[i] then
            if AE(M,N).u[i] = true and
            μ(AE(N,D_t(N)),AE(M,N)) is different from AE(N,D_t(N)) then
                add ( AE(M,N),(N,D_t(N)) ) to W
            else if AE(M,N).u[i] = false and
            μ(AE(N,D_f(N)),AE(M,N)) is different from AE(N,D_f(N)) then
                add ( AE(M,N),(N,D_f(N)) ) to W
            else if AE(M,N).u[i] = none then begin
                if μ(AE(N,D_t(N)),R((AE(M,N).s[1],...,true,...,AE(M,N).u[m])))
                is different from AE(N,D_t(N)) then
                    add ( R((AE(M,N).s[1],...,true,...,AE(M,N).u[m])),(N,D_t(N)) ) to W
                if μ(AE(N,D_f(N)),R((AE(M,N).s[1],...,false,...,AE(M,N).u[m])))
                is different from AE(N,D_f(N)) then
                    add ( R((AE(M,N).s[1],...,false,...,AE(M,N).u[m])),(N,D_f(N)) ) to W
                (true and false are the i-th elements of u) end
    end else begin
        remove K from W;
        if μ(AE(D_r(K),D(K)),AN(D_r(K))) is different from AE(D_r(K),D(K)) then
            add ( AN(D_r(K)),(D_r(K),D(K)) ) to W
    end
end
```

Algorithm R(V)

set R(V) <- V;
for every R(V).u[j] which is true or false and
every evaluation rule with a matching base expression in the antecedent do
    begin match other patterns against relational expressions; check conditions;
    if the antecedent is satisfied then
        update R(V).s[i]/R(V).s[i] represented by a consequent part if it was none end
for every R(V).s[j]/R(V).t[j] which is none and every evaluation rule
whose base part in the consequent matches the respective expression from Θ do
    begin match other patterns against relational expressions; check conditions;
    if the antecedent is satisfied then
        update R(V).s[j]/R(V).t[j] end
for every R(V).u[j] which is none and
every evaluation rule with a matching base in the consequent do
    begin match other patterns against relational expressions; check conditions;
    if the antecedent is satisfied then
        update R(V).u[j]] end

7 Analysis Properties

Let $A(I,S...N)$ denote an environment whose constituents are true, false, or constants. $A(I,S...N)$ is calculated for the actual values of program expressions at the end of execution of path $S...N$ which is exercised for input I. $A(I,S...N).u[j]$ is the boolean value of the respective predicate expression. For $s[j]$ representing $p(e,\_)$, $A(I,S...N).s[j]$ is the value of e. For $s[j]$ representing $\neg p(e,\_)$, $A(I,S...N).s[j]$ is some value of the respective type: $neq_p(e)$. It is not equivalent (w.r.t. p) to the value of e. For $t[j]$ representing $p(e,\_)$ or $p(\_,e)$, $A(I,S...N).t[j]$ is the value of expression e.

Let g be the number of edges in the program control flow graph. $\overline{AN}(N)$ and $\overline{AE}(N,M)$ will denote $AN(N)$ and $AE(N,M)$ after BC termination. Let t stand for the maximum time of transfer function execution. Apparently, t is at least $O(g)$. When calculating time complexity, we assume that the time of executing assignments and operations from expressions under consideration is bounded by a constant. Note that this typical assumption about language operations can be relaxed at the cost of a higher analysis complexity.

Theorem 1. Algorithm BC will eventually terminate on any control flow graph. The asymptotic time complexity of BC is $O(g^2*t)$.

Proof. The time to execute initialization steps of BC is proportional to the total number of nodes and edges in the program graph. Algorithm BC terminates when worklist W is empty. At most two new elements can be added to W at each iteration of BC's main loop. This happen only when AE(E) changes. AE(E).u[i] can only drop twice: from undef to true or false and then to none. Similarly, AE(E).s[i] and AE(E).t[i] can drop twice at most: from undef to a constant, and then to none. Values k, l, and m are proportional to g. Hence, the main loop may add $O(g^2)$ elements to W at most. Therefore, BC will terminate.

The time of executing operation μ and that of assigning an environment to AN(N) or AE(N) is proportional to g. Hence the running time of the initialization phase of BC is proportional to g^2. The time complexity of algorithm R is $O(g)$ because the time of a single execution of the body of each loop in R is bounded by a constant if the two tables are utilized. Since t is at least $O(g)$, the running time of a single iteration of the main loop of BC is proportional to t. The overall time of executing the main loop of BC is proportional to g^2*t. The asymptotic time complexity of BC is $O(g^2 * t)$. ∎

Note that the worst case is rarely achieved because $AN(N)$ and $AE(M,N)$ rapidly converge to fixed points (likewise other optimistic propagation algorithms behave). Actual running time is usually close to the best-case running time. The best-case running time of BC is $o(g * t)$. The asymptotic time complexity of preliminary actions including construction of tables is not higher than BC's asymptotic complexity.

Definition. Transfer function f_N is called *safe* if $\Phi(A(I,S...N)) \Longrightarrow \Phi(x)$ implies that $\Phi(A(I,S...NN")) \longrightarrow \Phi(f_N(x))$ for any x, any input I, and any execution path S...NN" resulting from the input.

Lemma 1. $\Phi(x) \longrightarrow \Phi(R(x))$ holds for any x without undef.

Proof. Validity of the rules implies the following statements about $R(x)$ constituents. If $x.u[i]$ is none and $R(x).u[i]$ is set up to true or false by R, then $\Phi(x) \longrightarrow \Phi(R(x).u[i])$ holds. If $s[i]$ is raised to a constant from none by R, then $\Phi(x) \longrightarrow \Phi(R(x).s[i])$ holds. Similarly, if $t[i]$ is raised to a constant from none by R, then $\Phi(x) \longrightarrow \Phi(R(x).t[i])$ holds. Therefore, $\Phi(x) \longrightarrow \Phi(R(x))$ holds because $\Phi(R(x))$ is conjunction of $\Phi(x)$ and formulas which are implications of $\Phi(x)$. ∎

Theorem 2. If all transfer functions are safe, then all $\overline{AN}$ and $\overline{AE}$ are conservative, that is, $\Phi(A(I,S...N)) \longrightarrow \Phi(\overline{AN}(N))$ for any input I and execution path S...N resulting from I, and $\Phi(A(I,S...NN")) \longrightarrow \Phi(\overline{AE}(N,N"))$ for any input I and execution path S...NN" resulting from I.

Proof. Suppose to the contrary. Consider a shortest execution path S...N such that: implications $\Phi(A(I,S...M)) \longrightarrow \Phi(\overline{AN}(M))$ and $\Phi(A(I,S...M'M)) \longrightarrow \Phi(\overline{AE}(M',M))$ hold for any node M on path S...N except N; either one or both of these implications are not valid formulas for N. N is not the start node because $\overline{AN}(S) = A(I)$ and $A(I) \leq A(I,S)$.

Suppose S...N has an edge which has never belonged to any pair from W. Let (M,M") be the first such edge on S...N. M is not the start node because $(S,D(S))$ is placed on W. Let M' be the predecessor of M on S...N. By our assumption, $\Phi(A(I,S...M'M))$ implies $\Phi(\overline{AE}(M',M))$. Thus $\overline{AE}(M',M)$ does not contain undef. If M is an assignment node, then a pair containing M's out-edge is placed on W each time when $AE(M',M)$ changes. $AE(M',M)$ changes at least once because $\overline{AE}(M',M)$ does not contain undef. In particular, a pair containing (M,M") is placed on W when $\overline{AE}(M',M)$ is attained. Similarly, if M is a call node, then a pair containing (M,M"), where M" is $D_c(M)$, is placed on W when $\overline{AE}(M',M)$ is attained. If M is a return node, then a pair containing (M,M") is placed on W when a mark in W is reached after attaining $\overline{AE}(M',M)$.

$\Phi(A(I,S...M))$ is a consistent formula [8]: it is true for the values obtained after execution of S...M on input I. If M is a branch controlled by the expression represented by u[i], then $\overline{AE}(M',M).u[i]$ is either equal to $A(I,S...M).u[i]$ or none. In both cases, a pair containing (M,M") is placed on W when $\overline{AE}(M',M)$ is attained. Hence every edge (M,M") from S...N belongs to a pair which is placed on W after $\overline{AE}(M',M)$ is attained.

Let N' stand for the predecessor of N on S...N. If N' is the start node, then $\overline{AE}(S,N) = A(I)$ and $\overline{AN}(N) \leq A(I)$. Hence both $\Phi(A(I,SN)) \longrightarrow \Phi(\overline{AN}(N))$ and $\Phi(A(I,SN)) \longrightarrow \Phi(\overline{AE}(S,N))$ hold, which contradicts our assumption. Let N" be the predecessor of N' on S...N. By our assumption, $\Phi(A(I,S...N"N'))$ implies $\Phi(\overline{AE}(N",N'))$. If N' is a call or return node, then $A(I,S...N"N')=A(I,S...N"N'N)$. If N' is a call node, then $(\overline{AE}(N",N'),(N'N))$ has been placed on W. If N' is a return node, then $(\overline{AN}'(N'),(N'N))$ has been placed on W, and $\overline{AN}'(N') \leq \overline{AE}(N'',N')$ by Proposition 1. If N' is an assignment node, then $(R(f_{N'}(\overline{AE}(N'',N'))),(N',N))$ has been on W, and $\Phi(A(I,S...N'N)) \Longrightarrow \Phi(f_{N'}(\overline{AE}(N'',N')))$ since all transfer functions are safe. By Lemma 1, $\Phi(f_{N'}(\overline{AE}(N'',N')))$ implies $\Phi(R(f_{N'}(\overline{AE}(N'',N'))))$.

If N' is a branch node, let u[i] represent the controlling expression of N'. If (N',N) is the then-edge of N', then either $(R((\overline{AE}(N'',N').s[1],...,true,...,\overline{AE}(N'',N').u[m])),(N',N))$ or $(\overline{AE}(N'',N'),(N',N))$ has been on W. $\overline{AE}(N'',N').u[i]$ is either true or none since $\Phi(A(I,S...N'))$ is a consistent formula. Note that $\Phi(A(I,S...N'N)) = \Phi(A(I,S...N'))$. Henceforth, implications $\Phi(A(I,S...N)) \Longrightarrow \Phi(\overline{AE}(N'',N'))$ and $\Phi(A(I,S...N)) \Longrightarrow \Phi((\overline{AE}(N'',N').s[1],...,true,...,\overline{AE}(N'',N').u[m]))$ hold. By Lemma 1, $\Phi((\overline{AE}(N'',N').s[1],...,true,...,\overline{AE}(N'',N').u[m]))$ implies $\Phi(R((\overline{AE}(N'',N').s[1],...,true,..., \overline{AE}(N'',N').u[m])))$.

If (N',N) is the else-edge, then either $(\overline{AE}(N'',N'),(N',N))$ or $(R((\overline{AE}(N'',N').s[1],...,false,...,\overline{AE}(N'',N').u[m])),(N',N))$ has been on W. $\overline{AE}(N'',N').u[i]$ is either false or none. Again, implications $\Phi(A(I,S...N)) \Longrightarrow \Phi(\overline{AE}(N'',N'))$ and $\Phi(A(I,S...N)) \Longrightarrow \Phi((\overline{AE}(N'',N').s[1],...,false,...,\overline{AE}(N'',N').u[m]))$ hold. By Lemma 1, $\Phi((\overline{AE}(N'',N').s[1],...,false,...,\overline{AE}(N'',N').u[m]))$ implies $\Phi(R((\overline{AE}(N'',N').s[1],...,false,..., \overline{AE}(N'',N').u[m])))$.

In all cases, such (V,(N',N)) has been on W that $\Phi(A(I,S...N)) \Longrightarrow \Phi(V)$. The second statement of Proposition 1 guarantees that successive values AN(M) and AE(E) form decreasing sequences for any given node M and edge E. Proposition 1 also guarantees that $\overline{AN}(N) \leq \overline{AE}(N',N)$. Thus, $\overline{AE}(N',N) \leq V$ and $\overline{AN}(N) \leq V$. By proposition 2, $\Phi(V)$ implies $\Phi(\overline{AN}(N))$ and $\Phi(\overline{AE}(N',N))$. This contradicts the assumption. ∎

8 Specialization

Consider the store-based specialization first. Polyvariant specialization techniques select program variables whose calculations can be done at compile time. Their values are computed for every program point in a driven program [16]. Thus, values of these variables belong to finite sets. Normally, loop indices are such variables. Suppose a technique for detection of these variables is selected. Let Λ be the set of the variables. Let store sets be given by $\overline{AE}(M,N)$: $\overline{AE}(M,N)$ represents all the stores that satisfy $\Phi(\overline{AE}(M,N))$. $\overline{AE}(M,N)$ is obtained from $\overline{AE}(M,N)$ in the two following steps. First, environment elements representing v-_ for variables from Λ are changed to the respective constants if the elements were none. Second, R is applied.

Each edge in the control flow graph is a specialization point. Edge (M,N) is specialized with respect to different environments $\overline{AE}(M,N)$. Apparently, there are finitely many different $\overline{AE}(M,N)$ for every edge (M,N). The store-based specialization runs through the control flow graph, calculates $\overline{AE}$ for current values of variables from Λ, changes expressions to constants on the basis of equalities represented by .s elements of $\overline{AE}$, executes static calculations, and generates code for dynamic nodes.

Polyvariant specializations may generate huge residual programs due to loop unrolling. When code size is a concern, the edge-based specialization below is a preference. The edge-based specialization utilizes $\overline{AE}$ and $\overline{AN}$ values. It is accomplished by the following steps.

1. Disjoint subgraphs are segregated. A subgraph is selected for every conditional branch

and every assignment which have multiple in-edges. The above node is the top node of the respective subgraph. All assignments and conditional branches that are immediate successors of any node from the subgraph and that have one in-edge are assigned to the respective subgraph along with their in-edges.

2. Each selected subgraph is replicated as many times as there were top node in-edges with different $\overline{AE}$ not containing undef before this replication process started. Then, out-links are added to each replicated copy. These edges lead to the same nodes as the original out-links do. The in-edges of subgraphs are distributed among copies so that all edges with the same $\overline{AE}$ lead to one copy. Edges whose $\overline{AE}$ contain undef are eliminated. Note that all in-edges which are also out-edges for a different subgraph lead to one copy.

3. $\overline{AE}$ of the in-edges of the top node of every subgraph copy is propagated across the subgraph to update $\overline{AE}$ and $\overline{AN}$ values within the subgraph. $\overline{AE}$ and $\overline{AN}$ are set by applying transfer functions and then R to propagate environments across assignments and by setting one .u element to true/false and then applying R to propagate environments across conditional branches. It is similar to what BC does.

4. Expressions from Θ occurring in nodes are replaced by constants if their respective equalities represented by .s elements of $\overline{AN}$ are set to constants. Conditional branches whose controlling expressions are static are eliminated. Identical nodes whose out-edges lead to the same nodes are merged. Unreachable code, i.e. the nodes whose $\overline{AN}$ contain undef and the edges whose $\overline{AE}$ contain undef, is eliminated.

It is assumed that the both specializations are followed by dead-store elimination [1]. Figure 2 exhibits the result of transformation of the control flow graph fragment in Figure 1 in the process of the edge-based specialization. Rectangles in figures depict assignments, calls, or their sequences. Triangles depict conditional branches.

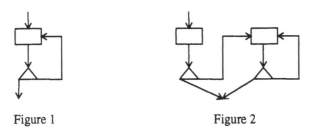

Figure 1   Figure 2

Theorem 3. $\overline{AN}$ and $\overline{AE}$ remain conservative after the edge-based specialization changes them. The number of nodes in the specialized program is $O(g^2)$ at most.

Proof. $\overline{AN}$ values for calls, returns, and other nodes with multiple in-edges in the source program and $\overline{AE}$ values for edges leading to the above nodes remain unchanged in the specialized program. Consider a shortest path S...N such that $\overline{AN}$ and $\overline{AE}$ are conservative for all nodes on the path but N. N should be an internal node of one of replicated subgraphs, i.e. it is either an assignment or a conditional branch with one in-edge, because the path is the same as it would be in the source program, and $\overline{AN}$ and $\overline{AE}$ are not changed for the other nodes.

Let N' be the immediate predecessor of N on the path, and let N'' be the immediate predecessor of N'. By the assumption, $\Phi(A(I,S...N''N')) \Longrightarrow \Phi(\overline{AE}(N'',N'))$. If N' is an assignment, then $\overline{AE}(N',N)=\overline{AN}(N)=R(f_{N'}(\overline{AE}(N'',N')))$. If N' is a conditional branch and (N',N) is the then-edge, then $\overline{AE}(N',N)=\overline{AN}(N)=R((\overline{AE}(N'',N').s[1],...,true,..., \overline{AE}(N'',N').u[m]))$. If (N',N) is the else-edge, then $\overline{AE}(N',N)=\overline{AN}(N) = R((\overline{AE}(N'',N').s[1],...,false,...,\overline{AE}(N'',N').u[m]))$. The above equalities hold because (N',N) is the only in-edge of N. Now, Theorem 2 reasoning applies to derive the following: $\Phi(A(I,S...N'N)) \longrightarrow \Phi(\overline{AE}(N',N))$; $\Phi(A(I,S...N'N)) \longrightarrow \Phi(\overline{AN}(N))$. This contradicts our assumption.

Let e_i be the number of in-edges for the top node of the i-th subgraph, and n_i be the number of nodes in this subgraph. The number of added nodes is fewer than $e_1*n_1+...+e_r*n_r$, where r is the number of replicated subgraphs. Apparently, the following inequalities hold: $e_1+...+e_r \leq g$; $n_1+...+n_r \leq g$. Since $e_1*n_1+...+e_r*n_r \leq (e_1+...+e_r)*(n_1+...+n_r)$, the number of added nodes is not more than g^2. ∎

In practice, the number of nodes in the residual program is not big. This happens because the subgraphs are disjoint and few edges lead into most subgraphs (see the proof above). Normally, the number of edges leading to a subgraph is reflective of the level of nesting conditional branches and loops. Since the nesting level is normally bounded by a small constant, code size growth due to the edge-based specialization is linear in practice. Dead code elimination further reduce code size. Examples from this paper exhibit residual code that is even smaller than the source.

9 Examples Revisited

Let us look at the two examples from the Motivation section again. Figure 3 below depicts the control flow graph of the first code fragment. The then-branches are to the right in the figures. The following table gives numbering for nodes in the graph:

1: state==off	2: event==on_off	3: state=on;	4: toggle();
5: vol_trg	6: event==vol_up	7: volume=1;	

Figure 4 illustrates the outcome of subgraph replication. Figure 5 shows the same code fragment after elimination of static conditional branches (lower 5 and 1 in Figure 4) and elimination of unreachable code (left lower 6 and 3-4-7). Copies of node 1 in the lower side of Figure 4 are static because assertions ¬state==off and state==off are propagated into the left and right copies, respectively, during the edge-based specialization. Note that this is a simple example that under-utilizes BC's capabilities. The power of inference procedure R is not used here at all.

The second example exhibits more power of our partial evaluation. The rules presented earlier help to derive that the controlling expressions b>=0 and a[i]*u+b>=2 are always true. Note that AE of the loop back edge is propagated solely to the else-branch of if (flag==1). The three following subgraphs are detected and handled by the edge-based specialization:

- if (flag==1) ... else t=1+2*v;   (2 copies)
- t=(t-0.01)*(1-t0);   (1 copy)
- s+=a[i]*t; ... while (++i<=n);   (3 copies, 2 merged)

If a polyvariant specialization does not use results of our analysis, then loop body instances in the respective residual code could be represented by the following pattern:

if (a[k]*u>= b) { { if (a[k]*u+b>=2) t=1; else t=1+4*v; } t=(t-0.01)*c; } else t=1+2*v;
s+=a[k]*t;

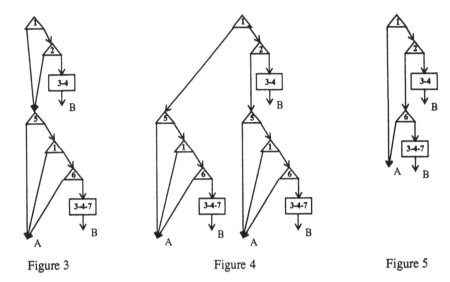

Figure 3   Figure 4   Figure 5

10 Related Work

Our analysis cumulates much more information than binding time analysis [17] does. It iterates over the static/dynamic division not only for variables but also for other program expressions. Moreover, our analysis exploits other relational expressions and controlling expressions of conditional branches as another source of information for finding static expressions. The inference procedure derives additional static information from that other source. Hence, more precise information is yielded by our analysis algorithm. Our analysis gives static information per program control flow edge, i.e. several classifications may be given for one node.

Blazy and Facon use constant propagation as a specialization enabler [4]. If a controlling expressions of a conditional branch reduces to an equality between a variable and a constant, then their method propagates the constant in the then-branch. Glueck and Klimov [13] developed a method for propagating assertions for the sake of program specialization in a simple functional language called S-Graph. The following assertions as well as their negations are propagated: equalities between variables and constants; equalities between structure components and constants, equalities between variables. A wider set of assertions is propagated in our analysis, and additional assertions are derived. Note that difficulties associated with using the operation meet for propagating assertions are missing from functional languages.

Meyer studied on-line partial evaluation for a Pascal-like language [21]. Andersen developed a partial evaluator for a substantial subset of C [2]. Baier, Glueck, and Zochling created a partial evaluator for Fortran [3]. Blazy and Facon created a Fortran specializer aimed at program understanding [4]. In contrast to these partial evaluation techniques for imperative languages, our specializations are done at the level of control flow graphs.

The structure of the residual code generated by our store-based specialization is similar to that of residual code resulting from the traditional polyvariant program point specialization [6,17,3]. Our residual code is potentially more efficient because of a more precise analysis. The store-based specialization can be combined with various versions of the traditional specialization, which may differ in the way they select variables whose calculations are unfolded. The edge-based specialization generates small residual programs as opposed to the store-based specialization that incorporates loop unrolling [3]. Still, some fragments of these small residual programs are more efficient then traditional residual code. Essentially, both the store-based and edge-based specializations are intermediate cases of driving [16].

Our framework does not fit the mold of existing static analysis formalisms [18,25,10,23]. The closest analysis frameworks to ours are the constant and assertion propagation framework from [24] and the framework utilizing logical expressions whose constituents are equalities about value numbers [15]. The class of formulas tracked in the intra-procedural framework of [24] is substantially narrower. Algorithm BC ignores impossible pairs in-edge/out-edge for conditional branches. Inference capabilities of the analysis algorithm from [24] are much weaker. The framework from [15] does not include interpretation of conditional branches and does not incorporate any inference mechanism. The analysis presented here subsumes conditional constant propagation [26, 7], and number interval propagation with widening [10, 5] (widening is embedded into meet).

Analysis and optimization algorithms for elimination of conditional branches in RTL are proposed in [22]. The analysis algorithm from [22] is applicable to well-structured programs only. The analysis from [22] incorporates 1-step inference which is substantially weaker than algorithm R. The analysis algorithm from [22] is a pessimistic algorithm. Generally, pessimistic algorithms are less powerful than optimistic ones. Yet another advantage of BC over the analysis from [22] is that BC ignores impossible pairs of in/out-edges for conditional branches. The optimization algorithm from [22] may lead to exponential growth of code size.

References

[1] A.V. Aho, R. Sethi, J. D. Ullman, *Compilers. Principles, Techniques, and Tools*, Addison-Wesley, 1986.

[2] L. O. Andersen. Partial Evaluation of C and Automatic Compiler Generation. *Lecture Notes in Computer Science*, v. 641, 1992, 251-257.

[3] R. Baier, R. Glueck, R. Zochling. Partial Evaluation of Numerical Programs in Fortran. *Proceedings of the ACM SIGPLAN Workshop on Partial Evaluation and Semantics-Based Program Manipulation*, 1994, 119-132.

[4] S. Blazy, P. Facon. Partial Evaluation for The Understanding of Fortran Programs. *International Journal of Software Engineering and Knowledge Engineering*, v. 4, 1994, #4, 535-559.

[5] F. Bourdoncle. Abstract Debugging of Higher-Order Imperative Languages. *Proceedings of the ACM SIGPLAN Conference on Programming Language Design and Implementation*, 1993, 47-55.

[6] M. A. Bulyonkov. Polyvariant Mixed Computation for Analyzer Programs. *Acta Informatica*, v. 21, 1984, 473-484.

[7] P.R. Carini, M. Hind. Flow-Sensitive Interprocedural Constant Propagation. *Proceedings of the SIGPLAN Symposium on Programming Language Design and Implementation*, 1995, 23-31.

[8] C.-L. Chang, R. C.-T. Lee. *Symbolic Logic and Mechanical Theorem Proving*, Academic Press, 1973.

[9] C. Consel, S.C. Khoo. Parameterized Partial Evaluation. *ACM Transactions on Programming Languages and Systems*, v. 15, 1993, #3, 463-493.

[10] P. Cousot, R. Cousot. Abstract Interpretation: A Unified Lattice Model for Static Analysis of Programs by Construction or Approximation of Fixpoints. *Proceedings of the ACM Symposium on Principles of Programming Languages*, 1977, 238-252.

[11] C.N. Fisher, R.J. LeBlanc, Jr. *Crafting A Compiler*, Benjamin/Cummings, 1988.

[12] Y. Futamura, K. Nogi. Generalized partial computation. In: *Partial Evaluation and Mixed Computation* (D. Bjorner, A.P. Ershov, N.D. Jones, Eds.), North-Holland, 1988.

[13] R. Glueck, A. V. Klimov. Occam's Razor in Metacomputation: the Notion of a Perfect Process Tree. *Lecture Notes in Computer Science*, v. 724, 1993, 112-123.

[14] M.S. Hecht. *Flow Analysis of Computer Programs*, Elsevier North-Holland, 1977.

[15] H. Johnson. Data Flow Analysis for 'Intractable' System Software. *Proceedings of the ACM SIGPLAN Conference on Programming Language Design and Implementation*, 1986, 109-117.

[16] N. Jones. The Essence of Program Transformation by Partial Evaluation and Driving. *Lecture Notes in Computer Science*, v. 792, 1994, 206-224.

[17] N.D. Jones, C. K. Gomard, P. Sestoft. *Partial Evaluation and Automatic Program Generation*, Prentice Hall, 1993.

[18] J.B. Kam, J.D. Ullman. Monotone Data Flow Analysis Frameworks. *Acta Informatica*, v. 7, 1977, 305-317.

[19] D.E. Knuth, P.B. Bendix. Simple Word Problems in Universal Algebras. In: *Computational Problems in Abstract Algebra* (J. Leech, Ed.), Pergamon Press, 1970.

[20] W. Landi, B.G. Ryder. A Safe Approximate Algorithm for Interprocedural Pointer Aliasing. *Proceedings of the ACM SIGPLAN Conference on Programming Language Design and Implementation*, 1992, 235-248.

[21] U. Meyer. Techniques for Partial Evaluation of Imperative Languages. *Proceedings of the ACM Symposium on Partial Evaluation and Semantics-Based Program Manipulation*, 1991, 94-105.

[22] F. Mueller, D.B. Whalley. Avoiding Conditional Branches by Code Replication. *Proceedings of the SIGPLAN Symposium on Programming Language Design and Implementation*, 1995, 56-66.

[23] S. Sagiv et al. A Logic-Based Approach to Data Flow Analysis Problems. *Lecture Notes in Computer Science*, v. 456, 1990, 52-65.

[24] A. Sakharov. Propagation of Constants and Assertions. *SIGPLAN Notices*, v. 29, 1994, #5, 3-6.

[25] B. Wegbreit. Property Extraction in Well-Founded Property Sets. *IEEE Transactions on Software Engineering*, v. 1, 1977, #3, 270-285.

[26] M.N. Wegman, F.K. Zadeck. Constant Propagation with Conditional Branches. *ACM Transactions on Programming Languages and Systems*, v. 13, 1991, #2, 181-210.

ML Pattern Match Compilation and Partial Evaluation

Peter Sestoft
sestoft@dina.kvl.dk

Department of Mathematics and Physics
Royal Veterinary and Agricultural University
Thorvaldsensvej 40, DK-1871 Frederiksberg C, Denmark

Abstract: We derive a compiler for ML-style pattern matches. It is conceptually simple and produces reasonably good compiled matches. The derivation is inspired by the instrumentation and partial evaluation of naïve string matchers. Following that paradigm, we first present a general and naïve ML pattern matcher, instrument it to collect and exploit extra information, and show that partial evaluation of the instrumented general matcher with respect to a given match produces an efficient specialized matcher.

We then discard the partial evaluator and show that a match compiler can be obtained just by slightly modifying the instrumented general matcher. The resulting match compiler is interesting in its own right, and naturally detects inexhaustive matches and redundant match rules.

1 Introduction

Consel and Danvy [3] studied a general string matcher, taking two inputs: a *pattern* string to look for, and an *object* string to look in. The matcher finds the first occurrence (if any) of the pattern in the object string. They showed that partial evaluation of a naïve string matcher with respect to a static pattern did not improve the algorithm. Then they instrumented the matcher to collect and exploit information about previous partial matches, taking care to make this information static, and showed that partial evaluation of the instrumented matcher would produce efficient Knuth-Morris-Pratt style matchers [11].

Jørgensen applied the same idea to tree pattern matching [9, 10]. He studied a general tree pattern matcher, taking two inputs: a *match*, which is a sequence of *patterns*, and an *object* term. The matcher finds the first pattern (if any) which is matched by the object. Jørgensen showed that the instrumentation approach carries over to the new setting, producing efficient specialized matchers from an instrumented version of the naïve matcher.

Continuing Jørgensen's work, we handle arbitrary ML-style pattern matches, present a general naïve matcher, and instrument it to collect positive and negative information. Initially we use a partial evaluator to specialize the instrumented matcher, but then observe that a specialized matcher implements a decision *tree*: it has no loops and no sharing — no memoization is needed. We therefore discard the partial evaluator, modify the instrumented matcher, and obtain a conceptually simple and fairly efficient ML match compiler.

In Section 2 we describe ML-style tree pattern matching, and in Section 3 we present a naïve pattern matcher, taking two inputs: a sequence of match rules to be tested, and an object term to match against the rules. In Section 4 we show how to represent positive and negative information about terms, and in Section 5 we instrument the naïve matcher to collect such information. In Section 6 we partially evaluate the instrumented matcher with respect to static match rules, and obtain a specialized matcher which performs no repeated tests. In Section 7 we construct the final match compiler by replacing dynamic variables and expressions of the instrumented matcher with symbolic terms. Section 8 discusses related work, and Section 9 contains the conclusion.

2 ML pattern matching

We assume that the object language is statically typed, so that the set of constructors that may appear at some point in a pattern or term is known at compile-time. This description fits e.g. Standard ML and Haskell, but not Scheme.

2.1 Constructors, patterns, terms, and matching

For the theoretical development, we use slightly generalized notions of constructor and pattern. A *constructor* is characterized by

- its *name*; in implementations this is typically a numerical tag;
- its *arity*, which is the number of arguments it takes (and is assured to get, by the type system);
- its *span*, which is the total number of constructors in its type.

A *pattern* is either a variable, or a constructor applied to a possibly empty sequence of patterns. Patterns must be *linear*: no variable may occur more than once in a pattern. A *(proper) term* is a pattern not containing variables. Constructors and patterns can be modelled as follows:

```
type con = { name : string, arity : int, span : int }
datatype pat = PVar of string | PCon of con * pat list
```

Example 1. For instance, the three constructors Null, Leaf, and Node declared by the Standard ML declaration

```
datatype 'a tree =
    Null | Leaf of 'a | Node of 'a tree * 'a * 'a tree
```

can be represented as follows:

```
val Nullc = {name = "Null", arity = 0, span = 3}
val Leafc = {name = "Leaf", arity = 1, span = 3}
val Nodec = {name = "Node", arity = 3, span = 3}
```

Then the SML term Node(Leaf 9, 12, Node(Leaf 4, 7, Null)) would be encoded by the following term:

```
PCon(Nodec, [PCon(Leafc, [9]), 12,
             PCon(Nodec, [PCon(Leafc,[4]),7,PCon(Nullc,[])])])
```

A *match rule* or *mrule* is a pair of a pattern and an (unspecified) right-hand side, and a *match* is a sequence of match rules:

```
type 'rhs match = (pat * 'rhs) list
```

A *match object* is the term to be matched against a pattern. A term *matches* a pattern if there is a substitution of terms for variables in the pattern which makes the term and the pattern equal. The problem of pattern matching, given an object and a match, is to find the first match rule (`pat`, `rhs`) for which the object matches the pattern `pat`, or to decide that the no such rule exists in the match.

2.2   Representing ML data

We assume the reader is familiar with Standard ML pattern matching [14].

In an ML datatype, such as `'a tree` above, a constructor `Null`, `Leaf`, or `Node` is encoded by taking its *arity* to be the declared number of arguments[1], and its *span* to be the number of constructors belonging to the datatype.

An ML tuple, such as `(1, Null, true, "abc")`, is represented by a single constructor with span 1 and arity equal to the number of components, e.g. the arity is 4 in this example, and 2 for the pair constructor.

The components of an ML record can be sorted by their labels, so records can be handled as tuples in an implementation.

The ML special constants of type `int`, `real`, and `string` are encoded by constructors with arity 0 and infinite span. Character constants of type `char` are encoded with arity 0 and span 256 (for the ASCII character set).

A vector[2] constructor `#[_, ..., _]` has arity equal to the number of listed arguments, and span 1. Its name must reflect the arity, so that vector constructors of different arities are distinct. The ML exception constructors, such as `Div` or `Io`, have arity 0 or 1 and have infinite span. The ML `ref` constructor has arity 1 and span 1.

Hence all matchable ML data can be represented by our notions of constructor, pattern, and term.

---

[1] In principle, an ML value constructor takes either zero or one argument, which may be a tuple. It is immaterial for the present development whether one follows this model strictly, or allows a constructor to take multiple arguments. For purposes of matching, there is no difference between the pattern $C(v)$ and the pattern $C(v_1, \ldots, v_a)$ where $a = arity(C)$ and $v, v_1, \ldots, v_a$ are variables.

[2] Character and vector constructors are extensions to Standard ML, implemented by Standard ML of New Jersey, Moscow ML, and other systems.

Example 2. ML booleans and tuple, pair, and list constructors, can be encoded as follows:

```
val tt = PCon({name="true",  arity=0, span=2}, [])
val ff = PCon({name="false", arity=0, span=2}, [])

fun tup args = PCon({name="", span=1, arity=length args}, args)
fun pair(x, y) = tup[x, y]

val nil     = PCon({name="nil",  arity=0, span=2}, [])
fun cons(a,b) = PCon({name="cons", arity=2, span=2}, [a,b])
```

3 A naïve ML pattern matcher

The general pattern matcher takes as input a match object (a term) and a match (a sequence of mrules), and produces as output the right-hand side of the first matching mrule, or fails.

It works by sequentially matching the object against the mrule patterns (the left-hand sides); if a pattern fails, then the next one is tried, etc., until the object matches some pattern, or there are no more patterns. As in a naïve string matcher, this is potentially inefficient, because tests of the same subterm may be performed repeatedly. The worst-case complexity is the product of the number of mrules and the size of the object term.

The naive matcher shown below takes two inputs: an object term `origobj`, and a match `allmrules`. It is implemented by three mutually recursive functions, with the following specifications:

- `fail(rules)` will attempt to match the original object term `origobj` against each pattern `pat` from a rule `(pat, rhs)` in `rules`; it succeeds with the `rhs` if the rule matches; it fails otherwise.
- `succeed(work, rhs, rules)` succeeds, returning the `rhs`, if for every pair `(pat, obj)` in `work`, the object `obj` matches the pattern `pat`; or succeeds if the original object `origobj` matches some rule from `rules`; fails otherwise. Actually, `work` is a stack of lists of `(pattern, object)` pairs; this saves some append operations.
- `match(pat1, obj1, work, rhs, rules)` succeeds, returning the `rhs` if `obj1` matches `pat1`, and for every pair `(pat, obj)` in `work`, `obj` matches `pat`; or succeeds if `origobj` matches some rule in `rules`; fails otherwise.

That is, `fail` expresses disjunction of matches, `succeed` expresses conjunction of matches, and `match` does the actual matching work. The `rules` parameter is a list of alternatives to backtrack to; and the `work` parameter is a stack of match hypotheses still to be checked. These parameters are first-order representations of the failure and success continuations, respectively. This is useful in connection with our representation of positive and negative information in the instrumented matcher; see Section 4.3. Jørgensen's matcher represented the continuations by functions [9]. The function `main` implements the matcher:

```
fun main (origobj, allmrules) =
let fun fail []                              = NONE
      | fail ((pat1, rhs1) :: rulerest) =
        match(pat1, origobj, [], rhs1, rulerest)
    and succeed([],              rhs, rules) = SOME rhs
      | succeed(work1 :: workr, rhs, rules) =
        case work1 of
            ([], []) => succeed(workr, rhs, rules)
          | (pat1::patr, obj1::objr) =>
                match(pat1, obj1, (patr,objr)::workr, rhs, rules)
    and match(PVar _, _, work, rhs, rules) =
        succeed(work, rhs, rules)
      | match(PCon(pcon,pargs),PCon(ocon,oargs),work,rhs,rules) =
        if ocon = pcon then
            succeed((pargs, oargs) :: work, rhs, rules)
        else
            fail rules
in fail allmrules end
```

Note that there are no arity tests; static typing ensures that if two constructor names are equal, then they are applied to the same number of arguments, whether occurring in a pattern or a term.

4 Positive and negative information about terms

We now instrument the naive matcher to record and exploit information about the match object. The only source of such information is the test ocon = pcon in the match function above. We shall record *positive* information from tests which succeed, and *negative* information from tests which fail.

4.1 Term descriptions

This information will be recorded in the form of a *term description*. A *positive* term description is a skeletal term, consisting of a constructor together with a tuple of argument term descriptions. A *negative* term description is a set of impossible constructors:

```
datatype termd = Pos of con * termd list | Neg of con list
```

The positive term description $\text{Pos}(c, [t_1, \ldots, t_a])$ describes any term whose topmost constructor is c, and whose components are described by t_1 through t_a. The negative term description $\text{Neg}\{c_1, \ldots, c_n\}$ describes any term whose topmost constructor is none of $c_1, \ldots, c_n$. In a negative term description $\text{Neg}(S)$, the cardinality of S must be strictly less than the span of any constructor in S. Otherwise the term description is contradictory, and describes the empty set of terms. Due to static typing, all constructors in S must belong to the same type and hence have the same span.

Example 3. For terms of type `'a tree`, the term description `Neg[Node]` describes terms which are either `Null` or `Leaf(a)` for some a. The positive term description `Pos(Node,[Neg [Node], Neg [], Pos(Null,[])])` describes terms of the form `Node(t, a, Null)` where t does not have form `Node(_,_,_)`, and a is some term.

The set of term descriptions is

$$TermD = \{ \text{ Neg}(S) \mid \forall c \in S.card(S) < span(c) \}$$
$$\cup \{ \text{ Pos}(c,[t_1,\ldots,t_a]) \mid a = arity(c), t_i \in TermD \}$$

There is a natural information preordering $\sqsubseteq$ on the set $TermD$ of term descriptions, defined as follows, where $\bot = \text{Neg}\{\}$:

$\text{Neg}(S_1) \sqsubseteq \text{Neg}(S_2)$	iff $S_1 \subseteq S_2$
$\text{Neg}(S) \sqsubseteq \text{Pos}(c,[t_1,\ldots,t_a])$	iff $c \notin S$
$\text{Pos}(c,[\bot,\ldots,\bot]) \sqsubseteq \text{Neg}(S)$	iff $card(S \cup \{c\}) = span(c)$
$\text{Pos}(c,[t_1,\ldots,t_a]) \sqsubseteq \text{Pos}(c,[u_1,\ldots,u_a])$	iff $t_i \sqsubseteq u_i$ for all $i = 1,\ldots,a$

The relation $\sqsubseteq$ is a preordering because $\text{Neg}(S)$ provides the same information as $\text{Pos}(c,[\bot,\ldots,\bot])$ when $card(S \cup \{c\}) = span(c)$; taking the quotient over the congruence induced by this equivalence gives a partial order. The least element is $\bot = \text{Neg}\{\}$, which describes any term, and represents the absence of information. A maximal element is an encoding of a proper term, describing just that term.

In the instrumented matcher, the information about the match object is $\bot$ initially, and grows monotonically during the execution of the instrumented matcher. The work stack of (`pat`, `obj`) pairs must be extended to a stack of (`pat`, `obj`, `dsc`) triples, which records a subterm description `dsc` along with every subterm `obj` of the object.

The auxiliary function `addneg: termd * con -> termd` adds negative information to a partial term:

```
fun addneg(Neg nonset, con) = Neg(con :: nonset)
```

It has two preconditions: `con` $\notin$ `nonset`, and $card(\text{nonset} \cup \{\text{con}\}) < span(\text{con})$.

4.2 Static matching

Static matching attempts to match a constructor `ocon` from the object against a constructor `pcon` from the pattern, using only the object term description which has been constructed by those matching steps already performed. Static matching produces one of three answers: `Yes`, `No`, or `Maybe`, as follows:

a. If the object constructor is (positively) known to be c, and $pcon = c$, then the answer is `Yes`.
b. If the object constructor is (positively) known to be c, and $pcon \neq c$, then the answer is `No`.

c. If the object constructor is (negatively) known not to be any of $c_1, \ldots, c_n$, and $pcon = c_i$ for some $1 \leq i \leq n$, then the answer is No.

d. If the object constructor is (negatively) known not to be any of $c_1, \ldots, c_n$ (all distinct), and $pcon \neq c_i$ for all $1 \leq i \leq n$, and $span(pcon) = 1 + n$, then the answer is Yes.

e. Otherwise the answer is Maybe.

For constructors with span 1, such as tuples and pairs, rule (d) ensures that matching succeeds unconditionally. Since inequality of SML exception constructors cannot be safely decided at compile-time, rule (b) never applies for exception constructors. This is easily ensured in an implementation, and we shall disregard exception constructors for the remainder of the paper. Constructors of type int, real, and string, and exception constructors, have infinite span, so rule (d) never applies for those.

Using the span to optimize matches is well-known in match compilers for typed languages, and was suggested also by Jørgensen [9, page 191].

Static matching of the object term description against a pattern constructor pcon is implemented by a function staticmatch: con * termd -> matchresult.

4.3 Context descriptions

During the matching of a composite object against a composite pattern, we need to manage partial term descriptions, describing the part of the term which is already matched at a given point. Since we match top-down and left-right, the part of the description already computed is above and to the left of the current subterm. Hence a left *context description* must describe the constructors on the path from the root to the current subterm, and those of their arguments which are to the left of the current subterm.

For example, assume we are matching the object

```
Node(Node(Null, 1, Leaf 2), 3, Null)
```

against the pattern

```
Node(Node(x, 1, Leaf y), z, Null)
```

and assume the current subterm is the rightmost occurrence of Null. Then the current context description should be

```
Node(Node(⊥, 1, Leaf ⊥), ⊥, [])
```

where $\perp$ denotes the absence of information, and [] is the 'hole' containing the current subterm.

This context is represented by the path of constructors from the current subterm up to the root, together with descriptions of those of their arguments which are to the left of the hole. Hence a context description is a list of constructors and argument descriptions:

```
type context = (con * termd list) list
```

In particular, the example context shown above is described by

```
[(Node, [⊥, Pos(Node,[⊥, 1, Pos(Leaf,[⊥])])])]
```

This represents the partial application of constructor Node to two arguments, described by Pos(Node, ...) and $\perp$. The general form of a context description is

$$[(c_n, [t_{nk_n}, \ldots, t_{n1}]), \ldots, (c_1, [t_{1k_1}, \ldots, t_{11}])]$$

where the t_{ij} are term descriptions, $k_i < arity(c_i)$ for $i < n$, and $k_n \leq arity(c_n)$. If $k_n < arity(c_n)$, then it represents the context

$$c_1(t_{11}, \ldots, t_{1k_1}, c_2(\ldots c_n(t_{n1}, \ldots, t_{nk_n}, [], \perp, \ldots, \perp) \ldots \perp), \perp, \ldots, \perp)$$

where information-less descriptions $\perp$ are added on the right to saturate the constructor applications. If $k_n = arity(c_n)$, then it represents a context of form

$$c_1(t_{11}, \ldots, t_{1k_1}, c_2(\ldots c_n(t_{n1}, \ldots, t_{nk_n}), [], \ldots \perp), \perp, \ldots, \perp)$$

In particular, the empty list [] of partially applied constructors (with $n = 0$) represents the top-level context [].

When the matching of a subterm succeeds, it produces a term description dsc which is an argument to the local-most constructor c_n. Hence we partially fill the hole with dsc, by adding dsc to the list of argument descriptions for the local-most constructor c_n. Function augment: context * termd -> context accomplishes this:

```
fun augment([],                dsc) = []
  | augment((con, args)::rest, dsc) = (con, dsc :: args) :: rest
```

When argument descriptions $[t_{na}, \ldots, t_{n1}]$ for all arguments of the local-most constructor c_n have been found, a positive term description $Pos(c_n, [t_{n1}, \ldots, t_{na}])$ is constructed, and the remainder of the context is augmented with this description. This is done by function norm:

```
fun norm ((con, args) :: rest) =
    augment(rest, Pos(con, rev args))
```

When the matching of a subterm fails, the current match rule must be abandoned and the next one tried, but first the object term description must be reconstructed. There are three components:

(1) the context description ctx, which describes the part of the object term to the left of the current subterm;
(2) the current subterm description dsc; and
(3) the term descriptions on the work stack, which together describe the part of the object term to the right of the current subterm.

These three components are reassembled to a term description as follows. If the context and the work stack are empty, then the current subterm description is the desired result. Otherwise both are non-empty, and the local-most partial constructor application (in the context) is further applied to the current subterm description, plus the top-most list of argument descriptions from the work stack, to obtain a term description. Then the rest of the context is recursively applied to this description and to the rest of the work stack.

This procedure is implemented by the builddsc function:

```
fun builddsc([], dsc, []) = dsc
  | builddsc((con, args)::rest, dsc, (_, _, dargs) :: work) =
      builddsc(rest, Pos(con, rev args @ (dsc :: dargs)), work)
```

Jørgensen used an occurrence environment, mapping occurrences (also called positions, or paths) of a term to term descriptions, to represent the knowledge acquired through partial matching of a term [9]. Hence he did not need a notion of context.

5   The instrumented ML pattern matcher

The instrumented matcher improves on the naïve one by (1) recording positive and negative information about the object term, also in the work list, and (2) attempting static matching using this information, resorting to actual tests on the object only when the static matching produces the result Maybe. The function main: pat * 'rhs match -> 'rhs option implements the instrumented matcher:

```
fun main(origobj, allmrules) =
  let fun fail(dsc, [])                            = NONE
        | fail(dsc, (pat1, rhs1) :: rulerest) =
          match(pat1, origobj, dsc, [], [], rhs1, rulerest)
      and succeed(ctx, [], rhs, rules)             = SOME rhs
        | succeed(ctx, work1::workr, rhs, rules) =
          case work1 of
              ([], [], []) => succeed(norm ctx, workr, rhs, rules)
            | (pat1::patr, obj1::objr, dsc1::dscr) =>
                  match(pat1, obj1, dsc1, ctx,
                          (patr,objr,dscr)::workr, rhs, rules)
      and match(PVar _, obj, dsc, ctx, work, rhs, rules) =
          succeed(augment(ctx, dsc), work, rhs, rules)
        | match(PCon(pcon, pargs), PCon(ocon, oargs),
              dsc, ctx, work, rhs, rules) =
          let fun args f = List.tabulate(#arity pcon, f)
              fun getdargs (Neg _) = args (fn _ => Neg [])
                | getdargs (Pos(con, dargs)) = dargs
              fun succeed' () =
                  succeed((pcon, []) :: ctx,
                            (pargs,oargs,getdargs dsc)::work,
                            rhs, rules)
              fun fail' newdsc =
                  fail(builddsc(ctx, newdsc, work), rules)
          in case staticmatch(pcon, dsc) of
              Yes   => succeed' ()
            | No    => fail' dsc
            | Maybe => if ocon = pcon then succeed' ()
                        else fail' (addneg(dsc, pcon))
          end
  in fail(Neg [], allmrules) end
```

If `allmrules` is static and `origobj` dynamic, only the underlined parameters and
test will be dynamic. In addition, `work` is a partially static list of triples (`pats`,
`objs`, `dscs`) where the patterns `pats` and the term descriptions `dscs` are static,
and the `objs` are dynamic. Hence all tests can be eliminated by the partial
evaluator, except the test `ocon = pcon`, performed when the static matching
returns `Maybe`. This is also the only place new information is born, by recording
the outcome of the dynamic test.

Two new auxiliary functions are used. Function `getdargs` returns the list of
argument descriptions from a term description: if it is positive, then the argument
descriptions `dargs` are explicitly provided; if it is negative, then all argument
descriptions are implicitly $\perp$.

Function `success'` is called after a successful match of a constructor; it
extends the context with positive information about the matched constructor.
Function `fail'` is called after an unsuccessful match of a constructor; if the match
is dynamic, then new negative information is added to the subterm description
before `builddsc` reconstructs the object term description.

6 Experiments with a simple partial evaluator

We rewrote the above instrumented ML program in a subset of Scheme, separating binding times by splitting the work list into three parallel lists. It was partially evaluated using the Scheme0 partial evaluator, a prototypical polyvariant program specializer for a first-order Scheme subset [8, Chapter 5]. The results are as expected, although clumsy, since the partial evaluator performs no postunfolding etc. Indeed, the simplicity of the Scheme0 partial evaluator ensures that the result is due to the recording and exploitation of static information, rather than powerful optimizations and transformations performed by the partial evaluator. This is important, as the ultimate goal is to write the match compiler without a partial evaluator.

Consider the following example datatype:

```
datatype lam =
    Var of int
  | Lam of int * lam
  | App of lam * lam
  | Let of int * lam * lam
```

and the following example match on this type:

```
  Var x                           => 111
| Lam(x, Var y)                   => 222
| Lam(x, Lam(y, z))               => 333
| Lam(x, App(y, z))               => 444
| App(Lam(x, y), z)               => 555
| App(App(x, y), z)               => 666
| Let(x, Let(y, z, v), w)         => 777
| Lam(x, Let(y, z, v))            => 888
| Let(x, y, App(z, v))            => 999
| App(App(Lam(x, Lam(y, z)), v), w) => 1010
```

The residual program contains 66 functions with a total of 10 conditionals, testing some subterm for equality with a constructor. The control structure is shown below, after unfolding of trivial function calls and removal of unused variables, and (ab)using the notation #con for extraction of the topmost term constructor. Observe that test is performed twice. The occurrences of FAIL show that the match was inexhaustive. The non-occurrence of the right-hand side 1010 shows that the last match rule is redundant (it is covered by the sixth rule):

```
fun f1 obj = if #con obj = Var then 111
             else if #con obj = Lam then f2 obj
             else if #con obj = App then f3 obj
             else f4 obj
and f2 obj = if #con(#2 obj) = Var then 222
             else if #con(#2 obj) = Lam then 333
             else if #con(#2 obj) = App then 444
             else 888
and f3 obj = if #con(#1 obj) = Lam then 555
             else if #con(#1 obj) = App then 666
             else FAIL
and f4 obj = if #con(#2 obj) = Let then 777
             else if #con(#3 obj) = App then 999
             else FAIL
```

7 ML match compilation without partial evaluation

7.1 Decision trees and access paths

Inspection shows that match will not be specialized twice with the same values of pat, work and rules — its first, fifth, and seventh parameters. Hence the call graph of a specialized matcher is a *tree*.

Thus memoization in the partial evaluator serves no purpose, and we can generate decision trees directly. We then obtain a match compiler which, given a match, generates a decision tree. The decision tree performs tests on subterms of the object term; such subterms are denoted by symbolic *access paths*. An access path is either Obj, meaning the entire object term, or Sel(*i*, *acc*), meaning the *i*'th component of the subterm pointed out by *acc*:

```
datatype access = Obj | Sel of int * access
```

A decision is either Failure, which immediately fails; or Success(*rhs*) which immediately succeeds, returning *rhs*; or IfEq(*acc*, *con*, d_t, d_f) which tests whether *con* equals the constructor at subterm *acc* of the object term, and then evaluates decision d_t or decision d_f according as the outcome was true or false:

```
datatype 'rhs decision =
    Failure
  | Success of 'rhs
  | IfEq of access * con * 'rhs decision * 'rhs decision
```

7.2 The match compiler

Now the match compiler itself is obtained from the instrumented matcher just by replacing the dynamic data and computations by symbolic data and computations. Namely,

- the value NONE returned by `fail` is replaced by the decision tree `Failure`;
- the value SOME `rhs` returned by `succeed` is replaced by `Success rhs`;
- a new function `getoargs` produces access paths into the object term;
- the dynamic parameter `PCon(ocon, oargs)` is replaced by access path `obj`;
- the dynamic test `if ocon = pcon then e1 else e2` is replaced by the generation of a node `IfEq(obj, pcon, e1, e2)` in the decision tree.

The resulting match compiler `compile: 'rhs match -> 'rhs decision` is strikingly similar to the instrumented matcher shown in Section 5. The differences are underlined:

```
fun compile allmrules =
let fun fail(dsc, [])                                = Failure
      | fail(dsc, (pat1, rhs1) :: rulerest) =
        match(pat1, Obj, dsc, [], [], rhs1, rulerest)
    and succeed(ctx, [], rhs, rules)                 = Success rhs
      | succeed(ctx, work1::workr, rhs, rules) =
        case work1 of
            ([], [], []) => succeed(norm ctx, workr, rhs, rules)
          | (pat1::patr, obj1::objr, dsc1::dscr) =>
              match(pat1, obj1, dsc1, ctx,
                    (patr, objr, dscr) :: workr, rhs, rules)
    and match(PVar _, obj, dsc, ctx, work, rhs, rules) =
        succeed(augment(ctx, dsc), work, rhs, rules)
      | match(PCon(pcon, pargs),obj,dsc,ctx,work,rhs,rules) =
        let fun args f = List.tabulate(#arity pcon, f)
            fun getdargs (Neg _) = args (fn _ => Neg [])
              | getdargs (Pos(con, dargs)) = dargs
            fun getoargs () = args (fn i => Sel(i+1, obj))
            fun succeed' () =
                succeed((pcon, []) :: ctx,
                        (pargs,getoargs (),getdargs dsc)::work,
                        rhs, rules)
            fun fail' newdsc =
                fail(builddsc(ctx, newdsc, work), rules)
        in case staticmatch(pcon, dsc) of
            Yes   => succeed' ()
          | No    => fail' dsc
          | Maybe => IfEq(obj, pcon,
                          succeed' (),
                          fail' (addneg(dsc, pcon)))
        end
in fail(Neg [], allmrules) end
```

7.3 Properties of the match compiler

The above match compiler produces a decision tree, the size of which is at most linear in the sum of the pattern sizes. However, the tree is not optimal, because we perform the matching in strict top-down, left-right order. The decision tree may be larger than necessary, and may perform more tests at runtime than necessary.

Example 4. This example from Baudinet and MacQueen shows that their algorithm may create more compact trees than ours:

```
datatype color = red | blue | green;

case ... of
   (true,  green) => 111
 | (false, green) => 222
```

Our match compiler produces the following code which tests the first component before the second one, thus duplicating the test on the **green** constructor:

```
IfEq(Sel(1, Obj), true,
    IfEq(Sel(2, Obj), green,
             Success 111,
             Failure),
    IfEq(Sel(2, Obj), green,
             Success 222,
             Failure))
```

Baudinet and MacQueen's algorithm would produce a decision tree which tests the second component first, leading to a smaller decision tree.

Example 5. Our match compiler will compile the following

```
case ... of
   (large_pattern, true)  => 111
 | ( _,            false) => 222
```

into a decision tree which attempts to match the first component to the large pattern, before it checks whether the second component is **true**. It seems more sensible to perform the latter simple test first: if the simple test fails, there is no need to check the large pattern.

We have not yet tested the match compiler on real programs, so it is unclear whether the non-optimal behaviour above is problematic in practice.

Example 6. The time and space consumption of the match compiler itself is exponential in n on matches with $n + 1$ rules, each a $2n$-tuple, of the following form:

```
datatype t = A | B
fun f x = case x of
   (A,A,_,_,_,_,_,_,_,_) =>  0
 | (_,_,A,A,_,_,_,_,_,_) =>  1
 | (_,_,_,_,A,A,_,_,_,_) =>  2
 | (_,_,_,_,_,_,A,A,_,_) =>  3
 | (_,_,_,_,_,_,_,_,A,A) =>  4
 | (A,B,A,B,A,B,A,B,A,B) => ~1
```

Simple practical experiments show that the match compilers used in Standard ML of New Jersey, Edinburgh ML, and the ML Kit take exponential time, and sometimes space, too.

The exponential space consumption can be avoided by using memoization while constructing the decision tree, as discussed in Section 7.5 below.

7.4 Inexhaustive matches and redundant cases

For every path through the generated decision tree, there is an object term which takes that path: all paths are feasible. Conversely, the decision tree is complete: for every object term there is a path through the decision tree, leading to a leaf (Failure or Success). This permits detection of inexhaustive matches and redundant cases, as required by e.g. the Definition of Standard ML [14].

Namely, a match can fail if and only if a Failure decision appears in the decision tree. Hence an inexhaustive match can be detected just by setting a global variable to true if a Failure decision is generated by the match compiler.

For the same reasons, the right-hand side of a match rule can be exercised if and only if it appears as a Success leaf in the decision tree. Hence the redundant match rules can be found by keeping a global set of match rules, initially containing all match rules. Whenever a Success(rhs) decision is being generated, remove rhs from the set. At the end of the match compilation, the set contains just the redundant rules.

7.5 Other refinements

A simple memoization scheme can be applied during the construction of the decision tree, turning the tree into a dag (directed acyclic graph), which will contain no two isomorphic subdags. An approach similar to hash-consing suffices. Whenever a branching node IfEq(acc, con, t1, t2) is about to be constructed, it is checked whether there is already a node with the same components, and if so, this node is used instead. An experimental implementation of this memoization works well and produces compact decision dags. It avoids the exponential space consumption problem on pathological matches discussed in Example 6 above.

The decision dag as constructed contains only binary equality tests. In practice, one wants to replace sequences of binary equality tests by more efficient switches, or indexed jumps through tables, whenever possible. A *switch* has the form Switch(acc, rules, default) where acc is a dynamic access path; rules is a list $[(c_1, dec_1), \ldots, (c_n, dec_n)]$ of pairs of constructors and decisions, where all constructors are distinct; and default is the decision to be evaluated if the constructor at acc does not occur in rules. The decision dag can be 'switchified' by a simple linear-time postprocessing.

Common subexpression elimination can be applied to the decision dag to avoid repeated extraction of the same object subterm.

7.6 Examples

Example 7. The match

```
(x, nil) => 111
| (nil, x) => 222
```

is compiled into the optimal decision tree

```
IfEq(Sel(2, Obj), nil,
    Success 111,
    IfEq(Sel(1, Obj), nil,
        Success 222,
        Failure))
```

Example 8. The example from Section 6 is compiled into the decision tree shown below. The match compiler detects that the match is inexhaustive and that rule 10 (the last one) is redundant. In the decision tree, sequences of binary equality tests have been replaced by switches, as proposed above. Its structure is identical to that of the residual matcher generated by partial evaluation in Section 6.

```
Switch(Obj,
        [(Var, Success 111),
         (Lam, Switch(Sel(2, Obj),
                        [(varc, Success 222),
                         (lamc, Success 333),
                         (appc, Success 444)],
                        Success 888)),
         (App, Switch(Sel(1, Obj),
                        [(Lam, Success 555),
                         (App, Success 666)],
                        Failure))],
        IfEq(Sel(2, Obj), Let,
            Success 777,
            IfEq(Sel(3, Obj), App,
                Success 999,
                Failure)))
```

8 Related work

Partial evaluation: Futamura and Nogi [4] showed that in principle, efficient string matchers à la Knuth-Morris-Pratt can be generated from a general naïve matcher. This required a generalized partial evaluator which would record the outcome of previous tests and use a theorem prover to decide subsequent tests. Apparently it was not implemented.

Consel and Danvy [3] demonstrated that even a simple partial evaluator could generate KMP-style string matchers from an *instrumented* naïve matcher.

Jørgensen [9, 10] applied the instrumentation approach to tree pattern matching, and showed that efficient compiled matches were generated; his work is a close precursor of the present work. Jørgensen also discussed several of the techniques presented here, but did not obtain a stand-alone match compiler by discarding the partial evaluator.

Glück and Jørgensen [5] achieved the programme outlined by Futamura and Nogi, generating a KMP-style string matcher from a general naïve matcher, using a specializer with positive and negative information, but without a theorem prover.

Match compilation: Augustsson described a top-down, left-right compilation algorithm for ML-style pattern matching in lazy functional languages [1]; see also Wadler's exposition in [16, Chapter 5]. It does not naturally discover inexhaustive matches and redundant cases.

In a lazy language, the order of testing of subterms affects evaluation order and hence termination, so terms are usually tested from top-down and left-right for simplicity and transparency. Our naïve matcher, and hence our match compiler, implements pattern matching as required by the Haskell report [6]. Our compiled matchers, like Jørgensen's, are more efficient than Augustsson's and Wadler's on non-uniform matches.

Jørgensen showed that some inefficiencies in matchers generated by Augustsson's and Wadler's method can be removed by a simple postprocessing, recording and using information from previous matches. The resulting compiled matches are always compact and usually efficient; however, the approach does not naturally detect inexhaustive matches and redundant rules.

Petterson [15] presented an improvement of the techniques of Augustsson and Wadler, based on finite automata, but retaining the top-down, left-right matching order. His match compiler has many similarities to that derived here; in particular, it naturally detects inexhaustive matches and redundant rules. Petterson compares the use of memoization (Section 7.5) to minimization of automata.

The top-down, left-right matching order does not produce optimal compiled matchers. Huet and Lévy [7] studied optimality for *unambiguous* matches (non-overlapping patterns only). However, programming languages usually allow patterns to overlap, but impose an order on them, and make the match deterministic by selecting the first matching one.

To adapt Huet and Lévy's work to programming practice, Laville [12] studied optimal compilation of ordered ambiguous pattern matches for lazy languages, relaxing the left-right matching order. As far as we know, his algorithms have not been used in a practical compiler.

Puel and Suárez [17] used constrained terms, similar to our term descriptions, instead of Laville's ordered patterns. An ordered collection of ambiguous patterns can be compiled into an unordered collection of unambiguous constrained patterns, from which one can construct a decision tree.

Augustsson's top-down, left-right match compilation technique is not optimal for strict languages, in which subterms may be tested in any order without compromising termination. Even so, the technique is being used successfully in e.g. the Caml Light system [13], which shows that the generated matchers are efficient enough in practice.

Baudinet and MacQueen [2] studied match compilation for Standard ML. Their goal was to construct as compact a decision tree as possible; according to the paper, this also generally minimizes the number of tests performed at runtime. Example 4 above shows that their method indeed may produce a more compact and efficient decision tree than ours. Since constructing a minimal decision tree is an NP-complete problem, heuristics are used to decide the order of subterm tests. The match compiler currently used in the Standard ML of New Jersey system was written by Bill Aitken and seems to incorporate the heuristics proposed by Baudinet and MacQueen [19].

Ramesh, Ramakrishnan, and Warren [18] studied automata-based match compilation for Prolog. Their results show that large procedures with complicated arguments benefit from the automata-based match compilation, whereas the usual simple 'indexing' on the first argument is preferable for small procedures with shallow argument terms.

9 Conclusion

We have developed a simple technique for compiling ML-style pattern matches, recording, as positive and negative information about the term being matched, the outcome of all tests previously considered in the match. Inexhaustive matches and redundant cases are discovered as a natural by-product of this approach. The match compiler is likely to be correct, since it was derived in a step-wise manner from a naïve general matcher. The compiled matchers are compact and as efficient as possible, given the fixed top-down, left-right matching order.

For strict languages, the match compiler is not optimal, but neither is it worse than some match compilers already in use. We expect to use it in the Moscow ML compiler [20, 21].

It may seem ironic that we first discard the partial evaluator because no memoization is needed, and then reintroduce memoization explicitly to obtain sharing of isomorphic subtrees in the decision tree. However, the memoization performed by existing partial evaluators is based on identity of available data (function arguments), not on the use made of these data (the corresponding function results), and would not lead to sharing of subtrees.

The present work can be considered a case study in program derivation. Although the resulting match compiler makes no explicit use of partial evaluation, it owes its existence to inspiration from that field.

Acknowledgement: Thanks to Stephan Diehl, Jesper Jørgensen, Jacques Noyé, Alberto Pettorossi, Sergei Romanenko, and the anonymous referees for helpful comments and pointers.

References

1. L. Augustsson. Compiling pattern matching. In Jean-Pierre Jouannaud, editor, *Functional Programming Languages and Computer Architecture, Nancy, France,*

September 1985. (Lecture Notes in Computer Science, vol. 201), pages 368-381. Springer-Verlag, 1985.

2. M. Baudinet and D. MacQueen. Tree pattern matching for ML (extended abstract). Draft paper, AT&T Bell Laboratories, 1985.

3. C. Consel and O. Danvy. Partial evaluation of pattern matching in strings. *Information Processing Letters*, 30:79–86, January 1989.

4. Y. Futamura and K. Nogi. Generalized partial computation. In D. Bjørner, A.P. Ershov, and N.D. Jones, editors, *Partial Evaluation and Mixed Computation*, pages 133–151. Amsterdam: North-Holland, 1988.

5. R. Glück and J. Jørgensen. Generating optimizing specializers. In *IEEE Computer Society International Conference on Computer Languages, Toulouse, France, 1994*, pages 183–194. IEEE Computer Society Press, 1994.

6. P. Hudak, S. Peyton Jones, P. Wadler, et al. Report on the programming language Haskell – a non-strict, purely functional language, version 1.2. *SIGPLAN Notices*, 27(5):R1–R162, May 1992.

7. G. Huet and J.-J. Lévy. Call by need computations in non-ambiguous linear term rewriting systems. Rapport de Recherche 359, IRIA Rocquencourt, France, 1979.

8. N.D. Jones, C.K. Gomard, and P. Sestoft. *Partial Evaluation and Automatic Program Generation*. Prentice-Hall, 1993.

9. J. Jørgensen. Generating a pattern matching compiler by partial evaluation. In S.L. Peyton Jones, G. Hutton, and C. Kehler Holst, editors, *Functional Programming, Glasgow 1990*, pages 177–195. Berlin: Springer-Verlag, 1991.

10. J. Jørgensen. Compiler generation by partial evaluation. Master's thesis, DIKU, University of Copenhagen, Denmark, 1992. Student Project 92-1-4.

11. D.E. Knuth, J.H. Morris, and V.R. Pratt. Fast pattern matching in strings. *SIAM Journal of Computation*, 6(2):323–350, 1977.

12. A. Laville. Implementation of lazy pattern matching algorithms. In H. Ganzinger, editor, *ESOP'88, 2nd European Symposium on Programming, Nancy, France, March 1988*, pages 298–316. Berlin: Springer-Verlag, 1988.

13. X. Leroy. The Zinc experiment: An economical implementation of the ML language. Rapport Technique 117, INRIA Rocquencourt, France, 1990.

14. R. Milner, M. Tofte, and R. Harper. *The Definition of Standard ML*. MIT Press, 1990.

15. M. Petterson. A term pattern-match compiler inspired by finite automata theory. In U. Kastens and P. Pfahler, editors, *Compiler Construction, Paderborn, Germany, October 1992 (Lecture Notes in Computer Science, vol. 641)*. Berlin: Springer-Verlag, 1992.

16. S.L. Peyton Jones. *The Implementation of Functional Programming Languages*. Prentice-Hall, 1987.

17. L. Puel and A. Suárez. Compiling pattern matching by term decomposition. *Journal of Symbolic Computation*, 15(1):1–26, January 1993.

18. R. Ramesh, I.V. Ramakrishnan, and D.S. Warren. Automata-driven indexing of prolog clauses. *Journal of Logic Programming*, 23(3):151–202, 1995.

19. J. Reppy. Personal communication, November 1995.

20. S. Romanenko and P. Sestoft. *Moscow ML Language Overview, version 1.31*, October 1995. Available as ftp://ftp.dina.kvl.dk/pub/mosml/doc/mosmlref.ps.Z.

21. S. Romanenko and P. Sestoft. *Moscow ML Owner's Manual, version 1.31*, October 1995. Available as ftp://ftp.dina.kvl.dk/pub/mosml/doc/manual.ps.Z.

Self-Applicable Online Partial Evaluation

Michael Sperber

Wilhelm-Schickard-Institut für Informatik
Universität Tübingen
Sand 13, D-72076 Tübingen, Germany
sperber@informatik.uni-tuebingen.de
phone +49 (7071) 29-5467, fax +49 (7071) 29-5958

Abstract. We propose a hybrid approach to partial evaluation to achieve self-application of realistic online partial evaluators. Whereas the offline approach to partial evaluation leads to efficient specializers and self-application, online partial evaluators perform better specialization at the price of efficiency. Moreover, no online partial evaluator for a realistic higher-order language has been successfully self-applied. We present a binding-time analysis for an online partial evaluator for a higher-order subset of Scheme. The analysis distinguishes between *static, dynamic,* and *unknown* binding times. Thus, it makes some reduce/residualize decisions offline while leaving others to the specializer. We have implemented the binding-time analysis and an online specializer to go with it. After a standard binding-time improvement, our partial evaluator successfully self-applies. Our work confirms the practicality of an idea by Morry Katz.

Keywords: online partial evaluation, offline partial evaluation, self-application, compiler generation, binding-time analysis

Partial evaluation is a program specialization technique based on aggressive constant propagation. During specialization, a partial evaluator reduces expressions with known values while residualizing those whose values are not known at specialization time. Partial evaluators can make the residualize/reduce decision in two different ways: *Offline* partial evaluators make the decision before specialization itself by performing an "offline" *binding-time analysis* which annotates each expression in the program as either reducible or subject to residualization. *Online* partial evaluators, on the other hand, make the decision during specialization, based on the actual values propagated.

Both techniques have respective advantages: The specialization phase of an offline partial evaluator merely follows the annotations made by the binding-time analysis. It is therefore comparatively simple and efficient. Moreover, it makes offline partial evaluators amenable to *self-application* which makes it possible to generate stand-alone compilers and compiler generators. However, the binding-time analysis can provide only an approximation of the true binding-time behavior of the subject program. That approximation is often crude, especially for programs not already optimized for effective partial evaluation, and makes for poor precision during specialization. The online approach, on the other hand, can generally perform better specialization at the cost of specialization efficiency. Also, the complex specialization phase and the lack of offline binding-time information make self-application of a naive online partial evaluator non-practical.

We show how to unify the advantages of both approaches by using an online specialization phase in conjunction with an offline binding-time analysis. As opposed to binding-time analyses in offline systems, our analysis admits when it cannot precisely determine a binding time; it distinguishes between binding time values *static*, *dynamic*, and *unknown*. Our "honest" analysis is able to determine that substantial parts of the specialization phase are indeed static which makes self-application possible.

To summarize:

- We have specified a binding-time type system for a higher-order functional subset of Scheme which allows for unknown binding times.
- We have implemented a constraint-based binding-time analysis which runs in quasi-linear time generalizing Henglein's work [19].
- We have implemented a specializer which works on binding-time-annotated subject programs; it handles higher-order functions, partially static data structures, and performs arity raising.
- We have performed single and double self-application of the specializer, generated stand-alone compilers, and run several benchmarks

Overview The next section gives a brief account of online partial evaluation. In Sec. 2, we explain why self-application is harder to achieve with the online approach, and how to correct the problem by using a binding-time analysis. Subsequently, Sec. 3 briefly explains the type system underlying our binding-time analysis. Section 4 explains how to use its results in a specializer and Sec. 5 shows how to improve the binding times of the specializer to achieve self-application. Some preliminary experimental results are contained in Sec. 6. Section 7 contains an overview of related work.

1   Online Partial Evaluation

Online partial evaluators propagate *symbolic values* through a program [41, 30]. A symbolic value is a description of a set of runtime values. and represents the specialization-time approximations of runtime values. Typically, it will either contain an actual value already computed at specialization time, or some code to compute a value not known until runtime, possibly with additional type information. Thus, symbolic values may have the following structure for a higher-order language with partially static data structures:

$$
\begin{aligned}
SVal ::=\ &Top(Code) \\
&|\ Scalar(Val) \\
&|\ PS(CTor, SVal^*) \\
&|\ Closure(Code, SVal^*)
\end{aligned}
$$

In this specification, *Code* is a representation for output code, *Val* is for first-order Scheme values, *CTor* is for constructors of partially static data (such as cons); a *Closure* object needs to contain code for its body, and the symbolic values of its free variables.

$$spec[\![(\texttt{if } E_0 \ E_1 \ E_2)]\!] =$$
$$\text{let } sval_0 = spec[\![E_0]\!]$$
$$\text{in}$$
$$\quad \textbf{case } sval_0 \textbf{ of}$$
$$\quad\quad Scalar(v_0) \rightarrow \textbf{if } v_0 \textbf{ then } spec[\![E_1]\!] \textbf{ else } spec[\![E_2]\!]$$
$$\quad\quad Top(c_0) \quad\rightarrow \textbf{ let } c_1 = \mathcal{C}(spec[\![E_1]\!])$$
$$\quad\quad\quad\quad\quad\quad\quad\quad\quad\quad c_2 = \mathcal{C}(spec[\![E_2]\!])$$
$$\quad\quad\quad\quad\quad\quad\quad \textbf{in} \quad Top((\texttt{if } c_0 \ c_1 \ c_2))$$

Fig. 1. Code fragment from an online partial evaluator for handling **if**

The specialization phase itself is a non-standard interpreter which executes a program on symbolic values. Hence, its environment also contains symbolic values. For each operation, the specializer checks if it can execute the operation at specialization time, and, based on that decision, creates either residual code via *Top* or reduces the expression, yielding a *Scalar*, a *PS*, or a *Closure* object. Figure 1 contains an example for handling **if** in an online partial evaluator. The $\mathcal{C}$ function used there generates code from a symbolic value. The example shows that an online partial evaluator, in contrast to its offline counterpart, need not lift[1] **if**s with branches that have different binding times. (We have omitted a possible pairwise generalization of the results of the **if** branches which could preserve information even on dynamic conditionals.)

Since an online partial evaluator can make reduce/residualize decisions at runtime, its specialization is necessarily more accurate than that of offline counterparts. Specifically, online partial evaluators are trivially binding-time polyvariant, and therefore more likely to perform useful specialization on programs not optimized for effective partial evaluation. Realistic programs, when subjected to a monovariant offline analysis, get most binding-times coerced to "dynamic" by binding-time-polyvariant calls [30, 34].

2 Self-Application and Compiler Generation

Researchers in online partial evaluation have traditionally favored specialization accuracy over the possibility of self-application [41]. The main motivation for

---

[1] We use "lift" for "move a value up the binding-time type lattice" (specifically coerce a static value to a dynamic one) and "generalize" for "find the least upper bound of several values in the binding-time lattice."

self-application is the generation of stand-alone compilers from interpreters [10, 24, 30]. However, self-application of realistic partial evaluators for higher-order languages so far has only been possible for the offline case—on the other hand, actually obtaining *optimizing* compilers requires some online specialization [30]. Consequently, it is certainly desirable to achieve at least compiler generation using the online approach.

The main problem in achieving compiler generation with the online approach is the lack of binding-time information in the specializer being specialized. In the offline case, compiler generation works as follows:

$$\text{comp} = [\text{pe}](\text{pe}^{sd}, \text{int}^{sd})$$

In the example, pe^{sd} and int^{sd} are binding-time-annotated sources for the partial evaluator and the interpreter, respectively.

Now, in the online case, there generally are no binding-time annotations on the subject program. In a naive application of the partial evaluator, there may not even be initial binding-time information about the arguments. In the absence of binding-time information, the specializer might have to specialize the interpreter with respect to a static program and dynamic input (the intended effect), or with respect to a static input and a dynamic program—a not very useful feature. Thus, the resulting compiler would suffer from excess generality [23], and exhibit little or no performance advantage, and usually significant bloat of the resulting program.

Consequently, the lack of binding-time information is at the heart of the problem. The question is therefore how to provide binding-time information without compromising the precision of the specialization process. Glück and Ruf [12, 31, 30] have succeeded in propagating that information during specialization, albeit only for simple partial evaluators for first-order languages. In contrast, we take an offline approach.

Standard offline binding-time analyses are crude approximations of the true binding-time behavior of a given program. However, they are only crude in the sense that binding times which they cannot prove to be static are coerced to "dynamic." The information about static values is precise. Since we are really interested in having our specializer recognize static operations, an analysis capable of distinguishing between static, dynamic and unknown binding times could help making an online specializer self-applicable. Bondorf has already applied this idea to the self-application of term-rewriting systems [2].

Then, any subject program would be amenable to a wide and well-researched variety of binding-time improvements [8, 35, 23, 22] which would not necessarily change the result of the specialization, but possibly improve specialization efficiency. Since we are really interested in specializing the specializer itself, and generating compilers from interpreters, both of which are typically specialized once and applied many times, we can afford to spend some effort on these improvements. Indeed, this effort has already been done for quite a few applications [25, 23], and turns out to be straightforward for the specializer itself.

3 Reconstructing Binding-Times for the Online Case

The first step towards such a specializer is obviously a suitable binding-time analysis. We use a monovariant type-based analysis. A polyvariant analysis could probably improve precision but is unnecessary for successful self-application.

Our type language for binding-time types τ is as follows:

$$\tau ::= B \mid S \mid \Lambda \mid \Upsilon \mid (\tau_1 \ldots \tau_n) \to \tau_0$$

Our analysis also treats partially static data. The extension is analogous to the handling of functions.

The type B is for first-order values of yet unassigned binding time, S is for static base values, Λ for dynamic values (first- or higher-order), and Υ for values of unknown binding-time. $(\tau_1 \ldots \tau_n) \to \tau_0$ is for partially static functions with argument binding times $\tau_1 \ldots \tau_n$ and result τ_0. The B binding time is present for technical reasons; it is used by the analysis algorithm to denote values which are known to be first-order (such as the conditional of an if) but whose binding time is not yet known. The specializer interprets all remaining B binding times as S.

The binding-time lattice is as follows:

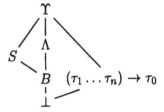

Figure 2 shows the syntax of the language treated by our analysis. It is a side-effect-free higher-order version of Scheme [21]. V denotes variables, K constants, O primitive operators.

$E \in$ Expr, $D \in$ Definition, $\Pi \in$ Program

$E ::= V \mid K \mid (\text{if } E\ E\ E) \mid (O\ E^*) \mid (P\ E^*) \mid$
$\qquad (\text{let } ((V\ E))\ E) \mid (\text{lambda } (V_1 \ldots V_n)\ E) \mid (E\ E)$
$D ::= (\text{define } (P\ V^*)\ E)$
$\Pi ::= D^+$

Fig. 2. Syntax

Figure 3 shows the type inference system underlying our binding-time analysis. Its judgements have the form $\Gamma \vdash N : \tau$, where N is either an expression, a procedure name, or a procedure definition. Γ is a set of typing assumptions of the form $N : \tau$. The first rules type expressions, the last two procedure definitions and procedure calls, respectively. $\bar{\tau}$ represents a tuple of binding-time types.

$$\frac{}{\Gamma \vdash K : S}$$

$$\frac{\Gamma \vdash E_i : S \text{ for all } i \in \{1, \dots, n\}}{\Gamma \vdash (O\ E_1\ \dots\ E_n) : S} \qquad \frac{\Gamma \vdash E_i : \Lambda \text{ for one } i \in \{1, \dots, n\}}{\Gamma \vdash (O\ E_1\ \dots\ E_n) : \Lambda}$$

$$\frac{\Gamma \vdash E_i : \tau_i}{\Gamma \vdash (O\ E_1\ \dots\ E_n) : \Upsilon}\ \tau_i \in \{S, \Upsilon\}$$

$$\frac{\Gamma\{V_i : \tau_i\} \vdash E' : \tau}{\Gamma \vdash (\texttt{lambda}\ (V_1\ \dots\ V_n)\ E') : (\tau_1 \dots \tau_n) \to \tau}$$

$$\frac{\Gamma\{V_i : \Upsilon\} \vdash E' : \Upsilon}{\Gamma \vdash (\texttt{lambda}\ (V_1\ \dots\ V_n)\ E') : \Upsilon}$$

$$\frac{\Gamma \vdash E' : (\tau_1 \dots \tau_n) \to \tau \qquad \Gamma \vdash E_i : \tau_i}{\Gamma \vdash (E'\ E_1\ \dots\ E_n) : \tau}$$

$$\frac{\Gamma \vdash E' : \Upsilon \qquad \Gamma \vdash E_i : \Upsilon}{\Gamma \vdash (E'\ E_1\ \dots\ E_n) : \Upsilon}$$

$$\frac{\Gamma \vdash E_1 : \tau_1 \qquad \Gamma\{V : \tau_1\} \vdash E' : \tau}{\Gamma \vdash (\texttt{let}\ ((V\ E_1))\ E') : \tau}$$

$$\frac{\Gamma \vdash E_1 : S \qquad \Gamma \vdash E_2 : \tau \qquad \Gamma \vdash E_3 : \tau}{\Gamma \vdash (\texttt{if}\ E_1\ E_2\ E_3) : \tau}$$

$$\frac{\Gamma \vdash E_1 : \Lambda \qquad \Gamma \vdash E_2 : \tau \qquad \Gamma \vdash E_3 : \tau}{\Gamma \vdash (\texttt{if}\ E_1\ E_2\ E_3) : \Lambda}\ \tau \in \{S, \Lambda, \Upsilon\}$$

$$\frac{\Gamma \vdash E_1 : \Upsilon \quad \Gamma \vdash E_2 : \Upsilon \quad \Gamma \vdash E_3 : \Upsilon}{\Gamma \vdash (\texttt{if}\ E_1\ E_2\ E_3) : \Upsilon} \qquad \frac{\Gamma \vdash E_2 : \Lambda \quad \Gamma \vdash E_3 : \Lambda}{\Gamma \vdash (\texttt{if}\ E_1\ E_2\ E_3) : \Lambda}$$

$$\frac{\Gamma \vdash E : B}{\Gamma \vdash (\texttt{static}\ E) : S} \qquad \frac{\Gamma \vdash E : B}{\Gamma \vdash (\texttt{dynamic}\ E) : \Lambda}$$

$$\frac{\Gamma \vdash E : S}{\Gamma \vdash (\texttt{forget}\ E) : \Upsilon} \qquad \frac{\Gamma \vdash E : \Lambda}{\Gamma \vdash (\texttt{smash}\ E) : \Upsilon}$$

$$\frac{\Gamma \vdash P : (\tau_1 \dots \tau_n) \to \tau \qquad \Gamma \vdash E_i : \tau_i}{\Gamma \vdash (P\ E_1\ \dots\ E_n) : \tau}$$

$$\frac{\Gamma\{V_i : \tau_i\} \vdash E' : \tau}{\Gamma \vdash (\texttt{define}\ (F\ V_1\ \dots\ V_n)\ E') : (\tau_1 \dots \tau_n) \to \tau}$$

$$\frac{\Gamma\{F_i : \overline{\tau}_i \to \tau_i\} \vdash (\texttt{define}\ (F_k\ V_1\ \dots\ V_n)\ E') : \overline{\tau}_k \to \tau_k}{\Gamma \vdash F_k : \overline{\tau}_k \to \tau_k}$$

Fig. 3. Type inference system

Note that we have omitted rules for operations dealing with partially static data as well as for special primitives such as * whose return value may be static even in the presence of dynamic arguments. The addition of the corresponding typing rules is straightforward.

The most obvious fundamental difference to offline analyses is the presence of four different implicit lifting operators to reflect the more complex binding-time type lattice.

Our analysis computes a binding-time annotation for any given program that is maximal with respect to the annotations with binding-time S. Obviously, it allows for if expressions with arms of different binding times without causing unnecessary liftings during specialization.

The type reconstruction algorithm is constraint-based and works along the same lines as Henglein's algorithm [19]. We have omitted details for brevity's sake.

4 Specialization Using the Binding-Time Information

Given a binding-time-annotated subject program, the actual specialization algorithm is straightforward: For binding times S and Λ, we employ offline, for Υ we use online techniques. Correspondingly, our symbolic value domain reflects the binding-time distinctions. Figure 4 shows the actual declarations[2] used in our specializer: Static stands for partially static data according to the binding-time analysis; its argument is a value of the val data type. For dynamic values, a code fragment is needed. Only for the uk (for "unknown") type, the full information normally present in symbolic values in online specializers is required.

```
(defdata sval
  (uk uk-sval uk-code)
  (dynamic dynamic-code)
  (static static-val)
  (lookup-error))

(defdata val
  (scalar scalar-value)
  (closure closure-native closure-label closure-free-svals)
  (ps ps-ctor ps-arg-svals))

(defdata uk-val
  (uk-top)
  (uk-scalar uk-scalar-value)
  (uk-closure uk-closure-native uk-closure-residualize
              uk-closure-label uk-closure-free-svals)
  (uk-ps uk-ps-residualize
         uk-ps-ctor uk-ps-arg-svals))
```

Fig. 4. Symbolic values

A static value may either be a fully static first-order value scalar, a closure represented by a procedure closure-native that performs an application, a unique label and the symbolic values of its free variables, or a partially static data structure declared by a defdata form. The corresponding fields in the uk-val type contain additional components uk-closure-residualize and uk-ps-residualize which are procedures that perform residualization when applied to symbolic values for their free variables. More on residualization can be found in the next section. A uk-val may also be (uk-top) which denotes an

---

[2] using a special form **defdata** to declare user-defined data types

unknown value; in that case, the uk-code field must contain code to compute the value. The closure-free-svals, ps-arg-svals, uk-closure-free-svals, and uk-ps-arg-svals fields are lists of symbolic values of the free variables captured either by constructors for partially static data or lambdas.

Figure 5 shows the fragment of the specializer that handles if expressions. The main specialization procedure is specialize-expr. If? tests if the expression to be specialized is a conditional, corresponding selectors extract its components. Expr-binding-time extracts the binding time from the annotated source expression. It can either be 'S for "static," 'D for "dynamic," or '? for "unknown." Lift lifts a symbolic value from the binding time specified by the first argument to the binding time specified by the second argument.

It is clearly visible how the branches for static and dynamic directly correspond to code commonly found in offline partial evaluators [23], whereas the case for uk code is similar to that found in online partial [30].

Unlike the specializers from the *Fuse* project [41, 30], our specializer generates code directly rather than using an intermediate graph representation. *Fuse* employs the graph representation to defer the questions of whether lets should be unfolded until after specialization proper. We employ a simple offline occurrence count analysis analogous to that in offline partial evaluators to decide whether a let should be unfolded. This does not always yield optimal code, but considerably simplifies code generation.

Memoization issues also deserve some explanation. To prevent non-termination, a specializer needs to introduce *specialization points* or *memoization points* [23, 30] which lead to procedures in the residual code. For our present implementation, we have chosen the simple strategy to insert memoization points at dynamic ifs and at user-introduced program points. Hence, the system never automatically inserts a memoization point that would lift a specialization-time value and thus incur information loss at specialization time.

On entering a memoization point, the specializer builds an entry in a memoization cache indexed by the name of the procedure being specialized and a projection of the static components of the free variables of the memoization point. Again, for free variables that are static or dynamic, the code corresponds to that in an offline partial evaluator. For uk symbolic values, the code is analogous to the online case.

On creating a memoization point, specialization must continue with a new environment composed of *instantiated* versions of the symbolic values of the free variables. Instantiation [30] replaces all dynamic components in symbolic values by fresh variables, which are then formal parameters of the residual procedure being constructed. The code expressions corresponding to the dynamic components being replaced become the actual parameters in the residual call. If partially static data structures are involved, this step performs *arity raising* [29]. After specializing a memoization point, the specializer generates code for the procedure call and updates the entry in the memoization cache with the residual procedure constructed from it.

This memoization strategy is simple-minded but has proven sufficient for

```
((if? expr)
 (let* ((expr-bt (expr-binding-time expr))
        (test-expr (if-test expr))
        (test-sval (specialize-expr test-expr f env cache prg))
        (test-bt (expr-binding-time test-expr))
        (then-branch (if-then expr))
        (branch-bt (expr-binding-time then-branch))
        (else-branch (if-else expr)))
   (cond
    ((equal? 'S test-bt)
     (if (scalar-value (static-val test-sval))
         (specialize-expr then-branch f env cache prg)
         (specialize-expr else-branch f env cache prg)))
    ((equal? 'D test-bt)
     (let ((then-sval (specialize-expr then-branch f env cache prg))
           (else-sval (specialize-expr else-branch f env cache prg)))
       (dynamic (make-if (dynamic-code test-sval)
                         (sval->code then-sval branch-bt)
                         (sval->code else-sval branch-bt)))))
    (else                              ; unknown
     (let ((test-val (uk-val test-sval)))
       (cond ((uk-scalar? test-val)
              (lift branch-bt expr-bt
                    (if (uk-scalar-value test-val)
                        (specialize-expr then-branch f env cache prg)
                        (specialize-expr else-branch f env cache prg))))
             ((or (uk-closure? test-val) (uk-ps? test-val))
              (lift branch-bt expr-bt
                    (specialize-expr then-branch f env cache prg)))
             (else                     ; (uk-top)
              (let* ((then-sval
                       (specialize-expr then-branch f env cache prg))
                     (else-sval
                       (specialize-expr else-branch f env cache prg))
                     (then-code (sval->code then-sval branch-bt))
                     (else-code (sval->code else-sval branch-bt))
                     (code (make-if (uk-code test-sval)
                                    then-code else-code)))
                (if (equal? 'D expr-bt)
                    (dynamic code)
                    (uk (uk-top) code)))))))))))
```

Fig. 5. Specializer fragment for handling if

ensuring termination of self-application. It does not give a termination guarantee in general. A number of other offline and online analyses detect potential loops in residual code unfolding and insert memoization points to break infinite recursion. The purely online generalization strategies used in variants of *Fuse* [41, 30] may perform pairwise generalization on any value at any time, thus often lifting it from static to dynamic. In our specializer, this would only be possible on values not annotated as static. Thus, a straightforward application of this technique is not possible in our framework. However, an offline analysis could make a prediction which values *may* be lifted at specialization time, again combining off- and online techniques. One such pair of an offline analysis and an online strategy has been successfully used in the generation of online specializers that must guarantee termination [38, 33, 39, 36]. It also seems applicable in our case.

5   Self-Application and Compiler Generation

In the context of our work, "successful" self-application means that specialization of the specializer removes at least the syntax dispatch and the binding-time dispatch on the annotations. In any case, we expect a substantial speed-up and practical sizes for the generating extensions.

To achieve successful self-application, it is necessary to ensure that the binding-time analysis will actually annotate the specializer in the desired way. Namely, the following values need to be static to obtain good results:

1. the annotated source program,
2. the expression being specialized, and
3. the names in the current environment.

The first item is trivial to propagate such that the binding-time analysis will recognize it as static. For the second and third item, the online capabilities of the specializer create a slight problem: Unlike in the offline case, closures and partially static data with binding time Υ are not immediately residualized—rather, the specializer creates uk symbolic values that preserve the full information, effectively postponing the reduce/residualize decision until later.

On self-application the value of the uk-closure-label field is dynamic—and this would lead to a dynamic abstraction body should the specializer decide to residualize the closure, and thereby make the expression argument to the specialization call dynamic. We have used a simple binding-time improvement from Bondorf's early work on Similix [4] to solve the problem: On the creation of the closure, the call to the specializer that would perform the residualization is eta-expanded, and the resulting abstraction becomes the value of the uk-closure-residualize field. Creation uk-ps partially static data works analogously; the residualization abstraction ends up in the uk-ps-residualize field.

With this single binding-time improvement in place, the specializer successfully self-applies. Somewhat perversely, our specializer is now also amenable to effective *offline* partial evaluation, which achieves the same desired effect, thereby confirming a suspicion by Ruf [30].

6 Experimental Results

We have achieved practical self-application of our online specializer leading to stand-alone compilers. The results mirror those of Ruf's work [31, 30]. For our experiments, we used an IBM 320 RS/6000 workstation running Scheme 48, a byte-code implementation of Scheme. We used the following example programs:

append The generic **append** procedure, specialized to a static first argument.
scheme0 An interpreter for a first-order subset of Scheme, specialized to a static program and dynamic inputs.
match A regular expression matcher, specialized to a static regular expression and a dynamic input.

Note that specifically the scheme0 example shows the additional power of the online approach over using an offline partial evaluator: Its generating extension is an *optimizing compiler* which itself performs constant propagation and specialization, an effect much more difficult to achieve with purely offline techniques [13, 14, 17, 39, 33, 36].

program	direct		online generator		offline generator	
	bta	no bta	bta	no bta	bta	no bta
append	29.90	32.03	1.59	2.51	1.60	2.52
scheme0	24.17	26.35	2.78	-	2.78	-
match	9.28	10.24	0.91	1.43	0.92	-

Fig. 6. Speedups due to using a generating extension. (All times in seconds.)

Figure 6 demonstrates the speedups through use of a generating extension instead of direct specialization. For every run, we have used both a fully annotated version ("bta") of the subject program and one with only unknown binding times ("no bta"). The first two columns contain the timings for direct specialization. The second two columns contain the result of using a generation extension obtained from specializing a regularly annotated version of the specializer. The final two columns contain timings resulting from using a generating exension obtained from a version of the specializer with a purely *offline* annotation, that is with all unknown binding times changed to dynamic. All timings represent purely specialization time, without time spent on binding-time analysis or post-processing. The columns not containing figures indicate that Scheme 48 was not able to compile the programs in a 4-megaword-heap.

Figure 7 shows the sizes of the programs and the corresponding generating extensions. Note the blowup in those generating extensions obtained from "no bta" programs.

Figure 8 shows the times used for generating the generating extensions.

program	direct of interpreter	online generator		offline generator	
		bta	no bta	bta	no bta
append	23	455	1405	474	1436
scheme0	692	7149	-	7169	-
match	552	4472	59847	4499	59900

Fig. 7. Sizes of the programs and their generating extensions (Sizes in cons cells.)

program	online generator		offline generator	
	bta	no bta	bta	no bta
append	9.50	25.52	9.40	25.10
scheme0	179.08	-	176.93	-
match	116.25	1004.31	115.39	995.75

Fig. 8. Generation times. (All times in seconds.)

We have also performed double self-application resulting in a stand-alone compiler generator. Unfortunately, the resulting residual program is presently too large to be compiled by Scheme 48.

The experiments and timings suggest the following conclusions:

- Using a generating extension results in realistic speedups comparable to other work in both the off- and the online world [31, 30, 24, 3]. Specialization removes the dispatch on syntax and binding-time annotations, some intermediate representation overhead through arity raising—specifically when dealing with argument lists—and the interpretive overhead for dispatching primitives. The latter two account for the major portion of the speedups.
- Little online specialization happens on generating the generating extensions, as supported by the near-identical sizes and times when using online- and offline-annotated specializers for self-application.
- Naive generating extensions perform not significantly slower than those generated from fully-annotated counterparts. However, the huge blowup in generation time and size makes generation (and sometimes compilation) impractical for realistic programs.

Furthermore, the results indicate the following avenues of future research:

- Real-world programs usually produce poor results when subjected to a mono-variant binding-time analysis which might make generating extension generation impractical. Consequently, it seems desirable to experiment with poly-variant binding-time annotations [27, 6, 20, 9].
- Almost no binding-time propagation happens during self-application. Presently, this is because most of the internals of the representation of the symbolic values is made opaque to the specializer. It remains to be examined if the information provided by the binding-time annotations could be combined with more accurate information obtained online.

- The *Fuse* project has implemented more sophisticated online specialization techniques [30], such as performing pairwise generalization (instead of lifting) on ifs with dynamic conditionals, and return and parameter value analyses. It should be investigated how they could be integrated with our approach.
- It remains to be seen what effects more sophisticated termination mechanisms have on the quality of the binding-time annotations and how well they would perform in this setting. As indicated above, we have already done some work in a different setting which could work here as well.

7 Related Work

The main work on online partial evaluation of functional languages has been done by the *Fuse* project at Stanford [41]. The standard reference on online partial evaluation is Ruf's Ph.D. thesis [30] which contains an excellent overview of current techniques in online specialization. Mogensen shows how to perform online partial evaluation of the pure lambda calculus using higher-order abstract syntax [26]. Glück and Jørgensen have discovered that is possible to automatically generate online specializers from interpreters [13, 14, 17]. Thiemann, Glück, and the author have recently extended the approach to higher-order languages [33, 36]. Online specialization techniques beyond constant propagation are supercompilation [40, 16, 37], and generalized partial computation [11].

Compiler generation and self-application have been among the main fields of interest for researchers in partial evaluation since Futamura's work [10]. This led to the discovery of offline partial evaluation and the construction of practical compilers and compiler generators [24, 25].

As mentioned above, research in the online world has focused on accurate specialization rather than self-application [41]. Weise and Ruf [31, 30] argue that compiler generation is desirable with the online approach because of the potential of gaining optimizing compilers which is much more difficult to achieve with the offline approach [36]. However, self-application is not crucial to compiler generation: Ruf specializes a small first-order online partial evaluator with a full-fledged version of *Fuse* [31, 30]. Even this easier task requires sophisticated analyses in the "outer" specializer. Ruf already suspected that offline methods might also be suitable to specialize online specializers [30]. Recently, self-application has also been achieved for the supercompiler [28].

Bondorf's TreeMix [2] also uses a binding-time analysis for term rewriting systems with an "unknown" binding time, but Bondorf does not give any information on how often that binding time occurs in practical programs.

Glück [12] has investigated multi-level self-application of online partial evalutors. However, his specializer performs an on-the-fly binding-time analysis which precludes some of the optimizations typical of the online approach, such as ifs with static condition and branches of differing binding times. Also, representation problems blow up the specializations to an impractical extent. Presently, Glück and Hatcliff are re-investigating multiple online self-application [18] with representation techniques from Glück and Jørgensen's earlier work on multi-level offline specialization [15], albeit still in a first-order context.

Mogensen achieves self-application of his online partial evaluator for the pure lambda calculus [26] by prescribing the position of the static and dynamic arguments, reducing the reduce/residualize decision to tuple selection.

The pioneering work on efficient binding-time analysis is by Henglein [19]. His type-based approach as well as his fast algorithm for performing the type inference have been used in many offline partial evaluators, most notably Similix [5]. A number of authors have investigated polyvariant and polymorphic binding-time analyses which could provide added accuracy for the binding-time annotations [27, 6, 20, 9]. The standard textbook on partial evaluation [23] contains an overview of binding-time improvements.

8 Conclusion

We have shown how to unify online and offline partial evaluation, retaining the specialization accuracy of the online approach, but making compiler generation and self-application possible and practical. Our main contribution is the use of a binding-time analysis which does not incur a loss of specialization accuracy. In fact, our approach also allows for compiler generation by applying an *offline* partial evaluator to our specializer. Thus, we have applied a weaker offline partial evaluator to a stronger online partial evaluator. Consequently, we have opened the door to the automatic generation of optimizing compilers and compiler generators, which is not easily possible with the offline approach. We believe that our approach is amenable to both offline and online approaches to increase termination of specialization and specialization accuracy, such as induction detection, termination analysis, or context propagation. We hope our results can induce more research in hybrid approaches to specialization, and some revived interest in online partial evaluation.

Acknowledgments I am grateful to Peter Thiemann for solid advice, and for his excellent CPS-based offline cogen which provided the front end for the specializer described here. Morry Katz who independently had come up with the same idea some years ago motivated me to convert it into practice. I am also grateful to the anonymous referees and the participants of the Dagstuhl seminar who provided additional insights and suggestions.

References

1. ACM. *Proc. 1991 ACM Functional Programming Languages and Computer Architecture*, Cambridge, September 1991.
2. Anders Bondorf. A self-applicable partial evaluator for term rewriting systems. In J. Diaz and F. Orejas, editors, *TAPSOFT '89. Proc. Int. Conf. Theory and Practice of Software Development, Barcelona, Spain. (Lecture Notes in Computer Science, Vol. 352)*, pages 81–95. Springer-Verlag, March 1989.

3. Anders Bondorf. *Self-applicable partial evaluation.* PhD thesis, DIKU, University of Copenhagen, 1990. DIKU Report 90/17.

4. Anders Bondorf. Automatic autoprojection of higher order recursive equations. *Science of Computer Programming,* 17:3–34, 1991.

5. Anders Bondorf and Jesper Jørgensen. Efficient analyses for realistic off-line partial evaluation. *Journal of Functional Programming,* 3(3):315–346, July 1993.

6. Charles Consel. Polyvariant binding-time analysis for applicative lanuages. In *Symp. Partial Evaluation and Semantics-Based Program Manipulation '93,* pages 66–77, Copenhagen, Denmark, June 1993. ACM.

7. Olivier Danvy, Robert Glück, and Peter Thiemann, editors. *Dagstuhl Seminar on Partial Evaluation 1996.* Springer-Verlag, 1996. LNCS.

8. Olivier Danvy, Karoline Malmkjær, and Jens Palsberg. The essence of eta-expansion in partial evaluation. *Lisp and Symbolic Computation,* 8(1):1–19, 1995.

9. Dirk Dussart, Fritz Henglein, and Christian Mossin. Polymorphic recursion and subtype qualifications: Polymorphic binding-time analysis in polynomial time. In *Proc. 2nd Int'l Static Analysis Symposium (SAS), Glasgow, Scotland,* Lecture Notes in Computer Science. Springer-Verlag, September 1995.

10. Y. Futamura. Partial evaluation of computation process—an approach to a compiler-compiler. *Systems, Computers, Controls,* 2(5):45–50, 1971.

11. Yoshihiko Futamura, Kenroku Nogi, and Aki Takano. Essence of generalized partial computation. *Theoretical Computer Science,* 90(1):61–79, 1991.

12. Robert Glück. Towards multiple self-application. In *Proc. Partial Evaluation and Semantics-Based Program Manipulation '91,* pages 309–320, New Haven, June 1991. ACM. SIGPLAN Notices 26(9).

13. Robert Glück. On the generation of specializers. *Journal of Functional Programming,* 4(4):499–514, October 1994.

14. Robert Glück and Jesper Jørgensen. Generating optimizing specializers. In *IEEE International Conference on Computer Languages,* pages 183–194. IEEE Computer Society Press, 1994.

15. Robert Glück and Jesper Jørgensen. Efficient multi-level generating extensions for program specialization. In *Programming Language Implementation and Logic Programming 1995.* Springer-Verlag, 1995. LNCS.

16. Robert Glück and Andrei V. Klimov. Occam's razor in metacomputation: the notion of a perfect process tree. In *Static Analysis,* volume 724 of *Lecture Notes in Computer Science,* pages 112–123. Springer-Verlag, 1993.

17. Robert Glück and Jesper Jørgensen. Generating transformers for deforestation and supercompilation. In B. Le Charlier, editor, *Static Analysis,* volume 864 of *Lecture Notes in Computer Science,* pages 432–448. Springer-Verlag, 1994.

18. John Hatcliff and Robert Glück. Reasoning about hierarchies of online program specialization systems. In Danvy et al. [7]. to appear.

19. Fritz Henglein. Efficient type inference for higher-order binding-time analysis. In FPCA1991 [1], pages 448–472.

20. Fritz Henglein and Christian Mossin. Polymorphic binding-time analysis. In Donald Sannella, editor, *Proceedings of European Symposium on Programming,* volume 788 of *Lecture Notes in Computer Science,* pages 287–301. Springer-Verlag, April 1994.

21. IEEE. Standard for the Scheme programming language. Technical Report 1178-1990, Institute of Electrical and Electronics Engineers, Inc., New York, 1991.

22. Neil D. Jones. What *not* to do when writing an interpreter for specialisation. In Danvy et al. [7]. to appear.

23. Neil D. Jones, Carsten K. Gomard, and Peter Sestoft. *Partial Evaluation and Automatic Program Generation*. Prentice-Hall, 1993.

24. Neil D. Jones, Peter Sestoft, and Harald Søndergaard. An experiment in partial evaluation: The generation of a compiler generator. In J.-P. Jouannaud, editor, *Rewriting Techniques and Applications*, pages 124–140, Dijon, France, 1985. Springer-Verlag. LNCS 202.

25. Jesper Jørgensen. Compiler generation by partial evaluation. Master's thesis, DIKU, University of Copenhagen, 1991.

26. Torben Æ. Mogensen. Self-applicable online partial evaluation of pure lambda calculus. In Scherlis [32], pages 39–44.

27. Torben Æ. Mogensen. Binding time analysis for polymorphically typed higher order languages. In J. Díaz and F. Orejas, editors, *TAPSOFT '89*, pages II, 298–312, Barcelona, Spain, March 1989. Springer-Verlag. LNCS 351,352.

28. Andrei P. Nemytykh, Victoria A. Pinchuk, and Valentin F. Turchin. A self-applicable supercompiler. In Danvy et al. [7]. to appear.

29. Sergei A. Romanenko. Arity raiser and its use in program specialization. In Neil D. Jones, editor, *European Symposium on Programming 1990*, pages 341–360, Copenhagen, Denmark, 1990. Springer-Verlag. LNCS 432.

30. Erik Ruf. *Topics in Online Partial Evaluation*. PhD thesis, Stanford University, Stanford, CA 94305-4055, March 1993. Technical report CSL-TR-93-563.

31. Erik Ruf and Daniel Weise. On the specialization of online program specializers. *Journal of Functional Programming*, 3(3):251–281, July 1993.

32. William Scherlis, editor. *ACM SIGPLAN Symp. Partial Evaluation and Semantics-Based Program Manipulation '95*, La Jolla, CA, June 1995. ACM Press.

33. Michael Sperber, Robert Glück, and Peter Thiemann. Bootstrapping higher-order program transformers from interpreters. In *1996 ACM Symposium on Applied Computing Programming Languages Track*, pages 408–413, Philadelphia, 1996.

34. Michael Sperber and Peter Thiemann. The essence of LR parsing. In Scherlis [32], pages 146–155.

35. Michael Sperber and Peter Thiemann. Turning an art into a craft: Automatic binding-time improvement. submitted, 1995.

36. Michael Sperber and Peter Thiemann. Realistic compilation by partial evaluation. In *Conference on Programming Language Design and Implementation '96*, Philadelphia, May 1996. ACM. to appear.

37. Morten Heine Sørensen, Robert Glück, and Neil D. Jones. Towards unifying partial evaluation, deforestation, supercompilation, and GPC. In Donald Sannella, editor, *Proc. 5th European Symposium on Programming*, pages 485–500, Edinburgh, UK, April 1994. Springer-Verlag. LNCS 788.

38. Peter Thiemann. Type-based termination analysis for partial evaluation. Technical Report WSI-95-XX, Universität Tübingen, September 1995.

39. Peter Thiemann and Robert Glück. The generation of a higher-order online partial evaluator. In Masato Takeichi, editor, *Fuji Workshop on Functional and Logic Programming*, pages 239–253, Fuji Susono, Japan, July 1995. World Scientific Press, Singapore.

40. Valentin F. Turchin. The concept of a supercompiler. *ACM Transactions on Programming Languages and Systems*, 8(3):292–325, July 1986.

41. Daniel Weise, Roland Conybeare, Erik Ruf, and Scott Seligman. Automatic online partial evaluation. In FPCA1991 [1], pages 165–191.

Metacomputation:
Metasystem Transitions plus Supercompilation

Valentin F. Turchin

Computer Science Department
The City College of New York *

Abstract. Metacomputation is a computation which involves *metasystem transitions*(*MST* for short) from a computing machine M to a metamachine M' which controls, analyzes, and imitates the work of M. Semantics-based program transformation, such as partial evaluation and supercompilation (*SCP*), is metacomputation. Metasystem transitions may be repeated, as when a program transformer gets transformed itself. In this manner MST hierarchies of any height can be formed.

The paper reviews one strain of research which was started in Russia in the late 1960s–early 1970s and became known for the development of supercompilation as a distinct method of program transformation. After a brief description of the history of this research line, the paper concentrates on those results and problems where supercompilation is combined with repeated metasystem transitions.

Keywords: program transformation, supercompilation, metacomputation, self-application, metasystem transition, MST-schemes, metacode, pattern-matching graphs, Refal.

First of all, I want to thank the organizers of this seminar for inviting me to review the history and the present state of the work on supercompilation and metasystem transitions. I do believe that these two notions should be of primary importance for the seminar, because they indicate the directions of further development and generalization of the two key notions most familiar to the participants: supercompilation is a development and generalization of partial evaluation, while metasystem transition is in the same relation to self-application. For myself, however, the order of appearance of these keywords was opposite: I started from the general concept of metasystem transition (MST for short), and my consequent work in computer science has been an application and concretization of this basic idea.

1 History

Consider a system S of any kind. Suppose that there is a way to make some number of copies of it, possibly with variations. Suppose that these systems are

---

* New York, NY 10031, USA. (`turcc@cunyvm.cuny.edu`)

united into a new system S' which has the systems of the S type as its subsystems, and includes also an additional mechanism which somehow examines, controls, modifies and reproduces the S-subsystems. Then we call S' a *metasystem* with respect to S, and the creation of S' a *metasystem transition*. As a result of consecutive metasystem transitions a multilevel hierarchy of control arises, which exhibits complicated forms of behavior.

In my book *The Phenomenon of Science: a Cybernetic Approach to Evolution* [39] I have interpreted the major steps in biological and cultural evolution, including the emergence of the thinking human being, as nothing else but metasystem transitions on a large scale. Even though my Ph.D. was in theoretical physics, I was so excited about my new cybernetic ideas that I shifted from physics to computer science and left the atomic center in Obninsk for the Institute for Applied Mathematics in Moscow.

An extra-scientific factor came into play in the late 1960s: I became an active member of the human rights movement. My book was written about 1970, but it could not be published in the Soviet Union solely because of the author's name. It took seven years to smuggle it to the West and have it published in the English language.

The first step towards MST in computers was to design an appropriate algorithmic language. I called the first version of such a language *meta-algorithmic* [36], since it was supposed to serve as a metalanguage for defining semantics of algorithmic languages. Then I simplified it into what was named REFAL (for REcursive Functions Algorithmic Language). Refal was conceived as the universal language of metasystem hierarchies, which is, on one hand, simple enough, so that the machine that executes programs in this language (the *Refal machine*) could become an object of theoretical analysis—and, on the other hand, is rich enough to serve as a programming language for writing real-life algorithms, unlike such purely theoretical languages as the language of the Turing machine or Markov's normal algorithms (the latter, by the way, was one of the sources of Refal). Even to this day Refal remains, in my (biased, no doubt) view, the most successful compromise between these two requirements.

An efficient interpreter for Refal was first written in 1968 [26]. At that time Refal was very different from other languages, being a purely functional language with built-in pattern-matching. Now that functional languages are common place, I need only to summarize Refal's distinctive features to make it familiar to the reader.

The most distinctive feature of Refal is its data domain. Refal uses *expressions* for symbol manipulation, not *lists* (skewed binary trees). Refal expressions can be seen as trees with arbitrary (unfixed) arity of nodes, or sequences of such trees. They are formally defined as:

term ::= *symbol* | *variable* | (*expression*) | < *function expression*>
expression ::= *empty* | *term expression*

Variables in Refal have their intrinsic types shown by a prefix e.g., s.1, t.2, e.x. Thus an *s-variable* s.i, where i is the index (name), stands for an arbitrary symbol, a *t-variable* t.i—for an arbitrary term, and an *e-variable* e.i—for any expression. In the case of an *e*-variable, the prefix may be dropped: x is the same as e.x.

We use angular brackets to form function calls: $<f\ x>$. A program in Refal is a sequence of mutually recursive *sentences* (rewrite rules) which are tried in the order they are written. Here is an example of a function f which traverses its argument from left to right and replaces every 'a' by 'b':

```
<f 'a'> = 'b'<f x>
<f s.1 x> = s.1 <f x>
<f > =
```

By the year 1970 I was lucky to have gathered a circle of young people, the Refal group, which met regularly, survived my emigration and is still alive and well. As in any informal group, some people went, new people came. I am deeply thankful to all of them, and especially to those most active and persistent: Sergei Romanenko (the first to have come), Nikolai Kondratiev, Elena Travkina, Andrei Klimov, Arkadi Klimov, Viktor Kistlerov, Igor Shchenkov, Sergei Abramov, Alexei Vedenov, Ruten Gurin, Leonid Provorov, Andrei Nemytykh, Vika Pinchuk. I will always remember Alexander Romanenko who died before his time in 1993.

Together with a smaller group at the Moscow Engineering and Physics Institute (Stanislav Florentsev, Alexander Krasovsky, Vladimir Khoroshevsky) we made Refal compilers for the most popular machines in the Soviet Union, and Refal became pretty well known in that part of the world (a bibliography on the development and use of Refal compiled a few years ago includes about 200 items). It is not my intention here to focus on Refal, but I want to mention two further outgrowths of Refal: The language FLAC for algebraic manipulation developed by Viktor Kistlerov [22, 4], and Refal Plus by Sergei Romanenko and Ruten Gurin [17], which is a kind of logical closure of the ideas on which Refal is based. In my later work I used the extended version of Refal named Refal-5 [44], which is operational under DOS and UNIX.

The next conceptual station after fixing the language was *driving* [37, 38]. Suppose we have the call $<f\ 'a'x>$ of the function f above. Obviously, it can be replaced by 'b'$<f\ x>$, because this is what the Refal machine will do in one step of function evaluation. *Partial evaluation* took place, which is a simple case of driving. Now take the call $<f\ x>$ where a partial evaluator has nothing to do. Driving, however, is still possible, because it is simulation of one step of computation in any circumstances. When we see equivalent transformation of programs as the use of some equations, our partial evaluation is the use of the equation $<f'a'x> = 'b'<f\ x>$, and this makes perfect sense. But, given the call $<f\ x>$, there is no equation in sight that would improve the program. Driving is a product of cybernetic thinking. We create a metamachine, and the first thing it must be able to do with the Refal machine is to simulate its behavior. Thus, the metamachine *drives* the Refal machine, forcing it to do something for which it was not originally prepared: make computation over expressions with free variables. Such computation should better be called *metacomputation*; its result is not the value of the function, but a graph of states and transitions of the Refal machine which describes one step of computation towards that value.

In our case driving will produce the graph:

```
[1]<f x>   x:'a'x;  [2]'b'<f x>
       + x:s.1 x;  [3] s.1 <f x>
       + x:[];  []
```

where the original call is the root node labeled by [1], and there are three edges, separated by +, which lead to three resulting expressions, according to the three cases (sentences) in the definition of f. By $e : p$ we denote the operation of matching expression e to pattern p; a pattern is a special kind of an expression (referred to as *rigid*), which guarantees the uniqueness of the operation. An expression E is rigid if (1) only s-variables may enter E more than once, and (2) no subexpression of E (including E itself) includes two e-variables separated by an expression. [] stands for an empty expression for readability.

From driving I came to supercompilation (SCP for short). Let me briefly describe this technique of program transformation, leaving aside many details and variations.

A supercompiler is an upgrade of a driver. While driving describes one step of the Refal machine, supercompilation may include any number of steps. When a new *active* (i.e., representing a function call) node C appears in driving, the supercompiler examines its ancestors and with regard to each ancestor C' takes one of the three decisions:

1. Reduce C to C' with a substitution; this can be done only if $C \subseteq C'$.
2. Generalize C and C', i.e., find such C^g that $C \subseteq C^g$ and $C' \subseteq C^g$; then erase the driving subtree which starts at C', reduce C' to C^g and go on driving C^g.
3. Do nothing on C' (the nodes C and C' are "far from each other"), and examine the next ancestor. If there are no more ancestors to loop back to, go on driving C.

Supercompilation ends when the graph becomes self-sufficient i.e., it shows, for every active node, how to make a transition to the next node which corresponds to at least one step of the Refal machine. This graph is a program for computing the function call represented by the initial node.

Note the difference between the principle of supercompilation and the usual idea of program transformation, where the program is changed step by step by applying some equivalences. In supercompilation we never change the original program. We regard it as a sort of "laws of nature" and construct a model of a computation process governed by these laws. When the model becomes self-sufficient, we simply throw away the unchanged original program. I see supercompilation as a computer implementation of the general principle of human knowledge, which, in my view, is the search for such generalized states in terms of which we can construct a self-sufficient model of some part of the world.

When we discussed supercompilation in the seminars of the Refal group, I always stressed my belief that metasystem transition is important in itself. If indeed it has been the key at all stages of biological and technical evolution, how can we hope to create really intelligent machines without the use of this principle? We should develop techniques of dealing with repeated metasystem transitions; applications are bound to follow.

The first confirmation of this belief came when I figured out that supercompilation of an interpreter is compilation, and supercompilation of the supercompiler that does compilation (second MST) yields a compiled (efficient) compiler. Moreover, making the third MST we can obtain a compiled compiler generator. I was very excited about my discovery, and told Andrei Ershov about it. Ershov at that time worked on partial evaluation—the first MST—but he did not know about the second MST, and he also got excited.[2] Neither he, nor I knew at that time that Yoshihiko Futamura [9] made this discovery a few years before me. Ershov saw a reference to Futamura's paper, but could not get the journal. In his big paper [7] he referred to my result as "Turchin's theorem of double driving".

That was in 1976. Since 1974 I had been jobless, home-searched, and periodically interrogated by the KGB. Meanwhile a book on Refal and its implementation was written by several members of the Refal group, including myself [3]. My friends managed to get permission for publishing it as a technical material of the institute where I worked before being fired—on the condition that I do not figure in the list of authors. To meet this requirement they decided not to mention any authors at all. The book was thus published anonymously. But I smuggled into it a few pages about my results on automatic production of compilers.

I emigrated in 1977, and it took some time to take roots in the new environment: a process which can never be fully successful. For a year and a half I stayed at the Courant Institute of NYU and used this time to write a 250 pages report [40], where I summarized the ideas and results of the past years and also sketched some new ideas to turn to them later. Then I got a position at the City College of the City University of New York.

I wrote the first supercompiler (SCP-1) in 1981-82 [41] with the help of Bob Nirenberg and my son Dimitri in carrying over the implementation of Refal from Russia to the US and upgrading it. From the examples in [41] one could see that supercompilation includes, but is much stronger as a transformation technique than partial evaluation (which takes place automatically in driving). The examples in [41] included program specialization, but when I tried self-application (2nd MST), I met a dozen of technical difficulties.

Partial evaluation is simpler then supercompilation, so automatic generation of a compiler from an interpreter was first achieved by self-application of a partial evaluator (2nd and 3rd MST). This was done by Neil Jones and co-workers at DIKU, Copenhagen [18, 27, 19, 20], and was an important step forward and a great success. Self-applicable partial evaluation became an established field of research. Of the members of the Moscow Refal group, Sergei Romanenko and Andrei Klimov contributed to this field [23, 30, 31], but I decided to concentrate

---

[2] Ershov describes our meeting in detail in his 1987 keynote speech [8].

on further development of techniques of supercompilation, and wrote a stronger and better supercompiler, SCP-2.

The fall semester of 1985 I spent at DIKU in Copenhagen invited by Neil Jones. This was a very important visit for me. I got a chance to discuss in detail my ideas on MST and SCP with Neil and other people at DIKU. Among other things, these discussions helped me to finalize and have published my paper on supercompilation [42]. Since then I visited DIKU on several occasions and always had useful discussions and enjoyed the friendly atmosphere there.

In 1988-89 Robert Glück, then at the Vienna Technical University, joined the MST-SCP Project. He spent a year and a half at the City College working with me on its various aspects. We managed to achieve self-application of SCP-2 in some simple cases, but it became clear that a thorough overhaul of the supercompiler is needed. After returning to Europe, Glück carried over the techniques of metacoding and doing MSTs, which was originally developed for the Refal supercompiler, to partial evaluation and list-based languages. In the early work on partial evaluation by Neil Jones with co-workers [20] it was stated that in order to achieve good results in self-application, a preliminary binding time analysis ("off-line") was necessary. However, Glück showed ([12]) that with a correct use of metacoding, partial evaluation is self-applicable without any binding time analysis: "on line".

Little by little, more people got involved in the work on MST+SCP. The Moscow Refal group has never ceased discussing and working on these ideas, but now their work began being published in English. Andrei Klimov found a mate in Robert Glück [14, 15, 16]; their paper [14] helped arouse interest towards supercompilation in the partial evaluation community by bridging the two methods. Alexander Romanenko started work on function inversion [28, 29]. Sergei Abramov did an excellent and potentially very important work [1] on program testing on the basis of *driving with a neighborhood* (see Sec.3.3), and wrote a monograph on metacomputation other than supercompilation, [2] (it is still in Russian, though).

Neil Jones [21] gave a thorough theoretical analysis of driving as compared to partial evaluation. More papers on supercompilation have appeared recently from DIKU [13, 32, 33, 34, 35]. The role of Glück in that, as one can see from the references, has been of primary importance.

Morten Sørensen wrote a Master's thesis on supercompilation [32]. Its title, *Turchin's Supercompiler Revisited*, symbolized the emerging interest to my work. Later Sørensen made a suggestion that the Higman-Kruskal theorem on homeomorphic embedding be used as the criterion for generalization in supercompilation [33], which probably will be judged as one of the most important contributions to the SCP techniques during the last few years; I discuss it in more detail in Sec.2.2.

In 1993 I decided to restrict Refal as the object language of SCP to its *flat* subset where the right side of a sentence cannot include nested function calls: it is either a passive expression, or a single function call. The purpose, of course, was to simplify the supercompiler for self-application to become possible. I started writing such a supercompiler, SCP-3. In September 1993 Andrei Nemytykh from the Programming Systems Institute (Pereslavl, Russia), came to CCNY for an academic year under a grant from the National Research Council. Working together, we have, at long last, made SCP-3 self-applicable [46, 47]. That was in the spring of 1994. Returning to Russia, Nemytykh continued the work on SCP-3 with Vika Pinchuk. I do not speak more on this because SCP-3 with some examples of its performance is presented in a separate paper at this symposium [25].

In the summer of 1993 Futamura invited me to spend a month in Tokyo to discuss supercompilation in relation to his concept of *generalized partial computation* [10, 11]. There are common aspects, indeed. In both approaches the information about the states of a computing machine goes beyond listing the values of some variables. The main difference is that Futamura relies on some unspecified theorem proving, while my point is to do everything by supercompilation, including theorem proving.

In July 1995, invited by José Meseguer, I spent a pleasant week at Stanford Research Institute in California explaining and discussing the details of SCP and MST. Meseguer and his graduate student Manuel Clavel are working on reflective logics and languages in the frame of Meseguer's theory of general logics [24, 5]. They set a goal of extending the techniques of supercompilation to their systems in order to improve their efficiency, and I know that they have already made some progress along this path.

My review of events and ideas concerning MST and SCP is, no doubt, incomplete, and so is my bibliography. I ask for forgiveness in advance.

In Sec.2 I discuss a few important aspects of supercompilation. In Sec.3 I give an outline of a few ideas which have not yet been properly translated into computer programs. My exposition is very informal and sketchy. I try to do it through a few simple examples. The field of MST+SCP has its own formalism, which I, obviously, cannot systematically present here. Yet I hope that the reader unfamiliar with it will still be able to figure out what it is all about, without going into formal details.

A word on terminology. In 1987 I suggested *metacomputation* as an umbrella term covering all computations which include at least one metasystem transition. By this definition, partial evaluation is also a variety of metacomputation. However, partial evaluation people have been in no hurry to use this term. In contrast, it is readily used by people in the field I denote in this paper as MST plus SCP (sounds barbarian, of course). Thus, for the time being, at least,

$$metacomputation \approx MST + SCP$$

2 Aspects of supercompilation

2.1 Pattern-matching graphs

I will reveal a small secret. Our supercompilers do not actually use Refal as the language of object programs; they use the language of *pattern-matching graphs*, also referred to as *Refal graphs*. The program in Refal to be supercompiled is first automatically translated into the graph form, and the output of the SCP is also a Refal graph.

Algebraically, a pattern-matching graph is a sum of products of three varieties of the operation of pattern-matching, with a product implying sequential, and a sum parallel, execution. A *contraction* is a pattern matching $v : p$, where v is a variable and p is a rigid pattern; we shall denote this contraction as $v \xrightarrow{c} p$. An *assignment* is a pattern matching $e : v$, where e is an expression and v a variable; we shall denote this assignment as $e \xleftarrow{a} v$. A *restriction* is $(\# G)$, where G is a contraction graph, i.e., a pattern-matching graph which consists only of contractions. It is evaluated either to $\mathbf{Z}$(impossible operation, failure), if at least one contraction path in G is successful, or to the identity operation $\mathbf{I}$ (do nothing) otherwise.

This notation may seem unusual (especially that of an assignment), but it is logical and quite convenient. It is derived from the following two principles. (1) On the left side we have *bound* (old, defined) variables; on the right side *free* (new, to be defined) variables. (2) When the operation is understood as a substitution, the arrow is directed from the variable to its replacement.

Examples. $x \xrightarrow{c} s.1\ x\texttt{'a'}$ is a contraction for x. If the value of x is 'koshka', after the execution of this contraction x becomes 'oshk', and a new variable s.1 becomes defined and has the value 'k'. If x is 'kot' the result is the impossible operation $\mathbf{Z}$ (failure of matching). Further, this contraction can be decomposed into a product of *elementary* contractions:

$$(x \xrightarrow{c} s.1\ x\texttt{'a'}) = (x \xrightarrow{c} s.1\ x)(x \xrightarrow{c} x\ s.2)(s.2 \xrightarrow{c} \texttt{'a'})$$

An example with a restriction:

$$(\texttt{'b'} \xleftarrow{a} s.5)\ (\#\ (s.5 \xrightarrow{c} \texttt{'a'}) + (s.5 \xrightarrow{c} \texttt{'b'})) = \mathbf{Z}$$

I have developed a set of relations of equivalency for the algebra of pattern-matching operations, and the programming of SCP-3 was based on it, but, unfortunately, this theory is not yet published; the initial stages of the theory can be found in [40].

The most important equivalence is a *clash* between an assignment and a contraction for the same variable, which is *resolved* in a matching:

$$(e \xleftarrow{a} v)(v \xrightarrow{c} p) = e : p$$

Thus the example above can be seen as the equation:

$$(\texttt{'koshka'} \xleftarrow{a} x)\ (x \xrightarrow{c} s.1\ x\ \texttt{'a'}) = (\texttt{'oshk'} \xleftarrow{a} x)\ (\texttt{'k'} \xleftarrow{a} s.1)$$

Here is an example of resolution which includes the contraction of a bound variable:

$$(\texttt{'kot'} s.2 \xleftarrow{a} x)\ (x \xrightarrow{c} x\texttt{'a'}) = (s.2 \xrightarrow{c} \texttt{'a'})\ (\texttt{'kot'} \xleftarrow{a} x)$$

To give an example of a function definition in the graph form, here is the graph for the iterative program of changing each 'a' to 'b', where nodes [n] correspond to configurations of the Refal machine:

[1] ([] $\overset{a}{\leftarrow}$ y) [2]
[2] (x $\overset{c}{\rightarrow}$ s.1 x) { (s.1 $\overset{c}{\rightarrow}$ 'a') (y'b' $\overset{a}{\leftarrow}$ y) [2]
           +(# s.1 $\overset{c}{\rightarrow}$ 'a') (y s.1 $\overset{a}{\leftarrow}$ y) [2] }
    +(x $\overset{c}{\rightarrow}$ []) [] $\overset{a}{\leftarrow}$ out

With Refal graphs, driving is an application of commutation relations for pattern-matching operations. A walk in the normal form, in which it appears in function definitions and represents one step of the Refal machine, has the structure CRA, where the letters stand for Contraction, Restriction and Assignment, respectively. A walk representing two steps is $C_1 R_1 A_1 C_2 R_2 A_2$. Resolving the clash $A_1 C_2$ and then adjusting contractions and restrictions according to commutation relations, we return the walk to the normal form CRA: we have made one step of driving.

2.2 Generalization

Generalization is one of the central problems of supercompilation. It breaks down naturally in two parts: (1) a decision to generalize the current configuration C with some of its predecessors C' trying to reduce C to it; we need a 'whistle' to warn us that if we do not try reduction, we may end up with infinite driving; and (2) the generalization proper, i.e., defining a configuration C_{gen} such that both C and C' are its subsets. A good generalization algorithm must find a balance between two extreme cases: a too willing generalization, which makes the resulting program interpretive and leaves it unoptimized; and a generalization postponed for too long so that the supercompilation process never ends.

In [43] I defined an algorithm of whistling for lazy supercompilation of nested function calls, and proved its termination. This algorithm was implemented in SCP-2, and it works very well, but only within its domain of usefulness.

It works with *stacks* representing nested function calls, and refers to an unspecified algorithm for generalization of *flat* configurations, i.e., ones without nested function calls.

In SCP-2 and SCP-3 we used several empirically found algorithms of generalizing flat expressions, but no termination theorems were proven.

Sørensen and Glück, [33] used the Higman-Kruskal theorem about homeomorphic embedding (HK for short) to define a whistle for supercompilation which is of a proven termination. The data domain in [33] is the set of functional terms with fixed arity of each functional symbol. This domain is sufficient for representation of lists, but not Refal expressions. Refal allows *concatenation* of terms, which can be seen as the use of a functional symbol of arbitrary arity (a *variadic* symbol). Fortunately, the Higman-Kruskal theorem allows variadic symbols. When I learned this, I defined a whistle for supercompilation in Refal along the lines of [33].

I will briefly outline the concept of embedding following the work by Dershowitz [6].

Let a finite set F of functional symbols be given. Consider the set $T(F)$ of all functional terms $f(t_1, \ldots, t_n)$ with functional symbols $f \in F$. Some symbols may be of arity $n = 0$; they are *constants*, and we shall write them without parentheses: f for $f()$. Some of the symbols may be variadic: different n in different calls.

Definition. The homeomorphic embedding relation $\trianglelefteq$ on a set $T(F)$ of terms is defined recursively as follows:

$$t = g(t_1, t_2, \ldots, t_n) \trianglelefteq f(s_1, s_2, \ldots, s_m) = s$$

if either

$$t \trianglelefteq s_i \quad \text{for some } i = 1, \ldots, m$$

or

$$f = g \quad \text{and} \quad t_j \trianglelefteq s_{i_j} \quad \text{for all } j = 1, \ldots, n$$

where $1 \leq i_1 < i_2 < \ldots < i_n \leq m$. $\square$

Note that in the second rule f and g must be identical, but their calls may have different number of terms: $n \leq m$; some of the terms in f may be ignored.

Theorem. (Higman,Kruskal) If F is a finite set of function symbols, then any infinite sequence $t_1, t_2, \ldots$ of terms in the set $T(F)$ of terms over F contains two terms t_j and t_k, where $j < k$, such that $t_j \trianglelefteq t_k$. $\square$

To use HK, we map the set of all Refal terms T_R onto the domain of functional terms $T(F)$ over some set F of functional symbols.

Definition. The set F is $S \cup \{s_e, s_s, s_n, f_{par}, f_{fun}\}$, where S is the set of Refal symbols except numbers; it is finite because only those non-numerical symbols that enter the program can appear in computation. Symbols from S, as well as the two special symbols s_e and s_s, are of arity 0, while the other two symbols are variadic. The mapping $M_{rt} : T_R \to T(F)$ is recursively defined by Table 1, where s stands for any non-numerical symbol, n is any number, t is a term, and e is an expression. $\square$

In Refal the most general data structure is that of expressions, not terms. But it is easy to reduce a relation on expressions to a relation on terms:

$$e_1 \trianglelefteq_R e_2 \Leftrightarrow (e_1) \trianglelefteq_R (e_2)$$

We define the homeomorphic embedding relation $\trianglelefteq_R$ on Refal terms as the mapping of the relation $\trianglelefteq$:

$$t_1 \trianglelefteq_R t_2 \text{ if and only if } M_{rt}[t_1] \trianglelefteq M_{rt}[t_2]$$

$$M_{rt}[\mathsf{s.i}] = s_s$$
$$M_{rt}[\mathsf{e.i}] = s_e$$
$$M_{rt}[n] = s_n$$
$$M_{rt}[s] = s$$
$$M_{rt}[(e)] = f_{par}(M_{rt}[e])$$
$$M_{rt}[<s\ e>] = f_{fun}(M_{rt}[s]\ M_{rt}[e])$$
$$M_{rt}[t\ e] = M_{rt}[t]\ M_{rt}[e]$$
$$M_{rt}[\ ] = \text{empty}$$

Table1. The mapping $M_{rt} : T_R \to T(F)$

Rewriting the definition of $\unlhd$ in terms of Refal, we have:

Definition. The homeomorphic embedding relation $\unlhd_R$ on the set T_R holds if either *term is embedded in term*:

$$t \unlhd_R (e_1 t' e_2) \tag{1}$$

where $t \unlhd_R t'$ and e_i for $i = 1, 2$ are some expressions; or *expression is embedded in expression*:

$$(t_1\ t_2 \ldots t_n) \unlhd_R (e_1\ t_1'\ e_2\ t_2' \ldots e_n\ t_n'\ e_{n+1}) \tag{2}$$

where $t_i \unlhd_R t_i'$ for $i = 1, \ldots, n$, and any of the expressions e_i may be empty. $\square$

This definition translates into the algorithm in Refal given in Table 2.

This whistle was not yet tested in the computer, but I believe it will work well.

I discovered, with some surprise, that the embedding relation on Refal expressions leads to a whistle different from that derived from the embedding relation on Lisp's lists, even though these two kinds of symbolic objects may look identical. I cannot go into detail here (see [48] for that). Just an example and a few words.

Consider this relation:

$$(a\ b\ c) \unlhd (a\ p(b\ c)q)$$

If it is understood as a relation between Refal expressions $\unlhd_R$, it does not hold. But if we see it as a relation between lists, it does hold. Moreover, the algorithm for Refal expressions above is linear with the size of expressions, while the corresponding recursive algorithm for lists is exponential (it can be converted, though, into a quadratic iterative algorithm). I must also notice that we can have the Refal whistle working with lists by exploiting a one-to-one mapping between these two domains.

A few words about generalization proper. With a given whistle algorithm, various algorithms of generalization proper may be used. For our whistle algorithm all variables of a given type (s or e) are the same, while for generalization proper this is not so, of course. Still the embedding relation which caused the

```
* <Emb t1 t2> results in T if t1 ⊴R t2,
* and in F otherwise.
Emb {eX = <Dec eX <Embk 1 eX>> }

* Decide if the second case must be considered
Dec { eX T = T;
      eX F = F;
      eX 2 = <Embk 2 eX> }

Embk {
  sN s1 s1 = T;
  sN t1 s2 = F;
  sN ()(e1) = T;
  1 t1 () = 2;
  2 t1 () = F;
  1 t1 (t2 e3), <Emb t1 t2>:
                 { T = T;
                   F = <Embk 1 t1 (e3)> };
  2 (t1 e2)(t.1s e.2s), <Emb t1 t.1s>:
                            {T = <Embk 2 (e2)(e.2s)>;
                             F = <Embk 2 (t1 e2)(e.2s)> };
  }
```

Table2. The Refal program for the embedding relation $\unlhd_R$.

whistle may serve as a starting point for generalization. In particular, if the relation $t_i \unlhd_R t_i'$ in the case *expression embedded in expression* happens, for some i, to be an equality, we can leave it as a common part in generalization. For example, the embedding:

$$a\,b\,c \unlhd_R p\,a\,b\,c\,q\,r$$

leads to the generalization:

$$gen[a\,b\,c,\ p\,a\,b\,c\,q\,r] = x_1\,a\,b\,c\,x_2$$

where x_1 and x_2 are some e-variables.

This method, though, works only for Refal expressions, not for lists. With lists as the basic data structures, generalization can preserve only that common substructure which is on the left, but not on the right side. Even though a list, such as $(a\,b\,c)$, looks like a string, it is, in fact, a binary tree which in the Refal representation is

$$(a(b(c\,nil)))$$

We can generalize it with a list which extends it on the right side, without losing the common part:

$$gen[(a(b(c\,nil))), (a(b(c(p\,nil)))) = (a(b(c\,x_1)))$$

but if the extension is on the left, the most specific generalization is a free variable. The common part is lost:

$$gen[(a(b(c\,nil))), (p(a(b(c\,nil)))))] = x_1$$

Unfortunately, when a program works by iterations (as opposed to programs where data is passed from the result of one function to the argument of another) it is exactly on the left side that the lists are growing. Because of this, a supercompiler working with lists may not perform partial evaluation in cases where a Refal supercompiler easily does it.

2.3 Theorem proving

Using formal logic is not the only way to prove theorems in computers, especially those of primary interest for computer scientists. Metacomputation provides an alternative method of automated theorem proving. We face here two different paradigms.

In the axioms-and-logic paradigm of mathematics, we deal with things which are completely undefined, true abstractions. We can know about these things only as much as we can extract from the axioms we have chosen to assume. Mathematical objects—as long as the mathematician is faithful to the proclaimed axioms-and-logic paradigm—do not really exist. The meaning of the statement that certain mathematical objects exist is simply that no logical derivation using these objects leads to contradiction.

In contrast, when we are doing computer science we deal with well-defined finite cybernetic systems, such as Turing machines or computers, and with computational processes in these systems.

Compare the treatment of the primary theoretical objects of all exact sciences—natural numbers—in the axiomatic and cybernetic paradigms. In axiomatic arithmetics, numbers are abstract entities operations on which meet requirements codified in a certain number of axioms. In particular, the operation of addition + is defined by two axioms:

$$x + 0 = x$$
$$x + y' = (x + y)'$$

where x' is the function 'next number' applied to x. To prove a proposition one must construct, according to well-known rules, a *demonstration*, which is a sequence of propositions.

In the cybernetic paradigm natural numbers are chains of some pieces of matter called symbols, and functions are machines which know how to handle symbols. The Refal program for + is:

```
<+ x,'0'> = x
<+ x,y'1'> = <+ x,y>'1'
```

Another function we want to compute is the predicate of equality:

```
<= '0','0'> = T
<= '0',y'1'> = F
<= x'1','0'> = F
<= x'1',y'1'> = <= x,y>
```

The strong side of the axioms-and-logic method is its wide applicability. A theory may be developed about objects (such as those of geometry or set theory) which are not easy to represent by symbolic expressions. Also, the same theorem can be used with different interpretations. Group theory is usually adduced as an example. However, in computer science it is exactly the world of symbolic expressions and processes that we are primarily interested in. For this world the cybernetic paradigm is pretty natural.

The obvious advantage of the cybernetic paradigm is the completely mechanized way to perform computations. To prove that $2 + 2 = 4$, we only have to compute the truth-value of the proposition:

$$<= <+ '011','011'>,'01111'>$$

When we give this job to the Refal machine, the results is a finite computation process. It ends with T, which proves the statement.

This has been a proposition without quantification. Can general propositions be proven by computation?

Not directly. But they can be proven by *metacomputation*. Let us take a simple example from arithmetics where the proof requires the use of mathematical induction. Consider the following statement:

$$\forall x \, (0 + x = x) \tag{3}$$

Let us see how this theorem is proven by a supercompiler. The translation of the statement into the cybernetic paradigm is as follows. The initial configuration:

[1]: $<= <+ '0',x>, x>$

evaluated by the Refal machine with any value substituted for x results in T; so we expect from the supercompiler that it will equivalently transform [1] into just T.

The supercompiler that makes this job uses the outside-in (lazy) driving. It attempts to drive the call of =, but the nested call of + is a hindrance, thus SCP switches to driving it. Two contractions are produced in accordance with the definition of +: $x \xrightarrow{c} \, '0'$ and $x \xrightarrow{c} x'1'$. With the first contraction the computation is straightforward and leads to T. With the second contraction the machine makes a step in the computation of $<+ '0',x'1'>$, which produces the configuration:

[2]: $<= <+ '0',x>'1', x'1'>$

The process returns to the outermost call and makes, in a unique way, one step according to the definition of =. The result is the same as [1]. Thus we have this transition graph:

$$[1] \quad x \xrightarrow{c} \text{'0'; T}$$
$$+ \quad x \xrightarrow{c} x\text{'1'; } [1]$$

The supercompiler easily recognizes such a graph as transformable to just T, since the only exit configuration is T; this is the form which mathematical induction takes in metacomputation. The theorem is proven. (We set aside the problem of termination. In our case it is secured by the fact that all functions involved are total).

The associativity of addition is also easily provable in this way. However, proving the commutativity of addition requires more sophisticated techniques, which I shall discuss in Sec. 3.1.

2.4   Metasystem hierarchies and jumps

Consider metasystem hierarchies of computing machines. After we have chosen a universal all-level programming language, such as Refal, a hierarchy of machines becomes a hierarchy of programs. We want to write functions which are defined on definitions of other functions.

In every programming language we distinguish *objects* which are manipulated, from certain special details, variables and function calls, which represent sets of objects and computation processes and cannot be directly treated as objects. Let the set of objects be S_{ob} and the set of variables and function calls S_{vf}. To write a program which manipulates programs, we must map the set of all elements of programs, i.e., $S_{ob} \cup S_{vf}$, on the set of objects S_{ob}. We call this mapping a *metacode*, and denote the metacode transformation of e as $\mu\{e\}$:

$$\mu : S_{ob} \cup S_{vf} \to S_{ob}$$

Obviously, metacoding must have a unique inverse transformation, *demetacoding*, so it must be injective:

$$\forall(e_1, e_2) \, (e_1 \neq e_2 \Rightarrow \mu\{e_1\} \neq \mu\{e_2\})$$

For convenience of reading metacoded expressions we require that $\mu\{e_1 e_2\} = \mu\{e_1\}\mu\{e_2\}$. Also, it is desirable that the image of an object expression be as close to the expression itself as possible. It would be nice, of course, to leave all object expressions unaltered under the metacode, but this is, unfortunately, impossible, because it contradicts to the requirement of injectivity. Not every expression e can be represented as $\mu\{e'\}$, where e is also an object expression. This creates a hierarchy of *MST domains*:

$$S^0 \supset S^1 \supset S^2 \ldots$$

where $S^0 = S_{ob}$, and $S^k = \mu\{S^{k-1}\}$, for $k \geq 1$.

The metacode for Refal which is used in the latest implementation of this language is given in Nemytykh, Pinchuk and Turchin [25] (see Table 2) in this volume.

Compare two function calls: `<F2 <F1 x>>` and `<F2 μ{<F1 x>}>`. The first call is a functional composition: `<F1 x>` is computed and its value is taken as argument in the computation of F2. In the second call there is no evaluation of `<F1 x>`, but the metacode of this expression is turned over for the computation of F2. If the metacode of [25] is used, we have: `<F2 ('!'F1('ex'))>`. This is an MST hierarchy of two levels: function F2 is supposed to manipulate F1 (its representation, to be precise). If this manipulation is *semantic* in nature, i.e., based on the definition of F1, as it is in all interesting cases, then the machine F2 must have access to the definition of F1. In order not to encumber our notation, we shall always assume that whenever a metamachine F_2 manipulates a machine F_1, it incorporates the definition of F_1, so we need not indicate this in each case.

We use *MST schemes* for a clear and metacode-invariant representation of metasystem hierarchies. [3] An MST scheme is built according to the rule: whenever a subexpression has the form $E_1\mu\{E_2\}E_3$, the metacoded part is moved one level down and replaced by dots on the main level:

$$E_1\mu\{E_2\}E_3 \Longleftrightarrow E_1.....E_3$$
$$E_2$$

This rule can be applied any number of times. To convert an MST scheme into an equivalent Refal expression, we must metacode each level as many times as long is its distance from the top.

MST schemes allow us to represent very clearly certain operations on variables which are necessary for correct construction and use of metasystem hierarchies. I shall show this using as an example the well-known procedure of converting an interpreter for some language into a compiler by partial evaluation (see [9, 41, 18]).

Let L be an interpreter for some language L written in Refal, and let it be used in the format `<L e.prog,e.data>`. Let PE be a partial evaluator for Refal written in Refal and having Refal as the target language, i.e., producing a Refal program at the output. We apply PE to the call of L where some program P is substituted for `e.prog`, while `e.data` remains free. This call is `<L P,e.data>`. We metacode it and submit to the partial evaluator:

```
<PE ............. >
    <L P, e.data>
```

In this MST scheme the call of L, which is submitted for partial evaluation, is a function of data only, since the value of `e.prog` is fixed at a specific expression P. After PE performs all operations which can be performed because the program P is known, it outputs a residual program which is nothing else but the translation of the program P into Refal. Function PE has worked as a compiler.

Now suppose we want a PE function which would accept an *arbitrary* program, not just P. If we simply put the variable program instead of P:

---

[3] I first introduced this notation in my lectures at the University of Copenhagen in 1985. Ever since, its various versions were used in seminars on Refal and metacomputation in Moscow and New York. In a published form it first appeared in [12].

```
<PE ................ >
    <L e.prog, e.data>
```

we will not get what we want. Here the variables for data and for program are on the same level and are treated in the same way. No partial evaluation takes place, because the value of e.prog remains unknown to PE. Even though e.prog is an argument of L, its value must be provided on the level of PE, so that when L is running (being driven by PE), the program is fixed. We represent this situation by raising e.prog to the top level, and leaving the bullet • in the place where this variable originated on the bottom level:

```
<PE .. e.prog ....... >
    <L     •,  e.data>
```

We shall call the variables like e.prog *elevated*. For such a variable, the *definition level*, at which its name is placed, is different from the *usage level* indicated by the bullet, and the difference h between the two is the variable's *elevation*. The value assigned to a variable on the definition level enters the configuration after being metacoded h times. Possible values of an elevated variable belong to the MST domain S^h, and this must be taken into account for correct driving.

The *rule of two levels* helps read MST schemes: The variables on the top level are *free*. Those on the next level are *bound*: they run over their domains as, e.g., integration variables, or the variables in a function definition.

Even though e.prog is used by L, it is not free for it. It is free on the level of the partial evaluation function PE; to run PE we must first substitute some specific program for e.prog. Hence L always receives a fixed program. The result of PE will be a transformed (partially evaluated) function L, which depends only on the variable e.data and is a translation of e.prog from L into Refal.

The translation, however, is made directly by PE, which can work with any definition of L (hidden in the function name L, as we agreed above). We can further optimize PE by partially evaluating it by itself according to the MST scheme:

```
<PE ...................... >
    <PE .. e.prog ........ >
        <L     •,    e.data>
```

This scheme is a scheme of generation of a compiler from the language L defined by a given interpreter L. Let us read it using the rule of two levels. There are no free variables on the top level: we run the upper PE only once and receive a program which is a function of e.prog: a compiler for L. Now we take one step down and again apply the rule of two levels. The lower PE (the compiler) is on the top. It asks for e.prog on the input and produces a function of e.data as the output. It is the translation of e.prog.

As I mentioned above, one must be aware of the narrowed domains of elevated variables when driving. It is interesting to note, though, that ignoring this leads to actual mistakes only when the MST scheme has at least three levels. In the two-level scheme of compilation above, e.prog is elevated. But it is, at the same time, free. When making a call of PE, we substitute for it a *metacoded* program (and cannot do otherwise since program is not in S_{ob}); hence the requirement to the value of e.prog becomes satisfied. However, with the third level, the upper PE drives expressions which include unreplaced (free for the lower PE) variable e.prog, and it will consider various contractions for it. If it is not informed that the variable's domain is S^1, not the full S_{ob}, it will consider non-existing contractions, which will make the program wrong, and will typically result in an infinite loop.

It often happens that a program transformer must transform a function call which, in fact, can be simply evaluated. The argument may include no free variables or yet uncomputed function calls or, if there are some, they may not be consulted at any stage of evaluation. Even more frequent is a situation where such independence of unknown data holds for a part of the evaluation process, even though not for the whole length of it.

Consider our two-level scheme of compilation. The interpreter L operates on a known program and unknown data. On some stretches of computation L will work on the program, but without consulting the data. An obvious example is the parsing of the program. Further, if the language L includes GO TO statements with jumps to a label, then it may be necessary to examine a big piece of program in search of the needed label. The work of the function PE in this part of computation will be nothing else but simulation of the work of L, which, of course, will take much more time than a direct run of the function L.

In our papers with Nemytykh and, later, Pinchuk [46, 25] we describe a supercompiler which makes automatic jumps from one level to another in order to avoid doing on the level n in the interpretation mode what can be done on the level $n - 1$ by direct computation. Before driving a configuration, the supercompiler passes control one level down by demetacoding the configuration and starting the execution of it. If it is possible to bring the computation to the end, the result is metacoded and control returns to the upper level. If at a certain stage of execution its continuation becomes impossible because of unknown values of variables, the configuration of the latest stage preceding the current is metacoded and control passes to the top level for driving.

To make this system work, it was necessary to modify the implementation of Refal by adding a feature which was called a *freezer*, see [44]. In tests we could see that the use of metasystem jumping can lead to very significant speedups, sometimes by a factor of more than twenty.

2.5 Expressions *vs.* lists

As mentioned above, the major difference between Refal and pure Lisp, as well as other languages working with lists, is the data domain. Refal expressions are strings of terms which can be processed both left to right, and right to left. They are trees with an arbitrary and unfixed arity. A list is a special kind of a Refal expression. There are several reasons why I stubbornly use Refal in metacomputation (beyond the main reason, which I am trying to conceal: I invented it).

1. I hope that sooner or later the methods of metacomputation will be used on the industrial scale for automatic development of big and fast programs. The efficiency of algorithms is, as we very well know, tightly bound to data structure. I cannot imagine that practical programmers will agree to abandon such an important data structure as string. Limiting ourselves to lists, we throw overboard a huge set of efficient algorithms.

2. As we saw in Section 2.2, Refal expressions allow generalizations that are inexpressible with lists. This makes supercompilation easier and more efficient. Data structures we use are, essentially, models of reality. More sophisticated data structures allow us to express more subtle features of the medium. A language based on graphs would have the same advantage over Refal as Refal has over a pure list-processing language.

3. When we create a metamachine for examining and controlling the operation of the object machine, we often want to trace its steps in both forward and backward directions. Histories of computation are naturally represented by strings of states. In Sec.3.1 I show how supercompilation can be enhanced by switching from configurations of the computing machine to histories of computation by it. Moreover, backward movement is part of the concept of supercompilation. It can be avoided, but not without paying some price—in conceptual simplicity, if not in anything else. Languages we use not only help express something we are doing; they suggest what we might do further. It is not an accident that the concept of supercompilation first appeared in the context of such a language as Refal.

4. Pure list-processing languages are good for programming in recursive style, but poor when the algorithms are iterative. Meanwhile, we often face the situation where a recursive algorithm is clear and elegant, but inefficient, so that we have to transform it into an iterative form. In functional languages, even a simple traversal without inverting the list is impossible when we do it iteratively. Refal is equally at ease with both recursive and iterative programming.

The use of lists, though, is not without its own advantages. As a data structure for analysis and manipulation, lists are simpler than Refal expressions, though in my view, the difference is not significant. Another advantage is the simple fact that people in computer science research are accustomed to this domain, and the languages based on it are widely used. One balances these two sets of advantages according to one's priorities.

3 Still to come

3.1 Walk grammars

Now I will show how to make one more—and maybe the most promising—metasystem transition in program transformation [40, 45].

As discussed in Sec.2.1, one step of the Refal machine is represented in the pattern-matching graph as a normal walk $C_1 R_1 A_1$. For driving we combine two steps by concatenating two normal walks: $C_1 R_1 A_1 C_2 R_2 A_2$, and normalize them into one walk again. We can postpone driving and combine any number of elementary walks into unnormalized walks of arbitrary length. Such walks will represent possible (but not necessarily feasible) histories of computation without performing the computation itself.

Take the graph

[1] $(\square \overset{a}{\leftarrow} y)$ [2]
[2] $(x \overset{c}{\to} s.1\ x)$ { $(s.1 \overset{c}{\to} \text{'a'})\ (y \text{'b'} \overset{a}{\leftarrow} y)$ [2]
$\qquad\qquad +(\# s.1 \overset{c}{\to} \text{'a'})\ (y\ s.1 \overset{a}{\leftarrow} y)$ [2] }
$\quad +(x \overset{c}{\to} \square)\ \square \overset{a}{\leftarrow} \text{out}$

from Sec.2.1. Denote the one-step walks in the graph as follows:

w_1 = $(\square \overset{a}{\leftarrow} y)$
w_2 = $(x \overset{c}{\to} s.1\ x)\ (s.1 \overset{c}{\to} \text{'a'})\ (y\text{'b'} \overset{a}{\leftarrow} y)$
w_3 = $(x \overset{c}{\to} s.1\ x)\ (\# s.1 \overset{c}{\to} \text{'a'})\ (y\ s.1 \overset{a}{\leftarrow} y)$
w_4 = $(x \overset{c}{\to} \square)\ \square \overset{a}{\leftarrow} \text{out}$

Now the set of all terminated walks (histories of completed computation) is described by the regular grammar:

[1] $\Rightarrow$ w_1 [2]
[2] $\Rightarrow$ w_2 [2]
[2] $\Rightarrow$ w_3 [2]
[2] $\Rightarrow$ w_4

or by the regular expression $w_1(w_2 + w_3)^* w_4$.

It is easy to see that for an arbitrary Refal program the set of all walks is defined by a context-free grammar, while if we restrict ourselves to *flat* Refal (no nested calls) the walk grammar becomes regular, hence the whole set is represented by a regular expression, which is a great advantage of the flat version. We shall work with a generalization of regular expressions where the number of iterations is denoted by a variable, so that such walk-sets as $w^n w^n$ are permitted.

Walk-sets are an alternative form of a program. We can define an interpreter *Int* which executes such programs, and transform *Int* calls by the supercompiler: an MST to the three-level hierarchy: $Scp - Int - Program$. But what do we achieve by this MST? Well, if *Int* does just driving, i.e., processes the walks in the strict order from left to right, we have achieved nothing. But we can create a clever interpreter which uses equivalence relations on the set of walks. It could *unwind* iterative loops both from the left, and from the right, i.e., use the relation $W^{n+1} = W W^n$ or $W^{n+1} = W^n W$ in order to achieve reduction in supercompilation. It could also reorder operations in walks using commutation relations and do other transformations. In [45] I show that with this technique we can make transformations which could not be done by direct supercompilation, such as function inversion and the merging of consecutive iterative loops.

The $Scp - Int$ technique can be very effectively used for *graph cleaning*. Suppose we finished supercompilation and have the resulting flat graph G. It does not mean that all exit nodes (expressions for output) are actually feasible. For each node in G we can write a regular expression for the set of all walks which lead to this node. Using the Scp-Int method we may discover that some walk-sets are reduced to $\mathbf{Z}$; then these nodes can be eliminated.

As an example, let us return to the proof of commutativity of addition, which we have found more difficult to prove than the other theorems in Sec.2.3. The proof requires a considerable analysis of the graph resulting from straightforward supercompilation. I will only sketch the proof.

The configuration to compute is

[1] <= <+ x,y>, <+ y,x>>

In the process of supercompilation, [1] is generalized, and reduced to the generalized configuration:

[1] $(x \overset{a}{\leftarrow} \bar{x}) (y \overset{a}{\leftarrow} \bar{y})$ [2] <= <+ x̄,y>, <+ ȳ,x>>

The graph for [2] has 15 exits. Four of them are T, eleven are F. To prove the theorem, the walks which lead to each of the eleven F ends must be proven unfeasible. As an example, I will do it for one of the walks, which is neither the least nor the most difficult:

$$w = (x \overset{a}{\leftarrow} \bar{x})(y \overset{a}{\leftarrow} \bar{y})(y \overset{c}{\to} y\text{'}1\text{'})^n (x \overset{c}{\to} x\text{'}1\text{'})^n (y \overset{c}{\to} y\text{'}1\text{'})(x \overset{c}{\to} \text{'}0\text{'})$$
$$(\bar{y} \overset{c}{\to} \bar{y}\text{'}1\text{'})(\bar{y} \overset{c}{\to} \bar{y}\text{'}1\text{'})^m (y \overset{c}{\to} y\text{'}1\text{'})^m (\bar{y} \overset{c}{\to} \text{'}0\text{'})(y \overset{c}{\to} y\text{'}1\text{'})$$

Here m and n are variables, so w represents an infinite set of walks, not a single walk.

Using commutation relations we reduce w to the form:

$$w = (x \overset{a}{\leftarrow} \bar{x}) \ (x \overset{c}{\to} x\text{'}1\text{'})^n \ (x \overset{c}{\to} \text{'}0\text{'})$$
$$(y \overset{a}{\leftarrow} \bar{y}) \ (\bar{y} \overset{c}{\to} \bar{y}\text{'}1\text{'})^p \ (\bar{y} \overset{c}{\to} \text{'}0\text{'}) \ (y \overset{c}{\to} y\text{'}1\text{'})^q$$

where we have introduced new variables p, q, which show the total number of iterations in the walk. Their relation to the loop variables m, n, namely $p = m+1$ and $q = n + m + 2$, will be treated as a restriction on p, q.

The unfeasibility of w results from the second line, i.e., y-part of it; so we ignore the first line (x-part). The call of the interpreter takes the form:

<Int $(y \overset{a}{\leftarrow} \bar{y})$ $(\bar{y} \overset{c}{\to} \bar{y}\text{'}1\text{'})^p$ $(\bar{y} \overset{c}{\to} \text{'}0\text{'})$ $(y \overset{c}{\to} y\text{'}1\text{'})^q$>

This is a function of p and q. Unwinding the p-loop means breaking it into a recursive call and the base:

$$W^p = (p \overset{c}{\to} p+1) \ WW^p + (p \overset{c}{\to} 0) \ []$$

and analogously for the q-loop.

Thus, driving produces branches to four cases:

[1] <Int w> $(p \xrightarrow{c} p\text{+}1)(q \xrightarrow{c} q\text{+}1)$ [2]
    $+ \ (p \xrightarrow{c} p\text{+}1)(q \xrightarrow{c} \text{'}0\text{'})$ [3]
    $+ \ (p \xrightarrow{c} \text{'}0\text{'})(q \xrightarrow{c} q\text{+}1)$ [4]
    $+ \ (p \xrightarrow{c} \text{'}0\text{'})(q \xrightarrow{c} \text{'}0\text{'})$ [5]

Let us consider the walk transformation in [2]. This is the case when recursion takes place in both p-loop, and q-loop:

$$(y \xleftarrow{a} \bar{y})(\bar{y} \xrightarrow{c} \bar{y}\text{'}1\text{'})(\bar{y} \xrightarrow{c} \bar{y}\text{'}1\text{'})^p \ (\bar{y} \xrightarrow{c} \text{'}0\text{'}) \ (y \xrightarrow{c} y\text{'}1\text{'})(y \xrightarrow{c} y\text{'}1\text{'})^q$$

Resolving the clash on $\bar{y}$, we have:

$$(y \xleftarrow{a} \bar{y}) \ (\bar{y} \xrightarrow{c} \bar{y}\text{'}1\text{'}) \ = \ (y : \bar{y}\text{'}1\text{'}) \ = \ (y \xrightarrow{c} y\text{'}1\text{'}) \ (y \xleftarrow{a} \bar{y}) \ (y\text{'}1\text{'} \xleftarrow{a} y)$$

Now the assignment $(y\text{'}1\text{'} \xleftarrow{a} y)$ travels to the right and clashes with contraction $(y \xrightarrow{c} y\text{'}1\text{'})$ to produce nothing. The contraction $(y \xrightarrow{c} y\text{'}1\text{'})$ is taken from the argument of Int and becomes a contraction on the input variable y (I cannot go here into formal details). The result is that [2] becomes identical to [1]: a reduction (folding).

It is easy to check, that configurations [3] and [4] are unfeasible. Configuration [5] is an exit from the loop where p and q are decreased by one in every cycle. If we denote the number of cycles as N, the restriction on p, q becomes:

$$p + N = m + 1, \quad q + N = n + m + 2$$

When $p = q = 0$, we have the restriction $m + 1 = n + m + 2$, which cannot be satisfied because $n \geq 0$. The graph for [1] becomes a loop without exits:

[1] <Int w> $(p \xrightarrow{c} p\text{+}1) \ (q \xrightarrow{c} q\text{+}1)$ [1]

This completes the proof of unfeasibility of the chosen walk. The other ten walks are handled analogously.

3.2 Alternating quantifiers

The logical formula for commutativity of addition is universally quantified over x and y. Now we want to find out how the computational paradigm tackles the cases of existential quantification and, especially, those where $\forall$ and $\exists$ alternate. As is well known, a sequence of identical quantifiers can be reduced to one by operating on tuples of variables, but there is no similar reduction when quantifiers alternate. We shall see that each placing of $\forall$ in front of $\exists$, or vice versa, requires, computationally, a metasystem transition.

Let All be a function which uses a supercompiler to prove universally quantified statements, as in the above examples. If the supercompiler comes with a graph where no branch ends with F, it outputs T, otherwise it outputs Z. Thus

$$\text{<All } \mu\{\text{<P } x\text{>}\}\text{>} = \begin{cases} \text{T; } \forall x \, P(x) \text{ is proven} \\ \text{Z; no information} \end{cases}$$

To introduce existential quantification we define the function **Exs** which constructs by driving the potentially infinite tree of configurations using the breadth-first principle. If it finds that some branch ends with T, it outputs T. Otherwise it works infinitely—or, realistically, till it is stopped:

$$\texttt{<Exs } \mu\texttt{\{<P x>\}> } = \begin{cases} \text{T; } \exists x\, P(x) \text{ is proven} \\ \text{is stopped; no information} \end{cases}$$

As always in Refal, a variable x may be an n-tuple (x1)...(xn). If all these variables take part in the driving implied in `<All `μ`{<P x>}>` or `<Exs `μ`{<P x>}>`, they are all appropriately quantified, e.g., computing

```
<All ........... >
     <P x, y, z>
```

is proving $\forall x \forall y \forall z P(x,y,z)$. We can fix the value of one variable, say x, by raising it to the top level (see Sec.2.4):

```
<All ...x ...... >
     <P •, y, z>
```

This computation requires some value of x be given, and for this value it tries to prove $\forall y \forall z P(x,y,z)$.

We can consider this function as a predicate depending on x and quantify it existentially by submitting it to function **Exs**:

```
<Exs ................. >
     <All ...x ...... >
          <P •, y, z>
```

This is the metacomputation formula for $\exists x \forall y \forall z P(x,y,z)$. In a similar manner we establish that the logical formula $\forall x \exists y \forall z P(x,y,z)$ is represented by:

```
<All ........................ >
     <Exs ..... x .......... >
          <All .. | y ... >
               <P •, •, z>
```

Following these lines it is easy to construct an MST scheme for every logical formula, after it has been reduced to the prenex form.

As an example, consider the theorem: there exists no maximal natural number: $\neg \exists x \forall y\, Less(y, x)$. Here the function **Less** is defined as follows:

```
<Less x'1',y'1'> = <Less x,y>
<Less x'1','0'> = F
<Less '0',y'1'> = T
<Less '0','0'> = F
```

To prove the theorem, we first reduce the proposition to the prenex normal form: $\forall x \exists y\, Less(x, y)$, (we have used the equivalence $\neg Less(y, x) = Less(x, y)$), then we form the corresponding MST scheme:

```
<All .................. >
     <Exs ..... x ... >
         <Less •, y>
```

Supercompilation of this simple configuration can be done manually, and I did it. I wrote a specialized version of Exs which does driving in the expectation that the only function called is Less. Then I did the supercompilation implied in All, and the result was T, which proves the theorem.

3.3   Neighborhood analysis

Consider the function fa which looks for the first 'a' in a string and returns T if it is found; otherwise it returns F:

```
<fa 'a'x> = T
<fa s.1 x> = <fa x>
<fa []> = F
```

Consider the computation of <fa 'kasha'>:

$$
\begin{array}{rl}
1. & \text{<fa 'kasha'>} \\
2. & \text{<fa 'asha'>} \\
3. & \text{T}
\end{array}
$$

One may notice that there is a part of the argument, namely 'sha', which did not take part in computation. It could be replaced by any expression, and the computation, as well as its final result, would not change a bit. One might guess that this kind of information about computational processes may be of interest for different purposes, such as debugging and testing programs. A variation of driving, *driving with neighborhood* [40], provides a general method for representing and extracting such information.

We define a *neighborhood* as the structure $(a)p$, where p is a pattern and a is a list of assignments for all variables in p, such that the result of substitution a/p is a ground expression (i.e., one without variables) referred to as the *center* of the neighborhood. Driving with a neighborhood is a combination of computation and driving. In computation the argument is a ground expression, and it defines the path of computation: which sentence is used at each step. In driving the argument is an arbitrary expression, and we analyze all possible computation paths for it. When driving with a neighborhood we drive its pattern, but consider only one path, namely the one taken by the neighborhood's center. At each step the center is the same as if the initial function call were directly evaluated. The free variables in the pattern p (which may be loosely called neighborhood) represent the part of information which was not, up to the current stage, used in computation.

Consider this driving:

	neighborhood	function call	contraction
1.	('kasha'$\overset{a}{\leftarrow}$y) y	<fa y>	y$\overset{c}{\rightarrow}$'k'y
2.	('asha'$\overset{a}{\leftarrow}$y) 'k'y	<fa y>	y$\overset{c}{\rightarrow}$'a'y
3.	('sha'$\overset{a}{\leftarrow}$y) 'ka'y	T	

In the initial neighborhood (column 2) the pattern has the maximal extension: anything, a free variable 'y'; the assignment makes the center 'kasha'. In column 3 is the call to compute the pattern. By driving under the definition of fa, we find that the contraction in column 4 is necessary in order to take the path the center will take (the second sentence of the definition). Modifying the neighborhood by this contraction, we have the next stage neighborhood in line 2. Proceeding further in this manner, we complete the computation of the initial call—it is T—and get the representation of the argument as a neighborhood with the pattern 'ka'y, which tells us that together with our argument, any argument which matches 'ka'y will lead to the same result of computation.

Sergei Abramov found a way to use neighborhood analysis for program testing [1, 2]. This may seem strange, because the neighborhoods give us information about unused parts of arguments, *data*, not about the program. But Abramov makes a metasystem transition: driving with neighborhood is applied not to program P working on data D, but to program Int which is an interpreter of the language in which P is written and works on the pair (P, D). Now the program becomes data. Fixing some input D—a test for P—we can, by neighborhood analysis, determine what parts of the program were used, and hence tested, in this run, and which parts were not.

On this basis Abramov built an elegant theory of program testing, which uses the following principle: choose each next test so as to check those features of the program which have not yet been tested. Abramov gives a precise mathematical definition to this intuitive principle and provides the necessary theorems and algorithms.

4 Conclusion

Supercompilation and partial evaluation belong to the same kind of program transformation, which we refer to as metacomputation. Supercompilation includes, but goes far beyond, partial evaluation. It may cause a deep transformation of a program, especially when combined with various metasystem transitions. Potential applications of driving, supercompilation, and other forms of metacomputation are numerous and include function inversion, program testing and theorem proving.

The boundaries of what is possible to do with metacomputation are not yet clear. Even though the principle of metacomputation is simple, its translation into working machines may be far from being simple. This is not unusual. The basic principles of flying are also simple, but a modern airplane consists of many thousands of details, and it has taken many years of work by many people, in order to develop air technology to the stage when the wonderful machines of today become possible. Metacomputation and, in particular, supercompilation are now at the technological stage of the brothers Wright. Let us hope that the process of technological improvement of supercompilers, which has just started, will produce software tools to be widely used in computer science and industry.

I want to finish by listing a few problems which could serve as milestones for the nearest stretch of the road towards reliable and widely used metacomputation technology.

1. The present supercompiler(s) must be rewritten so that its different parts be more clearly separated and defined by more formal comments. The goal: to help other authors to benefit from the existing experience.
2. To build and test a supercompiler with recursive restrictions on the configuration variables (it is partly done, but only non-recursive restrictions have been well tested). The second part of this problem is automatic computation of restrictions in the process of supercompilation.
3. To implement the generalization algorithm based on homeomorphic embedding relation (see Sec.2.2).
4. The present flat supercompiler in combination with a lazy interpreter works as a lazy supercompiler (see [25]). By making one more MST it should be possible to generate a compiled (and hence fast) lazy supercompiler.
5. To achieve the proof, *in the computer*, of commutativity of addition (see Sec.2.3 and 3.1) and similar theorems.
6. To use *in the computer* the method of theorem proving outlined in Sec.3.2. What kind of theorems can be proven using the existing SCP? How far can we go?
7. A theoretical analysis is needed of the theorem-proving method in Sec.3.2 in comparison with a formal logical proof.
8. To build a 'clever' interpreter of walk-sets as postulated in Sec.3.1 and test it in the combination with the flat supercompiler.
9. To use Abramov's neighborhood testing on some real-world problems.
10. We have done a few simple cases of automatic inversion of functions using SCP. The problem now is to determine the boundaries of this method and try it with more powerful supercompilers.

Acknowledgment

To avoid repetition of what I have said in the History section, let me simply express my deep gratitude to all those who worked with me or appreciated my work.

References

1. S. M. Abramov. Metacomputation and program testing, in: *1st International Workshop on Automated and Algorithmic Debugging*, Linköping, Sweden, pp.121-135, 1991.
2. S. M. Abramov. *Metavychisleniya i ikh Prilozhenija (Metacomputation and its Applications, in Russian)* Nauka, Moscow, 1995.
3. *Bazisnyi Refal i yego realizatsiya na vychislitel'nykh mashinakh, (Basic Refal and its implementation on computers, in Russian)*, GOSSTROY SSSR, TsnIPIASS, Moscow, 1977.

4. S. V. Chmutov, E. A. Gaydar, I. M. Ignatovich, V. F. Kozadoy, A. P. Nemytykh, V. A. Pinchuk. Implementation of the symbol analytic transformations language FLAC, DISCO'90, LNCS vol. 429, p.276, 1990.

5. Manuel G. Clavel and José Meseguer, Axiomatizing reflective logics and languages, *Proc. of Reflection'96*, pp.251-276 (1996).

6. N. Dershowitz. Termination in rewriting, *Journal of Symbolic Computation*, 3, pp.69-116, 1987.

7. A. P. Ershov. On the essence of compilation, *Programmirovanie* (5):21-39, 1977 (in Russian). See translation in: E. J. Neuhold, ed., *Formal description of Programming Concepts* pp 391-420, North-Holland, 1978.

8. A. P. Ershov. Opening Key-note Speech, in: D. Bjørner, A. P. Ershov and N. D. Jones, ed. *Partial Evaluation and Mixed Computation*, North-Holland, pp.225-282, 1988.

9. Y. Futamura. Partial evaluation of computation process—an approach to compiler compiler. *Systems, Computers, Controls*, 2,5, pp.45-50, 1971,

10. Y. Futamura and K. Nogi. Generalized Partial Evaluation, in: D. Bjørner, A. P. Ershov, N. D. Jones (eds), *Partial Evaluation and Mixed Computation, Proceedings of the IFIP TC2 Workshop*, pp.133-151, North-Holland Publishing Co., 1988.

11. Y. Futamura, K. Nogi and A. Takano. Essence of generalized partial evaluation, *Theoretical Computer Science*, 90, pp.61-79, 1991.

12. R. Glück. Towards multiple self-application, *Proceedings of the Symposium on Partial Evaluation and Semantics-Based Program Manipulation (Yale University)*, ACM Press, 1991, pp.309-320.

13. R. Glück and J. Jørgensen. Generating transformers for deforestation and super-compilation, in: B. Le Charlier ed. *Static Analysis, Proceedings*, Namur, Belgium, 1994, LNCS, vol.864, pp.432-448, Springer, 1994.

14. R. Glück and A. V. Klimov. Occam's razor in metacomputation: the notion of a perfect process tree, in: P. Cousot, M. Falaschi, G. Filè, and A. Rauzy, ed. *Static Analysis*, LNCS vol.724, pp.112-123, Springer 1993.

15. R. Glück and A. V. Klimov. Metacomputation as a tool for formal linguistic modelling, in: R. Trapple, ed. *Cybernetic and Systems '94* vol.2 pp.1563-1570, Singapore, 1994.

16. R. Glück and A. V. Klimov. Metasystem transition schemes in computer science and mathematics, *World's Future: the Journal of General Evolution*, vol.45, pp.213-243, 1995.

17. R. F. Gurin and S. A. Romanenko. *Yazyk Programmirovaniya Refal Plus (The Programming Language Refal Plus, in Russian)*, Intertekh, Moscow, 1991.

18. N. D. Jones, P. Sestoft and H. Søndergaard. An Experiment in Partial Evaluation: The Generation of a Compiler Generator. In: Jouannaud J.-P. (Ed.) *Rewriting Techniques and Applications*, Dijon, France, LNCS 202, pp.124-140, Springer, 1985.

19. N. D. Jones. Automatic program specialization: a re-examination from basic principles, in: D. Bjørner, A. P. Ershov and N. D. Jones, ed. *Partial Evaluation and Mixed Computation*, North-Holland, pp.225-282, 1988.

20. N. D. Jones, P. Sestoft and H. Søndergaard, Mix: a self-applicable partial evaluator for experiments in compiler generation, in: *Lisp and Symbolic computation* 2(1), 1989, pp.9-50.

21. N. D. Jones. The essence of program transformation by partial evaluation and driving, in: N. D. Jones, M. Hagiya, and M. Sato ed. *Logic, Language and Computation*, LNCS vol.792, pp.206-224, Springer, 1994.

22. V. L. Kistlerov. *Printsipy postroeniya yazyka algebraicheskikh vychislenij FLAC (The defining principles of the language for algebraic computations FLAC, in Russian)* Institut Problem Upravleniya, Moscow 1987.

23. A. V. Klimov and S. A. Romanenko. *A Meta-evaluator for the language Refal, Basic Concepts and Examples* (in Russian), Preprint 71 Keldysh Institute for Applied Mathematics, Moscow, USSR, 1987.

24. J. Meseguer. General logics, in: H.-D. Ebbinghaus et al ed. *Logic Colloquium'87*, pp.275-329, North-Holland, 1989.

25. A. P. Nemytykh, V. A. Pinchuk and V. F. Turchin. A Self-Applicable Supercompiler, *in this volume.*

26. V. Yu. Olunin, V. F. Turchin and S. N. Florentsev. A Refal interpreter, in: *Trudy 1-oi Vses. Konf. po Programmirovaniyu, (in Russian).* Kiev, 1968.

27. P. Sestoft. The structure of a self-applicable partial evaluator, in: H. Ganzinger and N. D. Jones, ed. *Programs as Data Objects (Copenhagen, 1985)*, LNCS, vol.217, pp.236-256, Springer, 1986.

28. A. Yu. Romanenko. The generation of inverse functions in Refal. in: D. Bjørner, A. P. Ershov and N. D. Jones, ed. *Partial Evaluation and Mixed Computation*, North-Holland, pp.427-444, 1988.

29. A. Yu. Romanenko. Inversion and metacomputation, in: *Proceedings of the Symposium on Partial Evaluation and Semantics-Based Program Manipulation* (Yale University), pp.12-22, ACM Press, 1991.

30. S. A. Romanenko. A compiler generator produced by a self-applicable specializer can have a surprisingly natural and understandable structure, in: D. Bjørner, A. P. Ershov and N. D. Jones, ed. *Partial Evaluation and Mixed Computation*, North-Holland, pp.445-464., 1988.

31. S. A. Romanenko. Arity raiser and its use in program specialization, in: N. D. Jones ed. ESOP'90, LNCS, vol.432, pp.341-360, 1990.

32. M. H. Sørensen. *Turchin's Supercompiler Revisited*, Master's thesis, Dept. of Computer Science, University of Copenhagen, 1994.

33. M. H. Sørensen and R. Glück. An algorithm of generalization in positive supercompilation, in: J. W. Lloyd ed., *International Logic Programming Symposium*, MIT Press, 1995, to appear.

34. M. H. Sørensen, R. Glück and N. D. Jones. Towards unifying deforestation, supercompilation, partial evaluation and generalized partial evaluation, in: D. Sannella ed., *Programming Languages and Systems*, LNCS, vol.788, pp.485-500, Springer, 1994.

35. M. H. Sørensen, R. Glück and N. D. Jones. A positive supercompiler, *Journal of Functional Programming*, 1996 (to appear).

36. V. F. Turchin. Metajazyk dlja formal'nogo opisanija algoritmicjeskikh jazykov (A metalanguage for formal description of algorithmic languages, in Russian), in: *Cifrovaja Tekhnika i Programmirovanie*, pp.116-124, Moscow 1966.

37. V. F. Turchin. Programmirovanie na yazyke Refal (Programming in Refal, in Russian), Preprints Nos. 41, 43, 44, 48, 49 of the Institute for Applied Mathematics, AN SSSR, 1971.

38. V. F. Turchin. Equivalent transformations of recursive functions defined in Refal (*in Russian*), in: Teoriya Yazykov I Metody Postroeniya Sistem Programmirovaniya (Proceedings of the Symposium), Kiev-Alushta (USSR), pp.31-42, 1972.

39. V. F. Turchin. *The Phenomenon of Science*, Columbia University Press, New York, 1977.

40. V. F. Turchin. *The Language Refal, the Theory of Compilation and Metasystem Analysis*, Courant Computer Science Report #20, New York University, 1980.

41. V. F. Turchin, R.M.Nirenberg and D.V.Turchin. Experiments with a supercompiler. In: *ACM Symposium on Lisp and Functional Programming*, ACM, New York, pp. 47-55, 1982.

42. V. F. Turchin. The concept of a supercompiler, *ACM Transactions on Programming Languages and Systems*, 8, pp.292-325, 1986.

43. V. F. Turchin. The algorithm of generalization in the supercompiler, in: Bjørner D., Ershov A.P., Jones N.D. eds, Partial Evaluation and Mixed Computation, Proceedings of the IFIP TC2 Workshop, pp. 531-549, North-Holland Publishing Co., 1988.

44. V. F. Turchin. *Refal-5, Programming Guide and Reference Manual*, New England Publishing Co., 1989.

45. V. F. Turchin. Program Transformation with Metasystem Transitions, *J. of Functional Programming*, 3(3) 283-313, 1993.

46. V. F. Turchin and A.P.Nemytykh. Metavariables: Their implementation and use in Program Transformation, CCNY Technical Report CSc TR-95-012, 1995.

47. V. F. Turchin and A.P.Nemytykh, A. A Self-applicable Supercompiler CCNY Technical Report CSc TR-95-010, 1995.

48. V. F. Turchin. On Generalization of Lists and Strings in Supercompilation, CCNY Technical Report TR-96-02, 1996.

Author Index

Subject Index

Lecture Notes in Computer Science

For information about Vols. 1–1053

please contact your bookseller or Springer-Verlag